Museums:
A Place to Work

PLANNING MUSEUM CAREERS

"This book meets a vital need; for planning museum careers is the key to better museums – hence, a richer cultural landscape – for the twenty-first century."

Y.R. Isar, Director, International Fund
for the Promotion of Culture, UNESCO

"The work you have done is monumental."

Paul N. Perrot, Director Santa Barbara Museum of Art

Museum work is becoming increasingly professionalized. The skills demanded by those who work in museums are increasing as technology advances and as society changes. This much-needed volume surveys the latest trends in museum work.

Museums: A Place to Work, Planning Museum Careers is the definitive guide to the museum profession. It outlines in detail more than thirty museum positions, incorporates extracts from interviews with experienced museum professionals from many backgrounds and includes sections on the origins and history of museums, the importance of ethics, training, preparation, job-seeking, and the future for museums.

Museums: A Place to Work, Planning Museum Careers provides indispensable information on how to find jobs in museums. It is aimed at those starting a museum career as well as experienced professionals wanting to change or advance their careers, museum studies and other university programs, and career counselors.

Jane R. Glaser is a special assistant for the Smithsonian Institution Office of the Provost and has been working in and writing about the museum profession for thirty-two years, particularly in the areas of museum training, education, management and career counseling. **Artemis A. Zenetou** is a museum associate for the Smithsonian Institution Office of the Provost, has written about the museum field; and has coordinated seminars and international exhibitions.

The Heritage: Care–Preservation–Management programme has been designed to serve the needs of the museum and heritage community worldwide. It publishes books and information services for professional museum and heritage workers, and for all the organisations that service the museum community.

Editor-in-chief: Andrew Wheatcroft

Architecture in Conservation:
Managing developments at historic sites
James Strike

The Development of Costume
Naomi Tarrant

Forward Planning: *A handbook of business, corporate and development planning for museums and galleries*
Edited by Timothy Ambrose and Sue Runyard

The Handbook for Museums
Gary Edson and David Dean

Heritage Gardens: *Care, conservation and management*
Sheena Mackellar Goulty

Heritage and Tourism *in 'the global village'*
Priscilla Boniface and Peter J. Fowler

The Industrial Heritage: *Managing resources and uses*
Judith Alfrey and Tim Putnam

Managing Quality Cultural Tourism
Priscilla Boniface

Museum Basics
Timothy Ambrose and Crispin Paine

Museum Exhibition: *Theory and practice*
David Dean

Museum, Media, Message
Edited by Eilean Hooper-Greenhill

Museum Security and Protection:
A handbook for cultural heritage institutions
ICOM and ICMS

Museums 2000: *Politics, people, professionals and profit*
Edited by Patrick J. Boylan

Museums and the Shaping of Knowledge
Eilean Hooper-Greenhill

Museums and their Visitors
Eilean Hooper-Greenhill

Museums without Barriers: *A new deal for disabled people*
Fondation de France and ICOM

The Past in Contemporary Society: Then/Now
Peter J. Fowler

The Representation of the Past:
Museums and heritage in the post-modern world
Kevin Walsh

Towards the Museum of the Future: *New European perspectives*
Edited by Roger Miles and Lauro Zavala

Museums:
A Place to Work

Planning Museum Careers

Jane R. Glaser with Artemis A. Zenetou

London and New York
published in association with
The Smithsonian Institution

First published 1996
by Routledge
11 New Fetter Lane, London EC4P 4EE

Simultaneously published in the USA and Canada
by Routledge
29 West 35th Street, New York, NY 10001

© 1996 The Smithsonian Institution

Typeset in Sabon by Florencetype Ltd, Stoodleigh, Devon

Printed and bound in Great Britain by
TJ Press Ltd, Padstow, Cornwall

British Library Cataloguing in Publication Data
A catalogue record for this book is available from the
British Library

Library of Congress Cataloguing in Publication Data
A catalogue record for this book has been requested

ISBN 0-415-12256-2
0-415-12724-6 (pbk)

Contents

Contents

Foreword

The growing literature on the history of museums, their management, and their social obligations and ethical concerns, has yet to include a comprehensive volume on museum careers. This lacuna is now superbly filled by an author who has devoted several decades to studying and defining the roles of the various specialties that make up what now can be described as the "museum profession." True, this profession does not have the canons of disciplinary rigor of medicine, the law, or the sciences. Nevertheless, over the years certain basic principles have emerged, the requirements of various positions have been defined, and, taken together, they do indeed constitute a profession whose specialties, depending on the size of an institution, interact for the common purpose of preservation, presentation, interpretation, and transmission.

Museums in the aggregate are keepers of a substantial part of the tactile evidence of the earth's evolution and of humanity's development, from millennia past to the present. Through an analysis of their holdings, we can set new discoveries within a historical continuum and leave to our successors, to an unfathomable future, the resources through which they will be able to gauge the validity of our assumptions, and the results of their own creativity and discovery.

Seen in this light, the role of museums and related organizations has enormous importance. The resources they collectively hold represent irreplaceable values. In fact, these institutions are trusts, and this function imposes upon them an awesome ethical burden and one that should permeate all of their activities. Their aim should be the search for truth, and their goal the highest integrity in all of their activities.

As preservers, presenters, interpreters, and transmitters, museums are also centers for lifelong learning. Their resources stimulate the young, instruct the mature, rejoice the eye, and for all ages provide opportunities for quiet contemplation, for discovery, for that knowledge that can only result from asking questions, making comparisons, and understanding interrelationships. These attributes pertain to all museums, whether dedicated to art, history, science, or nature.

Since the objects in most art and history museums are the products of earlier civilizations, they are testimony of cultural development, and because culture is the collective expression of a society, museums must be boundary-free for all in society to enjoy. Museum staff must recognize that what they hold in trust is not the product of this or that elite but the tactile manifestation of what previous and present societies have accomplished. Hence, as they preserve the creativity of past societies, museums have the obligation to share this creativity with everyone in the present society.

Those museums that are concerned with natural history – the zoos, the botanical gardens, aquariums and others – must be equally open, since all of us are part of the natural order and dependent on that order for our continued collective existence. Through these institutions, we can obtain a heightened understanding of this interrelationship and be connected to our origins, enriched by the beauty of the biota, and become more sensitive to the growing threats to its viable continuity, indeed to its and our very survival.

All these considerations suggest the importance of museum careers since these have one common theme: to foster understanding of the past, enrichment and enjoyment of the present, and to be, as it were, a vote of confidence in the future. Hence, the importance of the training and professional commitment of those who choose a museum career.

As we face the twenty-first century, and this is admirably evoked in the latter part of this book, there are large clouds on the horizon: shrinking resources, overpopulation, urban blight, pollution, and the uncertainty caused by new technologies, some of which, by their very name, such as artificial intelligence, are highly threatening. In this perspective, museums have a renewed need to be clear in the articulation of their purposes and principles and, most importantly, to create a climate that will attract the best minds and the most enthusiastic attitudes to the various branches of the profession which is charged with their care.

This volume superbly introduces potential staff to the vast array of professional opportunities that are open, but it does more through its organization and thoughtful contents: it is a guide to those who, now or in the future, may be involved in museum training. In this book, Jane Glaser and her associates have produced more than an introduction to museum careers; they have produced a manifesto on their meaning.

Paul N. Perrot
Former Director, Santa Barbara Museum of Art,
Santa Barbara, California

Preface

Though the first museums were established almost half a millenium ago, at least 90 per cent, possibly 95 per cent, of the world's museums have been created since the end of the Second World War. This explosive growth in the number, range, variety, and richness of museums has been paralleled by similar developments in museum employment. From just two traditional types of employees – the scholar–curators and the non-professional support workers (technical, maintenance, and security personnel) – the museum workforce now includes an almost bewildering range of positions and job titles (though there remain major cultural differences between countries in this). The range of new museum jobs reflects both the widening educational and social role of modern museums and (much though many may deplore it) a marked decline in the traditional dominance of curatorship in present-day museum policy and management. In relation to both the debate about the future of museums in the twenty-first century and the growing importance of human resources management, this book is a timely and significant study, reflecting more than two decades' close observation of the changing nature of museum employment around the world.

Professor Patrick J. Boylan
United Kingdom

It has been said that museums reinvent themselves endlessly. So, too, the people who work in them reinvent museum careers. That's part of what makes museum work so intriguing and interesting.

The museum "profession" has been evolving in the United States over the past two hundred years, so it is not easy to define clearly what people do who work in museums. An amalgam of many professions within the museum has caused some to deny that there is a museum "profession." But today, with an extensive body of literature, museological theories, professional and technical practices unique to museums, and codes of ethics, it is appropriate to take a closer look at museum careers as being in a profession.

It is time, as well, to assist those who contemplate museum careers in assessing their potential for success in the museum field. While many in the past have entered museum work "through the back door," there now is a new degree of sophistication among job-seekers. They are asking the questions of the museum "profession" that they ask of many other fields of endeavor. It is time to provide some of the answers, or at least to provide food for thought on what it entails to be a museum person. We approach this with a degree of flexibility so that our terminology and information will be adaptable for our international colleagues, their institutions, and individuals seeking museum careers throughout the world.

Research for this book included informal discussions with museum workers at all levels, in all sizes of museums, in all disciplines, "veterans" and newcomers, in all regions of the country and abroad. Many many museum professionals in various positions were formally and personally interviewed, most of them by Artemis Zenetou, for their museum life stories. They took time from their busy lives to share their experiences so that others might benefit from the lessons learned. You will hear their voices throughout the book (the quotes are extrapolated from the interviews), and we hope that this uniquely personalized approach will have a special impact on your decisions and plans.

In addition, we sent surveys to hundreds of museum people throughout the country asking them to help us develop descriptions of their positions. The response was overwhelming in their cooperation and enthusiasm for our project. We also sent questionnaires to administrators of museum studies programs and university career counselors asking them to tell us what questions are being asked about possible museum careers. Their prompt and supportive replies were extremely useful.

All current museological and career-related literature has been thoroughly searched and scrutinized for ideas, philosophy, data, statistics, and other opinions to share with you. We found very little on museum careers, reinforcing our views on the need for more basic information.

This book comes as a result of a thirty-two-year love affair with museums, what they are about, and, most important, the people who work in them. So many colleagues have demonstrated the special commitment and dedication, even passion, for public service that is required for a museum career. Their intellect, curiosity, good humor, and wit are not matched in any other field. They argue and debate the issues, and somehow reach a consensus when it is important to do so. They reinvent their jobs, and invent new ones as society and technology change.

Most important, the museum field has matured to a point of understanding the difference between having a "profession" and being "professional." The best of museum people are a source of tremendous pride for their accomplishments as leaders, managers, scholars, collectors, researchers, preservers, exhibitors, and educators of our cultural and natural heritage and for the publics we serve, and their work exemplifies the best in museum professionalism. They epitomize what we are trying to describe for you in this book.

Jane R. Glaser

Acknowledgments

A book of this scope draws heavily on resources and colleagues throughout the United States and abroad. Because it is written for and about the museum field, we reflected upon the accumulated experience of the happy and rewarding career of the author and those of hundreds of museum professionals who generously shared their views of what museum careers are all about. Their career paths, their interests, their goals, their problems, their successes, their sustained good humor, and their unusual exploits all contributed to the "drama" of writing about planning a museum career. We are extremely grateful to all of them.

We are especially deeply indebted to those who gave freely of their time for personal interviews and agreed to be taped for posterity. By sharing their insights, they demonstrated the meaning of professional service. Their words of wisdom appear throughout the book.

Of all the help received, no one has sustained commitment longer or more imperturbably than Artemis Zenetou, my associate. No one has worked more steadily, done more extensive research, carried more of the endless detail, responded more thoughtfully, maintained more stamina and good humor, and endured more of the author's frustrations – all with flexibility and grace. Her patience and energy in conducting a great number of interviews, her tireless efforts to research and write one of the chapters and a unit of another, her intelligence and devotion to getting the book on track and "right," made the project possible. I shall be forever grateful!

There is no one in the museum field to whom I am more indebted than to my friend and colleague Paul Perrot, who graciously agreed to write the fore-word for this book. My indebtedness goes back twenty years, when he persuaded me to work at the Smithsonian Institution. His example of professionalism, integrity, and ethical conduct in the museum world remains an inspiration. He believed strongly in a global museum village long before it was the popular or "correct" thing to do. He promoted and doggedly fought for the recognition and importance of conservation. His influence in believing in a strong code of ethics and that we must assist one another in the museum field is indeed evident throughout this book.

We have been blessed with an editor, Ann Hofstra Grogg, who has had unfailing interest, patience, faith in the project, a marvelously critical eye, professionalism, a keen sense of the museum field, and the amazing ability to make the sometimes unintelligible into a literate document. She has calmly and wisely shepherded the book to a final manuscript. Our eternal gratitude!

My deepest appreciation to my friends and colleagues Marie Malaro and Bob Macdonald, who shared their special talents and expertise by writing three chapters of this book. This book would not be complete without their thoughtful and wise advice on governance, legal concerns, and ethics. Their sense of professionalism is a beacon to those considering entering the field.

For her invaluable assistance in compiling the bibliographies and the appendix, Maria Magdalena Mieri deserves a special medal. Her diligence, skills in sorting through voluminous information, checking and rechecking references, abiding interest, unfailing good cheer, and thoughtful judgments deserve special recognition. She was aided by Maria Mescua, who launched these special sections of the book in its beginnings. We are very grateful to her as well. Colleagues and librarians helped greatly in identifying sources and suggesting others.

A number of people have read or listened to parts of this book, and many have commented on it and made suggestions for improvements. I and the book have profited substantially, and changes were made from their observations. Among those whom I thank for their invaluable appraisals are the Glaser clan, Alexis Papahelas, Paul Perrot, Mary Grace Potter, George Robinson, and Philip D. Spiess.

Many other individuals have been supportive and given information, assistance, or advice, and we thank Edward Alexander, Margaret Anderson, Joan Bachrach, Alan Bain, Helena Bain, James Blackaby, Patrick Boylan, Claudine Brown, Kathleen Burke, Robert Burke, Elizabeth des Portes, James Dodd, Philippe Dubé, James Early, Tom Freudenheim, Nancy Fuller, Dolly Goulandris, David Huntley, Maria Karaiskakis, Gerd Lavik, David Liston, Eleanor MacMillan, Jan Majewski, Pieter Meyers, Valerie Wheat, the Museum Reference Center, Marc Pachter, Maria Papageorge, Thomas Peyton, Bea Poole, Larry Reger, John Rumm, Jane Scholl, Jane Sledge, William Tompkins, Patricia Williams, Donald Moore, Karen Lee Davis, David Voelkel, Inka Vostrezova, and U. Vincent Wilcox.

Much appreciation to Gail Anderson, David Butts, Katherine Cooper, Linda Cotter, Jane des Grange, Gary Edson, Selma Holo, Nina Jensen, Flora Kaplan, Marie Malaro, Candace Matelic, Carol Stapp, and Bryant Tolles, who provided additional and very useful information from their museum studies programs.

Financially, the book would not have been possible without the support of the Smithsonian's Office of the Provost, Office of the Assistant Provost for Arts and Humanities, and grants from the Smithson Society, the Glaser/Mudie Fund, Huntingdon T. Block Insurance, the Education Outreach Fund, administered by the Office of the Assistant Provost for Education and Public Service, and the former Office of the Assistant Secretary for External Affairs.

We thank the following for permission to print their mission statements: the J. B. Speed Art Museum of Louisville, Kentucky, the Bucks County Historical Society of Doylestown, Pennsylvania, the Museum of Science and Industry of Chicago, Illinois, the Natural History Museum of Los Angeles County of Los Angeles, California, the Museum of the Rockies of Bozeman, Montana, the Institute of Texan Cultures of San Antonio, Texas, the Chicago Zoological Society–Brookfield Zoo of Brookfield, Illinois, and the Art Institute of Chicago, Chicago, Illinois.

For use of their organization charts as examples: the Queensland Art Gallery of Australia, the Milwaukee Public Museum of Milwaukee, Wisconsin, The Exploratorium of San Francisco, California, the Virginia Museum of Natural History of Martinsville, Virginia, the Kentucky Historical Society of Frankfort, Kentucky, and the Museum of Hispanic American Art, "Isaac Fernandez Blanco," of Buenos Aires, Argentina.

We are obliged to the American Association of Museums for permission to reprint the 1994 *Code of Ethics for Museums*, and to the American Association of Museum Volunteers for use of their first chapter as a starting-point for our chapter "Staff/Volunteer Relations." We are pleased to have the endorsement of the UNESCO International Fund for the Promotion of Culture.

For generously contributing photographs for consideration, we are most appreciative to the California Academy of Sciences, the Denver Museum of Natural History, the Asian Art Museum of San Francisco, the Kentucky Historical Society, the Goulandris Museum of Cycladic and Ancient Greek Art, the Society for the Preservation of New England Antiquities, the Smithsonian Office of Exhibits Central, the Smithsonian Institution Archives, the Smithsonian Conservation Analytical Laboratory, the Smithsonian Office of Photographic Services, the National Park Service, and Guy Hardy of the Quebec Federal Office of Regional Development.

To the hundreds of respondents to our surveys who rallied to the cause and shared their information we doff our hats. The hundreds who came for museum career advice and counsel over the years we salute for their inspiration for this book.

To those named and those unnamed (unintentionally) our deepest thanks. We found great satisfaction and enrichment throughout the process of writing this book. We have learned anew, and hope to continue the learning process for all our days.

Jane R. Glaser

Interviewees

Sylvia Mullaly Aguire, Multicultural Coordinator, The Exploratorium, San Francisco, California

Peter Ames, Museum Consultant, Boston, Massachusetts, former Vice-President for Programs, Boston Museum of Science

JoAllyn Archambault, Curator, American Indian Program, Department of Anthropology, National Museum of Natural History, Smithsonian Institution, Washington, DC

Malcolm Arth, former Director of Education, American Museum of Natural History, New York, New York (deceased)

Bruce Bartholomew, Collections Manager, California Academy of Sciences, San Francisco, California

Terese Tse Bartholomew, Curator of Indian and Himalayan Art, Asian Art Museum of San Francisco, The Avery Brundage Collection, San Francisco, California

Arthur Beale, Director of Research, Museum of Fine Arts, Boston, Massachusetts

Craig Black, former Director, Natural History Museum of Los Angeles County, Los Angeles, California

Claudine Brown, Director, Arts Division, Nathan Cummings Foundation, New York, New York, former Deputy Assistant Secretary for the Arts and Humanities, Smithsonian Institution, Washington, DC

Jeannine Smith Clark, Board of Regents, Smithsonian Institution, Washington, DC

Eleni Cocordas, Exhibition Coordinator, Museum of Modern Art, New York, New York

Marie Acosta Colon, Director, The Mexican Museum, San Francisco, California

Spencer Crew, Director, National Museum of American History, Smithsonian Institution, Washington, DC

Sue Dahling, former Director of Marketing, The Computer Museum, Boston, Massachusetts

Steve Di Girolamo, Exhibition Designer, National Portrait Gallery, Smithsonian Institution, Washington, DC

Janet Dorman, former Museum Shop Manager, The Phillips Collection, Washington, DC

Sally Duensing, Science and Museum Liaison, The Exploratorium, San Francisco, California

Joyce Elliot, former Head of Publications, National Building Museum, Washington, DC

Rex Ellis, Director, Centre for Museum Studies, Smithsonian Institution, Washington, DC

Chang Bo Feng, Professor of American History, Nankai University, Tianjin, People's Republic of China

Patricia Fiske, Deputy Director, National Museum of African Art, Smithsonian Institution, Washington, DC

Tom L. Freudenheim, former Assistant Provost for the Arts and Humanities, Smithsonian Institution, Washington, DC

Edmund B. Gaither, Director and Curator, Museum of the National Center of Afro-American Artists, Boston, Massachusetts

Amareswar Galla, Cross-Cultural Heritage Specialist, University of Canberra, Australia

Barbara K. Gibbs, Director, Cincinnati Art Museum, Cincinnati, Ohio, former Director, Crocker Museum of Art, Sacramento, California

Niki Goulandris, co-founder and Director, the Goulandris Natural History Museum, Kifissia, Greece

Glenn Gutleben, Exhibition Design, Electronics Engineer, The Exploratorium, San Francisco, California

Wilhelmina Cole Holladay, founder and President, National Museum of Women in the Arts, Washington, DC

Ellen Holtzman, Program Director for the Arts, The Henry Luce Foundation, New York City, former Managing Director, The New Museum of Contemporary Art, New York City

Donald Hughes, Director of Exhibitions, Monterey Bay Aquarium, Monterey, California

Ron L. Kagan, Director, Detroit Zoo, Royal Oak, Michigan

Darlene Labrero, Director of the PM Explainer Program, The Exploratorium, San Francisco, California

Laura Lester, Director of Public Affairs, The Phillips Collection, Washington, DC

Barbara Luton, Director of Development, Santa Barbara Museum of Art, Santa Barbara, California

Robert Macdonald, Director, Museum of the City of New York, New York

Jeanne McDonnell, Director, Women's Heritage Museum, Portola, California

Anna McFarland, Administrator of Collections and Exhibitions, Dallas Museum of Art, Dallas, Texas

Stacy Miller, Project Director, Museum School, Teachers, College, Columbia University, New York, New York, former Curator of Education, Isabella Stewart Gardner Museum, Boston, Massachusetts

Barbara Moore, Head of Education Publications Program, National Gallery of Art, Washington, DC, formerly the Corcoran Gallery of Art, Washington, DC

Thomas Moritz, Librarian, California Academy of Sciences, San Francisco, California

Paul N. Perrot, former Director, Santa Barbara Museum of Art, Santa Barbara, California

Elizabeth A.C. Perry, Executive Director, American Red Cross History and Education Center, formerly Corporate Relations Officer, National Gallery of Art, Washington, DC

Margaret Piatt, Assistant Director for Museum Education, Old Sturbridge Village, Sturbridge, Massachusetts

Philip Ravenhill, Chief Curator, National Museum of African Art, Washington, DC

Harry Robinson, Jr, Director, Museum of African American Life and Culture, Dallas, Texas

Belgica Rodriguez, former Director, Art Museum of the Americas, Organization of American States, Washington, DC

Carolyn Rose, Senior Research Conservator/Deputy Chairperson of Conservation, Department of Anthropology, National Museum of Natural History, Smithsonian Institution, Washington, DC

Magda Schremp, Docent Coordinator, National Museum of Natural History, Smithsonian Institution, Washington, DC

Tom Southall, Curator of Photographs, Amon Carter Museum of Art, Fort Worth, Texas

Kenneth Starr, author and former Director of the Milwaukee Public Museum, Milwaukee, Wisconsin

Patricia A. Steuert, Deputy Director, The Children's Museum, Boston, Massachusetts

Linda Thomas, Registrar, Museum of Fine Arts, Boston, Massachusetts

Edith Tonelli, former Director, Wight Gallery, University of California, Los Angeles, California

Bonnie VanDorn, Executive Director, Association of Science–Technology Centers, Washington, DC

William J. Voss, Chief Curator of Science, Fort Worth Museum of Science and History, Fort Worth, Texas

Susan Wilkerson, Collections Manager, National Building Museum, Washington, DC

Sarah J. Wolf, Director of Conservation and Collections Management, The Textile Museum, Washington, DC

Kenneth Yellis, Assistant Director of Public Programs, Peabody Museum, Yale University, New Haven, Connecticut

Part I
The museum world,
its works and wonders

The museum world, its works and wonders: prologue

You may be among the curious who have had an abiding interest in museums and are considering launching a museum career, but you're not sure why or where to start. There is also a great deal you would like to know about museums and their origins. With this in mind, let us introduce you to the museum world, its works and wonders. This world has a long and interesting history, as you will see, and over the centuries it has attracted the interest and commitment of many thoughtful, wise, creative, and innovative people. From the historic yesterdays of museums, we present for you the time frames as museums evolved into both the unusual and the traditional educational institutions they are today.

> Why are there so many museums? It may be as simple as that Americans are always at risk at being disconnected with their past, and creating museums is an effort to find a meaningful past. In a country whose history is as short as ours, and in a country whose attention span is as short as ours, I think that museums are part of our civic memory, and clearly people have that in mind. They are also making a statement of who they want to be so that museums are part of an affirmative proactive aspect of the American temperament which says we are not who we want to be or need to be, yet we are ready to make a down payment on that.
>
> Kenneth Yellis, Yale University Peabody Museum
> of Natural History

> The beauty of museums is that they are not part of the real world, and yet we have to make certain that in our museums what people see in our buildings has to relate to what they see outside – they can't be two worlds apart. If museums are meaningful, people are going to go to museums and say that the museum has some relationship to what people are doing outside the museum.
>
> Kenneth Starr, formerly
> Milwaukee Public Museum

Museums, first and foremost, should be educational institutions. We may be a storehouse too because it is one of our functions to locate, obtain, and maintain material culture that reflects history – and that means storing things in a positive sense. But dissemination of information is the key!

Spencer Crew, National Museum of
American History

I think it is the duty of the museum to use the research in its education and public programs. I think this is the basic justification for why we are here, why we have the collections, and why we do the research.

Craig Black, formerly Los Angeles County
Museum of Natural History

It's intellectually challenging and a tremendous privilege to work in a museum.

Barbara K. Gibbs, Cincinnati Art Museum

I like the environment of museums. People tell me how lucky I am – others spend their leisure time in museums, and I work there!

Janet Dorman, formerly The Phillips Collection

Outside people are fascinated by what museum work is – all *they* do is make money. They tell me that someday they wish they could do what I do.

Robert Macdonald, Museum of the
City of New York

Embarking on a museum career you should have an openness, and perseverance. Museums are exciting.

Belgica Rodriguez, formerly Art Museum
of the Americas (OAS)

If you are looking to do something that is useful to humankind, to make the world a better place, by all means, do it!! You should think about museums.

Glenn Guttleben, The Exploratorium, San Francisco

I find that the people who work in museums tend to be generally intelligent, sensitive, and well-intentioned people.

Peter Ames, formerly Science Museum
of Boston

Museums are recognized as powerful centers of learning: they are a positive social force in their communities, they enhance their communities' public reputation and economy, and they provide a place where diverse cultures can find values that unify them.

Susannah Simpson Kent, formerly
Institute of Museum Services

1

So you want to work in a museum. . . . Why?

You may have your answer already, but most people who ask about working in a museum are not sure *why*.

- Perhaps it sounds glamorous – it's different from ordinary run-of-the-mill kinds of jobs.
- You have been collecting "things" for years, so don't collectors belong in a museum?
- You have a solid background in a discipline, but you don't particularly want to teach.
- You are a scholar, primarily interested in research and writing – where do you fit in a museum?
- You have been working in another field for five or ten years, and it's time for a change.
- You have spent two summers working on an archeological "dig" and found it fascinating, but you want to see where those artifacts end up, and how, and by whom they are studied and cared for – is this a place for you?
- Butterflies and bugs had special places on the shelves in your room for years – if you work in a museum, will you be able to go out in the fields to collect and study the specimens you love?
- You are a computer "whiz" – do museums want you?
- You are passionate about the importance of education and are looking for an educational institution whose mission matches your drive – would a museum be a good place to work?
- You are artistic, so there must be something for you to do in a museum.
- You are curious about who does all the work in getting an exhibition together – what goes on behind the scenes?

"I think museums are in a marvelously interesting place in American society now. The largest issues that are in life center around values that have to do with things like tolerance, diversity, and freedom of expression which museums can translate against our own history."

Edmund B. Gaither, Museum of
the National Center of Afro-American Artists

"I am strong in my encouragement to people who are interested to come into the profession if they have a passion for it. If they have a serious interest in museums and museum work, then they are going to succeed."
Malcolm Arth, formerly American Museum of Natural History

- You are intrigued by all those works of art, objects, and artifacts, and, since you like to do research, you would like to get closer to them, study them and learn more about them.
- You are very well organized, methodical and neat – you would like to keep records and set up systems in a museum, you think.
- Perhaps you have a museum studies or an arts administration degree, and a museum should be for you, but you are not sure where you fit.
- You want to know if your training and skills in writing, public relations, teaching, law, marketing, management, computers, etc., are transferable to museum work.
- You have a high-school diploma or a technical-school certificate – what can you do in a museum?
- You are comparing the museum field potential with several other fields, and you want to know what the career tracks are and how well you would be paid.
- You have heard that museums are the "old boys' club," and you are anxious to know about gender equity in hiring practices.
- You want to know if senior-level positions are attainable for minorities in traditional museums – where do you start?
- You want to know if the Americans with Disabilities Act is really going to have an effect on hiring people with disabilities for many jobs in museums.
- You have a great imagination, are creative, and like people – shouldn't you be working in a museum?

These are among the many approaches to inquiring about museum work that we have encountered over the past thirty-two years. All are valid, and all require answers, even though the ramifications and variables are endless. Of course, there is no *one* answer to these questions.

This is why we have written this book

We hope it will serve as a definitive *guide*, nationally and internationally, for those embarking upon a museum career, for high-school and university students and career counselors, for those changing careers, for museum studies students and instructors, for all university disciplinary programs students and instructors, for museum staff (those who hire, those who advise, and those seeking new or different positions), for career-reference shelves in libraries, and for those merely seeking information about museum work.

"I work in a museum because I love the collections, the people – it's interesting, it's challenging, and there is always change."

Linda Thomas, Boston Museum of Fine Arts

The book provides factual and up-to-date information on the types of positions available, educational prerequisites, experience and on-the-job skills requirements, the nature of policy-making positions, important ethical considerations, diversity in the work-force, the use of new technologies, the importance of managerial acumen and entrepreneurship, museums as learning-environments, museum governance and its effect on museum operations, where training and professional development fit in, and the obligations of museum staff in the "global village." These and many other considerations are indicative of the higher standards and increasing complexities within museum work. These issues affect museum staff today and certainly tomorrow, and if you want to work in a museum, you need to be prepared.

You should love museums, of course, and you must be committed to the ideas they embody. Museum work is a life of dedication and public service. Careers are not nine-to-five positions; they require doing what it takes to get the job done. The rewards they offer are not generally financial, though salaries are better than they once were. If your goal is a very lucrative position, however, look elsewhere.

To give you some idea of the observations, philosophies, rewards, and satisfactions of museum work you will hear throughout this book from among the *many* museum professionals interviewed. This special feature brings you personal commitment and enthusiasm derived from their experiences as professionals in the museum field.

All of the information in this book can be of value to those seeking a career in museums, and who need to know about abilities and knowledge required for museum positions. For example, skills in marketing and fund raising are imperative in a contemporary society where museums are competing with a multitude of organizations for support, both private and governmental. Such skills, important as they are, are not necessarily a part of the traditional academic training which candidates for museum careers receive.

Planning and preparing for a museum career are relatively new courses of action, but wise ones. Competition for jobs is greater than in the past, when most people came into museums through other disciplines or accidentally and learned museum practices mostly by trial and error. Museums today have a whole new set of concerns and financial constraints in serving their vast communities, recognizing the diverse cultures and age groups as part of their constituencies, providing the public and the educational establishment with alternatives, and becoming agents of social change.

Despite current financial restraints, the museum field has been, and continues to be, a "growth industry." Changes in society, advances in technology, and

"I like working in a museum because it allows me to use more of my skills than any other position that I have ever had in my life, and it allows me more control over what I am doing. I love the job."

JoAllyn Archambault, National Museum of Natural History

the "information age" of the 1990s are opening new avenues in museum work. At the same time museums are reaffirming their basic functions – collecting, preserving, researching, exhibiting, and interpreting – and must also include those added dimensions of knowledge and skills to prepare candidates for their roles in the museums of the twenty-first century.

To understand the museum "profession," take a long look at museums themselves. What is a museum? How do museums differ from or resemble each other? Exhibitions are one of the most visible products of museums, a bridge between the museum, its ideas, its collections, its research, and the public. How do they reflect their institutions? What do a museum's public programs, special events, publications, and facilities reveal about its mission and philosophy? That should give you some idea about the people who work in them, what their jobs may be, and the manner in which the museum operates. One of the main objectives of museums, as individualistic and independent as they are, is to build a sense of unity in their institutions and in the individuals who comprise the museum work-force.

Then read this book. We hope you will find answers to your questions about museum careers, and we also hope you will draw inspiration from those already committed to this career path. Why do they like working in museums?

One of the assets in terms of being in museum work is that you meet diverse people, you meet specialists who know incredible things about their subject-matter, so that if you have an interest you have access to people that will enable you to learn in depth about issues that concern you. Museums are full of the most creative and innovative thinkers that I've encountered. I love working in the field. I think museums celebrate the very best humankind has endeavored to give.

Claudine Brown, formerly
Smithsonian Institution

I never regretted going into the museum field. It's wonderfully satisfying, endlessly satisfying. No two days are alike. It's like Alice in Wonderland. When you finish your book you will find that there will be a great variety of views, and this is one of the joys and satisfactions of the museum world in that we don't come out of a production line like doctors, attorneys, etc. You sit around a table with a group of museum people, and it's seldom that two come from the same background. That brings a great richness to the profession. There is great diversity and quality that adds immensely to the museum field.

Kenneth Starr, formerly
Milwaukee Public Museum

I love objects. I love looking at them, working with them, and most of all I like the people in the museum. They are dedicated to what they do. Very few, if any of them, are motivated by finances, and therefore . . . they are content in their jobs in the sense that there are other things about their jobs that satisfy them.

Arthur Beale, Boston
Museum of Fine Arts

I was lucky. I fell in the museum business, and I am enjoying it tremendously. It has given me the opportunity to live in different parts of this country, and travel around the world. It introduced me to interesting people from every walk of life, every situation. I encourage people to do it.

Robert Macdonald, Museum
of the City of New York

Becoming a part of the museum field today, no matter in what capacity, requires a dedication and commitment as never before, and thorough preparation and planning for a museum career will lead to an understanding of the high level of ethics and professionalism that is required of all of us in the field.

2

Museums – yesterday and today

"Isn't fascination as comforting as solace? . . . Isn't curiosity as wondrously and fundamentally human as compassion?"

Stephen Jay Gould, in his reflections on natural history, was referring to nature being "immeasurably more interesting for its complexities and its lack of conformity to our hopes."[1] We would transfer his message, to write of *museums* as immeasurably more interesting for curiosity, wonder, awe, and fascination. Full of complexities, and not necessarily conforming to any one set of rules, or even hopes, museums, past and present, offer a variegated and fundamentally human scene. We hope *you* will be fascinated by the world of museums as you ponder a museum career.

A logical first step in thinking about a museum career is to learn a little about the origins and the long past of museums and about the breadth of concerns these institutions embrace in the present. It is often said that museums relate and interpret the past so that we may understand the present in order to meet the challenges of the future. Similarly, if you plan a museum career, you will need to know where, how, and why museums began, in order to understand what and why they are today, in order to speculate on the ways they will meet the challenges in the future, in *your* future!

The origins of museums

The word "muse" means to cogitate, meditate, think, dream, ponder, contemplate, and deliberate. For more than two thousand years people have created places where very special and valuable objects, artifacts, and works of art provide the milieu for "musing."

In fact, the word "muse" is derived from the Muses in Greek mythology. These were the nine daughters of Zeus who presided over arts and learning, including history, epic and lyric poetry, music, tragedy, dance, comedy, astronomy, and religious music. From these Muses came the Greek word, *mouseion*, "place of the Muses," and our English usage of the word "museum."

The earliest museum may have been in third-century Alexandria, Egypt. In ancient Rome museums were temples, and the colonnades surrounding the marketplace (*agora*) were full of works of art and historical objects (including military "trophies" from the Crusades), where beauty stimulated philosophical discussion. Like the Greek *mouseion*, they were dedicated to the Muses and ideal for public and philosophical discussion.

The term "museum" was first used to describe a collection in Renaissance Florence. Museums in the fifteenth century were art and objects amassed by the church or by wealthy and princely families of Europe. At the same time, humanist popes in Rome and other clergy and lay people started collecting classical, medieval and Romanesque statues and antiquities in Italy.[2] Some collections were described as "cabinets of curiosity," others as "cabinets of the world" (the "world" indicated that they were trying to represent the world as perceived by the owners). The very wealthy Medici family in Florence was among the princely groups outside the church who amassed great art collections for the pleasure and enjoyment of family members and friends. It was a very exclusive and self-indulgent patronage (even though of benefit to the artists of the time), because the families themselves, along with perhaps some royal and well-educated peers, were the connoisseurs, the "keepers," and the only visitors. Eilean Hooper-Greenhill identifies the Medici Palace as the first "nodal-point"[3] in the development of museums. Objects were not exhibited in any planned way but were rather haphazardly hung or placed in luxurious surroundings. Their purpose was to signify the importance of the owner. Gradually, throughout the seventeenth and eighteenth centuries, budding scholarship was brought to bear on these collections, and some rudimentary organization, usually by object type, began to be employed.

In the sixteenth century there were Italian *gallerie* (galleries) of pictures and sculpture and *gabinetti* (cabinets) of natural history collections. In the seventeenth century botanical gardens began to appear, and the first university museum was founded in 1671 in Basel, Switzerland.

In the late eighteenth and early nineteenth centuries, many major European cities established museums of antiquities or created special galleries in existing museums. Most of the museums of that time were still exclusively for the noble, the elite, and the highly educated; they were not intended for the public. England's first public museum was the Ashmolean, based on John Tradescant's "cabinet of rarities," which opened in 1683 at Oxford University, charging sixpence admission. The British Museum, which opened in London in 1759, a bequest of Sir Hans Sloane, was only a little more accessible than the museums of the Renaissance, as entry was limited to sixty visitors a day. The first true national museum, it was 1879 before it was open to the public on a daily basis. The Danish National Museum, which opened to the public in 1819, made a concerted effort to educate the "peasants," as they would have been the ones most likely to discover the nation's prehistoric artifacts while tilling the soil.

In the nineteenth century art museums "open to the public" (providing some kind of public service) included the Louvre in Paris (established in 1793), the

Prado in Madrid (1819), the National Museum for Greek Antiquities on the island of Aegina (1829), and the Altes in Berlin, which opened its doors in 1830. Governments in these nations were already housing former royal collections, usually in former royal palaces, and they were conscious of the advantages and goodwill generated by opening them to the general public. Indeed, the French Revolution, engendered by the "masses," contributed to the rise of nationalism, conversion to "public" collections, and the great national museums of Europe. At the beginning of the nineteenth century buildings began to be specifically designed and constructed for museums, including the Schinkel-designed Altes museum in Germany, although the Mint in Munich can be traced back to the sixteenth century. Other notable national museums of the period were founded in Budapest (1802), Prague (1818), and Stockholm (1847).

The development of museums in the United States

Quite the opposite of European museum history, public museums in the United States preceded private collections. They were established beginning late in the eighteenth century in fashions similar to the "cabinets of curiosities" and, like them, were not very accessible to the general public. There was, of course, a limit to what was available to collect: namely, local natural history, and art by American painters. Joel Orosz has described the impetus of our earliest museums as "cultural nationalism." Excluding European influences, "they were founded, for the most part, by Americans, in response to American cultural needs, and developed according to the imperatives of the changing American culture."[4]

John Adams, second president of the United States, predicted the future of cultural life in America in a famous letter to his wife: "I must study politics and war that my sons may have liberty to study mathematics, philosophy, geography, commerce, and agriculture, in order to give their children a right to study painting, poetry, music, architecture, statuary."[5]

Reflecting the evolution of American society, museum development in the United States might best be described in its various phases, with obvious overlaps: the age of the private society (cabinets of curiosities), the age of "popular" or commercial museums (self-education through entertainment), the age of the academic museum (research and teaching), the rise of the public museum (more democratic), the emergence of the educational museum (increasing professionalism), and museums as they are today – in crisis and diversity.

The few museums of the late eighteenth century were collections of miscellaneous materials displayed largely for society's elite. These included the curios of the Library Company of Philadelphia (with preserved animals, fossils, and coins) and the Philosophy Chamber (which meant science at the time) at Harvard University in Cambridge, Massachusetts (with a telescope and "philosophical apparatus"). In 1773, three years before the Declaration of

Independence, the first museum for the public opened in Charleston, South Carolina, with natural history and other eclectic collections. It exists and flourishes today, though not with the same collections nor in the same building.

The unfamiliar flora and fauna of the New World inspired collectors, as did new patriotic sentiments for the new nation. Private committees and clubs, not governmental authorities, started museums in many areas of the country. Founders represented a broad spectrum of social, intellectual, and economic backgrounds; their efforts established historical societies and museums related to the natural sciences. Historical societies sometimes reflected religious interests as well as patriotic energies. The Massachusetts Historical Society is one example. Other states established historical societies in the eighteenth and early nineteenth centuries, and they amassed all sorts of collections. Art was not yet a focus for museum collections, as most art was still commercial, the product of an artist–dealer–patron nexus.

In 1785, Charles Willson Peale, an eminent portraitist who had an art gallery in his home, noticed that his visitors also took great interest in his shells, minerals, and mounted birds. Thus, the Peale Museum in Philadelphia was started for the purpose of displaying "natural curiosities;" it later evolved into the Academy of Natural Sciences, although most of the Peale collections are at Harvard University. More than that, and unique at the time, Peale's museum had a mission that included both scientific and historical research and public education. Peale had a difficult balancing act of educating and entertaining while being a repository for collections and increasing the wealth of information. As Gary Kulik observes:

> He was an artist, scientist, museum founder closer to the Renaissance. His long struggle for financial support, his efforts to create a museum that was both entertaining and scholarly, and his attempts to use it self-consciously as an instrument of democracy, compel him to us. His problems seem not unlike ours.[6]

Other museums of the period were the American Antiquarian Society in Worcester, Massachusetts, DuSumetière's American Museum in Philadelphia, and the Wadsworth Atheneum (atheneums were originally private libraries used as "gentlemen's clubs" to read and play chess) in Hartford, Connecticut in 1844. They were within the same tradition as Peale of presenting scholarly exhibitions, yet hoping to appeal to an, as yet, unknown or unidentified public.

The age of the popular or commercial museum

A significant development in the history of American museums occurred when the entrepreneur P. T. Barnum opened his American Museum in 1841 in New York City. With a bizarre collection of curiosities and exotic performers, Barnum exploited, in a commercial way, the demand for popular learning in the United States. In addition to collections of shells, rocks and minerals, and fish, he had performing midgets, fleas, snakes, whales, and a white elephant from Siam. We are inclined to forget that most of the zoo animals we take for granted today were really exotic, indeed monstrous, in Barnum's day. He also displayed wax figures and panoramic scenes – forerunners of dioramas perhaps. Harold Skramstad said of him:

> For Barnum, the curiosity, the excitement, and knowledge embodied in his strange museum was to be shared with visitors in an active way. Even in the exhibits that bordered on hoaxes, Barnum touched on what is still a touchstone of museum interpretation, the issue of authenticity. He realized that people took instinctive pleasure in uncovering process, and that learning, if properly administered in acceptable doses, was a major American pre-occupation with box office appeal.[7]

It is easy to understand how Barnum's traveling circus developed from his first "museum."

Barnum appealed to a public seeking both reality and pleasure. He invited one and all to observe and learn how these exotic and strange things actually worked. He openly invited skepticism, challenge, and debate, and was a genuine pioneer in his understanding of the educational and entertainment power of museums.

Initially a center of science in a frontier "boom" town, the Western Museum of Cincinnati, founded in 1820, was another venture intended to entertain rather than educate. It attracted few visitors or patrons, and the founding fathers lost control of its administration and purpose. Louis Leonard Tucker quotes an English visitor's comment: "A 'museum' in the American sense of the word means a place of amusement, wherein there shall be a theatre, some wax figures, a giant and a dwarf or two, a jumble of pictures, a few live snakes, and a stock of very dubitable curiosities."[8] Having been converted into a freak and horror show, the Western Museum became one of the best-known entertainment sites in the United States – the first "Disneyland" of the West, according to Tucker. These attractions, not museums in the professional sense of the word, had hustlers and promoters as "staff," crude forerunners of our sophisticated and talented marketing people of today.

The age of the academic museum

In the first half of the nineteenth century, "public" and educational collections were established in academies, universities, and learned societies; some had staff, but "museum" duties related to collections were secondary. The emphasis was on scholarly research, and objects were arranged categorically for those purposes, as in many university science museums today. Indeed, most classification systems grew out of the need to organize for research purposes. The Columbian Institute in Washington, DC was established in 1816 for the promotion of the arts and sciences. Collections brought back by government-sponsored expeditions (the world-wide Wilkes expedition,

1838–42, for example) were stored there, primarily because the government had nowhere else to put them.

Universities became enclaves for many collections, as that was where the scholars were located. At the same time, collections and the knowledge associated with them were considered important in a democracy. Ildiko Heffernan has observed:

> American museums have been closely allied with the concept of democracy. Many were inspired by a belief in egalitarianism achievable through education. The relationship of museums to educational aspirations and political ideals is exemplified by the university museum whose development has been an integral part of higher education since the very beginning of our country.[9]

While the first college art museum, the Trumbull Gallery, was founded at Yale University in 1832, fine arts were integrally intertwined with natural history. James Audubon with his paintings of flora and fauna, and the Hudson River School of landscape art, for example, constituted an important genre in the early days of the United States that made significant illustrative connections for American collectors. The pioneers in a new land sought information that was immediately useful to them. Their natural environment and related phenomena were of greater importance, and that type of art was more closely related to their daily lives.

One of the most influential in the development of museums in the United States has been the Smithsonian Institution, established in 1846 following a bequest in 1826 by James Smithson, an Englishman and scientist, who had never been to this country. Smithson directed that the institution should provide for "the increase and diffusion of knowledge among men." How the institution would fulfill that mandate was debated then and, in some quarters, is still debated today. While most people felt that research should play a prominent role, it has been argued over these many years that a balance with education should prevail, as museums have increasingly become major learning-resources for their communities.

The Smithsonian's first secretary, Joseph Henry, a scientist, adamantly stated: "There are at this time thousands of institutions actively engaged in the diffusion of knowledge in our country, but not a single one which gives direct support to its increase."[10] Congress' specific legislative interpretation of Smithson's will was confined to provisions for a library, museum, art gallery, and lecture rooms. In 1847 the Board of Regents modified Henry's elaborate research plan and, upon Henry's death in 1878, with help from Congress, eventually established a national museum. Still in the 1930s a sign outside of the Smithsonian Castle building read: "The Smithsonian Institution is not a museum."

It was said that Louis Agassiz, a scientist, dreamed of a museum that would be a library of the works of God. This dream was realized with the founding of the Gray Museum of Comparative Zoology at Harvard. Agassiz meant for the museum both to teach and research in science and simultaneously to popularize science by encouraging visitors, producing exhibitions, and providing teacher training for the public schools. His was an ambition to create a truly American museum.

Some referred to this movement in museums as the great American compromise. Scientists thought scholarship was being compromised in the interest of educating the masses. Others argued that exposure of the fascinating collections for the general public should be emphasized. The great compromise really never came about; museums simply went in different directions. As S. Dillon Ripley has expressed it:

> All of these science and art museums of the 19th century began to show the same signs of divisions of goals and of cross-purposes [as the Smithsonian]. Which came first, the scholar or the collection? And where did the collector fit in? If a scholar, not a collector, wished to work at research with the collections, would [she or he] be welcome? What were the collections for? With the development of museums as great public institutions, there came a sense of muzziness about their purpose.[11]

There was a "muzziness" too about the few museum staff positions that existed. They were mostly curatorial in function, but their purposes and responsibilities were not defined within the context of a profession.

The rise of the public museum (and big benefactions)

In the second half of the nineteenth century, actually after the Civil War, a building "boom" of public museums accompanied increasing industrialization. New industries, with their new technologies, hired great numbers of workers and made fortunes for their owners. They founded many of the nation's important art museums in this period, including the Boston Museum of Fine Arts, the Metropolitan Museum of Art (a private/public partnership) in New York, the Art Institute of Chicago, and the Detroit Institute of Arts. As private wealth accumulated, private art collecting expanded, and the captains of industry and finance became museum benefactors and trustees.

At the same time the educational nature and responsibilities of museums took on a greater importance. In New York, city tax support for museums was established, and the city fathers issued an edict that museums should be as important and beneficial an agent in the instruction of the people as any of the schools or colleges of the city. State governments began to help subsidize existing institutions and to establish some of the first state-operated museums, often as outgrowths of old-line private historical and philosophical societies. Increasingly, immigrants and working people were welcomed into museums, a sign and portent of American democracy in action.

Natural history museums continued to emphasize research, putting heavily classified topological and taxonomical exhibitions on display. History museums, receiving an impetus from the 1876 Centennial and the 1893 Columbian expositions, consistently increased in number faster than all other kinds of museums, but individually they remained small and local. While expositions were initially conceived as trade fairs, they contributed to the commemoration of our country's history. They also celebrated the newest developments in science and technology, art, and horticulture as practiced and promoted by the new and thriving private industries.

Changes in museum operations accompanied this museum "boom." Staffs increased, but they were not always paid. As collections grew, however, a new kind of expertise was required, and the position of curator – the "keeper" of the collections – came into being. Changes in museum governance took place as well, partly to satisfy the wealthy collectors who were donating collections establishing museums. These people wanted a voice in decision-making and assurances that the museums would care for and exhibit their collections. They became trustees, and many museums became what would later be called nonprofit corporations, governed by boards of trustees. The staff, directors, and curators became answerable and accountable to those boards. New museum organizational structures were being formed, forerunners of today's museum operations (see organization charts in Appendix). Funds, as well as a volunteer work force, mostly women, were provided by individuals, both traditions continuing today.

While women played an extremely important role as volunteers, they were not always recognized or even acknowledged by their male colleagues. Yet a number of outstanding women were important in the establishment of major museums in the late nineteenth and the first half of the twentieth century. Among them are the Cooper–Hewitt Museum in New York founded by Sarah and Eleanor Hewitt in 1897; the Isabella Stewart Gardner Museum in Boston in 1900; Juliana Force and Gertrude Vanderbilt Whitney founded the Whitney Museum of American Art in New York City in 1930, and Force became its first director; and the Museum of Modern Art in New York founded in 1929 by Abby Aldrich Rockefeller, Lizzie Bliss, and Cornelia J. Sullivan. Ellen Scripps Booth established the Cranbrook Museums of Science and Art in Michigan. Women served as founders, directors, and curators of some of America's most important museums.

The emergence of the educational museum

In the early years of the twentieth century museums became educational institutions in earnest, and museum work emerged from "club activity" to "public service." Henry Cole, director of the Victoria and Albert Museum (then called the South Kensington Museum) in London in 1852 exerted some influence on American museums with his "world's fair" types of displays, lectures, seminars, publications, parties, and night openings. His "popular education" was a forerunner of the modern American museum.

Museums began to cooperate with schools and to establish schools of their own. The first school museum was established in St Louis, Missouri, in 1903. On the east coast, the Newark Museum was an early educational institution, and its founder, John Cotton Dana, wrote in 1917:

> Communities are still taxing themselves to get, and are asking private benefactors to get for them, marble palaces with those so-called emblems of culture, rare and costly and wonder-working objects. We can only say that, frankly, we cannot discover advantages to any community, from the presence in it of one of these culture-fetishes, at all commensurate with its cost. It serves no definite and expressed needs. It is alien to its community in every respect of that community's life.[12]

Putting into practice his strong belief that museums should educate all elements of the public, Dana established a program at the Newark Museum for what was likely the first "community" museum in the United States, reaching out to minorities, the disadvantaged, and the uneducated.

As early as 1900, the third secretary of the Smithsonian, Samuel P. Langley, created a special children's room in the first Smithsonian building (known today as "the Castle"). With low cases to accommodate the small visitor, he presented live birds, fish, and turtles along with rocks and minerals and mounted animals. As the self-appointed honorary curator of the Smithsonian's children's room, Langley wanted children to enjoy a museum as much as adults did. Other individuals and groups shared Langley's concern with making museums serve children. Children's museums, an American phenomenon, actually trace back to 1899, when the Brooklyn Children's Museum was founded. More than three hundred such institutions currently offer youth- and family-oriented exhibitions and activities. Pioneers in contemporary public education and appealing to the often neglected tactile senses, children's museums – along with science centers later – offer a motivating learning environment.

During the first half of the twentieth century, museums emerged as truly public institutions. They initiated new collaborations with public and private schools and developed programs in elementary and secondary education. New publications were designed for the general public. A self-conscious professionalism in the conduct of museum work was advanced by the establishment of the American Association of Museums (AAM) in 1906.

Due in a large part to staff increases and the growing compartmentalization of duties, serious consideration was given to the organizational structure of museums. Staff were hired to care for the collections, to do research on the collections, and to educate and interpret them for the public. Displays became more sophisticated as collections were interpreted around themes. Period rooms, natural habitats, dioramas, live demonstrations, and outdoor living history museums all testify to the growing bank of knowledge that started to make museum work a profession. Many constructive ideas had come from the thinking of George Brown Goode, curator (1878) and assistant secretary

(1879) of the National Museum at the Smithsonian. Goode wanted museums "to be transformed from 'bric-à-brac' cemeteries to nurseries of living thought and to retain their vitality in a continuous process of evolution."[13] Although the mission and goals of museums were yet to be clearly defined, the aesthetic, historical, and scientific preservation of collections became an increasing concern. There was greater need for preservation, in fact, as increased display entailed increased handling, and increasing environmental pollution meant that collections were disintegrating more rapidly.

With the advent of the automobile, national parks, state parks, and historic landmarks drew unprecedented numbers of visitors, and they began to establish visitor centers that imitated and shared the educational responsibilities of museums. Theirs was a different kind of mission, however: to preserve and interpret our natural, as well as cultural, heritage. The National Park Service, and natural and historic sites managed by state and local governments, probably recognized the advantages (exposure for more visitors) and disadvantages (deterioration and damage to property) of "cultural tourism" long before museum people began to discuss it.

The automobile and other improvements in transportation also brought greater numbers of visitors to museums. Out-of-the-way historic houses, in particular, became popular destinations for motorists. Larger museums began lending collections to smaller ones, and schools received objects on loan for the first time. All these expanded activities increased the need for additional staff, although historic sites and historical societies continued to rely heavily on volunteers to meet and greet the public and to care for collections. Not even the Great Depression or World War II deterred museum visitors. In fact, in hard times people seemed to need museums more than ever. They were free, and they took one's mind off the problems and restrictions of daily life. As America's family farms and small towns disappeared, museums that preserved the past were sought out for the sake of both scholarship and nostalgia.

New types of museums were emerging. Following the lead of Sweden's Nordiska Museet in Stockholm, established in 1891, and with the impetus of the preservation movement, "living history" museums were established in the United States. Colonial Williamsburg in Virginia was restored and re-created, through the beneficence of John D. Rockefeller, Jr. and Greenfield Village was re-created in Michigan by Henry Ford. These "total environments" bestowed a sense of "community" upon static museum buildings and honored famous people and regional events. Just as important, they evidenced the continuation of private initiative in supporting museums. Edward Alexander observed: "Now the museum and the picnic could be combined and the whole family might share in enjoyment of the national heritage."[14]

The Museum of Modern Art in New York, founded in 1929, laid the groundwork for acceptance of contemporary art in the United States. The National Gallery of Art in Washington, DC, opened its doors in 1941, a gift to the United States from Andrew W. Mellon. Other donors to the Gallery followed suit, with collections based on the same standard of excellence stipulated by Mellon. These museums catered to elite audiences quite different from those nurtured by history and natural history museums.

Astute observers recognized the unique institution that America's museums had become. Francis H. Taylor explained: "The American museum is neither an abandoned European palace nor a solution for storing national wealth. It is an American phenomenon developed by the people, for the people and of the people."[15] There were still conflicting ideas about the educational role of museums, however. Some viewed museums as social instruments, change agents that could help to improve society. Others, such as Dana, argued that museums were an educational force contributing to the economic and cultural life of their communities. Yet others questioned whether education could solve society's ills. And still others believed every object of art should communicate to the viewer with as little interference (interpretation) as possible.

The increase in museum attendance also gave rise to questions about quality vs. quantity: were numbers a reliable indicator of excellence or success? The doubters were overwhelmed by the increasing proliferation of museum activities: conducted tours, loan collections, lectures, and special interest groups. More and more people, from all walks of life, came to museums, and increasing numbers became museum members, broadening the base of museum support.

The proliferating museum activities attracted the attention of behavioral psychologists, who assessed the learning experiences of museum visitors and examined the relationships between exhibitions and learning. In the late 1920s Edward D. Robinson, of Yale University, pioneered studies that led to the more recent surge of research and evaluation of visitor behavior. Skepticism of visitors' studies flourished (but has now abated), as many museum people felt that you don't have to kick a tire to know it's flat! Independent consultants have dominated the field, producing many beneficial visitor studies and prompting a few large museums to hire a staff evaluator.

About 1930, museums began to evidence a serious interest in conservation of objects, artifacts, and works of art in their care. Conservation began to be recognized as an integral part of a museum's mission. Despite conflicts between conservation (preservation, care, and treatment of objects) and curatorship (research, study, and writing about objects), and between conservation and exhibiting (public display of objects), the field of conservation has steadily progressed. Matter has finite life, and it is the role of the museum to minimize and delay the process. Conservators, previously recognized only as technicians, are now professionals and an integral part of the higher levels of the museum profession. So are conservation scientists, as scientific research in this field has been slowly accumulating important contributions for the preservation of collections. The role of scientific inquiry is virtually indispensable to historians and anthropologists, for example, to understand fully the materials of the objects in their care.

The emergence of professional organizations such as the American Institute for Conservation (AIC), the International Institute for Conservation (IIC), the National Institute of Conservation (NIC), and the International Conservation Center (ICCROM) in Rome underscores the importance of individuals pursuing conservation as a career. The AIC Code of Ethics is further testimony to the professional status of conservators and conservation scientists.

In tandem with emerging specialties is the proliferation of the *museum worker*, one whose primary goal is to carry out the mission of the museum. Some may be called generalists or museologists, but many others are those who are astute enough to value the purposes and goals of the museum above their narrower areas of interest.

Today: museums in crisis, and museum diversity

In Search of Excellence, written by Thomas J. Peters and Robert H. Waterman, Jr. in 1983, was not at all related to museums, but the title and contents inspired many in the museum field to explore and scrutinize the search for excellence among American museums. Museums were questioning the fulfillment of their missions and the means and methods utilized to carry out their goals and objectives. Was quantity superseding quality? Was entertainment superseding education? What is excellence in museums? By whose standards? Interest in the book presented an opportunity to examine excellence in the context of museums, a goal that had not always been on the agendas of museums as they zealously pursued their activities. The Kellogg Foundation/Smithsonian Educational Project, underway from 1982 to 1988, was an example of an initiative and major project to search for museum educational excellence. Similar Kellogg projects were conducted at the Exploratorium in San Francisco and the Field Museum of Natural History in Chicago. In 1968 Thomas Hoving, director of the Metropolitan Museum, had declared that the museum possesses "a great potential, not only as a stabilizing, regenerative force in modern society, but as a crusading force for quality and excellence."[16]

The second half of the twentieth century has seen museums making efforts to attract visitors, popularize their programs, and provide services for the disadvantaged and for special audiences. More attention is paid to professionalism (ethics and standards) in the ranks of staff, as well as to specializations,

---

"In a community the size of ours, [referring to the Crocker Art Museum in Sacramento, California] the museum seems to form in some ways the cultural heart of the community, and especially because of its historic content and building. I refer to the museum as the community's living room, and a place where people can come together in an atmosphere of mutual understanding, celebration, cultural achievement, with provocative questions that can be raised in a safe haven. In some ways, the museum is more accessible to a broader segment of the community than the university."

Barbara K. Gibbs, Cincinnati Art Museum

> "I think that museums like the Studio Museum and our museum are so important because it's through these museums that individuals from our community are going to become interested in museums, and potentially they may also go to other museums. Museums like ours are going to open up the museum field . . . and make sure jobs are available."
>
> *Marie Acosta Colon, The Mexican Museum*

institutional needs, and training. Museum studies programs began proliferating in the 1970s as more students became interested in museums, and as universities, facing declining enrollments, sought to add new programs. Their popularity also raised concern about the quality of the training (see Chapter 8). More and more professional organizations, institutions, and outside consultants began offering mid-career training. These programs emphasized expanding interpretive exhibitions with audiovisuals, using docents as guides, up-to-date registration methods, the basics of museum management, refining living history techniques, computer usage for record keeping, and participatory, experiential, and interactive exhibitions. Research again was strengthened as an integral aspect of museum pursuits.

In *Museums: In Search of a Usable Future*, Alma Wittlin recalled the 1960s as "a time for meandering questions more than for definite answers: what indeed were the primary functions of museums? Did all museums have to follow the pattern of a uniform purpose? If museums did not exist, would people of the 20th century feel the need to invent them?"[17] These questions have been examined and re-examined, and many new ones have been added. The museum field continues to seek answers, but during the last few decades museums in the United States have taken giant steps toward professionalism, quality, integrity, and, indeed, excellence.

The numbers of museums in the United States have increased enormously. In the 1960s, a new museum was established every 3.3 days. In 1967 there were approximately 5,000 museums. Many were due to either community business expansion, making cultural attractions more important, or to individual or collective special interests in specific collections. There were in 1994 8,200 museums of all sizes, disciplines, and types in the country. The most recent spurt of growth occurred during the Bicentennial in 1976, when communities, searching for their historical identities, established museums to reflect local pride and cultural heritage.

The museum universe, as defined by the AAM, expanded from the traditional art, history, and natural history disciplines to include art centers, science and technology centers, zoos, botanical gardens, planetariums, nature centers, aquariums, and children's museums. While differing greatly in their specialties and disciplines, there is a thread of commonality among them: most of them collect, preserve, research, exhibit, and interpret, though in very different ways. They are the tactile and material conscience of humankind for civilizations that are sometimes in great turmoil and adversity. They educate, enlighten, and uplift the human spirit in an uncertain and changing world.

During recent decades, the emphasis on cultural pluralism has resulted in the founding of numerous culturally specific museums. People from many backgrounds are interested in preserving their cultural heritage, and today there are more than 120 African American museums, more than 100 Native American museums, and Jewish museums in most major cities. Asian and Latino cultural centers and museums are appearing in areas with large representative populations, as are many Euro-centrist museums.

New technologies have had an impact not only in exhibition techniques and museum operations but as the focus of new museums – those of television, radio, computers, photography, aviation, space exploration, and the history of technology. Think of the staff specialties required to function in these settings!

In fact, there are museums in the United States to match every possible (and sometimes improbable) interest: museums of glass, railroads, electricity, maritime artifacts, jails, American crafts, folk art, deserts, the military, canals, coal, oil, fire, sports, decorative arts, and, most recently, women's history and art, and the Holocaust. The Andy Warhol Museum, the Lower East Side Tenement Museum, the Museum of the Titanic, the General Shale Museum of Brick, the Pony Express Museum, the Bicycle Museum, and the Cryptographic Museum have opened. The newest and newsiest is the planned Newseum in Arlington, Virginia. It is interesting to note that in the 1950s the growth of industry-sponsored museums promulgated outstanding intellectual examples such as the Corning Museum of Glass in Corning, New York, the Hagley Museum and Library in Wilmington, Delaware, founded by the DuPont Corporation, and more recently the Kellogg Museum in Michigan. Museums are, essentially, a cross-section of America.

Although museums have common purposes and functions, their diverse subject-matter has prompted increased specialization among staff. Background in the discipline of the museum is not as simple as it used to be when art, history, and the sciences were the focus of museums. Additional advanced and mid-career studies are sometimes required to keep pace with the ever-changing and developing museum field.

Geographic areas that have experienced population growth have also seen a rapid increase in numbers of museums. According to *Museums for a New Century*,[18] since 1964 thirty new art museums have been built or are in the advanced stages of planning in the western states, and the number of all types of museums in Texas has increased sixfold, from 106 to 650, in the last fifteen years. Florida had thirty new museums since 1964 – excluding Disney World – an increase of 67 percent. In the 1960s Oregon had twelve museums; in 1992 there were eighty. In California, the state-park system alone has 229 museums.

These diverse institutions are largely independent entities and not part of any governmental or organized system. They also are widely divergent in size, governance, and sources of funding. A majority of American museums are governed by private voluntary boards of trustees that establish policies, seek funding, and approve the budgets of their institutions. They hire the director and are responsible for any legal actions taken by or against the museum. These boards are subject to the laws of their states regarding nonprofit, charitable organizations (see Chapter 4).

Slightly more than two thousand museums are operated by governments, mostly at state, county or municipal levels. Another substantial number of museums are constituent parts of schools, colleges, and universities. The federal government provides tax dollars to help support the National Park Service museums, presidential libraries and museums, the National Gallery, various armed-forces museums (with military bases closing, some of these are being converted to the private sector), and the Smithsonian Institution. These museums usually depend very heavily upon private support as well. Federal grants are available to museums, upon submission and approval of proposals for specific needs and projects, from the National Endowment for the Arts, the National Endowment for the Humanities, the Institute for Museum Services, the National Science Foundation and a few other federal agencies (see Appendix C). All are being threatened with major cut-backs in 1995–6.

More than half of American museums are history museums, including historic houses and sites, historical societies, living history farms and villages, and state, county, and city historical institutions. The next largest discipline group in numbers – albeit the largest in attendance and budgets – are the science museums, which include natural history museums, science and technology centers, planetariums, nature centers, aquariums, zoos, and botanical gardens. Art museums place third in both attendance and numbers.

There are few reliable statistics on visitor attendance. In the last two decades, however, museums have made a far greater effort than before to attract new and special audiences, and there has been a boom in attendance. A poll in 1980 indicated that 68 percent of Americans go to museums, 3 percent higher than the numbers who go to sports events, and the percentage is higher in the 1990s. There have been a few short periods of decline in attendance owing to threats of crime or terrorism in some large cities, the financial recession, or the cost of gasoline and air travel. The Smithsonian alone, with its sixteen museums, attracts about 25 million visitors per year.

But are high attendance figures an indication of excellence? A. E. Parr of the American Museum of Natural History in New York warned that:

> the grossness of a purely quantitative self-esteem may also back-fire in the end. It should not be forgotten that the Roman circuses likewise enjoyed excellent attendance records. The question is not how many arrive, but how well they are served by what they find when they get there.[19]

The growth of professionalism

The size and scope of American museums must be considered when examining their quest for quality and excellence, and for understanding the diffuse staffing situations within their varied organizational structures. For the most part, their growth and development have been accomplished without government-mandated national policy, regulation, or central direction of any type. Obviously, there are advantages and disadvantages, strengths and weaknesses, in such a system. Jealously guarding their independence and autonomy, United States museums have enormous opportunities for innovation, creativity, and flexibility. Without central controls and bureaucratization, delays can be minimized and problem-solving and decision-making become more imaginative and resourceful. Long-range and strategic planning can take many forms. On the other hand, there is duplication of effort, there are few national arts initiatives, no national or international cultural policies, and no means yet of nationwide data collection. Most significant, the search for excellence must constantly adapt to the ongoing struggle for dependable funding sources. Our foreign colleagues, most of whose museums are supported by their governments, are now experiencing comparable financial problems and are approaching corporations and private individuals for support.

There is no mechanism for a central governmental museum authority in the United States and little desire for one. As a result, numerous voluntary professional associations have assumed a prominent role in promulgating the mission of museums. The AAM is the "umbrella" professional organization, with a membership in 1995 of approximately 11,000 individuals and 2,987 institutions. Other associations include the American Association for State and Local History (AASLH), the Association of Science–Technology Centers (ASTC), the Association of Art Museum Directors (AAMD), the College Art Association (CAA), the Association of Youth Museums (AYM), the Science Museum Directors Association, other specialized associations, and regional and state museum associations (see Appendix B).

In its search for excellence, the museum community is also attempting to define itself and its essential characteristics. The 1968 Belmont Report, a United States museums study by the National Endowment for the Arts, examined the services museums offer and called for the establishment of measurable standards. The report urged "that the AAM and its member institutions develop and agree upon acceptable criteria and methods for accrediting museums."[20] In response, in 1970 the AAM established the Museum Accreditation Program. After a careful examination and identification of all the functions and

---

"The museum is an educational resource, and not simply a storehouse ... with an intellectual capacity for research, education, and exhibitions."
JoAllyn Archambault, National Museum of Natural History

characteristics of museums, the AAM instituted a self-evaluation and peer-review process to recognize and promote professional standards. With the start of accreditation, United States museums finally had a means of measuring excellence. As a basis for accreditation, the AAM developed a definition of a museum to determine eligibility:

> For the purpose of the Accreditation program of the AAM, a museum is defined as an organized and permanent non-profit institution, essentially educational or aesthetic in purpose, with professional staff, which owns and utilizes tangible objects, cares for them and exhibits them to the public on some regular schedule.[21]

Almost simultaneously, the International Council of Museums (ICOM) devised a similar definition of a museum:

> A museum is a non-profitmaking, permanent institution in the service of society and of its development, and open to the public, which acquires, conserves, researches, communicates, and exhibits, for purposes of study, education, and enjoyment, material evidence of humankind and its environment.[22]

After two years of committee deliberations, the AAM membership accepted the basic definition with additional clarifications: "professional staff" meant professionals in a field relevant to museology and to the museum's discipline and with a capability for scholarship; "educational" required the "knowledgeable utilization" of objects through exhibitions and interpretation. Through accreditation, the commonality of functions among museums served as the criterion in the search for standards, quality, and excellence.

Joseph V. Noble, then director of the Museum of the City of New York, declared in 1970, in no order of priority:

> The five responsibilities: acquisition, conservation, study, interpretation, and exhibition are, of course, interrelated; together they form an entity. They are like the five fingers of a hand, each independent but united for a common purpose. If a museum omits or slights any of these five responsibilities, it has handicapped itself immeasurably, and I seriously doubt whether such a museum will survive in the challenging years that lie ahead. Conversely, if we each strengthen our own institutions in these five inseparable areas, we will fulfill our obligations to the past and present and our aspirations for the future.[23]

Acknowledging that Noble's analysis has been extremely useful as a sturdy framework, Stephen Weil believes that a superseding paradigm now appears to be emerging. In 1990, Weil, deputy director of the Hirshhorn Museum and Sculpture Garden, proposed three essential functions of museums: to preserve, to study, and to communicate. He wrote:

> If this emerging three-function paradigm appears to be of value, the effort to more fully articulate the range and consequences of its third term ought to be pursued. . . . We need to be able to define the purposes for

which a museum deals with its public in far finer and more precise ways than we thus far have.[24]

Since 1970, the AAM Accreditation Commission has regularly assessed, revised, and strengthened its guidelines and has added definitions for accreditation of planetariums, science and technology centers, art centers, historic sites, zoos, botanical gardens, and aquariums. A reaccreditation program, for those museums first accredited in the 1970s, was established in the early 1980s to assure the maintenance of the standards and criteria. By 1995, there were 746 accredited museums.

A new vision of the museum's role in society has emerged along with a renewed sense of responsibility to preserve and transmit cultural values for humankind. The methods, skills, techniques and practices used to fulfill these roles varies as greatly as the types, disciplines, and sizes of museums in the United States. The diversity of museum goals, objectives, and organization reflects the diversity of American society. As interests, directions, information, technology, and activities shift, the character of the museum may shift as well. Museums are pliable educational and social institutions and appear to move in several directions at the same time.

Nonetheless, museums of today are for the public, including all ages, disregarding economic wherewithal, educated or not, and from all segments of society – at least, that is the ideal sought by enlightened museum professionals who are working in museums, by the communities they serve, and by the other institutions that are closely involved with the museums.

The barometer for the search for excellence may be found in the great commonality among museums the world over that seek to collect and preserve, research, exhibit, interpret and, yes, to communicate. Transcending differences in political systems and cultures is an enthusiastic commitment to preserve and share the resources of our world and human history. People in countries everywhere are dedicated to ensuring a healthy and dynamic climate for museums.

Indeed, we may be returning to the philosophy of the *mouseion* in a way, but today the museum is the learning center and "academy" for the general public rather than for the elite, a place where everyone may "muse," inquire, cogitate, and communicate. Said S. Dillon Ripley, former secretary of the Smithsonian: "Somewhere within these realms [museums] there are clues to our understanding of ourselves, and, I suspect, our survival."[25]

Notes

1   Stephen Jay Gould, *Eight Little Piggies: Reflections in Natural History* (New York: Norton, 1993), p. 324.

2   Donald Horne, *The Great Museum: The Re-Presentation of History* (London, UK: Pluto Press, 1984), p. 14.

3   Eilean Hooper-Greenhill, quoted in Kevin Walsh, *The Representation of the Past* (London, UK: Routledge, 1992), p. 18.

4   Joel Orosz, *Curators and Culture: The Museum Movement in America, 1740–1870* (Tuscaloosa, Ala.: University of Alabama Press, 1990), p. 9.

5   John Adams, to his wife, Abigail Adams, 1780, *Familiar Letters of John Adams and his Wife, Abigail Adams, During the Revolution* (New York: Hurd & Houghton, 1876), p. 381.

6   Gary Kulik, introduction to *Mermaids, Mummies, and Mastodons: The Emergence of the American Museum*, ed. William T. Alderson, (Washington, DC: American Association of Museums, 1992), p. 11.

7   Harold Skramstad, address to International Research and Exchanges Board/German Democratic Republic Seminar, "Museums as Learning Resources," October 3, 1988, Gaussig, Germany.

8   Louis Leonard Tucker, *A Cabinet of Curiosities: Five Episodes in the Evolution of American Museums*, (Charlottesville, Va: University of Virginia Press, 1967), pp. 73–4.

9   Ildiko Heffernan, "The Campus Art Museum Today," *Museum News* 65, no. 5 (June, 1987): 26.

10 Joseph Henry, quoted in Tucker, *Cabinet of Curiosities*, p. 109.

11 S. Dillon Ripley, *The Sacred Grove: Essays on Museums* (Washington, DC: Smithsonian Institution Press, 1978), p. 51.

12 John Cotton Dana, *The New Museum* (Woodstock, VT: The Elon Tree Press, 1917), p. 32.

13 George Brown Goode, "The Principles of Museum Administration," *Annual Report of the U.S. National Museum, 1897* (Washington, DC, Government Printing Office, 1901), p. 206.

14 Edward P. Alexander, *Museums in Motion: An Introduction to the History and Functions of Museums* (Nashville, Tenn.: American Association of State and Local History, 1979), p. 86.

15 Francis H. Taylor, *Babel's Tower, The Dilemma of the Modern Museum* (New York: Columbia University Press, 1945), p. 21.

16 Thomas Hoving, quoted in Alexander, *Museums in Motion*, p. 19.

17 Alma Wittlin, *Museums in Search of a Usable Future* (Cambridge, Mass.: MIT Press, 1970), p. 217.

18 American Association of Museums, Commission on Museums for a New Century, *Museums for a New Century* (Washington, DC: American Association of Museums, 1984), p. 28.

19 A. E. Parr, "Museums and Realities of Human Existence," *Museum News* 45, no. 4 (December, 1966): 25.

20 *America's Museums* [Belmont Report] (Washington, DC: National Endowment for the Arts and American Association of Museums, 1968).

21 American Association of Museums, *Museum Accreditation: A Report to the Profession* (Washington, DC: American Association of Museums, 1970), p. 6.

22 International Council of Museums, *ICOM Statutes: ICOM Code of Professional Ethics* (Paris: International Council of Museums, 1990), p. 1.

23 Joseph V. Noble, "Museum Manifesto," *Museum News* 48, no. 8 (April, 1970): 20.

24   Stephen Weil, "Rethinking the Museum," *Museum News* 69, no. 8 (March/April, 1990): 60.
25   Ripley, *The Sacred Grove*, p. 13.

Bibliography: Museums – yesterday and today

Alexander, Edward P., *Museum Masters: Their Museums and Their Influence* (Nashville, Tenn.: American Association for State and Local History, 1983). A study of the men and women whose concepts fostered the establishment of museums as educational institutions and the ways they implemented their individual philosophies.

——, *Museums in Motion: An Introduction to the History and Function of Museums* (Nashville, Tenn.: American Association for State and Local History, 1979). The history of museums and their changing roles according to changes in society; explores the different functions of today's museums.

The American Museum Experience: In Search of Excellence (Edinburgh, UK: Scottish Museum Council, 1986). Puts in historical perspective and contemporary context issues important to American museums such as museum management, education, and fund-raising.

Horne, Donald, *The Great Museum: The Re-Presentation of History* (London, UK: Pluto Press, 1984). Discusses how European history is presented through its museums and monuments.

Lumley, Robert, ed., *The Museum Time-Machine: Putting Cultures on Display* (London, UK: Routledge, 1988). Chapter 3 treats the evolution and role of a museum in a community from a social history viewpoint.

Noble, Joseph Veach, "More Than a Mirror to the Past," *Curator* 16, no. 3 (1973): 272–5. Deals with the issue of cultural identity within the mission of history museums.

——, "Museum Manifesto," *Museum News* 48, no. 8 (1970): 16–20. Discusses the evolution of museums and their roles, functions, and responsibilities, including acquisition, conservation, study, interpretation, and exhibition.

Thompson, John M. A., ed., *Manual of Curatorship: A Guide to Museum Practice*, 2nd ed. (Oxford, UK: Butterworth–Heinemann, 1992). Manual on relevant museum issues including history and kinds of museums, management, conservation, research, and user services; part 1 focuses on the history of museums.

Wittlin, Alma Stephanie, *The Museum, its History and its Tasks in Education* (London, UK: Routledge, 1949). Discusses the history of the museum (collections in relation to museums) and the role of the museum as an educational institution (research, students' galleries, centers for training and services).

——, *Museums: In Search of a Usable Future* (Cambridge, Mass.: MIT Press, 1970). Discusses the emergence and history of collections and museums and suggests directions for museum renewal.

Suggested readings

Alderson, William T., ed., *Mermaids, Mummies, and Mastodons: The Emergence of the American Museum* (Washington, DC: American Association of Museums, 1992).

Belk, Russell, *Collecting in a Consumer Society* (University of Utah Press, 1995).

Brigham, David R., *Public Culture in the Early Republic: Peale's Museum and its Audience* (Washington, DC: Smithsonian Institution Press, 1995).

Burt, Nathaniel, *Palaces for the People* (Boston, Mass.: Little, Brown, and Company 1977).

Hudson, Kenneth. *Museums for the 1980's: A Survey of World Trends* (New York: Holmes and Meier, 1977).

Karp, Ivan, Christine Muller Kreamer, and Steven D. Lavine, eds, *Museums and Communities: The Politics of Public Culture* (Washington, DC: Smithsonian Institution Press, and American Association of Museums, 1992).

McClellan, Andrew, *Inventing the Louvre: Art, Politics, and the Origins of the Modern Museum in Eighteenth Century Paris* (New York: Cambridge University Press, 1994).

Pearce, Susan, *Museums, Objects and Collections: A Cultural Study* (Washington, DC: Smithsonian Institution Press, 1993).

Richardson, Edgar P. "The Museum in America, 1963," *Museum News* 62, no. 3 (1984): 41–5.

Schlereth, Thomas J., ed., *Material Culture Studies in America* (Nashville, Tenn.: American Association for State and Local History, 1982).

Shapiro, Michael Steven, ed., *The Museum: A Reference Guide* (New York: Greenwood Press, 1990).

Tucker, Louis Leonard, *A Cabinet of Curiosities: Five Episodes in the Evolution of American Museums* (Charlottesville, Va: University Press of Virginia, 1967).

Part II
Principles and standards
of museums

Principles and standards of museums: prologue

Museums are unique organizations with an array of philosophies, missions, and governing bodies that require a special kind of professionalism and ethical conduct. They are workplaces that demand adherence to codes of conduct, bylaws, and policies unlike most other types of professions. Most museums are governed by boards of trustees who volunteer their time, expertise, and energies for the betterment of their educational and cultural communities. These same museums function because of dedicated, committed, and professional staff who manage, administer, and program their institutions as services for their publics. The staff and trustees must abide by myriad laws that affect almost every aspect of their operations. In addition, they have a strong inner conscience and deep sense of integrity that go beyond the letter of the law. The mantle of success goes to those special people who honorably and professionally run our museums.

> There is a professional ethic that museums need to be responsible to their many publics. We are stewards, we are only going to be here for a brief period of time. It's our responsibility to make sure that our museum is meeting its obligation as a public trust to serve the public.
> Robert Macdonald, Museum of the City of New York

> I think one of the great things about museum careers across the board is *ethics*. It may be one of the last bastions where ethics is one of the top priorities that we strive to uphold.
> Barbara K. Gibbs, Cincinnati Art Museum

> Ethics is very important – there are many temptations as a curator. You have to be very truthful when you are asked to identify objects. If you don't know something, you just say you don't know! Art history is not something you can guess, and you never know what people will do with your comments outside the museum. Most of the time they want to know the value, but this is something we are not allowed to do.
> Terese Tse Bartholomew, Asian Art Museum of San Francisco

> There are changes in the mentality of the boards who are thinking 'business.' There are changes in the necessity of a museum being an entrepreneurial-type atmosphere. Boards are hiring university presidents and

"Almost all law firms feel the need to perform a certain amount of pro bono or free legal services for individuals and nonprofit organizations."

Sean P. Scally, Esq., Assistant Attorney General for Tennessee,
History News 48, no. 4 (July/August, 1993): 26

"The Americans with Disabilities Act of 1990 (ADA) has been called the most sweeping civil rights statute in decades. An estimated 43 million Americans have some form of disability, including hearing, sight, and mobility impairment."

James D. Douglas, ALI–ABA Conference, 1992

corporate managers to run museums. What it really takes is a bigger team of people to fulfill all of the demands, and the discipline person as the director.

Bonnie VanDorn, Association of Science–Technology Centers

I think that museum trustees should be involved in the long-range and strategic planning, as involved as the bylaws call for. I share the view that trustees should establish museum policies, should approve the budgets, and should assist with fund-raising. The most important I think continues to be setting sound policies for the institution.

Jeannine Smith Clark, trustee, Smithsonian Institution

3

Museum ethics: the essence of professionalism

Robert Macdonald

To be a professional requires more than the command of a body of knowledge and skills. Professionalism compels you to apply that expertise in the context of the traditional values of the profession you have chosen. It is important in considering museum work as a career to understand that professionalism means more than competence in a particular area of museum work. In addition to mastering the specific discipline, museum professionals need to master the ethical traditions that will guide their work.

One of the principal characteristics of professions as they developed in the United States has been the ability of individuals working in a particular field to establish self-regulating rules of conduct guiding their work-related activities. These canons evolve out of professional custom and practice developed over years of common experience. The term given these collective convictions is "professional ethics." Some professional standards are codified by outside agencies such as state legislatures and Congress, in which case the precepts become law. However, professional ethics usually call for standards of conduct higher than those required by the law; they are norms agreed to by those who understand and agree to abide by their dictates.

It was for the purpose of self-regulation that the American museum community first articulated its understanding of professional ethics in 1925 through the publication of the *Code of Ethics for Museum Workers*. It is notable that the code was adopted by the profession only nineteen years after the founding of the American Association of Museums in 1906. The promulgation of ethical values by museum workers early in their organizational history makes clear that they viewed themselves as belonging to a profession willing to formalize principles that would inform individual and collective activities. However, in 1925 the fledgling museum profession was unable to go beyond the promulgation of tenets; it did not establish mechanisms to enforce adherence of its members to the code.

"American museums have greatly increased their professionalism in the last half century by agreeing upon a code of ethics."

Edward P. Alexander in Museums in Motion

"All museums have a social responsibility, and it is very hard to balance the political issues from an ethical stance. I think that museums should not avoid issues just because they are controversial, but have a social and ethical balanced look at the issues."

Edith Tonelli, formerly Wight Gallery, UCLA

Fifty-three years would pass before the profession would again formally address the question of museum ethics, a half-century of momentous change in museums, the museum profession, and the society they serve. That society had seen economic depression, war, a communications revolution, changing patterns of wealth and population, increased concern about individual rights, recognition of cultural diversity, and struggles for empowerment by women, ethnic and racial minorities, homosexuals, religious fundamentalists, and a plethora of special interest groups. Between 1925 and 1978 the role of government had also changed dramatically through the New Deal, the Fair Deal, the New Frontier, and a conservative revival. These years also witnessed a dramatic transformation of America's museums. It is estimated that more than three thousand museums of every type and discipline were created in large cities, small villages, and in rural areas throughout the country. University training and specialization created a technically more proficient profession composed of individuals with diverse skills, interests, and approaches to their work. Museums had also become "big business," drawing large audiences, the infusion of public and private wealth, grand expansion plans, "blockbuster" exhibitions, and major collection acquisitions. Along with this tremendous growth came the occasional museum scandal and public controversy, leading to an increase in governmental scrutiny.

It was in this context that the AAM issued *Museum Ethics* in 1978. While not a code, *Museum Ethics* presented the current thinking on a variety of museum-related issues. Where the 1925 code was strong in presenting the philosophical underpinnings of museum work, the 1978 ethics statement focused on internal human and collection management concerns, addressing the "how" of museum work rather than the "why." Unlike the earlier code, the 1978 statement was not adopted by the AAM Council as the official position of the AAM, although in its application *Museum Ethics* was often referred to as if it were a code of ethics. Like the earlier ethics code, the 1978 statement did not provide mechanisms of implementation. The absence of an enforcement mechanism weakened the impact of the 1978 ethics statement on the operations of America's museums.

Even with these shortcomings, the 1978 statement on ethics served the profession well and was used both by the museum community and by others such as governmental agencies and the press. In its approach it reflected the growing stress on a profession faced with increased public pressure and the changing roles and relationships of volunteer boards of trustees and paid specialists. Because the statement presented professional prerogatives rather than professional responsibilities, it could be argued that the 1978 document was a reaction by a profession splintered by specialization, unsure of either its past or its future, and unable to find a common philosophical ground for its activities.

While *Museum Ethics* proved useful in fighting internal battles, many were dissatisfied with its inability to curb abuses by individuals and institutions and clearly enunciate a professional philosophy to the public. The rise in public criticism and controversy, as seen in increasing governmental oversight of museums and their activities, indicated that the museum community would be unable to avoid addressing ethical issues and establishing mechanisms for self-regulation for another fifty years.

The deficiencies of the 1978 statement were highlighted in 1986 when the International Council of Museums issued its *Code of Professional Ethics*. The ICOM code provided a philosophical foundation for museum work that closely paralleled the 1925 American code. A comparison of the two documents underscores their shared understanding of traditional professional values:

Museums, in the broadest sense, are institutions which hold their possessions in trust for mankind and for the future welfare of the race. Their value is in direct proportion to the service they render the emotional and intellectual life of the people. The life of the museum worker is essentially one of service.

(*Code of Ethics for Museum Workers*,
American Association of Museums, 1925)

A Museum is defined as a non-profitmaking, permanent institution in the service of society and its development. The museum professional should understand two guiding principles: first, that museums are the object of a public trust whose value to the community is in direct proportion to the quality of service rendered; and, secondly, that intellectual ability and professional knowledge are not, in themselves, sufficient, but must be inspired by a high standard of ethical conduct.

(*Code of Professional Ethics*,
International Council of Museums, 1987)

In 1987, as the president of the AAM, I appointed a committee to begin the work of creating a code of ethics for America's museums. A task force was formed to draft a document that could be reviewed by those the code was intended to serve and recommended to the elected representatives of

"A major prerequisite [for a museum director] is a commitment to the ethical aspects of the profession as well as a thirst for excellence, the only aspect of elitism that is acceptable."

Paul N. Perrot, formerly Santa Barbara Museum of Artt

museums and the museum profession for adoption. Early in its deliberations the members of the task force concluded that, while only individuals could be ethical, only institutions had the capacity to regulate the museum-related behavior of their governing authorities, staffs, and volunteers.

The code was therefore addressed to the nonprofit institutional members of the AAM. It was also recognized that, to be meaningful, the code would need to be enforceable. Enforcement would be voluntary and achieved by requiring that adherence to and application of the code be a condition of institutional membership in the association. This approach to implementing the code would compel the discussion of ethical issues among those working on a museum's behalf and within the context of the institution's mission, history, and resources. The principal goal of the AAM in establishing an ethics code for museums is to provide a framework for advancing the standards and self-regulation of America's museums.

As in the 1925 code and the ICOM document, the concept of public trust in the new American code is characterized as the ideal of stewardship and public confidence rather than a narrower legal definition. The code is directed to the museum community and, because it deals with ethics, is more than a guide for avoiding legal liability. It sets standards higher than the law and is founded on the values held by a majority of the museum field. Those values are not found in dictates from a "higher authority." Rather, they are the traditional perspectives and methodologies that developed over more than a century and a half in the experience of America's museums. Museum ethics are revealed in the declarations of America's museum founders, in the writings and practices of our professional predecessors, and in the conventions maintained by the majority of contemporary museum professionals and their institutions.

Following three years of drafting, debate, and extensive review, the AAM's board of directors adopted the *Code of Ethics for Museums* in May 1991. In its introduction the code states:

> The Code of Ethics for Museums that follows confirms the commitment to professional standards of the 1978 statement on ethics by placing it in the context of the traditional values that have always guided America's museums and were so eloquently expressed in the 1925 code. This new code is informed by a renewed emphasis on the historic American concepts of museums as public trusts and museum work as service to society.

The difficulty in implementing the Code was recognized when the same AAM board suspended the document six months after its adoption in Denver. What followed was an intensive two-year campaign by those opposed to the code to replace it with a document whose premises were that there are no professional museum principles that transcend time, place, and circumstance. As one of the advocates for doing away with the code stated, "The word 'museum' has lost its power to adequately define a coherent body of institutions that have similar missions, goals, and strategies – the only rule that will apply to all museums is that there are no rules that apply to all museums."[1]

Those opposed to the implementation of an effective, self-regulating code focused their attention on the section of the code dealing with the use of funds raised by the disposal of collections (the code restricted those funds to the replenishment of collections) and to the fact that the 1991 code would be implemented by making its adoption a condition of institutional membership in the AAM. It is revealing that no American museum professional had objected to the ICOM's 1987 *Code of Professional Ethics*, from which the AAM code's section restricting the use of disposal funds to replenishment was copied almost verbatim. But, unlike the ICOM document and the earlier 1978 AAM ethics statement, the 1991 code included a voluntary but meaningful mechanism for its implementation by museums of all sizes and types throughout the country. In other words, the 1991 code was a real ethics code that could not be ignored by those museums who wished to be members of the AAM and used only at a museum's convenience.

Fortunately, the AAM board ultimately rejected the attempt to do away with the 1991 code entirely. But they did amend the disposal section to allow for the application of funds raised from collection disposal to collection conservation in addition to acquisitions. The board also did something that may make the whole exercise moot. They made adherence to the code optional for the association's institutional members.

It will take a renewed effort and possibly a new generation of museum professionals to attempt again to advance the profession by implementing an effective ethics code. In that effort it will be necessary to ensure that the original mission of the AAM as a professional association is not replaced by a growing tendency of the AAM to act as a trade association more interested in advocating the needs of museums to elected bodies than advancing the professionalism of museum workers. In the final analysis, if museums and museum professionals are unable to regulate themselves, they will be regulated by government. By failing to carry forward the ethical traditions of their profession, they will diminish their professionalism and expose themselves to losing their most important asset, the trust of the public they were established to serve.

"In my own personal view, personal collecting is inappropriate. I consider it a serious conflict of interest and should not be permitted."
Kenneth Starr, formerly Milwaukee Public Museum

Notes

1   Harold J. Skramstad, Jr, "Excellent Inequities," *Museum News* 72, no. 1 (1993): 50–1

Code of Ethics for Museums

Introduction

Ethical codes evolve in response to changing conditions, values, and ideas. A professional code of ethics must, therefore, be periodically updated. It must also rest upon widely shared values. Although the operating environment of museums grows more complex each year, the root value for museums, the tie that connects all of us together despite our diversity, is the commitment to serving people, both present and future generations. This value guided the creation of and remains the most fundamental principle in the following Code of Ethics for Museums.

Dan Monroe, 1994, AAM President

Code of Ethics for Museums [Published by the American Association of Museums]

Museums make their unique contribution to the public by collecting, preserving, and interpreting the things of this world. Historically, they have owned and used natural objects, living and nonliving, and all manner of human artifacts to advance knowledge and nourish the human spirit. Today, the range of their special interests reflects the scope of human vision. Their missions include collecting and preserving, as well as exhibiting and educating with materials not only owned but also borrowed and fabricated for these ends. Their numbers include both governmental and private museums of anthropology, art history and natural history, aquariums, arboreta, art centers, botanical gardens, children's museums, historic sites, nature centers, planetariums, science and technology centers, and zoos. The museum universe in the United States includes both collecting and noncollecting institutions. Although diverse in their missions, they have in common their nonprofit form of organization and a commitment of service to the public. Their collections and/or the objects they borrow or fabricate are the basis for research, exhibits, and programs that invite public participation.

Taken as a whole, museum collections and exhibition materials represent the world's natural and cultural common wealth. As stewards of that wealth, museums are compelled to advance an understanding of all natural forms and of the human experience. It is incumbent on museums to be resources for humankind and in all their activities to foster an informed appreciation of the rich and diverse world we have inherited. It is also incumbent upon them to preserve that inheritance for posterity.

Museums in the United States are grounded in the tradition of public service. They are organized as public trusts, holding their collections and information as a benefit for those they were established to serve. Members of their governing authority, employees, and volunteers are committed to the interests of these beneficiaries.

The law provides the basic framework for museum operations. As nonprofit institutions, museums comply with applicable local, state, and federal laws and international conventions, as well as with the specific legal standards governing trust responsibilities. This Code of Ethics for Museums takes that compliance as given. But legal standards are a minimum. Museums and those responsible for them must do more than avoid legal liability, they must take affirmative steps to maintain their integrity so as to warrant public confidence. They must act not only legally but also ethically. This Code of Ethics for Museums, therefore, outlines ethical standards that frequently exceed legal minimums.

Loyalty to the mission of the museum and to the public it serves is the essence of museum work, whether volunteer or paid. Where conflicts of interest arise – actual, potential, or perceived – the duty of loyalty must never be compromised. No individual may use his or her position in a museum for personal gain or to benefit another at the expense of the museum, its mission, its reputation, and the society it serves.

For museums, public service is paramount. To affirm that ethic and to elaborate its application to their governance, collections, and programs, the American Association of Museums promulgates this Code of Ethics for Museums. In subscribing to this code, museums assume responsibility for the actions of members of their governing authority, employees, and volunteers in the performance of museum-related duties. Museums, thereby, affirm their chartered purpose, ensure the prudent application of their resources, enhance their effectiveness, and maintain public confidence. This collective endeavor strengthens museum work and the contributions of museums to society – present and future.

Governance

Museum governance in its various forms is a public trust responsible for the institution's service to society. The governing authority protects and enhances the museum's collections and programs and its physical, human, and financial resources. It ensures that all these resources support the museum's mission, respond to the pluralism of society, and respect the diversity of the natural and cultural common wealth.

Thus, the governing authority ensures that:

- all those who work for or on behalf of a museum understand and support its mission and public trust responsibilities
- its members understand and fulfill their trusteeship and act corporately, not as individuals
- the museum's collections and programs and its physical, human, and financial resources are protected, maintained, and developed in support of the museum's mission
- it is responsive to and represents the interests of society
- it maintains a relationship with staff in which shared roles are recognized and separate responsibilities respected
- working relationships among trustees, employees, and volunteers are based on equity and mutual respect
- professional standards and practices inform and guide museum operations
- policies are articulated and prudent oversight is practiced
- governance promotes the public good rather than individual financial gain.

Collections

The distinctive character of museum ethics derives from the ownership, care, and use of objects, specimens, and living collections representing the world's natural and cultural common wealth. This stewardship of collections entails the highest public trust and carries with it the presumption of rightful ownership, permanence, care, documentation, accessibility, and responsible disposal.

Thus, the museum ensures that:

- collections in its custody support its mission and public trust responsibilities
- collections in its custody are protected, secure, unencumbered, cared for, and preserved
- collections in its custody are accounted for and documented
- access to the collections and related information is permitted and regulated
- acquisition, disposal, and loan activities are conducted in a manner that respects the protection and preservation of natural and cultural resources and discourages illicit trade in such materials
- acquisition, disposal, and loan activities conform to its mission and public trust responsibilities

- disposal of collections through sale, trade, or research activities is solely for the advancement of the museum's mission. Proceeds from the sale of nonliving collections are to be used consistent with the established standards of the museum's discipline, but in no event shall they be used for anything other than acquisition or direct care of collections
- the unique and special nature of human remains and funerary and sacred objects is recognized as the basis of all decisions concerning such collections
- collections-related activities promote the public good rather than individual financial gain.

Programs

Museums serve society by advancing an understanding and appreciation of the natural and cultural common wealth through exhibitions, research, scholarship, publications, and educational activities. These programs further the museum's mission and are responsive to the concerns, interests, and needs of society.

Thus, the museum ensures that:

- programs support its mission and public trust responsibilities
- programs are founded on scholarship and marked by intellectual integrity
- programs are accessible and encourage participation of the widest possible audience consistent with its mission and resources
- programs respect pluralistic values, traditions, and concerns
- revenue-producing activities and activities that involve relationships with external entities are compatible with the museum's mission and support its public trust responsibilities
- programs promote the public good rather than individual financial gain.

Promulgation

This Code of Ethics for Museums was adopted by the Board of Directors of the American Association of Museums on November 12, 1993. The AAM Board of Directors recommends that each nonprofit museum member of the American Association of Museums adopt and promulgate its separate code of ethics, applying the Code of Ethics for Museums to its own institutional setting.

A Committee on Ethics, nominated by the president of the AAM and confirmed by the Board of Directors, will be charged with two responsibilities:

- establishing programs of information, education, and assistance to guide museums in developing their own codes of ethics
- reviewing the Code of Ethics for Museums and periodically recommending refinements and revisions to the Board of Directors.

Comment on ethics codes

It is important to note that the AAM Code of Ethics is addressed to museums as institutions. Several of the AAM's Standing Professional Committees (SPCs), the American Institute for Conservation (AIC) and the Association of Art Museum Directors (AAMD) have written and adopted codes of ethics for individuals. The ICOM, Museum Stores Association, and American Association for State and Local History (AASLH) codes apply to both institutions and individuals. The AAMD also publishes *Professional Practices in Art Museums*.

Codes completed by the SPCs include those for conservators, curators, educators, registrars, public relations officers, and training-program administrators, with more under way. Other staff in museums, such as librarians and archivists, abide by codes of ethics of their related professional organizations. In response to the AAM Code of Ethics for Museums, a major advance is that museums are writing their own codes of ethics. These are, in turn, reinforcing the recognition and strength of professionalism among museum staff.

So you can see that those who work in museums may be complying with and adhering to a number of hopefully compatible ethical standards: personal, position-related, institutional, organizational, and those from outside the museum environs. We should all be pleased that these efforts are being made, and it should be an excellent "sign of the times" for anyone contemplating a museum career.

Bibliography: Museum ethics

American Association of Museums, *Code of Ethics for Museums* (Washington, DC: American Association of Museums, 1994). Document codifying the common understanding of ethics and professionalism in the museum profession in the United States.

"The Ethical Behavior of Museum Professionals," *Guide to Museum Positions. Including a Statement on the Ethical Behaviour of Museum Professionals* (Ottawa: Canadian Museums Association, 1979). Includes statements on personal relationships with fellow workers and superiors; and institutional relationships with the public, and specific outside organizations.

International Council of Museums, *ICOM Statutes; ICOM Code of Professional Ethics* (Paris, France: International Council of Museums, 1990). Outlines the structure and component bodies of ICOM and ethics of museum governance, acquisitions, collections, professional conduct, and personal responsibilities.

Macdonald, Robert, "A Code of Ethics for United States Museums," *Museum* (UNESCO) 45, no. 1 (1993): 53–6. Discusses the factors and process of developing the AAM's 1994 Code of Ethics for Museums.

"Professional Code of Ethics," *Museum News* reprint package, 1991. Includes codes of ethics for curators, conservators, registrars, museum stores, and educators.

Weil, Stephen E., "The Ongoing Pursuit of Professional Status," *Museum News* 67, no. 2 (1988): 30–4. Discusses the origins and development of the "profession" phenomenon and explains how the American museum workers achieved such status.

Suggested readings

AASLH Statement of Professional Ethics (Nashville, Tenn.: American Association for State and Local History, 1993).

Archibold, Robert R., "The Ethics of Collections," *History News* 48, no. 3 (1993): 22–6.

Association of Art Museum Directors, *Professional Practices in Art Museums: Report of the Ethics and Studies Commission* (Savannah, Ga: Association of Art Museums Directors, 1981).

Duggan, A. J., "Ethics," *Museums Bulletin* 6 (1987): 103–4.

Macdonald, Robert R., "An Agenda of Opportunity," *Museum News* 64, no. 1 (1985): 15–25.

—— ,"Ethics: Constructing a Code for All America's Museums," *Museum News* 71, no. 3 (1992): 62–5.

Messenger, Phyllis Mauch, ed., *Ethics of Collecting Cultural Property: Whose Culture?, Whose Property?* (Albuquerque, NM: University of New Mexico Press, 1989).

Museums Association, *Code of Ethics* (London, UK: Museums Association, 1993).

Skramstad, Harold J., "Excellent Inequities," *Museum News* 72, no. 1 (1993): 50–1.

4

Governance

Marie C. Malaro

*Hum, a chapter on governance? Perhaps I can skip this for now.
I'm really not planning on starting at the top.*

Please do not turn the page. No matter what professional position you aspire
to in a museum, and even if you are only at the entry level, your ability to
function effectively is greatly enhanced by a knowledge of museum governance. This is so for two reasons. First, museums are truly team operations.
While each professional staff member may have a unique role, all ultimately
shape the core educational work of the museum. This interdependence underscores the need for good lines of communication and clear delegations of
responsibilities. Neither can come about without an appreciation of governance principles. Second, with an understanding of museum governance you
gain a much better perspective of the role of museums, and this perspective,
in turn, sets the proper tone for the day-to-day activities within a museum.
A knowledge of basic governance principles can be the glue that strengthens
all human effort within a museum.

Governance is distinguished from administration. Those who govern make
policy; those who administer carry out the established policy. Within a museum
the usual governing authority is a board of trustees (sometimes called a board
of directors), and the chief administrator is usually called the director. Because
our topic is governance, let us begin with a close look at the legal status of
a museum and the role of the board of trustees.

The nature of a nonprofit organization

A museum is defined as

> a public or private nonprofit agency or institution organized on a perma-
> nent basis for essentially educational or aesthetic purposes which, utilizing
> a professional staff, owns or utilizes tangible objects, cares for them, and
> exhibits them to the public on a regular basis.[1]

"When you get a good match with a director and the board of trustees, with open channels of communication, you have a wonderful chance for a fine working relationship."
Wilhelmena Cole Holladay, The National Museum of Women in the Arts

Most museums are organized as nonprofit corporations. Every state has statutory procedures for establishing nonprofit corporations – entities created by private individuals to carry out a described public purpose. Museums, as educational organizations, qualify for such status. Thus, any group interested in forming a museum can follow the procedures set forth in its state for establishing such a nonprofit corporation.

Nonprofit organizations play an important role in our society, and they are a uniquely American tradition. These organizations fill in gaps that are not served effectively by our government sector or our business sector. To enable them to fulfill their mediating role, the following restraints are placed upon them, restraints that become self-evident upon a careful study of the history of and justification for our nonprofit sector.

- A nonprofit organization must confine its activities to its particular mission. The mission is the public purpose described in its founding document.
- A primary obligation of a nonprofit organization is to serve its particular constituency – those who fall within its mission.
- While it is permitted to make and accumulate money, the nonprofit organization cannot distribute any profits (money left over after expenses are paid) to private individuals. Any profits that accrue must be turned back into furthering the mission of the organization.

By law, nonprofit organizations are governed by boards of trustees. While the size of a board, its composition, and the terms of its members may vary from one nonprofit organization to another, the law sets forth general standards of conduct expected of those who serve on boards. These standards of conduct reflect what society considers to be the proper role of such organizations. It is instructive, therefore, to look at these standards of conduct.

A public trust

Nonprofit organizations such as museums are considered under the law to be "trust-like" operations. A trust is a fiduciary relationship whereby a party (known as a "trustee") holds property that must be administered for the benefit of others (known as "beneficiaries"). A trustee, even though holding legal title to trust property in the sense of controlling its disposition, may not use that property for her or his own purposes. The law requires that the trustee use the property only to further the good of the beneficiaries to be served.

The board of a museum acts as a trustee. The board is usually composed of citizens who volunteer their time and who are selected by procedures set forth in the museum's founding documents. While the board has the legal authority to control the assets of the museum, it is required to use these assets to benefit the people it serves, and all activities must further the mission set forth in the museum charter. It is because of this "trust-like" status that museums are frequently called "public trusts." Though they may be privately organized and operated (privately in the sense that they are not part of government), museums are required by law to carry out their public purposes (their "missions") for designated segments of the public.

As trustees of a public trust, members of museum boards have certain legal obligations: they are responsible for setting policy within the museum, appointing the director of the museum, looking after the economic well-being of the museum, and checking periodically to see that policies are working well and that the director is doing her or his job. In addition, the law expects trustees to protect the integrity of the museum so that the public will have confidence in its work. Normally, to achieve this end the board of a museum establishes a code of conduct or code of ethics for the museum (see Chapter 3). Such a code offers guidance to all those associated with the museum regarding conduct that can reflect on the integrity of the museum.

Museums also place great stress on record-keeping. They keep records of all activities: they document all events that concern the acquisition, use, care, and disposition of collection objects; they maintain careful financial records; they keep records regarding board and staff decisions. This stress on record-keeping flows from the "trust-like" nature of the museum. As a "public trust" a museum should be in a position to prove (by its records) that it is operating properly. Moreover, the records regarding its collections are essential to the work of scholars and educators because the meaning of museum objects and questions of authenticity are researched through records associated with those objects. To the average person, say the word "museum" and objects come to mind. To the museum professional the word brings to mind both objects and records.

The interaction of board and staff

Although the board of a museum bears ultimate legal responsibilities for the conduct of the museum, it cannot function effectively without a close and confident relationship with professional staff. Board members are not chosen for their knowledge of museum work but rather because they bring a variety

---

"For cultural diversity, look at the boards of museums. You have to change from within. How can there be cultural diversity if those culturally diverse minds are not there?"
Marie Acosta Colon, The Mexican Museum

of talents and viewpoints that help make up a group capable of guiding a "public trust" organization. Board members may come with backgrounds in business, finance, law, accounting, or education, or with special knowledge of groups that make up the museum's public. A good mix of talents and viewpoints within the board encourages decision-making that is thoughtful and reflective of the community, but it is up to the professional staff, working through the director to bring appropriate information to the board for discussion and decision.

As the "policy-makers" for the museum, the board is responsible for:

- establishing guidance with regard to what the museum collects and how it collects
- approving major programs
- approving annual budgets
- making specific delegations of authority so it is clear what must come to the board and what can remain within the control of the director and subordinate staff
- engaging in long-range planning.

When making decisions on these major issues the board relies on the professional staff of the museum to bring it well-researched and thoughtful proposals designed to further the museum's mission. When board and staff understand this interaction and when lines of authority are clearly drawn and respected the system works effectively. There are built-in checks and balances. Staff must be well prepared so as to convince a "lay" audience that a proposal deserves support, and the board, with its broad expertise and control of the purse, can ask many practical questions. There are numerous opportunities also to evaluate whether a proposal furthers the mission of the museum and will effectively serve beneficiaries. The stress on record-keeping encourages full exploration of issues and careful articulation of decisions because all those involved in the decision process realize there must be tangible evidence that all steps reflect prudent action. When it is working well the board–staff process encourages full communication and respect for individual expertise. It also makes clear where the buck stops.

The director

The director, as the chief administrative officer of the museum, is concerned primarily with implementing board policy. She or he conveys board decisions to staff and sees that procedures are established to accomplish defined goals. The director also, in consultation with staff, prepares budgets and issues to be presented to the board. Often it is the talent of the director that determines the success of the museum because she or he plays the pivotal role by serving as the link between board and staff.

The director hires and fires the staff of the museum and oversees the delegation of duties to each employee. It is the director who has the most visible role to the average employee, but an awareness of the limitations of that office – that the director suggests and implements policy but does not set policy – avoids many unnecessary confrontations and helps staff work together effectively.

The changing role of the director

Years ago museum directors achieved their positions mainly by being knowledgeable about the academic subject related to the museum's collections. The director might have been first an art historian, for example, or an anthropologist. Such training served directors well in the days when museums were relatively protected from outside pressures, and few thought to question the quality of management. The director of old was free to spend most of her or his time shaping the collections.

As levels of education increased and the public generally became more interested in museums, people also became more conscious of the fact that museums were there to serve them. This awareness, in turn, prompted scrutiny of internal procedures, questions about the quality of programs, and pressures for more diversity. As museums were held more accountable, administrative burdens grew by leaps and bounds and often the scholarly trained director felt beleaguered. These outside pressures also dramatically increased the costs of administration, and museum boards worried about making ends meet. Some questioned whether the traditionally trained director was equal to modern management demands, and experimentation began.

Some museum boards sought directors among those with degrees in business administration who had proved themselves successful in the commercial world. It was reasoned that these individuals would bring efficiency of operation and cost-cutting procedures and thus relieve growing financial strains. Most of these experiments were disappointing because there was a communication gulf between the scholarly staff and the business-trained staff. In the commercial world the standard measurement of success is profit, because the whole purpose of a business venture is to make money. What product is produced or what service is provided is only a means to an end, and business judgments are made accordingly. But museums, as nonprofit organizations, have as their goal quality of service (the service described in the mission statement), and this

---

"A director of a museum must have the academic and scholarly knowledge of the subject of the institution. I do not believe that a CEO or President of a museum can be someone who comes into the profession like that. The director has to inspire, has to lead, has to be a visionary. If they don't know what the museum is all about and what the collections are, and what they mean, you cannot do that. I am a very strong believer that a museum director should come from within the field."

Robert Macdonald, Museum of the City of New York

51

"A university museum is quite different in governance. The university acts as a board of trustees."

Edith Tonelli, formerly Wight Gallery, UCLA

type of goal cannot be measured by techniques designed for the profit motive. It soon became evident why the business-school-trained director was experiencing difficulties.

Other museums experimented with dual administrators: one assigned to scholarly work in the mode of the traditional director, and the other assuming the more business-like administrative duties that continued to mount for museums. Some of these partnerships worked when the chemistry was right between the two individuals involved. Others served only to divide.

The question of the best training for a museum director is still debated. Much, of course, depends on the individual. Similar training does not produce identical candidates. But certain observations can be offered:

- To operate effectively within the nonprofit sector, one must first study why we have a nonprofit sector. This knowledge should be required of the museum director.
- Most board members come to their roles without any training in nonprofit governance. It usually falls upon the director of the museum to provide this training. Accordingly, it is essential for the director to know the basics of good nonprofit governance.
- The director should be trained in communication. A large portion of the job is communicating information.
- The need to understand what a museum does and the ability to judge the quality of the work produced have never gone out of style and never should.

These remain essential elements of the director's training.

Conclusion

This brief chapter on museum governance should expand your appreciation of what it means to work in a museum. The chapter explains the phrase "public trust," it highlights the fact that team effort within a museum is important, and it describes the lines of authority within a museum. All of these points remain relevant no matter how much experience one gains working in a museum.

Notes

1   Definition used in the Museum Services Act 20 USC Sec. 968 (4).

Bibliography: Governance

Ames, Peter J., and Helen Spaulding, "Museum Governance and Trustee Boards: A Good Engine That Needs More Oil," *International Journal of Museum Management and Curatorship* 7, no. 1 (1988): 33–6. Discusses the role of museum governance and evaluates how the system is working through an analysis of its problems.

Brown, Ellsworth, "Models for Board Responsibilities," *History News* 39, no. 6 (1984): 27–30. Analyzes the differences between boards and the implications for their legal responsibilities, administration, and professional standards.

Di Maggio, Paul, *Managers of Arts* (New York: Seven Locks Press for the American Council for the Arts, 1987). Examines the backgrounds, schooling, and career experiences of senior administrators of arts agencies.

George, Gerald, and Cindy Sherrell-Leo, *Starting Right: A Basic Guide to Museum Planning* (Nashville, Tenn.: American Association for State and Local History, 1986). Discusses the pros and cons of establishing a museum and outlines its management, staffing, and functions.

Malaro, Marie C., *Museum Governance: Mission, Ethics, Policy* (Washington, DC: Smithsonian Institution Press, 1994). Explores the issues facing administrators and trustees, and the importance of using a code of professional ethics, and discusses board education and its role.

Naumer, Helmuth J., *Of Mutual Respect and Other Things: Thoughts on Museum Trusteeship* (Washington, DC: American Association of Museums, 1989). Update on a personal viewpoint of trustee responsibilities and concerns, and the nature of the director–trustee relationship.

Pizer, Lawrence, *A Primer for Local Historical Societies*, 2nd edn (Nashville, Tenn.: American Association for State and Local History, 1991). A guide to organizing, financing, and publicizing historical societies. Discusses the roles of site-marking, preservation, restoration, oral history, tours, libraries, and museums.

Rosenbaum, Allen, "Where Authority Resides: A Look at the Governance of University Museums," *Museum News* 67, no. 2 (1988): 47–8. Discusses the role of governance in university museums, and the relationship with the institution.

Ullberg, Alan, with Patricia Ullberg, *Museum Trusteeship* (Washington, DC: American Association of Museums, 1981). Deals with museums and the structure, operation, accountability, liabilities, and policy-making functions of museum boards.

Wolf, Thomas, *Managing a Nonprofit Organization* (New York: Prentice Hall, 1984). A guide to every aspect of the nonprofit world: boards, work-force, personnel policies, marketing, financial issues, fund-raising, planning, and information management.

Suggested readings

Herman, Robert, and Richard Heimovics, *Executive Leadership in Nonprofit Organizations* (San Francisco, Calif.: Jossey-Bass, 1991).

Houle, Cyril, *Governing Boards: Their Nature and Nurture* (Washington, DC: National Center for Nonprofit Boards, 1989).

Kurtz, Daniel L., *Board Liability: Guide for Nonprofit Directors* (Mt Kisco, NY: Moyer Bell, 1988).

Malaro, Marie C., "Earning Their Keep: Alternative Uses for Museum Collections," *Courier* 15, no. 4 (1995): 1–3.

Marsh, Gordon H., "Governance of Nonprofit Organizations: An Appropriate Standard of Conduct for Trustees of Museums and Other Cultural Institutions," *Journal of Arts Management and Law* 13 (1983): 32–53.

Robinson, Olin, Robert Freeman, and Charles A. Riley II, eds, *The Arts in the World Economy: Public Policy and Primate Philanthropy for a Global Cultural Community* (London and Hanover: University Press of New England, 1994).

Steckel, Richard, *Filthy Rich and Other Nonprofit Fantasies: Changing the Way Nonprofits Do Business in the 90s* (Berkeley, Calif.: Ten Speed Press, 1989).

Legal concerns

Marie C. Malaro

Ms Jones is the director of the recently opened State Science Museum. She sits in her modern office glancing down at the lines of people streaming into the gleaming new structure. She is proud of the museum and very gratified by the warm reception it is receiving from both the public and the press. Her phone rings. It is the public-affairs officer explaining there is a crisis on the main floor. A visitor in a wheelchair is insisting that he be allowed to go up the escalator in his wheelchair, a maneuver he claims he has done many times before. The head of the guard force is insisting that he use the elevator provided primarily to accommodate individuals with disabilities. The visitor has brought with him members of the press, who are busily taking pictures of the confrontation. Even the usually calm public-affairs officer sounds flustered as he seeks the advice of the director. Should museum directors know something about using wheelchairs on escalators?

Across town, Mr Smith, the director of the art museum, is having a crisis too. His museum has recently been offered as a gift a very costly antiquity. The object is owned by a well-regarded benefactor of the museum, who is a retired foreign service officer. The curator of antiquities, who recently joined the museum staff, has just recommended to the director that the museum not only reject the gift offer but that it notify authorities that the object probably illegally left its country of origin many years earlier. The director is horrified. It would be hard enough to refuse the gift, but to expose the owner to investigation is, to him, unthinkable. Is the museum prepared for this type of occurrence?

We are a country of laws. Some would say we are awash with laws and lawyers, and what used to be simple matters are now subjects of costly litigation. Our society has grown more complex, and museums are not protected from mounting legal perils. In fact, museums are probably more affected by the changing legal climate than most institutions, because masses of people visit them daily (thus raising the possibility of certain types of liability) and museum objects are escalating in value (thus raising the possibility of other types of claims). A well-run museum needs good legal advice, and that advice is worth much more if it is used to avoid legal problems. An experienced legal adviser tries to educate a museum on how it can avoid liability so that assets can be put to uses more productive than fighting lawsuits.

Let us consider the two hypothetical situations mentioned earlier. Accommodating and integrating the disabled into everyday life has been the subject of considerable legislation over the past few decades. Without doubt the planners and architects of Ms Jones's museum followed detailed regulations concerning handicap access when designing and outfitting the museum. But physical accessibility is not the sum total of these laws. Most statutes require, among other things, integration of the disabled. This requirement means that organizations coming in contact with many visitors daily need to have well-thought-out and functioning procedures in place to handle unexpected questions concerning adherence to all facets of disability statutes. An experienced lawyer advising the museum would not only have checked the construction contracts for the new museum regarding accessibility but would also have guided the museum toward internal procedures for responding in an informal manner to questions concerning other obligations under the disability laws. A prepared museum would have had at least one knowledgeable person on call and a list of local handicap organizations that could offer advice on individual questions. If Ms Jones's museum had had such internal procedures in place, the public affairs officer, when confronted with the question, could have explained calmly her concerns about safety and then added that before the day was over she would consult with an appropriate handicap organization as to what a public institution's practice should be regarding wheelchair access to escalators. This response, rather than confusion, wards off any serious threat of legal action.

Mr Smith, the art museum director, would not be able to do his job if he were unaware of the complex questions that arise concerning valid title to antiquities. Such questions can be legal (liability will result if the wrong decision is made) or ethical (professional standards are at issue). If a substantial part of the art museum's activities center around the acquisition and exhibition of antiquities, the museum, under Mr Smith's guidance, should have sought legal advice years ago to inform itself on the legal and ethical issues that might arise and then set in place policies and procedures to guide staff in making sound decisions. Mr Smith would not now find himself in disarray, if these simple and rather obvious precautions had been taken. While his task is not a pleasant one, he can explain with confidence the museum's policies regarding clarity of title and the reasons for those policies. This explanation also offers the opportunity for discussion as to an appropriate way to resolve a difficult situation.

Using legal counsel efficiently is particularly important to nonprofit organizations such as museums. When counsel is used to avoid legal clashes the museum benefits doubly. Money is saved because litigation, even when one prevails, is costly. Equally or more important, this preventive approach preserves the good name of the museum by avoiding even claims of impropriety. A good reputation is important to a museum because as a nonprofit, educational organization it cannot sustain itself or function effectively without the confidence of the public.

The range of issues

If a law student interested in working with museums approached a knowledgeable attorney and asked which law school courses to take to prepare for museum clients, the most honest answer might be "Everything!" Museums have all kinds of legal problems. They are employers with exposure to the full range of issues that can arise because of this relationship: workmen's compensation claims, civil-rights violations, disputes over benefits, salary, or working conditions. They enter into all types of contracts for services and supplies. They have buildings that must conform to zoning, health, fire, and safety standards. They host many visitors who may suffer accidents while on their premises. These exposures are common to all for-profit and nonprofit organizations.

In addition, a museum has a long list of legal exposures that are tied directly to its collection. These matters include:

- the importance of being able to prove that it owns the objects in its collections; staff must understand the elements of "good title"
- the ramifications of copyright as it relates to the use of certain objects
- a basic knowledge of tax law as it relates to charitable contributions and to unrelated business income
- a knowledge of laws and treaties relating to stolen or illegally exported objects
- a knowledge of laws protecting endangered species, domestic antiquities, and Native American remains and sacred objects
- the ramifications of accepting restricted gifts
- legal restraints on the disposal of collection objects
- liability exposure when objects are lent or borrowed
- the role of insurance in managing liability
- the role of indemnification statutes
- immunity from seizure statutes applicable to international loans
- the legal consequences of a promised gift
- legal exposure when a museum gives an opinion on the provenance or value of an object
- the proper steps to take if an object is lost, damaged, or stolen
- legal responsibilities providing access to collections and records
- legal responsibilities for the care given to collections.

No matter what a museum collects – whether it is contemporary art, postage stamps, locomotives, costumes, natural history specimens, motion picture films, or the thousands of other possibilities – there is much that needs to be known about the law so that sound collecting practices can be put into place.

"Museums which become owners of contaminated property through purchase or donation are increasingly finding themselves caught in an environmental web. They can
prevent or at least minimize their liability through the exercise of due diligence prior to
acquiring property that may be contaminated."

Michelle D. Jordan, ALI–ABA Conference, 1992

"As if life wasn't sufficiently complicated enough, nonprofit organizations suffer from an
extra layer of rules with which they must comply in order to maintain their special status."

History News (May/June, 1993)

"Occasionally, a situation may present a potential problem that just requires careful
internal monitoring while another matter may require direct legal intervention by a skilled
and knowledgeable professional. You must know and understand the difference."

History News (May/June, 1993)

Another area of particular legal concern for museums is what is commonly
called "conflict of interest" restrictions. Museums, as "trust-like" organizations (see Chapter 4) are required by law to use their assets to benefit the
public, not individuals. Those associated with the museum, whether as board
members, staff, or volunteers, should not place themselves in situations in
which they actually benefit or even appear to benefit personally because of
their relationship with the museum. For example, it would be improper for
a museum curator to trade in objects of a type collected by the museum. Such
activity would place in question the objectivity of judgment exercised by the
curator when making decisions concerning acquisition or disposal of collection objects. There would always be the question: "Is this transaction being
undertaken to benefit the museum, or for the curator's personal gain?" Similarly, if board members were permitted to borrow museum objects to decorate
their homes, this activity would be improper, for in such instances objects
dedicated to public use would be appropriated for personal benefit. There are
many potential conflict-of-interest situations. It is important, therefore, for
museums to understand the legal ramifications of their trust status so that
clear guidance can be offered to all those associated with the museum.

Law and ethics

Adherence to the law is not a voluntary matter. If one fails to abide by the
law, civil or criminal liability results. The law, however, does not set a particularly high standard, because its goal is not to make us honorable, only
bearable. Museums, however, should aim to be honorable; they should do
more than simply avoid liability, and this is where the role of ethics enters
(see Chapter 3). Ethical standards, when applied to a profession, are standards considered essential in order to uphold the integrity of the profession.

Ethical standards, as a rule, expect more than the law because the goal is to maintain the confidence of those served by the profession. It is prudent for a museum, when considering the legal consequences of an act, to consider also the ethical consequences.

Bibliography: Legal concerns

Bender, Ivan R., "The Copyright Column," *Museum Source Marketplace* 2, no. 1 (1995). Presents copyright issues as they apply to the special concerns of museums.

Feldman, F., and Stephen Weil, *Art Law*, 2 vols (Boston, Mass.: Little, Brown, 1986). Discusses the bodies of law on visual arts concerning the rights of the artist and the rights of the collector.

Floyd, Candace, "The Repatriation Blues," *History News* 40, no. 4 (1985): 6–12. Explains the issues of legislating ownership and disposition of tribal materials.

Malaro, Marie C., *A Legal Primer on Managing Museum Collections* (Washington, DC: Smithsonian Institution Press, 1985). Examines the museum's legal obligations and responsibilities, collection-related problems, and legal entanglement issues.

Merryman, John, and Albert Elsen, *Law Ethics and the Visual Arts* (Philadelphia: University of Pennsylvania Press, 1987). Describes the rights of the artist, the collector, and the museum in the international art world by compiling case studies, laws, articles, and clippings.

MUSE Educational Media and Getty Art History Information Project, Sample CD-ROM Licensing Agreements for Museums (New York, NY, 1995).

Phelan, Marilyn, *Museums and the Law* (Nashville, Tenn.: American Association for State and Local History, 1982). A handbook on major legal concerns of public and private institutions; includes discussions of museums and the Internal Revenue Service, legal liability, acquisitions, and organizational structures.

Phelan, Marilyn E., *Museum Law: A Guide for Officers, Directors, and Counsel* (Evanston, IL: Kalos Kapp Press, 1994).

Responsibilities of Trusteeship [videorecording] (Boston, Mass.: New England Museum Association, 1994).

Weil, Stephen E., *Beauty and the Beasts: On Museums, Art, the Law and the Market* (Washington, DC: Smithsonian Institution Press, 1983). Discusses three interrelated subjects: the crisis in museums regarding its role, integrity, and management, and the way the law and the market are influenced.

Weil, Stephen E., *A Cabinet of Curiosities: Inquiries Into Museums and Their Prospects* (Washington, DC: Smithsonian Institution Press, 1995).

Suggested readings

ALI–ABA, *ALI–ABA Course of Study: Legal Problems of Museum Administration* Philadelphia, Pa: American Law Institute–American Bar Association Committee Continuing Professional Education, 1993). Annual.

D & O, *Directors' and Officers' Liability: A Crisis in the Making. An Examination of the Scope of the Problem and its Impact on the Quality of Governance of American Institutions*, national survey conducted by Opinion Research Corporation, (New York: Peat, Marwick, Mitchell & Co., 1987).

Darcy, Edgar, "Silence the Teller, Silence the Tale: Evidence Gathering in Law and Museums," *Muse* 8, no. 3 (1990): 43–5.

Darraby, Jessica L., *Art, Artifact, and Architecture Law* (New York: Clark, Boardman, Callaghan, 1994).

Weil, Stephen E., "A Checklist of Legal Considerations for Museums," *Journal of College and University Law* 3, no. 4 (1980): 346–52.

Part III
What museum workers do – theory and practice

What museum workers do –
theory and practice: prologue

Museums generate countless activities and services that scholars, educators, and the general public have come to expect. Their achievements are due, without equivocation, to the creative, capable, and productive staff members who make museums come alive for their diverse constituencies. Describing what museum people do to make their museums work could take many more pages than we have in this book. We here enumerate what is required to assume the various positions of responsibility within museums. And we *add* what has been actually practiced through the voices of some of the museum professionals who were interviewed for this book. Beyond the staff, of course, is the host of devoted volunteers who work, without pay, alongside the staff, to help museums reach their goals.

> I like museum work because of the variety of experiences, the variety of contacts I have and the chance to get information of other places and times through exhibitions, lectures, and programs. It is a chance to re-define ourselves, a social responsibility to have a role in that, and in our society.
>
> Spencer Crew, National Museum of
> American History

> One needs flexibility, a sense of humor, and to be a people person as well as an object person. You have to be a person who enjoys variety, has natural inquisitiveness, and has an ability to enjoy learning different things.
>
> Linda Thomas,
> Boston Museum of Fine Arts

> One of the things I appreciate in museums is that I find the staff is usually more energetic, more committed to what they are doing – their jobs mean making a difference, be it to society or to visitors, that they are making a positive contribution. People are more team-oriented because of the common goals.
>
> Sue Dahling, formerly
> The Computer Museum

There is no substitute for being able to use language effectively. Museums are about putting things that are inexplicable into words, and that is internally as well as it is externally.

Kenneth Yellis, Yale Peabody Museum
of Natural History

The one quality that I would call for everyone is to have the ability to solve problems, not to panic, not to procrastinate, not to dramatize, but really develop the mature ability to analyze and approach problems in an intelligent fashion.

Wilhelmina Cole Holladay, The National Museum
of Women in the Arts

Scholarship would be infinitely better in museums if people felt less responsibility for speaking as authorities on subjects that have been resolved, and were more willing to pose questions.

Edmund B. Gaither,
Museum of the National Center of Afro-American Artists

6

Museum professional positions: qualifications, duties, and responsibilities

The priorities assigned to the different museum functions are important in establishing the essence of any museum, and its trustees, director, curators, educational staff, conservators, designers, and other specialists should all ponder its basic purposes, as well as try to find ever more effective ways of achieving them.[1]

A. Introduction

From theory to practice is the theme of this chapter. We begin with some general comments and then present job descriptions for thirty professional positions in museums. We have gone beyond the traditional guide to careers by conveying a sense of the "museum atmosphere" by having you hear what some of those who have had successful museum careers have to say. For instance, Claudine Brown, former deputy assistant provost for arts and humanities, Smithsonian Institution, cautioned that learning about how to do the work in a profession was not enough. You also need to learn about the culture of the profession to see if you have the personality for it.

If you have the appropriate training and experience, museums may employ you in the positions we describe. In these roles you will oversee, supervise, and implement the museum's mission, policies, goals, and objectives. You will also become part of an integrated team of professionals who understand their roles in the context of the larger roles of the museum and the museum "profession." You may want to examine some of the organizational charts in Appendix D to determine where different positions may fit in the overall structure. But remember that each museum may differ somewhat in its organizational, reporting, collegial, and operating procedures. However, no matter the size of the museum there is always a "big" organizational team picture beyond just one position. Keep in mind, too, that if you are just starting out with *no* experience, you may enter at a lower level, then concentrate on advancing your career in increments toward your goal. Some assistant and support positions are listed at the end of this chapter.

With rapidly changing and increasingly technical aspects of being a museum careerist, there are still basic and common interests in the goals and objectives of museum professionalism. Despite highly diversified tasks and qualifications, museum professional positions fall into four broad categories: administrative, collections-related, public programming, and coordinate functions. Examples of administrative positions include director, deputy director, financial officer; curator, registrar, and conservator are collections-related; and those classified as public programming include educator, exhibition designer, and audiovisual manager. Examples of coordinate positions are archivist, librarian, and editor. Some positions are unique to museums, such as curator, collections manager and conservator; others are not exclusively museum positions, including public-relations officer, editor, and financial officer. Titles may differ, of course, particularly among federal, state, county, and city government classification systems, and among National Park Service jurisdictions that may require your adjustments to those described by the museum field. From one country to another there is a great variance in titles and terminology. Whatever the category, however, each museum staff member is integrated into a corps dedicated to scholarship, communications, and public service.

The number and variety of jobs in an individual museum depend on a museum's discipline, size, and financial structure. Some of the positions exist only in large, well-funded museums with extensive and diverse collections or wide-ranging exhibitions and broad programming. Medium-size museums usually omit or combine jobs in accordance with their resources. Natural history and history museums may hire collections managers, but art museums seldom do. A small museum may have only a few people on the permanent staff, who must be able to command a wide variety of skills and "double or triple in brass." These types of staff members may be referred to as "generalists."

Many of the professional positions described here are relatively new to the museum field, having been recognized as discrete positions and included as museum staff within the past ten years. Among the factors influencing the directions and, thus, the employment practices in museums include changes in society, advances in technology, an increased community awareness and recognition of community responsibilities, heightened accountability, renewed emphasis on professionalism and ethics, recent legislation, and growing environmental and multicultural concerns. Information managers, marketing officers, human-resources personnel, and education staff with social concerns are among the professionals whose positions reflect the newer trends.

The qualifications listed for each position are not meant to be exclusive for that position. Conversely, if you are qualified for one position you may not necessarily be appropriately trained for any or all of the others. Knowledge of all areas of museum practice, in addition to strong qualifications for a particular position, are valuable for any staff member. Serving as a generalist often proves to be good training but does not diminish the need for specialization for advancement later in your museum career.

Some of the staff positions described exist also on a contract or consultant basis. Museums of various sizes may hire temporary outside experts for specific one-time programs or projects, usually requiring experienced people with special expertise in fund-raising, editing, marketing, exhibition design, visitor studies, public relations, conservation, or museum strategic planning. There is even discussion in the field that, in the future, the trend may be to have a core staff only and hire outside experts and consultants for specific museum tasks.

Depending upon needs and finances, a museum may hire part-time, temporary, or seasonal employees (see Chapter 9). Additionally, museums of all sizes and disciplines use volunteers to supplement paid staff. Volunteers are supervised by the staff, but some very small museums rely almost totally on volunteers for their operations (see Chapter 7).

There are no established written "standards" for positions in museums, and, fortunately, no "standardization" of what every job should be. Museums in the United States are so individualized that it would be undesirable and virtually impossible for them to have rigid requirements. University museums, for example, may treat faculty as staff (and staff as faculty) of the museum, offering them tenure and other faculty privileges, also imposing certain academic requirements.

The relatively recent trend among some large museums has been to hire corporate or university presidents as directors, the rationale being that museums must be operated on a more business-like basis. While there is general agreement that business-like procedures are necessary for accountability and sound financial practices, there is very vocal resistance in the museum community to this movement. Most museum professionals continue to believe that a person trained in the discipline of the museum and/or a related discipline and with demonstrated management skills should be the director, with a second-in-command overseeing financial management. A specialist in a discipline is not only best suited to understand and guide the purpose and content of the collections, but also to respond to the museum's public and to lead, inspire, and motivate the staff. This type of director will understand the vital importance of the mission of the museum, represent the museum to the community, and have the vision for the future. Museums are looking for leaders who combine organizational, business, fund-raising, and marketing skills, *along with scholarship in the discipline.*

You may aspire to the generally accepted criteria described in this chapter as a measure of professionalism for people who work in museums. The qualifications presented here have been reviewed or written by practicing professionals in the field and by members of the standing professional committees of the AAM. It can also be expected that adjustments to position descriptions will continue in the future to meet specific needs and changes in the museum field.

These guidelines will be useful for students contemplating or planning museum careers and exploring avenues leading to them; for high-school and college counselors who may be suggesting and structuring coursework for programs leading to careers in museums; for universities planning programs or coursework in museum-related disciplines, or museum studies; for museum personnel who are considering the needs of their own institutions' hiring practices and who are often asked for advice and counsel from students and visitors; for those considering a career change; for libraries building their reference materials; for those developing, refining, and evaluating museum-studies programs; and for special populations, including minorities, women, and people with disabilities who are underrepresented in many categories of positions in the museum field.

While terminology may differ, these qualifications and guidelines may be useful and adaptable in many countries outside the United States. They will surely be useful for relevant comparisons. In developing countries with renewed interest and attention to museums as preservers of cultural heritage, these qualifications may serve as guidelines for advisory services and job training.

There are general and essential skills, personal attributes, and attitudes and work habits which have an impact on effectiveness and professionalism. Some of these are obvious and apparent within a position description, but some, as in the following list, are so general that they have not always been included in the specific position listings.

As a senior-level museum professional, you will be expected to have:

- familiarity with the history, goals and functions of museums
- understanding of nonprofit organization management
- knowledge of, and commitment to, the AAM and ICOM codes of ethics, as well as those codes developed by other organizations within the museum field
- willingness to improve your skills by study and attendance at training sessions (both in-house and outside), seminars, and professional conferences
- ability to communicate orally and in writing, and interpersonal skills that will enable you to work productively with other staff and associates
- awareness of legal issues affecting museums
- ability to prepare and interpret budgets and grant applications
- general organizational and financial management skills
- a collections and preventive conservation orientation and an understanding of the physical and historical nature of objects and artifacts (depending on the discipline of the museum)
- computer skills, a second language, knowledge of the international museum scene, and familiarity with the museum's community resources.

In addition to the qualifications listed, it is acceptable professional practice that museums must define for you the standards and parameters for each position, and the resources and support available. As staff or as a candidate for a position, you should be made aware of the museum's mission, by-laws, long-range plan, budget, policies, and programs.

Within each position description, **Education** lists the highest recommended degree. Many professional positions require formal coursework in an area of the museum's specialization. Excellence in the field of study relevant to the particular position may be a primary consideration. "Scholars with graduate degrees in art history often think exclusively of curatorial positions . . . but education departments also utilize scholarly expertise."[2] Formal mid-career museum practices training is always an asset. Of course the type of museum, its size, the scope of its collections and programs, and the salary offered will determine the educational level required in each case. Intangible factors such as the opportunity to continue professionally related research or practice unique skills may also influence the educational requirements.

Under **Experience,** the number of years listed usually represents the minimum considered desirable. Experience in an accredited museum would be considered an asset. The relevance of your experience outside the museum field will be evaluated by the director and other hiring authorities such as search committees. Fellowships, internships, apprenticeships, and volunteer service will be of major interest. The amount of supervisory experience expected of you should depend upon the position's responsibilities.

Only special requirements are listed under **References**. Professional, academic, and personal references are, of course, expected of you for all positions.

Items listed under **Knowledge, abilities, and skills** emphasize attributes usually required for the most important functions of each position. Highly specialized or unique knowledge, abilities, and skills for a specific position in a particular museum will be defined for you in the course of job interviews. The order of this listing does not necessarily represent individual museum priorities.

But working in a museum is more than performing the duties outlined on a position description. To move from theory to practice, we have also included remarks from many museum professionals from throughout the United States (and some from abroad). They represent the whole range of museums: art, history, natural history, historic houses, aquariums, planetariums, zoos, science centers, children's museums, and all the different positions within them. Some of these people entered the field forty years ago, others just recently. Their personal accounts and observations from their museum career experiences should give you special insights into what you may anticipate as you enter the field. They describe aspects of museum work you should know about before you make a decision. They also offer testimony as to what museum work means to them and what makes the profession so different and interesting.

> It has been about ten years since I started working in museums and I strongly believe that the museum profession is very privileged because it offers opportunities to experience humanism. It is a profession that opens

the way toward human contact and offers opportunities that carry you beyond a specific time and place. This aspect of museum work transforms museum professionals into social activists who get involved in people's lives while they try to broaden their perspectives, to educate them, to entertain them.[3]

During the interviews, when the personal qualities needed for pursuing a museum career (not necessarily qualities that are unique to museum work) were discussed, there was a consensus for adaptability, energy, commitment, dedication, flexibility, enthusiasm, sensitivity, perseverance, integrity, patience, passion, assertiveness, diplomacy, dependability, efficiency, a good sense of humor, openmindedness, the stamina for thoroughness and accuracy, resourcefulness, an ability to work collaboratively or as a team, and a willingness to see oneself as part of a larger whole. Sarah J. Wolf of The Textile Museum remarked that you have to be flexible and a creative problem-solver. It helps to be a "community service" type too, for, no matter what your position, you will need to be aware of the visitors and the larger audience the museum serves. It was agreed that it is important to have management, communication, and entrepreneurial skills, for even if you are not in a specified management position you will likely find yourself managing something.

We hope that as you proceed through this chapter, examining position descriptions and reflecting on the observations of some of those who have performed these tasks, you will find a place you would fit and a goal you would like to achieve.

Notes: Museum professional positions: Introduction

1   Edward P. Alexander, *Museums in Motion: An Introduction to the History and Functions of Museums* (Nashville, Tenn.: American Association for State and Local History, 1979), p. 15.
2   Smithsonian Institution, *American Art Network*, Newsletter, (Spring, 1992), 1.
3   Artemis A. Zenetou, "Report on Professional Interviews". Work in progress, Museum Reference Center, Smithsonian Institution, Washington, DC

B. Positions

Archivist

Archives contain the recorded history of an institution, and museums are aware of the importance of preserving their print and nonprint records and documents. The archival profession is a relatively new and important addition to the museum field. Unlike a library, the records in archives are stored and used as documentary evidence of the museum's mission, goals, objectives, and accomplishments. Oral-history projects are often the responsibility of the staff of an archive. All museums should establish archives, but many cannot afford to hire a full-time archivist, so that trained archivists, some of whom are working in larger museums, often serve as advisers and consultants to smaller institutions.

The archivist administers unique original documents in all material media (paper, film, tape, etc.). They are kept so that those who consult them for research may have unquestioning confidence in the evidence they provide. The archivist certifies that any document in the archives is the authentic original document or a faithful copy of the same.

The archivist advises museum staff on principles and methods for documenting museum activities and for creating orderly and useful filing-systems of records. The archivist also advises museum staff on the preservation of official museum records not directly under the archives' control and ensures the preservation of all the museum's permanent, valuable, and vital records. The archivist, in consultation with appropriate individuals, determines the legal and historical value of museum records for permanent retention and authorizes accountable and systematic disposal of those not worth keeping. In consultation with museum staff, the archivist schedules and transfers historically valuable records from active office files to the museum archives. The archivist identifies, or helps identify, potential document-collection acquisitions, appraises their evidential value in complementing the museum's object collections, and, in cooperation with museum counsel and management, works out terms and conditions of gifts or purchases.

The archivist accessions official records and acquired document collections into the archives. Using archival principles of provenance and integrity of original order, the archivist arranges and describes records series and document collections for future reference. The archivist researches administrative histories and biographies, writes and publishes finding aids to the archives, and works directly with users to locate unique evidence from the records. The archivist also conducts oral-history projects to complement documentary evidence for better understanding of the museum as an institution.

Archival outreach includes exhibitions and publications that use documentary evidence from the archives, affirming the museum's institutional identity and role in the community through publications and exhibitions on museum history. The archivist also shares archives management expertise with others in museums and related fields.

The archivist enforces all necessary restrictions on the use of records and works to keep restrictions to a minimum. The archivist manages unique inactive records generated by the work of all departments of the museum and document collections acquired from others. The archivist's duties are clearly distinguishable from the responsibilities of other museum professionals such as the registrar, who administers currently active collections-management case files; the librarian, who administers mass-produced information from many sources; and the information manager, who administers systems of acquiring, storing, retrieving, and communicating current information.

The archivist oversees preservation and treatment, and is responsible for proper handling and storage conditions for all documents, photographs, films, audio-tapes, and videotapes as records.

Education

A master's degree in history or another social science, such as anthropology, sociology, or political science, often with additional graduate work in library science, and associated graduate work in archives management.

Experience

Certification by the Academy of Certified Archivists, established by the Society of American Archivists. In the absence of certification, at least one year in a museum archive, or comparable experience in apprenticeship to senior archivists in addition to the education required.

Knowledge, abilities and skills

- Knowledge of archival principles and procedures
- knowledge of archives on-line automated cataloging
- knowledge of records management, information management, data processing systems, and filing-systems
- knowledge of systems of institutional organization, management, operations, and communications
- knowledge of the institutional history of the museum and of the museum's past operating procedures and departmental responsibilities
- knowledge of physical properties, conservation, and proper storage of records in paper, photographic film, magnetic tape, videotape, and other media
- knowledge of legal matters relating to gifts, copyright, freedom of information, and institutional proprietary rights
- ability to discern the future research value of large quantities of integrally related documents
- ability to discern logical patterns and arrangement schemes in large masses of documentation
- ability to distill and present in written narratives the essential significance of large groups of documents having widely divergent and often intellectually complex subject contents
- ability to discern and apply appropriate levels of service to clients
- ability to associate and retain content knowledge across many file series and collections
- ability to work with scholars and the interested public in locating sources for research projects.

Attorney

Museum staff attorneys are still a rare breed, as only large institutions have the financial wherewithal to employ them. The need for them remains, nonetheless. As new legislation is passed and as existing laws are more and more applicable to museum operations, museums find it imperative to consult with and obtain legal advice from attorneys in their communities. Most boards of trustees have at least one member who is an attorney (see Chapter 4).

The museum attorney interprets laws applicable to museum operations and administration and recommends legal policies and actions for the museum.

The attorney provides legal counsel to the board of trustees, the director, and the program and support officers on all areas of law involved in the administration of the museum; oversees the conduct of litigation and other adversarial proceedings to which the museum is a party; reviews administrative claims arising out of museum operations; and monitors all aspects of museum administration for legal implications regarding developments in the law. As the legal arm of the museum, the attorney has the responsibility for ensuring the legal soundness of museum operations. The attorney is responsible for preventive legal information dispensed to the staff and trustees of the museum.

The museum may present a wide range of legal matters for consideration and resolution, including: fiduciary obligations and responsibilities of the trustees and employees; fiscal policy and procedures for all funding; employment policies and procedures; civil rights and labor laws; conformance by employees and trustees with conflict-of-interest rules, as well as museum standards of ethics and conduct; national and international legal requirements pertinent to field studies and research and to the import and export of collections, specimens, exhibitions, artworks and other cultural property; the impact on museum activities of environmental and protected wildlife laws; contract awards and agreements, and related claims and disputes; collections and acquisitions management regarding purchases, gifts, loans, and bequests; federal and state taxes; intellectual-property rights arising out of publishing, performing arts, and collections-acquisition activities; and real and personal property transactions.

Education

A Doctor of Jurisprudence (JD) or an equivalent degree, and an active member of the Bar in good standing of the state in which the museum is located.

"But no dollar value can be placed on the sense of elation Del Valle says she experiences each day when she walks into the museum." ABA Journal, September, 1995

Christina Del Valle,
Associate Counsel,
Metropolitan Museum of Art

Experience

Normally, one to three years of professional legal experience or education beyond the first professional degree, and experience in administrative proceedings.

Knowledge, abilities, and skills

- Competent knowledge of specific areas of the law, such as nonprofit and charitable organizations, employee relations, copyrights, endangered species, contracts, etc.
- ability to communicate effectively, both orally and in writing
- ability to make sound, effective, and responsible professional decisions
- ability to negotiate effectively in situations in which there are competing interests
- ability to perform thorough legal research and express the results succinctly and clearly
- ability to initiate, manage, coordinate, and handle legal and policy matters pertaining to research and educational functions and regulations; use of funds, grants, and contracts; litigation in which the museum is a party; laws applicable to accessions by gift, loan, transfer, or purchase; all forms of service contracts and research agreements; land acquisitions by lease or purchase, including for museum construction; tort claims and settlements; excise, sales, and gift taxes and deductions and exemptions; patents, copyrights, and other forms of intellectual property rights; conflict-of-interest and standards-of-conduct cases, particularly with respect to outside work and personal collecting by curators and certain other employees; liability, life, and indemnification insurance, as well as risk management, catastrophe planning and emergency evacuation programs; discrimination, sexual harassment, employee adverse actions, and labor cases; publication contracts; federal, state, and local environmental laws.

Collections manager

Collections managers are most often found in natural history and in history museums because of the types, sizes, and varieties of their collections. Rocks and minerals, insects, political buttons, clocks, and clothing lend themselves to heavy scrutiny and challenges for sorting, cataloging, and storage. Collections managers work in partnership with the registrars when both of

---

"My job is basically to run all aspects of maintaining and developing a growing collection of 1.6 million specimens. Essentially the position is to relieve the curators from having to deal with the collection so that they can pursue their research specialty more effectively. We do have daily 'science in action' presentations in the galleries, and I do several of these per year. I also have written some semi-popular articles."

Bruce Bartholomew, California Academy of Sciences

these positions exist in large and medium-size museums. If registrars are documentation oriented, collections managers are object/artifact/specimen oriented, with hands-on object responsibility.

Collections manager positions now encompass a broad variety of responsibilities, many of which were historically those assigned to curators. Because of the large size of some museum collections, curators, historians, and research scientists often delegate authority and responsibility to collections managers, depending on their qualifications and skills and the museums's policies concerning such delegation.

Similar to registrars, they are involved with the development of policies and procedures related to collections, but in addition are directly involved with every aspect of objects/artifacts/specimens from collection, preparation, housing, through identification, accessioning and cataloging, data and records management (manual and automated applications); organization and maintenance of storage; planning for short- and long-term environmentally controlled storage and exhibition; security; stabilization and preventive conservation of objects; planning and developing collection facilities; improving collection content and scope; accessibility and use of collections; dissemina-tion of collection information to staff, researchers, and public; and general collection support in the form of administrative, personnel, and financial management.

Being a relatively new type of position, collections managers are not often found in small museums, which may employ only a registrar, and then only part-time. But the trend is toward hiring collections managers, primarily because the collections in museums are growing more rapidly than museums can handle them, and to provide proper care and maintenance.

Education

A bachelor's degree in a discipline of a department or division of the museum's area of research or in the museum's specialization. A graduate degree in a museum's discipline, or in museum studies with a concentration in a discipline may be desirable.

Experience

Three years of experience in a museum registration department or in a museum position in which the main functions are the technical duties relating to collections management, such as the handling, storage, preservation, and cataloging of objects, artifacts, and specimens.

Knowledge, abilities, and skills

- Knowledge of the organization, arrangement and nomenclature of objects, artifacts and specimens in the relevant academic field
- knowledge of file and information management techniques, including computerization used in museum registration and record-keeping

- ability to coordinate personnel and plan and administer programs for collections management, including financial planning and budget preparation
- ability to identify accurately objects, artifacts, and specimens, within the context of the museum's collections
- ability to handle objects appropriately with knowledge of the fundamental principles of conservation, security, storage, and environmental controls.

Conservation scientist

As the conservation and preservation of objects and artifacts becomes increasingly important to museums, the role of the conservation scientist takes on an added and important dimension. A scientific examination and analysis of the nature of the materials being conserved greatly assists the conservators in determining the treatment of the objects. However, budget constraints limit most museums from having conservation scientists on staff, and with the exception in some of the very large museums, they serve more often as consultants.

The conservation scientist has the responsibility for the activities of the conservation research section of the museum. The conservation scientist may serve as the immediate assistant to the chief of conservation and is responsible for the technical study of the objects in the museum.

The conservation scientist may assist the chief of conservation in planning and directing the work of the conservation laboratory. The conservation scientist examines objects visually, with the use of a stereo microscope, and under ultraviolet and infrared illumination to determine object condition, damages, authenticity, and repairs. The conservation scientist also determines appropriate methods of examination and, when necessary, obtains samples for testing or analysis.

To carry out required tests and analyses, the conservation scientist uses binocular and petrographic microscopes, scanning electron microscopes, X-ray fluorescence and spark-source mass spectrometry, thermoluminescence dating equipment, and infrared, visible, and ultraviolet spectrophotometry. The scientist interprets results. The scientist also determines macro- and microstructures of objects using X-radiography and metallography and performs measurements of physical characteristics using available testing equipment, again interpreting results. The scientist supervises maintenance of all scientific and technical equipment and apparatus and may act as laboratory-safety officer.

The conservation scientist collaborates with conservators and curators on the technical study of objects and treatment procedures and initiates, coordinates, supervises, and interprets technical and scientific studies by outside specialists. The scientist also designs, supervises, and conducts research in the field of conservation science, and scientific examinations of objects. Scholarly activities include publishing in the professional literature, maintaining contacts with colleagues, and participating in symposia, seminars, workshops, and other professional meetings.

Education

A Doctor of Philosophy (PhD), master's, or Bachelor of Science (BS) degree in chemistry, conservation science, or a related physical science. Fellowships or post-doctoral appointments in institutions conducting research in conservation are desirable.

Experience

With a PhD, two years of experience in the field of the technical study of objects or conservation science; with a master's degree, four years of such experience; and with a BS degree, six years of experience.

Knowledge, abilities, and skills

- Knowledge and ability to apply research to disciplinary issues
- knowledge in the selection of display and storage materials for optimum compatibility with the objects
- knowledge of specialists outside the museum in engineering, air pollution, and transport design for collaborative research
- knowledge and understanding of the history of materials
- knowledge of and a broad familiarity with the literature of conservation as well as that of the traditional sciences
- knowledge of and familiarity with museological literature
- in an art museum, knowledge of and experience in artistic techniques
- knowledge of one or more foreign languages is helpful
- working knowledge of a broad range of scientific instrumentation
- ability to collaborate with curators to illuminate the origins of objects and the techniques by which they were made
- ability and skills to define categories and trends of materials in a broad class of objects
- ability to support the ongoing treatment and preventive care of the collections by the conservators through the application of scientific testing methods
- ability to help establish environmental standards for exhibitions
- ability and skills necessary to design protective systems for objects with unusual display requirements
- ability to train and supervise laboratory assistants
- ability to maintain high-quality control standards
- skills in oral and written communications
- interpersonal skills for dealing effectively with other staff and with outside resources
- high level of skills in operating and maintaining a variety of scientific instruments
- skills in determining the authenticity or provenance of objects.

"It was true in the past, and it's also true today that conservators are pretty much in demand. It's a career that you are almost assured of getting a job. It's not a matter of luck, or even of perseverance. In my case there were jobs available from the beginning.
Anonymous

Conservator

The size and the budget of a museum determine whether it has its own conservation laboratory. Many museums function with one or two conservators with minimal equipment, while small museums contract their conservation work to independent private conservators or to regional conservation centers. Most museums have a huge backlog of objects that need cleaning or treatment, with a shortage of funds and personnel. Trained conservators are in demand at all levels.

The conservator is primarily responsible for the physical well-being of a collection. The responsibility is twofold: examination and treatment of collection material, and the protection of the collection from further deterioration. The conservator may be involved in pest control; packing and shipping; the control of temperature, relative humidity, and light; the design of exhibition cases; and the improvement of storage conditions. In the course of this work the conservator consults with other museum staff such as curators, registrars, designers, and collections managers.

Conservators are usually specialists in one or more types of objects, such as paintings, sculpture, textiles, ceramics, glass, metals, furniture and wood, books, photographs, and art on paper. They provide treatment and refer materials that cannot be treated in the museum laboratory to other specialists.

Education

A master's degree, or a PhD when available, from a recognized conservation program of three or more years in the theory, principles, and practice of conservation, including two years of training in the principles of general material conservation and a minimum of one year's training or internship in a specialized field, or equivalent training by apprenticeship with one or more qualified practitioners. Undergraduate training should include courses in cultural or art history, scientific studies (chemistry, physics, material science,

There are a lot of off-shoots in conservation. One can be a hands-on conservator, a conservation administrator (they apply concepts, look at the bigger picture, and do long-range and strategic planning), a conservation scientist, and the newest is that of developing as a collections care specialist.
Carolyn Rose, National Museum of Natural History

"As a conservation administrator, some of my projects are quite complicated, require writing proposals for grants, and involve many other museum staff . . . a totally different occupation from being a bench conservator. I also do some teaching, and lecturing, bringing scholarly research to the public."

Arthur Beale, Boston Museum of Fine Arts

biology), studio arts, and manual skills. Continuing education courses, seminars, and workshops are desirable.

Experience

Two years of postgraduate, on-the-job experience (beyond academic training or apprenticeship), under the supervision of a qualified conservator. Conservators generally keep portfolios of current and past work, including examination, condition, and treatment reports, and written, photographic, or original documentation for references.

Knowledge, abilities, and skills

- Knowledge of the technology and materials of artistic, historic, scientific and technological objects and of the chemical and physical processes of their deterioration
- knowledge of the procedures relating to the examination and the preventive and corrective treatment of objects and specimens
- knowledge of environmental requirements and of controls for handling, storage, exhibition, and travel of objects and specimens
- knowledge of conservation and other relevant literature to assure knowledge of new technology
- ability to write thorough and effective treatment reports, position papers, grant applications, and correspondence
- ability to communicate the required participation of other staff in the implementation of approved conservation practices throughout the institution
- ability to plan a basic or specialized conservation laboratory and to implement its development
- manual skills in the treatment of materials.

"Our task as conservation professionals is the protection of the human spirit as it manifests itself in the tangible, artistic products of culture."

Miguel Angel Corzo, Director, Getty Conservation Institute

"As for personal qualities, one should have a real love for material culture, and be very curious. It is important to convey research information into a format that people will digest. That's the big difference to me between working in academia and working in a museum. Our public does not come prepared to be tested."

Spencer Crew, National Museum of American History

Curator

Years ago the curator was known as the "keeper," the person in charge of the collections of the museum, the "keeper" of the holdings of a particular museum. Today, though called "curators," they are still keepers and caretakers of collections. But their responsibilities go far beyond caretaking, as they do extensive research, write both scholarly and popular monographs and books, compose the scenarios and select objects for exhibitions, and work closely with other staff. They are often *the* major subject-matter expert in a discipline in the museum. Thus, they have an important responsibility in keeping the museum on track toward its goals and objectives.

The curator is a specialist in a particular academic discipline relevant to the museum's collections. The curator is directly responsible for determining and overseeing all policies and procedures regarding collections and loans; the care, preservation and academic interpretation of all objects, manuscripts, materials, and specimens belonging or on loan to the museum; recommendations for acquisitions, loans, and deaccessioning; attribution and authentication; and research on the collections, and the publication of the results of that research. The curator is responsible for the exhibition of objects under the care of the curatorial department, participates in exhibition-planning teams, arranges for and monitors the care and security of objects on exhibition and in storage, and participates in data collection for evaluation of exhibitions. In all these duties the curator must practice sound conservation principles.

The curator may also have administrative responsibilities and provide staff support for a collections committee. The curator may be responsible for overseeing the activities of the conservator, the registrar, and the collections manager and should be familiar with the duties and responsibilities of these positions. The curator may recommend or evaluate merchandise to be sold in the museum shop.

"I am a strong believer in what I call synergy . . . getting the fruits of research out to the public through programs and exhibitions. I am in the camp that says that we can't have purely staff preference-driven research . . . it must be related to the mission of the museum. I would go so far as to say that, other things being equal, one should choose the research topic that might be of the greatest relevance of interest to the public."

Peter Ames, formerly Boston Museum of Science

"You must be able to get along with people – many in museums may be temperamental – you have to be flexible, with technical expertise. You have to like people, this should not be an 'ivory tower.' It sounds prestigious, but you end up doing everything, sweeping the floor and wiping glass. There aren't enough people to do everything all of the time."

Terese Tse Bartholomew, Asian Art Museum of San Francisco

The curator is directly responsible for the intellectual content of the interpretation of the collection for museum programming, including the programs organized by the education department.

Education

A master's degree or PhD with a concentration in a discipline related to an area of the museum's specialization. Coursework in museum studies is desirable.

Experience

Three years of experience in a museum or a related educational or research organization. The amount of experience required varies from institution to institution, depending upon the size of the staff and the collections. Hands-on experience with material culture is desirable, and sometimes mandatory. Evidence of scholarly research and writing is also important.

Knowledge, abilities, and skills

- Specialized knowledge (connoisseurship) in one area of the museum's collections
- knowledge of the techniques of selection, evaluation, preservation, restoration, and exhibition of objects
- knowledge of the current market, collecting ethics, and current customs regulations in the area of specialization
- knowledge of computerization of collections
- knowledge of legal regulations and ethical conduct relating to museum work
- ability to interpret the collections and to communicate knowledge relevant to the collections
- ability to recognize in research, collecting, or exhibiting either stereotyping or omissions relating to gender or ethnic groups
- ability to manage and supervise staff
- ability to work cooperatively as a team with other staff to further the public mission of the museum
- communications skills, both oral and written
- skills in sound financial and budget management.

"As a vice-president, I am concerned with learning resources, the library, the collections of the museum, with education both in and outside the museum, with the theater and the planetarium, and with temporary exhibitions. I spend a lot of my time planning, allocating resources, and supporting staff. I try to see problems before they get too bad ... I am into preventive measures a lot. I try to spend a fair amount of time brainstorming and creative thinking, seeing if there is anything else we should be doing. I spend a good percentage of time either fundraising or in support of fundraising, and deciding what to fundraise for."

Peter Ames, formerly Boston Museum of Science

Deputy director/Vice president/Assistant director/ Associate director

This position takes on a variety of configurations, depending upon the desires and disposition of the director and on the size and scope of the museum. Where there is just one deputy or assistant director, the duties and responsibilities are quite different from those in a very large museum in which there may be three or four vice-presidents or assistant directors. Some are financial experts, some attorneys, some business people, some education, exhibition, and public-program specialists, some curatorial experts, and some simply fine administrators and organizers. You will see by the description that this position, whatever it may be called, may be a many-splendored occupation in a museum.

This position is often designated as being in charge of a specific area of museum activities, such as administration, education, or exhibitions, curatorial and research departments, or general operations. This person is responsive to policy direction from the director and the board of trustees and assumes responsibility for planning, organizing, and implementing the programs and operations under assignment. This position supervises the staff who carry out the work, determines the proportion of work to be done by outside contract, and creates the controls necessary for satisfactory completion of the assignments. This person may supervise a program of cost estimation, and the controls necessary to ensure that costs are kept in reasonable relationship to projections. They may also oversee the annual budget for their assigned area of responsibility and report regularly to the director on operational and financial matters. Long-range planning may be the responsibility of the deputy or assistant director, and frequently this position reports, alongside the director, to the board of trustees.

Depending upon the area of responsibility, they may work in collaboration with the curatorial and education staff in developing exhibitions. They may compile the results of research and advise curators of areas requiring research for exhibitions. The position may supervise the production of publications and other results of curatorial research for scholarly and public consumption. They may also develop, direct, and oversee a program of museum education and

"My duties and responsibilities have expanded over the years . . . doing exhibit development, administrative responsibilities, pushing for us to try new ideas, and working with other museums who want information."

Sally Duensing, The Exploratorium

supervise and work with specialists at all levels of education to ensure that exhibitions support the museum's educational objectives.

In other areas, this person may provide oversight for the financial management of the museum, including budget preparation, long-range planning, facilities planning, financial analysis, preparation of financial statements, and administrative and operations management of the museum. Security, facilities, health and safety, custodial, engineering, and public services may all be the supervisory responsibility of this position.

The position may manage human resources and personnel matters, including conflict resolution and interdepartmental relations. All business conducted by the museum that generates products and income, including shops, eating facilities, and publications, may be the responsibility of this position. In museums with one deputy or assistant director, the duties may include acting in the director's stead.

Education

A master's degree or PhD in the discipline of the museum, arts management, museum studies, business administration, or law.

Experience

Five years of experience in museum administration, in museum education, in exhibition planning, or in a combination of all of these.

Knowledge, abilities and skills

- Knowledge of nonprofit organization and administration
- knowledge of sound financial museum management practices
- working knowledge of the museum's mission, functions, and operations
- knowledge of the team approach to planning and producing exhibitions
- knowledge of research techniques and practices
- knowledge of material culture, curatorial functions and practices
- knowledge of museum design functions and practices
- knowledge of museum education learning theories, policies, procedures, and practices
- knowledge of current museum visitor studies and the ability to apply appropriate results

- knowledge of building systems and operations, and security methods and techniques
- ability to use tact and diplomacy in professional relationships
- ability to manage creative people and projects
- leadership abilities and skills
- organizational skills
- skills in human-resources management
- communications skills, both oral and written
- conceptualization skills
- skills in strategic and facilities planning
- computer literacy.

Development officer

Museums of all sizes now seek a specialized person to help raise money, for museums need to secure more outside funding than they ever had to in the past! Fund-raising activities play an important role in the life of a museum, particularly in times of a sluggish economy and decreasing federal funding. Unless a museum has a very substantial endowment, it relies heavily on a development staff to help balance the budget. Even though the money crunch may be cyclical, a museum cannot afford to wait around for more prosperous times.

The development officer coordinates the fund-raising activities of the museum with a genuine commitment to its nonprofit mission. The officer must know the community, be familiar with funding sources (both local and national), and generate new and original ideas for fund-raising projects. These activities may include funding for capital outlay; purchase and operating endowments; membership drives; proposals to government, corporations, individuals, and private foundations; and special fund-raising events. In all these areas the development officer works cooperatively with all of the museum staff, and most particularly with the director, and the public-relations and marketing managers.

"My role is critical to the future of the museum, and it gives me a great feeling of accomplishment . . . not just for the day to day fundraising, but for the funds we raise over a long period of time. Everything we do in development now, in cultivating people and making friends for the museum, have implications for the museum for the future of five or ten years from now.

The personal qualities needed are great communications skills, both verbal and written . . . it also takes a lively personality. You have to like people, you have to work well under pressure because there is always a deadline . . . there is always a goal, and once you achieve this goal, there is always a new one. The people skills are probably right at the top."

Barbara Luton, Santa Barbara Museum of Art

Education

A bachelor's degree in an appropriate field such as business, arts administration, public relations, marketing, or advertising. A bachelor's degree or coursework in the discipline of the museum is also desirable.

Experience

At least three years of experience in fund-raising on a scale consistent with the needs of the museum. Experience in a museum or a nonprofit or research organization is desirable. A portfolio of current and past work is helpful.

Knowledge, abilities, and skills

- Functional knowledge of methods donors may use in giving to institutions, including deferred giving, endowments, and bequests
- knowledge of the mission, goals, and objectives of the museum
- knowledge of nonprofit organizational fund-raising techniques
- knowledge of corporate and foundation funding resources
- knowledge of marketing techniques
- knowledge of applicable computer technology
- demonstrated ability to organize, implement, and supervise an effective fund-raising campaign
- ability to plan and write effective fund-raising promotional materials and grant proposals and to coordinate staff-generated grant requests
- ability to communicate the required participation of other staff and to train and motivate volunteers in fund-raising activities
- ability to give attention to details
- ability to coordinate museum membership activities with membership officer
- oral, written, and interpersonal communications skills
- skills in discretion in handling sensitive financial and personal information
- supervisory skills if there is a development-office staff
- tact and diplomacy, and ability to approach potential donors.

Director

The director sets the "tone" for the museum. The incumbent's museological philosophy permeates the institution and the staff. The director is the "face" of the museum to the staff, the trustees, and the public. It is an enormous responsibility to manage, inspire, and motivate a team of competent staff, to share ideas with them, to have the ability to listen, and responsibly to represent the staff to the board of trustees. If leadership, diplomacy, integrity, management, a sense of humor, and interpersonal skills are some of your attributes, becoming a director may be one of your goals.

The director provides conceptual leadership through specialized knowledge of the discipline of the museum and, with the governing board, is responsible

"Some days I am totally fundraising, and making necessary contacts. Sometimes I am a diplomat and meeting people from different countries. Other days I am an academic and I spend time doing research and writing. I still teach. A lot of time is spent on management issues, working with the staff making sure that things are going well, and supervising people about the budget. I can describe my job as being manager of a small business on one side, and on the other side I need an academic and aesthetic sensitivity. There has to be commitment . . . despite all the hardships and setbacks, what museums do is very important."

Edith Tonelli, formerly Wight Gallery, UCLA

for policy-making, planning, budgeting and fund-raising. The director serves as liaison to the board of trustees and is responsible for initiating policies and for implementing those made by the board. The director has authority over all operations of the institution, including staffing. All staff, directly or indirectly, are accountable to the director. The director is responsible for professional practices and adhering to the museum's code of ethics in acquisition, deaccessioning, preservation, research, interpretation, and presentation, and is responsible for financial, organizational, and human-resources management.

The director should be both leader and manager. A command of a field of knowledge in a discipline of the museum, as demonstrated by publications or acceptable equivalents, is likely to be essential at large institutions. The director follows standards and ethics of the profession at large and assists staff in aligning theory with practice. The director must possess qualities of personality that earn the confidence and respect of the staff and the board of trustees.

If the museum is part of a larger organization such as a university or a city, county, or state government, the director must be conversant with the objectives and long-range plans and policies of the parent organization.

Education

A master's degree or PhD in an area of the museum's discipline or specialization. Coursework or evidence of training in nonprofit or museum management and administration is desirable. A certificate or degree in museum studies may be an important advantage.

"I spend most of my time as a director 'people managing.' One of the most important, if not the single most important, characteristic of a successful museum director is the ability to work with people . . . both staff and trustees. Those relationships have to be based on partnership, collegiality, trust, good will, civility, and a sense of where people are in their own professional careers. But, separate business from your personal life."

Robert Macdonald, Museum of the City of New York

"To be the director of a museum, it seems to me that one should have a primary grounding in the discipline in which one is interested. Without that disciplinary overview one cannot fully comprehend the philosophy of the discipline and the institution. Increasingly it is important to be a good manager. One can do that in several ways: one can have a degree in a discipline, and then take some additional training in management, or get an MBA. Another approach which I tend to favor, for directors who have the proper disciplinary training and broad philosophical, educational, intellectual, and scholarly overview . . . surround themselves with highly competent well-trained specialists in finance, management, and development."

Kenneth Starr, formerly Milwaukee Public Museum

Experience

Three years of management experience (as a director or deputy director or as head of a department), including human resources, organizational, and financial management, in a museum or related cultural institution. Additional administrative experience in a related field may be desirable.

Knowledge, abilities, and skills

- Specialized knowledge in at least one area of the museum's collections or in the management of a particular type of museum
- knowledge of nonprofit organizational management
- knowledge of the history, the philosophy, and the body of literature concerning museums
- demonstrated knowledge of financial development, skills in fund-raising, and the ability to interpret budgets and manage ongoing fiscal responsibilities
- knowledge of the legal and ethical aspects of museum operations and of current and prospective legislation affecting museums
- knowledge of and experience in understanding educational issues, and a grasp of museums' appropriate roles in communities with diverse constituents
- familiarity with computer applications to museum operations
- ability to recommend and implement the policy established by the museum's governing body and to encourage the active participation of

Most of my time is spent dealing with board of trustee matters, fundraising, general overall administration of the institution, but individual areas are left to individual administrators. Yes, you are pretty much a people manager . . . if you remove yourself from that you lose contact with the institution. I still think that the best museum administrator is one who understands the underlying philosophy of the institution, and has worked with it."

Craig Black, formerly Los Angeles County Museum of Natural History

the governing body, the museum staff, and the public in realizing the objectives and goals of the museum

- abilities in long-range and strategic planning
- ability to work in a team situation and provide participatory leadership
- ability to communicate the museum's mission, values, and vision
- ability to establish working relationships with other institutions, organizations, and individuals within a community, nationally and internationally
- specialized abilities and knowledge in the main activity of a parent organization (if there is one), including public administration, bureaucracies, and political relationships
- ability to manage creative and scholarly people and projects
- interpersonal skills, and abilities in human-resource management
- effective communications skills, both oral and written
- skills in organizational life, including understanding organizational structures and chains of command.

Docent (guide)

Docents, or guides, paid or volunteer, are in effect the "voices" of the museum. They are surrogates for the director, curators, and educators in relating and mediating the collections and exhibitions to the public. Their function is to serve as catalysts in the interaction between object and observer.

In England, the word "docent" came into usage during the 1600s as an adjective derived from the present participle of the Latin *docere*, meaning "to teach." In the United States, during the late 1800s, the word was employed as a noun and used by universities and colleges to denote a recognized teacher or lecturer not on the salaried staff but paid by students for their private instruction. This latter usage still prevails in Europe today in many universities.

In 1915, Benjamin Ives Gilman, of the Museum of Fine Arts in Boston, described how the word "docent" first acquired its present meaning in the context of museum education. "A museum performs its complete office as it is at once gardant, monstrant, and docent," (as it preserves, exhibits, and teaches), he said, and added, "the duty of the museums is to give oral instruction upon their contents." It was then that the Boston Museum "first applied the forgotten English adjective 'docent' to the future duty it had just proposed to undertake." Since then, the word "docent" has become widely accepted among museums throughout the United States in the newer sense of an official commentator on things shown.

"You should be open to new ideas, a self-starter, wanting to interact with lots of different people, be a learner."

Darlene Labrero, The Exploratorium

The docent becomes a museum educator in acquiring the ability to mediate, interpret, and encourage visitors to participate actively in learning. Through organized guided tours and programs, the docent leads visitors in encountering, experiencing, and enjoying objects and artifacts in exhibitions.

Docents serve in a public relations capacity, conveying to visitors the mission of the museum and alerting visitors to public programs such as lectures, films, concerts, and demonstrations. They may present slide-lectures to introduce the museum to outside groups. Docents also assist in planning and overseeing special events and activities such as outreach programs, festivals, children's days, teacher workshops, treasure hunts, self-tours, and informational handouts for the public.

The docent most often is a volunteer, but this description is included because there are a number of museums that employ docents as paid staff.

Education

Some museums require coursework in the discipline of the museum or in the field of education, but most museums have no specific educational requirements. Extensive training and evaluation of performance are usually offered by the museum. Docents are made aware of the policies and procedures of the various facets of the museum so they may assist in answering general inquiries or direct visitors to specialized staff.

Experience

Teaching experience may be desirable, but is rarely required, as museum learning is very different from the classroom experience. Familiarity with, or experience in, applying learning theories may be an asset.

Knowledge, abilities, and skills

- Knowledge and interest in the discipline of the museum
- commitment to the mission of the museum
- willingness to learn more about the discipline and to participate in continuing education related to and offered by the museum
- willingness to learn the methods by which the knowledge can be most effectively shared with others and presented with factual accuracy
- knowledge of the museum's code of ethics and professional standards
- knowledge and understanding of various cultural, educational and age groups among visitors
- ability to assess the interest of groups quickly and to modify tours accordingly
- ability to adapt to new or different audiences
- ability to relate with ease and understanding to children at their level
- ability to use different or innovative interpretive techniques for different audiences

- fluency in or knowledge of a foreign language may be desirable
- ability to master the required training materials
- ability to fulfill prescribed obligations diligently
- ability to keep to a schedule and to be punctual and reliable
- ability to adapt to changes or additions in schedules
- ability to learn security procedures and preventive conservation practices
- ability to accept constructive criticism and evaluation of performance
- oral communications skills, including effective voice control, body language, vocabulary, and grammar.

Editor

Editors for museums come in two modes: on staff in large museums, or on contract or consultancy to most of the others. Many museums, no matter the size, prefer to hire independent freelance editors for their projects. Sometimes it is a matter of financial prudence. Either way, professional competence is essential so that the museum may enjoy a reputation for well-written, well-edited and attractive publications. The image of the museum is often the image its publications project to the public who visits or does *not* visit.

The editor prepares and supervises the production of the printed material for the institution. The editor reads, corrects, rewrites, or revises such material to ensure that the language is clear and precise and in proper grammatical and stylistic form. Working with a graphics designer, the editor also strives to project the museum's desired image and relate to its audience. The editor may supervise all the mechanical processes of production, from submission of manuscript, to the desk-top publisher or printer, to the binding of the final product.

When the institution publishes a journal, the editor may research, identify, and recruit appropriate authors and reviewers. The editor works with the authors to carry out substantive revisions. The editor watches for and corrects errors in fact, interpretation, and citation.

The editor sometimes oversees calendars and newsletters, and may write these publications as well.

Some large institutions hire exhibition editors who, in addition to applying basic editorial skills, specialize in preparing texts and labels that function in conjunction with exhibition visuals. Such editors work closely with the exhibition designer, the educator, and the curator.

Education

Bachelor's or master's degree in English or journalism. Course work in the area of the museum's specialization is desirable.

Experience

Three years or more of editorial experience. Experience in a museum or related institution is desirable. Experience in the area of the museum's specialization may be required. A portfolio of current and past work helps establish experience and background.

Knowledge, abilities, and skills

- Knowledge of publishing practices, methods, and procedures
- thorough knowledge of correct grammar, writing styles, and sentence construction
- knowledge of the mission, philosophy, and objectives of the museum
- knowledge of the necessity to eliminate gender bias and stereotyping of any individuals or groups
- knowledge of design, graphic arts, and printing
- working knowledge of label writing
- extensive knowledge of editorial procedures necessary to meet the highest standards of publishing
- knowledge of copyright laws and other regulations
- ability to analyze, reorganize, rewrite, and proofread manuscripts
- ability to master technical and foreign language terminology common to the discipline of the museum
- ability to work collaboratively with other staff of the museum, including the curator, educator, designer, public-relations officer, and administrative staff, and to work cooperatively with a variety of people outside the institution who might write or prepare publications
- ability to organize time, coordinate multiple projects, and plan schedules to meet deadlines
- ability to ensure editorial consistency and clarity of language
- skills and ability to write clearly and concisely
- skills working with photographs.

Educator

Nonformal or informal education is the forte of programming activities in museums of all sizes and disciplines. The degree to which it is carried out is determined by the philosophical stance of the director and the trustees. As you will read in other chapters of this book, education in museums has taken on a much more significant role than in the past, even to the point that education departments, *per se*, are either less isolated or eliminated completely as everyone on staff assumes an educational role. Education in museums is "in," due in part to *Excellence and Equity*, a report by the AAM, and to the masterful drive of museum educators to be recognized as professionals and to bring museum education to the forefront of museum priorities.

"As for personal qualities, I look for people who can think conceptually and verbalize it. I want people who can look at an object and understand the meaning behind it, but who also can explain that to people who might not necessarily think about it that way, and to explain it with enthusiasm and joy. I want articulate and honest people who have an interest in people, tolerance for others, and thinking about and respecting visitors. The role of an educator in a museum is to help make the museum more accessible to the public, and get them excited about it."

Margaret Piatt, Old Sturbridge Village

Essentially, the museum educator provides a broad spectrum of learning experiences for museums' diverse public, leading the way to reach out to newly defined audiences who historically have not been museum-goers. Older adults, members of ethnic and racial groups, and disabled people are among the targeted audiences. All ages, income groups, and educational levels are being brought into the museum fold. The museum educator may indeed be the "Renaissance" person on the museum staff in the 1990s.

The educator (sometimes called the director of public programs) develops, implements, evaluates, and supervises the museum's educational programs, based on the mission of the museum, with the goal of enhancing public access to and understanding and interpretation of the collections, exhibitions, and resources. Educational programs employ a variety of media and techniques, including exhibitions, printed materials such as self-guides, demonstrations, improvisations, classes, tours, films, lectures, special events, workshops, teacher-training programs, and school or other outreach programs. The educator may have administrative responsibilities and be a member of the exhibition planning committee, as well as a member of the "team" of museum management. The educator is also responsible for docent or guide training.

Education

A master's degree in an area of the museum's specialization, with coursework in learning theories, or graduation from a museum studies program with a concentration in museum education. A combination of all of the above is desirable.

Experience

Two to three years of experience in a museum education department or other educational institution, with responsibility for informal education planning and programming. Organizational or administrative experience is desirable.

"My background was in philosophy and education. I was interested in the learning philosophy that was going on in museums. I thought that the museum was a place that had great respect for different kinds of learning."

Patricia A. Steuert, Boston Children's Museum

Knowledge, abilities, and skills

- Knowledge of the mission, goals, and policies of the museum
- knowledge of museum education techniques and resources
- knowledge of current learning theories and the developmental needs of museum audiences as learners
- knowledge of the objectives, curricula, and operation of school systems and other educational institutions
- knowledge in the area of the museum's collections
- knowledge of evaluation and visitor-studies techniques
- knowledge and understanding of the requirements of special audiences, including the disabled, diverse ethnic groups, and older adults
- knowledge of audiovisual and of computer technologies and of interactive educational techniques
- knowledge and ability to manage human resources
- knowledge of marketing strategies
- knowledge of long-range and strategic planning
- ability to devise and carry out education programs, including the preparation and use of publications and exhibitions
- ability to represent the museum to outside organizations, schools, and potential donors
- ability to work cooperatively with museum curators, designers, financial officers, public relations specialists, and membership and development staff, especially on teams for exhibitions and special projects.
- ability to supervise staff in the designated education or program department
- ability to formulate and implement a budget

"I am in charge of the written and spoken word, by and large. I am in charge of the relationship between what goes on inside the head of the museum, making the connection between that and the public mind, in order to enrich understanding, pleasure, and interest in culture. Also to pick up on the overarching goal for this country which is to increase understanding between and among races and cultures.

The education department is a defender of what the public deserves and needs. There must be sharing of what the scholar's points are, and their belief in the value of their scholarship being popularized, so that I may relate them to the public. If you have the kind of personality interested in serving you can do very well as a museum educator. In terms of being effective, you must have a level head and the ability to know who you are."

Barbara Moore, National Gallery of Art

- ability to recruit, train, supervise, and work with volunteers, including the attributes of tact and diplomacy
- skills in creative thinking and initiating new and special projects and events
- skill in oral and written communication techniques appropriate to various educational levels and objectives
- skill in research and writing
- ability to recognize the importance of eliminating stereotyping of gender or of ethnic groups.

Exhibition designer

A key player in the exhibition program of any museum, the exhibition designer makes it all come together as the whole planning team wants it. The designer has the "eye" to project how all the ideas of others, and the selected objects, will appear in an exhibition. As more and more museums take the team approach to planning exhibitions, the designer plays a critical role as part of that team. There is more open discussion now, less isolation, among the curators, educators, administrators, and designers as plans are laid out for forthcoming exhibitions. The designer provides the artistic component of visual communications.

Working with curatorial and educational staff members, the exhibition designer translates conceptual ideas into concrete form for the production of permanent, temporary, or traveling exhibitions through renderings, drawings, scale models, lighting, arrangement of objects, and signage. The exhibition designer serves on the exhibition-planning committee or team, supervises the production of exhibitions, and may have considerable administrative responsibilities.

Education

Bachelor's degree in graphic design, industrial design, commercial art, communication arts, architecture, environmental design, interior design, theater design, or studio arts, with course work in typography and audiovisual techniques. Two academic years of course work pertaining directly to museum exhibition design are desirable.

Experience

At least two years' experience in exhibition design, preferably in or for a museum. Additional experience in exhibition production, related construction work (cabinet-making or wood, metal, or plastics fabrication), model-making, or media (graphics, advertising, illustration, audiovisual presentations) may be desirable. Designers always maintain portfolios of current and past work to establish their experience and credentials.

Knowledge, abilities, and skills

- Knowledge of security and conservation requirements and practices
- knowledge of lighting systems
- knowledge of tools and techniques for exhibition preparation, shop practices, mechanical drawing, and the use of planning models and mock-ups
- knowledge of estimating, budgeting, bidding, and accounting practices, and ability to design within budget guidelines
- knowledge of the state of the art in exhibition design and related fields
- knowledge of communication media and materials
- knowledge of the nature of the material to be displayed
- knowledge of interactive computer potential in exhibitions
- knowledge of the purpose and principles of visitor studies and evaluation techniques
- knowledge of the requirements for visitors with disabilities
- knowledge of museum educational theories
- ability to conceptualize exhibition design and make refined esthetic judgments that are appropriate to the goals and style of the institution
- ability to specify designs in drawings and written instructions
- ability to supervise fabrication and installation of exhibitions
- ability to identify and solve problems
- ability to organize, represent, and communicate information effectively through design
- ability to communicate concepts and requirements to museum administration, museum boards, funding sources, production specialists, and other professionals who contribute to the design process
- ability to listen and respond to ideas and issues from other staff and colleagues in the field
- ability to take exhibitions through stages of development: concept, design, and fabrication
- skills in three-dimensional design and drafting
- communication skills, including sketching, model-making, writing, and graphic design
- a creative and imaginative mind.

Exhibition planner (developer)

Exhibition planning can be a cumbersome operation, replete with conflicts, unless there is a method to streamline the procedure. Exhibition planners are quite new to museums, but many medium-size and large museums are finding that the assignment of this responsibility to an appropriate individual works well in coordinating team planning for exhibitions. The planner works closely with curators, designers, and educators to develop comprehensive plans, and is responsible to the administration of the museum. In addition to administrative responsibilities, the exhibition planner also serves as the "third person" who can remain objective through any controversy that may arise and can lead others to consensus and decisions.

The exhibitions planner develops and recommends concepts and interpretive strategies for individual exhibitions, and exhibition complexes. The planner executes the research required to write exhibition story-lines and selects the artifacts, specimens, photographs, and graphics to visualize that story-line. The planner works closely with curatorial staff and content consultants to ensure that the scholarship and information are accurate, timely, and appropriate for delivering the educational objectives of the exhibition and of the museum. The ultimate product the planner is responsible for is a written script and an object and graphic inventory in a form and content appropriate to guide the design and production of the exhibition. During the planning process, the planner often works with a museum team consisting of a curator, a designer, and an educator. When appropriate, the planner works with the facilities staff and outside personnel to coordinate the scheduling and installation of exhibitions.

Education

Bachelor's degree in the discipline of the museum or a degree or course work in design or communication arts. Course work in museum education and interpretation and training in material culture are desirable.

Experience

At least three years of broad-based exhibition-development experience, a breadth of scholarly and research experience, and demonstration of a high level of organizational responsibility for a sustained period.

Knowledge, abilities, and skills

- Broad interpretive vision
- knowledge of preventive conservation
- knowledge of the mission of the museum
- knowledge of design and graphics
- awareness of gender concerns in exhibitions
- knowledge of accessibility needs in exhibitions
- knowledge of visitor research and studies
- knowledge of the importance of the care of collections
- knowledge of estimating, budgeting, and accounting practices
- knowledge of current technologies
- ability to conceptualize entire exhibition complexes
- ability to identify and solve problems
- ability to work in a team situation
- ability to communicate ideas in the creative process
- advanced writing skills

- skills in planning to attract a multicultural audience
- organizational skills
- skills in research techniques.

Exhibition preparator

You could easily say this position is where the really hard work in producing an exhibition takes place. The preparators are the backbone of the operation in completing the work that usually has been dreamed of, conceptualized, written, and designed by others. The preparator has very special skills that are required for all kinds of exhibitions in all kinds of museums. This is a hands-on position for people who do not mind getting their hands a little dirty at times. They may be artists, craftspeople, or tinkerers who like to be in the thick of activity.

The exhibition preparator advises on, administers, supervises, or performs work in the planning, construction, installation, and operation of exhibitions, the preparation of gallery space for exhibitions, and the preparation of items to be exhibited. Under the general supervision of an exhibition designer, who is responsible for assigning and reviewing projects for compliance with policies and planning, the preparator, using a variety of techniques and materials, produces models, information displays, and technical and special-purpose equipment. Working from layouts of approved designs, the preparator fabricates and installs museum exhibitions and may assist with the design when appropriate.

Exhibition preparation involves photography; cutting display panels with power tools and shop machinery; finishing and framing edges with hand tools; applying undercoats; mixing and brushing or spraying color coats; masking and spraying varied background patterns; laying out lettering; designing and executing complex maps; designing and executing illustrations; designing and executing diagrams; designing and fabricating special mounting devices; painting diorama backgrounds; constructing realistic diorama foregrounds; fabricating precise accessories in scale and perspective; modeling and casting human figures and natural life; building scale models of structures or equipment; devising and assembling lighting equipment; preparing comprehensive sketches and finished renderings of flat paintings that might be simple spot illustrations, or murals of considerable size and complexity. The preparator prepares time estimates and work schedules for projects and keeps time and cost records as required.

"If you are going to be an exhibits builder you need to be a 'tinkerer' too . . . play with things at home in your garage . . . and be curious about things and how they work."

Glenn Gutleben, The Exploratorium

Education

A high-school diploma or a bachelor's degree or equivalent in studio art, photography, woodworking, electronics or another art form appropriate to the position. Course work in museum studies is desirable.

Experience

Two years of experience in practice of artistic skills and techniques. Museum or gallery experience is desirable and may be required.

Knowledge, abilities, and skills

- Knowledge of construction materials
- knowledge of mechanical, electrical, and electronic mechanisms
- knowledge of audiovisuals and a variety of media equipment
- knowledge of exhibition development and production
- knowledge of current technological apparatus
- knowledge of the value, handling, and preventive conservation of objects and artifacts
- knowledge of standards of quality and sound workmanship
- working knowledge of the physical qualities of the museum materials – their uses, stability, and durability under varying conditions
- knowledge of pest-control techniques
- knowledge of security controls
- knowledge of the requirements for accessibility of exhibitions
- ability to understand the subject matter of the exhibition
- ability to understand visitor traffic-flow
- ability to work with a team from museum staff and outside contractors
- ability to experiment with new devices and techniques
- ability to read and translate designer plans
- ability to organize work based on a practical and realistic timetable
- ability to make aesthetic judgments and demonstrate artistic taste
- ability to estimate costs and schedule work assignments
- skills in accuracy, detail, and adherence to instructions in work assignments
- skills in lighting techniques, with consideration of conservation problems
- skills in manual dexterity, mechanical skills, artistic skills, and aptitude for learning exhibition techniques
- skills in working with power and hand tools
- skills in working with diverse media, including paints, pen-and-ink, water-colors, and photographs.

Facilities manager (Operations manager, Superintendent)

The facilities manager is in charge of the museum's facilities and responsible for coordinating the physical workplace with the people and work of the institution. This position integrates the principles of business administration, architecture, and the behavioral and engineering sciences. Facilities management combines proven management practices with the most current technical knowledge to provide humane, productive, and effective work environments. There are scaled-down versions of this position, and various titles as appropriate, depending upon the size of the museum. The importance of the job is not diminished, however, as the physical care and maintenance of the building and grounds reflect the importance of the museum's collections and public service and the responsible staff who work there.

Facilities managers are responsible for performing or supervising the functions of long-range facility planning; annual facility planning (tactical planning); facility financial forecasting and budgeting; real-estate acquisition and/or disposal; interior space planning, work space specification, and installation and space management; architectural and engineering planning and design; new construction and renovation work; maintenance and operations management of the physical plant; and integration of telecommunications, security, and general administrative services (food services, reprographics, transportation, etc.). The position may have added responsibilities for shipping and receiving, safety practices, duplicating and computer resources, energy management, and other basic support services.

Education

High-school diploma and appropriate certified technical training in physical plant management. A degree in civil engineering, business management, and/or architecture and design may be highly desirable if employed by a large museum. Hazards communications training is often required.

Experience

Three years of experience in facilities management, including two years supervising staff and contractual maintenance personnel. Experience in a museum or a cultural or educational institution is desirable.

Knowledge, abilities, and skills

- Knowledge of appropriate local, state, and federal regulations and codes governing building operations and personnel management, particularly as related to historic structures
- knowledge of issues and techniques in space management
- knowledge of the appropriate United States Department of Labor job descriptions and the differentiation of craft skills
- knowledge of specification writing, bid procedures, cost accounting, and budget preparation
- knowledge of security systems and procedures and of their special capacities

- knowledge of safety laws and regulations and the records and reports required
- knowledge of the means of protecting collections during construction and renovation work
- knowledge of appropriate cleaning solutions related to museum procedures and other preventive conservation techniques
- knowledge of environmental issues and safeguards
- knowledge of legal means of disposing of hazardous materials
- knowledge of laws and regulations for accessibility for people with disabilities
- awareness of the institution's mission as an educational entity, a strong familiarity with all the special functions of a museum, and an appreciation of the impact of museum goals on the facilities services of the museum
- ability to formulate long-range and strategic plans
- ability to coordinate disaster planning for the museum
- ability to read blueprints and other drawings and diagrams and to use planning models
- in a small museum, custodial skills will be required.

Financial officer

Money is important to every organization, but sound fiscal management of a museum is crucial. The financial officer of a museum must often work under constraints while retaining accountability for the accurate financial condition of the museum to the director and to the trustees.

The financial officer reports to and works closely with the director or with a deputy or assistant director if so designated. Fundamental responsibilities vary according to the size of the museum, but they generally include oversight of budgeting, accounting, purchasing, personnel procedures, salaries and fringe benefits, insurance, operation of the physical plant, security, contracts, taxes, and membership, endowment, and fund-raising records. The officer may be responsible for revenue-producing activities such as sales shops and food services. If the incumbent also serves as treasurer, day-to-day management of endowment and investment income is an additional responsibility. The financial officer prepares reports to the board of trustees concerning financial status, management, and controls. In a large institution, the financial officer may be an assistant director, with a comptroller handling day-to-day record-keeping and accounting functions.

Education

For a small institution, a bachelor's degree in business or accounting; for a larger museum, an advanced degree in business or public administration.

Experience

Minimum of three years of administrative or directly relevant experience. Experience in a museum or a nonprofit cultural organization is desirable.

Knowledge, abilities, and skills

- Knowledge of fund accounting and general fiscal practices, including grants administration as applicable to nonprofit organizations
- knowledge of the legal aspects of museum operations
- knowledge of personnel management procedures
- knowledge of insurance requirements and risk management
- knowledge of required office and museum equipment, data-processing systems, physical plant management, and security needs
- knowledge of and experience in specification writing, contracts, bid procedures, cost accounting, and budget preparation
- working knowledge of computerized financial record keeping
- knowledge of sound investment policies and procedures
- knowledge of all aspects of the museum's operations
- ability to prepare and analyze budgets
- ability to prepare and analyze financial statements
- skills in communicating financial issues to staff and trustees
- skills in supervision of assistant staff.

Health officer

Nurses may not often think about working in a museum, but opportunities are increasing as recent legislation stipulates that any institution employing 132 people or more must have a health officer on staff. While this is an indicator only for large museums, many medium-size museums assign healthcare to a staff member, at least part time. Smaller institutions depend on the trusty first-aid kit and know of a doctor or nurse who might be available on short notice in case of emergencies. Larger institutions, however, have broader responsibilities. They must be prepared to handle the potential health hazards for staff who work with chemicals or toxic materials, the inevitable minor accidents, and a wide variety of visitor health needs. Here is another position, not unique to museums certainly, but increasingly a part of the expanding museum field.

The health officer is usually a registered nurse who is responsible for providing first aid for injured or ill employees and visitors and a comprehensive and appropriate occupational health program for all museum employees. The health officer supports the objective of providing a safe and healthy work environment for all employees and is responsible, in addition to emergency first aid, for applied toxicology, industrial hygiene, safety, food and sanitation regulations, health screening, health education, and counseling. The health officer initiates treatment of occupational and nonoccupational illnesses and injuries, makes doctor referrals, and supports a well-rounded workplace employee health program.

Education

A nursing degree and current registration as a nurse in the state where employed. Current certifications in Cardiac Pulmonary Recussitation (CPR), in audiometric testing, and in pulmonary function testing are required. Board certification in occupational-health nursing is highly recommended.

Experience

At least one year of experience as an occupational health nurse. A diverse nursing background, particularly in clinical, medical, surgical, and emergency-room nursing, is highly desirable.

Knowledge, abilities, and skills

- Knowledge of occupational health problems and issues, including physical and chemical hazards, toxicology, industrial hygiene, and epidemiology
- knowledge of medical care and treatment of common illnesses and injuries, as well as special and infrequently used drugs for the life-threatened, seriously ill, or injured patient
- knowledge of the relationship and impact of illnesses, injuries, medications, and treatments on worker performance
- knowledge of Office of Safety and Health Administration and local guidelines, regulations, and standards to assure compliance within the workplace
- knowledge of accessibility requirements for the disabled as staff and as visitors
- knowledge of professional nursing principles and procedures
- knowledge of international health and vaccine requirements for staff travel
- knowledge of physician contacts for referral
- ability to communicate effectively with all levels of museum staff
- ability to function well independently
- ability to administer vaccines for staff travel, and routine flu shots
- ability to recommend environmental modifications to allow a worker to remain productive or to recommend that the worker be moved to another environment when required by physical or health problems
- ability to evaluate and interpret laboratory and X-ray reports, pulmonary-function tests, audiograms, and other tests in relation to potential work-site stresses on the basis of the degree of exposure and the medical status of the worker
- ability to recognize an employee's personal medical and emotional problems, and sufficient knowledge and skill in counseling, so as to assist and refer employees

- communications skills, both oral and written, to conduct appropriate educational programs related to health and safety
- managerial and administrative skills.

Information manager

Cyberspace, the "information age," and the "information highway" are upon us, and the new technologies present new challenges to museums to manage, store, utilize, and retrieve information. As a result, an information manager is a relatively new position for museums, but one of great importance for efficient operations and record-keeping. Museums need to incorporate the latest developments in information management, and a highly motivated person with specialized computer knowledge and skills is in demand either as a full-time staff person (in large and medium-size museums) or more frequently as a consultant on contract.

The information manager is responsible for facilitating the flow of information within an institution and between the institution and the public. Narrowly interpreted, the information manager's activities might be confined to overseeing the institutional applications of technology such as computers with the attendant concerns for standards, training, and access. Broadly interpreted, the activities include ongoing analysis and implementation of the ways in which the institution collects, stores, and disseminates information. This responsibility might include coordination of collections-documentation activities with educational offerings, exhibition-planning with the business office, conservation with the maintenance staff, or publications programs with membership and public relations. The information manager may create home pages for World-Wide Web, CD-ROMs, or other new electronic means for education, promotion, or communications. Collaboration with other institutions may be an important facet of the responsibilities.

Education

Bachelor's degree in a discipline that emphasizes analysis and communication, coupled with training in current technologies. Training in museum studies would be beneficial.

Experience

Three years of experience in technology, communication, education, or management. Additional experience with cultural institutions is desirable.

Knowledge, abilities, and skills

- Knowledge of the opportunities and limitations of the information technologies available to the institution

- knowledge of the creative ways in which cultural institutions utilize or might utilize information
- knowledge of the standards employed in information exchange, including those of practice (archival finding-aids or membership lists), of content (audits), of medium (computer configurations), and of form (data exchange protocols and typesetters' conventions)
- knowledge of the care and use of information-exchange technologies, including routine maintenance and security of computers, microfilm readers, and cash registers; proper storage of information; design of retrieval systems; and programming
- knowledge of inventory control, desk-top publishing, and local, national, and international electronic networks
- ability to analyze the informational needs of an institution and develop strategies for meeting those needs
- ability to plan and oversee the implementation of information strategies
- ability to communicate, educate, and facilitate understanding in a variety of media – through focus groups, training programs, or design of intuitive interfaces (relating one program to another)
- ability to explore the possibilities of public access to museum information, and knowledge of media applications such as microfiche, CD-ROM, home page, laser, and videodisc
- ability to manage implementation of museum information policies and plans
- skills in state-of-the-art techniques and methods
- verbal and written communications skills are essential.

Librarian

Museum libraries are an important source of information for staff, visiting researchers, and volunteers. Some museum libraries are also open to the public. Their size, scope, and personnel depend heavily on the financial resources of the museum. Some small museums have used professional librarians from a local university or the public library to set up a cataloging system, then assign its management to volunteers. But the numbers of museum librarians are growing, and museum libraries are recognized by the American Library Association as "special libraries," a category that also includes libraries in universities and hospitals.

The librarian administers the museum library and performs services such as selection (often upon recommendations from other museum staff), acquisition, cataloging, classification, circulation, and maintenance of library materials. The librarian also furnishes reference, bibliographical, and readers' advisory services. Most museum libraries now have access to computer databases and can readily locate materials repositories. In museums the librarian may have special responsibilities for slides, graphics, or manuscripts. Some museum librarians are also in charge of the museum's archives.

"My role here at the Academy has been as a librarian, but that is only my nominal title. My activity has been far broader than that. I am serving on national and international committees in the systematics community having to do with computerization of collections and a whole range of activities. There has been a fortunate confluence in my training in natural history and my background in international affairs."

Thomas Moritz, California Academy of Sciences

Education

Master's degree in library science. An undergraduate degree or additional course work in the area of the museum's specialization or museum studies is desirable.

Experience

Two years of experience in a museum or specialized library. Experience with archival administration or with information retrieval in a research-oriented cultural or arts organization may be desirable or required.

Knowledge, abilities, and skills

- Knowledge of the special needs and purposes of a museum library
- knowledge of all the support services inherent in librarianship: acquisitions, cataloging, reference, and administration
- knowledge of various storage and retrieval systems for printed materials and other media, including slides, reference photographs, and other archives
- a working knowledge of at least one foreign language
- knowledge of fundamental issues of book preservation for maintenance of library collections
- knowledge of relevant resources in other libraries
- ability to provide bibliographic support, including knowledge of foreign-language sources and the use of computerized bibliographic services
- interpersonal skills, and the ability to work with research scholars, museum staff, volunteers, and the general public
- skills in cataloging, cross-referencing, and indexing
- skills in computer usage in a library environment for on-line search and retrieval.

Marketing manager

Marketing for museums is a relatively recent phenomenon, as museums strive to cope with financial crises, prove their accountability, make their services and "products" for the community better known, and reach new and diverse audiences. Museums now realize the value of marketing in projecting an image

"This job requires both skills and creativity. The challenges are the same as at a private company . . . get the message out, try to provide the services, and make the customer happy. You have to respond to balancing your educational and your social mission with the fact that you need to stay alive to do that."

Sue Dahling, formerly Computer Museum

of service and education, along with their scholarship, research, and care of the cultural patrimony.

The marketing manager is responsible for conducting market research, developing a marketing plan, and organizing the staff to accomplish it. The marketing manager usually reports directly to the director of the museum and works closely with the development and public-relations officers. This position exists primarily in large museums, in some medium-size museums; smaller institutions may use marketing consultants.

The marketing manager targets high-potential consumers for a museum "product": an exhibition, an education program, a special event, a concert series, a membership program, the museum shop, and publications. The manager advises museum staff with an interest in audience-based marketing on how to develop promotional strategies that will reach those groups and individuals.

The marketing person may be responsible for a membership campaign; the campaign for a single event; special offers, such as discounts and multiple-event purchases; mass mailing and all types of advertising. The incumbent may conduct or assist in the negotiation of museum tours for member and nonmember groups, special tours for visiting dignitaries, events preceding special programs and lectures, and sales related to these events such as concessionary items, souvenir programs, mail-order shop items, or legal raffles. The museum marketer is a very creative "salesperson" for the unique offerings of museums, but remains within the ethical and professional boundaries of museums as nonprofit and cultural "public trust" institutions.

Education

A bachelor's or master's degree in marketing, public relations, advertising, or communications, or a Master's in Business Administration (MBA).

Experience

Three years of experience in marketing, preferably with a museum or a related cultural organization.

Knowledge, abilities, and skills

- Knowledge of all aspects of the museum's operations and programs
- knowledge of the mission and the code of ethics of the museum

- knowledge of the methodologies for bringing the public and the museum, its services and products, together
- knowledge of public-relations techniques
- knowledge of the media in all formats
- ability to research and analyze public attitudes toward the museum
- ability to understand and communicate the mission and objectives of the museum
- skills in oral and written communications
- skills in data analysis
- skills in entrepreneurship, and intuitive acumen
- computer literacy.

Media manager

This position is relatively new to museums and currently enjoying popularity in medium-size and large museums because of the explosion of new computer, audio, and visual techniques. Museums have jumped on the bandwagon of visual exhibitry and programming, and need specialists to create and activate these images for the public (see Chapter 11 for more details on new media). Small and medium-size museums may employ media contractors or consultants for special projects.

The media manager is responsible for developing policy and planning strategies for all educational media programs, for media as part of exhibitions, and for broadcast media for the museum. The media manager serves as the liaison for technical and audiovisual information to all members of the museum staff who consider the use of media in the museum operations and programming. The media manager supervises all purchases of technical equipment, oversees the maintenance and storage of the equipment, and controls the usage for appropriate purposes.

The media manager may propose the creative use of media in exhibitions and programs, write scripts, and produce and direct slide-tape, videotape, and film productions. The manager may also be responsible for introducing innovative techniques such as interactive computers, virtual reality, and CD-ROMs. The media manager conducts research into new technologies and tests their effectiveness in a museum setting. Especially when planning new endeavors, the media manager works closely with museum staff and may work with outside contractors and consultants when needed, occasionally in collaboration with other museums and organizations. The manager provides orientation or training in media as needed for museum staff.

Education

A bachelor's or master's degree in communications, education, or the discipline of the museum. Course work in media technology is desirable.

Experience

At least two years of responsible media experience, including producing, directing, and scripting for various types of programs. Experience with media equipment is required.

Knowledge, abilities, and skills

- Knowledge of the museum's operations, exhibitions, and programs
- knowledge of the history of film and other media
- knowledge of state-of-the art developments in videotapes, film, computers, television, and slide programs
- knowledge of additional state-of-the-art media technology, including interactive computerization and video, virtual reality, and holography
- knowledge of and working skills in use of media equipment
- creative, and willing to experiment with new ideas
- knowledge of and participation in appropriate professional organizations
- ability to work in a team situation
- ability to meet production deadlines
- ability to recognize standards of quality and good taste
- ability to work with outside contractors
- ability to budget and control costs
- ability to interpret and prepare financial reports
- skills in organization
- skills in oral and written communication
- writing and editing skills for scripts and other documents.

Membership officer

Museums of all sizes and disciplines have membership programs for three closely aligned reasons: to raise funds for operations, to solicit community support, and to ensure an interested audience for program activities. Members are an extremely important arm of the museum as they represent the constituent community of the museum. They often raise additional funds, serve as volunteers, and generate community interest and support. When membership programs are large and complex, museums hire a special membership officer to coordinate the varied services. From organizing many educational programs in large museums to sending out notices for dues and keeping records in smaller ones, the membership officer may be at different levels in different museums.

The membership officer works closely with the development and public-relations officers and with the museum educator to attract and retain the interests of a broad and diverse public. Responsibilities include recruitment and retention of members, and planning, promoting and supervising special events and educational programs such as classes, films, workshops, lectures, and exhibition openings as benefits to museum members. The membership officer may have administrative responsibilities, including a database for maintenance of membership files and records; recruit and manage volunteer assistants; design and publish membership brochures and other promotional literature; and develop and be responsible for a budget for membership activities.

Education

Bachelor's degree in business, public relations, marketing, public administration, or liberal arts. Course work in the discipline of the museum or museum studies is desirable.

Experience

Two years of experience in programs of public involvement or in a museum or related nonprofit or cultural institution.

Knowledge, abilities, and skills

- Knowledge of the history, philosophy, and mission of the museum
- knowledge of the techniques used to attract, maintain, and benefit organizational membership
- knowledge of media resources
- knowledge of financial management, record-keeping and data-processing systems
- knowledge of and ability in computer technology for membership records
- ability to develop and carry out participatory programs for the museum's audiences and sponsors in support of the objectives of the museum
- ability to enlist staff and volunteers in membership activities
- interpersonal skills, and the ability to meet and work with the public, the media, staff, and trustees.

Personnel (human resources) director

Usually this position as described here is found only in medium-size and large museums, but in some form these responsibilities for hiring and employment practices are carried out in all museums. In a small museum it may be the director who makes the decisions for employment, but those museums with large staffs require recruitment, screening, and recommendations by specialized people. This is a "people-person" job because it involves regular contacts with staff members who are looking to hire and with people who are seeking to be hired. The director of personnel also often serves as a counselor or adviser to those who need more information about the museum, the types of positions and openings, the special requirements they may entail, and potential vacancies.

The primary purpose of this position is to provide professional expertise in the area of human-resources administration. The director of personnel advises senior and supervisory staff on personnel decisions, including hires, terminations, promotions, reclassifications, performance appraisals, and disciplinary actions. The director also interprets museum policy on personnel-related activities to all staff levels. The position coordinates selection and staffing activities, including recruitment, applicant evaluation, interviewing, and recommendations. At the policy level, the director of personnel writes all personnel-related policies and submits them to the museum director and board for approval.

The personnel director also represents the museum to external agencies, such as the Equal Employment Opportunity Commission, state commissions on human relations, city commissions on human relations, the Workers Compensation Commission, and the unemployment office.

The personnel director administers the museum benefit program, including dissemination of information about benefits to employees. The position is also responsible for preparing and analyzing equal-opportunity data, highlighting areas of underutilization, and identifying minority and disabled recruitment sources. The personnel director analyzes employee and volunteer injury reports and works with the workers' compensation insurance carrier to reduce accidents and insurance premiums.

The personnel director plans and conducts orientation for new staff members, drafts all correspondence and documentation in regard to personnel administration, monitors the leave status of staff, supervises the museum payroll in cooperation with the financial officer, and manages the budget for the personnel office.

Education

A bachelor's or master's degree in liberal arts.

Experience

Three years' combined personnel-policy and benefit-administration experience.

Knowledge, abilities, and skills

- Knowledge of museum departments and daily operations
- knowledge of city, county, state, and federal laws governing employment, benefits, and equal opportunity
- knowledge of accommodations in the work environment for disabled and older adults
- knowledge of sources for advertising and recruitment for staff
- knowledge of the mission, goals, and objectives of the museum
- knowledge of records management, methods, and techniques
- ability to work effectively with people on a personal level
- ability to structure a yearly budget for the office
- ability to develop, establish, implement, and analyze personnel policies and procedures

- ability to enforce the ethical standards of the museum
- ability to plan and implement training programs
- computer skills for records management
- skills in oral and written communications
- skills in organization and management, especially financial and human resources
- skills in supervision, decision-making, and leadership
- skills in tact and diplomacy.

Photographer

Photographs in a museum are much more than just for exhibition. Essential to record-keeping, research, and publications, a sensitive-to-museum-needs staff photographer is often hired by large and some medium-size museums. Those museums with limited budgets, however, usually hire a freelance photographer to perform the tasks as outlined here. Either way, there are needs in museums for well-trained and professional photographers.

The photographer produces documentary prints of objects, and details of objects, on loan or in the collection, for the registrar's or conservator's records, for curatorial research and publication, for educational (interpretive) materials, for public information and for promotional literature or uses. Museum program activities, special events, new exhibitions, and other publicity-related activities are among the promotional responsibilities of a museum photographer. The photographer may be required to make use of specialized techniques and may be responsible for photographic files.

Education

High-school diploma and certified technical training in photography with an emphasis on studio photography and use of larger format (up to 4 × 5″ film) equipment. Apprenticeship training may be acceptable or desirable.

Experience

Experience in commercial photography and processing. Studio experience is essential for all but public-relations photographer positions. Photographers maintain portfolios of current and past work.

Knowledge, abilities, and skills

- Knowledge of studio practice, portable lighting equipment, and use of view cameras
- knowledge of photocopy and macro- and micro-photography equipment and techniques
- knowledge of preventive care of photographic collections

111

- ability to photograph a variety of two- and three-dimensional subjects for both record and publication uses
- skill in photographing objects requiring special handling, such as museum objects and artifacts
- skills in developing and enlarging techniques.

Public relations officer

The public-relations officer is often the person who *is* the museum to newspapers, television, radio and other media. The "PR" person must not only know the media but be totally familiar with the community, and – most importantly – know *everything* about the museum.

The public relations officer is concerned with the public image of the museum and is responsible for media strategy, including relations with newspapers, radio, television, magazines, and other media, and for museum promotional projects such as special events and special publications. The public relations officer develops and issues news releases, conducts media and news events, and serves as a resource, especially responding to media inquiries.

The function of this position is to establish useful relationships between a museum's substance and goals and the perceived needs and interests of its various publics. To this end, the public relations officer coordinates media relations with all museum departments and staff and is responsible for the content and development of public information brochures and publications about the museum, especially for fund-raising promotions.

The public relations officer establishes community relations for the museum and monitors issues of interest so that the museum may participate in shaping them. The public relations officer represents the director and staff, as well as the board of trustees, to the media; and has a keen sense of timing for media appearances of the director or the trustees. The officer promotes and markets (with the marketing manager, if there is one) the museum and its programs and exhibitions, for the purpose of stimulating attendance, membership, and financial support. The incumbent also manages the public relations and advertising budget of the museum. If the museum is a constituent part of a governmental unit or a university, the public relations officer serves as liaison between the museum and its parent organization.

Education

Bachelor's degree in public relations, journalism, English, or communications. Course work in the discipline of the museum or museum studies may be desirable.

Experience

Two years of experience in public relations. Experience in a museum, nonprofit, or research organization is desirable. Additional experience in journalism, marketing, advertising, or communications may also be very helpful. A portfolio of current and past work can help establish credentials.

Knowledge, abilities, and skills

- Knowledge of the mission, code of ethics, goals, and policies of the museum
- knowledge of the discipline that the museum serves
- knowledge of media outlets
- knowledge of writing, editing, layout, and standard media formats
- knowledge of the print media
- knowledge of the appropriate use of photography
- knowledge of the interests and needs of diverse ethnic groups, persons with disabilities, and older adults within the community, and the ability to develop strategies to attract them
- ability to communicate to museum staff the needs of media, and to the media the standards and needs of the staff
- ability to implement effective public relations programs
- ability to represent the museum to the media, to potential donors, to community organizations, and to the public
- ability to coordinate all promotional efforts within the museum, including exhibition planning, education, special events, membership and development, audience development, and tourism
- skills in marketing techniques
- skills in the management and administration of budgets
- interpersonal skills, and the ability to work with colleagues, the media, and the public
- skills in oral and written communications
- skill in understanding the necessity of elimination of gender or ethnic bias or stereotyping in all formats of the museum's public relations
- computer literacy.

Registrar

One of the most responsible positions in a museum, the registrar controls the flow of all information concerning the collections, and is responsible for the

---

"I always sort of joke and say a registrar's office is a cross between a library and an air traffic controller. We keep the records of the collections and record all movements within or outside the building. Then we also become air traffic controllers because we work world-wide with multiple kinds of shipping, customs, insurance, packing, crating . . . all of these things with a strong basis in record-keeping and records management. We also do legal work, financial tracking, logistics, and budgeting. We play travel agents for the objects and the people associated with them."

Linda Thomas, Boston Museum of Fine Arts

113

development and enforcement of the museum's collections policies and procedures. Registration departments were among the first in museums to use computers, recognizing the value of computerized records for accurate and efficient cataloging and retrieval. The registrars are the official "keepers of the records," but they are much more than that.

Pursuant to the care, custody, and control of objects in perpetuity, the registrar is responsible for an information system comprising forms, legal documents, and files associated with acquisitions, condition reports, accessioning, cataloging, loans, packing, shipping, inventory, insurance, and storage. The registrar organizes, documents and coordinates all aspects of borrowing and lending objects, including responsibility for handling and packing objects, negotiating insurance coverage, processing insurance claims, making shipping arrangements, arranging for security, handling customs procedures, processing incoming and outgoing loans, and processing requests for rights and reproductions. In essence, the registrar organizes data so that facts and ideas may be usefully extracted. Other collections responsibilities include accession records, marking objects, inventory and storage records. This position is responsible for monitoring deaccession procedures in compliance with the museum's collections management policies.

Education

A bachelor's degree in the area of the museum's specialization or in liberal arts. A master's degree in museum administration, in an area of the museum's specialization or in museum studies may be required.

Experience

Two years of experience in a museum registration department or in a museum position in which registration is an ongoing responsibility.

Knowledge, abilities, and skills

- Knowledge of accepted museum manual and automated registration techniques
- complete computer literacy
- knowledge of the museum's collections
- knowledge of preventive conservation, including object-handling and storage practices
- knowledge of legal matters related to the collections, of copyright laws, and of policies governing rights and reproductions
- knowledge of computerized records and information management and data-processing systems
- knowledge of insurance requirements for the collection, and for loans, packing techniques, and transportation methods
- knowledge of inventory methods

- knowledge of collections-policy development and implementation, and monitoring compliance
- knowledge of computerized museum information exchange and networking systems, and collaborative projects
- ability to be flexible in originating sound solutions or adapting proven ones to special situations and problems
- ability to plan and implement multiple projects
- skills in organization and management.

Security chief

Museum protection is everybody's business, and every museum and all museum staff have a stake in protecting the building, the collections, the exhibitions, the staff, and the public who visit. Museums, large and small, have some means for security. From a sizable corps of guards to a few uniformed volunteers, museums have procedures to protect themselves from emergencies of all kinds. The person ultimately responsible for coordinating these activities is often called the security chief. *The following description would be modified for smaller institutions.*

The security chief is responsible for the protection of the building, its collections, and its visitors and staff from theft, fire, injury, and other damage. The position is responsible for establishing security procedures; planning for emergencies; disaster planning; personnel training; evacuations; around-the-clock security coverage; crowd control; access control; parcel control; and fire and intrusion alarms and their applications. The security chief must have knowledge of applicable law and is responsible for investigations. The chief is responsible for adherence to a professional code of ethics.

Education

A Bachelor of Arts (BA) or a Bachelor of Science (BS) degree in the field of law, criminal justice, or police science is desirable. Completion of courses in these fields, with a college degree in another discipline, is acceptable. Required courses may be substituted by a degree in another discipline and eight years' experience in the museum security field, the Federal Bureau of Investigation, the United States Secret Service, military security, or a major police department. Sometimes experience may be substituted for education requirements.

Experience

At least five years in an active supervisory and leadership position managing an operational law-enforcement unit. Security experience in the field of protection of high-value or cultural property is highly desirable. Prior experience in investigations, fire protection, and occupational safety is also desirable.

References

Portfolio listing current and past security positions as well as specialized training and recommendations from members of national and international security organizations is helpful.

Knowledge, abilities, and skills

- Basic knowledge of criminal law and security procedures
- knowledge of intrusion alarms, central monitoring needs, computerized security, and associated electronics
- broad general knowledge of national fire-prevention standards as outlined by the National Fire Prevention Association (NFPA)
- broad general knowledge of Occupational Safety and Health Administration standards
- knowledge of protection requirements for museums
- knowledge of guard-force employment needs, recruitment, and procurement
- knowledge of access controls and barrier systems
- knowledge of closed-circuit television and its use in security
- knowledge of locks and security hardware
- ability to develop and articulate budget and resource requirements for security
- ability to work with employees, staff of the museum, and the public
- ability to conduct crime-prevention security surveys and risk analysis
- ability to develop training programs and to train guard and staff personnel
- ability to formulate and implement disaster plans
- ability to conduct criminal and administrative investigations
- skill in preparing and executing emergency plans.

Museum shop manager

The museum shop is often the first or last stop for the museum visitor. The people who work in the shop are sometimes the only staff the visitor encounters, except for the guards. These people must put the museum's "best foot forward" in communication with the public. The museum shop manager oversees this operation, including training staff and monitoring its public relations style. The sales approach must be friendly and dignified, while persuasive. In addition, sales of shop merchandise may contribute significantly to the financial stability of the museum. Income cannot be the primary goal, however. The shop manager must be fully aware of the mission of the museum so that the shop becomes an extension of the museum's exhibition and educational programs. Depending upon the size and budget of the museum, the shop manager may be paid staff or an experienced volunteer.

The museum shop manager is responsible for the operation of the museum shop in a retail environment. The manager oversees all phases of operations,

"I think it is very important for a museum shop manager to know the institution . . . being sensitive to art as educational and aesthetic, not just a product. Management skills are really important in my job, being good with numbers and budgets."

Janet Dorman, formerly The Phillips Collection

merchandising, sales, and management controls. The manager supervises a staff of paid workers and volunteers and is responsible for the sale of merchandise based on quality and on relationship and relevancy to the museum collections and exhibitions. The manager prepares and oversees the annual shop budget and submits financial reports to the director or the financial officer of the museum. The manager attends all relevant trade shows and merchandise markets and is the principle buyer for the shop.

The museum shop manager supervises the shop's appearance and display, emphasizing aspects of the merchandise relating to the museum's exhibitions, collections, and programs. The incumbent prepares all advertising and promotion for the museum shop, including coordinating special events with other museum departments; prepares an annual merchandise inventory and maintains orderly inventoried storage facilities for merchandise.

When appropriate, the museum shop manager develops and directs a program of new merchandise production based on the museum's collection or new exhibition. In such programs the manager, in consultation with the museum director, curators, and education staff, researches and oversees product development. In a large museum, the shop manager may develop and oversee a mail-order division. Such responsibilities include ordering supplies, publishing a mail-order catalogue, and supervising its marketing and distribution.

Education

A bachelor's degree in business, marketing, or accounting. Additional coursework in the discipline of the museum is desirable.

Experience

Three to five years of experience in retailing in a museum shop, or in a department or specialty store.

Knowledge, abilities, and skills

- Knowledge of the mission, goals, and objectives of the museum
- knowledge of museum shop operational procedures, policies, and vendors
- knowledge of federal, state, and local laws and regulations affecting museum shops

- knowledge of inventory-control techniques and standard retail concepts and practices
- knowledge of accounting procedures and financial management
- knowledge of sources of supply for merchandise, including appropriate trade journals
- knowledge of the requirements for accessibility for the disabled
- ability to manage, control, and prioritize multiple activities smoothly in a busy atmosphere
- ability to assess product relevancy in concert with the director and curatorial and education staff
- ability to translate the museum code of ethics into the shop operations
- ability to meet and greet the public in a diplomatic and tactful manner
- skills in retail and merchandising techniques, including price comparisons, trends, and styles
- skill in managing a diverse work-force to achieve maximum productivity from staff and volunteers
- skills in computer usage for shop records and management
- oral and written communications skills.

Volunteer coordinator

Museums of all sizes depend on volunteers (see Chapter 7). Because of the great variety of assignments and tasks undertaken by this corps of dedicated individuals, many museums find it necessary to have a person on staff to recruit, coordinate, and oversee their myriad activities. This is a "people-person" job, requiring tact, diplomacy, sensitivity, and thorough knowledge of the museum's staff and operations. The volunteer coordinator may be either paid staff or, in smaller museums, an experienced volunteer.

The volunteer coordinator is responsible for the development, organization, operation, supervision, evaluation, and maintenance of museum volunteer activities. The coordinator develops volunteer programs and services responsive to the needs of the museum and defines the parameters, organization, and responsibilities of the volunteer programs and services. In so doing the coordinator works with museum staff at all levels, observes established museum policies and procedures, and promotes the professional use of volunteers.

The volunteer coordinator recruits, screens, and selects volunteers, utilizing methods that assure appropriate program placement and a balance of age, gender, and ethnicity within the volunteer corps. The coordinator establishes or facilitates training appropriate to the program and services to be provided by volunteers.

The volunteer coordinator supervises volunteer activities, reviewing individual performance and providing supplemental training and counseling as needed. The coordinator evaluates volunteer programs and services to determine their viability. The incumbent seeks to maintain volunteer programs and services by securing administrative support, volunteer recognition and appreciation activities, and benefits to volunteers commensurate with museum unpaid employee status.

The volunteer coordinator formulates an annual budget, maintains administrative oversight, and carries out assigned personnel functions in accordance with museum policies and procedures.

Education

A bachelor's degree in liberal arts. Course work in museum studies or the discipline of the museum is desirable.

Experience

Two years' supervisory or administrative experience in a museum or related organization, preferably working with volunteers and a variety of staff. Volunteer service in a museum is very useful.

Knowledge, abilities, and skills

- Knowledge and skills in human-resources management
- knowledge of the mission, goals, and objectives of the museum
- knowledge of all museum departments and operations
- knowledge of the community as a source for recruits
- knowledge of accessibility requirements for the disabled
- knowledge of records-management methods and techniques utilizing computer technology
- ability to develop, establish, implement, and analyze policies, procedures, and programs
- ability to define and interpret volunteer systems and goals for the staff
- ability to enforce ethical standards for the volunteers
- ability to apply principles of group dynamics
- ability to plan and implement training programs
- ability to establish good working relationships with staff
- writing skills for development of resource materials
- skills in oral communications for training and promotional activities
- skills in tact and diplomacy
- interpersonal skills
- skills in making decisions, with leadership abilities.

C. Assistant and support positions

Art or objects handler

Pack and unpack objects, artifacts, and works of art for storage, lending, borrowing, and travel. May work into an assistant registrar's or collections-manager's position.

Artist

Use artistic skills to paint backdrops for exhibitions, do silk screening or graphics, sketch for planning exhibitions, sculpt for reproductions, or paint walls. Many studio artists become heads of exhibition departments.

Cataloguer

Record-collections information either manually on cards or by computerization. Keep the records well organized and assist the registrar with storage and handling of objects. A valid opportunity to becoming a registrar.

Conservation aide

Follow instructions of a conservator in routine cleaning and preventive care of objects and artifacts, and assist with treatment as requested. You may become a conservation technician, or with additional required education (or a lengthy apprenticeship), a conservator.

Development assistant

Research funding sources, utilizing directories, computerized data, libraries, and resource centers. Provide appropriate staff with information, and assist with proposal writing. A good training ground for a future development officer.

Exhibitions assistant

Take photographs, do silk screening, mount pictures, make labels, use a hammer and screwdriver, glue props, and maybe even run errands for the designer and production crew. With demonstrated abilities, any or all of these duties may lead to positions of authority or full design responsibility.

Financial clerk or administrative assistant

Keep financial records, have a working knowledge of the budget of the museum, write purchase orders and travel-request forms, and generally assist the financial officer. With competence and experience, a financial whiz can move up a career ladder in a museum.

Interpreter or explainer

Work in the galleries or out-of-doors to answer questions of the visitors and make suggestions for better understanding and interpretation of exhibitions and surroundings. A logical entry into a museum education department or a senior position in the National Park Service.

Library technician

Assist the librarian with cataloging, indexing, cross-referencing, and keeping books and journals shelved properly. Help researchers retrieve materials. Enter and retrieve information on the computer. With required education, you may become a museum librarian.

Objects processor

Assist a registrar, collections manager, or curator in examining and storing objects, particularly in a natural history museum. With perseverance and abilities you may have their job some day.

Proofreader

Assist an editor or an information officer with press releases, copy for catalogues, bulletins, newsletters, and other printed materials. With acquired skills and training, you may move up the editorial or public relations career ladders.

Researcher

Assist in a curatorial department to gather information about specific objects or a forthcoming exhibition. With the appropriate education, it may lead to a curatorial position. Large museums may hire researchers for a journal staff.

Secretary

Hone your computer skills, file, write correspondence, take notes at meetings, type reports, and more. It may work into becoming a program, editorial, or curatorial assistant.

Shop assistant

Price and mark merchandise, keep display areas attractive and storage areas orderly, serve as a salesperson, and generally assist the shop manager.

Technician

Work on computers, audiovisual equipment, video production, or exhibitions. There are promising career ladders in museums for highly skilled technical people in this age of sophisticated technologies.

Tour scheduler

Assist in an education department, taking telephone and written requests, responding to inquiries, and scheduling tours for children and adults. An opportunity to learn the museum education business from the ground up, and you may achieve your museum education goals.

Assistant to the assistant

Wherever there is an opening!

Other support positions

Guard

Every museum must protect its objects, its building, its grounds, its staff, and its visitors. Alert, knowledgeable, well-trained, and responsible guards make the difference. Large museums have senior-level jobs in protection services and guards may serve as "ambassadors" for the museum.

Custodian

Keep the museum and its collections in good shape, cleaning, polishing, waxing, sweeping, repairing, and often keeping a watchful eye for potential damage to objects and equipment. Proper maintenance is obligatory for a first-rate museum, and the skilled person will be recognized and promoted accordingly.

Gardener

Planting, hoeing, raking, transplanting, mowing, weeding, and keeping the grounds of the museum attractive, and in some places educational. You may be a future horticulturalist.

Mechanic

Repair everything from the heating system, the telephones, the museum bus, the lighting, to the exhibition gone awry. Highly skilled and well-organized maintenance work may lead to senior jobs in facilities management.

Woodworker

Construct parts of exhibitions, build cabinets, repair furniture, and use wood-working skills throughout the museum. You may become a supervisor for other museum artisans.

Bibliography: Museum professional positions

Adams, Donald, *Museum Public Relations* (Nashville, Tenn.: American Association for State and Local History, 1993). Guide to marketing, fund-raising, and public relations management.

Alexander, Edward P., *Museum Masters: Their Museums and Their Influence* (Nashville, Tenn.: American Association for State and Local History, 1983). A study of the men and women whose concepts fostered the establishment of museums as educational institutions and the ways they implemented their individual philosophies.

American Association of Museums, *Excellence and Equity: Education and the Public Dimension of Museums* (Washington, DC: American Association of Museums, 1992). Report on the educational role of museums and their responsibilities as public education institutions.

Burke, Robert, and Sam Adeloye, *A Manual of Basic Museum Security* (Leicester, UK: International Council of Museums and International Committee on Museum Security, 1993). Covers security needs, responsibilities, guard-force operations, collections' security, building security (internal and external), fire protection, alarm devices, and personal safety.

Case, Mary, ed., *Registrars on Record: Essays on Museum Collections Management* (Washington, DC: American Association of Museums, 1988). Defines the museum registrar's role and describes collection management issues.

Chenhall, Robert, and David Vance, *Museum Collections and Today's Computers* (Glenview, Ill.: Greenwood Press, 1992). Explanation of the nature of museum records, database management, and computer programming, for executives, museum staff, and computer scientists.

Daniels, Maygene, and Timothy Walch, eds, *A Modern Archives Reader: Basic Readings on Archival Theory and Practice* (Washington, DC: National Archives and Records Service, 1984). Brings together essays of archival literature and articles with basic concepts of archival principles.

Davis, Jessica, and Howard Gardner, "Open Windows Open Doors," *Museum News* 72, no. 1 (1993): 34–7, 57–8. Discusses issues related to education in schools and museums, the learning process, and the unique role of museums.

Finley, G., *et al.* "Being a Curator Is the Most Impossible Profession on Earth," *Muse* 3, no. 4 (1986): 15–18. Conversation among four experienced curators discussing their role.

Friedman, Renée, "Museum People: The Special Problems of Personnel Management in Museums and Historical Agencies," *History News* 37, no. 3 (1982): 14–18. Discusses issues in managing personnel in museums, including personnel problems, volunteers, equal employment opportunities, compensation, labor relations, training, and discipline.

Glaser, Jane R., "Museum Careers in the United States: a Non-System," *Museum International* 45, no. 4 (1993): 18–21. Explains the variety of museum structures and jobs and discusses why no overarching museum classification system exists in the United States.

Kavanagh, Gaynor, "Curatorial Identity," *Museums Journal* 92, no. 10 (1992): 27–33. A series of articles dealing with the curator's profession and the conflicts curators face in today's museums.

—— , ed., *The Museum Profession: Internal and External Relations* (Leicester, UK: Leicester University Press, 1991). Discussions on the museum profession, museum tradition and culture, marketing, performance standards, museums and the economy, and museum theory.

Larsen, John C., *Museum Librarianship* (Hamden, Conn.: Library Professional Publications, 1985). Manual on the museum library's role and functions, including staffing, building, organizing collections, care of collections, and relations with other museum functions.

Liston, David, ed., *Museum Security and Protection* (London, UK: Routledge with ICOM Committee on Security, 1993).

Oddy, Andrew, ed., *The Art of the Conservator* (Washington, DC: Smithsonian Institution Press, 1992). Surveys the skills, techniques, and ethics of museum conservators; includes case studies.

Rose, Cordelia, *Courierspeak* (Washington, DC: Smithsonian Institution Press, 1993). Multilingual (English, French, German, Japanese, Russian, and Spanish) sourcebook and reference on protecting and caring for museum objects during transit.

Theobald, Mary Miley, *Museum Store Management* (Nashville, Tenn.: American Association for State and Local History, 1991). Guide to every phase of museum-store management: includes merchandise and its educational role, product development on budget, security, and inventories.

Thompson, M. A., *Manual of Curatorship: A Guide to Museum Practice,* 2nd edn (Oxford, UK: Butterworth–Heinemann, 1992). Manual on relevant museum issues, including history and kinds of museums, management, conservation, research, and user services.

Suggested readings

Bellow, Corinne, ed., *Public View: The ICOM Handbook of Museum Public Relations* (Paris, France: International Council of Museums, 1986).

Darrogh, Joan, and James S. Snyder, *Museum Design: Planning and Building for Art* (New York: Oxford University Press, 1993).

Dean, David, *Museum Exhibition: Theory and Practice* (London, UK: Routledge, 1994).

A Guide to Museum Positions, Including a Statement on the Ethical Behaviour of Museum Professionals (Ottawa: Canadian Museum Association, 1979).

Hoachlander, Marjorie E., *Profile of a Museum Registrar* (Washington, DC: Academy for Educational Development, 1979).

ICOM Committee for Conservation, *The Graduate Conservator in Employment: Expectations and Realities* (Amsterdam, Netherlands: Opleiding Restauratoren, 1990).

Jones, Walter, *Exhibit Planning, Development, and Implementation Procedures* (Jacksonville, Ala.: Jacksonville State University, Psychology Institute, 1986).

Kavanagh, Gaynor, *History Curatorship* (Leicester, UK: Leicester University Press, 1990).

Lawrence, J., ed., *Museum, Archives, and Library Security* (Woburn, Mass.: Butterworth Publishers, 1983).

Lord, Barry, Gail Dexter, and John Nicks, *The Cost of Collecting: Collection Management in Museums* (London, UK: HMSO, 1989).

Munley, Mary Ellen, *Catalysts for Change: The Kellogg Projects in Museum Education: The Exploratorium, San Francisco, Field Museum of Natural History, Chicago, Smithsonian Institution Office of Museum Programs, Washington, DC* (Chicago and San Francisco: Kellogg Projects in Museum Education, 1986).

"Museum Careers," *Museum International* 45, no. 4 (1993): entire issue.

"Museum Store Management," *History News* 47, no. 5 (1992): entire issue.

National Committee to Save America's Cultural Collections. Caring for Your Collections (New York: N. H. Abrams, 1992).

Naumer, Helmuth, "Evaluating the Museum Director," *Museum News* 65, no. 5 (1987): 61.

Recruiting and Retaining a Diverse Staff (Washington, DC: American Association of Museums Technical Information Service, 1994).

Roberts, David Andrew, *Planning the Documentation of Museum Collections* (Duxford, Cambridge, UK: The Museum Documentation Association, 1985).

Solinger, Janet, ed., *Museums and Universities: New Paths for Continuing Education* (New York: Macmillan Publishing Company for American Council on Education, 1990).

Teather, Lynne, *Professional Directions for Museum Work in Canada: An Analysis of Museum Jobs and Museum Studies Training Curricula* (Ottawa: Canadian Museum Association, 1978).

Tolles, Bryant F., Jr, ed., *Museum Curatorship: Rhetoric vs. Reality* (Newark, Del.: University of Delaware, 1987).

Ward, Philip R., *The Nature of Conservation: A Race against Time* (Marina del Rey, Calif.: Getty Conservation Institute, 1986).

D. Interviews with museum professionals

Artemis A. Zenetou

In a period of two years museums across the country were visited and informal interviews were conducted with many museum professionals at various levels from museums of different sizes and disciplines. They talked about their work in museums, how they became interested in the field, their first jobs, their experiences, and their views and ideas on the profession. This process was an invaluable research and learning experience, a challenging exercise that reinforced beliefs about the profession, at the same time helping to reevaluate museum career development. Through the interviews it was clear that museums have gone through changes during the last ten years; they have become much stronger and much more important in society. The ways that museums exhibit have changed dramatically. Spears or butterflies are no longer simply hung on the wall, but are displayed in their cultural or historical context, or in their natural environment. Museum work has evolved as well. Those who have devoted their careers to the field were proud of the standard of performance incorporated in accreditation programs, the promulgation of codes of ethics, the emergence of formal programs of academic training for those who aspire to museum careers, and the growing body of literature on museum philosophy, theory, and practice.

In the following pages you will read a number of these interviews, which will put in context what you have read so far.

Kenneth Starr, author, and former Director of the Milwaukee Public Museum, Milwaukee, Wisconsin

"Unlike the university people who have books and ideas, in the museum field we have books and ideas and the objects that make it a totality.

I was drawn to museums through my interest for the outdoors; I have always enjoyed the natural world. My undergraduate work was mainly in Asian history, particularly China, my master's degree in Chinese language and literature, and my doctorate in anthropology.

My approach to museums was through natural history museums. I went to museums as a child as one of the fortunate ones, but it wasn't until graduate school that I had a fellowship at the Yale Peabody Museum of Natural History and so formally entered the museum profession. From that point on, for forty years, I have been in museums.

My first real job was at the Field Museum of Natural History, where I was in charge of the Asian collection, curator of anthropology and ethnology, for seventeen years. There I had the chance to combine natural history and human history. I did a great deal of exhibit work. I always had many friends in the art world, and I've always spanned all the disciplines and tried not to be parochial. Some of the people in the museum profession that I most admire are those who understand the goals and purposes of those in other disciplines – "Renaissance" people with diverse backgrounds who provide perspective.

My next position was director at the Milwaukee Public Museum, which is one of the largest museums of natural and human history in the country. Milwaukee was the center for cyclorama painting, in the late nineteenth century, so many artists worked in diorama painting for the museum. . . . Carl Akeley, the famous taxidermist, also was at the museum at that period. Instead of just using stiff poses, with the animals standing on four legs, he was able to put them in lifelike poses. He did his work, and then these cyclorama painters painted the background of the dioramas. So two traditions and two techniques came together there in Milwaukee.

In 1987 I retired, but I received an invitation from the National Science Foundation to work for two years in science education. I dealt particularly with natural history museums, and with botanical gardens and zoological parks, which had not been active in searching for funding. In retirement I am on the board of the Historical Society of Frederick County, Maryland, and I am pressing for professional standards as one of my salient interests."

Barbara K. Gibbs, Director, Cincinnati Art Museum, Cincinnati, Ohio, former director, Crocker Museum of Art, Sacramento, California

"I was an art student at Brown University, with a major in English. I loved art and was lucky in getting my first job. I knew someone who allowed me to work on a contract basis at the Museum of Art, Rhode Island School of Design. I gave Sunday lectures for the public, I wrote a column for the *Providence Journal Bulletin* featuring different objects from the collection, and I helped with the educational brochures.

Later on I went to Vancouver, British Columbia, and there, through a personal connection I got an entry-level job at the Vancouver Art Gallery. I worked in the education department, where I was assigned the organization of the slide library. Once I started working at the museum I volunteered in different areas, so eventually I lectured to docents, I gave public tours, etc.

I went back to the United States, where I applied for lots of arts-related jobs, and I didn't get any. Because I did not have a graduate degree, didn't have connections, in general not much to offer, I started working on various other jobs. I was ready to bail out of the arts field and go to business school when I learned about the University of California at Los Angeles (UCLA) arts management program and applied. That was a turning point for me. It was very exciting. The students in the program were top-notch. The program itself was dedicated to building the students' confidence and using every avenue to open doors and place students. It suited my experience and my personality really well. I did my internship at the Guggenheim in development and then had the nerve to turn down the first job that was offered to me after school, which was to run a community arts program. I knew I wanted to work in museums and I felt that job would get me further from my goal.

My first professional job was deputy director of the Portland Art Association in Oregon. I worked there for four years, and I was able to establish a strong administrative department serving the three areas of that institution: the museum of art, the art school, and the film-study center. It was a wonderful experience, but did not have direct involvement with the artistic end of the institution, and that was not really going to change. So I applied for several other museum jobs, and I was surprised but delighted to be hired as the director of the Crocker Art Museum. I've been here for almost nine years. I have had the opportunity to build the collection, the staff, the building, and the endowment. It's been a complete joy."

Peter Ames, Consultant, former Vice-president for Programs, Boston Museum of Science, Boston, Massachusetts

"I answered an ad in *The Wall Street Journal* for an assistant counsel in a major New York museum [the Metropolitan Museum of Art], which was essentially for the number-two lawyer. I got the job within a couple of months, and after a number of years I am still working in the field.

I went to law school and I hadn't been thinking of working in a museum, but if you look a little deeper it wasn't really accidental, as I grew up in "museum mile" in Manhattan. My mother also worked in a museum, so I was going to museums all the time. I had a predisposed positive attitude for museums, which is very important and may be the real reason I entered museums. I did not attend any museum studies programs, and I would say the only part of my education that seems particularly germane to museums is that skill that one develops in law school of identifying and framing critical issues. I have worked in three different museums – an art museum, an aquarium, and a science museum – and I have consulted for many others. In terms of preparing for a museum career, I think I am one of the relatively few people in the field, whom I know, who have been in charge of programs but is not a subject matter expert in the respective field. My undergraduate degree was in modern European history, and my postgraduate work in international affairs and international law. The only thing I might have done differently would be to get an MA earlier on in the subject-matter that interested me the most.

In my current job at the Boston Museum of Science, I have been concerned with learning resources – the library, the collection – with education both in and out of the museum, with the theaters (Planetarium and Omni), and with temporary exhibitions. I spend a lot of my time planning, allocating resources, supporting. I try to see problems before they get too complicated. I am into preventive measures. I try to spend a fair amount of time brainstorming and in creative thinking to see if there is anything else we should be doing. I also spend a good part of my time either fund-raising or in support of fund-raising."

Joyce Elliott, former Head of Publications, National Building Museum, Washington, DC

"My background is in education and freelance writing. At some point in my career I stopped and was looking for something else. I came across a newspaper ad that a local museum was looking for volunteers. It sounded so interesting, so very different. I applied and got the job immediately. I was asked to work on the first issue of the newsletter, and now, ten years later, I am still with the museum, heading the publications office. I started as a volunteer and later became paid staff. I think it's a case of being at the right place at the right time. In the beginning we were mainly a group of volunteers, most of us having come to learn about museums by being here. Now several people from the staff come from museum studies programs.

Trends seem to be changing. Depending on what kind of work you are looking for within a museum determines what kind of background is needed. I am currently planning to hire an assistant, and I want someone with a publications, design, and graphics background and at least a general idea of what museums are and what they do. I need someone who will come in and be able to take on responsibilities and do things immediately. Things have changed a lot since I came on board."

Barbara Luton, Director of Development, Santa Barbara Museum of Art, Santa Barbara, California

"I have been working in this museum for five and one half years now. Although I did not come to this job through normal museum channels, the transition from my previous position to this one was very smooth. I held a similar position in a small liberal arts college, having worked my way up by doing a variety of different jobs – grant writing, public relations, publications, direct mail, etc. When I came to the museum my main task was to manage a staff that had specialists in all those areas. I was a generalist; I knew about all the areas of development since I have worked in all of them at some point.

The biggest difference that I have encountered working in a museum is the fact that there is much more emphasis on federal grant-seeking. However, in our museum the majority of the support is from individuals, on a local basis. In a college or university support tends to be more widespread since you have alumni all over the country.

My academic background is in psychology. In the beginning, when I started working at the college, I was involved with the public relations area. The typical professional path in a development career is to begin in public relations as it is the low end of the totem. To grow beyond that you need to become more involved with development and fund-raising. While I was working at the college, I got an MBA degree. In order to prepare for a career in development, I would suggest starting with a liberal arts background. In development work you don't really need to have a fine-arts background, and you learn the development-related skills on the job. However I would advise a student to take some museum courses to obtain a well-rounded education in how museums work. In my case the master's degree also helped a great deal, and I would strongly recommend it."

Glenn Gutleben, Exhibit Designer/Electronics Engineer, The Exploratorium, San Francisco, California

"If you are looking for something that is really going to make a difference in the world or educate people, by all means you should think about working in a museum.

I am an electronics engineer by training, and I worked in research and development electronics, doing basically medical and biological work. The company I was working for moved out of town, and I did not want to follow. I looked around for jobs but I did not find anything that interested me; I was getting tired of the corporate world. One night this movie came on PBS; it was about The Exploratorium and Frank Oppenheimer, the founder. It was really interesting, but I thought it was probably impossible to work there since I did not have a museum background. However, I went in the next day and found my way to the electronics shop office. I spoke to the supervisor, as the museum needed an electronics engineer to design exhibits. For the following three weeks I was there practically every other day. I guess that indicated my strong interest. Finally, they called me up and they had a job for me. That was it!

As you realize, I came to the museum field totally cold; I had no background or museum experience in any sense. I liked The Exploratorium, and I thought it was doing a neat thing with hands-on science education – teaching people that the world around them is understandable to everyone and that you don't need mathematics or a lot of science background to understand.

I think if you are interested in a museum career you have to visit as many museums as you possibly can . . . even if you have the traditional museum training. If that involves taking time and traveling, just do it . . . take your camera with you, take a notebook, and look at the exhibits very closely. What are they about . . . what are they trying to tell me . . . if I were going to do it, how I would have done it differently . . . what don't I understand about it? Professional background and education will certainly make a difference. It is important to know what you like and what intrigues you about museums . . . if a particular area interests you or some type of exhibit, that is what you should concentrate on, think about that, and develop the skills you need to do that."

Edith A. Tonelli, former Director, Wight Art Gallery, UCLA, Los Angeles, California

"It was through my art-history professor, Linda Nochlin, with her enthusiasm and energy, that I got . . . interested in art and museums. Growing up, I was never in a museum as far as I can remember. In our community there was no museum of art. It was a real eye-opener to take her class and work as her research assistant.

I started in museums with an internship at the Boston Museum of Fine Arts, which was very helpful and gave me a lot of contacts. My first full-time job was at the De Cordova Museum, Lincoln, Massachusetts, where I got a whole sense of how the museum works from the ground floor up. I was the one and only curator. Because it was a small museum, everything was done in house. There were not many on staff, so I did everything from painting pedestals to writing the essays in the catalog and hanging the work. It was a good introduction to what a museum does.

Other than the internship and the De Cordova, I have worked in two university museums during the past fifteen years. A museum at a university campus is perceived to be unlike any other unit on campus. It is not usually seen by the administration as being in the core of the educational instruction of the university. It is often a second-class citizen, so we always have to fight and justify our existence and needs. Mine is a multifaceted job that is sometimes hard to understand. Some days I am only fund-raising and making the necessary contacts; sometimes I am a university ambassador who hosts people from different countries. I still teach. I spend a considerable amount of time in management issues, working with the staff, making sure that things are going well, supervising people and budgets. I have a very good administrative manager, but I still need to know day by day how the budget stands. I describe my job as being the manager of a small business on one side because I need all these skills to run the institution, and on the other side I need an academic and aesthetic sensitivity, and a strong commitment to the arts."

Sarah J. Wolf, Director of Conservation and Collections Management, The Textile Museum, Washington, DC

"My starting in museum work was a result of my graduate work. I was doing archeological fieldwork in Italy, where I met Carolyn Rose [conservator at the Smithsonian's Museum of Natural History]. I was not enthusiastic about continuing in archeology, and she encouraged me to pursue the conservation field. I became one of the first students at the George Washington University program in conservation [it no longer exists].

I have spent my entire career working in museums, beginning with internships and then moving into jobs of greater responsibility. While my graduate work prepared me to conserve objects, it did not teach me the management skills necessary to be an effective team member of a museum staff. These were skills I had to learn on the job.

I think that management issues, issues about collections care, and the integration of conservation principles into the daily operations of a museum are important for a conservator to understand. It is also important to recognize that conservation is only one part of what takes place in a museum, and that the needs of the collection have to be balanced with the needs of exhibition, research, and education.

131

Having worked in large institutions like the Smithsonian, and in smaller institutions as well, I have come to appreciate the opportunity for creativity that smaller institutions have to offer. I also have taken the opportunity to work in several different kinds of institutions, feeling that I arrive at a museum with a set of skills and a goal to use those skills for the betterment of the collection. Once I have achieved that goal, I have moved on to undertake new challenges.

At present, I no longer spend much time as a bench conservator, although I do teach interns. My current job is administrative; I am responsible for a large department of people who do conservation treatment, collections management and exhibition preparation. In addition to contributing to institutional long-range planning, I participate in the exhibitions task force that plans the exhibition program for the museum, and I chair the collection management task force that deals with policies and procedures as well as the museum's daily operations relating to the collections.

More and more conservators are becoming managers in addition to their collection treatment responsibilities. Communication skills are important as more of us are asked to participate in institution-wide activities, and as the museum community continues to integrate conservation and preservation principles more fully into all aspects of daily operations. My job description may not be typical of most conservators, but I enjoy the opportunity to have an impact on my museum beyond my hand-skills."

Kenneth Yellis, Assistant Director of Public Programs, Peabody Museum, Yale University, New Haven, Connecticut

"For me, starting to work in a museum was definitely a case of luck. I had just finished graduate school in history and I was trying to get a job teaching. I did not have a detailed sense of what museum careers were or whether, indeed, there were any for historians. There was an announcement from the National Endowment of Humanities for a museum fellowship at the National Portrait Gallery. Since my academic possibilities were coming up empty, I decided to send in an application. Within a couple of weeks I was called and asked for an interview and shortly after I was offered a fellowship.

When I went to the museum for the first time, I fell in love with it. I think I loved the building as a building, but I don't think that was what won me over so much as the labels. I don't think I ever went to a museum in which the labels took the visitor quite so seriously as a learner. There was so much effort to ... frame for the visitor what he or she was seeing and provide a sense of context and appropriate detail. The museum treated me as an adult, and, of course, it was about history, and especially biography, in which I have always been interested.

I did not study to become a museum professional, although the fellowship was an extraordinary preparation for a museum career. During the year at the museum I worked in virtually every department. The director of the museum had assembled a group of young, talented people, and I had a chance to be tutored by every one of them in some dimension of museum work. It was a museum that was thinking about what its role in the community was and, in general, permeated by an idea of professionalism. It was a really good place to learn your craft.

I spent a lot of time in the education department doing elementary and secondary school programs, going through docent training, education training, and, in general, trying to get the hang of what museum education was about. We also did a lot of work in exhibitions, everything from objects research to dismantling the show. There were various shows that were in different stages of development and during the course of a year I was involved in one or more phases of each of them. I also did research, uncrated objects, built a show-case for an object, and walked through the galleries taking off dust. Not every moment was wonderful, but it was a great experience and I am still in the museum field.

Since then I have worked in three museums [for a total] of almost twenty-one years. As a consultant for a period of time, I provided creative management services for museums and other cultural organizations, which ranged from exhibition curation, to development, to program and needs assessments, to writing and editing. I have migrated from history and biography to living history (Plymouth Plantation) to natural history (Yale Peabody Museum), where I am now, telling stories in exhibits and programs about the earth, its past, and its people. It's fun."

Marie Acosta Colon, Director, The Mexican Museum, San Francisco, California

"When I was in high school and in college I used to go to museums, but I did not feel comfortable, I never felt welcomed, never felt a relationship with the work; I felt intimidated.

I entered the museum field from the theater, where I was an actress and an arts administrator for many years. I come to the field more with an arts-administration background rather than museum training. Probably I would have never considered working in a museum except that it is The Mexican Museum. My own personal philosophy is that the arts and in extension, museums, need to serve society and if they don't, then I am not interested. I think in this country, for our community, the museum needs to be saying something about who we are, reinforcing it, providing our people with our history, with our culture, with the accomplishments of Mexican people both in Mexico and the US. For that reason, I agreed to work at The Mexican Museum.

It has been three years since I joined the museum and it has been rewarding and a lot of hard work. Last year a teacher approached me from an elementary school in Oakland, that was having a career day. The school had never had anyone from the museum field, and would I be interested? I thought it was a great opportunity to tell kids that museums were actually workplaces where someone could make a living. People don't realize that. They look at museums and because they don't see what is going on in the background, because of what people consider traditional jobs, it's hard to think of a museum job. I think a lot depends on how you market museums so that they become a viable option. The field itself has built this aura of "sacred place" around museums, a unique, mysterious entity. So if you can't break through, how can people find out that there are indeed job opportunities? Museums have to open up. At The Mexican Museum we have started this demystification.

My own priority and responsibility right now [is] to build the new facility. When I started the budget was $549,000, and had five staff, and gallery attendants. This year [1992] we have a $1.5 million budget and nineteen staff members – phenomenal growth."

Edmund B. Gaither, Director, Museum of the National Center of Afro-American Artists, Boston, Massachusetts

"We must know what the museum is and what it can do. We should come with more questions than answers and think of it as an enterprise which has a 'people' dimension as well as an 'object' dimension. You have to be prepared to embrace change as a value, and to enjoy participating in change.

I grew up in a very small town in South Carolina, in an area with no museums. My first encounter with museums was at the college level. I had a great interest in art and got a lot of support and encouragement. I knew there was a high probability that I would end up doing something in the arts. I had to think what I would do for a livelihood. So as an undergraduate I was trying to put together a major in art history at a college that didn't really offer that. So my option was to try general humanities, and I ended up taking English literature with history and art as minors, and that was the best balance of humanities course work I could get. I did very well in academic subjects. I was very interested in issues – iconography and philosophy – so art history seemed the best way to go. I still didn't think about museums. I thought more about teaching, and I thought I might contribute by developing literature in American art history focusing on Afro-American issues.

I went to Brown University in Providence, Rhode Island, where in the program I had the chance to take some courses in museum work; a methods course involved organizing exhibitions was one. That particular program gave me a footing to go either direction, teaching or museum work. I taught art history in Atlanta, and as I considered my return to go to school in New York City, I got an invitation to be considered for a new post which was not yet defined with the Boston Museum of Fine Arts. The museum had been pressed to respond to the 'black presence' and to be the national center for Afro-American artists. A professor of mine from Brown University had submitted my name, and I guess that's how I was considered.

I got the job, and I thought I would be in Boston for a couple of years and then return to school. I came to Boston, and I found myself in this absolutely unusual circumstance of being able to work for a very large, very well-established museum, and being free to develop the African American Center in a museum, which existed only as a vague idea. So I had the chance to create the idea, shape it, and then bring it to being. When I actually started to work it was necessary to think a lot more of what being in the museum world really meant, in terms of what kinds of museums will be useful, and what their purposes ought to be, and what it might demand. It was about that time that I met John Kinard, who was, to a very considerable degree, a mentor. He was very well rounded in what he thought museums ought to do, and I was very influenced by that."

Bonnie VanDorn, Executive Director, Association of Science–Technology Centers, Washington, DC

"I was an elementary school teacher. As a teacher I took my students to the Pacific Science Center every year for three years, and I fell in love with the place. When I decided that I wanted to leave teaching in the public schools, I couldn't think of anything I wanted to do more than explore the possibility of working in a science museum. It would allow me to use my educational background, but at the same time it would give me a lot of freedom to do interesting educational things with a whole range of people. I was fortunate that at the time there was an opening at the Science Center. The Center was looking for someone with a master's in education and experience in curriculum development and teaching. I had had contact with the staff and the director while I was teaching at a public school. I got the job. If I had known that someday I would be working in a science museum I would have probably gotten a stronger science background. It was on-the-job training. I never missed not having a museum studies background. The science center where I worked . . . was not into collecting; there weren't any curators on staff, and we never had anyone called a docent. It was truly an informal education institution, and so coming through the school system was probably better for me than coming from a museum background."

Ellen Holtzman, Program Director for the Arts, The Henry Luce Foundation, New York; former Managing Director, The New Museum of Contemporary Art, New York

"When I was in high school, I fell in love with art museums through my Spanish class. We were exposed to art, and I discovered Picasso, Dali, and El Greco. I had to go to the Metropolitan to research my Spanish paper. It was through this class that I got hooked on museums.

I was preparing for a career in art. As an undergraduate I majored in art history. I wasn't quite sure what I was going to do with that, so I went straight

135

to graduate school, figuring that it would all become clear. Then I started a doctoral degree. In graduate school I expected to teach or get a job in a museum.

While I was in undergraduate school I worked in a very important commercial art gallery, and I was exposed to the best artists in the area. That was very interesting, but I still did not know whether I wanted to go work in a museum or in a commercial gallery or teach, so I continued my studying and went part way through my doctoral program. At some point I decided to get into the real world. All my friends with doctoral degrees were jobless. I felt it was time to get out there, so I did not complete my doctoral degree. I was on the west coast and I was trying to get a job teaching at a junior college or to break into the museum world. I had absolutely no luck for one year. I knew no one, no connections, no strings. I went back to the east coast, where eventually I got a job in a gallery. I had started developing my own eye and got interested in having my own shop. I did that for almost two years as I was dealing with selecting artists and organizing shows. After a couple of years I had to assess the fact that this wasn't going to be a very fruitful career for me or my artists, so I had to give it up.

I found a job out of the newspaper classified as the assistant to the director of a New York museum. It was basically a secretarial position but the director's *righthand person*. I was miserable that I had to take this job, but at least it was in the director's office. It was an instinct I had. I hit it off with the director and he immediately knew I was overqualified. For one and one-half years I was his special assistant, and frankly that is where I learned what museums are all about. If I could make every aspiring museum professional work for a while in a director's office, I would strongly recommend it. In my experience as a managing director I found that most people in the museum are focused on their own areas – be it education, curatorial or conservation department – and they don't necessarily have an overview of all the things a museum and a director have to deal with.

There was no guarantee that this job was going to lead me somewhere, but I was able to prove myself. About two years later a job opened in the education department. It was called assistant manager. The job was actually head of public programs, which involved doing all the interpretive programs for special exhibitions, lectures, etc. I applied and got the job. It was a great job. With my art history background I got to work with the curators about the concept of the exhibitions, but not to curate them. I liked the variety, it was a lot of running around, you got feedback from the public. It was autonomous in the sense that the public wanted programs, and I did programs. It was an enormously rewarding experience.

About three years later I saw an announcement for a job as the assistant director of a museum in Queens, New York, and, to be perfectly honest, I wanted to see at the time how I could fly. How I could be received if I was looking for that level job. Evaluating my skills, I had become very good in conceiving programs, but I was also a good manager, and it was clear that that was something that I could build on, having learned what I did in the director's office, then becoming an assistant director started making sense. That was the next step. Then I became the managing director of a contemporary art museum, which basically meant that I dealt with policy, implementation, working with the staff, overseeing everything. Although I did not have my own projects, I monitored other people's projects and some of the day-to-day issues that came up in the museum."

Harry Robinson, Director, African American Life and Culture Museum, Dallas, Texas

"My formal academic training was in history and library science. I sort of stumbled into museum work not knowing what I was doing. When I was a student in college I accidentally met a dean of academic affairs who was working in the college archives. I would go on Saturday afternoons and work with him on old pictures and old material; I just had a natural liking for that kind of work, so I went to library school and got a master's in library science, got involved with special black history collections. I left Atlanta University, went to Kentucky State University, where I did some more work on a smaller scale with archival material. I went back to graduate school, where I became more interested in this line of work. I went to the University of Illinois, where I was instrumental in organizing an archival program. My next move led me to Alabama State University as dean, where I was responsible for special-collections archives, the gallery – the works as you may say. I stayed there for a while and got involved with a lot of museum-type activities.

I left Alabama and came to Texas, to Bishop College, where I started a museum. The museum I direct now was originally part of Bishop College. In 1979 we became independent, established our own board but remained on campus. Our museum's collections focus on African American art, African American folk art, and African art. We're in the process of building a new museum based on our collection [and completed it in 1994]. Our goal is to become a regional museum. Right now we're concentrating, from a history point of view, on Texas history, and we deal with African and African American art from a more global perspective.

If I didn't go into museum work I probably would have been a college librarian or a university administrator. I decided to let all that go and stay in museums. In the black community most of us came from backgrounds other than museums. It was not our tradition, but now it's changing. Young people are now preparing. When I came into the field, I came through the back door, but now young people want to plan for a career, and I think we have an obligation to tell them how. If we can expose more kids to museum work and help them see the value of museums, we will be able to attract more of them into the field."

Thomas Moritz, Librarian, California Academy of Sciences, San Francisco, California

"One of the things I am really proud of is that, during my six years at the academy, we've had three nonprofessional library assistants who gained experience through this library and decided to go to Berkeley to earn degrees in librarianship.

Growing up, I spent a lot of time in the American Museum of Natural History in New York. My background is in international affairs, and then I went to library school in New York. When it was time to do an internship, I decided that the library of the American Museum of Natural History would be a very good place, partially because I had this long-standing love for the museum. From that point on I went to work for the federal government in Washington, DC.

I was not trained as a scientist, but I have been working in the sciences for about fifteen years. My first library job was shelving books at the United States Department of the Interior Library in Washington, DC, while I studied Chinese at George Washington University (GWU), and I continued working for the government in a variety of positions, and then for the University of Washington. The reasons I applied for my current job was that I love museums, and in particular natural history museums, and I also loved San Francisco. My passion and interest in museums are what eventually led me here.

I don't think that there was specific academic training for the work I am doing here. Many of the skills that I acquired in the process have full application in my current job. In fact, a lot of the skills that I developed in a whole variety of areas, personally and professionally, have application now that I am in this setting. My role here at the Academy has been as a librarian. That's my nominal title, but my activity has been far broader than that. I am serving on national and international committees in the systematics community having to do with computerization of collections and a whole range of other activities. There has been a fortunate confluence in my training in natural history and my background in international affairs.

Ron L. Kagan, Director, Detroit Zoo, Royal Oaks Michigan

"Zoos have more of a social conscience than they used to. Our public is finally demanding more; people are becoming more sophisticated, and they're expecting us to be more sensitive. Zoos have an incredible nitch to fill because we are *nature* offered in the middle of an urban environment. We are a place for all cultures, people from different backgrounds to visit. In a way, we're a melting pot, which gives us unique opportunities that other places don't have. A lot of people argue that museums don't necessarily have a broad enough appeal, but, fortunately, you find everybody at the zoo.

I loved animals from a very early age. When I went to college I studied zoology. My working in a zoo happened in a very strange way. In 1973, when the war in Israel broke out, I left the United States and went there to volunteer. When I arrived the Israelis needed help at the zoo because all the people that worked there normally were away in the army and the reserves, so within two days I was working in the zoo. If this incident had not happened I had been thinking more of becoming a veterinarian.

I completed my studies and for a while taught at a university. I don't know whether what I learned in college helped me that much in my current job [Dallas Zoo], and, in fact, when we recruit people to work in zoos often we don't look as closely at zoology majors as we do at majors such as animal science and wildlife science, because that is a more applied approach. I should stress that my academic training has been critical in developing scientific programs. So that prepared me for one particular aspect of working in a zoo, but in terms of administration and animal management these are not things you learn with a zoology degree. Practical experience is very important. For someone interested in working in a zoo I would recommend . . . working with animals while you're studying. It could be working for a veterinarian or volunteering at the local zoo or with a wildlife organization."

JoAllyn Archambault, Curator, American Indian Program, Department of Anthropology, National Museum of Natural History, Smithsonian Institution, Washington, DC

"I don't think I have a career in a museum. I have a career as an anthropologist, and I happen to work in a museum. I think that young people should be counseled with a very honest portrayal of job opportunities in the museum field. We should be up front in telling them that there are so many job openings per year, it's a small field, and it does not pay all that well. If they are still interested and have the passion, they should pursue it. The next thing they should do is find out about the different kinds of positions within the field and what kind of museum they think they would like to work in. Once they figure out these things and they know what kind of career they want to have, they can make the correct choices regarding their education and practical experience that will facilitate their goal. They need to pose questions such as: Do I really want to be in an education office, or be a curator? What does it really mean to be a curator? Do I want to be a conservator or an exhibit designer?

It's really ironic that my first job was in a museum, on the University of California Berkeley campus. I was a freshman in anthropology, and it was just sheer luck. It was a small museum where everybody did a bit of everything. I was painting backdrops, preparing cases, cleaning glass, working with the text – a little bit of everything. I worked there for almost two years. Then the museum lost funding, and I had to get another job. I never thought I would work in a museum again. I have always enjoyed museums but never

139

thought of being a museum professional. I started out to become an anthropologist, and that's what I've been. I never studied to become a museum professional. My major in graduate school and all my degrees were in anthropology. Then this job happened; it was serendipity. I had been teaching for almost ten years, and I was getting tired of it. I was asked to apply for this job, and I got it. It has turned out to be the best job I've ever had in my life. It has allowed me to use more of my skills than any other position I've ever had and it allows me more control over what I am doing. I am a program director/curator, where I engage all of my skills in ways that simply having a teaching position never did before. It allows me to be around the kinds of objects that I love, plus be in a setting where I could do lots of research, if I only had the time."

Janet Dorman, former Museum Shop Manager,
The Phillips Collection, Washington, DC

"It has been on-the-job training, although many of my shop colleagues have straight retail backgrounds or book selling. I think a lot of those merchandising ideas are very helpful as museums today depend upon the net profit a shop can provide.

Straight out of college I got a job as a museum assistant, which was essentially a guard position in one of the galleries. I had a background in art history and studio art. I studied painting and drawing and came to this museum because lots of artists were coming to the galleries sitting and working. At some point the museum started to change rapidly, and a lot of positions were opening up. The position that I ultimately started working in after about a year was photographic services. I coordinated all of the reproduction of paintings and filled orders to lenders who wanted photographs and rights to reproduce images from the collection. Through that job I became assistant to the administrator. I worked on grant proposals and assisted in preparing the museum operating budgets. I stayed in that position for about three years while I continued doing all photographic work, so I learned a little about publishing. There was an opening in the museum shop, and I was one of the people who was considered. I got the job, and later on became the museum-shop manager. I do all the buying, handling all publishing except exhibition catalogues, and all new product development.

I think that one of the reasons I am good for this job is because I know every object in the collection. I have good visual knowledge, but I also think it is very important for a museum shop manager to know the institution. You have to be sensitive to the museum's collection as educational and aesthetic and not only as a product. In my case it was more on-the-job training; I never received an advanced degree either in museum studies or in art history. For my specific job, I had to learn all the laws (copyright, trademark, Unrelated Business Income Tax), attend seminars, and learn a lot by talking to my colleagues in other museums. I found the latter very helpful because even if they didn't know the answer, they would put me in touch with people who would. There is a strong collegiality."

One of the most important things the interviewer and interviewees shared was the excitement of discovering museum work, the willingness to act collaboratively and a passion for museums. There are many different kinds of people needed in the museum world – *detail* people, *big picture* people, *idea* people and *practical* people. We hope that you will be able to discover yourself among them.

7

Volunteer–staff relations

"Volunteerism is a strongly established American institution, and the creative, self-fulfilling nature of museum work will continue to attract volunteer women and men with strong cultural and community interests. Indeed, many museums could not exist without their talented and devoted volunteers."[1]

Whatever course your museum career takes in the United States, you will have the pleasure of meeting and working with volunteers. (Less so in other countries of the world, but that is changing.) You will, in some capacity, work for and alongside them. Museum trustees are volunteers; so, too, are docents. In fact, volunteers work in nearly every aspect of museum operations. It is very important for you who may be planning a museum career to understand the vital contributions volunteers make to museums, and the special outlook working with them demands.

The most amazing fact about museum staffing is that volunteers actually outnumber paid museum staff by three to one. They come in both genders and from all educational and cultural backgrounds. According to the AAM 1990 survey, some 376,020 Americans volunteer in museums, and they contribute in countless ways. Some serve in museums' public arenas – answering questions at information desks, leading tours, and clerking in museum shops. Many contribute professional skills – keeping hands-on science exhibits in working order, researching an artist's career for a catalog chronology, or leading a workshop for children. In all these capacities, volunteers are committed to the importance of museum work and dedicated to the museums they serve.

Museums recognize the vital contributions of volunteers; but to be effective, they must be trained, directed, and supervised by staff (and sometimes by more experienced volunteers). You may need to devote many hours to the well-being of the corps of volunteers. In most museums, volunteers, the same as paid staff, are interviewed, are hired, work on a regular basis, and can be "relieved of their duties" (more often transferred to another assignment) when their work is not satisfactory. Their work schedules may vary from eight hours per week to once per month. Some volunteers work full-time. Adjusting

"Volunteers are critical for museums. I think they deserve all the support they can get, but I would put some emphasis on training of volunteers to make sure that their abilities and knowledge are up to speed, with goodwill, in making things happen."

Peter Ames, formerly Boston Museum of Science

volunteer schedules to meet the needs of the institution is never easy. Many museums now have a paid staff volunteer coordinator (see Chapter 6) who keeps the program running smoothly so that other staff members are free to supervise the work performed by volunteers in their particular areas. Tact and diplomacy are, of course, important in working with volunteers, who need to be encouraged, motivated, and rewarded for their services outside the employer–employee framework. There are sometimes frustrations for staff who hesitate to make demands on volunteers or who encounter conflicts among paid and unpaid staff (or among the volunteers themselves) who must work together amicably. But most museum people find volunteers an inspiration. Their willingness to devote their efforts and talents to museums is testimony to the strong ties museums have with the communities they serve.

Trustees

Although the volunteers you work with on a daily basis will command your attention to schedules and necessary skills required, in a larger sense your role in your museum itself will be shaped by policies made by volunteers on the board of trustees (see Chapter 4). Many museums owe their existence to groups of private citizens who crafted a mission and purpose for the institution, formed the first board of trustees, and then administered the museum's operations as volunteers until paid staff could be hired. Today trustees contribute time and expertise to the governance of their institutions, and they assume significant legal obligations when they agree to take on the responsibilities of board members. Although unpaid and part-time, trustees wield influence and power that affect all aspects of the museum's operations. They formulate policies, approve budgets, raise money, and oversee the director as executive officer, but they do not interfere with the director's administration and management of the museum. (This is where problems may arise within a museum's governance.)

Trustees should be carefully selected to represent different facets of the community, and many museums are making special efforts to be certain that trustees do reflect the entire diverse community the museum serves. Many trustees come to boards uninitiated in the museum's mission, operations, ethics, and cultural and educational purposes, and they are devoting just *part* of their busy lives to the museum. Thus, trustee orientation – the responsibility of the director and sometimes of other staff as well – ensures that trustees understand the museum's mission, goals, and objectives, the nature of a nonprofit institution, and the avoidance of any conflict of interest. At the same time,

"It is primarily a labor of love, both for staff and volunteers. I think students must be made aware of the fact that without volunteers, museums generally cannot exist."

Jeannine Smith Clark, regent, Smithsonian Institution

orientation of trustees gives you, as staff, reinforcement as to what it means to serve a volunteer board as opposed to the hierarchy of a for-profit organization. The bottom line in a nonprofit organization is adherence to the mission, budget, policies, and procedures, and compliance with the museum's code of ethics and its goals for services approved by the trustees – not the number of widgets produced and the end-of-the-year profit margin. Whatever your relationship with trustees may be – collegial, subordinate, or even distant at times (depending heavily on personalities involved and the director's initiatives) – you are ultimately, directly or indirectly, responsible to them.

As a staff member, your primary relationship with the board of trustees will be through the director of the museum, who will seek to maintain a complementary and cooperative working relationship in both directions. The director is the liaison to the board for the staff and should endeavor to represent your point of view and that of other staff members fairly and forcefully. If you are "senior staff," you may be called on occasion to meet with the board and present your views on, for example, funds required for a special project, a legal problem that has arisen, or requests for acquisitions not already included in the budget. Staff members at all levels may be called on to help formulate policies on collections, education, administration, accessibility, staff training, and other issues that will be presented and recommended by the director to the trustees for approval. The same is true for the annual budget, and the director must justify and defend all items for the board to consider. Other staff may not have direct access to the trustees, but they nonetheless are affected by all board actions.

Internationally, for the most part, a national, provincial, or local governmental unit serves in a similar capacity as a board of trustees, providing oversight, monitoring, and assuming financial responsibilities.

Trustees today generally take their responsibilities seriously – not merely lending their names and positions, but participating actively and networking with other trustees through the professional museum associations and the Museum Trustee Association's meetings and newsletters.

"I strongly believe in volunteers. I actually don't want to use the term 'volunteers.' They are people who are competent, and can work. There are people who are on the payroll, and there are people who are not. This has nothing to do with competence. I don't like the contrast between 'professional' versus 'volunteer.' I believe there are professional volunteers."

Tom L. Freudenheim, Smithsonian Institution

"I think it is especially important for adolescents to work as volunteers in museums. I would love to see more emphasis for work-like experiences that enrich and broaden their career possibilities and their own ability to envision a museum career. The 'explainers' positions in science centers are often the road into a science museum career."

Bonnie VanDorn, Association of Science–Technology Centers

Beyond the board room, some volunteers – gallery guides (or docents) or information-desk and shop volunteers, for example – work directly with visitors. Others are involved in less visible, but equally valuable, services behind the scenes – in administrative offices, exhibition departments, libraries, curatorial departments, registrar's offices, and conservation laboratories.

Visitor services and public programs

The work of volunteers is most visible in a museum's public arenas – visitor services, and public programs – and often volunteers are the only people with whom museum visitors come in contact. For this reason, if it is your responsibility to select and train volunteers for these areas, you will need to screen all applicants for their special motivation, talents, and skills, including a desire and willingness to research, study, and learn, and to be outgoing, with good communications skills. Staff must understand the philosophy of "hiring" unpaid workers so that volunteers understand the professional standards of the museum. Some museums even go through the formality of having a contract or written agreement outlining the responsibilities of both parties.

One major responsibility the museum has to volunteers is training. Because volunteers at information desks are usually the visitor's first contact with the museum, other than security officers, they must be trained by the staff to meet, greet, and welcome a diverse public on behalf of the museum and respond to needs, questions, and interests. Volunteers at membership sales desks and in museum shops must receive training in their specific responsibilities, and be equally knowledgeable about the museum's exhibitions, collections, and mission as a whole.

In interpretive programs volunteers may be called docents, interpreters, gallery guides, or explainers (animateurs, in some countries) and work in a highly visible, sensitive, and critical part of a museum's public educational programming. They usually undergo extensive training conducted by staff, often lasting a year or more. You may be asked to develop such a training program that ensures volunteers have a strong knowledge of content related to the museum's collections and exhibitions, and that also emphasizes communications and inquiry skills. Following training, the work of volunteers needs to be monitored carefully. To many museum visitors, they will be the "museum staff."

Sometimes volunteers in public programs concentrate their efforts on working with schools and schoolchildren. These volunteers serve as educators, and they

145

may have had previous experience working with young people. Following additional training by staff, they may offer previsit classroom presentations, lead museum tours, conduct participatory activities or special demonstrations, and assist museum educators in evaluating the effectiveness of museum–school programs. Other public program volunteers specialize in are cultural activities, presenting music, theater, dance, demonstrations, and film as part of the museum's offerings, or conducting neighborhood or ethnic festivals to promote the image of the museum to a broad community audience. Staff designing programs for audiences such as older adults, high-school students, people with disabilities, and people from a variety of ethnic and cultural backgrounds may find it helpful to draw on the assistance and advice of volunteers representing similar segments of the community who can offer special insights as to program emphasis and direction.

In all their work, these volunteers make programs happen at the museum that might otherwise be impossible. They not only fill slots in staff-developed activities, but their enthusiasm and special interests generate activities that staff may have overlooked. Those who work in museums must be ready to recognize and foster the resources volunteers can offer and to pursue the many ways volunteers can bring the museum into closer contact with the public it serves.

Behind-the-scenes activities

If your job in the museum is behind-the-scenes, you may not have as many opportunities to work with volunteers as staff involved in public programs, but you may encounter volunteers in collections management, collections care, and exhibition preparation and maintenance. Often these volunteers are highly skilled; some may be professionals in their own right. Small institutions in particular often depend on volunteers for support in cataloging collections, designing and constructing exhibitions, and carrying out routine preventive conservation work. In larger museums, unpaid professionals work behind the scenes as highly trained volunteer scholars, researchers, technicians, and scientists. Of course these volunteers will need direction and supervision, but you as a museum professional may also share your own work with them. They can contribute, for example, to one very fundamental activity in most museums by researching, under the tutelage of a curator, a part of the collection or a specific subject-area in the museum's discipline, often in conjunction with an exhibition or publication.

Fund-raising, special events, and community relations

The administrative objectives of a museum may be supported by volunteer assistance in offices such as public relations, development, membership, education, and financial affairs. Museum educators who are conducting visitor research often train volunteers to assist with interviewing, collecting, compiling, and analyzing data. Again, staff must be assured that these volunteers are either previously trained or receive a solid orientation at the museum.

Museum directors and senior staff often solicit volunteer assistance from corporate, professional, and business executives in the community for marketing, sales, financial management, public relations, and legal matters. Organizations such as the Business Committees for the Arts and Volunteer Lawyers for the Arts also provide professional assistance, and these volunteer projects must be clearly defined by the museum, with specific goals and a mutually agreeable predetermined timetable.

Fund-raising in museums would not be possible without volunteers, and the museum director and the development office work closely with, in addition to the trustees, "guilds," collectors, and "friends'" groups to raise money for specific projects, acquisitions, and general operating expenses. As these groups are independent, but not autonomous, the director may ask them to help fund unbudgeted expenditures such as an important acquisition, renovation of a storage area, a special or commemorative public program, a conservation project, or a new exhibition. Support comes not only as monetary contributions from these groups, but in the form of in-kind donations of equipment, new museum members, new volunteers, and donations of objects. "Friends'" groups can be numerous, even within a single institution: women's and men's councils, collectors' clubs, business volunteers, "young" friends, and special-interest groups supporting particular collections or galleries. Comparable groups are appearing in museums outside the United States as an increasing number of museums are turning to private sources for funding. As these groups become a mainstay of the museum's needs beyond the annual budget, they will require understanding and respect from staff, and you may need to learn the art of cultivating these types of community supporters.

Being a strong and vital link between the museum and its community, volunteers promote and profile the museum through special programs, involvement in civic organizations, and contacts with community leaders. They give promotional speeches to civic organizations, work to expand the museum's audiences, increase the numbers of members, and strengthen the museum's base of support. Volunteers can have a major impact when testifying before a legislative body on the museum's behalf. When those with political contacts speak for or against proposed legislation that affects the museum or lobby against possible reductions in financial support for the museum, they provide a service that is critical to the museum's effectiveness. In all these capacities, volunteers raise the public consciousness about the museum's contribution and services to community life. These activities require close coordination among the museum's director, the public relations staff, and the involved volunteers.

"You should be a volunteer in some museum, or school, or town, or anywhere first before applying for a job. Working to serve (as a volunteer) is a desirable quality that enhances your ability to work for money."

Wilhelmena Cole Holladay, founder and president,
The National Museum for Women in the Arts

Volunteerism

As American society changes, the face of volunteerism, a uniquely American phenomenon, is changing too. One contributing factor to change is that there are many more working couples, and working people of necessity opt to volunteer for evening and weekend museum duties. Thus, these volunteers are increasingly independent and responsible for their own actions and their relations with the public. While supervision has decreased, the need for training has increased. Another factor is a growing number of retired people and older adults with years of experience and exceptional expertise who are lending their talents to museums, and this dynamic resource should be encouraged and nurtured. High-school and university students are finding museum volunteer work challenging and stimulating: researching a discipline of special interest, assisting with challenging projects, serving their community, and a means by which they may make more knowledgeable career choices. What an opportunity for museums to contribute to raising standards for the educational future of this country! These newer types of volunteers are often filling the gap left by young and middle-aged women who used to form the nucleus of the museum volunteer work force, but are now working full time.

Museum volunteers have organized themselves on a broad basis, and it behooves museum staff to nurture and encourage these organizations. The World Federation of Friends of Museums[2] is the largest organized group of museum volunteers in the world. Established in Barcelona, Spain, in 1972, the brainchild of Luis Monreal, the former Director-General of the International Council of Museums (ICOM), the membership exceeds 650,000 from countries throughout the world. Its goal is to work with museum staff to promote and develop museums as institutions in the service of humanity by encouraging mutual understanding, the exchange of information and services, and the sharing of past experiences. The Federation holds international conferences every three years, fosters new national federations of friends, manages an international documentation fund, and collaborates with international organizations such as ICOM on behalf of museums and museum visitors. Written guidelines have been developed for voluntary workers. The Federation has sponsored educational activities, promoted legislation favorable to donations to museums, published a newsletter, implemented an exchange program, and encouraged young people to join. Fifteen countries are represented in the vast numbers of members, and each member country has its own schedule of activities. The American Association for Museum Volunteers in the United States (AAMV) is an active member.

The AAMV was organized in 1976 by several volunteers who understood the value of groups of people with common interests that can share experiences, exchange information, and devise ways to enhance their museum activities that will benefit museums and their staffs. A working relationship with the AAM has resulted in sessions pertaining to volunteers being conducted at the national and regional meetings. In 1993 the AAMV published, with the American Council for the Arts, a manual for both staff and volunteers, *Volunteer Program Administration*. Another group, the Organization of Art Museum Volunteers was founded in 1952 and meets annually to discuss common interests, concerns, and problems.

The Museum Trustees Association conducts meetings twice a year which are attended by both trustees and directors of museums, and holds sessions during or prior to the AAM annual meeting and regional museum meetings. One of the important purposes of these meetings and of a membership newsletter is to help museum leaders, both trustees and directors, keep abreast of current legislation and regulations affecting museums.

You, as museum staff, must have a clear perspective on the valuable services volunteers provide. You must be sensitive to the ways volunteers share in the life of the museum and take pride in a volunteer corps that experiences with you a sense of accomplishment, intellectual growth, and the development of interpersonal relationships. Working side by side, museum staff and volunteers influence future generations by contributing time and talents to an important and vital cultural institution in their community.

Notes

This chapter was prompted by chapter I in *Volunteer Program Administration: A Handbook for Museums and Other Cultural Institutions*, Joan Kuyper, ed., Ellen Hirzy and Kathleen Huftalen (New York: American Council for the Arts and American Association for Museum Volunteers 1993).

1　Edward P. Alexander, *Museums in Motion: An Introduction to the History and Functions of Museums* (Nashville, Tenn.: American Association for State and Local History, 1978), p. 235.
2　Anna Grandi Clerici, "The World Federation and How It Grew," *Museum* (UNESCO) 176, no. 4 (1992): 193–5.

Bibliography: Volunteer–staff relations

Chadwick, Alan, "Volunteers in Museums and Galleries: A Discussion of Some of the Issues," *Museums Journal* 84, no. 4 (1985): 177–8. Discusses issues and conflicts in using volunteers in museums.

Cook, Gillian E., *et al.*, "Preparing Community Volunteers for Museum Education," *Curator* 26, no. 1 (1983): 37–57. A case study about a program developed by the Institute of Texan Cultures performed entirely by community volunteers.

Kuyper, Joan, *et al. Volunteer Program Administration: A Handbook for Museums and Other Cultural Institutions* (New York: American Council for the Arts, and American Association for Museum Volunteers, 1993). Guidelines and options for volunteer-program administration, intended for museum volunteers, volunteers' administrators, volunteer-program officers, directors, and trustees.

Millar, Sue, "Volunteers," *Museums Bulletin* 28, no. 5 (1987): 87. Refers to problems in museum-volunteer management.

National Docent Symposium: Documentation of Presentations (Indianapolis, Ind.: Indianapolis Museum of Art, 1981). Collection of essays discussing topics such as the volunteer as professional; incentives, awards, and bonuses; recruitment and training; and the docent contract.

Nickerson, Ann T., "Is It Fun? Is It History? A Teen-age Volunteer Corps Learns History and Lightens the Workload at Old Economy Village," *History News* 40, no. 4 (1985): 30–3. Case study of a program (Old Economy Village in Ambridge, Pennsylvania) that uses teenage volunteers in a museum setting, with emphasis on career opportunities they might pursue from these kinds of programs.

Suggested readings

American Association for Museum Volunteers, *A Directory of Museum Volunteers Programs* (Washington, DC: American Association for Museum Volunteers, 1988).

Grinder, Alison L., *The Good Guide: A Sourcebook for Interpreters, Docents, and Tour Guides* (Scottsdale, Ariz.: Ironwood Press, 1985).

Kipps, Harriet Clyde, ed., *Volunteerism: The Directory of Organizations, Training, Programs and Publications* (New Providence, NJ: R. R. Bowker, 1991).

Lewis, Joyce, "Volunteer Support Groups," *Museum Quarterly* 15, no. 2 (Summer, 1986): 20–7.

Lord, James Gregory, *A Guide for the Professional: A Collection of Ideas and Techniques to Aid the Professional in the Management of Volunteers and the Development Program* (Cleveland, Ohio: Third Sector Press, 1985).

McBee, Shar, *To Lead is to Serve: How to Attract Volunteers and Keep Them* (Washington, DC: Points of Light Foundation, 1994).

Measham, Terence, *Voluntary Guide Training* (Canberra, Australia: Council of Australian Museums Association, 1986).

"Minds in Motion," *Docent Educator: The Quarterly Journal for Dedicated Docents* 1, no. 1 (1991): entire issue.

O'Connell, Brian, *Volunteers in Action* (New York: Foundation Center, 1989).

Thirteenth Triennial Conference Report of the Volunteer Committees of Art Museums of the United States and Canada (Richmond, VA: The Virginia Museum of Fine Arts, 1988).

Part IV
Museum careers –
where to start

Museum careers – where to start: prologue

Actually, you have already "started" your pursuit of a museum career because you are reading this book. Now the preparation really begins. Making decisions about training for the museum field is complex because of the diversity of the disciplines and the numerous types of positions even within just one museum. That is why it is extremely important to explore the entire spectrum of museums before making your training decisions. This completed, study and consider the various routes into the museum world. Your educational options are many until, and if, you decide on a particular or specific career. Even then, there are more choices to make before you reach your educational goals. Competences and degrees challenge you to a balancing act for your future.

Then the job search is on! During your preparation, we hope you have visited numerous museums, so when the time has come to seek that first job in a museum, to change museum jobs, to re-enter the field, or to change careers entirely, you will know what you want or are getting into. You have the "big" picture. There is no *one* step-by-step process to finding a position, just as there is no *one* route into museum work. But there are ways and means of making the search easier and more productive. Read on, and perhaps heed our advice and counsel – a job may be waiting for you around the corner.

> I think it is very important to get on-the-job training and what you learn through internships and various other projects rather than through the study of how to do that job.
>
> Tom Southall, Amon Carter Museum of Art

> I think that if you are going to do only a museum-studies program you are going to be limited in your career as to what you can do, at least in the major museums. If you have a combination of a master's in museum studies and an advanced degree in a discipline, you are then prepared to do almost anything in a museum. I would recommend to young people to pursue a doctorate in a discipline if you have a particular desire to make a name for yourself as a curator or a scholar, and even for administrative purposes.
>
> Craig Black, formerly Los Angeles County Museum of Natural History

I would really recommend to people to take those museum studies classes, but also get into an internship program somewhere. It is also valuable for your resumé – it counts as museum experience when you are looking for a job.

Glenn Gutleben, The Exploratorium

While there are the graduate programs in conservation, apprenticeships are still another route into the conservation field, but one needs to have a strong background in the sciences. You have to have a core discipline to work in a museum. You cannot just take museum studies in a vacuum, you need a working knowledge of the museum's discipline. I think that exposure to a museum-studies program is very important, however. I think more of a problem exists that there are a lot of people who are doing straight discipline studies, and they don't have enough museum-studies exposure at all, a lack of understanding of objects and artifacts, their uses and their care.

Carolyn Rose, National Museum of
Natural History

Science centers are rapidly growing in numbers as well as growing in size. We have a huge shortage of people, especially in positions as exhibits designers, exhibits developers, and directors of educational programs. We hope very much that there will be many trained and attracted to the field, and certainly the challenge of getting more minority people in the field is wonderful.

Bonnie VanDorn, Association of Science–Technology Centers

One needs energy, commitment, dedication, ability to work for not much money, and still not burn out. Know before you start that passion is crucial. Many of us are here because we love the idea of being able to work within these disciplines and with the general public. Be clear about the realities of working in the nonprofit world.

Thomas Moritz, California Academy of Sciences

I think that salaries in museums are no worse than some other nonprofit organizations – and museums are more exciting.

Harry Robinson, Museum of African American
Life and Culture

Networking is extremely important within the institution, within the office, with the greater museum professional community, and also the international museum community.

Linda Thomas, Boston Museum of Fine Arts

Small museums give you a generalized sense, and they give you infinitely more opportunity to talk, and talking is important. It's the basis for sharing and forming ideas about what the potential is. There is more latitude for their own creative input, much more dialogue, and they have a higher probability to see the impact of their presence.

Edmund B. Gaither, Museum of the National
Center for Afro-American Artists

Yes, I feel museums have a social responsibility, and that's why I work as hard as I do. But you can't be everything to everybody, so perhaps there are particular kinds of things to be done for particular groups of people. Many museums are doing a very good job of showcasing and legitimizing the cultures of non-European ethnic groups, or even different kinds of non-English European groups. Obviously, museums should have staff that reflects the diversity of the society.

JoAllyn Archambault, National Museum
of Natural History

Salaries have gotten a lot more competitive over the last five to ten years, particularly at the high levels. I don't think they are satisfactory in education yet.

Peter Ames, formerly Science Museum of Boston

The important personal qualities to be a museum person are adaptability, willingness to be totally open and have everything examined because you are a public institution. Depending on the job, you need a commitment to objects, but you have to appreciate people as much as objects, and you have to know how to respond to the public's interest.

Craig Black, formerly Los Angeles County
Museum of Natural History

I believe it is always best to try to get a position in a major institution. The opportunities for professional development, advancement, and mobility to other institutions are far greater.

Bruce Bartholomew, California Academy of Sciences

I believe you both make your own luck and take advantage of opportunities.

Tom Southall, Amon Carter Museum of Art

In my case, starting a career in museums was definitely a case of luck, being in the right place at the right time.

Kenneth Yellis, Yale Peabody Museum of
Natural History

It's very important to have a mentor, someone you respect who has the experience. My first boss is still a friend today.

Robert Macdonald, Museum
of the City of New York

I had an art history professor as a mentor. It was her example and her energy and joy with the material that inspired me.

Edith Tonelli, formerly Wight Gallery of UCLA

I think it's really important to go to an institution where you may think you may find a mentor. What I learned from my mentor was who I am, what my gifts are, and how to insist on quality. I learned a lot about personal strength and integrity.

Barbara Moore, National Gallery of Art

You can go to a large museum and have an overview and learn a great deal about the organizational structure of the museum. In a smaller one, it's really hands-on – you are doing everything. Each one offers different advantages.

Kenneth Starr, formerly Milwaukee
Public Museum

I think starting in a small museum is better, judging on my own experience. A large museum ought to be more interesting and have more to see, but people get pigeon-holed so they don't see the whole picture.

Tom L. Freudenheim,
Smithsonian Institution

There is really no substitute for working in a small museum because you do more, you learn more about the basics, and you have the opportunity to investigate other jobs. I would not have known initially that I wanted to be a registrar.

Linda Thomas, Boston Museum of Fine Arts

There are a lot of things that you may not realize are part of a museum operation – so you have to find out what the jobs are, and the different varieties of those jobs that require a lot of different skills.

Anna McFarland, Dallas Museum of Art

I started in museums by a fluke. I came from a media and teaching background. I was working in a radio station, and I learned about this job through a friend.

Sylvia Mullaly Aguire, The Exploratorium

I had been teaching history in college for two years after graduate school when I heard of opportunities at this museum. My first job was as an administrative assistant. This was not a planned approach to a career in museums, and I hope most people do it in a more planned fashion than I did.

Spencer Crew, National Museum of
American History

I was lucky in getting my first job – I knew someone who allowed me to work on a school-contract basis in the education department of a museum.

Barbara K. Gibbs, Cincinnati Art Museum

I come to museums from the theater where I was an actress for many years. Probably I would have never considered working in a museum except this Mexican Museum.

Marie Acosta Colon, The Mexican Museum

I tell people that it is very competitive, which is a very good sign. It means that we are finally reaching people who really are focused on what the mission is.

Ron L. Kagan, Detroit Zoo

I had never been in a museum until I went to college. African American kids today have a lot more exposure, taking field trips to museums. We need to expose them at early ages. I guess it would not have anything to do with race, it is more of a class problem. I think the white people in my home town were just as unexposed as I was.

Harry Robinson, Museum of African
American Life and Culture

I tell people that if there is a particular museum that they like, it really helps to be there, even if it means volunteering or just helping out. Then you get a sense of the direction of the museum – then you decide what you want to do, and what works for you.

Sally Duensing, The Exploratorium

We are still at a point that jobs can be defined by the individual, at least at the lower levels. Get your foot in the door, position yourself to be in the right place at the right time. Don't compromise too much. My working in a museum is more the result of a metamorphosis rather than a direct decision. It grew out of a desire to be in a museum more than anything else.

Stacy Miller, formerly
Isabella Stewart Gardner Museum

8

Training and preparation

"*Most museum careerists I know in my generation came into the museum field accidentally, or through the 'back door.'" ["Quoth the raven, NEVERMORE!"]*

Back-door entries still may happen, but today's job-seekers are, for the most part, a sophisticated and realistic lot, planning and preparing for careers in a very competitive job market.

Unlike many other professional fields of endeavor, there is no *one* training route into the museum field. Depending upon the discipline, the type of position, the specialization, and sometimes the size of the museum, training and education requirements may vary from a high-school diploma, a bachelor's degree, a master's degree, to a PhD or a LLD (or JD) (see Chapter 6).

One reason there is no *one* training route into the museum field is that there are great numbers and varieties of disciplines within the "discipline" of museology. Incidentally, there are many in the field in the United States who do not accept "museology" – the theory, history, and role of museums – as a separate discipline. Nor do they accept the term "museography", which includes documentation of collections, preventive conservation, and exhibition techniques. These terms and philosophy are much more widely accepted in other parts of the world. But there *is* a body of museological and museographical knowledge and literature that defines and illustrates the types of professional theories and practices unique to museums. Flora Kaplan has observed: "Common ideas and values connecting those who work in museums form a social science."[1] Whether it is called museology or museography, the body of information is there for your elucidation!

Depending upon to whom you talk, the answers to your questions about training will run the gamut from a strict disciplinary approach, to museum studies programs, to internships, to "learning by doing" on the job, or a combination of different methods.

To clarify the issues for your decision-making, this chapter presents training options for you to consider in preparing for a museum career. Museum studies programs are emphasized, but internships, graduate, and undergraduate degrees

"The best preparation is to have a specific subject area of expertise that you are particularly excited about. Then you apply that interest to the particular museum that you are entering, and then you begin to acquire the other skills."

Spencer Crew, National Museum of American History

in disciplines, and professional development after being on staff are also discussed. You should consider all the possibilities.

Museum studies programs

Skepticism about museum studies programs as one route into the museum field was once the norm, but has now virtually disappeared. While some museum professionals still recommend discipline-based entry training, they accept museum studies as valid training for many positions, if accompanied by an internship in a museum as well as by rigorous study in a discipline. Many of the best programs offer master's degrees in a discipline with a certificate in museum studies. Job announcements are increasingly mentioning museum studies as a desirable qualification.

Some museum studies programs in United States museums and universities began in the early twentieth century. Even at that time disagreement centered on the core issue of whether there was any point in training individuals for a field as diverse and diffuse as museums. Frederic A. Lucas of the Museums of the Brooklyn Institute took the following position: "A curator is born and not made. I do not believe you can train a man [indeed, almost all were men] to be a curator. He is the result of the combination of natural ability and circumstances."[2] There were those who thought differently, however, as Karen Cushman points out.[3] Among them was George Brown Goode of the Smithsonian, one of the first American museum leaders to suggest principles and standards for museum workers. Goode believed that "intelligence, a liberal education, administrative ability, enthusiasm, and that special endowment which may be called 'the museum sense,' are all prerequisite qualifications." His constructive ideas were to transform museums "from bric-à-brac cemeteries to nurseries of living thought."[4]

"If they are looking toward the administrative side of a museum career, then I think they do need probably more exposure to legal and business practices. If you are coming in to be a curator or to work with collections, or even to be an educator, coming in through a discipline approach is really the best way. I got a lot of training on the job, and I think that's where it's important. Communications skills are very important because you spend a lot of time writing and speaking to groups asking for money and telling what your museum is all about. For most jobs in museums you need to communicate."

Craig Black, formerly Los Angeles County Museum of Natural History

159

In 1908, a continuing increase in the number of museums, and a shortage of trained museum workers, inspired Sarah Yorke Stevenson, assistant curator of the Pennsylvania Museum in Philadelphia, to offer the first known museum-training program in the United States. Her intent was to produce curators for art museums through training that combined theory and practice. The program continued until her death in 1921.

Sarah Stevenson's example, together with an increase in new natural history museums suffering from staff shortages, caused Homer Dill, director of the Museum of Natural History of the State University of Iowa, to establish a four-year program with degrees in a major discipline and a minor in museum science. The program still exists. Neither of these first two efforts offered training in museum administration, education, or documentation. They graduated people with a "new calling," primarily curators.

The Farnsworth Museum of Wellesley College began in 1910 to train women in education and in library, clerical, and exhibition skills for art museums, even though art museums were few in number. Thus three programs were in place at the 1910 meeting of the American Association of Museums (AAM), when Dr A. R. Crook of the Illinois State Museum of Natural History, after a survey of museum leaders, presented a list of fifty examination-type questions to determine the proper qualifications for museum work. They included topics such as general education, museum skills, museum history and philosophy, exhibition techniques, and talent for museum administration (example: "Explain in detail the age, intelligence, and occupation of the people to whom a museum should appeal and how it can best benefit them").[5] Museum leaders added that a candidate must "be in good health, be able to handle a canoe, and be inured to the hardships of camp life and work of exploration."[6] The AAM soon adopted resolutions recommending the Iowa and Wellesley College programs. However, Mr Dill could not provide enough candidates for the jobs available, while the Wellesley graduates found difficulty in obtaining placements. In 1917, the AAM established the first committee to survey museum studies.

Two of the most renowned museum-training programs began in the 1920s. Paul Sachs, assistant director of the Fogg Museum at Harvard University and a man of unique talents and personality, established the first model for contemporary museum training, specifically for candidates interested in art museums. Dr Sachs included in his one-year course the history and philosophy of museums, organization and management, education, buildings, collections, installation, restoration, storage, record-keeping, museum policies, and museum ethics. Visits to museums, a practicum, and presentation of an exhibition were integral parts of the curriculum. Dr Sachs actively assisted the students in finding positions, sometimes accompanying them to job interviews, and required students to buy a work of art for their own collections. He conducted the course for twenty-five years, and it was a truly amazing and creative program for just one year of study!

The other program was offered by director and librarian John Cotton Dana at the Newark Museum in New Jersey. Dana's emphasis was on museum education and the museum's responsibility to its community. He once said that so long as museums felt their duty was done if they gathered objects, identified and preserved them, and occasionally, at hours inconvenient to most busy people, displayed them, they needed only two kinds of help – that of the expert for identification and labeling, and that of the unskilled worker – of the porter and watchman. He believed that workers should be skillful, by reason of experience, study and observation, in the practice of the arts of explaining, suggesting, stimulating and even, at times, instructing. The program developed into apprenticeships, primarily for college graduates, emphasizing in-museum, hands-on experiences. Dana included all aspects of museum operations, informal talks by department heads on their disciplines, and visits to other museums; students were paid fifty dollars per month. The program was considered extremely successful until its demise due to World War II.

In 1926, the AAM formally accepted the necessity of training for museum work and proposed cooperation between universities and museums, with stated goals and objectives. The proposal demonstrated, even with general opposition in the field to museum training, increasing recognition that standards for training must be reckoned with.

Museum studies programs and courses began appearing in universities and colleges in unexpected and alarming numbers, and have proliferated at a rapid pace since the early 1970s. Some of the relatively recent ones – and there have been literally hundreds of them – were started without regard to professional criteria or standards, and many times without any affiliation with museums. The changes and improvements have been significant since, however, primarily due to investigations and major efforts in developing standards by the AAM Museum Studies Committee (MSC), formally established in 1976. A first effort was made in 1972 with the publication of a suggested museum-studies curriculum. In 1978–80, *Minimum Requirements* was written and published, a *A Self Evaluation for Universities* in 1982, and *Criteria* in 1984 (see Bibliography). Although there are a few well-administered undergraduate museum studies programs, only graduate programs have been discussed by the MSC.

The MSC has recommended the types of courses to be offered, such as the history and philosophy of museums, ethics, management, curatorship, education, collections management, exhibition design and production, preventive conservation, and evaluation techniques. Other recommendations include a mandatory internship, a close affiliation with at least one museum, a museological library, faculty that reflect museum experience, advisory and placement services, and clarification to the students as to what they would be prepared to do in a museum upon completion of their studies.

The MSC has been functioning as the Committee for Museum Professional Training (COMPT) since 1991 and is a standing professional committee of the AAM. Periodic reports from the MSC have included information about basic principles, standards, qualifications, self-study guidelines, criteria, and the results of surveys. Conference proceedings and the recommendations of a special task-force appointed by COMPT have also been distributed. The feasibility of

161

"As a graduate student in art history I still didn't think about museums, more about teaching or developing literature in American art history, focusing on African American issues. I had the chance to take some courses in museum work, methods involved in organizing exhibitions. That gave me a footing to go either direction."

Edmund B. Gaither, Museum of the
National Center for Afro-American Artists

accreditation or recognition procedures for museum-studies programs at the graduate level has been studied, and proposals have been presented to the AAM for consideration. No official action has been taken, however. New attempts toward a training assessment program were initiated in 1992. In the UK, the Museum Training Institute has been established to set high professional standards for training for museums and for the Museums Association.

Museum studies programs, and courses as well, are conducting self-evaluations and generally are abiding by guidelines established by the AAM MSC. There is still room for measuring success, however, and you should investigate carefully before entering a program. The best programs will withstand scrutiny!

The most comprehensive listing of museum-studies programs, courses, workshops, and internships, *Museum Studies International* (*MSI*), was published in 1988 by the Smithsonian Institution (Office of Museum Programs) and the International Council of Museums' Committee for the Training of Personnel (ICTOP). You will find that every region of the United States has at least one program, and some have many more. *MSI* can be found in libraries and museums throughout the country; and the new edition from ICTOP, *The International Directory of Museum Training* was published by Routledge in 1995. A condensed version of *MSI* describing United States programs has been published by the AAM.

As a general rule, museum studies programs have areas of specialization, and you must decide where you may fit best with your interests and background. Programs may be oriented toward history, the sciences, anthropology, or art, for example, or they may have important strengths in such work areas as curatorship, museum education, or management. Such specialization is usually apparent from the list of course offerings and should be considered in making a selection, with a caution that many would-be curators discover that they really prefer management (or the reverse), and many would-be educators have changed their minds once they have a broader exposure to the real world of job opportunities. Of course, in addition to your special interests, you should assess the job market when considering a specialization (see Chapter 9).

Many museum studies students are already experienced in museum work and want to obtain an advanced degree or feel that they need more specific museum-related training than they received previously in an academic discipline. These students are not necessarily making a career change but are enhancing their chances for advancement and acquiring additional knowledge and skills. Others have completed their undergraduate work in a discipline and choose to continue their education progressively.

Saroj Ghose, President of ICOM, at the Museums – 2000 Conference, stressed "the need for the closest possible links between museum training and the leading museums in order to ensure the continued relevance of professional training, and the feedback of best practices from museums to training programs."[7] As you consider the museum studies route generally and attempt to decide if a particular program is right for you, conversations with students, graduates, museum staff, and faculty of these programs can be helpful. They can be especially revealing about the emphasis and quality of a particular program.

Questions to ask in considering museum-studies programs[8]

What is the degree offered?

> If the answer is a master's in art history or anthropology, with a certificate in museum studies, for example, that may be what you want. Or do you want a master's in museum administration or museum studies? Consider all the components of the program before making your decision. There are some undergraduate programs, but the BA degree is usually in a discipline.

Does the program have a particular emphasis such as museum education, administration, or curatorship?

> This emphasis may be a key factor as you consider your options or if you have already decided what you want to do in a museum.

What are the academic requirements for admittance to the program?

> If undergraduate majors are specified (perhaps in history, art, biology, or archeology), are you prepared, or do you still have time to take the required courses?

Is an applicant interview required?

> Are you geographically close enough to go for an interview? Can the requirement be waived?

What are the requirements for graduation? How many credit hours? A thesis? An internship or apprenticeship?

> These are very important considerations; compare programs. A thesis and an internship are essential to a complete and comprehensive program.

What is the duration of the program? Is there a residency require-ment? Can you complete it as a part-time student?

> If the program is two years, as most are, and you are working, can you take the time off to enroll, or can the duration be extended to a longer period so you may complete the program as a part-time student? Is there an off-campus program where you may work full time while pursuing the degree? (There are several, such as the University of Oklahoma, the Bank Street College in New York, the John F. Kennedy University in California, and the University of Victoria in British Columbia, Canada.)

How many students are enrolled in the program at any one time?

> Enrollment will give an indication of the size of classes and seminars. It also may give you a clue as to the quality of the program unless the number of students is restricted and accep-tance is highly selective, as are programs in conservation training.

What is a reasonable estimate of the cost for the program? Tuition? Books and materials? Living expenses?

> The costs may be a determining factor in your selection of a program.

What is the availability of scholarships, fellowships, assistantships, and other types of student financial assistance?

> Is financial support or a travel stipend for instance available to enable students to attend professional meetings and workshops? This kind of support is a plus, an indicator that the program understands the value of supplementary education and training. Some programs do not have the financial ability to give this sup-port, however. Assistantships in museum studies are rare.

Is there a full-time coordinator or director of the museum studies program?

> It is extremely important that the university views the museum studies program as equal with other academic programs. The director may also teach some classes, but the program should be top priority. In some instances, the director of the program is also the director of the campus museum, an arrangement that may facilitate practical experiences for the students but may also overload the director unless there is a sizable staff to assist.

Is there a required core program with opportunities for specialization in a discipline or museum job category?

> This type of curriculum will assist you in evaluating the museum career outcome of the program for you.

Among those courses required for completing the degree, how many are museum theory and practice courses? How many are in some other academic discipline?

> A balance of theory and practice will give you the best of both, depending upon the career you have selected. For example, if you are on a curatorial track, you will need *more* of an emphasis on a discipline than if you are planning to be a registrar or an administrator.

How broad an exposure to the museum field is provided? What is the extent of that exposure?

> An opportunity to spend more than the required hours of an internship in a museum is a great advantage. Some programs offer field trips to a variety of museums for exposure to institutions of different sizes and disciplines.

What specific skills does the student develop?

> As you review the qualifications required for different positions in Chapter 6, check the programs and correlate position requirements and course work.

Is the program geared to both traditional museums and to museums as agents of change; that is, is the program innovative and visionary?

> You will ascertain the innovativeness of the program from courses offered, from discussions with the director and faculty, and from current students. Does the program include aspects of environmental concerns as they affect museums? Are the students exposed to the latest technologies? These are among the key questions to ask.

"I wish I had known there would be a lot of public speaking, I would have taken more courses in that."

Terese Tse Bartholomew,
Asian Art Museum of San Francisco

What is the mode of instruction – lectures, seminars, field trips, practicums?

> You will probably look for a good mix and balance for individualized advantages for problem solving and free and open discussions.

How flexible is the program? Can it be structured to individual needs?

> Will you have the freedom to elect courses from another department of the university, such as management in the business school, education, communications? This kind of flexibility will help you design a curriculum to meet your interests and needs.

Is there direct affiliation with a museum? Is there a museum on campus? Are students given an opportunity for the actual use of museum facilities to study or research? How close is the museum? Is it accredited?

> These questions relate to the museum as a direct resource, in order to realize a balance of theory and practice in addition to the essential internship.

Faculty

How well qualified is the faculty?

Who are the faculty members? Are they full-time or part-time?

What is their background? Have they worked in museums? When, and to what extent?

How long has each faculty member been involved in the program? How many are university faculty? How many are museum professionals? What subjects do they teach?

What is their commitment to the museum field? Have they published or participated in museum activities on a national, regional, or international level?

"I think the only thing I wish I had had more training in is the business, management, financial, and fundraising side of museums."

Edith Tonelli, formerly Wight Gallery, UCLA

What is the extent of exposure the students will have to each faculty member?

> The answers to all of these questions, and discussions with faculty and students, will reveal to you the quality of the leadership in the program.

Internships

Is there a required internship?

> There must be!

How is it organized?

> Find out in which museums the students are placed, and if the program places them, or students find their own internships.

How much time must the students commit? Is that a meaningful amount of time?

> At least one semester should be committed and required for a solid internship experience with an assigned project.

What is the commitment of participating museums?

> The best situation is one in which an assigned staff supervisor in the museum has written the intern job description, monitors and advises at all stages of the internship, and evaluates the performance of the intern upon completion. The intern may be asked for an evaluation as well.

"It is absolutely invaluable to get the information from an internship. I really wish I could have done that. Getting into the museum as an intern really gets you tuned in to the workings of the place or what it takes to make an exhibition, if that is what you are interested in. It gives you the feeling of what works and what doesn't work. I am a real believer that what you learn out of a textbook is OK, but you really need to get out there and do it!"

Glenn Gutleben, The Exploratorium

What types of projects are assigned?

It varies, of course, with the size of the museum, and if it is in a specialized department. In a small or medium-size museum, the intern may have the opportunity to work in several areas such as curatorial, education, exhibitions, administration, and collections management. Exposure to the entire museum may be a very rewarding and useful experience. In a large museum the assignment may be very departmentalized, researching a specific topic or planned publication, doing artwork for an exhibition, inventorying a collection, or organizing a conference for the management office. If you request it, contacts and/or interviews may be arranged with other departments or offices so that you can become familiar with the whole operation.

How much practical museum experience is provided?

A meaningful internship project should have, after an orientation to the museum, a project or assignment, a beginning or start-up, a working middle, and a completion, all of which include specific practical jobs to perform that will be beneficial for both the intern and the museum.

What is the mechanism for internship review?

There should be written and oral final reviews by the intern, the supervisor, and the university program. An interim report by all concerned is advisable, especially if there are problems or the internship turns out to be not "as advertised."

Are interns ever hired by the participating museums after completion of the internships and the program?

There is never a guarantee, but it happens sometimes if the museum has a vacancy in the area in which you have worked and have been successful. Or it may happen at a later date,

"My internship was an extraordinary preparation for a museum career. I worked in virtually every department of National Portrait Gallery, and had experiences with all facets of exhibition development. I had a chance to be tutored by all the team of young and talented staff in some dimension of museum work. It was a museum thinking about what its role was in the community of museums, and in general permeated by the idea of professionalism."

Kenneth Yellis, Peabody Museum of Natural History, Yale University

or the museum may serve as a reference for another job. With an internship, you are a proven quantity!

Resources

Will field trips in which students visit museums and related institutions be offered?

> Field trips are important for a broad perspective on the museum field. Find out where the museums, historic houses, science centers, zoos, and other museum-related facilities are in the vicinity of the university. Visit them and talk to staff at every opportunity, even if field trips are planned.

Will you have access to a library of museological literature?

> It is extremely important that you have access to the current literature, both books and periodicals, for your reading assignments, for references, and for additional research. Your instructors will no doubt distribute bibliographies, and you will need a source for obtaining the materials.

Does the program offer opportunities for students to meet visiting specialists, connoisseurs, etc.?

> These, in themselves, are valuable learning-experiences by providing exposures to a variety of points of view, future contacts, mentoring, and the possibilities for networking.

Are career counseling and job-placement assistance provided for students enrolled in the program?

> Of course, they should be, and most often are. Take advantage of them, by all means.

"I think before applying for a museum job a student is well advised to take an internship. The value is that you learn, and if a person is smart and has creative skills, you see both the attractions and the limitations of the museum world. You need to assess how good the environment is for you, how committed you are to the things that are available in it, proximity to objects, the relationships between culture and people . . . which is what thrills me, having the public mind turned on by unique objects and experiences with cultures."

Barbara Moore, National Gallery of Art

169

> How successful have graduates of this program been in securing employment in the museum field? What kinds of positions do they hold?
>
> This information will require some research on your part, but most of the programs keep graduate records on file. Ask the school for lists of their graduates, then inquire as to their positions and their achievements in the museum field. Generally, the programs report about 80 percent of the graduates are employed by museums.

Although a PhD in Museum Studies is rarely offered, you may design your own doctoral program around a discipline with museum studies at a cooperating university.

Other graduate programs

Because of the many disciplines engaged in museum work, there are those who advocate an education in a specific discipline (art history, paleontology, anthropology, history, and many others) for entry into museums. Many museum people in the sciences are proponents of this route. By the same token, the large art museums stress the importance of advanced degrees in art history for curatorial and education department positions. The history field too has many who argue that a strong disciplinary background is necessary for becoming a "public historian," as historians in the museum field are often called. These major courses of study may be combined, of course, with courses in museum theory and practices, if museum courses are offered by your university. If not, those with graduate degrees in a specific discipline learn museum practices through internships or on the job, a route that appears to be very satisfactory to many curators and directors. This route was established long before museum studies programs became popular, and it continues to be preferred in many museum and disciplinary circles.

If you choose this route, the questions you should ask are those appropriate for any university graduate program within a special discipline: Who are the faculty? How large is the library? What is the depth of the courses? Is there emphasis on the aspect of the discipline that interests you? If you know your career goal is museum work, you will want to inquire, as well, about university courses in museum practices and museum internships.

We desperately need some sort of graduate training program to help educators in science museums. The present graduate programs do not get science-oriented students.
Bonnie VanDorn, Association of Science–
Technology Centers (ASTC)

"There are lots of people that are really good in our field on developing hands-on exhibits who came through the industrial design programs, but somewhere along the line people have to learn about museums, and get excited about them."

Bonnie VanDorn, Association of Science–Technology Centers

If you already know, too, what aspect of museum work you want to specialize in, then your questions may be fewer but even more specific. For example, if conservation of objects and artifacts is your abiding interest, there are a limited number of universities that offer graduate programs, and a very limited number of students are accepted into them each year. The programs have various prerequisites, such as undergraduate courses in chemistry and physics, and some are even more specialized within the conservation field. A relatively new doctoral program at the University of Delaware/Winterthur prepares those who wish to become conservation scientists. If your intent is to practice in a museum, as opposed to being a private conservator, you should find out if there are museum-related courses within the programs you are considering.

If you have an artistic bent, and exhibition design and production appeal to you, you may want to consider a design school (theater, industrial, interior) that includes some training in museum-exhibition design. The latter component will take some searching, as there have been very few such programs. Exhibition designers are graduates of all types of design schools, however, or they are studio artists in the other part of their lives. Two examples of university programs specifically for museum exhibition design in the United States are the University of the Arts in Philadelphia and the University of California at Fullerton (see listings in *MSI* and in *The International Directory of Museum Training*).

After you complete your graduate degree, you may want to consider an internship in a museum before applying for that first job (see Chapter 9). Internships are an excellent way to learn by doing, and most of them are not tied to museum studies programs. Museums of all sizes and disciplines welcome and seek interns, and a small percentage of them offer limited stipends. In evaluating the quality of independent internships, ask the same questions listed earlier in in this chapter for internships as part of programs.

Many positions in museums are not unique to museums. These include jobs in public relations, development, financial management, the practice of law, librarianship, archives, computer science, audiovisual communications, publications, and others. Most positions in these areas require an advanced degree for professional practice, and skills and experience are readily transferable to a museum setting. If any of them are of your choosing, pursue their educational and training requirements. Again you may want to correlate your selection of a graduate program with the position qualifications outlined in Chapter 6.

Keep in mind that, in addition to graduate programs in arts administration and public administration and MBAs in arts management, some schools will permit you to design your own curriculum to include museum-related courses.

171

As cultural organizations and institutions, including museums, have recognized the importance of management training in the education of their leadership, new courses and programs have been established by universities, organizations, and museums. The accountability factor has reinforced the need for management training among nonprofit institutions. Many universities have integrated the management of cultural organizations into existing public administration curricula, but the emphasis is usually on management of performing-arts organizations. Some of them include museum-related courses, however. Newer ones may have an emphasis on nonprofit management. You will need to investigate a variety of programs to find the right one for your needs and interests. Some museum staff have chosen to add a straight MBA degree to their previous education in a discipline or in museum studies, to improve their qualifications for leadership positions. Others elect to enroll in management courses while completing masters' degrees in a discipline or museum studies.

One *major recommendation*: no matter the route you may select, the vast majority of experienced museum professionals strongly suggest electing courses in management (financial, organizational, and human resources) and communications (both oral and written). We are compelled to add computer science as a very desirable preparatory course for museum work in the 1990s and beyond. These are not only vital to all positions in museums, but they are also preparation and training for "life!"

Preparation at other levels

While we have been discussing graduate training for museum positions, keep in mind that there is room in the museum business for those with bachelors' degrees, or, in some support positions, with a high-school diploma.

There is nothing like a solid undergraduate liberal arts program, with a major in a special interest, as the basis for almost any career. A liberal arts background is appropriate for many positions in museums – large, medium, and small – that are in themselves fulfilling and meaningful careers (see Chapter 6). An undergraduate degree, combined with some experience, often qualifies a person to be a registrar, an editor, a photographer, an exhibitions specialist or designer, a collections manager, a museum educator, or for other positions in small and medium-size museums. The downside is that, as more and more people pursue graduate degrees, you will find yourself in stiff competition for scarce job openings.

Experience is often equated with education, however, and many museums consider an established track-record more convincing potential. This preference

---

If there are individuals who don't have the credentials, they can still contribute and provide vision and drive to museums."

Marie Acosta Colon, The Mexican Museum

should be heartening for you "career changers" who have amassed quite a bit of experience in another field but have no advanced degree. Again, internships, which count for both training and experience, may be a useful avenue to explore.

Some people pursue a higher degree while on the job, with the full support of the museum. Consider attending classes in the evening, or enrolling in one of the off-campus programs we mentioned earlier in this chapter. Pursuing a degree as a full-time employee and part-time student is not easy, and will take longer than a conventional program, but it will enable you to keep many options open.

While not the particular focus of this book, many technical and support positions in museums may require no more than a high-school diploma – clerk-typists, guards, exhibition preparators, museum aides, receptionists, museum-shop staff, maintenance crew, to name a few. Education is extremely important, however, and those with limited resources, but with ambition and resourcefulness, may find a way to realize their potential within museums.

Professional development

Mid-career programs, or continuing education, for museum workers have largely taken place outside the university setting. A notable exception is the Distance Learning Program of the University of Victoria in British Columbia in Canada, which successfully conducts "correspondence" courses by videotape and literature. Associations, organizations, and museums have assumed the professional responsibility to meet the needs of this changing and growing market. Large numbers of individuals who have entered the museum field without any previous training or knowledge of museum practices and operations need or want training to enhance their skills. Others want to increase and update their abilities to perform well in their positions and ensure their upward mobility. Increasing numbers of workshops, institutes, and courses offer myriad topics about museum functions – everything from management and legal problems, to the use and care of collections, to protection services.

In this realm, as with other museum training, there have been some serious concerns as to the quality of the offerings. In 1980, under the authority of the National Museum Act, the Smithsonian's Office of Museum Programs (now the Center for Museum Studies) convened a meeting of twenty-four representatives of museum professional-development training programs in the United States and Canada, to discuss the quality of training opportunities for museum personnel. This was the first such conference specifically to consider the state and future directions of mid-career museum training. Participants examined the needs of both individuals and institutions for mid-career training. They assessed the breadth of present programs attempting to respond to these needs; examined the methodology of existing programs, including content,

"I think in some areas skills are more transferable than others. Take public relations, for example. If you come in as a good public-relations person from the corporate or business world, you take 6 months to learn the museum before you start doing things. I think you can become very successful. Security people is another example. Educators? It's as difficult to come from formal education into museums as it is for museum educators to train teachers because you really do two entirely different things. Teachers use the written word in two-dimensional approaches, they don't use three-dimensional approaches as museum people use . . . participation, hands-on, and three-dimensional objects. It's really quite different."

Craig Black, formerly Los Angeles County Museum of Natural History

faculty, and evaluation; made recommendations for guidelines and criteria; and recommended follow-up activities. The result was improvements in many programs, but there was no official action by any professional association. However, the subject of mid-career training became a regular topic on the agendas of national, regional, and international meetings and conferences and in numerous museum-related journals and periodicals. Increased awareness was followed by a tremendous increase in the numbers of programs.

There is a new trend nationally and internationally to "train trainers," so that those responsible for conducting mid-career courses and workshops are properly prepared in the most effective methods and techniques for communicating substantive information. The Training Committee of ICOM (ICTOP) is preparing a pilot program for training trainers in developing countries so that there may be a cadre of local or regional trainers which, in turn, will produce more skilled workers in their museums.

National and international museum leadership continue to recognize the importance of professional development, mid-career training, and upward mobility. Both AAM and AASLH have renewed initiatives to provide sophisticated training models. Some long-standing programs, such as the Seminar for Historical Administration (AASLH), the Winedale Seminar, Texas Historical Commission (THC), the Mather Training Center of the National Park Service (NPS), and the Museum Management Institute of the American Federation of the Arts (AFA) and the Getty Trust, continue to flourish. On-the-job training, museum support for released time for further education, sabbaticals, and opportunities for attendance at conferences, seminars, institutes, and workshops, contribute to advancement in a museum career. Learning new skills, sharing problems, problem-solving, and networking are among the many long-term benefits to both the individual and the institution. Modern management and the implementation of current museum theories and practices are goals for institutions of all sizes and resources. Continuing education and career-long learning are encouraged and supported, and it is up to you to take advantage of them.

Professional development enhances professionalism, performance, and self-worth. It is also a measure of the individual's value that the museum has chosen to invest in their competence. John M.A. Thompson once commented that a planned training program to meet the recognized needs of the institution, and as a way of developing the potential of staff at each stage of their careers, is one of the most important responsibilities of heads of museums and senior staff, if museums are to develop a common sense of purpose to meet the challenges of a changing society. In a policy document of the Museums and Galleries Commission of the United Kingdom, it is pointed out that much of what needs to be done to improve museums hinges on museum training, and training is not a luxury but an essential investment.

Museum training may make, but will seldom break, your career. Still, education and training appear as very positive items on your resumé. Their benefits are visible in your self-confidence and your performance in whatever museum path you choose to follow.

Notes

1   Flora Kaplan, "Growing Pains," *Museum News* 71, no. 1 (January/February 1992): 49.
2   Frederic A. Lucas, from A. R. Crook's "The Training of Museum Curators," Proceedings of the fifth annual meeting of the American Association of Museums, Washington, DC, 1910.
3   Karen Cushman, "Museum Studies: The Beginnings, 1900–1926," *Museum Studies Journal* 1, no. 3 (Spring, 1984): 8–16.
4   George Browne Goode, "The Principles of Museum Administration," in *Annual Report of the US National Museum*, 1897, pt 2 (Washington, DC: Government Printing Office, 1901), p. 206.
5   A. R. Crook, "The Training of Museum Curators," in *Proceedings of the 5th Annual Meeting of the AAM* (Washington, DC: American Association of Museums, 1919), p. 64.
6   "Report of Committee on Training of Museum Workers," *Museum Work* 1 (June 1918–May 1919): 89.
7   Saroj Ghose, Discussion during *Museums – 2000: Politics, People, Professionals and Profit*, ed. Patrick Boylan (London, UK: Museums Association and Routledge, 1992), p. 18.
8   Questions adapted and revised from *Museum Studies Committee Report II* (Washington, DC: American Association of Museums, 1980).

Bibliography: Training and preparation

American Association of Museums, *Museum Studies and Training in the United States: A Resource Guide* (Washington, DC: American Association of Museums, 1993). Includes a listing and description of museum studies programs by state, and information on resource organizations.

American Association of Museums, Museum Studies Committee, *Museum Studies Programs: A Guide to Evaluation* (Washington, DC: American Association of Museums, 1987). Report on the curricula and quality of museum studies programs; assesses and compares different programs.

Belmont Conference on Mid-Career Museum Training: Abstract of the Proceedings, May 9–11, 1980 (Washington, DC: Office of Museum Programs, Smithsonian Institution, 1981). Report discussing goals, objectives, organization, and format of mid-career training; includes needs assessment and recommendations.

Danilov, Victor J., *Museum Careers and Training: A Professional Guide* (Westport, Conn.: Greenwood Press, 1994). Describes more than 700 courses, undergraduate and graduate programs, internships, fellowships, and mid-career training programs in the United States and countries around the world. Discusses requirements for many types of museum positions.

Glaser, Jane R., "Museum Studies in the United States: Coming a Long Way for a Long Time," *Museum* (UNESCO) 39, no. 4 (1987): 268–73. Discusses the beginnings and development of museum training-programs, their consequences, and their implications in the United States.

International Committee on Training of Personnel. Museum Training as Career-Long Learning in a Changing World, Proceedings of the ICOM–ICTOP Annual Meeting (Washington, DC: Smithsonian Institution, 1990). Essays discussing the future of museums, societal and technological changes, and their impact for professional museum training.

International Directory of Museum Training, ed., Gary Edson (London, UK: Routledge and ICTOP, 1995).

Introduction to Museum Studies, 3 vols (Victoria, BC: University of Victoria, Faculty of Fine Arts, Department of History in Art, 1986). Study guide divided into six sections: introduction to museums, collection management, conservation, museum education, exhibitions, and museum management.

Learning Goals for Museum Studies Training, 4th edn (Leicester, UK: University of Leicester, Department of Museum Studies, 1984). Basis for a short course; provides objectives and key elements on topics such as museum context, collections management, museum management, and museum services.

Malt, Carol, "Museology and Museum Studies Programs in the United States: Part One," *International Journal of Museum Management and Curatorship* 6, no. 2 (1987): 165–72. Describes different discipline-related museum-studies programs in the United States.

Matelic, Candace Tangorra, and Elizabeth Marie Brick, eds, *Cooperstown Conference on Professional Training: Needs, Issues, and Opportunities for the Future* (Nashville, Tenn.: American Association for State and Local History, 1989). Includes reports of the working groups on training providers and training consumers; also reports on museology, cultural diversity, and institutional issues.

van Mensch, Peter, ed., *Professionalizing the Muses: The Museum Profession in Motion* (Amsterdam, Netherlands: AHA Books, 1989). Collection of essays considering the development of professional museum workers, training, ethics, and the role of museology as a scientific basis for the museum profession.

Museum Studies International (Washington, DC: Office of Museum Programs, Smithsonian Institution, 1988). Directory of all museum studies programs in the United States and abroad; includes four appendices with articles of interest.

Woodhead, Peter, and Geoffrey Stansfield, *Keyguide to Information Sources in Museum Studies* (New York and London: Mansell, 1989). Overview of information sources concerning museums and museum studies programs in the United Kingdom, Canada, and the United States.

Suggested readings

Ambrose, Tim, and Crispin Paine, *Museum Basics* (London, UK: Routledge, 1993).

August, Raymond, "So You Want to Start Your Own Profession! Fable, Fulfillment or Fallacy?" *Museum Studies Journal* 1, no. 2 (1983): 16–24.

Bandes, Susan J., *et al.*, "Interns Ins and Outs," *Museum News* 68, no. 4 (1989): 54.

Blackmon, Carolyn, *et al.*, *Open Conversations: Strategies for Professional Development in Museums* (Chicago, Ill.: Field Museum of Natural History, Department of Education, 1988).

Conaway, Mary Ellen, *Student Projects and Internships in a Museum Setting*, Technical Leaflet 184 (Nashville, Tenn.: American Association for State and Local History, 1993).

"Criteria for Examining Professional Museum Studies Programs," *Museum News* 61, no. 5 (1983): 70.

Dailey, Charles, *Museum Training Program: Institute of American Indian Arts Museum* (Fort Worth, Tex.: Institute of American Indians, 1984).

Guide to Arts Administration Training Programs, 1993–1994 (New York: American Council for the Arts Books, 1993).

ICTOP, "The ICOM Common Basic Syllabus for Professional Training," *ICOM News* 41, no. 2 (1992): 5–8.

van Mensch, Peter, *et al.*, "Methodology of Museology and Professional Training," *ICOFOM Study Series* 1 (1983): 81–94.

Museum (UNESCO) 39, no. 4 (1987): entire issue.

Report of the Study Committee on Education and Training (Washington, DC: National Conservation Advisory Committee, 1979).

9

Where the jobs are – or are not

"The past is my heritage, the present is my responsibility, the future is my challenge."[1]

Your future in a museum may be a challenging opportunity to make a difference in our society as we approach the twenty-first century. But how do you begin? Where do you look for museum jobs? What should you do to prepare yourself so that you will be the one selected when you find an opening you want?

How, where, what? Already the questions resemble those a journalist asks when collecting and reporting the news. What about "Who?" "When?" (If you've read this far in this book you already know *why*.) Let's use these questions as a framework for a chapter offering some insights and practical advice into the sometimes daunting task of seeking – and landing – a museum job.

Who?

When you consider a museum career, the major "who" is *you*. You must calculate *who you are*. You will want to identify your skills, the roles and experiences you find interesting and enjoyable, and the achievements in your life, so far. Think about your interests, your work habits, what motivates you, and your character type in relation to museums. How quickly do you get at the crux of a matter, and how do you solve problems? Are you well organized, or is "casual" your style? Do you like being around people, or do "things" interest you more? Would you rather work alone? How well do you handle instruction and authority? Would you rather *be* the instructor or the authority? Do you like providing people-to-people services, or would you rather be researching information? Do you prefer being creative by working with your hands? How well can you communicate your ideas, orally or in writing? How strong are your powers of persuasion? What are your levels of enthusiasm, energy, and pizzazz? Are you more introspective and reserved? Are you known to be assertive or aggressive? Do you intuitively come up with the right answers? Do you have some unique talents? Are you a team player?

178

Can you laugh at yourself a bit? The driving force in museums today is education – are you suited to that emphasis? When you weigh your assets and liabilities, how can you relate them to the museum field?

There are no right or wrong answers to these questions, but it is a good idea to gain perspective about yourself before heading out on a museum job search. The great variety of positions in museums requires many different types of people, so you will save a lot of time, energy, and frustration if you have some ideas regarding where you might best fit and be happy. Of course, you can accommodate and adjust to new, different, and unexpected experiences, particularly if it means getting a job! (It may also broaden your horizons.)

Richard Bolles, author of a book on job-searches called *What Color Is Your Parachute?*, proposes: "You flourish in some job environments, but wither in others. Your twin goals should be to be as happy as you can be at your job, while at the same time you do your most effective work."[2]

As you examine your credentials and analyze your skills, ask yourself and others how long it might take to prepare for and realize your goals. Consider what is lacking in your education or your experience. Ponder where you are now, where you might like to be in five years, even in ten years. But keep in mind that sometimes the best-laid plans go awry because of changing circumstances in your life. An unexpected job offer may come along that completely changes your museum career directions. You may decide later to move to a different part of the country where the museum job-market is different (sometimes more, sometimes fewer jobs). You may discover skills and talents you didn't know you had. You may meet your mentor and rethink what you want to do with your museum life.

The other "whos" are the people who counsel and mentor you, who give you moral support during your job search, who may recruit you, who will interview you, who will supervise you, who will be your "audiences." Some will be human resources managers, some will be colleagues; some may turn out to be the most important people in your life. *Listening* may become your newest skill if previously you were the talker. That is not to say that you should not speak up, state your views, exude self-confidence, and ask questions. But listening to the "whos" in your life can give you some of the clues (their questions and suggestions) you need to understand and sell yourself.

What?

What is the nature of museum work? Much of it has been described in other chapters, but here are some other "whats" to explore.

What is the museum job market? We know that museums are a relatively small occupational field. There are approximately 8,200 museums in the United States (according to the AAM survey), the majority of which are small, with staffs often of one to three people. In 1991 there were some 148,225 full-time and part-time people employed in museums, and 376,020 full-time and part-time *unpaid* employees, that is, volunteers or employees serving without compensation. On the surface, those appear to be large numbers. But, by doing your arithmetic you will see that the number averages out to about eighteen paid employees per museum, which includes everyone from the director to the custodians. Continuing your mathematics, consider the numbers of museums in each discipline; approximately 1,214 art museums, 4,484 history, 991 science (includes aquariums, arboretums, zoos, natural history, science and technology, nature centers, and planetariums), 704 general, 350 children's, and 586 on specialized themes. Of all of those, approximately 746 (1995) are accredited by the AAM.

Then, look at the numbers of vacancies. These, of course, fluctuate from month to month and year to year. When you do your homework, checking out placement services, and announcements of openings in *Aviso* (the AAM newsletter), the *Chronicle of Higher Education*, and the newsletters of the American Association for State and Local History (AASLH), the College Art Association (CAA), the Association of Youth Museums (AYM), announcements in regional and state museum associations and in government publications, you will have a general idea of the job market. Placement announcements and publications may be found at a local museum or a library (the Museum Reference Center at the Smithsonian Institution is a major source of museological information) or by writing to the organizations (see Appendix B for addresses). Staff members in museums also will usually share job announcements.

Keep in mind that within the job market there are many options. In addition to full-time permanent positions, you will find temporary, part-time, seasonal, contract, or consultant jobs, and paid internships. What kind of a job is right for you?

Temporary jobs are often available when a museum has a time-limited special project or when the museum does not have a permanent job "slot" (particularly in government-related museums). These jobs may last for a few months or even as long as two years. A temporary job may be attractive to you if you are undecided about your direction and want to keep your options open, or if you have time or family limitations, or if the type or size of museum that may interest you is still a mystery. Temporary jobs are also good "foot-in-the-door" positions; they may lead to full-time work. Be aware, however, that they offer no guarantees and that temporaries are unlikely to be eligible for benefits such as health insurance and retirement plans.

Part-time positions are especially good for the people who are going back into the work force after a hiatus, say, of pursuing an advanced degree, being enrolled in courses or teaching at a college or university, having been ill or retired, staying at home with children, preferring time-sharing (sharing one job with another person), are changing careers, or are just not wanting to work full-time. Museums with financial constraints often seek individuals who can enhance museum activities but who cannot or do not want to work full-time.

Seasonal jobs are most often available within national or state parks, or museums closed to the public for several winter months each year, or in areas that depend heavily on tourist seasons for large numbers of visitors. Opportunities at these places provide valuable learning experiences for the newcomer to museum work, particularly those right out of school, or still in school, who do not have families to support. In many cases seasonal jobs require more physical stamina, as they may be in the out-of-doors, perhaps guiding groups through unusual terrain, or may involve demonstrating physical skills, as in living history museums, farms, and villages.

Independent contracting or consulting is an especially good route for someone with special skills who may be making a career change, likes freelancing, is semi-retired, is between jobs, or is, for some reason, not otherwise available for a permanent position. A museum may have decided to undertake a special project, or it may have received funds to conduct a unique program; if there is no one on staff with the time or capability for the work, the museum may be looking for your skills. (There is discussion in the field that contracting and consulting may be the wave of the future.) Such contracts might be to organize a project, write a proposal or a script, design a brochure or an exhibition, edit a manuscript, raise money, conduct a publicity campaign, transcribe, computerize, conduct a visitor study, or produce an audiovisual (film, video, or slides). To undertake contracting or consulting, you must make sure, of course, that your credentials are sound, your references are available, and your resumé is well prepared and current. These kinds of assignments are difficult to find without an established reputation in a field of expertise. Success in independent contracting also depends heavily upon personal contacts or referrals by people who know your work. Cultivating contacts is the key to finding contracts. Some freelancers have advertising brochures for distribution.

A number of museums offer a few paid internships that are essentially "apprenticeships." Several large art museums have curatorial internships, for example, and there are some internships specializing in museum education as well. Some are designed to facilitate the entry of minorities into museum work. Internships are limited in length of time, usually to six months or a year. Some may, with rarely a guarantee, lead to employment by the museum. More likely they will serve as a positive referral to another museum.

Some internships are paid, but most are not. Most of those that are affiliated with a university graduate program are unpaid. In either case, they offer excellent work experience toward a museum career by enabling you to learn by doing. Internships are mutually beneficial. While the intern gains skills and experience, the museum gets a task or a project completed, and museum staff get to know a new practitioner and foster a museum career. As an intern you will be assigned a specific project or specific task to complete; even the dreary and routine can be exciting in their newness and for their insights into the nature of museum work. You should be well supervised, and you will have an opportunity to visit other departments and offices of the museum and get to know a variety of museum people. The internship may or may not lead to

181

"I would say that opportunities for minorities in museums are unbelievable. I teach a course in museum studies, and if a minority person figured out early enough in life – which few of us do – that they might want to work in a museum, and got a master's in museum studies and interned in a museum, I think they would be one of the hottest items in the employment field of museums. There isn't a museum I know of that isn't desperately looking to put minorities into professional and management positions."

Peter Ames, formerly Boston Museum of Science

a staff position, but it will put you on the "inside," in a good position to hear about job openings. You may even find your mentor during an internship. Even with several degrees under your belt, an internship can give you on-the-job training and invaluable experience that will serve you well when you apply for a job. (For more information about internships, see Chapter 8.)

There are a number of other "whats" to consider. Are you a minority? (This question is a "who," too.) Minorities are generally underrepresented in traditional museums, although this situation is changing and improving, albeit slowly. Many museums are looking, in good faith, for qualified minorities. You will want to know about the museum's equal-opportunity, affirmative action, and upward-mobility practices. Look for clues of bias or omissions in public programming and exhibitions, and whether conditions exist under which you want to work. Do you want to be the one to set a precedent, break the barrier, or be the "first"? It's up to you. There even may be an advantage for you in museums challenged to take affirmative action. ("Official" affirmative action is undergoing scrutiny by Congress in 1995–6.) That is not the ideal, certainly, as "tokenism" rarely produces job satisfaction. All of us want to be considered for our qualifications, not for our race or ethnic origins. Still, museums are becoming much more aware of issues on cultural representation, equity and parity, thanks to the efforts of organizations that have done a fine job of consciousness-raising. A number of museums now have diversity task forces or committees to activate and promote inclusiveness and pluralism. Changes are also due to the changing fabric of American life, but that is the subject of another discussion.

This "who" question leads, in fact, to a number of other "whats."

If you have strong feelings about ethnic identity, you may want to explore the possibilities of working in an ethnic museum. In the United States there are 120 African American museums, 200 Native American museums, and a sprinkling of Latino and Asian museums.

The Association of African American Museums (see address in Appendix B) can give you information on the locations, sizes, purposes, and number of staff in those types of museums. They range in size from small (the majority) to medium-large in cities all over the United States. Most are discipline-based in history or art. Opportunities for positions are somewhat limited, however, as African American museums are relatively recent to the museum scene and most have small staffs. The Smithsonian Institution has established a National African American Center for History and Culture.

The tribal museums of Native Americans are primarily on reservations, and they tend to hire members of their own tribal affiliations. They are eager, however, to find and obtain training for enthusiastic and aspiring museum people to conduct their programs and activities. They, too, have been established only in the past fifteen to twenty years and, in many cases, are still struggling financially and programmatically. The newly established National Museum of the American Indian at the Smithsonian Institution, planned for opening at the turn of the century, presents possible opportunities for "ground-floor" employment. Staff is being hired in advance of the actual construction and opening. The Smithsonian adjunct American Indian Museum has opened in New York City.

Asian museums and cultural centers and the Latino museums (representing a variety of Spanish-speaking countries), with collections from or representing countries of origin, are for the most part art museums that require professional qualifications similar to those of the traditional United States art museums, with specializations in particular disciplines.

The other numerous ethnic museums are one-or-few-of-a-kind, each depicting their cultural histories and often located in communities with a concentration of people with those ethnic origins, including Chinese, Czech and Slovak, Dutch, Irish, Italian, Japanese, Jewish, Lithuanian, Norwegian, Polish, Russian, Swedish, Ukrainian and Hellenic museums, among others. Jewish art and history museums may be found in most large cities in the United States (New York, Chicago, San Francisco, Los Angeles, Washington, DC, Philadelphia, Baltimore, Cincinnati); some are affiliated with universities and/or libraries. Some smaller communities have Jewish historical societies. The Council of American Jewish Museums will provide additional information (see Appendix B).

Other "whos" can lead to more "whats." If gender inequities are particular concerns of yours, do probe and consider your options. Women are hired in museums, without question – but for which jobs and with what chances for promotion? These are the key questions. Check the museums you are considering for stereotypical female positions and investigate the possibilities for lateral or upward movement. Find out how many women are on staff and at what levels, and if there is pay equity among women and men. A recent ASTC survey reported that wages in science museums in 1993 for men were 11 percent higher than those for women in the same job category. If you are qualified, don't hesitate to investigate and ask! Women today are challenging the subtle and hidden agendas of the recent past. Look also for clues of gender equity in the museum's research projects, collections, and exhibitions. Conversations with staff may be helpful as well. It is up to you to decide what kind of a museum environment exists for women where you are looking.

The 1990 Americans with Disabilities Act is having an impact on museums, making them much more accessible in job placement for people with disabilities. Organizations actively representing the interests of visitors with different disabilities are also encouraging museums to be more inclusive in hiring. Which types of positions are available to you depends a great deal upon your interests, but there are enormous possibilities to be explored. The more information you have about job qualifications, the better your chances.

If you meet the required qualifications for a job opening, you should volunteer information concerning the extent of your disability. Legally, an employer or potential employer cannot ask you about the disability, but your being forthright will establish an open and honest relationship. The employer must know what accommodations you will need, such as a Text Telephone (TTY) – a special telephone for people who are deaf or hard of hearing. Other accommodations may include interpreters, computers for electronic mail for communications, desks of a certain height to accommodate wheelchairs, and adequate lighting and audio equipment for the people with visual impairments. Are there ramps, parking facilities, visual fire alarms, and rest room accommodations? By law, if an individual is hired (a person cannot be rejected only for the reason of a disability), the employer must provide such accommodations. Innovative plans for disabled visitors may indicate to you a museum's concern. Audio descriptions for people with visual impairments, raised models of objects and maps for those who are blind, renovations for those with physical limitations, and complete captioning are significant "signposts".

An increasing number of people, by choice, law, or otherwise, retire but wish to stay in the work force. If you are one of them, many museums will recognize your special qualifications and rich experiences and may choose you for positions at many different levels. Others of you may encounter age discrimination, which is illegal. If, however, you recognize your own value, identify your assets and convince your potential employer of the contributions you can make, you may be able to capitalize on unusual opportunities.

For the most part, museums today understand "inclusiveness," and no matter what your "special" qualities and abilities, you should be in a competitive position for a museum job.

When?

The "whens" are up to you and your life requirements. So much depends at what point in your life you are thinking of a museum career. Have you recently graduated from high school or college? Have you just completed your master's degree or earned your doctorate? Have you worked at another job for five or ten years? Are you thinking of retirement? All these questions contribute to the quandary and quagmire of decisions that you must make. When you stop working and go back to school to qualify for a higher-level job is a major decision, for example. The considerations are financial, academic, professional, and personal. Much depends on the qualifications required for the career path you may choose; more depends on whether you have to earn a living (and how much money you need to meet your obligations). Much also depends on your inclination to study further.

"Interestingly, we find when we are hiring, that people are not interested to leave the East Coast or the major centers. I would strongly urge young people or career changers who think that they are just going to die in the boondocks to reconsider if they do want to begin a career path in museums."

Barbara K. Gibbs, Cincinnati Art Museum

Other "whens" may be a little less clear, or related to the progression of job-hunting. Accepting an internship, for instance, may depend upon your academic status or simply on the availability of such a position. Internal "whens" are, of course, affected by external factors having to do with the job market at any particular time. People in the museum field move from place to place quite often, so the timing of your opportunities, and your adaptability to circumstances may have to be flexible, sometimes depending on the moves of others.

Can anyone predict how long it will take from "when" you start looking until you find the job? Of course not! It may take two weeks (unlikely), a few months (probably), or even a year (we hope not). It depends heavily upon how much time each day or each week you devote to "looking," your perseverance, your resourcefulness, and, sometimes, being in just the right place at the right time!

Where?

Where are the jobs? They are around the corner, in the next town, in the nearby state, three hundred miles away, and across the country. That's what looking is all about. It depends on when you start looking, when you read the ads, or when you talk to a counselor. Keeping current on where the jobs are will keep you busy, but it is extremely important as you begin your job-search.

Where you want to live is your choice, but if your range is too limited you may lose opportunities. Geographic preferences can also narrow down the possibilities and concentrate your search. You may not have as many choices as you might think! If you or members of your family have health problems, by all means check the climate. But don't miss the *big* opportunity for unnecessary reasons.

First, look in your own backyard. No matter where you live, there are museums. Most are in cities, of course, and the majority of all kinds of museums are east of the Mississippi River. But the ads in the various museum newsletters indicate that there are openings in museums all over the country. Attractive areas abound, and interesting museums exist where you may never have thought of locating before. Even isolated and rural communities have made efforts to preserve their heritage. If there is a historical society, there is often a house or historical landmark museum, or an interest in one by the community. These museums may be very small, but they are more likely to offer jobs to newcomers to the field. If you are in or near a large city, the possibilities for working in large or small museums are, of course, the greatest. The fields are not necessarily greener farther away.

In fact, if you want to learn how a total museum operates, small or medium-size museums are where you should look first. These kinds of museums offer great opportunities for you if you are not ready to specialize, and they are, in fact, a good experience for anyone. The downside is that these museums usually have a small (but dedicated) staff and there are fewer openings. Salaries are also likely to be lower. But, if the museum is in a small or medium-size community, the cost of living is also likely to be less, and, again, the museum may be willing to hire someone with little or no experience. (See Appendix B for the listing of the Institute of Museum Services 1992 *Study of the Needs of Small, Emerging, Minority, and Rural Museums.*) The IMS study identified 75 percent of America's museums as small, 52 percent as emerging, 5 percent minority, and 43 percent as rural. The study defines the terms as IMS determined them.

If you already know you want to specialize – in a discipline, in research, in education, in design, in collections management, in public relations, in writing and editing, in financial administration, or in conservation, a large museum might be the best place to start. If you have had the relevant education or possibly some experience in another field, you will find many opportunities in a large museum to work with and learn from experienced specialists.

The type of environment – small, medium, or large – is your decision and, again, it is based partly on your "who," your self-assessment. The factors to ponder are the type of city, the size of the museum and its staff, and if you want to be a specialist or a generalist. Do you need an office of your own? Or can you share a cubicle in a "factory?" Can you be productive in shared space with just a few people, or do you need faces everywhere? Are you most effective in a well-equipped lab, or do you have the facility to "make do?" Do you need state-of-the-art tools, or can you improvise? Working with a small staff, can you double-or-triple-in-brass if occasions and needs arise?

"You can learn in a small museum because you are often in a position that you have to do and be exposed to many things such as exhibition design, exhibit installation, public programming, research, etc. It depends how well formed you are at the time. For someone who has a Ph.D. in a specialized field and interested in doing research, then it would be a terrible mistake to go to a small museum. It would be better for them to direct their career from the start to a large museum."

Malcolm Arth, formerly American Museum of Natural History

While you are looking, consider some "wheres" that are closely related to museum environments. Many private foundations, corporations, and government agencies have established art or historical collections, some with public programming, as part of their operations. They may have galleries, traveling exhibitions, and lending programs, thus creating museum-related job opportunities. Government agencies at the federal, state, and local levels, such as the United States Senate, the Library of Congress, most state houses, or historic county courthouses are examples. Libraries, school systems, national and state parks, and historic preservation organizations have exhibition, education, and museum-related positions on staff.

How?

How you go about looking for a museum job depends partly on "who," "when," and "where" you are starting from, and "what" you are seeking. But whether you are right out of school, changing museum jobs, or a career changer, you can find assistance from career counselors, professional organizations, museum staff, personnel managers, and search firms. Begin by gathering information, check all the resources we have mentioned, and meet and talk with as many museum people as you can.

More people than ever are changing careers. In the 1960s, control over your destiny was emphasized and one vocation for life was somewhat abandoned. What has evolved is that today the desire for intellectual challenges and the drive for more career satisfaction motivate many to change directions. Others are responding to necessity – a move, or a job being phased out. Whatever your motivations, timing may be an important factor. Frequent and legitimate questions to ask yourself are: "How old am I?" "Where am I in my life?" Successful career changers evaluate and re-evaluate throughout their lives the personal visions and values that are important to them.

"The mobility is greater in a large museum. In a small museum you may be tucked away in a small county museum and you may go to state, regional, and national meetings maybe once a year. But in a large museum there is a constant flow of people coming in, and you keep up with what is happening in the world. You are much more in the mainstream."

Kenneth Starr, formerly Milwaukee Public Museum

"I would argue to start in a small museum. You can get fast exposure to all aspects of the process, you cannot specialize in just one thing."

Spencer Crew, National Museum of American History

The keys to making a successful change are flexibility and thorough preparation for and investigation into the new field. For career changers, moving into museums may involve assessing transferable skills and previous work experience, learning a whole new vocabulary, and becoming familiar with a very different work environment. Career changers may be able to enter the museum field at a higher level than those with no experience, but an orientation period or a beginning level may still be necessary.

Even within a museum, you may want to change positions for new challenges. Moving up or laterally will require becoming familiar with other positions, their levels of responsibility and salaries, and the education and experience you must have to qualify. A move of this kind may require some additional education, and you may decide to enroll in courses at a university in the evening or on weekends.

Your research, curiosity, and stamina, and the inquiries you make when looking for a museum job, will be crucial to the search process. Begin by making sure you have all the background information you will need. Consult the publications of the professional organizations (see Appendix B), and request information or lists of other publications they have available. Visit your library, or contact the Smithsonian Museum Reference Center (see Appendix B). Ask for bibliographies. For a complete listing of all museums in the United States, consult the *Official Museum Directory*,[3] available in local libraries and museums.

If you are in school, either a high school or a university, find out about your school's career counseling, vocational testing, and job-placement services. Take advantage of these opportunities and make appointments to discuss your individual case. Visit museums wherever you are and talk to the staff. Professional museum organizations can put you in touch with individuals in your vicinity who may be of assistance. The search firms, or "head-hunters," in museum-related fields, recruit and often provide advice and counsel. Explore all the possibilities.

Whether you are looking for a first job or a career change, make appointments with museum people for "research" or informational interviews. The purpose of

"I think if you are interested in a museum career you have to visit as many museums as you possibly can . . . even if you have the traditional museum training. If that involves taking time and traveling, just do it! Take your camera with you and take a notebook, and look at the exhibits very closely. What are they about? What are they trying to tell me? If I were going to do it, how would I have done it differently? What don't I understand about it? Professional background and education will certainly make a difference."

Glenn Gutleben, The Exploratorium

"I think starting in a mid-size museum is a good experience because although your job may be fairly specific, it's small enough so that you get a sense of what is going on in the museum. Interns here can learn all aspects of the museum."

Barbara Luton, Santa Barbara Museum of Art

a research interview is to gather as much information as you possibly can about jobs in museums – so go to the source. Large museums with personnel departments sometimes have people on staff who will be willing to counsel and advise you about their museum and the museum field generally. Sometimes museum directors will see you. In fact, museum people of all types, and in most positions, are quite generous with their time for providing advice and counsel.

State clearly that you are not asking for a job, but that you are seeking information about museum jobs, about a specific type of job in the museum, about the museum, or about museums in general. If you are granted a research interview, plan to stay no more than thirty minutes – museum people are also busy! Ask appropriate questions, based upon your knowledge, education, and experience (you may take along a resumé for reference only) – then *listen*. Let the museum people do most of the talking, and perhaps they will have some questions or suggestions for you. You will learn a great deal from them. Do not expect a job offer, but if you make a good impression, they may remember you when there is a job available. Research interviews can be the beginning of networking. If you are unemployed or "between jobs," try to have at least one research interview with a prospective employer per day. A difficulty, of course, will be the travel that these interviews entail.

During research interviews or through your other contacts, try to talk to people who have been hired in museums recently, and ask them how they conducted their job search. There are many methods of job-hunting, and you can learn from the experiences of others – from answering ads to word-of-mouth connections.

Obviously your job search will depend on how old you are, how high you are aiming in the museum infrastructure, the state of the economy and its effect on museums, and how mentally prepared you are to plan for a new or different career.

While you are finding out about museums and museum work, ask museum people what they like to see on a resumé (or curriculum vitae), and prepare your own accordingly. If possible, obtain samples of resumé guides, and

"Before applying for a museum job, visit the museum, but get an annual report before you visit. Find someone there to talk to so that you can get a sense of the direction the museum is going, and perhaps find out the kinds of qualities that the supervisor of the position might be looking for beyond the obvious. Think hard whether this is the field, or section thereof, that you want to be in."

Peter Ames, formerly Boston Museum of Science

189

"The best thing they can do is to volunteer . . . to really get an experience that sets you apart from the bulk of applicants. It strengthens personal initiative to demonstrate what your abilities and skills are."

Barbara K. Gibbs, Cincinnati Art Museum

rules for resumé writing, from a career counselor, a library, or a museum association. List and explain everything you have ever been employed to do, including volunteer work. A potential employer in a museum may be keenly interested in the fact that you worked at a community playground one summer, teaching youngsters how to play volleyball or how to make something out of an orange juice can. The employer may be especially impressed that you are fluent in more than one language, have traveled extensively as an "army brat" or served in the Peace Corps, volunteered to read to the elderly at a community center, went on an archeological excavation when you were in college, have tutored immigrants in English, are adept at using power tools or skilled in computers, or have been actively involved in community theater. These interests, skills, and activities tell more about you as a person than you might think. Museums often look to hire people with broader interests than a specific job may suggest or require, particularly if these interests relate to the museum's endeavors. You may be applying for the assistant registrar's position, for instance, but you also write poetry and short stories as an avocation. If the museum has a publishing program and would be pleased to have an aspiring writer on staff, you will stand out among the applicants.

Your resumé should, of course, concisely present personal data, education, experience, career goals, museum-related accomplishments, and a list of publications in a logical sequence. List job titles, but specify too what you accomplished in each position. Emphasize personal attributes applicable to the type of museum position you are seeking and select the skills that may support future tasks.

Some applicants rewrite their resumé to fit the specific requirements of a potential job, but a well-written cover letter may serve the same purpose. All of the conventional wisdom for good resumés applies to job searches in the museum field. Write your resumé with confidence in your abilities to perform well at whatever museum position you are after.

If you want to apply for positions in museums funded by the federal government, you may go to your nearest federal building or write to the Office of Personnel

"I think a student should have the opportunity to work behind the scenes, as an intern or even as a volunteer for six weeks. There is no substitute for being there and working with museum professionals. You need to have the chance of seeing people at work in different activities, and how they do things. I think that museums are apprentice-oriented, and a person will have to adapt to that particular system. I got an entry-level position, and worked my way up."

Linda Thomas, Boston Museum of Fine Arts

"First try to find a way to understand what the museum is. I try to encourage volunteerism so they can really see what it is all about. People who are highly motivated will find a way in."

Ron L. Kagan, Detroit Zoo

Management (OPM) in Washington, DC, and ask for an optional Form No. OF-612 or a Form SF-171 (no longer mandatory due to "reinventing government"). Most museums that are funded by the federal government will have copies of these forms as well. Complete the form, or you may now submit a resumé. The resumé or application must contain, in addition to specific information requested in a job vacancy announcement, the following:

- job information such as the announcement number, title, and grade of the job for which you are applying (only if you know of a specific vacancy)
- personal information, including full name, mailing address, and day and evening telephone numbers; social security number, country of citizenship (most federal jobs require United States citizenship); veteran's preference (if you served on active duty in the United States military); reinstatement eligibility; and highest federal civilian grade held
- education, including high school, technical school, colleges, and universities with type and year of any degrees received
- work experience, paid and nonpaid, related to the job for which you are applying; include job titles, duties and accomplishments, employer's name and address, supervisor's name and phone number, starting and ending dates, hours per week, and salary; indicate if your current supervisor may be contacted.
- other qualifications to be listed are job-related training courses, special skills such as other languages, computer technology, machinery and tools, typing speed, certificates and licenses, job-related honors and awards, and publications and public-speaking engagements
- similar information is required for positions in the private sector.

You then submit the application or form to OPM and to the museum or agency you are interested in. Then you patiently wait (because the process usually moves slowly), though it doesn't hurt to make some telephone inquiries to museums while you are waiting as long as you don't make a nuisance of yourself, until the museum asks you for an interview (in person or by telephone), or tells you that there are no positions available at that time.

For state, county, or city museums, there are many different application procedures. It is best to inquire directly of the governmental unit or to the museum. Testing for jobs is fairly obsolete, but some government jobs still require it.

With your resumé or forms in hand, you are now ready to look for vacancies. Consult the newsletters with the ads for museum positions, and visit or write to museum placement centers (see Appendix B). To inquire about vacancies and application procedures, contact museum personnel managers (sometimes called human-resources managers) or the hiring authorities in museums. Look through the *Official Museum Directory* (in your local library or museum) for descriptions, addresses, and names of some of the staff in museums throughout the United States. Or call, fax, or write to the museums where you might like to work for names of the hiring authorities. Not all museums have a personnel manager, however. The hiring may be by the director, the deputy director in charge of a particular aspect of the museum's operations, or the head of a department or office. It is always best to know a name.

Explore or re-establish museum contacts and begin networking in earnest by introducing yourself and talking to as many museum people as possible, in their museums and at conferences. Attend annual meetings, and join museum-related organizations of interest to you, such as the American Association of Museums (AAM), the American Association for State and Local History (AASLH), the Association of Science–Technology Centers (ASTC), the College Art Association (CAA), the National Association of Museum Exhibitors (NAME), the Association of Youth Museums (AYM), and regional and state museum associations (see Appendix B). Meetings and conferences provide an opportunity to scrutinize the positions described in the organization's place-ment services and to learn by word of mouth of recent or potential openings. You may have the opportunity to meet recruiters, as some museums conduct interviews with potential staff at these meetings.

Try especially to make contact with museum people whose interests you share. Museum educators have museum education roundtables, for example. Cura-tors have discipline-based professional organizations; women in museums in some locales have a network (e.g. Women in Museums Network in the DC area); women museum directors meet annually at AAM meetings; and the standing professional committees of the AAM (registrars, curators, educators, media and technology managers, museum training people, security personnel, exhibition designers and producers, public relations and development officers, small museums, etc.) have publications and meetings. You can become involved in all those that interest you. And don't forget your classmates and instruc-tors from college. Get in touch with friends, relatives, and teachers who may have contacts in the museum field.

Learning about job openings while still employed severely limits your time for looking. This is the perfect time to make the most of museum contacts and networking. A search firm may be very helpful if you are looking for a senior-level professional position. Consultants in the search firm have institutional listings and will be able to tell you what is currently available in your areas of interest and expertise. They will also contact museums about your avail-ability and will keep you apprised as to the progress of the recruitment for a particular job that interests you.

Confidentiality will be important if you do not want your present employer to know you are looking for another job. It is less of a problem if you are transferring from another field of endeavor. Remember that professionally you still have a responsibility to your present employer and that you must give adequate notice before leaving in order to fulfill your present obligations. Your new employer will respect that. It is always a good idea to obtain your next job before resigning from your present one, especially if you cannot afford a gap between jobs.

Of course, that first entry-level museum job is often the most difficult to obtain. How often have you heard or said: "Every time I apply for a museum job, they tell me I must have some experience. How can I get experience without getting that *first* job? How can I apply my education to that *first* job in a museum?"

These are valid questions for entry into the museum field. Know and assess your museum-related skills. A positive attitude is paramount, but no one owes you a job. Recognize your limitations, but don't sell yourself short. For example, if art education is your strength and background, you may not think you would find work in a science museum, but a multidisciplinary education program in a natural history museum may have a niche for you. Just remember that entry level means that *first* job, no matter what your goals or what professional position you hope to attain. Keep in mind, too, that a first job in a museum for those right out of school may be very different from the first museum job for an experienced professional from another field who is changing careers, or for an experienced museum person who wants to change career directions and is looking for a first job in another museum career track.

Let's look at your options. What considerations should you weigh, what compromises should you make, to get started?

"But I don't want to be a clerk-typist!" "ME, with a degree, do an internship?" "I don't think I can live on that salary!" "But I wanted to be in charge of something or someone." "Just counting objects and running errands?" "But I want to design, not just use a hammer and nails." "That research sounds boring." "Scheduling group appointments was not what I had in mind for museum education." "Aren't storage areas kind of dark and musty?" "But I wanted to make a lateral move." "Stuck in an office? But I'm a *people* person!" And on and on.

Such apprehensions and attitudes are common, and even reasonable. But keep in mind that it is rare to be able to start at or near the "top" in a museum unless you have spent years in service. Each year more and more people are taking risks, or compromising a bit, and coming into the museum field in all sorts of jobs or internships because of the unique challenges and unusual opportunities museums have to offer. And they are willing to "pay their dues." Museums are a coherent whole made up of very diverse jobs. They provide a broad base for gaining knowledge in a variety of ways and for exploring your own abilities and skills.

If you happen to be in the right place at the right time, depending on your skills and your positive attitude, you might be hired to assist with cataloging collections, to help organize the storage area, to research sources of funds, to

"My first job in a museum was as a clerk-typist in the membership department, and I assisted the bookkeeper and the receptionist. After getting my master's in oriental art, I was hired as an administrative aide for exhibitions, and worked into this job [exhibitions coordinator] because I was logical and well organized."

Anna McFarland, Dallas Museum of Art

do secretarial work for the director, to paint or construct something for an exhibition, to handle the telephone for appointments for group visits and to answer inquiries, to help with the gardens or landscaping, or to work in the museum library. Or there may be an internship available, paid or, more likely, unpaid, and a fine opportunity to prove yourself. You are no doubt already aware that the museum field has become very competitive, and even with an advanced degree, but with no work experience, people often have to settle for a "foot-in-the-door" position.

The point is, of course, to get that first job, then to demonstrate how overqualified you are by performing well and going that "extra mile" above and beyond the duties outlined in the position description. Have enthusiasm, show an interest, and ask questions about all aspects of the museum's operations. Whatever the job or internship, the experience of working in a museum will be invaluable for your future. The contacts you make in your first job may lead to everything else you accomplish.

It will be even more compelling to settle for a less important first job if it is in a department or office that particularly interests you. It may be only a matter of time and hard work as an assistant to the assistant curator, for example, before you are a full curator. Also, to demonstrate your keen interest in working in a particular museum, you may decide to take a temporary, part-time, or seasonal position, or possibly volunteer your services.

Keep in mind, also, that museums rely heavily on "support" or assistant positions to keep their operations humming. Senior-level staff need skilled and competent support to do their jobs effectively. These positions are all vital to the life of the museum. There is satisfaction, pride, and even glory in doing any job well, and support people are highly regarded by all who work in museums. Some of those positions, when you lack experience, may be the first rung of the career ladder for you. See a list of some of these positions in Chapter 6.

You are in a somewhat different position if you approach museums for employment for the first time after having a number of years of work experience,

"The entry level jobs here are, for example, handling donor receipts, the computer, the thank-yous, the tracking of pledges ... another is the assistant for special events, lectures, films, and concerts."

Barbara Luton, Santa Barbara Museum of Art

although in a different profession. Your years of teaching history, art, or one of the sciences in a university, working in an advertising firm, being a newspaper reporter, doing radio or television production work, writing or editing for a reputable journal, being an engineer, being a chemist in a research laboratory, designing for theater, fund raising for a nonprofit organization, or managing a small business may help you obtain that first museum position at a senior level. You may not start at the top, but there are many layers in medium-size and large museums, and museums will recognize the applicability of your experience to a museum situation. You may be rewarded with one of the senior-level professional positions described in Chapter 6 or, at least, as a top-level assistant in the beginning.

Remember that the job market in museums is relatively small, and many museums' economic stability reflects the economic health of the nation at any point in time. But with luck, perseverance, talent, skills, and goodwill, you may have the good fortune to find that *first* museum job!

Actual hiring and selection processes differ from museum to museum, depending upon differences between government-supported museums and those in the private sector, and upon the size of the museum, the special requirements of particular types of museums, individual idiosyncrasies of directors and managers, and financial resources. Application procedures differ as well.

When you hear of an opening for which you would like to apply, send your resumé with a cover letter stating why you are particularly interested and what your qualifications are for that position. Your letter should be positive in tone and demonstrate a serious interest in that museum. Emphasize the special skills or job requirements you may possess.

If you are invited to be interviewed, be as well prepared as possible. Investigate the reputation of the museum in its community. Read as much as you can about it and its mission, and try to discuss it with people who live in the community. If it is feasible, make an advance visit to the museum. The facilities, exhibitions, and public spaces will give you information and a feeling about what it may be like to work there. Look for other clues about the museum as a workplace from staff members you may encounter. Inquire about the involvement of the board of trustees in museum activities.

You will want to be advised about the cost of living in the locale of the museum. Contact the local chamber of commerce and, if possible, current residents or local real-estate agents. Inquire about costs of housing and recreation. Find out, too, how the educational system ranks in the state, in the region, or nationally. The quality of the school system will certainly affect the quality of programming in the museum. Compare salaries at the museum with those at educational institutions and with professionals in other fields in the community. (See Appendix A for museum salary surveys.)

If you can, find out about the benefits before the interview – health insurance, retirement, annual and sick leave, and moving expenses. With these concerns out of the way, the interview can focus on substantive topics about you and the specific job in the museum.

It is always interesting to know the museum's "track record" on employment and terminations. Check with current or former staff on the museum's methods and practices in both hiring and terminating. Will the museum be under unusual financial constraints for the near future? If so, your job may depend on the outcome of downsizing or cutbacks. Or you may be hired to solve financial problems. Is that what you want? Try to get some background information, if possible, on the person who will interview you so that the discussion may be congenial. Having done your homework, ready with informed questions, you will be all the more impressive.

Sometimes a telephone interview precedes a personal one to determine the interest of both parties and to answer some fundamental questions. If you are expected to interview for a senior-level position, the museum probably will pay for your travel, meals, and lodging. You will be on the short list of candidates, and the museum will be willing to subsidize the interview.

On the day of the interview, arrive early, but not too early. Your appearance will be important. "Clean and neat" reflects orderliness in your work, which may be essential to the type of museum job you are seeking. Modish clothes may fly in some museums, but in others they may be frowned upon. Appropriate dress also depends on whether the job you are applying for involves meeting the public and on the general attitude of your interviewer. Again, be prepared. If a portfolio or records of your previous work in exhibition design, editing, or public relations, for example, are required, have a clear and well-presented demonstration ready.

Answer questions succinctly, truthfully, and without hesitation. Exude self-confidence, but don't overdo it. Ask incisive and knowledgeable questions about the job and the museum, and listen carefully to the answers. Emphasize your unique qualifications and your potential contributions. Know yourself – what makes you different from other applicants. Describe your work habits and methods of problem-solving as suited to museum operations. Explain your adaptability to many different situations and your willingness to pitch in to

"Museum salaries are better than they used to be, but not as competitive as they should be. There is a big difference with the business world; not so much with the academic world. When hiring, basically I am looking for people who are so committed that they are here for reasons beyond the financial ones."

Edith Tonelli, formerly Wight Gallery, UCLA

assist with work other than your own. Flexibility and adaptability may be deciding factors in a small museum.

If the museum is looking for qualifications you do not have, be honest with yourself and the interviewer, but do not sell yourself short. If you are willing to learn, say so. Convert potential disqualifications (your age, your gender, your disability, your ethnicity, your lack of museum experience) into assets by pointing out how they can be new resources for the museum. Age, for instance, connotes maturity and many cumulative life experiences, encounters, and relationships with people that can be very important in museum work, for museums are "people" places. As a woman, your knowledge of women's role in history can rejuvenate the museum's collections and its exhibitions by depicting the *complete* human story. Your ethnic origins can bring whole new audiences into the museum, and create a new approach to programming. Your new ideas may foster experimentation within the museum.

Interviews are, of course, two-way streets. During the interview not only will you be evaluated by the interviewer, but you will form impressions of the museum and perhaps your potential supervisor as well. How do you assess the interviewer? Listen carefully to the interviewer's approach to the job in question. What aspects of the job are emphasized? What attitudes are expressed toward employees. You will want to know if the potential supervisor's theories, ethics, and museum philosophy are compatible with yours.

Some basic questions you may want to ask include:

- What is the museum's mission? Nothing is quite so basic as the mission statement. Read it carefully. It should tell you the major purpose and goals of the institution. What is the emphasis on research and public programming, for instance?
- If you are interested in a senior-level position, you will want to see the museum's by-laws, policies, code of ethics, annual report, and current budget. If you meet resistance without satisfactory explanation, there may be something amiss.
- What aspects of the museum's operations demonstrate potential for newer types of jobs? Find out if the museum is computerizing its collections and memberships, using multimedia and interactive computers, marketing programs and services, initiating new multicultural programming, devising a new strategic plan, planning an expanded facility, or streamlining its publications. Does the museum often apply for grants? Are plans underway for implementing new ideas? Museum operations can reveal much

about progressive attitudes and practices or, conversely, indicate financial straits.

- What opportunities exist for professional development? Does the museum recognize the importance of ongoing training of staff, and does it have funds allocated in the budget for staff attendance at workshops, institutes, and conferences? The answers to these questions may affect your promotion potential as well as your professional growth.

- What is the promotion potential for this position? Based on the response, can you envision where you might be in two to five years? Occasionally chances for advancement are stated in the advertisement for the job. If not, ask.

What about salaries? If one of your goals is to become a millionaire, look elsewhere for employment. Salaries in museums have been notoriously low, though the situation is improving.

Negotiating for salary depends on how experienced you are. For your first job, the salary is probably set unless you want to negotiate for part-time work because the salary is not adequate for you to live in that community and you will need to find a second job. For a senior-level position, you should have a predetermined idea of what salary scale is satisfactory to you. The benefits may influence your decision – health insurance (and how much the museum pays of it), retirement, museum-related travel, and sick and annual leave are the common and expected ones, and some museums offer moving costs, life insurance, the use of a car, and even living quarters (not too many, and primarily for directors, although some outdoor museums and parks offer, or may require, on-site residence). Often the benefits are more negotiable than the salary, and they may even compensate for lower wages.

You may be encouraged if the interviewer appears to be impressed with you and asks you more questions than other interviewers have, such as: "How would you solve our current problem?", "How soon can you start?", or "Would you like us to help you find a place to live?" Other encouraging signs are a willingness to negotiate salary or benefits, a behind-the-scenes tour of the museum, and introductions to staff members.

Be courteous throughout the interview. When it is over, thank the interviewer for her or his time, and write a thank-you note the next day. Museum people are sensitive to the courtesies shown by colleagues.

If you are among the lucky ones who receive a job-offer (or several) assess, estimate, and speculate on what the job may mean to you. Can you use your

---

"I think that salaries are probably adequate if your goals and objectives are that salaries are not everything! I think that everyone working in museums acknowledges that there are more things about the job that are important than the actual money you make. You do it because you love it, you enjoy it, and you get a lot of satisfaction from your job."
Linda Thomas, Boston Museum of Fine Arts

"When I entered the field twenty-six years ago, luck played an important role, and probably still does today, but perseverance is certainly an essential – more so today."
Arthur Beale, Boston Museum of Fine Arts

education, experience, skills, and talents to the greatest advantage? Where can you be most effective? Can you grow professionally? Is this a museum with a social conscience, one that is willing to be an agent for change? What are your chances for advancement? Where will you be headed?

How do you know if you will be "comfortable" in a particular museum? The people, the physical setting, the programs, the exhibitions, the collections, the research, the care, the mission – all are contributing factors, depending on what makes you comfortable. You may sense compatibility on your first visit to the museum, or you may recognize that it will take you a while to settle in. Careful decision-making cannot be rushed. List pros and cons, use your common sense. Properly fitting the pieces of your life together, with the problems and the "price tags," can be a fascinating experience.

If the job you have been looking for just doesn't materialize, refocus your search. Perhaps your skills and abilities will fit into another position in the museum, or into an opening in another museum. Don't be discouraged. If the museum is of special interest to you, be gently persistent; check back a few times, just in case there is a new opening. Or if you can afford the time and are close by, volunteer for weekends at that special museum, or for one day a week for awhile. Your capabilities will be observed.

Entering the museum field can be one of the best choices you will ever make. The rewards for you in museums are satisfaction, challenging work, creativity, imagination, scholarly pursuits, accomplishments, and educational services to community and society. They, and the people you will work with, are worth your perseverance.

Notes

1   Anonymous.
2   Richard Nelson Bolles, *What Color is Your Parachute?* (Berkeley, Calif.: Ten Speed Press, 1971), p. 224.
3   *Official Museum Directory*, (New Providence, NJ: American Association of Museums and National Register Publishing Co., 1995). Annual.

Bibliography: Where the jobs are – or are not

Bolles, Richard Nelson, *What Color Is Your Parachute?* (Berkeley, Calif.: Ten Speed Press, 1971). Describes how to plan a career and search effectively for a job.

Canham, Michèle, *Museum Careers: A Variety of Vocations* (Washington, DC: American Association of Museums, Technical Information Service, 1989). Provides a broad overview of professional career opportunities in museums, including qualifications, experience, internships.

Careers Opportunities in Art Museums, Zoos and other Interesting Places (Washington, DC: US Department of Labor, Employment and Training Administration, 1980). Provides an occupationally oriented overview of employment in museums, etc., for career counselors and students, with job descriptions, entry level, requirements, opportunities, and promotions.

Federal Career Directory (Washington, DC: US Office of Personnel Management, 1990). Lists all resources and information about federal employment; offers guidance to people making career decisions.

A Guide to Museum Positions, including a Statement on the Ethical Behaviour of Museum Professionals (Ottawa, Ont.: Canadian Museums Association, 1979). Describes fourteen position titles with duties, responsibilities, and qualifications.

Internship Opportunities at the Smithsonian Institution 1994 (Washington, DC: Office of Museum Programs, Smithsonian Institution, 1992). Guide to the behind-the-scenes work of the Smithsonian Institution, listing all internship opportunities, projects, and skills required.

Jobs in the Arts and Arts Administration, 4th edn (New York: Center for Arts Information, 1984). Guide to resources available for finding employment in the arts; includes organizations that provide job-placement, career counseling, and job-referral.

Langley, Stephen, and James Abruzzo, *Jobs in Arts and Media Management: What They Are and How to Get One* (New York: American Council for the Arts, 1990). Guide to the job market and career development in arts management; includes topics such as career planning, training, and the job-search.

Lew Wang, C. M., "On Internships in Museums," *Curator* 25, no. 3 (1982): 173–86. Based on a survey of thirty-six museums in New York; examines internship programs and describes supervision, program content, and selection criteria for interns.

Mindlin, Freda, "Writing a Resumé That Opens Doors," *Museum News* 57 no. 6 (1979): 54. Explains and gives "tips" on how to write a resumé that will help to find a job.

Smithsonian Opportunities for Research and Study in History, Art, Science (Washington, DC: Office of Fellowships and Grants, Smithsonian Institution, 1994). Gives information on fellowships, internships, grants and research activities at the Smithsonian Institution.

The Sourcebook – 1995 Annual Meeting (Washington, DC: American Association of Museums, annual). Includes a variety of articles and resources about the topic of the meeting, and materials of general interest to the museum community.

Zhering, John William, "Careers in Museums: Twelve Ways to Break into a Field Where Most of the Jobs Are for Generalists and Where Much of the Work Goes Unseen," *Journal of College Placement* 40, no. 2 (1980): 26–31. Contains interviews that answer the questions: Which jobs exist? How can you get those jobs? What courses and skills are needed? What are future trends in museums?

Suggested readings

Baker, Barbara, and Garret Martin, eds, *The National Directory of Internships* (Raleigh, NC: National Society for Internships and Experiential Education, 1993).

Berger, Melvin, *Jobs in the Fine Arts and Humanities* (New York: Lothrop Lee and Shepard, 1974).

Career Choices for Students of Art (New York: Walker & Co. for Career Associates, 1985).

Career Choices for Students of History (New York: Walker & Co. for Career Associates, 1985).

Eggins, Heather, ed., *Arts Graduates, Their Skills and Their Employment: Perspectives for Change* (Washington, DC: The Falmer Press, 1992).

Finding a Job in the Nonprofit Sector (Rockville, Md: Taft Group for Fundraising Institute, 1991).

"Focus on Women," *Museum* (UNESCO) 43, no. 3 (1991): entire issue.

Frey, Woody, *Student Employment and Internship at Botanical Gardens and Arboreta* (Wayne, Pa: American Association of Botanical Gardens and Arboreta, annual).

Glaser, Jane R., and Artemis A. Zenetou, eds, *Gender Perspectives: Essays on Women in Museums* (Washington, DC: Smithsonian Institution Press, 1994).

Goldfarb, Roz, *Careers by Design: A Headhunter's Secrets for Success and Survival in Graphic Design* (New York: Allworth Press, 1993).

Haubenstock, Susan H., and David Joselit, *Career Opportunities in Art* (New York: Facts on File Publications, 1988).

ICOM Committee for Conservation, Working Group on Training in Conservation and Restoration, *The Graduate Conservator in Employment: Expectations and Realities* (Amsterdam, Netherlands: Opleiding Restauratoren, 1990).

Jobst, Katherine, ed., *1988 Internships: 38,000 on the Job Training Opportunities for College Students and Adults* (Cincinnati, Ohio: F & W Publications, 1987).

McDaniels, Carl, *Counseling for Career Development: Theories, Resources, and Practice* (San Francisco, Calif.: Jossey-Bass Publishers, 1992).

"Making a Difference: Women in Museums," *Museum News* 69, no. 4 (1990): entire issue.

Museum Professional Training and Career Structure: Report, Working Party (London, UK: HMSO, 1987).

Stitt, Susan, "The Search for Equality," *Museum News* 54, no. 1 (1975): 17–23.

Washington DC Internship Directory (Washington, DC: Congressional Youth Leadership Council, annual).

Women's Changing Roles in Museums, Conference Proceedings March 16–19, 1986 (Washington, DC: Smithsonian Institution, 1986).

Wright, John W., *The American Almanac of Jobs and Salaries* (New York: Avon, 1984).

Part V
Global perspectives

Global perspectives: prologue

You well know we live in a global village and that the concerns of our international colleagues are our concerns too. Museums throughout the world have a commonality of interests and problems, goals and objectives. The responsibility for the preservation of the cultural patrimony and natural heritage of all peoples rests with all of us, and the condition of the global environment affects us, motivating us in museums to action wherever we may live. The trouble spots in the world cannot be isolated from any of us in museums who care about the cultural, physical, and natural world. There must indeed be cooperation, collaboration, ministry of services from the developed to the developing, and reinforcement of the ties that bind us together as cultural institutions.

Museums have for more than a century, and especially during the past twenty years or so, demonstrated the world over that they have a specially important role in recording, preserving, and above all communicating to their own people the overall natural and human environment of their own defined territory, whether this is a whole nation at one extreme or the smallest of villages at the other.

I am quite convinced in my own mind that many of the independence leaders decided that the four most vital symbols of independent nationhood, and most vital instruments for trying to keep the peoples together and create a true nation, have been in this order of priority: (1) a national defense force, (2) a national broadcasting service, (3) a national museum, and (4) a national university.

Museums certainly can be, and in many cases already are, the deepest embodiment and expression of the cultural identity of any nation or more local territory. I appeal to the ordinary people, the museum profession, and those in government at all levels, to understand them, cherish them, and work in an effective and genuine partnership with their national or local communities to conserve, develop, and communicate that patrimony and cultural identity.

Professor Patrick J. Boylan, City University, London, UK,
from "Museums and Cultural Identity," address to annual
conference of the Museums Association, 1992

10

Museums around the world

Artemis A. Zenetou

"No country has within its people a broader representation of world cultures than the United States. Hence, it is especially appropriate that the American museum profession maintain, not only linkages with their colleagues abroad, but develop a better understanding of their resources and aspirations."[1]

In a world in which people speak hundreds of languages and dialects, and in which many people cannot read or write at all, museums offer an avenue for international communication. Whatever their differences, all museums are keepers of a patrimony that belongs not only to the countries in which they are located but, in a larger and philosophical sense, to all humankind. As George Salle, president of the International Council of Museums in the 1950s, explained,

> UNESCO's aim is to bring people together through cultures and the exchange of their spiritual heritage. And museums are most advantageously placed to help in the good work. They are the only place in the world where, with the objects as interpreter, a language is spoken that everyone understands."[2]

Global issues

We live at a time in which patrimony is threatened by military operations, terrorist actions, natural disasters, and environmental degradation. The end of the Cold War and the two-superpower era did not end the threat of destruction of cultural property. In fact, with the eruption of numerous regional and ethnic conflicts, the world may be a more dangerous place to preserve our heritage. Of special concern to the museum profession is the continuing potential for damage to movable, immovable, and irreplaceable cultural monuments. Armed conflicts such as the Iraqi occupation of Kuwait, the Persian Gulf War, and internal struggles within the former Soviet Union and People's Republic of Yugoslavia clearly demonstrate that centuries-old archeological sites, museums, monuments, church treasures, and important townscapes can be lost in an instant. Museums and other cultural institutions in the Republic of

"Networking is extremely important within the institution, within the office, and with the greater museum professional community, and also the international museum community."
Linda Thomas, Boston Museum of Fine Arts

Croatia are among the victims in the bloody civil war between age-old enemies, the Croats and the Serbs. According to the Museum Documentation Center in Zagreb, about 160 churches, old castles, and other national monuments, including at least ten museums, have been destroyed or damaged in the fighting. In a different context but with similar results, the Uffizi Gallery in Florence suffered a terrorist attack in the spring of 1993.

Cultural property that is destroyed is lost forever and is a loss for all human-kind. In these times especially, museums need to build bridges of understanding across national boundaries and work together to preserve the cultural and natural heritage that belongs to us all. As we prepare for the beginning of a new century, museums must broaden and intensify their efforts at safeguarding, preserving, and interpreting for all people human art and artifacts and the natural world. In even the smallest museums, both trustees and staff members must have a global perspective.

Organizations such as the United Nations Educational Scientific and Cultural Organization (UNESCO), the International Council of Museums (ICOM), the International Council of Monuments and Sites (ICOMOS), the International Center for the Preservation of Cultural Property (ICCROM), and the World Monument Fund have long sought to protect cultural property. International agreements such as the Hague Convention for the Protection of Cultural Property in the Event of Armed Conflict (1954, under review in 1993) and the Convention on the Means of Protecting and Preventing the Illicit Export, Import and Transfer of Ownership of Cultural Property (1970) have been signed by more than seventy-five nations.

International cooperation in the prevention of illicit trade has already had considerable impact. The 1970 Convention, as it is usually referred to, encour-aged the adoption of a code of ethics by ICOM and has encouraged many museums throughout the world to adopt ethical acquisition policies, forbidding transactions of objects illicitly collected or traded with uncertain ownership. But there is room for interpretation, and different countries, even those with similar legal systems, have enforced the code in different ways. The Conven-tion on The Return of Stolen and Illegally Exported Cultural Objects is referred to as the "UNIDROIT Convention" after the Institute for Unification of Private Law (UNIDROIT) based in Rome. The United States is an active member of UNIDROIT, an international organization with seventy member states. The organization exists to promote the reconciliation of the private laws of nations, which is needed because of the differences in common and civil law. In the case of stolen property, common and civil law systems view the rights of true claimants and good faith purchasers differently, civil law favouring the former and common law the latter. The UNIDROIT Convention seeks to create a unified code whereby claimants in countries that are party to the convention may sue in courts of another signatory nation for the return of stolen or illegally exported cultural objects. In June 1995 the UNIDROIT Convention was completed at a Diplomatic Conference in Rome. The trend is toward cooperation. A case in point is the so-called Lydian Hoard antiquities. Following a lawsuit and settlement, the Metropolitan Museum of Art returned to the Turkish government more than 200 antiquities that were illegally excavated from Turkey in the 1960s and acquired by the Metropolitan from established dealers in New York. As a result:

> the museum and the Turkish government have announced that they intend to consider collaborating on projects of mutual benefit, including art conservation, reciprocal loans, archeological excavation in Turkey, and the establishment of study fellowships both in Turkey and at the museum.[3]

In 1982, after ten years of debate, the United States Congress passed the Convention on Cultural Property Implementation Act, which was signed by the President in January 1983. Primary responsibility for support of the executive and advisory functions under the act is assigned to the United States Information Agency (USIA), which provides technical and administrative support to the Cultural Property Advisory Committee. Even though the United States withdrew as a member of UNESCO in 1984, it continues to uphold its legal obligation and moral commitment to implement the Convention.

UNESCO also issues notices of missing cultural property for countries who are party to the Convention and to the International Criminal Police Organization (INTERPOL). INTERPOL has a specific program of action to deal with art theft and the destruction of archeological objects and sites. The police forces of its 169 member countries, representing all regions of the world, cooperate in circulating descriptions of stolen art. Notices in INTERPOL's four official languages (Arabic, English, French, and Spanish) alert galleries, museums, pawnbrokers, antique dealers, auctioneers, and customs authorities to stolen cultural property, and all thefts are logged in a database that is also distributed to ICOM, UNESCO, the International Foundation for Art Research (IFAR), the International Art Loss Register, and *Trace* magazine.

Another important issue demanding international cooperation is protection of the environment. As early as 1969, A. E. Parr, director of the American Museum of Natural History in New York, warned:

"How far can we go with the public concerning the threats for the environment? We need to have more exhibition exchanges between countries so that we become aware of the way different countries and cultures treat the same subject."
Niki Goulandris, Goulandris Natural History Museum, Greece

We are faced with an urgent need to protect the environment, on behalf of man, for his present enjoyment and his survival in the future. In this struggle it falls to the natural sciences to try to defend the human condition and its supporting milieu against the damage inflicted by the exact sciences and the technologies they breed. . . . The natural history museums are, or could and should be, among the strongest bastions of this defense and therein lies a mission greater than any they have had before, since the beginning of their history.[4]

Since that time people all over the world have become more keenly aware of the consequences of pollution, loss of biodiversity, destruction of the rain forests, the ozone layer's dangers, and species extinction. Natural history museums and zoos are already assuming responsibility to increase public awareness on these issues. In Greece staff of the Goulandris Natural History Museum studied the most effective ways to engage the public's interest in their research results, and, working along with exhibits specialists, they turned scientific studies into educational exhibits. The museum organized an exhibition on the importance of protecting Greece's wetland areas that traveled in more than thirty provinces in the country and has influenced re-evaluation of environmental laws.[5]

International organizations and collaborations

In the face of such global issues, more and more museums around the world have responded to the call to work together. Museums learn from one another. More important, their joint efforts can increase their service to society throughout the world. Increasing numbers of museum professionals are benefiting from exhibition exchanges, personnel exchange, joint publications, and exchange of information regarding all aspects of museum operations and practice. Among the international museum-related organizations making cooperation possible are ICOM, UNESCO, ICCROM, and ICOMOS.

ICOM, a nonprofit organization dedicated to the improvement and advancement of museums and the museum profession, provides a worldwide communications network to assist museums in sharing information and a code of ethics important for their operations and development. ICOM also promotes the professional advancement of staff by making available a network of experts and training programs, publishes museum-related literature, conducts symposia and conferences, and has established a major information center with UNESCO whose print and computerized resources are available on a worldwide basis. Today the ICOM Information Center in Paris is the world's largest repository of information on all aspects of museum operations and practices. ICOM publishes *ICOM News*, a quarterly bulletin with current news of committees and reports of stolen artifacts. Paul Perrot, former director of the Santa Barbara Museum of Art, has explained:

ICOM is in an ideal position to channel an understanding *of*, and a concern *in* museums at the highest governmental levels. Its role has been critical in the establishment of now generally accepted international norms and in assisting developing countries in the creation of their own museum networks.[6]

Every three years, ICOM's general meeting enables museum leaders from 120 member countries from around the world to become acquainted, to discuss theoretical and practical issues involving museums, and to visit museums in the region of the meeting-site. The triennial conferences began in 1948 at the same time UNESCO published *Mouseion*, now renamed *Museum International*, a quarterly journal which serves as a forum for information and reflection on museums of all types throughout the world. To communicate with their members, most of the international committees publish newsletters, and some definitive books and periodicals. ICOM functions primarily through twenty-four international committees focusing on specific topics such as applied art, archeology and history, architecture and museum techniques, audiovisual and new technologies, conservation, costume, documentation, education and cultural action, Egyptology, ethnography, exhibition exchange, fine art, glass, literary museums, management, modern art, museology, musical instruments, natural history, public relations, regional museums, science and technology, security, and training of personnel. These committees meet annually to exchange information, plan publications and training, and consider pertinent issues; at the triennial conference they report and make recommendations to the general membership. The international committees of ICOM testify to a strong trend toward innovation within the museum profession. Researchers, trainers, administrators, audiovisual specialists, Egyptologists, historians, and architects now work in their various capacities with professionals in more traditional areas such as museology, education, security, and regional museums.

ICOM's current membership is 11,000 professional museum staff and institutional members in 120 countries. It has national committees in 93 different countries. The responsibility of these committees is to promote ICOM's activities nationally, with a particular emphasis on international activities and programs. They often work in close collaboration with their national museum associations, but they cannot assume responsibilities of a national museum association if one does not exist, or dictate policy if such an association does exist.

Programs within ICOM promoting exchange of museum personnel include the International Partnership Among Museums (IPAM). Proposed and administered by the United States National Committee (AAM/ICOM), IPAM provides American and foreign museums with an opportunity to establish inter-institutional ties through the exchange of staff members. Similar programs include the Swedish–African Museum Program (SAMP), implemented by the Swedish National Committee for collaboration among Swedish and African museums, and the Professional Enrichment Program, proposed by the ICOM Pacific Regional Organization (ASIA/ICOM) to develop joint training programs for professionals of the region. A recent initiative to "train trainers" in various regions of the world is being developed by the ICOM Committee for the Training of Personnel (ICTOP).

UNESCO, established in Paris in 1946, initially set up a Museums Division that partially subsidized ICOM. In 1949 UNESCO enlarged this division to include the Division of Museums and Monuments, and in 1950 it established ICCROM, now an inter-governmental organization independent from UNESCO. ICCROM has ninety-one member states and sixty-four associate members (nonprofit conservation institutions) throughout the world. The organizational headquarters are in Rome. ICCROM's functions are to collect and disseminate documentation on scientific problems of conservation, to promote research in this field, to provide advice on technical questions, to train conservators and technicians, and to raise the standards of restoration work. ICCROM also organizes symposia on conservation topics and works closely with other organizations committed to the conservation of cultural property.

In 1965 ICOMOS was developed to parallel ICOM. Its primary concern is the conservation, preservation, and restoration of buildings, monuments, historic sites, and cultural resources in countries worldwide. With headquarters in Paris, ICOMOS has eighty-seven constituent national committees, with about 5,000 members, throughout the world, including US/ICOMOS.

Museums around the world

Over the past twenty years, there has been a significant growth of museums worldwide, not only in numbers but in types. Different kinds of museums have been established to address new concerns and issues: community or ecomuseums, theme museums, interactive museums, museums of discovery and reflection, children's museums, nature centers, science–technology centers – indeed, museums of the future. Museums are no longer just storehouses or preservation agents; in many countries they perceive themselves as powerful instruments of education in the broadest sense of the word. This fact again serves to emphasize the need for worldwide cooperation. Another impetus to collaboration is the assistance sought by developing countries as they seek to professionalize their museums and provide educational resources for their populations, not just to preserve their cultures, but to train and educate their people.

Despite decades of international cooperation, the organization of museums and the nature of museum work vary greatly from one country to another. Museums, of course, reflect their national and local cultures, traditions, values, and national laws. In countries throughout Europe, Latin America, Africa, Asia and the Middle East, museums are largely government-subsidized and government-controlled. Museum workers are state-qualified civil servants whose primary professional interests focus on an academic discipline related to the traditional care of collections. Exhibition design, finances, human resources management, conservation, and other museum-related services are usually provided by other branches of government service or by independent practitioners and businesses. In these countries entering museum work is often very competitive, achieved through a difficult public examination; an

"Children in Latin America are preoccupied with museum education . . . they start going to museums at a very early age."

Belgica Rodriguez, formerly Art Museum of the Americas

appointment usually guarantees a lifelong career in public service as a museum specialist. In other countries appointment to museum work is political, made by the current administration, national, regional, or local, and may change as heads of government change. Sometimes both methods exist.

In the United States (and only somewhat in the United Kingdom, Canada, and Australia), museums are usually established and run through strong private initiatives. There is less government influence and a wider range of professional and technical positions among museum staff. Recruitment is overseen by the individual museum, and large numbers of museum workers have skills and qualifications that are usable outside the museum environment. Government-run museums in these countries organize their staffs and recruitment procedures in the same way.

The economic uncertainties of the 1990s have put museums throughout the world, regardless of sources of financial support, in difficult positions. They must compete for public and private funds against a host of pressing needs like health, housing, literacy, and hunger. Most are adopting diverse strategies to survive, relying less on government funding and seeking to attract money from a wider range of private sources by becoming more vigorous in serving their communities.

The following overview of museums in various countries and regions emphasizes issues of interest to those embarking on museum careers.

Latin America

In Latin America the core museum collections were drawn from the local culture and environment and became the symbol of cultural identity. After the wars of independence in the nineteenth century, the newly formed governments recognized the significant role museums could play in national consolidation and the development of new ideologies. Museums have long been instruments of communication and education, and the founding documents of new national museums explicitly mention this function.

> Professionals have been brought out of their isolation, at least in part, with the help of regional associations. In the Latin American arena, the number of meetings and exchanges of discussion papers among professionals has mushroomed over the past six or seven years.[7]

Museum training programs have been introduced and are widely accepted.

In Mexico museums that formerly enjoyed plentiful government funding are now adjusting to the country's economic downturn. But they have not let the crisis deter them from their one passion – education. More than 80 percent of the country's museums are managed by the Office of the Secretary of Public Education. Still, the government is struggling to maintain them. One problem is rapid growth. Most of Mexico's existing museums were built in the last twenty years, and many of them in remote areas, as the government has sought to decentralize the country's cultural resources, formerly concentrated in Mexico City. A second problem is private financial support. Mexican industries and private institutions are not accustomed to donating money to museums or to any government project, and individuals are equally hesitant to donate money to museums for fear it will be lost in the bureaucracy. In addition to a lack of economic resources, Mexican museums are lacking in trained personnel. Many of those on museum staffs are scholars, but few know museum work, and they are learning on the job. Recently the Getty Conservation Institute sponsored conservation training programs in Mexico, and Mexican-sponsored conferences, seminars, and workshops have brought in outside experts for professional development.[8]

In Argentina, where about 90 percent of the museums depend for funding on the national, provincial, and municipal governments, budgets for cultural affairs and museums are small. As in many Latin American countries, museums struggle to survive in the face of scarce state resources and a lack of incentives for private donations. Because museum administration depends heavily on government, museum directors have to contend with large bureaucracies and long delays. Practical problems are enormous: museum buildings are in danger of collapse, objects in many storage areas are deteriorating because temperature and humidity are not controlled, and staffing is inadequate. Generating income and privatizing museums are the major issues that the museum community and the government are currently discussing. The government will continue to own the patrimony but will no longer support and administrate them. The privatization program is very much in agreement with the museum community. It will provide them with a more effective administration and will bring independence from government politics. Another positive step Argentinian museums are taking involves strengthening their emphasis on education to overcome an image of catering to the artistic and aristocratic elite. As museums are recognized as "potential powerful educational tools," they are increasing their services to the general public.[9]

Middle East

Few countries in the world can rival the splendor and wealth of cultural heritage that is found in Egyptian museums. Like Italy, Spain, and Greece, Egypt has more museum objects than it can satisfactorily handle, and many of its museums have become mere storehouses. The Egyptian Antiquities Museum, the most important national museum, is an example: thousands of masterpieces are piled in exhibit areas that do not differ significantly from storage rooms. Modernizing exhibition techniques is just one of the challenges facing Egyptian museum professionals and cultural administrators today. Others include improving lighting, documentation, labeling, conservation practices; developing catalogs and guidebooks, and training professional staff. Financial support for museums is a problem, but much deeper is the problem of cultural apathy among Egyptians themselves. The ongoing effort to build a relationship between the public and museums and to create a commitment to museum life in general includes building small, local museums in each of Egypt's governorates, where the antiquities found in the region can be displayed. This decentralization effort is aimed at stimulating local pride and making Egyptians more aware of and interested in their history. On a smaller scale, the introduction of educational programs such as slide shows, films, and lectures, particularly for younger audiences, is helping museums overcome their "storehouse" image.

Is a museum career possible in Egypt? There are no schools or institutions in which you can study museum practices and museology, but numerous museums would benefit from the services of trained or experienced museum professionals. ICOM has conducted several museum training programs for museum staff. There is still hope that Egyptian museums will match the marvel of their contents.[10]

In Israel, museums are a cornerstone of cultural life and an essential component of the educational system. The country has approximately 180 museums, most of them in the central and northern areas. In recent years since the founding of the State of Israel dozens of new museums have opened. The nation's first museum is said to have been in the Greek Orthodox monastery in the Valley of the Cross in Jerusalem, which opened in 1865, and many other museums similarly developed from the archeological collections of monasteries. These early museums were established by dedicated people who taught themselves how to organize and run their institutions. The majority of the museums in Israel are archeological. They vary considerably in size and arrangement, period, subject matter, region, and site. Most of Israel's museums are public and belong either to the government or to the municipality, like those in Tel Aviv and Haifa; others are private, like the Israel Museum. Each private museum has different sources of funding, both local and foreign. Only recently has the role of museums been defined, and with the increase in numbers of museums has come a greater need to create a system for supervision and training to guide continuity and development.

In 1975, the minister of education and culture appointed a special commission to study museums in Israel. Its work led to the passage of the Museums Act (1983) and Museum Regulations Act (1984), which set standards for museum operations and personnel training. In 1993 thirty-four Israeli museums are recognized under the Museums Act, and museums studies programs offering professional training for museum personnel are being developed.[11]

Europe

Europe is experiencing enormous social and political changes. It is shrinking or widening, depending on how you look at it. Borders are opening up, and culture may be introduced into the official European Community (EC) policy via the Maastricht Treaty. These changes all put museums in a different light, and museum people cannot afford to be inactive. So far no umbrella museum organization exists within the EC, but there is need for such a network that could function as an advisory group for museum associations in European countries and eventually promote cooperation among museums in education, personnel exchange, and European-wide museum policy. Such hopes were expressed at a meeting in Copenhagen that brought together representatives of museum associations from the EC and associated countries.

Museums in the United Kingdom are different from those in the rest of Europe in the organization, qualifications, and status of museum personnel. Competence-based skills and advanced education and research are the prerequisites for professional museum work. The movement for the professionalization of museums and museum work began in Great Britain at the end of the nineteenth century. Emphasizing the notion that museums of all types faced many of the same practical problems, this movement led to the founding of the first museum association in the world in 1889 and the beginning of museological literature. In 1901 the Museums Association launched the *Museums Journal*, the first national journal for the museum field as a whole. Well-known museum training programs are in place at the University of Leicester and the University of Manchester, and the Museum Training Institute in London is conducting initiatives to set standards for mid-career training programs in the United Kingdom. Still, most museum staff in Great Britain learn "on the job."[12]

Over the past decade, French museums and related institutions have been undergoing a cultural renaissance. The French have caught the world's attention with the Institut du Monde Arabe, the Musée Picasso, the Musée d'Orsay, the Center for Science and Industry at Parc La Vilette, which features interactive exhibits on nature as well as technology, new media libraries, study centers, learning laboratories and the "Grand Louvre." Museums are being expanded and reorganized on the model of the American museum. In addition to the established Ecole de Louvre, which is now drawn together with the Ecole Nationale du Patrimoine, new museum training programs are emerging. The Ecole du Louvre was long the only entrée in France to a museum career as a curator in art, archeology, or ancient monuments and historic buildings.[13]

The Czech Republic has a great number of museums, the majority being technical, natural history, and history. The museums exhibiting art are called *galleries*, making a distinction between museums and galleries. Most museums and galleries are controlled by the ministry of culture or by a specific city, region or municipality. Few are private or self-supported. There are several different types of museums such as ethnic, open-air museums, automobile museums, and some that reflect a specialization of the country such as costume jewelry, beads, and hats. Most museums are understaffed, with inadequate facilities, but the situation may be soon changing. The ministry of culture is undergoing a major reorganization and review in order better to manage its museums and galleries. Volunteerism is not part of the museums and galleries in the Czech Republic, with the exception of smaller regional museums, where volunteers are usually responsible for special projects. Some museums and galleries offer programs to the public, such as lectures, concerts, films, etc. The Czech Republic has a long tradition in museological and teaching activities. A lectureship for museum affairs was established at Brno University in 1921, and in 1963 the University created a department of museology. Since 1965, in collaboration with the Moravian Museum in Brno, they have organized postgraduate courses in museology for professional museum workers from the Czech Republic (Brno Center has been collaborating closely with ICOM/ICOFOM, the ICOM Committee on Museology, and has established an International School of Museology). A few other museum-studies programs focus on museum conservation and museology, primarily for museum personnel.[14]

Norway

There are approximately 500 museums and historical collections in Norway, 300 of which are members of the two National Museum Associations (Association of Museums of Art and Social History and the Association of Museums of Natural History). There are a few large national institutions located in large cities, but most Norwegian museums started at a local level, where there are museums even in the smallest communities. Regional museums serve larger geographical areas throughout the country. Museums in Norway are divided into three main categories: (1) museums of social history; (2) museums of art and applied art; and (3) museums of natural history. They are also divided into different categories according to ownership and financing: (a) university museums; (b) state-owned and municipal museums, funded by the ministry to which they belong; (c) semi-public museums; and (d) private museums and collections.

A great number of professional groups are specifically trained for museum work such as (a) curators who are involved in collections, documentation, research and often procurement; (b) technical curators involved in conservation and restoration work; and (c) museum teachers, "educational staff" involved in instruction. Museum job openings are advertised in the newspapers, most being for curators. The applicants are assessed by a professional committee, but such a committee is not a requirement. The University of Oslo offers a one-semester specialization in museology, the four Norwegian universities each offers a one-year museum scholarship, and there are a number of other museology courses.[15]

Greece

The History of Greek museums is related to the establishment of the new state of Greece in 1830 after the War of Independence. In 1829 one year before the officicial recognition of Greece as an independent state the provisional government had established the first National Museum for Greek Antiquities in the capital then located on the island of Aegina. Among the first preoccupations of the new state was the care of its antiquities which clearly demonstrates their priority to preserve their cultural heritage. Today in Greece there are about 420 museums, half of which are archaeological and under the supervision of the Ministry of Culture. After archeological museums, the second largest category is ethnographic museums, followed by ecclesiastical art, historical, modern art, natural history, Byzantine, and Christian art museums. All of Greece is a vast archeological field; treasures are constantly unearthed. The National Archeological Museum in Athens is officially "full," not able to add to its collections. The new finds are deposited in Greece's regional museums, most of which do not have any security system and do not have a systematic record of what they own – factors heavily contributing to thefts. The older museums do not have either the organizational structure or the exhibition techniques that most of the contemporary Greek museums have. The majority of museum professionals, appointed by the Ministry of Culture, are either archaeologists or specialists in a particular discipline, and have learned about museums either on the job or attending museology programs abroad. Greece now has its first museology course. The course is offered at the Ionian University on the island of Corfu, within the department of archives studies and librarianship. Most of the students are expected to take up curatorial or administrative posts in Greek museums where there is a great shortage of suitably trained people. During the last decade museums in Greece have become an integral part of the cultural life of the country. There are ideas and potential for innovation that should eventually take all Greek museums into the twenty-first century, but there must be some serious reorganization that will protect museums from being victims of political instability, allow more autonomy and private initiative, and less dependency on government funding. There are many exhibition exchanges between Greece and museums abroad. As part of an innovative EC program on Remote Access to Museum Archives (RAMA), seven European museums will be connected electronically and share information on their collections and archives. The Goulandris Museum of Cycladic and Ancient Greek Art in Greece is one of the seven.[16] A new addition to the Greek museum scene is the Hellenic Children's Museum, located in two houses which have been specially transformed for a children's museum's needs. Although inspired by museums in the US, it is focused on children's experiences in Greece.

Canada

Canadian museums are in many ways similar to those in the United States. Compared to most other countries, Canada has a high museum density: museums or related institutions number over 2,200, scattered across a large, geographically diverse nation, and supported by a relatively small population of approximately 27 million. The nation's museum system is very advanced.

217

Its facilities are among the finest anywhere: staffs have an exceptional level of professionalism; conservation standards are extremely high; and sophisticated communications networks (such as the Canadian Heritage Network) link museums and their collections. The Canadian museum system has developed and flourished as the result of far-sighted public policy. In a country relatively lacking in private wealth, most museums were developed at the community level and subsidized by various levels of government as instruments of social policy. While heavily funded by the public purse (except at times of a weak economy), museums are operated "at arm's length" from the hand that feeds them. The Canadian Museums Association was formed during the 1947 meeting of the American Association of Museums in Quebec City. Since then it has grown dramatically, paralleling the increase in the size of the museum community. Training programs for museum work have proliferated and succeeded in Canada, and professional development is considered essential, even though an attempt at certification of individuals was abandoned.[17]

Pacific Region and Asia

In Australia, the government views large museums and art galleries as key elements in the nation's economic strategy and in attracting tourism. Still Australian museums are not equipped to negotiate more support from government; nor is government always responsive to museum needs. As in countries around the world, museums in Australia are having to become more entrepreneurial. To continue enjoying community support, these museums are looking for new ways of being both educational and entertaining to a wider cross-section of people. A study conducted for the Museum of Victoria found that public expectations of museums are changing, and museums are catering to a public that is better educated and increasingly interested in actively participating in museum affairs. Increased participation will, it is hoped, attract money from a wider range of sources. Australian museums and their associations have important recent initiatives under way in the areas of outreach to indigenous populations, women's issues, and professional training. There are a number of museum-studies programs in Australia, some requiring prior museum experience.[18]

China

Museums were first established in China in the late nineteenth century, almost two hundred years after their emergence in the West. Western missionaries brought the concept of the museum to China and established the first group of museums in the coastal areas. In 1905 the Nanatong Museum was the first to be established by Chinese people. Since then museums and museum studies have experienced different stages of growth, all shaped by political and social changes. The period between 1905 and 1949, like revolutionary eras elsewhere, saw a group of intellectuals demanding the opening of royal collections to the public. In 1925 the Palace Museum in the Forbidden City opened to the public and has remained open ever since. In 1928 there were only ten museums in China; by 1936 that number had risen to seventy-seven. Collections grew as well, and so did museum studies and museology. The Chinese Museum Association, the first of its kind in China, was formally founded in 1935 to conduct research on museology, develop museums, and promote cooperation among museums. It made contact with the rest of the world by participating in ICOM and engaging in international traveling exhibitions. The Sino-Japanese war of 1937–45 ended this vigorous growth period, and many collections were damaged during the conflict. After the establishment of the People's Republic in 1949, the Chinese government supported museums and the preservation of cultural heritage. Almost overnight hundreds of museums came into existence, but without buildings, collections, or professional staff, and most dissolved during the economic recession and natural disasters between 1959 and 1961. During the 1960s museum-studies programs were set up in a few educational institutions. The political function of museums was primary but, following 1978, with a policy of internal reform and an "open door" to the outside world, the nation's academic community and museums experienced a renaissance.

Currently there are more than 1,000 museums in China, and branch museum organizations on the provincial and municipal levels have been operating since the early 1980s. During that decade the Ministry of Culture set up a training center for museum studies, and on-the-job training programs by large museums and universities have proliferated. There are nine museum studies programs in institutions of higher learning, and China has sent many emissaries to Western countries to observe museum practices. Some serve as interns, and they are expected to return with beneficial information for Chinese museums.[19]

Japan

The decade of the 1980s was a boom time for museums in Japan. The growth of museums reflects the cultural aspirations of the newly affluent nation. Japan's economic strength is more apparent at local-government level than in the national government, and as a result there is greater support for local and state museums than for national museums, according to Tadashi Inumaru, director of the National Museum of Modern Art, Tokyo, and head of Japan's ICOM National Committee. Government-sponsored museums benefit from a tax law provision that allows an exemption from inheritance tax if objects are given to the government, but there is no law allowing tax deductions for contributions or donations. Many museums, particularly the national museums, participate in international exchanges of exhibitions, and some Japanese museums have developed collaborations with United States museums that also involve exchanges of museum professionals. An example is the Museum of Fine Arts, Boston, which will act as a consultant to the new Nagoya/Boston

Museum of Fine Arts in Japan, and will eventually develop both long-term and temporary exhibitions, and will also make itself available in all areas of the new museum's operations.

Still, Japanese museums are unlike museums in the United States in practices and infrastructure, in that they offer few memberships or special activities for members, and a limited number of educational programs and volunteer opportunities; museum shops are often restricted to selling catalogs and postcards. Part of the differences has to do with the cultural traditions and mores of Japanese society.[20]

Africa

Most museums in Africa are based on colonial collections gathered for the benefit of European settlers and to serve the interests of the colonial regime. These collections reflected external perceptions of Africa, and the principles that guided their acquisition and display were those practiced in Europe. This colonial outlook drew sharp boundaries between traditional and modern, primitive and civilized, inefficient and efficient, past and present, and these dichotomies of thought still permeate African museums. Today in various African nations responsibility for cultural heritage falls under a number of different ministries – culture, education, tourism, youth, sports, or recreation. The ministry with this responsibility is often one of the weakest. In Djibouti, Liberia, and Somalia there are no agencies in this role. Most nations in sub-Saharan Africa do not have adequate financial and human resources to protect their cultural property.

In November 1991, a conference sponsored by ICOM brought together museum professionals from forty African countries, as well as colleagues from Europe and the United States, to discuss the museum's role in the future education of African publics. Participants agreed that there is a real need to collect, preserve, and interpret not just the generic, albeit fascinating, objects of a folkloric past, but the specific objects, historically constituted, that bear witness to systems of knowledge, both past and present. Preservation must be motivated by more than simple nostalgia; it must promote a critical understanding of both the cultural past and the present. The "cultural" orientation of museums in Africa must be expanded to embrace environment, history, technology, urban culture, and archeology. The challenge is twofold. On the one hand, those who undertake research in the above-cited areas must be invited into the museum to communicate with the national public. On the other hand, the inherited model of the single "national" museum in the national capital must be augmented by a "local museology" in which smaller, local museums become critical venues for public education. If one accepts the idea that the museum can, and must, function as a place of learning, one school per nation simply cannot suffice. The "school" must be decentralized; museums must become key institutions at the local level. The conference made three recommendations for moving African museums forward: autonomy, regional collaborations, and specialized training. A clear consensus emerged that museums in Africa must free themselves from the vagaries of politics and the inadequacies of central funding. They must take their own management, planning, income-generation, and fiscal responsibility. At the same time they must become active agents of public education in a range of exhibition and outreach activities.[21]

> The museum in Africa, I am convinced, is a privileged arena for dialogue and communication. It allows **things** to speak, to bear witness to past experiences and future possibilities – to cause one to reflect on how things might otherwise be.[22]

Despite their different cultures, sources of funding, organizational structures, and staffing patterns, museums throughout the world have commonalities in purposes and goals, and in the future they will continue to work together. The issues affecting museums in one country now affect museums in another, and a global perspective will increasingly permeate all aspects of museum work. Throughout the world museum professionals will be influenced by developing multicultural concepts, and they will strongly advocate interdisciplinary cooperation. Evidence of the new spirit of international awareness and cross-cultural orientation is the emphasis museums and museum people everywhere are placing on international cooperation, community consciousness, public-oriented actions and the accessibility of museums to all people. Museums indeed are part of the global village for the promotion of peace, understanding, education, scholarship, and communication.

Notes

Research for this chapter involved extensive discussions with colleagues from different countries as well as the United States, the review of *Museum International*, *Museums Journal*, *Museum News*, and other museum-related journals and periodicals.

1 Paul N. Perrot, interviewed by Artemis A. Zenetou, Spring 1991 and 1993.
2 Edward Alexander, *Museums in Motion: An Introduction to the History and Functions of Museums* (Nashville, Tenn.: American Association for State and Local History, 1979), p. 249.
3 "Istanbul: Lydian Hoard Restored," *Art News* 92 no. 10 (December, 1993): 47.
4 Victoria Dickerson and Jeff Harrison, "Museums and Environmental Issues," *Muse* (Winter, 1991): 2.
5 Artemis A. Zenetou, "An Isle of Mediterranean Museology: The Goulandris Museum of Natural History," *Exhibitionist* (Spring, 1992): 16–17.
6 Paul N. Perrot, interviewed by Artemis A. Zenetou, Spring 1991 and 1993.
7 Hugues de Varine, "Where Are We Now? What Should We Follow?" in *Museums: Rethinking the Boundaries*, ICOM Proceedings 1992 (Quebec, Ont.: ICOM, 1992), 66
8 Yani Herreman, "Museums in Latin America," *Museum* (UNESCO) 44, no. 1 (1992): 5–6; "Museums: A Global View; Mexico," *Museum News* 67, no. 1 (September/October, 1988): 24.

9   "Museums: A Global View; Argentina," *Museum News* 67, no. 1 (September/October, 1988): 35.

10   "Museums: A Global View; Egypt," *Museum News* 67, no. 1 (September/October, 1988): 44.

11   Judith Inbar, "On the History and Nature of Museums in Israel," in *The Museum and the Needs of People*, CECA Conference, Jerusalem, Israel, October 15–22, 1991 (Quebec, Ont.: ICOM Committe for Education and Cultural Action, 1993), 28–34.

12   *Museums Journal* 93, no. 1 (1993), Peter Van Mensch, "Museology, Museum Training and the Challenge of a New Century," presented at ICOM meeting, Quebec City, 1992; International Report, "The Welfare of British Museums," *Museum News* 66, no. 4 (March/April, 1988) 12.

13   Patrick J. Boylan, "Museum Policy and Politics in France, 1959–91," in *Museums and Europe 1992*, ed. Susan Pearce (London, UK, and Atlantic Highlands, NJ: Athlone Press, 1992), 87–115; "Museums and the French State," ibid., 23–31; and Timothy Clifford, "Le Grand Louvre," *Museums Journal* (August, 1989): 44.

14   Information provided by the cultural affairs section of the Embassy of the Czech Republic.

15   Information provided by the Norwegian Ministry of Culture and the Cultural Affairs Section of the Royal Norwegian Embassy.

16   Discussions with Greek colleagues, and M. Andronikos, *The Greek Museums* (Athens: Ekdotike Athinon, 1974); and A. Kokkou, *The Care of Antiquities in Greece and the First Museums* (Athens: Hermes, 1977).

17   "The State of the Canadian Museum Community," *Muse* 10, nos 2 and 3 (Summer/Fall, 1992); and "A Window on Quebec Museums," *Musées* 14, no. 3 (September, 1992); and "Museums: A Global View; Canada," *Museum News* 67, no. 1 (September/October, 1988); and information exchanged with colleagues during the 1992 meeting in Quebec City.

18   M. Anderson, "Heritage Collections in Australia Report," Heritage Collections Working Group, Melbourne 1991; A. Galla, "Training Towards Tomorrow," *Bulletin of the Conference of Museum Anthropologists* 23 (April, 1992): 68–72; and "Museums: A Global View; Australia," *Museum News* 67, no. 1 (September/October, 1988): 33–4.

19   Interview with Chengbo Feng, professor of American History at Nankai University, Tianjin, People's Republic of China while visiting the NMAH as a Fulbright Scholar, and also Chengbo Feng, "China's Museums Reveal a Dynamic Past as Well as Future," *Museum News* 70, no. 6 (November/December, 1991): 16–19; Ji-Min Lu, director of the Palace Museums, president of Chinese Society of Museums and chairperson of ICOM China National Committee, "Training of Professionals of Chinese Museums," and Joanna Shaw-Eagle, "A Sackler for Beinjing," *Museums News* 72, no. 4 (1993): 15–16, 65.

20   "Japan, From Local-Government Prosperity: Regional Museums Enjoy New Popularity," *Museum News* 67, no. 1 (September/October, 1988): 41–2; "Department Store or Museum, Corporate Sponsorship Japanese Style," *Museum News* 66, no. 3 (January/February, 1988): 12–14; information from the Museum of Fine Arts, Boston Office of Public Affairs and Mizushima, Eiji; "What is an Intelligent Museum? A Japanese View," *Museum* (UNESCO) 41, no. 4 (1989): 241–3.

21   P. Ravenhill, "Public Education, National Collections, and Museum Scholarship in Africa," *Culture and Development in Africa* (Environmentally Sustainable Development Proceedings), eds Ismail Serageldin and June Taboroff, no. 1 (1994); Lucille M. Chaveas, "Autonomy for African Museums: More Than a Question of Reorganization;" Philip L. Ravenhill, "What Museums for Africa?", *Museum News* 71, no.

2 (March/April, 1992); Silas Okita, "From Patronage to Partnership: Establishing International Training Dialogues with African Museums in the 1990's," paper presented at *Museum Training in the 1990's*, AAM Annual Meeting, May 16–20, Fort Worth, Texas.
22 P. Ravenhill, "What Museums for Africa?" *Museum News* 71, no. 2 (March/April, 1992): 78, 79, 90.

Bibliography: Museums around the world

Berck, Brenda, "Museums: Rethinking the Boundaries," *Museum* (UNESCO) 44, no. 2 (1992): 69–72. Discusses the role of museums in the new world order; analyzes current museum limits and boundaries.

Hudson, Kenneth, *Museums of Influence* (New York: Cambridge University Press, 1987). Describes thirty-seven museums around the world that focus on archeology, history, science, art, and nature as "pointers of the future."

Kaplan, Flora E. S., ed., *Museums and the Making of Ourselves* (Leicester, UK: Leicester University Press, 1994). This volume presents fourteen case studies from many countries, placing museums in an historical perspective, and as part of democratization.

Museum Abstracts International (Edinburgh: Scottish Museum Council, monthly information service). Monthly compilation of abstracts of worldwide articles on museum administration, finance, conservation, legal issues, collections management, training, exhibitions, marketing, and development.

"Museums: A Global View," *Museum News* 67, no. 1 (1988): entire issue. Series of articles describing the current status of museums in Mexico, Canada, the Soviet Union, Australia, Argentina, Western Europe, Japan, Egypt and Nigeria.

UNESCO, *The Organization of Museums: Practical Advice* (Paris: United Nations Educational, Scientific and Cultural Organization, 1960). Manual on museum functions; gives practical advice to small museums, and museums with limited budgets.

Suggested readings

Ardouin, Claude Daniel and Emmanuel Arinze, eds, *Museums and the Community in West Africa* (London, UK: J. Currey, 1995).

Asian Cultural Centre for UNESCO, *Educational Activities for Museums* (Tokyo: UNESCO, 1991).

Bourdieu, Pierre, and Alain Darbel, *The Love of Art: European Art Museums and Their Public* (Stanford, Calif.: Stanford University Press, 1990).

Cossons, N. "The New Museum Movement in the United Kingdom," *Museum* (UNESCO) 35, no. 2 (1983): 83–9.

Feilden, Bernard, and Jukka Jokilehto, *Management Guidelines for World Cultural Heritage Sites* (Paris: ICOM–UNESCO–ICOMOS, 1993).

"Focus on Women," *Museum International* 171, no. 3 (1991): entire issue.

Hawes, Edward L., *et al.*, "After the Fall," *Museum News* 71, no. 3 (1992): 52–7.

Herreman, Yani, "Museums in Latin America," *Museum* (UNESCO) 44, no. 1 (1992): 5–6.

Hudson, Kenneth, *1992: Prayer or Promise?*, Museums and Galleries Commission (London, UK: HMSO, 1992).

International Journal of Cultural Property (Berlin and New York: De Gruyter).

Mizushima, Eiji, "What Is an Intelligent Museum? A Japanese View," *Museum* (UNESCO) 41, no. 4 (1989): 241–3.

The Museum and the Needs of People, CECA Conference, Jerusalem, Israel, October 15–22, 1991.

Museum International 180, no. 4 (1993): entire issue.

Museums Journal 93, no. 1 (1993): entire issue.

"Museums and the French State," *Museums Journal* 89, no. 5 (1989): 23–31.

Pearce, Susan, ed., *Museums and Europe* 1992 (London, UK: Athlone Press, 1992).

Roth, Evan, "Romania's Revolution Rocks Museum – For Good and Ill," *Museum News* 69, no. 3 (1990): 24–6.

Scottish Museums Council, *Museums Are for People* (Edinburgh: Scottish Museum Council, 1985).

Shaw-Eagle, Joanna, "A Sackler for Beijing," *Museum News* 72, no. 4 (1993): 15–16, 65.

Trucco, Terry, "The Welfare of British Museums," *Museum News* 69, no. 4 (1988): 12–14.

Trudel, Jean, *Formation et Perfectionnement en Muséologie* (Ottawa, Ont.: La Société des Musées Quebecois, 1983).

"A Window on Quebec Museums," *Musées* no. 3 (1992): entire issue.

Part VI
Views on the future
in museums

Views on the future in museums: prologue

No seers are we, but, despite financial constraints of the 1990s, the societal and technological changes taking place in the world promise exciting and innovative museums of the future. Museums are heading for the twenty-first century with open minds as to how best they may serve their diverse communities, how information management will streamline their operations and communications, how they may take advantage of the inventive and imaginative techniques for enhancement of exhibitions, and how, most importantly, they may be resolute educational institutions. Without sacrificing their traditional roles of scholarship and conservation, museums may be in the forefront as masters of communications and as agents of change.

Those who work in museums in the future will have a wonderland of opportunities. They will also have significant challenges to utilize the abundance of resources available to them. And they will need to concentrate additional energy on knowing and serving their communities.

Museums will be forceful institutions with "thinking" and "caring" staff to move them forward. What a delight it will be to work in them!

> We have dealt with the social issues and cultural diversity more in the form of debates than in exhibits. The AIDS exhibit is actually one of our first social things for presenting issues, and it is risk-taking.
>
> Sally Duensing, The Exploratorium

> As for discrimination, I think there is a culture within museums that has to change to make more people feel welcome to come as visitors. It's helpful for museums to establish relationships with community-based organizations who represent various minority groups involved in cooperative projects.
>
> Bonnie VanDorn, Association of
> Science–Technology Centers

> We plan to establish a multicultural advisory committee. Another goal is to have bilingual signage and labels throughout the museum.
>
> Barbara Luton,
> Santa Barbara Museum of Art

227

We are into an age now that the ozone layer, the global warming, and saving the rain forests provide an opportunity for zoos to be the perfect messengers for all those messages about the environment, about recycling, and about ecology. Zoos have more of a social conscience than they used to. Our public is finally demanding more, and is becoming more sophisticated. Zoos have an incredible niche to fill because we are nature offered in the middle of an urban environment, and we are a place where all cultures and people from different backgrounds come. It gives us so many unique opportunities that other places don't have.

Ron L. Kagan, Detroit Zoo

Museums are places for women to really excel, and I think they are taking over the profession! You don't see as many women directors as men, but I think it may be a matter of time. Some of their natural abilities – openness and a more team-oriented approach – seem to work well. We can learn from these examples.

Donald Hughes, Monterey Bay Aquarium

I think the major challenge for museums in this decade is how they are going to adapt vis-à-vis the financial situation of the country at large, and how they are going to incorporate exciting technology into museums' public educational functions, assuming they can afford the technology. In museum collections you need to start collecting initiatives for them [minorities] in order to show their objects, and you also need to change your public education programs to deal with the growing majority groups. As society changes, obviously museums have to change to reflect the population.

JoAllyn Archambault, National Museum of Natural History

I think we will have real difficulty, and will require more intensity, dealing with the difference between a museum as a storehouse and as an educational and social institution.

Edith Tonelli, formerly Wight Gallery of UCLA

I don't think the employment opportunities in museums will dry up, despite the current economy. Museums have been promoted, everyone likes them, and they are part of everyday life because of public and educational programming.

Janet Dorman, formerly The Phillips Collection

I think that people are seeing museums as an essential part of their lives and as centers for learning. I tend to be optimistic about the future of museums, particularly with their expanding role in education – I think there will be more positions available.

Arthur Beale, Museum of Fine Arts of Boston

It's hard to predict the future, but I wonder if interactivity and communications won't take over museums, and if they won't become "you are there" virtual-reality experiences, which may be a good thing, but drawing a line between simulated reality and reality makes me a little nervous.

American education is in trouble – the forte of museum object-based education is needed! I see museums much more as a resource than store-houses.

Peter Ames, formerly Science Museum of Boston

I think that more work will be done in museums by fewer people, and that museums will carefully shape their priorities, and it will be more toward public programs and public education. The public is more demanding as to what they get for their money.

Margaret Piatt, Old Sturbridge Village

Museums have to develop ways to be more competitive for funding, they have to think of ways of being creative in order to attract good staff – they have to take these positions seriously, and offer salaries that are comparable with the skills and experience they are requiring. They have to think of marketing and development that were not traditionally associated with museums. No museum today can be without staff computer literacy.

Carolyn Rose, National Museum of Natural History

In the future we have to find diversity in presenting material with all the technological changes. When people visit they should become engaged, and not just more perplexed. People learn certain things from Disneyland, and only that knowledge stays with them, and that is why we need to compete.

Spencer Crew, National Museum of American History

If we don't have money for the blockbusters, our idea is that we have such wonderful collections – why don't we just select pieces from these and create a show!

Terese Tse Bartholomew, Asian Art Museum of San Francisco

It takes some courage in our cultural institutions to really take the position of wanting to be social activists or wanting to lead or challenge their communities. Sometimes people cannot really afford to risk their jobs to take up causes.

Malcolm Arth, formerly American Museum of Natural History

Natural history museums which have large systematic collections are the documentation for the biological diversity of the earth. With the current concerns for deterioration of the environment and extinction of various species, natural history museums are becoming increasingly important. This importance may help the financial outlook of these institutions. What is important is that the storehouse aspects of the museum are driven by the desire to be a resource.

Bruce Bartholomew, California Academy of Sciences

I think the major change I see in the next ten years is that museums are going to have to find ways to earn more of their income because I don't see the corporate and private support increasing enough to do it.

Craig Black, formerly Los Angeles
County Museum of Natural History

We are into an era of heightened expectations by communities, and rightfully so. We are in a period of creative transition to make our museums relevant to all parts of those communities, all classes of our society. This expansion of museums is an opportunity to really fulfill the educational mission of museums in a meaningful way.

Barbara Moore, National Gallery of Art

11

Museums – today and tomorrow

"Today, to survive one must be skilled not only in politics and war, but also in poetry, music, and mathematics, lest the urgent clangor of our environment deafen us to the very meaning of life itself. We risk being dehumanized in a single generation, so that every generation must be all things to itself. There is no waiting, no putting off. In order to preserve anything at all, we must seek total personal integration. The perfect vantage point for this integrative point of view is the museum of the future."[1]

The future of museums, and of those who work in them, is closely aligned with the future of the society or cultures in which they exist. As the twenty-first century approaches, we are encouraged to consider how the world and society may be restructured, how civilizations and their cultural characteristics may evolve, and what impact the evolutionary changes may have on our traditional institutional structures and content.

Interestingly, we can look back to the 1980s and evaluate the predictions in George Orwell's *Nineteen Eighty-Four*. What credibility did futurists and their predictions have anyway? As we have observed, *studying* the future has become a serious and largely respected profession that allows us to predict with some accuracy the shape and characteristics of societies and civilizations and their respective values and cultural institutions in decades and generations that will follow. We have an opportunity to look hopefully to the future for a better, or at least a different, world.

During the latter part of the twentieth century significant and remarkable changes have been occurring. American society is emerging as more culturally diverse than ever, and we are getting better at recognizing and acknowledging diversity. The population as a whole is aging, with proportional shifts in population age groups. There are demographic regional realignments, with people moving to the west, southwest, and southeast areas of the United States. Public education is under increasing criticism as inadequate to meet new and better standards and cultural needs; some believe public education requires a major overhaul. Astounding new technologies are being developed with almost frightening speed. The information explosion is here. The planet earth's ecosystem

"Museums are not our tradition in the black community, but now that is changing and they are planning their careers. We have an obligation to tell them how they can make a contribution. I hope in the next ten years the kids will not be as money-driven. I am optimistic about that."

Harry Robinson, Museum of African American Life and Culture

is seriously threatened and endangered, and social problems of poverty, health, drug abuse, AIDS, and homelessness persist. Gender equity has taken on renewed importance, and people with special disability needs are newly empowered. Financial instability will continue to be a problem for the country and its institutions, but may taper off as the economy improves. Political influences are attempting indirectly to reshape, perhaps temporarily, cultural and educational institutions in the United States.

As society and lifestyles are restructured and new social values evolve, so the institutions that reflect them will also change, including our museums. Indeed, individuals who can initiate changes, or adapt to them quickly, will staff those institutions. Tomislav Sola of Croatia has observed that "we have to analyze institutions in order to make assertions concerning their professional staffs."[3] Indeed, if museums as institutions are changing we must examine what types of individuals are best suited to work in them.

Can museums be barometers of the future while traditionally preserving the past? Are they indeed catalysts for change? Should they be? What are the roles for museums in managing and coping with the problems and changes of society that they may provide even more meaningful environments for study, education, and interpretation? Lorena San Roman of Costa Rica argues: "Today, museums cannot be useless, because if they are, they will disappear. They must play a role in the polemics of the country and in its socio-economic development."[4] The time for reflection and action is upon us. Museums must embrace new social and educational roles in their communities. Attempted external controls of museums cannot prevent museums from raising social issues, presenting alternatives, and finding past and present truths for our lives. "Cabinets of curiosities," if ever they were that, will become agents of change.

Cultural diversity

Marcia Tucker describes the opportunities museums must seize as they become institutions of tomorrow:

> As we begin this final decade of the century – with the upheaval, disruption, and opportunities for reflection that the fin de siècle provides – museums have an ideal opportunity to radically revise ethnocentric ideas of art, culture, history, politics, and social relations. We have a chance to challenge and remake the structures that create profound inequities in our field, and to face the enormously rewarding task of adapting our

232

artistic, intellectual, and scholarly practices, and our museums themselves, to the global and vastly heterogeneous world we inhabit.[5]

We may call it cultural democracy, cultural diversity, multiculturalism, ethnicity – whatever term we choose, *Crossroads*[6] tells us it is inherent in every culture its relationship to history, and culture is a product of multiple generations, and that institutions such as museums are building blocks of cultural life. Museums evolved as European institutions, preserving European culture and displaying other cultures as "curiosities." Now they are attempting to incorporate those other cultures in their structures. Doing so will remake them as institutions.

Minority populations in the United States are growing at a much faster rate than the white population, according to the 1990 census, and the country's cultural profile is changing. Leon Bouvier[7] of Tulane University predicts that minorities will outnumber non-Latino whites nationally by the year 2060. Asians will exceed 8 million by the end of this decade. If present trends continue, Latinos will outnumber African Americans and become the country's largest minority group sometime in the next twenty years.

Museums, as institutions that represent, display, and interpret cultures, should assume a leadership role in shaping awareness of and attitudes toward the nation's increasing cultural diversity. Robert McC. Adams, former Secretary of the Smithsonian Institution, 1984–94, stated:

> Museums can – and the Smithsonian must – play a unique and increasingly vital part in learning about and finding ways to communicate and represent the pluralism that has always deeply characterized this country, as well as the increasingly multi-faceted and problematical character of cultural knowledge itself.[8]

Museums are in a position to exemplify and reinforce the ways in which various cultures within a society enrich each other. Increasingly, many museums are perceiving themselves as "laboratories" of cultural transformation. Recent exhibitions and programs are depicting reality in our society, leading to the humanization of museums. Art exhibitions are featuring minority artists; history museums are examining the role of minorities in the past with all the conflict, and challenging the traditional consensus of what constitutes American history; natural history museums are updating their Native American exhibitions by representing life as it is today, depicting the true image of the past, and removing sacred objects from display. Examples of the newer trends are *Native [American] Visions* from the Heard Museum in Phoenix, *Kids' Bridge* (children are important links in building bridges of understanding among all ethnic groups) from the Boston Children's Museum, *Mining the Museum: Artists Educate the Community* (an artist makes a statement about the omissions in the depiction of history by displaying underutilized museum objects that relate the "whole story") at the Maryland Historical Society in Baltimore, and the Oakland, California Museum exhibition on the strength and diversity of Japanese-American women. *Field to Factory* and *Japanese*

American Internment in World War II are two at the National Museum of American History of the Smithsonian. One of the newest museums on the scene is the Lower East Side Tenement Museum in New York City, a depiction of a housing condition in its bare reality.

While exhibitions are offering broader and bolder interpretations of society, museums are expanding their collections to include diverse cultures previously not represented. Researchers and curators from those cultures are pressing for reappraisals of the past. Oral-history projects are helping to preserve various perspectives of community heritage. Advisory groups from many ethnic communities are assisting museum staff as they incorporate diverse cultures into exhibition and program planning. And the complexion of museum boards and staffs is changing as greater consideration is given to community and cultural representation. Museums are beginning to understand themselves as agents of history in the making. Museums are taking those first steps, toddling a bit, but should be "walking" soon.

It is interesting to note that, according to the AAM 1989 survey, among the approximately 1,200 museums with a cultural or ethnic focus in their collections there are 419 historic sites, 409 history museums, 221 art museums, and 90 general museums. For specific ethnic audiences, the survey shows 149 history museums, 59 historic sites, 33 art museums, and 21 general museums.[9] There appears to be some disparity between ethnic collections in museums, and ethnic audiences who visit them. An analysis of those figures may indicate that minorities do not visit any museums in large numbers. Museum service to minorities is not a new issue, but it is a problem that museum staffs are now recognizing and attempting to resolve. The statistics also do not necessarily reflect the national interest in the 200 Native American, the 120 African American, the scattering of Latino and Asian, and the myriad other ethnic museums.

Museum people are looking for ways to illustrate, through cultural diversity, our common humanity. Museums seek to educate how people can live and work together, without separatism and divisiveness, and be enriched and enlivened by one another. In 1994, the New York Jewish Museum produced an exhibition that looked at the combined history of the Jewish and the African American movements in the US. Even as they explore diverse origins and cultures, museums are hoping, along with author Alex Haley, to move beyond *Roots*, to break down what he called the artificial lines of race, lines that too often are walls. It is the vision of inclusiveness that motivates museums. B. Gaither has said: "We must honor the comprehensive character of the American experience. We belong inseparably both to ourselves and to the whole. We are our own community while also being part of the larger community."[10] He adds that the stories museums tell will have to be richer and more inclusive, without paternalism or condescension. A new kind of sensitivity will be required of museum staff, who must go beyond passive response, philosophical acceptance, and be proactive in programming cultural democracy.

Reporting on a session on "Multicultural Management and Conflict Resolution for Museums" at a meeting of the Museum Association of Arizona in

1992, Carol Leone reported that "Americans have a tendency to feel that all people are basically the same, and if we can get together and talk about it, everything will work out." Her report continues:

> Unfortunately, we often fail to realize that conflict lies in the very act of communication between different ethnic and cultural groups. Cross-cultural training, developing a sensitivity to different, yet legitimate, patterns of communication takes time, time to learn, to apply the methods, process the experience, and receive feedback.[11]

Two examples of the ways museums are working to achieve the consciousness they must exemplify, the Virginia Association of Museums conducted a workshop as a training exercise for cultural democracy; and the Lake County Museum in Illinois is committed to change through research fellowships, independent study projects, board and staff recruitment, and building new audiences.

As the infrastructures of museums change, increased awareness and cultural diversity will be evident among policy-makers, funders, and those in positions of authority in museums. They will recognize that all people want to see themselves reflected in these institutions. They will also seek to remake their own profile. On the cusp of the new century, museums are in a unique position to build multicultural bridges by presenting the collective human experience with mutual respect.

Growth of the older adult population

America is aging. According to Heather Paul, a futurist:

> The greatest growth in the next decade [1990s] will be among ages thirty-five to fifty-four. The second fastest growing group includes those over sixty-five. This group will grow by 28 percent in this same period. As seventy-seven million "baby boomers" [those born between 1946 and 1960] move into their middle and later years, they will have as dramatic an effect on aging as they have been having, politically and economically, on other phases of the life cycle. Museums of the twenty-first century will be much more conscious of these aging Americans' special needs.[12]

In the next decade the "baby boomers" will be reaching their peak earning and spending years, and they have the potential to be major sources of private financial support for museums. For that reason, museums must be strongly accountable, both financially and programmatically, for this generation is sophisticated in the business and cultural worlds. That accountability is in the hands of the staff (and trustees) of museums.

But the baby boomers will have even more to offer museums in the way of human resources. Retired or semi-retired people will use their experience, talents, skills and education to become a major force for fund-raising, volunteerism, trusteeship, financial management, marketing, and many other types of services for museums. Creative and imaginative museum staff members should be aware of these rich resources that can carry out museum functions in times of financial constraint. Simultaneously, they must examine why persons 60 and older are underrepresented in their audiences. They must tend to the "Woopies" (well-off older people) as they are now tending to the "Yuppies" (young urban professional people) for their future alliances. We must remember too that the Elder Hostel Programs will increasingly use more museums for their intellectual bases.

Paul also believes that "along with the very anxious policy analysts in the Social Security Administration, there are others of us who are fascinated by the prospect of reinventing aging, [especially for women]." "Better health and adaptability to new circumstances could mean a totally new way of growing old."[13] If they are wise, museums will exploit these energies, talents, and skills to their advantage. They will also "develop marketing strategies for the new demographic profiles."[14]

Population shifts

Americans are on the move; not just the people who are retiring and moving to warmer climates, but all sectors in our society. Since 1980, growing segments of the population have been moving to the West, the Southwest, and the Southeast of the United States. Other shifts have been to suburban or rural areas from the troubled large cities.

A 1989 AAM Survey[15] confirms the connection between population shifts and museums. Between 1980 and 1989 there were 889 new museums established, a growth of 10.87 percent. The increases were, in descending order of percentages, in the Southeast, Midwest, Mid-Atlantic, Mountain–Plains, West, and New England – the six regions of the AAM.

According to *Museums for a New Century*,

> It is clear that as people build new communities, they build new museums. The Census Bureau projects continued growth in the Sun Belt. Between 1980 and 2000 the western states, Texas, and Florida are expected to show population increases of 45, 46, and 79 percent respectively. Their residents can look forward to more and better museums.[16]

In the fairly small community of Sun City, Arizona, outside of Phoenix, for example, a group of newly arrived residents decided they wanted their own art museum, and proceeded to raise the money and build one. Often bringing with them an interest in an expanded cultural life, new residents bring new support to existing museums, too. If you are wondering where museum jobs are most likely to be in the future, look south and west.

Prospects for museum positions, in small and medium-size museums, in suburban areas are also strong, but don't overlook possibilities in the inner

236

cities. For the past twenty-five years pioneering and creative inner-city museums (often established by larger and traditional museums in the area) have addressed the problems in these areas and have worked hard to involve their communities in the museum, i.e., the Boston Museum of Fine Arts, the Whitney in New York City, the Museum of Contemporary Art in Los Angeles, the Smithsonian, and museums in Stockholm and London. In the twenty-first century, these may be the most challenging jobs of all. On the other hand, recent turmoil in the inner cities is prompting population shifts to the suburbs and rural communities. The small and medium-size museums in those suburban areas may experience a renewed vitality and opportunities for expansion and support. They, too, if financially viable, may provide new job opportunities.

The state of education

As the country examines the shortcomings of its public educational system, museums, as educational institutions, and their staff are recognizing that they have enormous potential as alternative educators and as "parallel schools." Science museums and children's museums have pioneered innovative educative techniques for many years, providing imaginative learning experiences for people of all ages. Their experiential, participatory, and hands-on methods of presentation have had an impact on museum visitors. The 1989 AAM Survey[17] shows that the greatest growth of new museums during the 1980s was in children's museums, followed by specialized museums (about one specific topic such as automobiles, soaring, electricity, jails, potatoes), and planetariums. Other museums are now following the lead of the children's museums and science centers, emphasizing informal, family, and lifelong learning and incorporating innovative methodologies and practices.

With their renewed commitment to education, society in general and local communities particularly are looking to museums to complement and even replace the weakened formal classroom education. Some museums have functioning schools within their walls. Consortiums of museums in Brooklyn, New York City, and Philadelphia are establishing floating school classrooms, taking up temporary residence in several area museums, or in a unique public high school. The Pacific Science Center in Seattle, the Franklin Institute in Philadelphia, the Smithsonian Institution, and the Fernbank Science Center in Atlanta are among the *many* museums offering teacher training, and these services are being sought by local and state governments as never before, particularly in the sciences. Museums are becoming an integral component in the formal curriculum of school systems in Detroit, San Antonio, New York, Indianapolis, and Portland, Oregon. They are changing the way traditional subjects are taught, introducing new and different subjects, and offering access to objects and to learning from exhibitions. Joel Bloom, former Director of the Franklin Institute in Philadelphia, upon accepting an achievement award from Mid-Atlantic Association of Museums, said, "We are educational institutions which offer rich encounters with reality, a chronicle of human creativity, a window on the world."

The trend toward lifelong learning has expanded and redefined the role of the museum educator. No longer do museum education departments focus narrowly or only on school programs. Expectations of personal growth and learning and the needs for "mid-career" and "mid-life" information by the adult population, have expanded the concept of museum education, and education staff are developing programs that serve these new audiences. As an example, the National Gallery of Canada may be in the forefront among art museums in presenting "theme rooms," didactic areas adjacent to main galleries, that enhance the educational content of exhibitions for adults. The Seattle Art Museum has "resource" rooms for visitors on two floors, and the J. Paul Getty Museum in Malibu, California has "browsing rooms" with interactive computers to pose and answer the questions visitors may have after viewing an exhibition. Interactive computers in many museums were not created exclusively for children, but offer adults an opportunity for in-depth examination of subject matter. The Museum of Science and Industry in Parc La Villette in Paris even requests the visitors to evaluate their museum experience on computers.

In these educational efforts, museums are collaborating with schools, other museums, universities, local organizations, businesses, and the corporate community. A new international initiative called "Collaborations" emanating from Hawaii, is linking museums, schools and universities in an exhibition-based virtual community. Indeed, additional financial support for museums may hinge on their educational agendas and accountability. New programs of formal and informal education challenge schoolchildren to discover, to question, and to seek additional information. University museums have always collaborated with their parent institutions, but scientists in other museums are now encouraged to share their research with university colleagues, which will ultimately benefit a broader audience. Local organizations and businesses are co-sponsoring festivals, concerts, films, lectures, rock and mineral shows, international and ethnic days, and many other special events that enhance and reaffirm the museum's commitment to public service and to the educational quality of museum activities.

An emphasis on professional development and training of both museum educators and the entire staff will be required to fulfill the current obligations and responsibilities of museums. The AAM report *Excellence and Equity*[18] stresses the need for *all* museum staff members to be concerned with education. Curators, designers, administrators, registrars, conservators – in short, people in every position – have a responsibility to fulfill the museum's educational mission. The curator who researches and writes for peer groups, for example, must also share that information with the public and make sure it is accessible to museum visitors. To change attitudes and long-existing practices that are contrary to this approach, museums will need to budget for and offer staff training. Workshops and seminars in educational theory and practice will help foster new approaches and contemporary skills.

To be effective in their educational mission, museums will need to augment their efforts in recognizing and assessing public perceptions of museums, and audience needs and interests. The field of visitor studies, perhaps reconsidering their techniques, will be important here. Staff, too, will need to be trained to assess the impact of museum exhibitions and activities, from conceptual stages through completion. Museum educators have generally been in the forefront in recognizing the contributions visitor evaluation can make to improving museum programs.

Museum educators also have been in the forefront of networking among their peers. Museum Education Roundtable (MER), initiated in the Washington, DC area about 1973, now publishes the *Journal for Museum Education* for worldwide distribution, still meets regularly, and has been emulated throughout the country.

The energy with which museums have responded to what has been described as a nationwide crisis in education exemplifies the ways in which these institutions are connected to society. Not only have museums stepped into an expanded role they have been asked to fill; they have taken it on themselves to define that role.

> The community of museums in the United States shares the responsibility with other educational institutions to enrich learning opportunities for all individuals, to nurture an enlightened, humane citizenry that appreciates the value of knowing about its past, is resourcefully and sensitively engaged in the present, and is determined to shape a future in which many experiences and many points of view are given voice. In this endeavor, museums will play a powerful, beneficial role for the people of the next century.[19]

This statement in the 1992 AAM report *Excellence and Equity* emanated from a task force that spent three years compiling information, discussing issues with a large cross-section of people, and writing. For museums, it is a landmark document, reinforcing what many museum people already believed and practiced, but also introducing a new dynamic in bold statements as to what museum education should be. Dan Monroe has commented:

> *Excellence and Equity* marks a turning point for American museums. Important as the role of preservation is, it is no longer the prime or sole mission of museums. Our primary enterprise must now be ideas, values, and learning. Preservation serves to make this enterprise possible in the future. It is not an end in itself.[20]

The report has generated nationwide discussions, and the AAM has launched a national research demonstration project, with thirteen test sites, to expand education and public service in museums. Those contemplating careers in museums will surely need to be in concert with an emphasis on education. For those who love interpreting and offering learning in the broadest sense, museums in the twenty-first century will be exciting places to be.

"New technologies have changed our jobs . . . no museum today and in the future can be without computer literacy. One cannot minimize the technologies that people are familiar with from other dimensions of their lives."

Carolyn Rose, National Museum of Natural History

Technologies

The years into the next century will continue the revolutionary challenges of the information age, with amazing advances. Museums' abilities to participate, and to infuse technology wisely into all aspects of museum operations, will determine their success.

Dramatic technological innovations by the year 2000, some predicted by Paul,[21] are:

- 90 percent of work now done on computer mainframes will be done on the desk-top, a boon to smaller museums with limited budgets.
- Erasable storage is likely, and data compression may increase optical storage density by six times, whereby a compact disk could hold the equivalent of 6,000 books. Think how records of museum collections and inventories may be stored and easily retrieved and shared with other institutions.
- Phone systems will have end-to-end digital-carrying text, data, graphics, pictures, and full-motion video as well as voice. Communications among museums will be revolutionized, and communications specialists will be in demand.
- Speaker-independent speech-recognition systems will recognize 5,000–15,000 words of continuous speech. Voice-recognition software is coming, and the lives of researchers and writers will be altered beyond our present dreams.
- It is likely that the museum community will institute a national series of computer-based inventories of museum collections along with an information-sharing system, indeed, a "national museum catalog." [Canada has already made advances in this arena].
- For museums that have international communications needs, there will be fonts in eighteen languages.
- Museum computerized inventories will not be bound to the printed word but will offer capacity for image, color, sound, and categorization. The Victoria and Albert Museum in the United Kingdom is involved in an image database program. The Whitney Museum of Art in New York is planning a pay-per-view digital bank for people to access art from home.

"What needs to be articulated, regardless of the format of the man–machine relationship, is the goal of humanism through machines."

Nicholas Negroponte, The Media Lab

"The same technology that offers the promise of breathtaking new research methods, can also facilitate easy high-quality and high-volume piracy of these electronic images. Unauthorized duplication presents similar problems in conventional publishing and the computer software industry. Intellectual property protections, both technical and legal, are being proposed by a number of ad hoc image rights consortia. The entire Museum rights and reproductions machinery will continue to ferment until there is solid precedent for image security measures."

Agnes Tabah, ALI–ABA Conference, 1992

- "Learning about learning" is emerging from neuroscience and the cognitive and social sciences. Museums will feel the impact as they investigate how people learn in museums.
- Artificial-intelligence techniques will be used to create intelligence tutoring systems that can diagnose defects in what a person understands and help people see the reasoning processes involved in solving problems. These systems will also respond to questions instead of simply presenting information in some sequence predetermined by a programmer. The informal education procedures in museums will greatly benefit as learning experiences are provided in this mode for the public.
- "Artificial or virtual reality" is one of the hot technologies of the 1990s, and a technique museum exhibitors applaud. It may be applied to museums by creating computer simulations of cultural democracy, ideal environments, an Alice in Wonderland make-believe setting, or current exhibitions for instance. The Connecticut Museum of Natural History features fifty variations on reality. Visitors can assemble a space station in "outer space" and turn a deaf person's signing into speech.
- Virtual reality will bring more museum exhibitions into your homes through your computers.
- Have you been to Cybersmith, a "cyber-cafe?" One opened in Cambridge, MA and one in New York City, in 1995, and they operate similar to a video store with refreshments. They may be a boon to museum home pages.
- The Pompidou Center in Paris is planning a new publication with both print and CD-ROM editions.
- In August 1995, over 500 (and increasing daily) museums around the world had "home pages" on world wide webb.
- The computer wizard Myron Kreuger has built a prototype "videodesk" that responds to human gestures without touching a keyboard or a glove.

"I think in the future we are going to see a lot more computer-based exhibits . . . use of video disks, and bringing virtual reality spaces into the museum. I worry a little that we are not really training people to appreciate the real world out there, the natural world. We are separating them somehow by showing pictures or computer demonstrations of it. It is nice to go to the planetarium to look at the stars, but it is important and we should encourage them to go out and look at the real sky. It is a little worrisome to me that museums are getting to a kind of video mentality, computer games kind of mentality.

Glenn Gutleben, The Exploratorium

- Advanced computer simulations that use images, sounds, and text will lend realism and allow visitors in museums (among the many museums now employing interactive media are the Valentine, the Walker Art Center, the Denver Art Museum, and the Art Gallery of Ontario) to learn by following their own interests and blazing their own paths through large areas of knowledge. The National Gallery of Art has established a "Micro Gallery," patterned after the one in the National Gallery in London, consisting of an interactive computer system linked to seventeen work stations. Think about the changes taking place in the attitudes of art museum staff.
- In hypermedia systems, visitors in museums will be able to move easily among information in any form: text, data, sound, pictures, or video.
- Knowledge navigators or "knowbots" will help people to find the exact "needles" of information they need within the vast "haystacks" of information available in electronic databases. The registrars and collections managers will welcome this innovation, as will almost all staff in museums who use computers and store information.
- Artists' use of computers is stirring the creative juices in sight and sound.
- Multi-sensory coding of objects will be possible, aiding museum staffs and also museum users.
- Linked to an international network of museums, users will be able to construct their own "museum without walls" by gathering together objects and artifacts for the purpose of analysis, research, or mere pleasure. Computer networking will continue to expand through INTERNET and other new systems.
- New theories of "multiple intelligences" (spatial, bodily–kinesthetic, musical) have major implications for learning and interpreting in museums. Out of these theories can come stimulating interactive software that will enable people to appreciate the arts, humanities, and sciences more fully.
- Museums may publicize their programs, exhibitions, and even building plans through distribution of discs in their communities, as was done successfully by the new National Maritime Center in Norfolk, Virginia.
- You will be exploring museum career possibilities through WWW and internet.

What a splendid menu of possibilities for museums! It is extremely important that equal electronic access to information be provided to museums by the controling companies and regulators of the "information highway."

Some museums have already adopted state-of-the-art technologies. Communications technology has led museums to a new mechanism of story-telling: three-dimensional animation. The Pacific Science Center entertains with it, and at the St Louis Zoo a lifelike animated Charles Darwin welcomes visitors. The Missouri Botanical Garden has a talking orchid; in Jacksonville, Florida, the Science and History Museum has an animated space creature; and an animated three-dimensional old-time postman tells his tales at the Smithsonian's Postal Museum in Washington, DC The use of electronic mail and automated systems has exploded to the extent that the Computer Museum in Boston offered its visitors an opportunity to call the President or Vice-President of the United States on e-mail. The Exploratorium has introduced a "Multimedia Playground" as a roadside attraction along the "information highway."

Museums will have to be discerning, however, to avoid being overwhelmed. George Grant warns: "Technology is a power that drives us to do things just because it is possible to do them."[22] Digital depiction is very different from first-hand viewing, for instance, unless it is for the purposes of history and understanding. Museums will have to decide what is usable for them and not embrace technology for its own sake.

Many museologists caution that our zeal to popularize our institutions and make them viable financially must not allow them to become imitation "Disneylands," theme parks, or mega-malls. Museums have unique functions as keepers and interpreters of real objects and artifacts of our cultural patrimony, or "systems of knowledge," and, while increasing their educational appeals to people and promoting tourism, they should retain their universal function of scholarly research and educational responsibility to their communities.

Michael Ames, director of the Museum of Anthropology at the University of British Columbia in Vancouver, offers an instructive example:

> I take my lead from a Hindu sage who, many centuries ago, considered the importance of such worldly attractions. "I like sugar," this old philosopher one day remarked to his students, "but I don't want to become sugar." That is my first point: I like the West Edmonton Mall and Epcot, but I wouldn't want the museum I work in to be like them. I like sugar, but I don't want to become sugar.[23]

Ames's ideas are echoed, but with a twist, by George MacDonald, director of the Museum of Civilization in Ottawa:

243

The integrated theme park approach is setting the tune to which we will all ultimately have to dance. Although this may appear to be a dire and hopeless prediction, it can also be viewed as an exciting series of challenges to museologists. In fact, I believe we can pre-empt their techniques and outclass them with the resultant product, which will have value-oriented content they cannot match. I believe we have to bring our own skills and training to bear on this problem. Museums have a unique place in the formation of an individual's reality and experiential grids.[24]

The new technologies have already greatly influenced the ways in which people spend their leisure time (television, VCRs, CD-ROMs, and home computers), and museums will, of course, apply them to facilitate public access to information. The use of technology and, yes, even entertainment does not necessarily preclude research, scientific data, or collections information. Analytical skills for computer records, for instance, are the same used for paper documents. In the twenty-first century technology may help more people find more authentic ways to participate in the public and social arena of museums.

Those who work in museums will surely need to be computer and technology literate. There is a dynamic quality to the technology revolution, and the new technologies will offer them new options too, for some staff may work for the museum at home as "telecommuters." Computer linkages will also facilitate shared time and flex-time. Technology will have the added benefit of freeing up work and exhibit space in the museum.

The endangered earth and other social problems

Global environmental and social problems seriously endanger the survival of the earth's flora and fauna, cultural artifacts, and *homo sapiens*. Museums' heightened role as educators presents them with the added responsibility and obligation to society to research, explore, and present pressing environmental and social issues factually and to offer possible solutions.

From documenting the effects of automobile emissions on outdoor sculpture and monuments to recounting the destruction of rain-forests in Brazil, to model recycling programs, to energy efficiency, museum staffs are already engaged in conservation and educational endeavors. The Association of Science–Technology Centers (ASTC) and the Franklin Institute in Philadelphia have developed "Greenhouse Earth," an interactive exhibition; the Milwaukee Public Museum and the Smithsonian Institution have mounted major exhibitions on saving the rain forests; the Denver Museum of Natural History has an exhibition on the problems with "trash;" the New England Science Center in Massachusetts explores the fundamentals of energy and energy transformation in its exhibition, "Abiding Locally, Thinking Globally;" and the Denver Zoo has "Tropical Discovery," a two-acre glass-domed re-creation of a tropical rain-forest. "Ocean Planet" is the newest environmental effort by the National Museum of Natural History, Smithsonian Institution.

While musing on museum education during an interview, Claudine Brown stated: "I would hope that we will use our entire world as a classroom." Environmental problems are global, and museums throughout the world share responsibility for making people aware of the dangers of overpopulation, global warming, ozone depletion, pollution, and deforestation. Staffs of science museums, particularly in natural history, science and technology, and zoos, have a special obligation not only to alert the public to species extinction but to help preserve endangered species and be environmentally responsible in their research, collections policies, conservation, exhibitions, and educational programming. Zoo and natural history museum curators are strong proponents of biodiversity research.

Environmental issues are likely to be only one arena in which the increasing social relevance of museums is played out. Their unique position as educational institutions permits museums to address controversial topics in non-threatening ways. About twenty years ago the Museum of the City of New York mounted two landmark exhibitions, one on drugs (with former addicts as docents), and another on venereal disease. The Metropolitan Museum of Art exhibition *Harlem on My Mind* explored black and hispanic culture and the plight of disadvantaged minority youth. The American Museum of Natural History did a shocking-to-the-senses exhibition on pollution and how the public was responsible. These were pioneering efforts by museums in social consciousness-raising. The "causes" were profoundly serious, and some museums were courageous enough to make statements. The problems have persisted, and there are critical new ones today. Museums are examining the devastation of AIDS (at the Gray Art Gallery at New York University, the Brooklyn Historical Society, the Experimental Gallery of the Smithsonian, the Franklin Institute, and the Exploratorium), the effects of the Exxon oil spill (at the Pratt Museum in Homer, Alaska), and the self-portraits of those who have been sexually abused (at the Johnson Gallery of the University of New Mexico in Albuquerque). The controversial Falklands War is being discussed and displayed at the Manchester City Art Gallery in the UK. "Mating Games" at the Monterey Bay Aquarium; the Waco issue at the Baylor University Museum; and "From Here to Maternity" at the Glasgow Museum are among the diverse "issue" exhibitions. The Pacific Northwest Museum in Oregon is using a "whole learning" approach to reveal "larger truths" in the "Passport to the Pacific Northwest" exhibition. The homeless, the continuing and alarming drug abuse among our youth, hunger and poverty, enormous health care inequities – these stories, too, are being told in museums. But how much can museums do? Many compassionate and community-conscious museum people are struggling with these questions, and the museum professionals of the future will find these problems on their doorsteps. As agents of change, do museums have an obligation to educate the public and increase awareness? Museums *can* fill an educational void. If they don't, who will?

Those in leadership and fund-raising positions may discover that some of their financial problems will be eased as their institutions provide the intellectual and educational leadership that society needs and is seeking.

245

At a Canadian Conference in 1990, Duncan Cameron stated:

> These are demanding times, critical times, but above all these are times that give us the opportunity to create a community of cultural institutions with contemporary social values. In so doing there is no need to surrender our essential values or our ethics. There is only the need to accept change in the interest of all.[25]

Neil Postman's comments at an ICOM meeting in 1989 were:

> A museum, then, must be an argument with its society. And more than that, it must be a TIMELY argument. A good museum always will direct attention to what is difficult and even painful to contemplate. Therefore, those who strive to create such museums must proceed without assurances that what they do will be appreciated.[26] [Dr Postman could not foresee the 1994–5 controversy concerning the "Enola Gay" exhibition at the National Air and Space Museum, Smithsonian Institution, in Washington, DC.]

Those efforts will be necessary, nonetheless.

Gender equity

Women in museums today are challenging the historically male bastion of museums. Some are feminists, some are not, but today's feminists are intellectually and very thoughtfully active in proposing and implementing change, and those in museums represent a positive force to be reckoned with. They have indeed benefited from the activists of the 1970s (more than they sometimes admit or even realize) and are now challenging the antiquated and outdated male theories and practices in institutions, including museums. Refusing to be excluded, more women are entering and becoming notable in the sciences. Women are rewriting history so that it is inclusive, and women are demanding that women artists are not only exhibited but are recognized historically. Reinterpretation of material culture will make gender perspectives more explicit.

During a 1990 seminar at the Smithsonian Institution on "Gender Perspectives: The Impact of Women on Museums,"* the thirty-two women and men speakers and 180 participants discussed, among other topics, how the feminist perspective has a significant impact on the scholarly and educational pursuits of museums. When, for example, a woman historian plans and produces an exhibition on politics of the nineteenth century, the role of women will be introduced and clearly depicted, and the point of view or "angle of vision" may be entirely different from the traditional male perspective. The speakers assessed the leadership role of women as museum professionals (are they properly represented as directors of large museums?), examined the philosophical and psychological

---

* Gender Perspectives: Essays on Women in Museums was published in 1994 by the Smithsonian Press. The presentations at the seminar are presented as essays.

empowerment of women, and shared experiences demonstrating the efforts, past and present, that offer challenges for museum women in the future.

The historical fact is that the feminist movement of the 1970s bypassed museums. Only a few concerned women challenged the comfortable male world of museums, and their numbers were not great enough to have an impact. The "old boys' club," if not openly acknowledged, continued to perpetuate itself.

A new generation of women, entering museum work from 1970 to the present, have had highly professional training and look upon museum work as a serious career. Today's museum women enter the field with an agenda of goals and objectives. They are aware of achievements that formerly went unrecognized, and their backgrounds and dedication should place them in high-level policy and decision-making positions.

Museum women can now relate to those in academia who have been involved in women's studies for a number of years. At the 1990 seminar Lois Banner said:

> Feminist scholarship has moved through a three-stage process: emphasis on documenting both discrimination and liberation; identifying and investigating separate female traditions and cultures; questioning the theoretical bases of all the disciplines, and including men much more directly as a subject of study under the rubric of gender.[27]

Most museum women are coming to it late, however, and are now only beginning to understand how the museum world fits into this historic mold. They are attempting to cram all three of the stages of feminist scholarship into one major accomplishment, and there are sufficient numbers of strong and dynamic women in museums to do it!

The role and character of women in museums were topics that generated discussions of women as civilizers, nurturers, socializers. As they apply their expertise and perspective, there may be fewer exhibitions of "boys and their toys:" male-dominated displays of tools, engines, and weapons. There may be more exhibitions oriented to social realities of our system, dealing with all human beings. There has been a general neglect of women as theorists and interpreters of the visual arts, but that too is changing. Gradually, more women will study, enter, and be accepted in museum-related scientific fields.

The gradual changes are already evident. Successful, dynamic, and thoughtful museum men understand and acknowledge the importance of the contribution women bring to institutions. Women's issues are of public concern now, and it is crucial that their arguments for appropriate positions in society may not be merely self-serving ones. Gender will make a difference, and the real question may be how museums respond. Will they, in time, be agents of this change too? Leadership in museums by women is the key if it achieves consensus and brings people together, and that is something women do well.

Museum women are aware of the views of Gloria Steinem, Susan Faludi, and Nan Robertson[28] on the strengths of women in the marketplace, to which

247

"The 90s look tough financially, but it will swing back. Museums are many things to many people, and I think that will be acknowledged in the future."
Linda Thomas, Boston Museum of Fine Arts

modern women can easily relate and which are relevant to their lives. Women are taking strong positions in the workplace, initiating lawsuits for unfair practices, both for gender equity and gender parity. Museum women will take advantage of the growing opportunities to invent their own preferred futures for leadership, for scholarship, and for equal pay – futures quite different from the past and even the present. The operative words are "choices" and "options." If the experience of the past twenty years is any indicator, there will be a new generation of intelligent, assertive museum women who will not accept the *status quo*, but will change and advance the status of women in museums considerably in the next century.

Accessibility

As noted in Chapter 9, the Americans with Disabilities Act (ADA), passed in 1990, is having a dramatic impact on programming and hiring practices in museums. Most museums are already physically accessible to visitors and staffs, with ramps, accessible parking locations, reachable drinking fountains and telephones, larger-type labels, increased seating arrangements in exhibition areas, and appropriate rest-room facilities. Many of these facilities have the added benefits of accommodating children and the elderly.

Still to come on a comprehensive scale, and there may be many more, are barrier-free principles throughout facilities planning. It is less expensive to ensure accessibility at the earliest possible moment when planning for new facilities and exhibitions or renovating old spaces. Universal design for full access to all staff and visitors will be the goal all museums will strive for. Visual fire-alarm systems for people who are deaf and hard of hearing, assistive devices for the deaf, hard of hearing, and visually impaired; sign language interpreters and captioning for conferences, staff meetings, and lectures; captioned films and video (an innovative touchscreen in an exhibition at the Asian Art Museum in San Francisco has captioning in both English and Chinese); captioned note-taking for staff members; adjustable desks and turn-around spaces for wheel-chairs; wheelchair lifts in eating areas; more enlarged signage and labels; audio-tape interpretation for the visually impaired; various height levels of labels; and fairness in consideration of people with disabilities for all types of positions in museums. Staff and volunteers will be trained to understand and respond to the needs of people with disabilities. Job-seekers with disabilities will find a wider and more welcoming reception in museums, for there are many positions that can be available if accommodations are made (see Chapter 9).

Accommodations for both wider audiences *and* for staff hiring must be priorities for professional reasons as well as to be in compliance with ADA.

Intellectual access is as important as physical access, and museums need to create public-access policies as part of their management operations. Attitudes are changing, and an exhibition about deaf and hard of hearing people at the Capitol Children's Museum in Washington, DC, is but one example of an innovative attempt to enhance understanding of one type of disability.

Financial constraints

The 1990s are reeling from the excesses of the 1980s in the business and corporate communities. Museums and other nonprofit institutions are feeling the indirect effects of a recession. Former donors are cutting back or eliminating contributions while at the same time expecting more services from museums. As the *Midwest Museums Conference Newsletter* pointed out:

> This is a time when the nonprofit community, [including museums], has been rocked by cutbacks and escalating needs at the same time as government has turned increasingly to nonprofits to provide community services, and when business and other private donors face constraints in giving.[29] Proposed federal government cutbacks (1995–6) to grant-making federal agencies will have an enormous negative impact on museums in serving the widest possible constituencies.

Economic efficiency through sound management practices will produce more secure financial structures within museums. While maximizing programs and services, human and financial resources will be used more wisely. Museums are already attracting in-kind services from businesses and corporations that can enhance their management practices. More museum–business relationships will be forthcoming, most often through the communities' Business Committees for the Arts. In addition to subsidizing museum exhibitions, some corporations such as IBM, Kellogg, Hallmark, and Corning have their own museums. In the European Community (EC) plans there is a committee for business, art, and culture.

Competition for museum jobs will be keen, and those seeking those jobs must be exceptionally well prepared. When hiring directors and deputy directors as well as managers and administrators, museums will be seeking people with training and experience in fiscal responsibility. These qualifications will be in addition to, and *not instead of*, knowledge of the discipline of the museum. While reduced resources may be a barometer for the types of fiscal skills required of some museum staff in the future, it also may indicate that the museum-job market may shrink. Creativity, resourcefulness, commitment, and imagination will be even more in demand.

In this era of diminishing resources, museum staff members will have to concentrate on generating more institutional earned income, establishing and building endowment funds (the *real* safeguard for constancy in financial management), collaborating programmatically and sharing collections with other museums, increasing selectivity in collecting, strengthening public awareness of the value of museums to the quality of life and to the economy of the community, and increasing efforts to gain public and private support. Articulate appeals for stronger government partnership will be undertaken aggressively. Being a line item in the city, county, or state budget is reassuring as long as the governmental unit is fiscally sound.

Earned income, often controversial for its commercial connotations, will likely increase in importance for budget stability. "Here at the New England Aquarium," explains John Prescott, "book publishing, commercial radio and television production, fee-based educational programming, and an annual changing exhibition schedule all serve to enhance revenue while promoting our messages to the broadest audience possible."[30] The Vanderbilt House in Asheville, North Carolina operates a cattle farm, a winery, and a furniture-reproduction factory.

But most important will be continued service to the community. "The challenge for museums," says Alan Ray, "is to make their case to their constituents – including the general public – before the budget ax falls. If they do, they may be able to live up to their potential in the next decade. If not, their role in the 21st century may be that of caretakers and showpeople, instead of practitioners."[31] Museums must clarify their positions in their communities, not as "Epcots" or "mega-malls," but as significant and unique educational institutions, contributing to the quality of life that cannot be lost to the next generations.

Other aspects of museums in the future

In addition to the trends this chapter has identified, there are other signposts of what museums may be like in the future. Here are some predictions:

- Museums, staffs, and trustees will follow the lead of the AAM and ICOM Codes of Ethics (and that of AASLH) and develop their own codes, emphasizing professionalism, integrity, and ethical conduct.
- All standing professional committees of the AAM will have a code of ethics for individuals.
- In addition to collections policies, the leadership in museums will develop educational, environmental, communications, professional development, and public access policies.
- Museums will have an expanded international role, including exchanges of staffs, collections, and exhibitions, expanded international computer networks, training exchanges for new or inexperienced staff members, training of "trainers," bilingual (or more) labels and signage, staff fluency in more than one language, collective efforts in environmental awareness, increased membership and activism in ICOM, less competitiveness, and more collaboration (see Chapter 10).
- Museums will be at the forefront of social change as agents of change; they will be more proactive and will play a stronger role in publicizing and helping to solve society's social problems. Some believe that museums have the obligation to present the facts for the public to find their own

solutions. We may become "moral educators," as Robert Sullivan and Michael Ames propose.[32]

- Board of trustees membership will more realistically reflect the cultural diversity of their communities.
- All museum staff will be positioned to understand their unique role as educators. More research will be put on display and published in "popular" formats.
- New discoveries in the sciences will have an impact on curatorial research, education, exhibitions, and the need for more storage and research space. For example, while solving the mysteries of the universe, exploration of living and working in space may lead to the first museum in space! One artifact has already been collected. The National Aeronautical and Space Administration (NASA) has announced that the satellite on Mars will be given to the Smithsonian as the first artifact for the first museum on Mars.[33]
- There will be stronger efforts and programs to encourage public understanding of science, with a focus on young people. The Exploratorium has been a pioneering example.
- Cultural tourism, becoming "attractions" and entertainment for the traveling public, will become a national industry, and museums, pressed by financial constraints, will have increasing difficulty resisting the temptation to jump on the bandwagon. The problem for museums, as educational and cultural institutions, will be to avoid compromising their professional integrity, ethics, and values.
- More experiential, theatrical, and hands-on exhibitions will appear in all types of museums, along with objects displayed in a meaningful contextual framework, rather than as isolated artifacts.
- Exhibition planners, curators, designers, and educators will employ interactive computers, television, film, and virtual reality to provide a framework for the collections and enhance the visitor experience in the best McLuhan ("the medium is the message") tradition.
- More multi-disciplinary exhibitions will appear in all types of museums with an enriching cross-fertilization of the arts, sciences, and humanities. Six international museums were selected to participate in the "AT & T: New Experiments in Art and Technology" initiative.
- Because of the financial and managerial burden of housing vast collections, and with the advent of national and international databanks and systems, objects and artifacts may be distributed on long-term loan to many different museums. Repatriation and return of sacred objects and human remains to Native American museums and tribes is already occurring for legal, moral, and humanitarian reasons. This trend toward decentralization will be accelerated by changes in communications and cultural connections that will, in turn, affect the duties and responsibilities of directors, curators, registrars, and collections managers.
- Visible storage facilities will increase public and scholarly access to collections and initiate a reassessment of the use of space.
- Contemporary collecting by museums will expand, but with a greater emphasis on selectivity, with quality over quantity. The "disposable"

culture is giving way to the "ecological" culture, making for far more discrete collecting as well.

- By the same token, the success and accountability of museums will be measured by the quality of their presentations, services, and programs rather than by statistics on the *numbers* of visitors. Measurement devices for quality will be carefully honed by staff to meet the needs of museums and their publics.
- Museum "teams" for planning exhibitions will be reassessed, refocused, and strengthened.
- Traditional barriers between program and curatorial staff will crumble and disappear, albeit slowly, because the individual roles of museum staff will be reinvented.
- Curators, educators, and designers will present alternate views of issues contained in exhibitions to galvanize discussion leading to new and different ways of seeing and understanding an era, an artist, or a discipline. (Creators of exhibitions will sign their work.)
- There will be more critical peer-review of museum exhibitions.
- New materials in contemporary artifacts will present a preservation challenge to conservators and conservation scientists, and new techniques will emerge for the continuous revision and updating of conservation of collections.
- More conservation management and museological training will be offered in conservation training programs, with a renewed effort for preventive conservation.
- Public and staff awareness of the importance of conservation will be promoted by institutions.
- The accreditation process may be expanded to include museum studies programs and professional development. The process itself will be re-examined to reflect museums as agents of change. Owing to general financial constraints, AAM accreditation of institutions may become a criterion for funding by governments, private foundations, and corporations.
- There will be a continuing search for professional standards and excellence in individual performance. While certification of museum workers is a far-off goal in the United States, it will become more of a reality in other countries.
- Efforts to establish ecomuseums will increase. These museums, sometimes called "community" museums, depict relationships among the natural and made culture of a particular and defined area or region in its living and working habitat. They were conceived by Georges-Henri Rivière, the "father" of French museology, at the Bretagne Museum in Rennes twenty-five years before Hugues de Varine coined the term "ecomuseum" at an ICOM meeting in 1971. Heritage associations in Canada organized their first eco-museums. In the United States they may include existing, living, and working communities such as Native American reservations and Shaker villages.
- Innovative building designs and techniques will appear such as the Pointe á Calliere in Montreal, constructed over an archaeological site, and providing see-through walkways.

252

- Folklife methodology of studying cultures through their language and lore, their music, dancing, and crafts may be increasingly employed in museums. Robert Baron has asserted: "Folklife can contribute to a fuller understanding of the cultural experience of classes and social groups."[34] Storytellers may help to bridge the gap between the collection and the general public.

- An increase in employment of people with disabilities will take place as their skills become better understood and recognized; and there will be a dramatic increase in captioning of video, computers and film, and large-letter signage in exhibitions.

- Future outreach programs may be redirected toward making direct connections with a diverse public and educating it on how to use museums as learning environments. The "movable museums" of the American Museum of Natural History in New York, and the Staten Island Children's Museum, are prototypes.

- More museums will cross disciplinary lines to form consortia and collaboratives to enhance and enliven their community services. An example is "A Glimpse of Five Towns" organized by the five historical societies as an exhibition to celebrate their bicentennials.

- There will be a new emphasis on educational programming for adolescents in museums, emulating the "Youth Alive" project of ASTC.

- Teleconferencing will alter and improve the methods for professional development, distance learning, and teacher training.

- Distance learning and off-campus museum studies programs will be strengthened and expanded to accommodate working museum staff.

- Art museums of all sizes will reassess their roles as arbiters of aesthetic judgments, and offer themselves more as art mediators for public learning and appreciation.

- New arts and humanities cable channels on television supported by museums, will provide cultural outlets. In 1994 a history television network, "History Alive," was initiated, which screens documentary films and produces miniseries.

- The museum community will be formally involved in the education-reform movement, and museum educators will conduct more research about how people learn in museums.

- Museums will be swathing paths to new paradigms such as Farmparks in the US and industrial outdoor museums in the UK in the next century.

- Museum studies programs will reassess their roles in an inter-disciplinary environment and in a changing societal role for museums.

- Watch for the signposts for changing position descriptions and new responsibilities to accommodate the changes within museums.

Perhaps what we need to do, as suggested in the film, *Dead Poets' Society*, is to stand on our desks to see the museum world from a different vantage point. Speculating about the future makes it clear that museums face some dramatic changes. But these changes will not alter the basic tenets and values of museums as institutions and of the individuals who work in and for them.

253

New skills in technologies, adaptability, special talents, knowledge, and abilities may be required, but the commitment and dedication to the important mission of museums remain the same.

"The future for museums requires flexible, motivated, and technologically competent staff," claims Jane Sledge. "Museums will need to take greater care to ensure the development of their staff in a more aggressive and competitive environment. They will need to commit to the constant education, training, and retraining of their staff."[35] Neil Cossons has suggested that there will be fewer but more highly trained people on museum staffs of the future, with consulting professionals brought in and out as they are needed. The existing core staff will have managerial qualities based upon scholarly understanding and a passion for museum collections.

Planning museum careers with informed thinking and an "integrative point of view" will require an examination of your principles and goals, a balance of self-realization and the facts of a changing museum life in both a local and a global perspective, and commitment and dedication to the exciting, lofty, and incomparable strengthened future of education and social responsibility in museums: "The true source of professional strength lies in the people employed in museums."[36]

Notes

1   S. Dillon Ripley, foreword to Alma Wittlin, *Museums: In Search of a Usable Future* (Cambridge, Mass.: MIT Press, 1970), p. xiii.

2   American Association of Museums, Commission on Museums for a New Century, *Museums for a New Century* (Washington, DC: American Association of Museums, 1984).

3   Tomislav Sola, "Professionals – The Endangered Species," in *Museums – 2000: Politics, People, Professionals, and Profit*, ed. Patrick Boylan (London, UK: Museums Association, and Routledge, 1992), p. 110.

4   Lorena San Roman, "Politics and the Role of Museums," in *Museums – 2000*, p. 9.

5   Marcia Tucker, *Different Voices: A Social, Cultural, and Historical Framework for Change in American Art Museums* (New York: Studley Press, and Association of Art Museum Directors, 1992), p. 15.

6   Don Adams and Arlene Goldbard, "Taking a Long View," in *Crossroads* (Talmadge, Calif.: DNA Press, 1990), 4.

7   Leon Bouvier, *The Washington Post*, June 12, 1991, p. A3.

8   Robert McC. Adams, "Statement by the Secretary," *Smithsonian Year* (Washington DC: Smithsonian Institution Press, 1991): 8

9   American Association of Museums Survey, 1989, Table B-15.

10   Edmund Barry Gaither, "Hey, That's Mine," keynote paper presented at ICOM Committee for the Training of Personnel Conference, Washington DC, August 10, 1990.

11   Carol Leone, Report on "Multicultural Management and Conflict Resolution for Museums," *Museums Association of Arizona Newsletter* 10, no. 1 (Summer, 1992): 1.

12   Heather Paul, "In Preparation for the Future," paper presented at the Smithsonian Seminar on "Gender Perspectives: The Impact of Women on Museums," Washington,

DC, March, 1990). A book, based on the 1990 seminar, *Gender Perspectives: Essays on Women in Museums*, ed. Jane R. Glaser and Artemis A. Zenetou, was published by the Smithsonian Institution Press in April, 1994.

13 Ibid.

14 Stephen L. Gerritson, "Is the Boom Over?" *Museum News* 68, no. 5 (September/October, 1989): 64.

15 *AAM Survey of Compensation Practices Among Museums: A Report* (Washington, DC: American Association of Museums, 1991).

16 American Association of Museums, *Museums for a New Century*, p. 28.

17 *AAM Survey of Compensation Practices*.

18 American Association of Museums, *Excellence and Equity: Education and the Public Dimension of Museums* (Washington, DC: American Association of Museums, 1992).

19 Ibid., p. 22.

20 Dan Monroe, "Excellence and Equity," *Inside SEMC*, Southeastern Museums Conference Newsletter, 1992, p. 2.

21 Heather Paul, "In Preparation for the Future."

22 George Grant, *Beyond Industrial Growth* (Toronto, Ont.: University of Toronto Press, 1976), pp. 117–31.

23 Michael Ames, "Daring To Be Different: An Alternative," *Muse* 6, no. 1 (Spring/April, 1988): 38.

24 George MacDonald, "Chronicle," *Museum* 39, no. 3 (Winter, 1987): 211.

25 Duncan Cameron, "Values in Conflict and Social Re-Definition," *Muse* 8, no. 3 (Fall/November, 1990): 16.

26 Neil Postman, "Extension of the Museum Concept," paper presented at ICOM Triennial, The Hague, August 28, 1989, p. 6.

27 Lois Banner, "Three Stages of Development," paper presented at the Smithsonian Seminar, "Gender Perspectives: The Impact of Women on Museums," Washington, DC, March, 1990.

28 Gloria Steinem, *Revolution from Within* (Boston, Mass.: Little, Brown, 1991); Susan Faludi, *Backlash: The Undeclared War Against American Women* (New York: Crown, 1991); Nan Robertson, *The Girls in the Balcony: Women, Men, and the New York Times* (New York: Random House, 1993).

29 "Newsbrief," Editorial in *Midwest Museums Conference Newsletter* 4, no. 4 (May/June, 1992): 3.

30 John H. Prescott, letter to the editor, *Museum News* 72, no. 2 (March/April, 1993): 6.

31 Alan Ray, "Science on Display," *Science* 256 (May, 1992): 1271.

32 Robert Sullivan, "Evaluating the Ethics and Consciences of Museums," paper presented at Smithsonian Seminar, "Gender Perspectives: The Impact of Women on Museums," Washington, DC, March, 1990; Robert Sullivan, "Trouble in Paradigms," *Museum News* 71, no. 1 (January/February, 1992): 42; Ames, "Daring To Be Different," p. 39.

33 George S. Robinson, "A Museum on Mars," *Futurist* 19, vol. XIX no. 5 (October, 1985): 42.

34 Robert Baron, "Folklife in the American Museum," in *Folklife and Museum*, ed. Patricia Hall and Charlie Seeman (Nashville, Tenn.: American Association for State and Local History, 1987), p. 25.

35 Jane Sledge and Marguerite d'Aprile-Smith, "Present Needs and Future Trends," in *Common Databases Task Force Final Report to the Field* (Nashville, Tenn.: American Association for State and Local History, 1989).

36 John M. A. Thompson, ed., *Manual of Curatorship: A Guide to Museum Practice*, 2nd edn (London: Butterworth, 1992), p. 492.

255

Bibliography: Museums – today and tomorrow

Ames, Michael M., *Cannibal Tours and Glass Boxes: The Anthropology of Museums* (Vancouver, BC: University of British Columbia Press, 1992). Series of essays exploring museums as windows and looking-glasses to see what can be discovered about museums and the anthropological profession.

Boylan, Patrick, ed., *Museums – 2000: Politics, People, Professionals and Profit* (London, UK: Routledge, 1992). Survey of political, economic, and cultural issues affecting all museums in the twenty-first century, from an open discussion in 1989.

"The High Tech Museum," *Museum News* 71, no. 4 (1992): entire issue. Articles on ways technology can serve museum functions.

Hudson, Kenneth, "The Dream and the Reality," *Museums Journal* 92, no. 4 (April, 1992): 27–31. Analysis of ecomuseums and ecomuseology in historical perspective, and their roles and mission.

Lumley, Robert, ed., *The Museum Time-Machine: Putting Cultures on Display* (London, UK: Routledge, 1987). Analyzes recent issues such as sponsorship, political interference, and fees, with special reference to the relationship between museums and the public, and the role of conservation in contemporary societies.

Mayo, Edith P., "Contemporary Collecting. Collecting in the 20th Century Requires More Work and a New Philosophy," *History News* 37, no. 10 (1982): 8–11. Discusses the commitment to collecting contemporary historical artifacts, the costs of collecting, and collections policies and their implications for the museum profession.

"Museums and the Enviroment," *Muse* 8, no. 4 (1991): entire issue. Articles about science centers and natural history museums, with case studies related to enviromental concerns.

Rivard, René, *Opening up the Museum, or Toward a New Museology: Ecomuseums and "Open" Museums* (Quebec City, Ont.: 1984). An interim report on the role of open versus closed museums, includes case studies and a special discussion of the dynamics of museums.

Suggested readings

Coates, J. F., "The Future and Museums," *Museum News* 62, no. 6 (1984): 40–5.

"Enviromental Impact," *Museum News* 71, no. 2 (1992): 50–2.

Horne, Donald, *The Great Museum: The Re-Presentation of History* (London, UK: Pluto Press, 1984).

Mann, Donna, "Digital Imaging: An Introduction to the New Technology," *ICOM News* 45, no. 3 (1992): 14.

Tolles, Bryant, Jr, ed., *Leadership for the Future: Changing Directorial Roles In American History Museums and Historical Societies* (Nashville, Tenn.: American Association for State and Local History, 1991).

Wallace, Michael, "The Future of History Museums," *History News* 44, no. 4 (1989): 5–8, 30–3.

Wood, Wilma, "The Cowichan and Chemainus Valleys Ecomuseum: The Ecomuseum Concept as a Successful Planning Tool for Government and the Governed," *Muse* 8, no. 4 (1991): 10–11.

Appendices

Maria Magdalena Mieri

Appendix A

General bibliography, directories, list of bibliographies, museum-related journals, and salary and other surveys

This appendix consists of bibliographic citations of books, articles, and monographs concerning relevant general museum topics (beyond the chapter citations), and sources used for this book; it also serves as a referral to other bibliographies and directories. It provides a listing of United States and international journals about museum-related issues that are not included in Appendix B and of surveys from museum organizations related to museum salaries, functions, and development.

General bibliography

ALI–ABA, *ALI–ABA Course of Study. Legal Problems of Museum Administration* (Philadelphia, Pa: American Law Institute–American Bar Association Committee on Continuing Professional Education, and the Smithsonian Institution, annual).

Alexander, Edward P., *Museums in Motion: An Introduction to the History and Functions of Museums* (Nashville, Tenn.: American Association for State and Local History, 1979).

Ambrose, Timothy, and Crispin Paine, *Museum Basics* (New York: Routledge, 1993).

——, and Sue Runyard, *Forward Planning: A Handbook of Business, Corporate and Development Planning for Museums and Galleries* (London, UK: Routledge, 1992).

American Association of Museums, Evaluation and Research Committee, *Current Trends in Audience Research and Evaluation* (San Francisco, Calif.: The Committee, 1987).

American Association of Museums, Technical Information Service, *Museums and Consultants: Maximizing the Collaboration* (Washington, DC: American Association of Museums, 1994).

——, *Native American Collections and Repatriation* (Washington, DC: American Association of Museums, 1994).

Ames, Michael M., *Cannibal Tours and Glass Boxes: The Anthropology of Museums* (Vancouver, BC: University of British Columbia Press, 1992).

Association of Science–Technology Centers, *A Status Report on the Role of Minorities, Women, and People with Disabilities in Science Centers* (Washington, DC: Association of Science–Technology Centers, 1992).

Basic Museum Protection: A Conference on the Protection of Cultural Property (Washington, DC: National Conference on Museum Security, Smithsonian Institution, 1990).

Benefield, Arlene, Stephen Bitgood, and Harris Shettel, *Visitor Studies: Theory,*

Research and Practice, 1991 Visitor Studies Conference (Jacksonville, Ala.: Center for Social Design, 1992).

Bloch, Milton, "Growing Pains: The Maturation of Museums," *Museum News* 62, no. 5 (1984): 8–14.

Boylan, Patrick, ed., *Museums – 2000: Politics, People, Professionals and Profit* (London, UK: Routledge, 1992).

Burcaw, Ellis, *Introduction to Museum Work*, 2nd edn (Nashville, Tenn.: American Association for State and Local History, 1983).

Butcher-Youghans, Sherry, *Historic House Museums* (New York: Oxford University Press, 1993).

Butler, Barbara H., and Marvin B. Sussman, eds, *Museum Visits and Activities for Family Life Enrichment* (London: Haworth Press, 1989).

Capstick, B. "Museums and Tourism," *The International Journal of Museum Management and Curatorship* 4, no. 4 (1985): 365–72.

Deiss, William A., *Museum Archives: An Introduction* (Chicago, Ill.: Chicago Society of American Archivists, 1984).

Edson, Gary, and David Dean, *The Handbook for Museums* (London, UK: Routledge, 1994).

Falk, John, *Leisure Decisions Influencing African American Use of Museums* (Washington, DC: American Association of Museums, 1992).

—, and Lynn D. Dierking, *The Museum Experience* (Washington, DC: Whalesback Books, 1992).

Franco, Barbara, Kenneth L. Ames, and Thomas Frye, eds, *Ideas and Images: Developing Interpretive History Exhibits* (Nashville, Tenn.: American Association for State and Local History, 1992).

Gaffin, Adam, "Visiting Museums on the Internet," *Internet World*, March/April (1994).

Gartenhaus, Alan Reid, *Minds in Motion: Using Museums to Expand Creative Thinking* (Davis, Calif.: Caddo Gapp Press, 1991).

George, Gerald, and Cindy Sherrell-Leo, *Starting Right: a Basic Guide to Museum Planning* (Nashville, Tenn.: American Association for State and Local History, 1986).

Harrison, Richard, ed., *Manual of Heritage Management* (Boston: Butterworth-Heinemann, 1994).

Hein, Hilde S., *The Exploratorium: The Museum as Laboratory* (Washington, DC: Smithsonian Institution Press, 1990).

Hooper-Greenhill, Eileen, *Museums and the Shaping of Knowledge* (London, UK: Routledge, 1992).

—, ed., *Museum Media Message* (London, UK: 1995).

Hudson, Kenneth, *Museums of Influence* (New York: Cambridge University Press, 1987).

Insights, Museums, Visitors, Attitudes, Expectations: a Focus Group Experiment (Los Angeles, Calif.: J. Paul Getty Trust, 1991).

Karp, Ivan, Christine Muller Kreamer, and Steven Lavine, eds, *Museums and Communities: The Politics of Public Culture* (Washington, DC: Smithsonian Institution Press and American Association of Museums, 1992).

Kavanagh, Gaynor, *History Curatorship* (Washington, DC: Smithsonian Institution Press, 1990).

—, ed., *Museum Languages: Objects and Texts* (Leicester, UK: Leicester University Press, 1991).

Lewis, Ralph, *Handbook of Museum Technology* (New York: Research and Education Association, 1982).

Liston, David, ed., *Museum Security and Protection* (London, UK: Routledge, 1994). Publication of ICOM Committee on Museum Security.

Loomis, Ross J., *Museum Visitor Evaluation: New Tool for Management* (Nashville, Tenn.: American Association for State and Local History, 1987).

Majewski, Janice, *Part of Your General Public Is Disabled: A Handbook for Guides in Museums, Zoos, and Historic*

Houses (Washington, DC: Smithsonian Institution Press, 1987).

Marketing the Arts: Every Vital Aspect of Museum Management (Paris, France: International Council of Museums, 1992; distributed in North America by UNIPUB).

Museum Handbook: Part I, Museum Collections (Washington, DC: National Park Service, Department of the Interior, 1990).

Museums Matter (Newhaven, UK: King Publishing, for Museums and Galleries Commission, 1992).

Museums without Barriers: A New Deal for the Disabled (London, UK: Routledge for ICOM and Fondation de France, 1991).

Patterns in Practice: Selections from the Journal of Museum Education (Washington, DC: Museum Education Roundtable, 1992).

Roberts, Andrew D., ed., *Terminology for Museums*, Second Annual Conference of the Museum Documentation Association (Cambridge, UK: Museum Documentation Association, 1990).

Runyard, Sue, *The Museum Marketing Handbook* (Newhaven, UK: King Publishing, for Museums & Galleries Commission, 1994).

Sherman, Daniel J., and Irit Rogoff, eds, *Museum Culture: Histories, Discourses, Spectacles* (Minneapolis, Minn.: University of Minnesota Press, 1994).

The Sourcebook, 1995 Annual Meeting "Museums: Educating for the Future" (Washington, DC: American Association of Museums, annual).

Southeastern Registrars Association, *Steal this Handbook! A Template for Creating a Museum Emergency Preparedness Plan* (Columbia, SC: Southeastern Registrars Association, 1994).

Steele, James, ed., *Museum Builders* (London, UK: Academy Group Ltd, 1994).

Thompson, John M. A., ed., *Manual of Curatorship: A Guide to Museum Practice*, 2nd edn (Oxford, UK: Butterworth–Heinemann, 1992).

Vergo, Peter, ed., *The New Museology* (London, UK: Reaktion, 1989).

Walsh, Kevin, *The Representation of the Past: Museums and Heritage in the Post-Modern World* (London, UK: Routledge, 1992).

Ward, Philip R., *The Nature of Conservation: A Race Against Time* (Marina del Rey, Calif.: Getty Conservation Institute, 1986).

Waterfall, Milde, *Where is the Me in Museums: Going to Museums With Children* (Arlington, Va: Vandamere Press, 1989).

Weil, Stephen E., *Rethinking the Museum and Other Meditations* (Washington, DC: Smithsonian Institution Press, 1990).

——, *A Cabinet of Curiosities: Inquiries into Museums and Their Prospects* (Washington, DC: Smithsonian Institution).

Williams, David, *A Guide to Museum Computing* (Nashville, Tenn.: American Association for State and Local History, 1987).

Directories

Aircraft Museum Directory (New York: Quadrant Press.
Lists aircraft museums of the United States and Canada by locality.

American Art Directory, 1993–1994 (Providence, NY: R. R. Bowker, biennial).
The directory covers 6,800 museums, art libraries and arts organizations, and 1,700 art schools. Lists state directors and suvervisors of art education in schools; exhibition booking agencies; corporations having art for public viewing; newspapers with notes on art; art scholarships and fellowships; and 190 national, regional, and state open art exhibitions.

American Museum Guides (Riverside, NJ: Macmillan, 1983).
Includes 100 fine-arts museums and 100 science museums: name, address, hours, description of holdings, publications, research facilities.

Art Museums of New England (Boston, Mass.: David R. Godine, 1982).

ASTC–CIMUSET Directory (Washington, DC: Association of Science–Technology Centers, annual).
Yellow pages of the science-museum profession. Includes ASTC and CIMUSET (ICOM International Committee of Science and Technology Museums) members (400 institutions in 40 countries), contact information and e-mail addresses.

California Museum Directory: A Guide to Museums, Zoos, Botanic Gardens, and Historic Buildings Open to the Public, 2nd edn (Sacramento, Calif.: California Institute of Public Affairs, 1991).

Children's Museums, Zoos, and Discovery Rooms: An International Reference Guide (Westport, Conn.: Greenwood Press, 1987).
Covers 235 zoos, aquariums, and children's museums worldwide: name, location, historical information, description of exhibits, subject specialities, personnel information, funding sources, publications.

Cummins, Alissandra, *Directory of Caribbean Museums* (Paris: ICOM, 1994).

Dale, Peter, ed., *Directory of Museums and Special Collections in the United Kingdom* (London, UK: Association for Information Management, 1993).

Directory of Asian Museums (Paris, France: UNESCO–ICOM Documentation Center, 1983).

Directory of College, University, Craft and Trade Programs in Cultural Resource Management (Washington, DC: National Park Service Cultural Resources, 1992).
Provides information about training or education programs, describes 75 programs with information on faculty, tuition, curriculum, and length of programs.

Directory of Library and Information Professionals (Detroit, Mich.: Gale Research, 1988).
Two-volume set, covers about 43,000 reference librarians, library administrators, authors, publishers, database producers, and others in the information industry: name, address, phone number, current position and employer. Contains Employer Index of libraries, information firms, and other institutions employing information professionals.

Directory of Museums in Japan, ed. Kunio Aoki (Tokyo, Japan: Japanese Association of Museums, 1980).

Directory of Natural Science Centers (Roswell, Ga: Natural Science for Youth Foundation, annual).

Directory of North American Indian Museums and Cultural Centers, ed. Simon Brascoupe (Niagara Falls, NY: North American Indian Museums Association, 1981).

Directory of Special Libraries and Information Centers (Detroit, Mich.: Gale Research, annual).
Three volumes: (1) directory of special libraries and information centers; (2) geographic and personnel indexes; (3) new special libraries. Covers more than 19,000 special libraries (including museum libraries), information centers, documentation centers in the United States, Canada, and 80 other countries. Gives information about services, facilities, availability of holdings, and staff.

Directory of Training Opportunities in Cultural Resource Management (Washington, DC: National Park Service Cultural Resource, Preservation Assistance Division, 1995).
Listing of workshops, seminars, and courses in cultural resource management topics, held in forty-four states, District of Columbia, and Puerto Rico).

Forest History Museums of the World (Santa Cruz, Calif.: Forest History Society, 1983).

The Glass Guide and International Directory of Galleries and Museums (New York: Experimental Glass Workshop, 1989).

Guide to Multicultural Resources, 1989–90 edn (Madison, Wis.: Praxis Publications, 1990).
Minority resource directory of the United States. Features a comprehensive collection of organizations, agencies, services, businesses, and related information from African Americans, Hispanic, Native American, and Asian communities).

Hispanic American Information Directory, 1994–1995, 3rd edn (Washington, DC: Gale Research Inc, 1994).

A Guide to organizations, agencies, programs, museums and publications concerned with hispanic-American life and culture.

Hudson, Kenneth, and Ann Nichols, *The Cambridge Guide to the Museums of Europe* (Cambridge, UK: Cambridge University Press, 1991).

Howe, Edward Hartley, *North America's Maritime Museums: An Annotated Guide* (New York: Facts on File, 1987).

ICCROM and Getty Conservation Institute, *International Directory on Training in Conservation of Cultural Heritage* (Santa Monica, Calif.: Getty Trust Publications, 1994).

International Council of Museums, *Membership Directory* (Paris, France: ICOM Secretariat, 1992.

International Council of Museums, International Committee of Museums of Science and Technology, *Guide-Book of Museums of Science and Technology*, 2nd edn (Prague: Narodni Technike Museum, 1980).

International Directory of Arts (Frankfurt, Germany: Art Address Verlag Müller GmbH and Co. KG, 1991).
Two volumes: (1) museums and galleries, universities, academies, colleges, associations, and artists; (2) art and antique dealers, numismatics, galleries, auctioneers, restorers, art publishers, antiquarian, and art booksellers; useful for finding the current telephone numbers and names of directors of art museums.

International Directory of Museum Training, ed. Gary Edson (London, UK: Routledge, 1995).

International Handbook of National Parks and Nature Reserves, ed. Craig W. Allin (New York: Greenwood Press, 1990).

International 2000 Yearbook, vol. 33 (London, UK: Zoological Society, 1994).

Museums and Galleries of Croatia, ed. Ministry of Culture and Education of the Republic of Croatia (Zagreb: Museum Documentation Centre, 1993).

Museums Studies International, ed. Robin Fogg (Washington, DC: Office of Museum Programs, 1988.

Museums Yearbook 1993–1994, ed. Sheena Barbour (London, UK: Rhinegold Publishing Ltd for Museums Association, 1993).

Museums of the World, 4th edn, ed. Karl H. Strasser (New York: K. G. Saur, 1992).

The Official Directory of Canadian Museums and Related Institutions (Ottawa, Ont.: Canadian Museums Association, 1990).
Lists museum associations, arts organizations, government departments and agencies; including the name of each museum, the year of opening, address, location, staff members, description of the collection, publications, and the governing authority.

The Official Museum Directory (New Providence, NJ: R. R. Bowker for the American Association of Museums, annual).
A basic listing and resource information about museums and museum-related organizations in the United States).

Pharmacy Museums and Historical Collections on Public View in the United States and Canada, ed. Sami K. Hamarneh and Ernst W. Stieb (Washington, DC: American Institute of the History of Pharmacy, and National Museum of American History, Smithsonian Institution, 1981).

Taylor, William, *Auto Museum Directory USA* (Butte, Mo.: Editorial Review Press, 1983).

Thompson, Bryce D., *US Military Museums, Historic Sites and Exhibits* (Falls Church, Va: Military Living Publications, 1989).

Zoological Parks and Aquariums in the Americas, ed. Linda Boyd (Wheeling, WVa: American Association of Zoological Parks and Aquariums, 1992).

List of bibliographies

Cushman, Karen, *Widening the Borders of the Museum World: Part II: A Bibliography* (California: JFK University, 1994).

International Council of Museums, *International Museological Bibliography for the Year 1985* (Paris, France: ICOM Secretariat, 1988).

Knell, Simon J., compiler and ed., *A Bibliography of Museum Studies*, 11th edn (London, UK: Scolar Press, 1994).

Legget, Jane A., *Learning Goals and Bibliography for Museum Studies Training: Archaeology Option* (Leicester, UK: University of Leicester, Department of Museum Studies, 1985).

McLean, Kathleen, ed., *Recent and Recommended: A Museum Exhibition Bibliography with Notes from the Field* (Washington, DC: National Association for Museum Exhibition, 1991).

"Museum Education Bibliography," *Journal of Education in Museums* 11 (1990), 12 (1991), 13 (1992).

Museum Studies Library Shelf List, 2nd edn (San Francisco, Calif.: John F. Kennedy University, Center for Museum Studies, 1986).

Shapiro, Michael, ed., *The Museum: A Reference Guide* (New York: Greenwood Press, 1990).

Spiess, Philip D., *Museums and Their Operations: A Basic Bibliography*, 5th edn (Washington, DC: Smithsonian Institution, 1988).

University of Leicester, *A Bibliography for Museum Studies Training* (Leicester, UK: Department of Museum Studies, University of Leicester, 1984).

Museum-related journals*

Archives and Museum Informatics (Pittsburgh, Pa: Archives and Museum Informatics).

Art Education (Reston, Va: National Art Education Association).

Arts Management and Law (Washington, DC: Heldref Publications).

The Art Newspaper (London, UK: Umberto Allemandi & Co. Publishing).

Comunique (Washington, DC: International Society for Intercultural Education, Training, and Research (SIETAR)).

Curator (New York: American Museum of Natural History).

The Docent Educator (Seattle, Wash.: The Docent Educator).

Exhibit Builder (Great Neck, NY: Sound Publishing Co.).

International Journal of Museum Management and Curatorship (Guildford, UK: Butterworth Scientific Limited).

Journal of Education in Museums (London, UK: Group for Education in Museums).

Journal of Material Culture (London, UK: Sage Publications).

Museum National (Fitzroy, Australia: Council of the Australian Museum Association).

Museum Roundup (Victoria, BC: British Columbia Provincial Museum Association).

Museum International (UNESCO) (Cambridge, Mass.: Blackwell Publishers).

Museum Source Marketplace (Milwaukee, Wis.: Museum Source).

Prologue (Washington, DC: National Archives).

Smithsonian (Washington, DC: Smithsonian Institution).

Spectrum (Cambridge, UK: Museum Documentation Association).

Studies in Conservation (London, UK: International Institute for Conservation of Historic and Artistic Works (IIC)).

Surveys

AAM, *1991 Survey of Compensation Practices Among Museums* (Washington, DC: American Association of Museums, 1991).

A summary of a survey done prior to a financial management seminar held at the

---

* See also Appendix B for publications from national, regional, and state associations.

1991 Annual Meeting of the American Association of Museums. Covers benefits, human resource management, planning and personnel development.

——, *Museums Count* (Washington, DC: American Association of Museums, 1993). A comprehensive report of the museum profession's national data-gathering).

AAMA, *Analysis of Curatorial Roles in African American Museums and Curators of African American Collections*, ed. Brenda Brown (Wilberforce, Ohio: African American Museums Association, 1986). Report on African American curators' education, training, location, occupational responsibilities, and personnel concerns.

——, *Survey of the African American Museum Field* (Wilberforce, Ohio: African American Museum Association, 1995). Information on size and type of institutions, collections, staffing and training needs.

AAMD, *1992 AAMD Salary Survey* (New York: Association of Art Museums Directors, annual). Information on 37 professional positions in art museums in the United States, with salaries analyzed on a national scale, regional scale, population of the area, and the size of the budget of the institution.

——, *1989 AAMD Statistical Survey* (New York: The Association of Art Museum Directors, 1989).

AASLH, *The Wages of History* (Nashville, Tenn.: American Association of State and Local History, 1984. Identifies state and local institutions likely to hire history professionals, salary ranges, and employment trends.

ASTC, *The 1993 ASTC Salary Survey* (Washington, DC: American Association of Science and Technology Centers, 1993). Salary information based on job descriptions, museum budgets, region of the country, and sex of employees.

Black and Hispanic Art Museums: A Vibrant Cultural Resource, ed. Azade Ardali (New York: Ford Foundation, 1989). Survey and needs assessment of 30 Black and Hispanic art museums. Information on sources of funding, staff size and composition, and on the condition of museum's facilities and collections.

CAM, *1993 Salary Survey of Museum Personnel* (Los Angeles, Calif.: California Association of Museums, 1993). Biennial survey of approximately 750 museums and related institutions in California. Information is based upon actual paid salaries and benefits).

Canadian Museums Association, *National Salary Study* (Ottawa, Ont.: Canadian Museums Association, 1983).

Ekos Research Associates Inc., *The Museum Labour Force in Canada: Current Status and Emerging Needs* (Toronto, Ont.: Lord Cultural Resources, February 1989. Comprehensive study based on a survey of a Canada-wide sample of museum workers. It examines the composition of the museum labor force: occupational characteristics, opportunities for professional training, potential impact of social and economic trends of supply and demand, perceptions of the quality of working life, and the implications for public policy.

Emmick, Nancy J., "The Jobline: A Valuable Resource for Librarians," *Special Libraries* 75 (December, 1984): 44–50.

IMS, *Institute of Museum Services National Needs Assessment of Small, Emerging, Minority and Rural Museums in the United States* (Washington, DC: Institute of Museum Services, 1992).

MMA, *Salary Survey* (Flint, Mich.: Michigan Museum Association, 1985). Information about Michigan museums, including job-descriptions, salaries, and benefits.

National Coordinating Committee for the Promotion of History, "A Survey of New Training Programs for Historians," *National Coordinating Committee for the Promotion of History*, Supplement 3 (May, 1981).

NEMA, *1992/1993 NEMA Salary and Benefits Survey* (Boston, Mass.: New England Museums Association, annual). Information about New England museums: report on 35 professional positions, including statistics by years in the job, gender, and education.

NYSAM, *1989 Salary Survey* (New York: New York State Association of Museums, 1989).
Findings organized by museum location, museum budget, museum discipline, gender of employee; includes position descriptions.

SEMC, *Southeastern Museums Conference Compensation Benefits Practices Survey, 1992* (Baton Rouge, La: Southeastern Museums Conference, 1993).
Includes compensation, benefits, wage and salary information, and staffing information about art, history, science and general museums).

SLA, *SLA Biennial Salary Survey* (Washington, DC: Special Libraries Association, 1991).

TAM, *Salary Survey* (Austin, Tex.: Texas Association of Museums 1984).
Includes position classification, budget size, and kind of museum; also a section on benefits.

"The State of Pay," *Museums Journal* 4 (1989): 26–8.
Survey of salaries paid to museum and gallery staff in the United Kingdom).

Zeller, Terry, "Art Museum Educators: Who Are They?" *Museum News* 67 (June, 1986): 53.
Reports the results of a 1983 survey on undergraduate majors, training orientations, teaching experience, and main responsibilities of art-museum educators.

Appendix B

State, regional, national, and international professional museum-related organizations and their services

This appendix is intended to be a quick reference to sources of information on where and how to find job opportunities, and also serves as a referral for professional services.

It consists of three sets of information about professional organizations categorized as national, regional, or state; identifying placement services, publications, professional development, and information about museums, and related organizations.

All of the national, regional, and state organizations listed have annual conferences. For dates and places of conferences, contact the organization direct. State museum association addresses may be obtained from the American Association of Museums, or from its regional association.

It lists international museum-related organizations, with addresses, newsletters published, and the International Council of Museums' international committees. Most Committees have newsletters or bulletins; consult current ICOM News for names of chairpersons and secretaries' addresses and phone numbers, or contact ICOM headquarters.

State museum and related professional organizations

Organization	Newsletters and bulletins	Placement	Professional development
Alabama Museums Association	*Alabama Museums Association Quarterly Newsletter*		Mid-career training programs
Arkansas Museums Association	*AMA Report* (quarterly)	Job announcements	Workshops and seminars during annual meetings
Museums Association of Arizona	*Museums Association of Arizona Newsletter* (quarterly)		Mid-career training programs. Workshops
California Association of Museums	*CAM News* (bimonthly)	Job announcements	Mid-career training programs

Organization	Newsletters and bulletins	Placement	Professional development
Colorado/Wyoming Association of Museums	*Highlights* (quarterly)	Job announcements	Workshops for museum professionals and for volunteers year round
Connecticut Museums Association	*Connecticut Humanities* (monthly)	Job referral service	Mid-career training programs
Florida Museums Association	*Florida Museums Association Newsletter* (quarterly)	Job announcements	Mid-career training programs
Gallery Association of New York State, Inc.	*Gallery Association Bulletin* (three times a year)	Job announcements	Mid-career training programs
Georgia Association of Museums and Galleries	*GAMG Newsletter* (quarterly)		Mid-career training opportunities. Workshops held at the annual meetings.
Hawaii Museums Associations	*NUHOU Newsletter* (quarterly)		Mid-career training program
Idaho Association of Museums	*IAM Newsletter* (quarterly)		Workshops during annual meetings
Association of Illinois Museums and Historical Societies	*Dispatch News* (quarterly)	Job announcements	Mid-career training programs
Illinois Heritage Association	*Illinois Heritage Association Newsletter* (bimonthly)	Career advice	Mid-career training programs, workshops in fall or spring. Library specializing in museum issues
Association of Indiana Museums	*Bulletin* (bimonthly)	Job announcements	Three workshops per year
Iowa Museums Association	*IMA Newsletter* (quarterly)	Job announcements	Mid-career training programs, pre-conference workshops every two years
Iowa Local Historical and Museum Association	*IMA Newsletter* (quarterly)	Job announcements, informal career counseling service	Pre-annual meetings workshops
Kansas Museum Association	*Exchange* (quarterly)		Mid-career training programs
Kentucky Association of Museums	*KAM Newsletter* (three times per year)	Job announcements	Mid-career training programs. Annual workshops
Louisiana Association of Museums	*LAM Quarterly*	Job announcements	Mid-career training programs. Workshops
Maine Association of Museums	*Maine Association of Museums Newsletter* (quarterly)		

Organization	Newsletters and bulletins	Placement	Professional development
Michigan Museums Association	*MMA Newsletter*	Job announcements	Mid-career training programs. Video-lending program
Minnesota Association of Museums			Mid-career training program
Mississippi Museums Association	*Artifacts* (quarterly)		
Missouri Museums Association	*Missouri Museum Association Newsletter* (bimonthly)		
Montana Association of Museums			
Museums Alaska, Inc.	*Network* (quarterly)	Job announcements	Workshops during annual meeting
Nebraska Museums Association	*Phoenix* (quarterly)	Job announcements	
New Jersey Association of Museums	*Monitor* (quarterly)	Job announcements	Mid-career training programs
New Mexico Association of Museums	*NMAM Newsletter* (quarterly)	Job announcements	Mid-career training programs
New York State Association of Museums	*Update* (quarterly)	Job referral service	Mid-career training programs
North Carolina Museums Council	*NCMC Newsletter* (quarterly)		
Ohio Museums Association	*Scrip* (quarterly)	Job announcements	Mid-career training programs
Ohio Association of Historical Societies and Museums	*The Local Historian* (bimonthly) *Echo* (monthly)	Job announcements	Mid-career training programs
Oklahoma Museums Association	*Muse News* (quarterly)	Job announcements	Mid-career training programs
Oregon Museum Association	*OMA Dispatch* (quarterly)		Mid-career training programs
Pennsylvania Federation of Museums	*Tapestry* (quarterly)	Job referral	Mid-career training programs
Rhode Island Museum Network			
South Carolina Federation of Museums	*Good Muse!* (quarterly)	Job announcements and job counseling	Workshops
Association of South Dakota Museums	*ASDM Newsletter* (quarterly)	Job announcements	Seasonal workshops

Organization	Newsletters and bulletins	Placement	Professional development
Tennessee Association of Museums	*TAM Exhibitor* (bimonthly)	Informal job referral service	Mid-career training programs
Texas Association of Museums	*Museline* (bi-monthly)	Job announcements	Mid-career training programs
Utah Museums Association	*Newsletter of the Utah Museum Association* (quarterly)	Job announcements	Mid-career training programs. Workshops and seminars
Vermont Museum and Gallery Alliance	*VMGA Newsletter* (quarterly)	Job announcements	Mid-career training programs
Virginia Association of Museums	*VAM Quarterly Newsletter* (quarterly)	Job announcements	Mid-career training programs
Washington Museums Association	*WMA News* (quarterly)	Job announcements	
West Virginia Association of Museums	*WVAM Newsletter* (three times per year)	Job announcements	Workshops
Wisconsin Federations of Museums			Mid-career training programs

Regional museum and related professional organizations

Organization	Newsletters and Bulletins	Placement	Professional development
Arts Midwest Hennepin Center for the Arts 528 Hennepin Ave, Suite 310 Minneapolis, MN 55403	*Agency Newsletter* (bimonthly		Fellowship programs in minority arts administration
Consortium for Pacific Arts and Cultures (CPAC) 2141C Atherton Rd Honolulu, HI 96822	*Tradewinds* (Two or three times a year)		
Cultural Alliance of Greater Washington 410 8th Street NW Washington, DC 20004	*Arts Washington* (monthly)	JoBank (job referral service), free first time	Educational assistance. Monthly workshops on arts management
Greater Philadelphia Cultural Alliance 320 Walnut Street Philadelphia, PA 19106	"Short subject" monthly	Job bank	Seasonal workshops. Resource library.
Mid-Atlantic Association of Museums (MAAM) PO Box 817 Newark, DE 19715-0817	*Courier* (bimonthly)	Job announcements	Mid-career training programs

Organization	Newsletters and bulletins	Placement	Professional development
Mid-America Arts Alliance 912 Baltimore Ave Suite 700 Kansas City, MO 64105	*Newsletter*		Education programs. Workshops
Mid-Atlantic Arts Foundation 11 East Chase St Suite 2A Baltimore, MD 21202	*Arts Ink* (quarterly)		Fellowships and residency programs
Midwest Museums Conference (MMC) PO Box 11940 St Louis, MO 63112	*Midwest Museum Conference Quarterly* *News Brief* (bimonthly)	Job announcements	Mid-career training programs
Mountain Plains Museum Association (MPMA) PO Box 335 Manitou Springs, CO 80829	*Newsgram* (bimonthly)	Job announcements	Mid-career training opportunities
Museum Council of Philadelphia and the Delaware Valley Mutter Museum 19 S 2nd St. Philadelphia, PA 19103		Job announcements and internship opportunities published bimonthly with minutes from meetings	Mid-career training programs
New England Museum Association (NEMA) Boston National Historical Park Charleston Navy Yard Boston, MA 02129	*NEMA News* (quarterly)	*Nema News Job* (quarterly supplement with job listings)	Mid-career training programs
Northern California Association of Museums (NORCAM) Museum of Anthropology California State University Chico, CA 95929	*NORCAM Newsletter* (quarterly)	Job announcements	Workshops, consultant services
Southeast Museums Conference (SEMC) PO Box 3494 Baton Rouge LA 70821-3494	*SEMC Newsletter* (quarterly)	Job announcements	Mid-career training programs
Regional Council of Historical Agencies 1400 North State St Syracuse, NY 13208	*Newsletter*	Job announcements	
Southern Arts Federation 1293 Peachtree St NE Suite 500 Atlanta, GA 30309	*Folk Art News* (quarterly)	Job announcements	Training programs

Organization	Newsletters and bulletins	Placement	Professional development
Western Museums Association 700 State Dr., Room 130 Los Angeles, CA 90037	*WMA Newsletter* (quarterly)	Job announcements	Mid-career training programs. Workshops and videotapes.
Western New York Association of Historical Agencies 230 Rochester St Avon, NY 14414	*Association Update* (bimonthly)	Job announcements	Mid-career training programs
Western States Arts Federation 236 Montezuma Ave Santa Fé, NM 87501	*ArtJob* (monthly)	Job announcements	Seminars and technical assistance service
Federation of Historical Services PO Box 71 Troy, NY 12181-0011	*Roundtable* (quarterly)	Job announcements	Mid-career training programs and seasonal workshops

National museum-related professional organizations

Organization	Newsletters and bulletins	Placement	Professional development/ sources of information
American Anthropological Association (AAA) 4350 North Fairfax Dr. Arlington, VA 22203	*Anthropology Newsletter (monthly) Museum Anthropology* (three times per year)	Placement services	Workshops for anthropologists and museum professionals
American Association of Botanical Gardens and Arboreta (AABGA) 786 Church Rd Wayne, PA 19087	*AABGA Newsletter* (monthly)	Job announcements	
American Association of Museums (AAM) 1225 Eye St NW Suite 200 Washington, DC 20005	*Aviso* (monthly) *Museum News* (bimonthly)	Careers booklet. Job announcements	Mid-career training programs. Workshops and seminars. Bookstore. Technical Information Service. *Standing Professional Committees*: Audience Research and Evaluation (CARE), Curators, Development and Membership, Education, Exhibition (NAME), Media and Technology, Museum Administration and Finance, Museum Professional Training (COMPT), Public Relations and Marketing, Registrars, Security, Small Museums Administrators

Organization	Newsletters and bulletins	Placement	Professional development/ sources of information
African-American Museum Association (AAMA) PO Box 548 Wilberforce, OH 45384	*Scrip* (quarterly) *AAMA Update* (published between Scrip editions)	Job announcements	
Association of Art Museum Directors (AAMD) 41 East 65th St New York, NY 10021	*The Director's Post*		Workshops and seminars for members
American Association for Museum Volunteers (AAMV) 1225 Eye St NW Suite 200 Washington, DC 20005	*American Association for Museum Volunteers* (quarterly)		
American Association for State and Local History (AASLH) 530 Church St Suite 600 Nashville, TN 37219	*History News Dispatch* (monthly) *History News* (bimonthly)	Job announcements	Mid-career training programs. Workshops and seminars. Slide-tapes on museum registration, security, conservation
American Association of Zoological Parks and Aquariums (AAZPA) Oglebay Park Wheeling, WV 26003	*Communique* (monthly)	Job announcements	Long- and short-term training programs
American Council for the Arts 1285 Avenue of the Americas New York, NY 10019	*ACA Update* (monthly) *ACA Reports* (monthly)		
American Historical Association 400 A St. SE Washington, DC 20003	*Perspective* (monthly)	Job announcements	
American Institute for Conservation of Historic and Artistic Work (AIC) 1717 K St NW Suite 301 Washington, DC 20006	*AIC Newsletter* (bimonthly) *Directory* (annual)	Job announcements	Sub-groups on specializations
Art Table 270 Lafayette St Suite 608 New York, NY 10012	*Art Wire* (biannual)	Career counseling	
Association of College and University Museums and Galleries University Museum Southern Illinois University at Edwardsville Edwardsville, IL 62026-1150	*ACUMG Newsletter* (quarterly)	Job announcements	Seminars and workshops during annual meetings

Organization	Newsletters and bulletins	Placement	Professional development/ sources of information
National Association for Interpretation PO Box 1892 Ft Collins, CO 80522	*Legacy* (bimonthly) Regional bimonthly newsletters	Job announcements: call DIAL-A-JOB. Internships information	Regional workshops. National and regional conferences
Association for Living Historical Farms and Agricultural Museums Route 14 PO Box 214 Santa Fé, NM 87505	*Bulletin* (quarterly)	Job announcements	Seminars and workshops during annual meetings
Association of Railway Museums, Inc. PO Box 3311 City of Industry, CA 91744	*Report to You* (quarterly)	Job announcements	Workshops, lectures and courses with an emphasis on conservation
Association of Systematic Collections (ASC) 730 11th St NW 2nd Floor Washington, DC 20001	*ASC Newsletter* (bimonthly)	Job announcements	
Association of Science Museum Directors (ASMD) Carnegie Museum of Natural History 4400 Forbes Avenue Pittsburgh, PA 15213	*Science Museums News* (twice a year)		
Association of Science– Technology Centers (ASTC) 1025 Vermont Ave NW Washington, DC 20005- 3516	*ASTC Newsletter* (bimonthly)	Placement services available. Job announcements	Training programs. Workshops
Association of Youth Museums (AYM) 1775 K St NW Suite 595 Washington, DC 20006	*AYM News* (bimonthly)	Job announcements	Workshops
Center for Museum Studies Smithsonian Institution Arts and Industries Building Room 2235 Washington, DC 20560 http://www.si.educ/organiza/ offices/musstud/	*Bulletin* (quarterly)		Workshops, museum reference center, print and non-print information
College Art Association 275 7th Ave New York, NY 10001	*CAA Newsletter* (bimonthly)	Job announcements. Job fair at annual conference	

274

Organization	Newsletters and bulletins	Placement	Professional development? sources of information
Council of America Jewish Museums (CAJM) Spertus Museum of Judaica 618 S. Michigan Avenue Chicago, IL 60605	*CAJM Newsletter* (twice per year)		
Council of American Maritime Museums South Street Seaport Museum 207 Front St New York, NY 10038		Job announcements circulated among members	Seminars during annual meetings. Internship program. Fellowships for young developing professionals.
Council for Museum Anthropology 4350 North Fairfax Drive Suite 640 Arlington, VA 22203	*Anthropology Newsletter* (monthly)	Job announcements	Workshops
Intermuseum Conservation Association Allen Art Building Oberlin, OH 44074	*ICA Newsletter* (twice per year)		Educational programs. Internship program in conservation
Institute of Museum Services 1100 Pennsylvania Ave NW Washington, DC 20506	*Access* (monthly)		Grant review workshops. Grant-writing training
Museum Computer Network 8720 Georgia Ave Suite 501 Silver Spring, MD 20910 http://world.std.com/~mcn/	*Spectra* (quarterly	Job announcements	Workshops at annual meetings. Internship programs
Museum Education Round-table 3000 Connecticut Ave Suite 237D Washington, DC 20008	*Network* (three times a year) *Journal of Museum Education* (quarterly		Workshops and colloquia
Museum Store Association 1 Cherry Center Suite 460 501 South Cherry St Denver, CO 80222	*Membermemo* (quarterly	Job Source (job referral service), job announcements	
Museum Trustee Association 1101 Connecticut Ave Suite 700 Washington, DC 20036	*Museum Trusteeship* (quarterly)		
National Association of Museum Exhibitors (NAME) PO Box 876 Bristol, CT 06011-0876	*Exhibitionist* (quarterly)	Job announcements	Workshops

Organization	Newsletters and bulletins	Placement	Professional development/ sources of information
National Center for Non-Profit Boards 2000 L St NW Suite 411 Washington, DC 20036	*Board Members* (bimonthly)		Board development services
National Park Service Cultural Resources PO Box 37127 Washington, DC 20013-7127	*Cultural Resource Management* (monthly)		Workshops. Training programs
Natural Science for Youth Foundation (NSYF) 130 Azalea Dr. Roswell, GA 30075	*Natural Science Center News* (quarterly) *Opportunities* (bimonthly)	Employee opportunities, information and placement services	Training courses in museum and nature-centers management
National Trust for Historic Preservation 1785 Massachusetts Ave NW Washington, DC 20036	*Preservation News* (monthly) *Historic Preservation* (bimonthly)	Job announcements	Audiovisual collections about historic preservation
Print Council of America The Baltimore Museum of Art Art Museum Dr. Baltimore, MD 21218		Placement services	Sponsor educational and research programs
Society of American Archivists (SAA) 600 S. Federal St Suite 504 Chicago, IL 60605	*SAA Newsletter* (bimonthly) *American Archivist* (quarterly)	Employment opportunities, placement services	Training programs
Special Libraries Association (SLA) 1700 18th St NW Washington, DC 20009	*The SpeciaList* (monthly) *Special Libraries* (monthly)	Career services. Employment opportunities, and advisory brochure on careers in special libraries	
US/ICOMOS 1600 H St NW Washington, DC 20005	*US/ICOMOS Newsletter* monthly		
Volunteer Committee of Art Museums (VCAM) The Philbrook Museum of Art 2727 S. Rockford Rd Tulsa, OK 74114-4104	*VCAM News* (twice per year)	Referral service	Regional meetings and triennial conferences

International professional museum-related organizations

International Council of Museums (ICOM)
Maison de L'UNESCO*
1 rue Miollis, 75732 Paris
CEDEX 15, France.
Publications: *ICOM News* (quarterly),
*Directory of Museum Professionals in
Africa*, publications from workshop on
Illicit Traffic of Cultural Property, and
Security Handbook
http:www.icom.nrm.se/icom/html

   International Council of Museums
     Committee of the American
     Association of Museums
     (AAM-ICOM)
   1225 Eye St NW
   Washington, DC, USA

   ICOM Agency for Asia and the Pacific
   Divan Devdu Palace
   Salarjung Museum
   Hyderabad 500002, India
   Publications: Newsletter and directories

   ICOM Secretariat for Latin America and
     the Caribbean
   Apt 1124
   San Jose 1000, Costa Rica
   Publications: *Chaski*, bulletin

International Centre for the Study of the
   Preservation and Restoration of Cultural
   Property (ICCROM)
13 Via di San Michele
Rome, Italy 00153
Publications: *ICCROM Newsletter* (annual);
listing of conservation training programs

International Council of Monuments and
   Sites (ICOMOS)
75 rue du Temple
F 75003 Paris, France
Publications: *Monumentum* (quarterly)
http://hpb1.hwc.ca.10002/

International Congress of Maritime
   Museums
Norsk Sjofartsmuseum
Bygdoynesv. 37
0286 Oslo 2, Norway

---

* There are 93 national committees of ICOM (see
Chapter 10).

International Institute for Conservation of
   Historic and Artistic Works (IIC)
6 Buckingham St
London WC2N 6BA, UK
Publications: *Studies in Conservation*
(quarterly)
Technical Papers (annual)

International Foundation for Art Research,
   Inc.
46 East 70th St
New York, NY 10021

International Museum Theatre Alliance
Museum of Science
Science Park
Boston, MA 02114
Publications: *IMTHAL* (quarterly)

UNESCO
Division of Cultural Heritage
7 place de Fontenoy
75700 Paris, France
Publications: *Museum International*
(quarterly)

World Monuments Fund
949 Park Ave
New York, NY 10028
Publications: *Newsletter*

International museum associations by country

Argentina

Colegio de Museologos de la Republica
   Argentina
Soler 4187
Casilla de Correo 318, Sucursal 25B
(1425) Buenos Aires
Publication: *Boletin Informativo*
(bimonthly)

Australia

Art Museums Association of Australia
GPO Box 2015 S
Melbourne, Victoria 3001
Publications: *AMAA News* (quarterly)

Council of Australian Museums
    Association
National Gallery of Victoria
St Kilda Rd
Melbourne, Victoria 3000
Publications: *Museums Australia*

Museums Association of Australia
Museum of Victoria
328 Swanston St
Melbourne, Victoria 3000
Publications: *Muse News*

Austria

Arbeitsgemeinschaft der Museumbeamten
    und Denkmalpfleger
Österreich Kunsthistorisches Museum
Neue Burg, A1010 Vienna
Publication: *Mitteilungsblatt der Museen
    Österreichs* (quarterly)
Österreichischer Museumsbund
Burgring 5, 1010 Vienna 1

Belgium

Vlaamse Museumvereniging
Museum voor Sierkunst
Jan Breydelstraat 5
9000 Ghent
Publications: *Museumleven*

Association Francophone des Musées de
    Belgique
Musée des Beaux Arts
Hotel de Ville, place Charles II,
B. 6000 Charleroi
Publications: *Vie des Musées*

Brazil

Sistema Nacional d Museus-Sphan
Central Brasilia 3-andar, Sala 301
Brasilia

Canada

Canadian Museum Association
280 Metcalfe St Suite 202
Ottawa, Ontario K2P 1R7
Publications: *Muse; Muséogramme*

La Société des Musées Quebecois
CP 758, Succarsale C
Montreal, Quebec H2L 4L6

Commonwealth Association of Museums
Glenbow Museum
130 Ninth Ave SE
Calgary, Alberta T2G 0P3

China

Chinese Society of Museums
29, May 4th St
Beijing

Colombia

Asosiacion Colombiana de Museos
Museo del Oro
Calle 16, n 5-41
Bogota

Denmark

Dans Kulturhistorisk Museumsforening
Nr. Madsbadvej 6, DK 7884 Fur.
Publications: *Arv og Eje* (annual)

Foreningen af Danske Museumsmaend
The Royal Collection at Rosenberg Castle
Oster Volgade 4 A, 1350 Copenhagen K

Finland

Skandinavisk Museumsforbund, Finnish
    Section, Finnish Museums
National Museum of Finland, PB
913, 00101 Helsinki 10
Publications: *Nordens Museer*

Finnish Museum Association
Suomen Museoliito-Finlands Museifoor-
    bund
Annankatu 16B50, 00120 Helsinki
Publications: *Osma, Suomen Museoliiton
vuosikirja-Finlands Suomen Museoliito
tiedottaa* (newsletter)

France

Association Generale des Conservateurs
    des Collections Publiques de France
6 rue des Pyramides, 75041 Paris, Cedex 01
Publications: *Musées et Collections
Publiques de France*

Réunion des Musees Nationaux
49 rue Etienne Marcel
75039 Paris
Cedex 01

Germany

Institut fur Museumswesen, Information-
Dokumentation
Muggelseedam 189, 1162 Berlin
Publications: *Schriftenreihe*

Deutscher Museumsbund
Colmantstrasse 14-16, 5300 Bonn 1
Publications: *Museumskunde*

Staatliche Museen Preussischer Kulturbe-
sitz, Institut für Museumskund
In der Halde 1, D-1000 Berlin 33
Publications: *Materialien aus dem Institut
Museumskunde, Berliner Schriften zur
Museumskunde*

Iceland

Felag islenskra safnmanna
c/o Byggoa-og listasafn Arnesinga a
Selfossi
Tryggvagotu 23, 800 Selfoss

India

Museums Association of India
Salarjung Museum
Hyderabad, India

Indonesia

Research Center for Archaeology and
History
Djalan-Cilacap #4
Djakarta

Israel

Museums Association of Israel
PO Box 33288
Tel Aviv

Italy

Associazione Nazionale dei Musei Italiani
Piazza S. Marco 49
00186 Roma
Publications: *Musei e Gallerie d'Italia*

Japan

Nihon Hakubuutsukann Kyokai
Syoyu-Kaikan, 3-3-1 Kasumigaseki,
Chiyoda-ku
Tokyo
Publications: *Museum Studies*

Netherlands

Nederlandse Museumvereniging
Oudezijds Voorburgwal 1G5
PO Box 3636
1001 AK Amsterdam
Publications: *Museumvisie*

New Zealand

Art Galleries and Museums Association of
New Zealand
National Museum
Private Bag, Wellington
Publications: *AGMANZ News*

Northern Ireland

Irish Museums Association
The Ulster Folk and Transport Museum
Cultra Manor, Hollywood, Co. Down
BT18 OEU
Northern Ireland

Norway

Norske Kunst- og Kultur historische
Museer
Ullevalsnv 11
0165 Oslo
Publications: *Museumsnytt*

Skandinavisk Museumsforbund; Norwegian Section
Oslo Bymuseum, Frognerveien 67
0266 Oslo 2
Publications: *Nordens Musee*

Pakistan

The Museums Association of Pakistan
National Museum of Pakistan
1 Frere Hall, Karachi
Publications: *Museums Journal of Pakistan*

Poland

Zarzad muzeow i ochrony zabytkow
Krakowskie Przedmiescie 15-17
Warsaw 00-171
Publications: *Biblioteka Muzealnictna i
ocheonyzabytkow, Biuletyn informacyjny
Zarzadu muzeow i ochrony zaytkow*

Portugal

Associação Portuguesa de Museologia-
APOM
c/o Museu de Arte Popular
Avenida de Brasilia 1400
Lisbon
Publications: *APOM-Informacoes*

Romania

Confederatia Asociatiilor de Muzeografi
din Romania
Consiliul culturii si educatie socialiste
Calea Victoriei nr 174
Bucureşti
Publications: *Revista muzeelor si monu-
mentelor-muzee*

Slovak Republic

Ustredna Sprava Muzei a Galerii
Lodna 2, 81577 Bratislava

South Africa

South African Museums Association–Suid-
Afrikaanse Museums–Assosiasie
PO Box 61
Cape Town 8000
Publications: *SAMAB–South African
Museums Association Bulletin*

Spain

Spanish Association of Museologists
Universidad Complutense de Madrid,
Facultad de Geografia e Historia,
Ciudad Universitaria
28040 Madrid NIFG – 80726599
Publications: *Revista de Museologia*

Generalitat de Catalunya, Departament de
Cultura-Servei de Museus
Portaferrissa 1, 08002 Barcelona
Publications: *De Museus, Informatiu
Museus*

Sweden

Skandinaviska Museiforbundet, Swedish
Section
Nordiska Museet
Djurgaden, Stockholm
Publications: *Nordens Museer*

Svenska Museiforeningen
Alsnogatan 7, VII
S-11641, Stockholm
Publications: *Svenska Museer*

Switzerland

Verband der Museen der Schweiz
Baselstrasse 7
4500 Solothurn
Publications: *VMS–AMS Information*

United Kingdom

British–American Arts Association
43 Earlham St
London WC2 9LD

Museum Documentation Association
Lincoln House
347 Cherry Hinton Road
Cambridge CB1 4DH

The Museums Association
34 Bloomsbury Way
London WC1A 2SF
Publications: *Museums Journal, Museums
Association Information Sheet*

Scottish Museum Council
Country House
20–22 Torphichen St.
Edinburgh EH3 8JB

International Council of Museums' international committees*

Applied Art (ICAA)
    Publishes *ICOM/ICAA Newsletter*

---

*ICOM International Committees have internal
working groups with specific interests and
projects. Many publish the proceedings of their
conferences.

Archeology and History (ICMAH)
Publishes *ICMAH Information*, bilingual bulletin

Architecture and Museum Techniques (ICAMT)
Publishes *Brief*, newsletter

Audiovisual, Image, and Sound: New Technologies (AVICOM)
Publishes *AVICOM-Flash* bulletin

Conservation
Publishes *ICOM Committee for Conservation Newsletter*, working groups, and *Triennial Preprints*

Costume
Publishes *Costume News* and bibliographies

Documentation (CIDOC)
Publishes *CIDOC Newsletter*

Education and Cultural Action (CECA)
Publishes *ICOM CECA Newsletter* and an annual review

Egyptology (CIPEG)
Publishes an annual newsletter

Ethnography (ICME)
Publishes *ICME News*

Exhibition Exchange (ICEE)
Publishes bibliographies

Fine Art (ICFA)

Glass
Publishes *Newsletter*

Literary Museums (ICLM)
Publishes *Newsletter* and an *International Handbook*

Management (INTERCOM)

Modern Art (CIMAM)

Museology (ICOFOM)
Publishes *Museological News*, and *ICOFOM Regional Bulletin for Latin America and the Caribbean*

Musical Instruments (CIMCIM)
Publishes *CIMCIM Bulletin, International Directory*, and bibliographies

Natural History
Publishes *Natural History Newsletter*

Numismatics

Public Relations (MPR)
Publishes *MPR News*
http://www.inhb.co.nz/icom.mpr

Regional Museums (ICR)
Publishes *ICR Informations*

Science and Technology (CIMUSET)
Publishes a *Newsletter* and *directory*

Security (ICMS)
Publishes *Newsletter* and *Manual*

Training of Personnel (ICTOP)
Publishes *It*, newsletter
http://kafka.uvic.ca/~maltwood/ictop.html

International Council of Museums' affiliated organizations

International Association of Agricultural Museums (AIMA)

International Association of Arms and Military History (IAMAM)

Association of European Open-Air Museums

International Confederation of Architectural Museums (ICAM)

International Congress of Maritime Museums (ICMM)
Publishes a *Newsletter*

International Movement for a New Museology (MINOM)

Museum Association of the Caribbean (MAC)
Publishes a *Newsletter*

International Society of Libraries and
Museums of Performing Arts (SIBMAS)

International Association of Transport
Museums (IATM)
Publishes a *Newsletter* and yearbook

South Africa Development Coordination
Conference Association of Museums
(SADCCAM)

World Federation of Friends of Museums
Secretariat of Presidency
Via Goito 9
20121 Milano, Italy
Publishes a *Newsletter*

Appendix C

Sources of funding for internships, fellowships, and research

This appendix lists sources of funding for internships, fellowships, and research activities. Includes addresses, and a brief description of the organization's service.

Paid and nonpaid internships are available at many museums throughout the United States and abroad. Contact the museums directly for further information. See bibliography in Chapter 8, "Training and Preparation," for additional information on internships.

Center for Museum Studies, Smithsonian Institution
Arts and Industries Building,
Room 2235
900 Jefferson Dr.
Washington, DC 20560
Internship Opportunities at the Smithsonian Institution.
Fellowships in Museum Practice, enables museum professionals to undertake research in museum theory and operations. Museum Intern Partnership program, partnership project between Smithsonian Institution and African American, Native American and Latino community focused museums.

The Foundation Center
79 Fifth Avenue
New York, NY 10003
There are about 100 locations in the US.
Grants for Arts and Cultural Programs, annual publication.
Offers assistance in locating grants.

The J. Paul Getty Museum
Education and Academic Affairs Department
PO Box 2112
Santa Monica, CA 90407-2112
Offers graduate and undergraduate paid internships in museum practices.

The Getty Grant Program
401 Wilshire Blvd, Suite 1000
Santa Monica, CA 90404-1455
Offers non-residential postdoctoral fellowships in art history; senior research grants for art-history and museum professionals.

National Endowment for the Arts (NEA)
1100 Pennsylvania Avenue NW
Washington, DC 20506
Guide to the National Endowment for the Arts.
The *Guide* gives an overview of the NEA's programs and projects, the funding categories for grants and fellowships, and eligibility criteria for each category. Individual booklets, called "Guidelines," for each program contain application forms and procedures for applying for each specific program. Currently employed full-time museum professionals may apply for individual fellowships.

National Endowment for the Humanities (NEH)
1100 Pennsylvania Avenue NW
Washington DC 20506
Overview of Endowment Programs; Division of Education Programs; Division of Research Programs; Division of Preservation and Access.

Individuals, nonprofit associations, institutions and organizations may apply. For information call or write the appropriate division to obtain guidelines and application forms. The Division of Fellowships and Seminars offers fellowships to museum employees for independent study, summer stipends, and travel collections. http://www.neh.fed.us

National Historical Publications and Records Commission (NHPRC)
National Archives Building
Washington, DC 20408
The Records program funds projects to train archivists, and has a fellowships program in archival administration.

National Research Council
Ford Foundation Fellowship Program
2101 Constitution Avenue, NW
Washington, DC 20418
The Ford Foundation sponsors doctoral fellowships for minorities in the humanities.

National Science Foundation (NSF)
Public Information Office
4201 Wilson Blvd
Arlington, VA 22230

The Directorate of Science and Engineering Education supports the Research and Informal Science Education program. The Career Access Program (CAP) is a joint program with ASTC that recruits members of minority groups into science-related careers in museums.

Office of Fellowship and Grants, Smithsonian Institution
955 L'Enfant Plaza
Suite 7300
Washington, DC 20560
Smithsonian Opportunities for Research and Study in History, Art and Science, annual publication.
The Smithsonian Fellowship Program includes fellowships for graduate, pre- and postdoctoral students and senior postdoctoral. Other fellowships in a field of specialty, and for minorities and Native Americans are also available.

US/ICOMOS
1600 H St NW
Washington, DC 20006
International summer intern program; professional-level, paid internships abroad for young preservationists.

Appendix D

Mission statements and organizational charts

This appendix includes samples, not necessarily "models," of museum mission statements and organizational charts which may serve as guides and for general information on organization structures and purposes. Mission statements and organizational charts vary greatly in all types of institutions, are very individualized, and must be regarded as references only.

The J. B. Speed Art Museum, Louisville, Kentucky

[Its collections house works from antiquity to the present of European and American decorative arts, paintings, sculpture, graphic arts, African art, and Native American art.]

The mission of the J. B. Speed Art Museum is to collect, research, conserve, exhibit, and interpret art of the highest quality for the enjoyment and enlightenment of its public. Through these activities the Speed celebrates the joy and power of visual images for the enrichment of human experience. By balancing concerns for collections with those of education, the Museum provides for the cultural heritage of future generations, and for the stimulation of its current audiences. Its continued existence and its constant activities are the dual concerns of those charged with stewardship of the J. B. Speed Art Museum. The Museum strives for excellence in building and preserving its collection of ancient to contemporary art, with particular emphasis on the fine and decorative arts from the Renaissance to the present. The artistic traditions of Kentucky are a special interest of the Museum. Our research and our exhibitions aspire to present works of art in a context of heightened appreciation and clear understanding. Educational and interpretive programs focus on instruction, inspiration and pleasure relating to the permanent collection and special exhibitions.

The Museum takes pride in being the foremost visual arts institution in Kentucky and in our region. It welcomes the public and is committed to serving all possible constituencies.

(*Courtesy of the J. B. Speed Art Museum*)

Bucks County Historical Society, Doylestown, Pennsylvania

[Its collections consist of tools and products of early handcraft, artifacts of everyday life, folk art, and local history items.]

The Bucks County Historical Society which administers the Mercer Museum, Fonthill Museum and the Spruance Library promotes an understanding of history through objects, architecture, art and documents. Inspired by the collections and creative achievements of Henry C. Mercer, the Society preserves and interprets through programs and exhibits the rich history and culture of Bucks County, the Delaware Valley and America before the Age of Industry.

(*Courtesy of the Bucks County Historical Society*)

Museum of Science and Industry, Chicago, Illinois

The mission of the Museum of Science and Industry is to:

- Excel in the communication of the knowledge of science, technology, and industry, as a non-traditional educational institution;
- Develop superior, innovative, and measurably effective methodologies and practices to further that communication and scientific education;
- Communicate the changes in science, technology, and industry while preserving and presenting the heritage of technological progress;
- Provide a public forum for issues raised by the impact of scientific and technological change on humankind;
- Participate in the formulation and implementation of a national science policy directed toward strengthening America's science resources;
- Collaborate with the community and with civic, educational, and scientific organizations to achieve shared goals through museum programs and activities.

(*Courtesy of the Museum of Science and Industry*)

Natural History Museum of Los Angeles County, Los Angeles, California

[The museum collections are about ethnology, anthropology, archeology, botany, geology, mineralogy, paleontology, mammalogy, and invertebrate zoology.]

Acquire, conserve and interpret collections of objects pertaining to natural and human history that document our planet from its origin to the present day. Serves both the local and international community through public and academic programs including exhibitions, education, research and publications. These resources are made available so that society may learn from the past, better understand the present and plan for the future.

(Courtesy of the Natural History Museum of Los Angeles County)

Museum of the Rockies

[Houses a collection of geology, astronomy, paleontology, archaeology, living history, and textile objects.]

The Museum of the Rockies seeks to understand, preserve and interpret the natural and cultural history of the Northern Rocky Mountain region. The Museum accomplishes its mission through research, care of collections, exhibits and educational programs consistent with the theme One Place Through All of Time for the education and enjoyment of people of all ages.

(Courtesy of the Museum of the Rockies)

Institute of Texan Cultures, San Antonio, Texas

[Houses a collection of 1,875,000 photographs.]

The Institute of Texan Cultures is a university educational center dedicated to the enhancement of historical and multicultural understanding through exhibits, programs, and publications that encourage acceptance and appreciation of our differences as well as our common humanity. Operating on the premise that people are stronger citizens when they know more about themselves and each other, the Institute serves as a forum for multicultural education efforts in the state and symbolizes the state's strength in diversity.

(Courtesy of the Institute of Texan Cultures)

Chicago Zoological Society–Brookfield Zoo, Chicago, Illinois

The mission of the Chicago Zoological Society is to help people develop a sustainable and harmonious relationship with nature. In doing so, the Society shall provide for the recreation and education of the people, the conservation of wildlife, and the discovery of biological knowledge.

(Courtesy of the Zoological Society–Brookfield Zoo)

The Art Institute of Chicago, Chicago, Illinois

It is the purpose of The Art Institute of Chicago to collect, conserve, research, publish, exhibit, and interpret an internationally significant, permanent collection of objects of art. It is the role of The Art Institute of Chicago both to provide the experience of original works of art and to maximize the richness of that experience. In addition, it is the responsibility of The Art Institute of Chicago to encourage interest in, and appreciation of, those objects of art. In recognition of that role, The Art Institute of Chicago will concentrate its efforts on increasing the appreciation and understanding of both our permanent collection and loan exhibitions, enriching the visitor experience, and encouraging broader participation in the Museum.

The emphasis in the coming decades will be on better utilizing The Art Institute of Chicago's exceptional permanent collections. To capitalize on these collections, the Museum will:

– Enhance the intellectual accessibility and aesthetic experience of the collection and exhibitions through an increased focus on presentation, interpretation, and integration of curatorial and educational efforts.
– Present selected loan exhibitions with a high degree of curatorial involvement and with well-developed, focused support programs. Encourage the creative use of the permanent collections in exhibitions.
– Increase the commitment to the highest standards of collection conservation and management through informed and responsible techniques and procedures, suitable facilities, and a capable staff.
– Establish priorities and specific goals for research in each curatorial department. Develop a publication strategy that increases the accessibility of the collection and meets the specific interests of a range of audiences.
– Maintain our commitment to building high quality collections through donation and selective acquisition. Develop new strategies

to attract donations and focus acquisitions on areas where our limited resources can make the greatest contribution to the institution as a whole, as well as best meet the needs of the expanded audience we intend to serve. In addition, maintain the currency of The Art Institute of Chicago's internationally renowned art library.

- Strive to create a comfortable and inviting environment for visitors, throughout the museum, by better understanding visitor's needs, providing responsive service, and emphasizing the Museum's human, comprehensible scale. The Art Institute will seek to broaden participation in the Museum through improved understanding of our audiences and their interests, expanded community interaction (outreach), improved service, and the development of programs targeted to specific audiences.

(Courtesy of the Art Institute of Chicago)

THE EXPLORATORIUM
San Francisco, California, USA

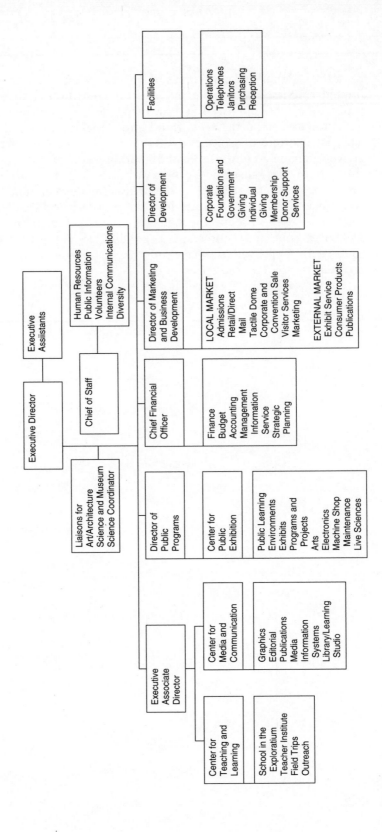

Courtesy of The Exploratorium

THE VIRGINIA MUSEUM OF NATURAL HISTORY
Martinsville, Virginia, USA

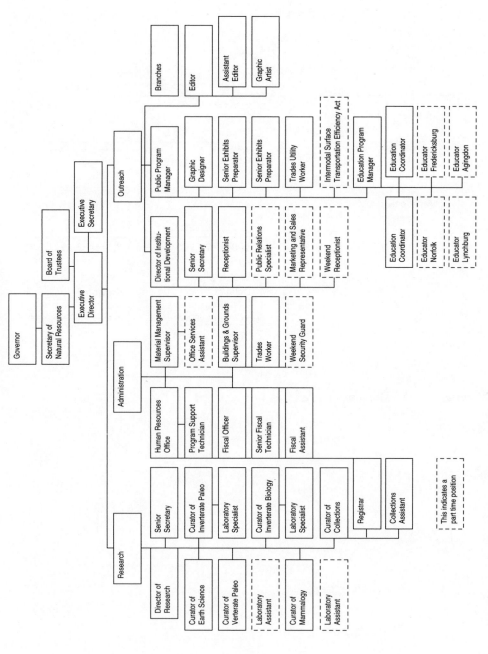

Courtesy of the Virginia Museum of Natural History

THE MUSEUM OF HISPANIC-AMERICAN ART
"ISAAC FERNANDO BLANCO"
Buenos Aires, Argentina

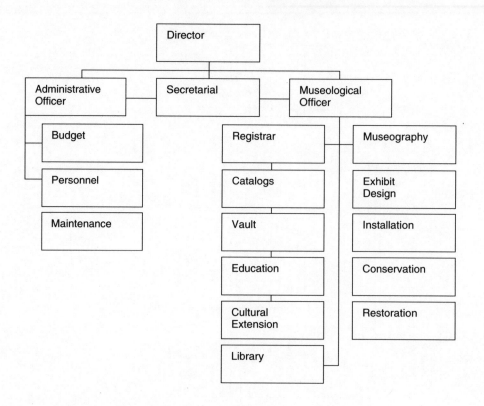

Courtesy of the Museum of Hispanic-American Art

KENTUCKY HISTORICAL SOCIETY
Frankfort, Kentucky, USA

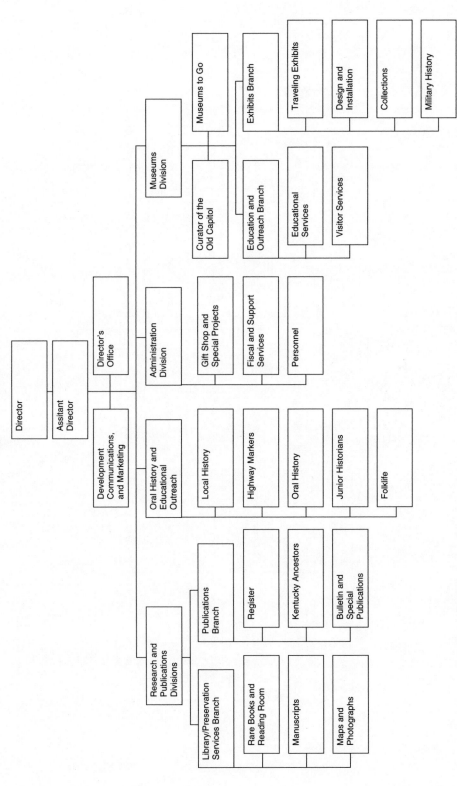

Courtesy of the Kentucky Historical Society

THE MILWAUKEE PUBLIC MUSEUM, INC.
Milwaukee, Wisconsin, USA

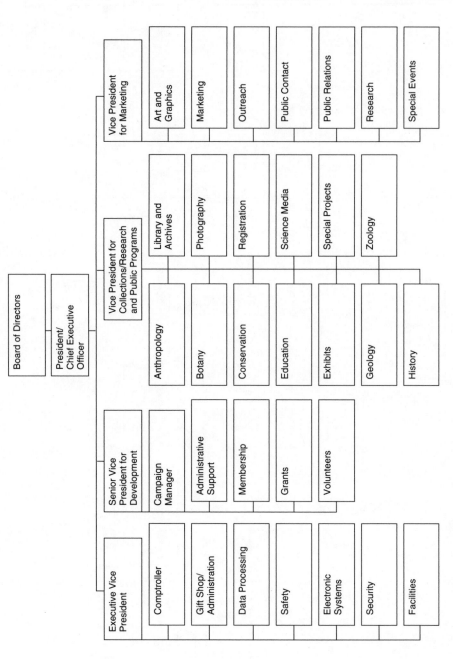

Courtesy of the Milwaukee Public Museum, Inc.

THE QUEENSLAND ART GALLERY
Brisbane, Queensland, Australia

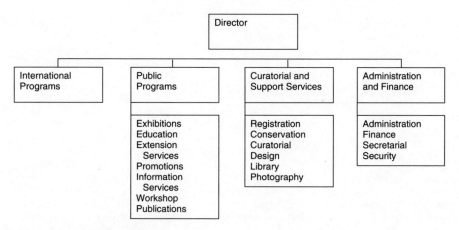

Director

International Programs	Public Programs	Curatorial and Support Services	Administration and Finance

	Exhibitions
	Education
	Extension
	  Services
	Promotions
	Information
	  Services
	Workshop
	Publications
		Registration
		Conservation
		Curatorial
		Design
		Library
		Photography
			Administration
			Finance
			Secretarial
			Security

Courtesy of the Queensland Art Gallery

Index

296

Current Topics in Microbiology and Immunology

151

Editors

R. W. Compans, Birmingham/Alabama · M. Cooper,
Birmingham/Alabama · H. Koprowski, Philadelphia
I. McConnell, Edinburgh · F. Melchers, Basel
V. Nussenzweig, New York · M. Oldstone,
La Jolla/California · S. Olsnes, Oslo
H. Saedler, Cologne · P. K. Vogt, Los Angeles
H. Wagner, Munich · I. Wilson, La Jolla/California

Bacterial Adhesins

Edited by
K. Jann and B. Jann

With 23 Figures

Springer-Verlag
Berlin Heidelberg New York
London Paris Tokyo Hong Kong

Prof. Dr. Klaus Jann
Dr. Barbara Jann

Max-Planck-Institut für Immunbiologie
Stübeweg 51, 7800 Freiburg, FRG

ISBN 3-540-51052-4 Springer-Verlag Berlin Heidelberg New York
ISBN 0-387-51052-4 Springer-Verlag New York Berlin Heidelberg

© Springer-Verlag Berlin Heidelberg 1990
Library of Congress Catalog Card Number 15-12910
Printed in Germany

Phototypesetting by Thomson Press (India) Ltd, New Delhi
Offsetprinting: Saladruck, Berlin; Bookbinding: B. Helm, Berlin
2123/3020-543210 – Printed on acid-free paper

Preface

The great majority of bacterial infections are initiated by the adhesion of pathogenic bacteria to cells and mucosal surfaces of the host. The sequela of adhesion may range from the action of toxins outside target cells to their penetration into or through tissue. Besides the consequences of bacterial adhesion related in infection, the result may be colonization of mucosal surfaces with normally harmless bacteria, which in stress situations may become virulent, a phenomenon known as nosocomial infections.

With very few exceptions, adhesion is carbohydrate specific. It is mediated by bacterial recognition proteins that are, according to the phenomenon studied, termed adhesins or hemagglutinins; the term "lectin" is sometimes also used. The chemical nature of the adhesins and their organization on the bacterial surface have been studied intensively in many laboratories. The application of genetic and biochemical techniques has led to substantial progress in the molecular characterization of adhesins in recent years. We now know that adhesins may occur as structural subunits of fimbriae and that they may form fimbriae which can be considered as mono- or multifunctional linear adhesin polymers. Other adhesins do not form recognizable structures and are tentatively called nonfimbrial. Adhesins may even be components of bacterial cell walls. Adhesin-receptor specificities have been unravelled. The study of the distribution of receptors in tissue has created implications about the possible susceptibility to infections. The genetics of adhesins provide insight into the biogenesis of adhesins and into the relationships between structure and function. Thus, a comprehensive view of bacterial adhesins is now available, revealing vistas about the molecular details of adhesins, both about pathogenicity in general, and on possible applications of the findings to medicine and the abatement of infections. The observer of the field will, however, also find many hitherto unanswered questions, for instance regarding protein–protein and protein–carbohydrate interactions. This will certainly be a stimulus for further research.

In this volume important aspects of adhesin research are presented, covering the most pertinent areas of genetics, serology, and biochemistry, and the approaches to medical applications. Since these areas overlap, we have encouraged the authors to present not only their most pertinent data but also more general outlooks on their field and to expound principles behind the facts. Although the book is restricted to the adhesins of *E. coli*, one of the genera on which the most information is available today, the principle findings will doubtlessly also be applicable to other systems. We feel that focussing on one system in this way will ensure a more concise and coherent presentation of general principles and their molecular basis.

Klaus Jann
Barbara Jann

July 20, 1989

Table of Contents

Indexed in Current Contents

List of Contributors

You will find the adresses at the beginning of the respective contribution

ANDERSSON, B.
ANIANSSON, G.
DE GRAAF, F. K.
EVANS, D. G.
EVANS, JR., D. J.
HACKER, J.
HOLTHÖFER, H.
HOSCHÜTZKY, H.
JANN, K.
KORHONEN, T. K.
LEFFLER, H.
LINDSTEDT, R.
DE MAN, P.

MOON, H.
NIELSEN, A.
OFEK, I.
ØRSKOV, F.
ØRSKOV, I.
PARKKINEN, J.
SCHMIDT, M. A.
SHARON, N.
SVANBORG EDÉN, C.
VIRKOLA, R.
WESTERLUND, B.
WOLD, A.

Genetic Determinants Coding for Fimbriae and Adhesins of Extraintestinal *Escherichia coli*

J. Hacker

1 Introduction

Extraintestinal *Escherichia coli* are a frequent cause of urinary tract infection (UTI), sepsis, and newborn meningitis (NBM) (ØRSKOV and ØRSKOV 1985; SVANBORG EDEN and DE MAN 1987). Uropathogenic *E. coli* produce different factors involved in pathogenicity, i.e., O antigens (e.g., O4, O6, O18, and O75), capsule antigens (e.g., K5, K12, and K13; ORSKOV et al. 1977), and cytotoxic proteins, termed hemolysins (Hly, HUGHES et al. 1983). It has often been shown that strains causing meningitis and sepsis belong to particular serotypes, e.g., O1:K1, O2:K1, O7:K1, O83:K1, or O75:K1 (KORHONEN et al. 1985; ACHTMAN and PLUSCHKE 1986; HACKER et al. 1989). In addition, extraintestinal *E. coli* strains produce adhesins which enable the isolates to attach to eukaryotic cells (SVANBORG EDEN et al. 1977; OFEK and SILVERBLATT 1982). The majority of adhesins produced by extraintestinal *E. coli* are associated

Institut für Genetik und Mikrobiologie, Röntgenring 11, D-8700 Würzburg, FRG

Table 2. Cloned fimmbrial and adhesin determinants of extraintestinal *E. coli* strains

Adhesin/fimbria type (gene abbreviation)	Receptor specificity	F-type	Subunit (kd)[a]	Parental strain	Serotype	References
Fimbrial adhesins						
Type 1 fimbriae (*fim*) (*pil*)	α-D-Mannose	F1A	17	PC31	K-12	KLEMM et al. 1985
	α-D-Mannose	F1A	17	J96	O4:K6	HULL et al. 1981; ORNDORFF and FALKOW 1984a
(**KS71D**) (*pil*)	α-D-Mannose	F1A	17	KS71[b]	O6:K2	RHEN 1985
		Non-F1A	17	536	O6:K15	HACKER (unpublished)
P fimbriae (*fso*)	α-D-Gal-(1-4)-β-D-Gal	$F7_1$	20	AD110[b]	O6:K2	VAN DIE et al. 1985
(*fst*)	α-D-Gal-(1-4)-β-D-Gal	$F7_2$	17	AD110	O6:K2	VAN DIE et al. 1983; VAN DIE et al. 1984b
(*fei*)	α-D-Gal-(1-4)-β-D-Gal	F8	19.5	2980	O18:K5	HACKER et al. 1986b
	α-D-Gal-(1-4)-β-D-Gal	F9	21	C1018	O2:K5	DE REE et al. 1985c
(*fel*)	α-D-Gal-(1-4)-β-D-Gal	F11	18	C1976	O1:K1	DE REE et al. 1985a
	α-D-Gal-(1-4)-β-D-Gal	$F12_{rel}$	16.8	20025	O4:K12	HIGH et al. 1988
(*pap*)	α-D-Gal-(1-4)-β-D-Gal	F13	19.5	J96	O4:K6	HULL et al. 1981; NORMARK et al. 1983
	α-D-Gal-(1-4)-β-D-Gal	F13	18.8	20025	O4:K6	HIGH et al. 1988
	α-D-Gal-(1-4)-β-D-Gal	F14	20.5	20025	O4:K6	HIGH et al. 1988
(**KS71A**)	α-D-Gal-(1-4)-β-D-Gal	$F7_1$	22	KS71	O6:K2	RHEN et al. 1983a; RHEN et al. 1985b
(**KS71B**)	α-D-Gal-(1-4)-β-D-Gal	$F7_2$	20	KS71	O6:K2	RHEN et al. 1983; RHEN et al. 1985b
(**pDC1**)	α-D-Gal-(1-4)-β-D-Gal	F11	20	IA2	O6	CLEGG 1982; CLEGG and PIERCE 1983
S fimbrial adhesin (*sfa*)	α-Sialyl-(2-3)-β-Gal		16	536	O6:K15	BERGER et al. 1982; HACKER et al. 1985
G fimbriae	GlcNac		19.5	IH11165	O2	RHEN 1986a
P-related sequence (*prs*)	GalNac-α-(1-3)-GalNac	F13	19.5	J96	O4:K6	LUND et al. 1988b

5

	Receptor specificity		MW	Strain	Serotype	Reference
A (non)-fimbrial adhesins						
M agglutinin (*bma*)	Glycophorin A^M		21	IH11165	O2	RHEN et al. 1986a
D hemagglutinin (previously O75X)	IFC blood group complex		21	IH11128	O75:K5	NOWICKI et al. 1987, 1988
A fimbrial adhesin (*afaI*)	Unknown		16	KS52	O2	LABIGNE et al. 1984
(*afaII*)	Unknown		?	A22	O15	LABIGNE and FALKOW 1988
(*afaIII*)	Like D hemaggl.?		?	A13	O75	LABIGNE and FALKOW 1988
Nonfimbrial adhesin (*nfaI*)	Unknown		21	827	O83:K1	HALES et al. 1988
Nonadhesive fimbriae						
Pseudo type 1 fimbriae (*foc*)	?	F1C	17	AD110	O6:K2	VAN DIE et al. 1984a
(KS71C) (*foc*)		F1C	17	KS71	O6:K2	RHEN 1985
(*foc*)		F1C	16.5	20025	O4:K6	HIGH et al. 1988
S/F1C-related fimbriae (*sfr*)	?		17	BK568	O75:K1	PAWELZIK et al. 1988
P-related fimbriae (*prf*)	?		22	536	O6:K15	HACKER et al. 1989b

[a] The molecular masses of fimbrial subunit proteins or, in the case of A-fimbrial adhesins, of the adhesive proteins are given on the basis of SDS–PAGE experiments;
[b] Strain AD110 is identical to strains C1212 and KS71 (see ØRSKOV 1983; I. VAN DIE, personal communication)

eight of the ten serologic variants of P fimbriae were ligated into suitable vector molecules. The same was done for the gene clusters coding for S fimbriae and G fimbriae and for the determinants coding for different nonfimbrial adhesins and for nonhemagglutinating fimbriae. It is interesting to note that more than two adhesins or fimbrial determinants were cloned from the chromosomes of wild-type strains J96 (O4:K6), AD110 (O6:K2), KS71 (O6:K2), 20025 (O4:K6), and 536 (O6:K15).

2.3 Molecular Characterization of Cloned Adhesin Determinants

In order to characterize the different cloned adhesin and fimbrial determinants more accurately the coding regions were subcloned and physical maps were established. In addition, their gene products were elucidated by the expression of the proteins in minicell and maxicell systems and by DNA sequence studies. With the help of subclones and transposon insertional mutants the gene organization of several gene clusters was determined. The generation of operon and protein fusions together with the detection of promoter regions and the characterization of mRNA species yielded new insights into the regulation of expression of adhesin determinants (see UHLIN et al. 1985b; BAGA et al. 1988).

It has been shown that the genetic composition of different adhesin determinants is similar. Different regions of the determinants which code for the major fimbrillin (pilin) subunits and for minor fimbrillin proteins, including the corresponding adhesin proteins, can be distinguished. In addition, sequences necessary for transport and assembly functions as well as regions involved in the regulation of transcription can be observed (KLEMM 1985; HACKER et al. 1985; NORMARK et al. 1986). These different regions of adhesin determinants are described below.

3 Genes Coding for Major Fimbrial Subunits

The intact fiber-like structures, consisting of about 500–1000 identical subunit proteins, seem to be necessary for the presentation of the adhesive molecules since they bridge the distances between adhesins and eukaryotic receptor structures. In addition, at least in particular E. coli wild-type strains fimbriae may function as carriers to help the adhesins overcome the shielding effect of the LPS-O side chains (VAN DIE et al. 1986c).

The genes coding for the major fimbrial subunit proteins have been mapped at the proximal (5′) end of the determinants analyzed. The nucleic acid sequences and the predicted amino acid sequences have been established from nine different fimbrial structural genes (BAGA et al. 1984; VAN DIE and BERGMANS 1984; VAN DIE et al. 1984a, 1986a; ORNDORFF and FALKOW 1985; RHEN et al. 1985a; KLEMM 1984; SCHMOLL et al. 1987). On the basis of the sequence data summarized in Fig. 1 the degree of homology between the mature fimbrial proteins has been calculated (Fig. 2). Five P fimbriae show a sequence homology of about 60% to each other. The

```
                            20 |              40 |              60              80
F11:         MIKSVIAGAVAMAVVSFGVN  AAPTIPQGQGKVTFNGTVV DAPCSISQKSADQSIDFGQL SKSFLEAGGTSKPNDL DIE
F13: (PapA)  MIKSVIAGAVAMAVVSFGVN NAAPTIPQGQGKVTFNGTVV DAPCSISQKSADQSIDFGQL SKSFLEAGGVSKPMDL DIE
F7₁/KS71A:   MIKSVIAGAVAMAVVSFGAN  AAASIPQGQGEVSFKGTVV DAPCGIETQSAKQEIDFGQI SKSFLQEGGETQPKDL NIK
F7₂:         MIKSVIAGAVAMAVVSFGAY  AAPTIPQGQGKVTFNGTVV DAPCGIEAQSAGQSIDFGQV SKLFLENTGESQPKSL DIK
SfaA:        MKLKFISMAVFSALTLGVAT NASAVTTVNGGTVHFKGEVV DAACAVNTNSANQTFS GQV RSAKLANTGEKSSPVGFSIE
F1C:         MKLKFISMAVFSALTLGVAT NASAVTTVNGGTVHFKGEVV NAACAVNTNSFTQTVNLGQV RSERLKVTGAKSNPVGFTIE
PilA:        MKIKTLAIVVLSALSLSSTT ALAAATTVNGGTVHFKGEVV NAACAVDAGSVDQTVQLGQV RTASLAQEGATSSAVGFNIQ
FimA:        MKIKTLAIVVLSALSLSSTA ALAAATTVNGGTVHFKGEVV NAACAVEAGSVDQTVQLGQV RTASLAQEGATSSAVGFNIQ
             ◄      Leader     ►I◄     N-Terminus     ►I◄            C-C-loop
```

```
             |             100            120            140            160
F11:         LVNCDITAFK  QGQAAKN GKVQLSFTGPQVTGQAEELA TNGGTGTAIVVQAAGKNVSF DG TAGDAYPLKDGDNVLHY
F13: (PapA)  LVNCDITAFK  GGNGAKK GTVKLAFTGPIVNGHSDELD TNGGTGTAIVVQGAGNNVVF DG SEGEANTLKDGENVLHY
F7₁/KS71A:   LVNCDITNLKQLQGGA AKK GTVSLTESGVPAENADDMLQ TVGDTNTAIVVTSSGKRVKF DGATETGASNLINGDNTIHF
F7₂:         LINCDITNFKKAAGGGGAKT GTVSLTFSGVPSGPQSDMLQ TVGATNTAIVVTPHGKRVKF DGATATGVSYLVDGDNTIHF
SfaA:        LNDCSSATAG  HASIIFA GNVIAT HNDVLSLQNSAAG SATNVGIQILDH TGTAVQF DGVTASTQFTLTDGTNKIPF
F1C:         LNDCDSQVSA  GAGIVFS GPAV TGKTDVLALQSSAAG SATNVGVQITDH TGKVVPL DG TASSTFTLTDGTNKIPF
PilA:        LNDCDTNVAS  KAAVAFL GTAIDAGHTNVLALQSSAAG SATNVGVQITDR TGAALTL DGATFSSETTLNNGTNTIPF
FimA:        LNDCDTNVAS  KAAVAFL GTAIDAGHTNVLALQSSAAG SATNVGVQITDR TGAALTL DGATFSSETTLNNGTNTIPF
             ►I◄                                   Hydrophilic region
```

```
             |    180
F11:         TALVKK  ANGGTVSEGAFS AVATFNLSYQ*
F13: (PapA)  TAVVKKSSAVGAAVTEGAFS AVANFNLTYQ*
F7₁/KS71A:   TAFVKKDNS GKNVAEGAFS AVANFNLTYQ*
F7₂:         TAAVRKDGS GNPVTEGAFS AVANFNLTYQ*
SfaA:        QAVYYAT   GKS TPGIAN ADATFKVQYQ*
F1C:         QAVYYAT   GQA TAGIAN ADATFKVQYQ*
PilA:        QARYFAT   GAA TPGAAN ADATFKVQYQ*
FimA:        QARYFA    GAA TPGAAN ADATFKVQYQ*
             ►I◄ C-Terminus ►
```

Fig. 1. Comparison of the amino acid sequences of the fimbrillin subunit proteins of P fimbriae (serotypes F11, F13 Pap, F7₁/KS71, F7₂), S fimbriae, F1C fimbriae, and type 1 fimbriae (PilA, FimA). The amino acids sequences are given in single letter code. The five main regions of the proteins are indicated (for references see text). The amino acids of the premature protein counted

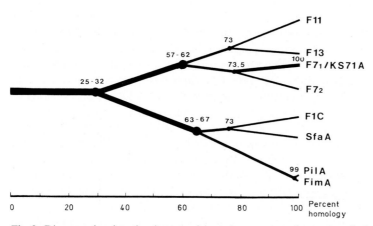

Fig. 2. Diagram showing the degrees of homology among the mature fimbrillin subunit proteins presented in Fig. 1

fimbriae of the serotypes F13 and F11 on the one hand and those belonging to serogroups $F7_1$ and $F7_2$ on the other form two "subgroups" (homology of about 73%) within the P family.

The two type 1 fimbrial proteins, FimA and pilA (see above), exhibit 99% homology. The type 1 proteins in general are more related to pseudotype 1 (F1C) and S fimbrial adhesins (homology of 63% and 67%) than to the P fimbrial proteins (homology 25%-32%). The F1C- and Sfa-specific proteins, which show a degree of homology of 73%, form another related group of fimbrial antigens (OTT et al. 1988). Thus on the basis of the sequence homologies three groups of fimbriae can be determined: P fimbriae, type 1 fimbriae, and a group consisting of Sfa and F1C fimbrillin proteins.

An analysis of the fimbrillin protein sequences shows that five different regions can be discriminated (for details see VAN DIE et al. 1987). These parts differ with respect to sequence homologies observed and to their putative functions.

1. The leader sequences necessary for the transfer of the proteins across the inner membrane show a homology of up to 90% within each of the three groups of fimbriae mentioned above. As demonstrated in Fig. 1, the length of the leader peptides also differs between the three putative groups.

2. The N-terminal sequences are the most homologous among all nine proteins. It is interesting to note here that a synthetic peptide consisting of seven amino acids of the N-terminus of the F13 fimbrillin protects animals against infection by P fimbriated strains of different F-types (SCHMIDT et al. 1988). These data confirm the view that the N-terminal sequences represent well-conserved parts of the major fimbrial subunits.

3. The two cysteine residues of the molecules which form a Cys-Cys bridge in native proteins (JANN et al. 1981) are located exactly at the same place in all nine molecules. Some of the differences in the primary protein structure of the Cys-Cys loops have no relevance to the secondary structure of the proteins because they reveal conservative amino acid exchanges (VAN DIE et al. 1987).

4. The regions between the second cysteine residue and the C-terminal end of the proteins consist of a remarkably high amount of hydrophilic amino acids (therefore they have been termed "hydrophilic regions") and show several differences in their amino acid composition. In these regions five to six "hypervariable parts," which should represent the immunodominant domains of the proteins, can be found (HOPP and WOODS 1981). This was confirmed by the isolation of site-specific mutants with altered protein sequences of the $F7_1$ and F11 fimbrillin molecules; these led to differences in the serologic properties of the proteins (VAN DIE et al. 1988a). The hypervariable parts also may be important for the stability of fimbriae because deletions of corresponding pieces of DNA led to a total absence of fimbriae. Furthermore, foreign antigenic determinants like peptides specific for foot-and-mouth disease virus can be incorporated into the hypervariable region of the fimbrial subunits (VAN DIE et al. 1988b). It is also suggested that the hyper-variable regions may play a role in the escape of fimbriated bacteria from the immune system (DE REE et al. 1985b).

5. The C-terminal regions of the proteins which carry some hydrophobic and aromatic amino acids exhibit a high degree of homology. In all cases the two amino acids at the C-terminal end of the proteins (tyrosine and glutamine) are identical (see

Fig. 1). It is suggested that the C-termini are involved in the interaction of the fimbrial protein subunits and the formation of an intact fiber-like structure (KLEMM 1985).

4 Genes Coding for Minor Fimbrial Subunits and Adhesins

It is generally accepted that fimbriae of extraintestinal *E.coli* isolates do not represent the adhesive proteins per se. Rather it has been shown that "minor fimbrial proteins" are incorporated into the fiber-like structures. Evidence revealed that one of these minor proteins represents the actual adhesin of P fimbriae (LINDBERG et al. 1984; UHLIN et al. 1985b; VAN DIE et al. 1985; HOSCHÜTZKY et al. 1989), S fimbriae (HACKER et al. 1985), and type 1 fimbriae (MAURER and ORNDORFF 1985; MINION et al. 1986), whereas another two minor proteins are involved in anchoring and/or presentation of the adhesins and in initiation of fimbrial polymerization (RIEGMAN et al. 1988; NORMARK et al. 1988; see also sect. 5). The major and minor fimbrial proteins form a structure termed "fimbria–adhesin complex" (see HOSCHÜTZKY et al. 1989).

4.1 P Type

Three minor components are detected for P fimbriae of serotype F13 which are encoded by the *pap* (pili associated with pyelonephritis) operon (NORMARK et al. 1983; LUND et al. 1985) and for fimbriae of the serotypes $F7_1$ (*fso* determinant; VAN DIE et al. 1985) and $F7_2$ (*fst* determinant; VAN DIE et al. 1984b). The genes are termed *papE*, *papF*, and *papG* and are analogous to *fsoE, F, G* and *fstE, F, G* (RIEGMANN et al. 1988). As indicated in Fig. 3a, these proteins have comparable molecular weights and in each case the corresponding genes are located at the distal (3′) end of the determinants. Genetic complementation data argue that the PapG protein represents the adhesin protein of the *pap* determinant (LUND et al. 1987, 1988a). It has also been suggested that the proteins FsoG, FstG, and FelG (for the F11 determinant) mediate adherence to the Gal-Gal receptor.

DNA sequence studies have shown that the putative adhesin proteins are nearly 32 kd in size. The genes *fstG* and *felG* are rather similar to each other, whereas the *papG* gene differs from the other two cistrons (only 45% sequence homology). The corresponding protein sequences, however, show similarities to the C-terminal part of the major P fimbrial subunits and they all carry four cysteine residues at well-defined positions. Very recently Hoschützky et al. (1989) isolated the adhesin proteins of three different P fimbrial adhesin complexes. The identity of the isolated proteins to the proteins extrapolated from DNA sequences was demonstrated by these authors.

It is interesting to note that the adhesin-specific genes may vary among fimbriae of the same F serogroup. LUND et al. (1988b) described two different binding specificities, Pap [α-D-Gal-(1-4)-β-D-Gal specificity] and Prs [P-related sequences, GalNAc-α-(1-3)-GalNAc specificity; see also Table 2] which are associated with

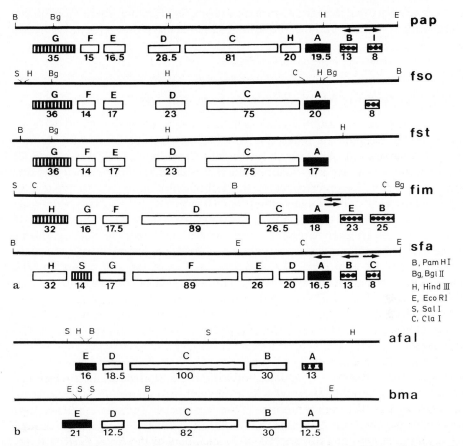

Fig. 3. a Comparison of the physical maps and the gene products of different fimbrial adhesin determinants. Gene clusters coding for P fimbriae (F13-*pap*, F71-*fso*, F72-*fst*), type 1 fimbriae (*fim*), and S fimbriae (*sfa*) are given. The *black boxes* represent fimbrial structural proteins; the *shaded boxes* represent adhesin proteins and the *boxes with closed circles* represent proteins involved in regulation of expression. The *arrows* indicate putative promoter regions and transcriptional orientations. The main direction of transcription is from right to left. The two *arrows* in the 5′ region of the *fim* determinant reflect the phase variation process (for further explanations and references see text). **b** Comparison of the physical maps and the gene products of two nonfimbrial adhesin determinants. The *black boxes* represent adhesin proteins; the *box with closed circles* represents a protein which seems to be involved in regulation of transcription. The main direction of transcription is from right to left (for references see text)

fimbriae of serotype F13. A similar observation was made with fimbriae of serotype F12, which may be associated with P-specific adhesins as well as with adhesins which recognize a different receptor located on canine erythrocytes (GARCIA et al. 1988a,b). In addition, it was shown that the genes coding for the nonadhesive minor proteins E and F but not those coding for the G proteins are *trans*-complementable between *pap* and *prs* determinants, a fact which also argues for a specific heterogeneity of the adhesin-specific genes of these two gene clusters.

While mutations in the *papG* gene (and also in the *fsoG* and *fstG* cistrons) abolished hemagglutination, *papE* mutants showed a reduced adherence (NORGREN et al. 1984; LINDBERG et al. 1984, 1986, 1987). Incubation of F_{71} and F_{72} fimbrial

adhesins with anti-FsoE as well as anti-FstE antibodies also inhibited hemagglutination (RIEGMAN et al. 1988). It is therefore suggested that the E gene products directly anchor the adhesins (G proteins) to the fimbriae. Mutants in the F genes of the three determinants, however, show a reduced number of fimbriae per cell. The corresponding proteins (and also the FstG product) seem to act by initiating the assembly of new fimbriae and may be necessary for the determination of the degree of fimbriation (LINDBERG et al. 1987; RIEGMAN et al. 1988).

Electron micrographs which show Pap-positive cells incubated with G-, F-, and E- specific polycolnal antisera indicate the presence of this complex at the tip of the fimbriae (LINDBERG et al. 1987). On the other hand data on the use of FstE- specific monoclonal antiserum argue for the presence of at least the FstE protein in the fimbrial structure, with a preference for the tip of the fiber (DE REE et al. 1987; RIEGMAN et al. 1988; Jann and Hoschützky, this volume).

4.2 Type 1

At the terminal parts of the genetic determinants *fim* and *pil* specific for type 1 fimbrial adhesins, three cistrons, which code for minor fimbrial proteins, were determined (KLEMM and CHRISTIANSEN 1987; MAURER and ORNDORFF 1987). The largest protein encoded by this region (FimH with a size of 32 kd, which is equivalent to pilE with a size of 31 kd) is indicated to be the adhesin mediating a mannose-specific binding to eukaryotic structures. Very recent chemical and immunologic data (HANSON and BRINTON 1988; HANSON et al. 1988) provide evidence that this protein represents the actual adhesin which is located at the tip of fimbriae as well as being interspersed at intervals along the fimbriae (KROGFLD and KLEMM 1988). It is interesting to note that the FimH protein seems to be conserved not only among different *E. coli* strains but also among other members of the *Enterobacteriaceae* family (ABRAHAM et al. 1988b). Mutations in the *fimG* but not in the *fimF* gene result in a hemagglutination-negative phenotype. In addition, both proteins seem to be involved in length modulation of the fimbriae, a fact which was also demonstrated for the *pilF* gene, the equivalent locus to *fimG* in strain J96 (MAURER and ORNDORFF 1987).

The DNA sequence of the *fimE*, *fimF*, and *fimG* cistrons and the predicted amino acid sequence of the proteins show a high degree of homology to the *fimA* (*pilA*) structural gene (KLEMM and CHRISTIANSEN 1987). It is interesting to note that the *fimA* gene products must be present on the cells to confer an adherence-positive phenotype to the strains. This is in contrast to what has been found for P and S fimbriae. In these cases subcloned plasmids can be isolated which are devoid of any fimbrial production but still exhibit hemagglutination (see HACKER et al. 1985).

4.3 S Type

The S-specific adhesin has been isolated and characterized as a 12- to 14-kd protein (depending on the gel system used; MOCH et al. 1987; SCHMOLL et al. 1989a). The gene *sfaS* is located next to the 3' end of the *sfa* determinant (see Fig. 3a). The DNA

sequence of this cistron (SCHMOLL et al. 1987; SCHMOLL et al. 1989a) shows homology to the sequence of the S fimbrial gene. A comparison of the SfaS sequence to the sequences specific for other sialyl-binding proteins (see JACOBS et al. 1986) shows a putative sialyl-binding site which includes a stretch of positively charged amino acids. Electron microscopic data show the presence of the SfaS adhesin protein at the fimbria with a predominance at the tip of the fiber (MOCH et al. 1987).

In contrast to the regions coding for the adhesins of the P fimbrial and type 1 fimbrial determinants, *sfaS* is not located at the extreme 3′ end of the *sfa* determinant. Another cistron (*sfaH*) is located distal to the *sfaS* gene (Fig. 3a). Mutations in the *sfaH* gene result in adhesin-positive but low fimbriated phenotypes, as also observed for P and type 1 fimbrial determinants (*papF* and *fimF* genes, see above).

It can be concluded that the functions of the minor components of the *sfa, pap,* and *fim* determinants resemble each other; their corresponding genes, however, are located at different positions in the determinants.

4.4 A (Non)-fimbrial Adhesins

Two of the cloned A(Non)-fimbrial adhesin determinants (see Table 1) have been analyzed in detail. The determinant coding for the A fimbrial adhesin I (*afaI,* LABIGNE-ROUSSELL et al. 1984, 1985; LABIGNE-ROUSSELL and FALKOW 1988) consists of five genes (Fig. 3b). One gene (*afaE*) located at the 3′ end of the gene cluster is the adhesin structural gene coding for the 16-kd adhesin protein found in the culture supernatant of AfaI-positive strains (see WALZ et al. 1985). The deduced amino acid sequence of AfaE has no homology to the sequence of any of the fimbrial subunit proteins show in Fig. 1. Another two genes, *afaB* and *afaC*, coding for proteins of 30 kd and 100 kd, respectively, are necessary for the expression of AfaI-specific hemagglutination (LABIGNE-ROUSSELL et al. 1985).

The gene organization of the blood group M agglutinin (*bma* described by RHEN et al. 1986a, b) resembles that published for *afaI* (Fig. 3b). The gene specific for the agglutination property is also located at the 3′ terminal end of the determinant and the putative amino acid sequence does not show any homology to the sequences of *afaE* and of fimbrial subunits.

5 Genes Involved in Transport and Assembly

As demonstrated in Sects. 3 and 4, major and minor fimbrial components are involved in assembly of fimbrial structures. In addition mutants have been isolated that show a low but significant intracellular pool of fimbrial subunit proteins but no fiber-like structures (NORGREN et al. 1984; HACKER et al. 1985; KLEMM et al. 1985; VAN DIE et al. 1984b; ORNDORFF and FALKOW 1984a). In all such mutants two or three gene products were abolished, a large protein of about 75–90 kd and

polypeptides 20–30 kd (see Fig. 3a). These proteins are involved in the transport of the fimbrillin subunits and minor proteins to the periplasm and across the outer membrane. In the case of type 1 determinants the genes *fimC* and *fimD* (equivalent to *pilB* and *pilC*; ORNDORFF and FALKOW 1984a; KLEMM et al. 1985) seem to be involved in these functions. The *sfa* determinant codes for three proteins of 20, 26, and 89 kd which are necessary for transport functions (Ludwig and J. Hacker, unpublished observations).

In the *pap* system, the *papD* gene product, which is found in the periplasmic space, the PapC protein, which is part of the outer membrane, and the PapH product are involved in transport and assembly functions (NORGREN et al. 1987). The PapD protein seems to transport the major and minor subunits into the periplasm. The PapD protein forms complexes with PapA, PapE, and PapG and presumably also with other fiber-like proteins (NORMARK et al. 1988). The PapC protein, however, functions as an anchor for the fimbriae in the outer membrane, as demonstrated recently for the FaeD protein encoded by the K88 adhesin gene cluster (MOOI et al. 1986). The *fsoC* gene product, a 75-kd protein encoded by the F_{71} determinant, seems to have the same effect on fimbrial assembly as PapC, while *fsoC* frame shift mutants do not completely block fimbrial biogenesis (RIEGMAN, personal communication). Another Pap fimbriae-like protein, termed PapH, has been analyzed recently (BAGA et al. 1987). Mutants of this gene show a high degree of intact fimbriae in the supernatant. It is therefore suggested that PapH acts as terminator for fimbrial development. The PapH protein itself seems to be located at the base of the fiber which is in contact with the PapC outer membrane protein.

In *trans*-complementation experiments transposon-induced mutations in the regions involved in the transport and assembly of S fimbriae were reexpressed by *foc*-specific plasmids (coding for F1C fimbriae, see OTT et al. 1988). Similar experiments are described for both P fimbrial determinants and type 1-specific gene clusters (RHEN et al. 1985b; CLEGG et al. 1985a,b). In addition, DNA hybrid molecules which consisted of DNA fragments derived from plasmids coding for P fimbriae of different serotypes or for Sfa and F1C fimbriae were isolated (VAN DIE et al. 1986b; OTT et al. 1988). These hybrid DNAs, which were ligated in the transport/assembly regions, were able to produce intact fimbriae. This result suggests a functional complementation of the corresponding proteins. The complementation data support the idea that the determinants coding for Sfa/F1C, type 1, and P fimbriae form related classes of gene clusters, as already suggested on the basis of the fimbrillin-specific DNA sequence data (see Sect. 3).

6 Regulation of Expression

6.1 MR Fimbrial Adhesins

DNA-DNA hybridization studies have shown that the proximal (5′) ends of the determinants coding for MR fimbrial adhesins of P- and S-type and for F1C fimbriae are well conserved (OTT et al. 1987). Transposon-induced mutations in this

region, which is located upstream of the fimbrial structural genes, led to a completely negative phenotype of the corresponding clones. Therefore, it was suggested that regulatory proteins which may act as *trans*-activators are encoded by this region (see Fig. 3a; UHLIN et al. 1985a; HACKER et al. 1986a). To substantiate this observation, *pap-lacZ* and *sfa-lacZ* operon fusions were constructed to map active promotors. In both cases (*pap* and *sfa*) two promotors, which were arranged in opposite orientations, were identified (BAGA et al. 1985; HACKER et al. 1986a). In addition, a week promotor was identified in front of the *sfaA* structural gene (see also Fig 3a).

Two gene products are encoded by the regulatory regions of *pap* and *sfa*. As demonstrated in Fig. 4, these proteins show a very high degree of homology to each other, thereby suggesting a similar function in the regulation of transcription. Another gene encoded by the adhesin determinant *fso* of serotype $F7_1$ shows nearly the same structure as the *papI* and *sfaC* genes (Fig. 4; see RHEN and VÄISÄNEN-RHEN 1987; see also LOW et al. 1987). It was further shown that the gene products encoded by these regions are *trans*-complementable between P, S, and F1C determinants (RHEN et al. 1985b; GÖRANSSON et al. 1988; SCHMOLL 1989).

The fact that the two proteins encoded by the 5′ region of the *sfa* determinant act as positive regulators was further confirmed by the construction of *sfaA-phoA* operon fusions (see Table 3). Using the promoter-probe vector plasmid pCB267, *sfaA* was fused to the gene coding for the enzyme alkaline phosphatase (SCHNEIDER and BECK 1986). The amount of PhoA activity was used as an indicator for the transcriptional activity of the *sfaA* cistron. It is obvious from the data presented that both proteins SfaB and SfaC are necessary for transcriptional activity of *sfaA*. A positive *trans*-complementation of $sfaA$-$phoA^+$, $sfaB^+$, $sfaC^-$ clones was possible following cotransformation of a $sfaC^+$-specific plasmid.

```
            10          20          30          40          50
SfaB:  MAQHEVITRG GTAFLLKLRE SALSSGSMSE EQFFLLIGIS SIHSTRVILA
PapB:  MAHHEVISRS GNAFLLNIRE SVLLFGSMSE MHFFLLIGIS SIHSTRVILA

            60          70          80          90         100
SfaB:  MKTYLVSGHS RKTVCEKYQM NNGYFSTTLG RLTRLNVLVA RLAPYYTDSV
PapB:  MKTYLVGGHS RKTVCEKYQM NNGQFSTTLG RLIRLNALAA RLAPYYTDES

           110
SfaB:  SAIAEAASL*
PapB:  SAFD*


            10          20          30          40          50
SfaC:    MQNEIM GFLSRHNVGK TAEIAEALAV TDYQARYYLL LLEKEGMVQR
PapI:  MSEYMKNEIL EFLNRHNHGK TAEIAEALAV TDYQARYYLL LLEKEGMVQR
Ks71:  MSEYMKNEIL EFLNRHNGGK TAEIAEALAV TDYQARYYLL LLEKAGMVQR

            60          70
SfaC:  SPLRRGMATY WFLKGEMQAG QSCSSTT*
PapI:  SPLRRGMATY WFLKGEMQAG QNCSSTT*
Ks71:  SPLRRGMATY WFLKGEKQAG QSCSSTT*
```

Fig. 4. Comparison of the amino acid sequences of proteins involved in the regulation of transcription of P fimbrial (PapB, PapI, KS71) and S fimbrial (SfaB, SfaC) determinants. The amino acid sequences are given in single letter code. Homologies are indicated by *boxes*

Table 3. Operon fusions between *sfa*-specific cistrons and the gene *phoA* coding for alkaline phosphatase

Resident plasmid	Genotype	Complementary plasmid	Genotype	PhoA units
pTTS267-38	*sfaA-phoA, B⁺, C⁺*	pACYC184		859
pTTS267-38ΔC	*sfaA-phoA, B⁺, C⁻*	pACYC184		306
pTTS267-38ΔC	*sfaA-phoA, B⁺, C⁻*	pANN801-15ΔN	*sfaC⁺*	1017
pTTS267-69	*sfaA-phoA, B⁻, C⁻*	pACYC184		146
pTTS267-69	*sfaA-phoA, B⁻, C⁻*	pANN801-15	*sfaA⁺, B⁺, C⁺*	121
pTTS267-84	*sfaB-phoA, A⁻, C⁺*	pACYC184		2215
pTTS267-1/5	*sfaB-phoA, A⁻, C⁻*	pACYC184		658
pTTS267-1/5	*sfaB-phoA, A⁻, C⁻*	pANN801-15ΔN	*sfaC⁺*	1230
pTTS267-1/8	*sfaC-phoA, B⁻, A⁻*	pACYC184		579
pTTS267-1/8	*sfaC-phoA, B⁻, A⁻*	pANN801-ΔEN	*sfaA⁺, B⁺*	2890
pCB267[a]	*phoA*			5

[a] Vector pCB267 was used for the cloning experiments (see SCHNEIDER and BECK 1986)

A positive *trans*-regulatory effect of PapB and PapI (equivalent to SfaB and SfaC) to the expression of the structural gene *papA* was also observed by Uhlin and co-workers (BAGA et al. 1985; UHLIN et al. 1985a). The intergenic regions between the two regulatory genes and the structural gene are necessary in *cis*-orientation for the thermoregulation of fimbrial production and they also play a role in the repressive effect of trimethoprim on P fimbrial expression (VÄISÄNEN-RHEN et al. 1988). In addition a putative Crp binding site was detected in the intergenic region which should have an influence on catabolic repression of the transcription of the *pap* operon (GÖRANSSON and UHLIN 1984; BAGA et al. 1985). Recently, it was reported that the differences in the expression of the genes *papB*, *papA*, and *papH*, which are all part of the same transcriptional unit, may result from different half-lives of the corresponding mRNA molecules (BAGA et al. 1988). This possibility, together with the presence of a teriminator downstream of *papA*, may explain why the amount of protein produced by the structural gene *papA* is somewhat larger than that produced by *papB* or papH.

6.2 Type 1 Fimbrial Adhesins

The region which regulates the expression of transcription of type 1 fimbrial determinants is also located at the proximal (5′) end of the gene cluster, upstream of the fimbrial structural gene. Sequence studies have shown that the regions involved in regulation of MR and MS fimbrial adhesins are completely different (BAGA et al. 1985; KLEMM 1986; SCHMOLL 1989). In addition it was demonstrated that the regulatory region of the type 1 determinant directs the process of phase variation, i.e., the on-off expression of type 1 fimbriae (EISENSTEIN 1981; FREITAG et al. 1985; ABRAHAM et al. 1985). An invertible DNA element of 314 base pairs (bp) located immediately upstream of the *fimA* gene is responsible for type 1 expression. This element, which is flanked on each side by a 9-bp inverted repeat sequence, carries the *fimA*-specific promoter region. Depending on the direction of integration of this promoter element, the *fimA* gene, together with the whole determinant, will

either be transcribed or not (see Fig. 3a). Two genes, *fimE* and *fimB*, located upstream
of the invertible element are also necessary for phase variation and seem to be
transcribed by their own promoters (KLEMM 1986). The respective proteins of 23 kd
and 25 kd seem to bind to the invertible DNA region and they switch the promoter
element in "on" (FimB) or "off" (FimE) orientation. Both proteins are highly basic
and have a high degree of homology to each other (48% identical amino acids).

It was shown that the type 1 phase variation process is independent of the action
of site-specific recombinases which mediate DNA inversion in *Salmonella typhimurium* (FREITAG et al. 1985). These recombinases, termed Hin proteins, are
involved in phase variation of the *Salmonella* H-antigen (SILVERMAN and SIMON
1980). Another *trans*-acting protein, the integration host factor (IHF), which is
encoded by the *E. coli* genes *himA* (map position at 37) and *hip/himD* (map position
at 20) and which is essential for phage integration and excision, is required for the
phase variation of type 1 fimbriae. Mutants in the gene loci *himA* and *himD* reduce
the frequency of switch events from 10^{-2}–10^{-3} to 10^{-5} per cell per generation
(EISENSTEIN et al. 1987). In addition, a sevenfold reduction of the transcriptional
activity of the *fim* determinant was observed in IHF negative strains as compared
with strains carrying intact IHF coding genes (DORMAN and HIGGINS 1987). It was
shown by sequence analysis that two IHF consensus sequences are located in the
type 1 regulatory region. It is suggested that the IHF protein shows recombinase
activity during the fimbrial switch (KLEMM 1986; EISENSTEIN et al. 1987; DORMAN and
HIGGINS 1987). Recently another DNA region involved in regulation of expression
of the type 1 determinant was identified (ABRAHAM et al. 1988a). A deletion located
downstream of the *fim*-specific structural genes led to an overproduction of the
adhesin protein FimH and the generation of so-called fimbriosomes, thereby
indicating the presence of a repressor presumably encoded by this DNA region.

The observations reviewed here were made for avirulent *E. coli* K-12 strains.
ABRAHAM et al. (1986) have shown however, that phase variation depending on the
switching activity of the invertible element also occurs in clinical isolates. In
addition, a locus termed *hyp* which is similar to the *fimE* gene of *E. coli* K-12 was
analyzed in the *pil* determinant of the pyelonephritic strain J96 (ORNDORFF and
FALKOW 1984b). Furthermore a gene coding for the PilG protein was described for
J96 and may also act as another *trans*-acting factor in type 1 fimbrial expression
(SPEARS et al. 1986). Therefore, it seems that processes similar to that found in *E. coli*
K-12 also occur in wild-type strains, thereby helping the bacteria to bind to mucosal
surfaces (in an "on" status) but preventing their adherence on phagocytic cells (in an
"off" status) which also carry mannose-specific receptor molecules (see OFEK and
SILVERBLATT 1982).

7 Adhesin Determinants Within Virulence Gene Blocks

7.1 Analysis of Structural Virulence Gene Blocks

Using adhesin-specific DNA probes it has been shown that the coding sequences responsible for one particular fimbrial adhesin may be homologous in *E. coli* strains

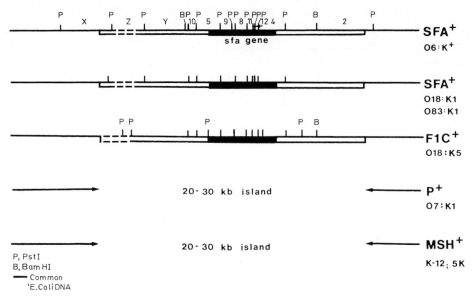

Fig. 5. Genetic maps of S fimbrial (*sfa*) and F1C fimbrial (*foc*) determinants and their flanking regions. The structural genes are indicated by *black boxes*. The *open boxes* represent homolog DNA belonging to the respective structural virulence gene blocks. The strains tested belong to serotypes O6:K⁺, O18:K1, O83:K1, and O18:K5. As controls Sfa⁻ F1C⁻ strains exhibiting P fimbriae or type 1 (Msh) fimbriae were used

derived from different sources. Such an observation was made for DNA sequences which code for S fimbrial adhesins and F1C fimbriae of uropathogenic strains and meningitis isolates and for P adhesin determinants of uropathogenic *E. coli* (OTT et al. 1986, 1988; EKBÄCK et al. 1986). It is remarkable that the homology between the *sfa* and *foc* determinants is not restricted to their coding sequences. It is obvious that the regions flanking the *sfa* and *foc* determinants at both sides are also homologous to each other (see Fig. 5). These DNA regions, which consist of the structural genes for the fimbriae and the flanking sequences (regions of about 25 kb were tested), were termed "virulence gene blocks" because they seem to be specifically inserted into chromosomes of pathogenic *E. coli* isolates but are missing on the chromosomes of non-pathogenic strains (OTT et al. 1988; HACKER et al. 1988).

The flanking regions of the *sfa* and *foc* determinants consist of noncoding DNA sequences. Other adhesin determinants are, however, closely linked to gene clusters which also code for virulence factors. This has been described for sequences which code for G fimbriae and the M agglutinin, which are located very close to each other on the chromosome of a particular *E. coli* 02 strain (RHEN et al. 1986a). Such DNA regions are termed "structural virulence gene blocks" because the different virulence determinants are structurally linked on the chromosomes.

Very often P or P-related fimbrial genes are linked to gene clusters coding for the α-hemolysin, another virulence factor of *E. coli* (HULL et al. 1982; for review see HACKER and HUGHES 1985). Such a linkage of P and Hly determinants has been described for different *E. coli* serotypes, including O4, O6, and O18 strains (Low

et al. 1984; HACKER et al. 1989b; HULL et al. 1988; M. OTT, L. BENDER and J. HACKER, unpublished observations). HIGH et al. (1988) described the linkage of five different adhesin determinants coding for P fimbriae of serotypes $F12_{rel}$, F13, F14, and an unknown F type, F1C fimbriae, and α-hemolysin (see also Table 2). The virulence gene block which is located on the chromosome of a particular O4:K12 strain encompasses a stretch of 50-kb DNA. It can be speculated that the physical linkage of six potential pathogenicity factors may have occurred by transpositional events between the chromosome and plasmid molecules (see Sect. 2).

7.2 Excision of Structural Virulence Gene Blocks from Chromosomes

The observation was made that structural virulence gene blocks are able to disappear from the chromosomes of different strains. It was shown that fimbriated, hemolytic *E. coli* strains are able to generate nonhemolytic, non-fimbriated mutants with relatively high frequencies (HACKER et al. 1983; KNAPP et al. 1984). As shown for the *E. coli* O6 strain 536 and for strains of serotypes O18:K1 and O4:K6, the structural genes coding for P (and P-related) fimbriae and for hemolysin were completely deleted from the chromosomes of the mutant strains (see Fig. 6).

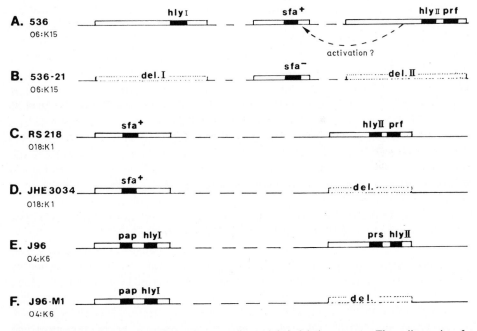

Fig. 6. Model of the chromosomes of wild-type strains and their deletion mutants. The coding regions for fimbriae or hemolysin are indicated by *black boxes*; the entire virulence gene blocks are indicated by *open boxes*. Strain 536 and the mutant 536-21 show structural and functional virulence gene blocks. In contrast the strains IHE 3034, RS218, J96, and J96-M1 only carry structural virulence gene blocks on their chromosomes. The *boxes with broken lines* represent chromosomal deletions (for references see text). *Abbreviations: hly,* hemolysin; *sfa,* S fimbrial adhesins; *prf,* P-related fimbriae; *del.,* deletion; *pap,* pili associated with pyelonephritis; *prs,* P-related sequence

Using DNA probes specific for the flanking sequences of the P-Hly coding regions it was demonstrated that at least in the case of the O6 strain 536 DNA regions of about 70–100 kb can be deleted from the chromosomes of the respective isolates (KNAPP et al. 1986). The deletion events are specific processes which include the left and right boundary sequences of the P-Hly virulence blocks. Such deletions of fimbrial determinants together with gene clusters coding for α-hemolysin from the chromosomes of wild-type strains may also occur in nature. It is generally accepted that the longer a patient suffer from a UTI, the greater the chances of isolating non-virulent strains from the urine. The non-virulent variants may be "deletion mutants" of former fully virulent strains which may have lost structural virulence gene blocks (see HACKER et al. 1989b).

7.3 Occurrence of Functional Virulence Gene Blocks in Strain 536

As already mentioned above, strain 536 carries gene clusters which code for two different α-hemolysins (hemolysin I and II) and P-related fimbriae (Prf). Mutants like strain 536-21 have lost these three determinants by deletional events. As indicated in Table 4, the production of S fimbrial adhesins and of type 1 fimbriae was also absent in these mutants.

Mutants which have lost the HlyII/Prf coding region but retained the HlyI coding region exhibited a negative phenotype for the two adhesins S fimbriae and type 1 fimbriae, whereas HlyI-negative, HlyII/Prf-positive strains were also Sfa and type I positive. Therefore, it can be concluded that the expression of the latter two fimbrial gene clusters is strongly associated with the presence of the HlyII/Prf coding DNA region. It was further demonstrated that the regulation, at least for the S fimbrial adhesin determinant, takes place at the transcriptional level (KNAPP et al. 1986). These data argue for the presence of a factor, encoded by the *hlyII/prf* virulence gene block, which functions as a positive *trans*-regulator, promoting the transcription of *sfa*. The fact that a region coding for two linked pathogenicity factors (Prf and Hly) directs the expression of another two nonlinked pathogenicity determinants (Sfa and type I) lends support to the existence of functional virulence gene blocks (see Fig. 6).

Similar phenomena were described for pathogenic strains of *Vibrio cholerae* and *Bordetella pertussis* (WEISS and HEWLETT 1986; MILLER et al. 1987). In such strains

Table 4. Properties of *E. coli* strain 536 and its mutants

Property	Strain			
	536	536-21	536-114	536-25
Hemolysin I	Active	Deleted	Deleted	Active
Hemolysin II	Active	Deleted	Active	Deleted
P-related	Active	Deleted	Active	Deleted
S fimbrial adhesin	Active	Reduced expression	Active	Reduced expression
Type 1	Active	Reduced expression	Active	Reduced expression

also *trans*-acting factors were necessary for the expression of different pathogenicity determinants, including gene clusters which code for adhesins. It therefore seems that the occurrence of functional virulence gene blocks is not restricted to *E. coli*.

8 Concluding Remarks

In the last decade, and especially the last 5 years, numerous determinants coding for fimbriae and adhesins have been cloned and genetically characterized (see Table 2). Despite this the following aspects have yet to be resolved.

1. Which sequences are necessary for the binding specificity of adhesins? It has been speculated that "consensus sequences" exist and these would explain the constant binding behavior of adhesins consisting of non-homologous proteins (e.g., different P fimbriae).

2. How do adhesin-specific gene products interact in the processes of transport and assembly? Different gene products involved in these processes have been determined but their complex interplay which leads to functional fimbrial adhesins has yet to be resolved.

3. How are adhesin genes regulated in wild-type strains? Studies on the regulation of transcription were performed with cloned determinants. The genetic "background" of the strains, however, seems to be important for regulatory events. In addition the copy effects of plasmids may influence the regulation of genes. Therefore the regulation of adhesin determinants should be studied in wild-type strains see (SCHMOLL et al. 1989b).

4. What kinds of molecular event are responsible for the phase variation of determinants other than type1? In the case of P and S fimbriae an on-off production of the fimbriae was described (RHEN et al. 1983b; NOWICKI et al. 1986; SAUKKONEN et al. 1988). The processes which lead to phase variation of these gene clusters seem to be different from those which are described for type 1 determinants.

5. How do *trans*-acting regulatory factors influence fimbrial expression? It has been shown that the expression of S fimbriae depends on factors which are encoded by genes not linked to the adhesin gene clusters. Factors like the IHF protein involved in type 1 expression also have to be determined and described for other adhesins.

6. What kinds of environmental signal play a role in fimbrial production? In order to describe the role of adhesins in infections more precisely the conditions of expression in wild-type strains and also in vivo have to be determined.

7. Does the genetic structure of *E. coli* adhesin determinants fit the "cassette model" of *Neisseria gonorrhoeae*? Some data, showing a conservation of special regions located next to sequences which are completely different among two or three adhesin determinants (e.g., regulatory genes in the case of P and S determinants or adhesins and minor proteins in the case of *pap* and *prs*), argue for an occurrence of processes similar to the generation of pili of *Neisseria gonorrhoeae* by a rearrangement of "cassettes" (see STERN and MEYER 1987). Do inactive copies of cassettes also exist on the *E. coli* chromosome?

8. How have adhesin-carrying strains evolved? Some data indicate a special development of extraintestinal *E. coli* pathogens which may include a "gene pick up" of fimbrial and hemolysin determinants (perhaps from plasmids or from different parts of the chromosomes, see HACKER et al. 1989b), the activation of genes during the acute phases of infection, and their subsequent loss (by deletion) in late phases of infectious processes. The dynamics of such processes have to be further elucidated.

In addition it is suggested that molecular studies with adhesin determinants should be yield new practical applications in order to improve diagnostic tools and to develop better drugs and vaccines for prevention.

Acknowledgments. I wish to thank many colleagues, too numerous to mention, who provided me with unpublished results, reprints, and helpful comments. In addition I thank Irma Van Die (Utrecht), Balakrishna Pillay (Würzburg), and Colin Hughes (Cambridge) for critical reading of the manuscript and Angelika Zirngibl (Würzburg) for editorial assistance. The work was supported by the Deutsche Forschungsgemeinschaft (Ha 1434/1-6).

References

Abe C, Schmitz S, Moser I, Boulnois G, High NJ, Orskov I, Orskov F, Jann B, Jann K (1987) Monoclonal antibodies with fimbrial F1C, F12, F13and F14 specificities with fimbriae from *E. coli* O4:K12:H⁻. Microb Pathogen 2: 71–77

Abraham JM, Freitag CS, Clements JR, Eisenstein BI (1985) An invertible element of DNA controls phase variation of type 1 fimbriae of *Escherichia coli*. Proc Natl Acad Sci USA 82: 5724–5727

Abraham JM, Freitag CS, Gander RM, Clements JR, Thomas VL, Eisenstein BI (1986) Fimbrial phase variation and DNA rearrangements in uropathogenic isolates of *Escherichia coli*. Mol Biol Med 3: 495–508

Abraham SN, Goguen JD, Beachey EH (1988a) Hyperadhesive mutant of type 1-fimbriated *Escherichia coli* associated with formation of FimH organelles (fimbriosomes). J Bacteriol 56: 1023–1029

Abraham SN, Sun D, Dale JB, Beachey EH (1988b) Conservation of the D-mannose-adhesion protein among type 1 fimbriated members of the family *Enterobacteriaceae*. Nature 336: 682–684

Achtman M, Pluschke G (1986) Clonal analysis of descent and virulence among selected *Escherichia coli*. Annu Rev Microbiol 4: 185–210

Bachmann BJ (1987) Linkage map of *Escherichia coli* K-12, Edition 7. In: Neidhardt FC, Ingraham JL, Low BK, Magasanik B, Schaechter M, Umbarger HE (eds) *Escherichia coli* and *Salmonella typhimurium*. Cellular and molecular biology, vol II. Washington, pp 807–876

Baga M, Normark S, Hardy J, O'Hanley P, Lark D, Olsson O, Schoolnik G, Falkow S (1984) Nucleotide sequence of the *papA* gene encoding the Pap pilus subunit of human uropathogenic *Escherichia coli*. J Bacteriol 157: 330–333

Baga M, Göransson M, Normark S, Uhlin BE (1985) Transcriptional activation of a Pap pilus virulence operon from uropathogenic *Escherichia coli*. EMBO J 4: 3887–3893

Baga M, Norgren M, Normak S (1988) Biogenesis of *E. coli* Pap Pili. PapH, a minor pilin subunit involved in cell anchoring and length modulation. Cell 49: 241–251

Baga M, Göransson M, Normark S (1988) Processed mRNA with differential stability in the regulation of *E. coli* pilin gene expression. Cell 52: 197–206

Berger H, Hacker J, Juarez A, Hughes C, Geobel W (1982) Cloning of the chromosomal determinants encoding hemolysin production and mannose-resistant hemagglutination in *Escherichia coli*. J Bacteriol 152: 1241–1247

Clegg S (1982) Cloning of genes determining the production of mannose-resistant fimbriae in a uropathogenic strain of *Escherichia coli* belonging to serogroup O6. Infect Immun 38: 739–744

Clegg S, Pierce JK (1983) Organization of genes responsible for the production of mannose-resistant fimbriae of a uropathogenic *Escherichia coli* isolate. Infect Immun 42: 900–906

Clegg S, Hull S, Hull R, Pruckler J (1985a) Construction and comparison of recombinant plasmids encoding type 1 fimbriae of members of the family *Enterobacteriaceae*. Infect Immun 48: 275–279

Clegg S, Pruckler J, Purcell BK (1985b) Complementation analysis of recombinant plasmids encoding type 1 fimbriae of members of the family *Enterobacteriaceae*. Infect Immun 50: 338–340

De Ree JM, Schwillens P, Van den Bosch JF (1985a) Molecular cloning of F11 fimbriae from a uropathogenic *Escherichia coli* and characterization of fimbriae with polyclonal and monoclonal antibodies. FEMS Microbiol Lett 29: 91–97

De Ree JM, Schwillens P, Van den Bosch JF (1985b) Monoclonal antibodies that recognize the P fimbriae $F7_1$, $F7_2$, F9 and F11 from uropathogenic *Escherichia coli*. Infect Immun 50: 900–904

De Ree JM, Schwillens P, Promes L, Van Die I, Bergmans H, Van den Bosch JF (1985c) Molecular cloning and characterization of F9 fimbriae from a uropathogenic *Escherichia coli*. FEMS Microbiol Lett 26: 163–169

De Ree JM, Schwillens P, Van den Bosch JF (1987) Monoclonal antibodies raised against Pap fimbriae recognize minor component(s) involved in receptor binding. Microb Pathogen 2: 113–121

Dorman CJ, Higgins CF (1987) Fimbrial phase variation in *Escherichia coli*: dependence on integration host factor and homologies with other site-specific recombinases. J Bacteriol 169: 3840–3843

Duguid JP, Smith IW, Dempster G, Edmunds PN (1955) Non-flagellar filamentous appendages ("fimbriae") and hemagglutination activity in *Bacterium coli*. J Pathol Bacteriol 70: 335–348

Eisenstein BI (1981) Phase variation of type 1 fimbriae in *Escherichia coli* is under transcriptional control. Science 214: 337–339

Eisenstein BI, Sweet DS, Vaughn V, Friedman DI (1987) Integration host factor is required for the DNA inversion that controls phase variation in *Escherichia coli*. Proc Natl Acad Sci USA 84: 6506–6510

Ekbäck G, Mörner S, Lund B, Normark S (1986) Correlation of genes in the *pap* cluster to expression of globoside-specific adhesin by uropathogenic *Escherichia coli*. FEMS Microbiol Lett 34: 355–360

Evans DJ, Evans DG (1983) Classification of pathogenic *Escherichia coli* according to serotype and the production of virulence factors, with special reference to colonization factor antigens. Rev Infect Dis 5 (S4) S682–S701

Freitag CS, Abraham JM, Clements JR, Eisenstein BI (1985) Genetic analysis of the phase variation control of expression of type 1 fimbriae in *Escherichia coli*. J Bacteriol 162: 668–675

Garcia E, Bergmans HEN, Van den Bosch JF, Orskov I, Van den Zeijst BAM, Gaastra W (1988a) Isolation and characterization of dog uropathogenic *Escherichia coli* strains and their fimbriae. Antonie van Leeuwenhoek 54: 149–163

Garcia E, Hamers A, Bergmans H, Bernard A, Van der Zeijst B, Jaastra W (1988b) Adhesion of canine and human uropathogenic *Escherichia coli* and *Proteus mirabilis* to canine and human epithelial cells. Curr Microbiol 17: 333–337

Goldhar J, Perry R, Golecki JR, Hoschützky H, Jann B, Jann K (1987) Nonfimbrial, mannose-resistant adhesins from uropathogenic *Escherichia coli* O83:K1:H4 and O14:K?:H11. Infect Immun 55: 1837–1842

Göransson M, Uhlin BE (1984) Environmental temperature regulates transcription of a virulence pili operon in *E. coli*. EMBO J 3: 2885–2888

Göransson M, Forsman K, Uhlin BE (1988) Functional and structural homology among regulatory cistrons of pili-adhesin determinants on an *Escherichia coli*. MGG 212: 412–417

Hacker J, Hughes C (1985) Genetics of *Escherichia coli* hemolysin. In: Current topics in microbiology and immunology, vol 118 Springer, Berlin Heidelberg New York, pp. 139–162

Hacker J, Knapp S, Goebel W (1983) Spontaneous deletions and flanking regions of the chromosomally inherited hemolysin determinant of an *Escherichia coli* 06 strain. J Bacteriol 154: 1146–1152

Hacker J, Schmidt G, Hughes C, Knapp S, Marget M, Goebel W (1985) Cloning and characterization of genes involved in production of mannose-resistant, neuraminidase-susceptible (X) fimbriae from a uropathogenic O6:K15:H31 *Escherichia coli* strain. Infect Immun 47: 434–440

Hacker J, Jarchau T, Knapp S, Marre R, Schmidt G, Schmoll T, Goebel W (1986a) Genetic and in vivo studies with S-fimbrial antigens and related virulence determinants of extraintestinal *Escherichia coli* strains. In: Lark D (ed) Protein–carbohydrate interactions in biological systems. Academic, London, pp 125–133

Hacker J, Ott M, Schmidt G, Hull R, Goebel W (1986b) Molecular cloning of the F8 fimbrial antigen from *Escherichia coli*. FEMS Microbiol Lett 36: 139–144

Hacker J, Ott M, Bender L, Schmittroth M, Tschäpe H, Achtmann M (1989a) Distribution of genetic determinants coding for hemolysin, aerobactin and adhesin production in *Escherichia coli* K1 isolates. Infect Immun (to be published)

Hacker J, Schmoll T, Ott M, Marre R, Hof H, Jarchau T, Knapp S, Then I, Goebel W (1989b) Genetic structure and expression of virulence determinants from uropathogenic *E. coli* strains. In: Kass E (ed.) Host–parasite interactions in urinary tract infections; Studies of infectious disease research, Univ of Chicago Press, pp. 144–156.

Hagberg L, Hull R, Falkow S, Freter R, Svanborg-Eden C (1983) Contribution of adhesion to bacterial persistence in the mouse urinary tract. Infect Immun 40: 265–272

Hales BA, Amyes SGB (1986a) Acquisition of a gene encoding mannose-resistant haemagglutionation fimbriae by a resistance plasmid during long-term urinary tract infection. J Med Microbiol 22: 297–301

Hales BA, Amyes SGB (1986b) The transfer of genes encoding production of mannose-resistant haemagglutinating fimbriae from uropathogenic *enterobacteria* J Gen Microbiol 132: 2243–2247

Hales BA, Beverley-Clarke H, High NJ, Jann K, Goldhar J, Boulnois GJ (1988) Molecular cloning and characterization of the genes for a non-fimbrial adhesin from *Escherichia coli*. Microb Pathogen 5: 9–17

Hanson MS, Brinton CC (1988) Identification and characterization of *E. coli* type I pilus tip adhesion protein. Nature 323: 265–268

Hanson MS, Hempel J, Brinton CC (1988) Purification of the *Escherichia coli* type I pilin and minor pilus proteins and partial characterization of the adhesin protein. J Bacteriol 170: 3350–3358

High NJ, Hales BA, Jann K, Boilnois GJ (1988) A block of urovirulence genes encoding multiple fimbriae and hemolysin in *Escherichia coli* O4:K12:H⁻. Infect Immun 56: 513–517

Hoekstra WPM, Felix HS, Theilemans M, Pere A, Korhonen TK (1986) Chromosomal location of P fimbrial gene clusters in uropathogenic *Escherichia coli* strains. Proceedings of the 14th International Congress of microbiology, IUMS, Manchester, England

Hopp TP, Woods KR (1981) Prediction of protein antigenic determinants from amino acid sequences. Proc Natl Acad Sci USA 78: 3824–3828

Hoschützky H, Lottspeich F, Jann K (1989) Isolation and characterization of the α-galactosyl-1, 4-β-galactosyl-specific adhesin (P adhesin) from fimbriated *Escherichia coli*. Infect Immun 57: 76–81

Hughes C, Hacker J, Roberts A, Goebel W (1983) Hemolysin production as a virulence marker in symptomatic and asymptomatic urinary tract infections caused by *Escherichia coli*. Infect Immun 39: 546–551

Hull RA, Gill RE, Hsu P, Minshew BH, Falkow S (1981) Construction and expression of recombinant plasmids encoding type 1 or D-mannose-resistant pili from a urinary tract infection *Escherichia coli* isolate. Infect Immun 33: 933–938

Hull SI, Hull RA, Minshew BH, Falkow S (1982) Genetics of hemolysin of *Escherichia coli*. J Bacteriol 151: 1006–1012

Hull S, Clegg S, Svanborg Eden C, Hull R (1985) Multiple forms of genes in pyelonephritogenic *Escherichia coli* encoding adhesins binding globoseries glycolipid receptors. Infect Immun 47:80–83

Hull R, Bieler S, Falkow S, Hull S (1986) Chromosomal map position of genes encoding P adhesins in uropathogenic *Escherichia coli*. Infect Immun 51: 693–695

Hull SI, Bieler S, Hull RA (1988) Restriction fragment length polymorphism and multiple copies of DNA sequences homologous with probes for p fimbriae and hemolysin genes among uropathogenic *Escherichia coli*. Can J Microbiol 34: 307–311

Jacobs AAC, van den Berg PA, Bak H, de Graaf FK (1986) Localization of lysine residues in the binding domain of the K99 fibrillar subunit of enterotoxigenic *Escherichia coli*. Biochim Biophys Acta 872: 92–97

Jann K, Jann B, Schmidt G (1981) SDS polyacrylamide gel electrophoresis and serological analysis of pili from *Escherichia coli* from different pathogenic origin. FEMS Microbiol Lett 11: 21–25

Jones GW, Rutter JM (1974) The association of K88 antigen with hemagglutination activity in porcine strains of *Escherichia coli*. J Gen Microbiol 84: 135–144

Källenius G, Möllby R, Svenson SB, Winberg J, Lundblad A, Svensson S (1980) The pᵏ antigen as receptor of pyelonephritic *E. coli*. FEMS Microbiol Lett 7: 297–300

Keith BR, Maurer L, Spears PA, Orndorff PE (1986) Receptor-binding function of type I pili effects bladder colonization by a clinical isolate of *Escherichia coli*. Infect Immun 53: 693–696

Klemm P (1984) The *fimA* gene encoding the type 1 fimbrial subunit of *Escherichia coli*. Eur J Biochem 143: 395–399

Klemm P (1985) Fimbrial adhesins. Rev Infect Dis 7: 321–340

Klemm P (1986) Two regulatory *fim* genes, *fimB* and *fimE*, control the phase variation of type 1 fimbriae in *Escherichia coli*. EMBO J 5: 1389–1393

Klemm P (1987) Three *fim* genes required for the regulation of length and mediation of adhesion of *Escherichia coli* type 1 fimbriae. MGG 208: 439–445

Klemm P, Jorgensen BJ, Van Die I, De Ree H, Bergmans H (1985) The *fim* genes responsible for synthesis of type 1 fimbriae in *Escherichia coli*, cloning and genetic organization. MGG 199: 410–414

Knapp S, Hacker J, Then I, Müller D, Goebel W (1984) Multiple copies of hemolysin genes and associated sequences in the chromosome of uropathogenic *Escherichia coli* strains. J Bacteriol 159: 1027–1033

Knapp S, Hacker J, Jarchau T, Goebel W (1986) Large instable regions in the chromosome affect virulence properties of a uropathogenic *Escherichia coli* O6 strain. J Bacteriol 168: 22–30

Korhonen TK, Väisänen-Rhen V, Rhen M, Pere A, Parkkinen J, Finne J (1984) *Escherichia coli* fimbriae recognizing sialyl galactosides. J Bacteriol 159: 762–766

Korhonen TK, Valtonen MV, Paarkkinen J, Väisänen-Rhen V, Finne J, Orskove I, Orskov F, Svenson SB, Mäkelä PH (1985) Serotype, hemolysin production and receptor recognition of *Escherichia coli* strains associated with neonatal sepsis and meningitis. Infect Immun 48: 486–491

Krallmann-Wetzel U, Ott M, Hacker J, Schmidt G (1989) Chromosomal mapping of genes encoding mannose-sensitive (type I) and mannose-resistant F8 (P) fimbriae of *Escherichia coli* O18:K5:H5. FEMS Microbiol Lett 58: B15–B22

Krogfeld KA, Klemm P (1988) Investigation of minor components of *Escherichia coli* type I fimbriae: protein chemical and immunological aspects. Microb Pathogen 4: 231–238

Labigne-Roussell AF, Lark D, Schoolnik G, Falkow S (1984) Cloning and expression of an afimbrial adhesin (AfaI) responsible for blood group-independent, mannose-resistant hemagglutination from a pyelonephritic *Escherichia coli* strain. Infect Immun 46: 251–259

Labigne-Roussell A, Schmidt MA, Walz W, Falkow S (1985) Genetic organization of the afimbrial adhesin operon and nucleotide sequence from a uropathogenic *Escherichia coli* gene encoding an afimbrial adhesin. J Bacteriol 162: 1285–1292

Labigne-Roussell A, Falkow S (1988) Distribution and degree of heterogeneity of the afimbrial-adhesin-encoding operon (*afa*) among uropathogenic *Escherichia coli* isolates. Infect Immun 56: 640–648

Lindberg FP, Lund B, Normark S (1984) Genes of pyelonephritogenic *E. coli* required for digalactoside-specific agglutination of human cells. EMBO J 3: 1167–1173

Lindberg FP, Lund B, Normark S (1986) Gene products specifying adhesion of uropathogenic *Escherichia coli* are minor components of pili. Proc Natl Acad Sci USA 83: 1891–1895

Lindberg F, Lund B, Johansson L, Normark S (1987) Localization of the receptor-binding protein adhesin at the tip of the bacterial pilus. Nature 328: 84–87

Low D, David V, Lark D, Schoolnik G, Falkow S (1984) Gene clusters governing the production of hemolysin and mannose-resistant hemagglutination are closely linked in *Escherichia coli* serotype O4 and O6 isolates from urinary tract infections. Infect Immun 43: 353–358

Low D, Robinson EN, McGee ZA, Falkow S (1987) The frequency of expression of pyelonephritis-associated pili is under regulatory control. Mol Microbiol 1: 335–346

Lund B, Lindberg FP, Baga M, Normark S (1985) Globoside-specific adhesins of uropathogenic *Escherichia coli* are encoded by similar transcomplementable gene clusters. J Bacteriol 162: 1293–1301

Lund B, Lindberg F, Marklund BI, Normark S (1987) The PapG protein is the α-D-galactopyranosyl-(1-4)-β-D-galactopyranose-binding adhesin of uropathogenic *Escherichia coli*. Proc Natl Acad Sci USA 84: 5898–5902

Lund B, Lindberg F, Normark S (1988a) Structure and antigenic properties of the tip-located P-pilus proteins of uropathogenic *Escherichia coli*. J Bacteriol 170: 1887–1894

Lund B, Marklund BI, Strömberg N, Lindberg F, Karlsson KA, Normark S (1988b) Uropathogenic *Escherichia coli* can express serologically identical pili of different receptor binding specificities. Mol Microbiol 2: 255–263

Marre R, Hacker J (1987) Role of S- and common type I fimbriae of *Escherichia coli* in experimental upper and lower urinary tract infection. Microb Pathogen 2: 223–226

Maurer L, Orndorff PE (1985) A new locus, *pilE*, required for the binding of type 1 piliated *Escherichia coli* to erythrocytes. FEMS Microbiol Lett 30: 59–66

Maurer L, Orndorff PE (1987) Identification and characterization of genes determining receptor binding and pilus length of *Escherichia coli* type I pili. J Bacteriol 169: 640–645

Miller VL, Taylor RK, Mekalanos JJ (1987) Cholera toxin transcriptional activator ToxR is a transmembrane DNA binding protein. Cell 48: 271–279

Minion FC, Abraham SN, Beachey EH, Goguen JD (1986) The genetic determinant of adhesive function in type 1 fimbriae of *Escherichia coli* is distinct from the gene encoding the fimbrial subunit. J Bacteriol 165: 1033–1036

Mooi FR, Claasen I, Bakker D, Kuipters H, De Graaf FK (1986) Regulation and structure of an *Escherichia coli* gene coding for an outer membrane protein involved in export of K88ab fimbrial subunits. Nucleic Acids Res 14: 2443–2457

Moch T, Hoschützky H, Hacker J, Krönke KD, Jann K (1987) Isolation and characterization of the α-sialyl-β-2,3-galactosyl-specific adhesin from fimbriated *Escherichia coli*. Proc Natl Acad Sci USA 84: 3462–3466

Norgren M, Normark S, Lark D, O'Hanley P, Schoolnik G, Falkow S, Svanborg-Eden C, Baga M, Uhlin

BE (1984) Mutations in *E. coli* cistrons affecting adhesion to human cells do not abolish Pap pili fiber formation. EMBO J 3: 1159–1165

Norgren M, Baga M, Tennett JM, Normark S (1987) Nucleotide sequence, regulation and functional analysis of the *papC* gene required for cell surface localization of *pap* pili of uropathogenic *Escherichia coli*. Mol Microbiol 1: 169–178

Normark S, Lark D, Hull R, Norgren M, Baga M, O'Hanley P, Schoolnik G, Falkow S (1983) Genetics of digalactoside-binding adhesin from a uropathogenic *Escherichia coli* strain. Infect Immun 41: 942–949

Normark S, Baga M, Göransson M, Lindberg FP, Lund B, Norgren M, Uhlin BE (1986) Genetics and biogenesis of *Escherichia coli* adhesins. In: Mirelman D (ed) Microbial lectins and agglutinins: properties and biological activity. Wiley, New York, pp 113–143

Normark S, Hultgren S, Marklund BI, Strömberg N, Tennent J (1988) Biogenesis of pili adhesins associated with urinary tract infectious *Escherichia coli*. Antonie Van Leeuwenhoek 54: 405–409

Nowicki B, Vuopio-Varkila J, Viljanen P, Korhonen TK, Mäkelä PH (1986) Fimbrial phase variation and systemic *E. coli* infection studied in the mouse peritonitis model. Microb Pathogen 1: 335–347

Nowicki B, Barrish JP, Korhonen TK, Hull RA, Hull SI (1987) Molecular cloning of the *Escherichia coli* O75X adhesin. Infect Immun 55: 2268–2276

Nowicki B, Moulds J, Hull R, Hull S (1988) A hemagglutinin of uropathogenic *Escherichia coli* recognizes the Dr blood group antigen. Infect Immun 56: 1057–1060

Ofek I, Silverblatt F (1982) Bacterial surface structures involved in adhesion to phagocytic and epithelial cells. In: Schlessinger D (ed) Microbiology 1982. American Society for Microbiology, Washington, pp. 296–300

O'Hanley P, Lark D, Falkow S, Schoolnik G (1985) Molecular basis of *Escherichia coli* colonization of the upper urinary tract in BALB/c mice. J Clin Invest 75: 347–360

Orndorff PE, Falkow S (1984a) Organization and expression of genes responsible for type 1 piliation in *Escherichia coli*. J Bacteriol 159: 736–744

Orndorff PE, Falkow S (1984b) Identification and characterization of a gene product that regulates type 1 piliation in *Escherichia coli*. J Bacteriol 160: 61–66

Orndorff PE, Falkow S (1985) Nucleotide sequence of *pilA*, the gene encoding the structural component of type 1 pili in *Escherichia coli*. J Bacteriol 162: 454–457

Orskov I, Orskov F (1983) Serology of *Escherichia coli* fimbriae. Prog Allergy 33: 80–105

Orskov I, Orskov F (1985) *Escherichia coli* in extraintestinal infections. J Hyg Camb 95: 551–575

Orskov I, Orskov F, Jann B, Jann K (1977) Serology, chemistry and genetics of O and K antigens of *Escherichia coli* Microbiol Rev 41: 667–710

Ott M, Hacker J, Schmoll T, Jarchau T, Korhonen TK, Goebel W (1986) Analysis of the genetic determinants coding for the S-fimbrial adhesin (*sfa*) in different *Escherichia coli* strains causing meningitis or urinary tract infections. Infect Immun 54: 646–653

Ott M, Schmoll T, Goebel W, Van Die I, Hacker J (1987) Comparison of the genetic determinant coding for the S-fimbrial adhesin (*sfa*) of *Escherichia coli* to other chromosomally encoded fimbrial determinants. Infect Immun 55: 1940–1943

Ott M, Hoschützky H, Jann K, Van Die I, Hacker J (1988) Gene clusters for S fimbrial adhesin (*sfa*) and F1C fimbriae (*fod*) of *Escherichia coli*: comparative aspects of structure and function. J Bacteriol 170: 3983–3990

Parkkinen J, Rogers GN, Korhonen TK, Dahr W, Finne J (1986) Identification of the O-linked sialyloligosaccharides of glycophorin as the erythrocyte receptors for S-fimbriated *Escherichia coli*. Infect Immun 54: 37–42

Pawelzik B, Heesemann J, Hacker J, Opferkuch W (1988) Cloning and characterization of a new type of fimbriae (S/F1C related fimbria) expressed by an *Escherichia coli* O75:K1:H7 blood culture. Infect Immun 56: 2918–2924

Pere A, Leinonen M, Väisänen-Rhen V, Rhen M, Korhonen TK (1985) Occurrence of type 1C fimbriae on *Escherichia coli* strains isolated from human extraintestinal infections. J Gen Microbiol 131: 1705–1711

Rhen M (1985) Characterization of DNA fragments encoding fimbriae of the uropathogenic *Escherichia coli* strain KS71. J Gen Microbiol 131: 571–580

Rhen M, Väisänen-Rhen V (1987) Nucleotide sequence analysis of a P fimbrial regulatory element of the uropathogenic *Escherichia coli* strain KS71 (O4:K12). Microb Pathogen 3: 387–391

Rhen M, Knowles J, Penttila ME, Sarvas M, Korhonen TK (1983a) P fimbriae of *Escherichia coli*: molecular cloning of DNA fragments containing the structural genes. FEMS Microbiol Lett 19: 119–123

Rhen M, Mäkelä PH, Korhonen TK (1983b) P-fimbriae of *Escherichia coli* are subject to phase variation. FEMS Microbiol Lett 19: 267–271

Rhen M, Van Die I, Rhen V, Bergmans H (1985a) Comparison of the nucleotide sequence of the genes encoding the KS71A and F7 fimbrial antigens of uropathogenic Escherichia coli. Eur J Biochem 151: 573–577

Rhen M, Väisänen-Rhen V, Korhonen TK (1985b) Complementation and regulatory interaction between two cloned fimbrial gene clusters of Escherichia coli strain KS71 MGG 200: 60–64

Rhen M, Klemm P, Korhonen TK (1986a) Identification of two hemagglutinins of Escherichia coli, N-acetyl-D-glucosamine-specific fimbriae and a blood group M-specific agglutinin, by cloning the corresponding genes in Escherichia coli K-12. J Bacteriol 168: 1234–1242

Rhen M, Väisänen-Rhen V, Saraste M, Korhonen TK (1986b) Organization of genes expressing the blood-group-M-specific hemagglutinin of Escherichia coli: identification and nucleotide sequence of the M-agglutinin subunit gene. Gene 49: 351–360

Riegman N, Van Die I, Leunissen J, Hoekstra W, Bergmans H (1988) Biogenesis of F7$_1$ and F7$_2$ fimbriae of uropathogenic Escherichia coli: influence of the FsoF and FsoG proteins and localization of the Fso/FstE protein. Mol Microbiol 2: 73–80

Saukkonen KMJ, Nowicki B, Leinonen M (1988) Role of type I and S fimbriae in the pathogenesis of Escherichia coli O18:K1 bacteremia and meningitis in the infant rat. Infect Immun 56: 892–897

Schmidt MA, O'Hanley P, Lark D, Schoolnik GK (1988) Synthetic peptides corresponding to protective epitopes of Escherichia coli digalactoside-binding piling prevent infection in a murine pyelonephritis model. Proc Natl Acad Sci USA 85: 1247–1251

Schmoll T, Hacker J, Goebel W (1987) Nucleotide sequence of the sfaA gene coding for the S fimbrial protein subunit of Escherichia coli. FEMS Microbiol Lett 41: 229–235

Schmoll T (1989) Molekulargenetische Analyse einer Adhäsin–Determinante von Escherichia coli. Phil Diss Univ Würzburg

Schmoll T, Hoschützky H, Morschhäuser J, Lottspeich F, Jann K, Hacker J (1989a) Analysis of genes coding for the Sialic acid–binding adhesin and two other minor fimbrial subunits of the S fimbrial adhesin determinant of Escherichia coli. Mol Microbiol in press.

Schmoll T, Ott M, Hacker J (1989b) Environmental signals controlling the expression of the S fimbrial adhesin of an Escherichia coli pathogen: construction of a site specific wild-type fusion. J Bacteriol (to be published)

Schneider K, Beck CF (1986) Promoter probe vectors for the analysis of divergently promoters. Gene 42: 37–48

Silvermann M, Simon M (1980) Phase variation genetic analysis of switching mutants. Cell 19: 845–854

Spears PA, Schauer D, Orndorff PE (1986) Metastable regulation of type 1 piliation in Escherichia coli and isolation and characterization of a phenotypically stable mutant. J Bacteriol 168: 179–185

Stern A, Meyer TF (1987) Common mechanism controlling phase and antigenic variation in pathogenic Neisseriae. Mol Microbiol 1: 5–12

Väisänen-Rhen V, Saarela S, Rhen M (1988) Mutations in cloned Escherichia coli P fimbriae genes that makes fimbriae production resistant to suppression by trimethoprim. Microbiol Pathogen 4: 369–377

Svanborg-Eden C, Eriksson B, Hanson LA (1977) Adhesion of Escherichia coli to human uroepithelial cells in vitro. Infect Immun 18: 767–774

Svanborg Eden C, de Man P (1988) Bacterial virulence in urinary tract infection. Infect Dis Clin North Am 1: 731–750

Swaney LM, Liu YP, To CM, To CC, Ippen-Ihler K, Brinton CC (1977) Isolation and characterization of Escherichia coli phase variants and mutants deficient in type 1 pilus production. J Bacteriol 130: 495–505

Uhlin BE, Baga M, Göransson M, Lindberg FP, Lund B, Norgren M, Normark S (1985a) Genes determining adhesin formation in uropathogenic Escherichia coli. In: Current topics in microbiology and Immunology, vol 118 Springer, Berlin Heidelberg New York, pp. 163–178

Uhlin BE, Norgren M, Baga M, Normark S (1985b) Adhesion to human cells by Escherichia coli lacking the major subunit of a digalactoside-specific pilus-adhesin. Proc Natl Acad Sci USA 82: 1800–1804

Väisänen-Rhen V, Elo J, Väisänen E, Siitonen A, Orskov I, Orskov F, Svenson SB, Mäkelä PH, Korhonen TK (1984) P-fimbriated clones among uropathogenic Escherichia coli strains. Infect Immun 43: 149–155

Van Die I, Bergmans H (1984) Nucleotide sequence of the gene encoding the F7$_2$ fimbrial subunit of a uropathogenic Escherichia coli strain. Gene 32: 83–90

Van Die I, Van den Hondel C, Hamstra HJ, Hoekstra W, Bergmans H (1983) Studies on the fimbriae of an Escherichia coli O6:K2:H1:F7 strain: molecular cloning of a DNA fragment encoding a fimbrial antigen responsible for mannose-resistant hemagglutination of human erythrocytes. FEMS Microbiol Lett 19: 77–82

Van Die I, Van Geffen R, Hoekstra W, Bergmans H (1984a) Type 1C fimbriae of a uropathogenic

Escherichia coli strain: cloning and characterization of the genes involved in the expression of the 1C antigen and nucleotide sequence of the subunit gene. Gene 34: 187–196

Van Die I, Van Megen I, Hoekstra W, Bergmans H (1984b) Molecular organization of the genes involved in the production of $F7_2$ fimbriae, causing mannose resistant hemagglutination, of a uropathogenic *Escherichia coli* O6:K2:H1:F7 strain. MGG 194: 528–533

Van Die I, Spierings G, Van Megen I, Zuidweg E, Hoekstra W, Bergmans H (1985) Cloning and genetic organization of the gene cluster encoding $F7_1$ fimbriae of a uropathogenic *Escherichia coli* and comparison with the $F7_2$ gene cluster. FEMS Microbiol Lett 28: 329–334

Van Die I, Dijksterhuis M, de Cock H, Hoekstra W, Bergmans H (1986a) Structural variation of P fimbriae from uropathogenic *Escherichia coli*. In: Lark D (ed) Protein-carbohydrate interactions in biological systems. Academic, London, pp 39–46

Van Die I, Van Megen I, Zuidweg E, Hoekstra W, de Ree H, Van den Bosch H, Bergmans H (1986b) Functional relationship among gene clusters encoding $F7_1$, $F7_2$, F9 and F11 fimbriae of human uropathogenic *Escherichia coli*. J Bacteriol 167: 407–410

Van Die I, Zuidweg E, Hoekstra W, Bergmans H (1986c) The role of fimbriae of uropathogenic *Escherichia coli* as carriers of the adhesin involved in mannose-resistant hemagglutination. Microb Pathogen 1: 51–56.

Van Die I, Hoekstra W, Bergmans H (1987) Analysis of the primary structure of P fimbrillins of uropathogenic *Escherichia coli*. Microb Pathogen 3: 149–154

Van Die I, Riegman N, Gaykema O, Van Megen I, Hoekstra W, Bergmans H, De Ree H, Van den Bosch H (1988) Localization of antigenic determinants of P fimbriae of uropathogenic *Escherichia coli*. FEMS Microbiol. Lett 49: 95–100

Van Die I, Wauben M, Van Megen I, Bergmans H, Riegman N, Hoekstra W, Pouwels P, Enger-Valk B (1988b) Genetic manipulation of major P-fimbrial subunits and consequences for formation of fimbriae. J Bacteriol 170: 5870–5876

Virkola R, Westerlund B, Holthöfer H, Parkkinen J, Kekomäki M, Korhonen TK (1988) Binding characteristics of *Escherichia coli* adhesins in human urinary bladder. Infect Immun 56: 2615–2622

Walz W, Schmidt A, Labigne-Roussell A, Falkow S, Schoolnik G (1985) AFA-I: a cloned afimbrial X-type adhesin from a human pyelonephritic *Escherichia coli* strain. Eur J Biochem 152: 315–321

Weiss AA, Hewlett EL (1986) Virulence factors of *Bordetella pertussis*. Annu Rev Microbiol 40: 661–686

Genetics of Adhesive Fimbriae of Intestinal *Escherichia coli*

F. K. DE GRAAF

1 Introduction

Escherichia coli is a normal inhabitant of the intestinal tract of man and animals. Colonization by *E. coli* takes place soon after birth and once established, *E. coli* remains part of the fecal flora. In addition, *E. coli* has been recognized as an important pathogen involved in a variety of intestinal and extraintestinal diseases.

Relatively little is known about the factors that promote intestinal colonization in the newborn. It is likely that type 1 fimbriae, found on the majority of *E. coli* strains, play a role in the colonization process, but other less "common" adhesins, including M, S, P, and X fimbriae, are also frequently detected in the fecal flora of healthy individuals.

A wide variety of adherence factors have been identified in relation to pathogenicity and it has become evident that adhesins play a significant role in

Department of Molecular Microbiology, Biological Laboratory, Vrije Universiteit, de Boelelaan 1087, 1081 HV Amsterdam, The Netherlands

the synthesis of CFA/II, ST, and LT all reside on a single plasmid which varies from 54 to 90 Md (PENARANDA et al. 1980, 1983). These plasmids are nonconjugative but can be mobilized into *E. coli* K-12 by co-conjugation with a drug resistance plasmid.

Studies on the expression of CFA/II-positive ETEC strains belonging to serotype O6:H16 using CFA/II antisera have shown that within this serotype three different antigenic components are detectable, designated as coli surface-associated antigens CS1, CS2, and CS3 (CRAVIOTO et al. 1982; SMYTH 1982). CS1 and CS2 are morphologically indistinguishable but are serologically distinct types of fimbriae (SMYTH 1984). In contrast to the rigid, 6–nm-wide CS1 and CS2 fimbriae, the CS3 antigen is composed of thinner and flexible fibrillae (LEVINE et al. 1984). Strains of serotype O6:H16, biotype A (rhamnose-negative) produce CS1 and CS3 whereas strains of biotypes B, C, and F (rhamnose-positive) possess the antigens CS2 and CS3. CFA/II-positive strains belonging to other serogroups usually produce CS3 only (CRAVIOTO et al. 1982; SMYTH 1982).

When CFA/II-ST-LT plasmids from O6:H16 strains of biotypes A, B, or C were transferred to *E. coli* K-12, all exconjugants produced CS3 only; when plasmids contained in *E. coli* K-12 were transferred back into wild-type *E. coli* O6:H16 strains of different biotype these strains again produced CS1 and CS3 (biotype A) or CS2 and CS3 (biotype B or C) (MULLANY et al. 1983; SMITH et al. 1983). Apparently, plasmids coding for the production of CFA/II, ST, and LT are very similar, if not identical, but the ability to synthesize the different CFA/II components depends on the serotype and biotype of the host. All CFA/II-positive strains, regardless of their serotype or biotype, produce CS3 but CS1 and CS2 are expressed exclusively by strains of serotype O6:H16 belonging to biotype A or to biotype B, C, or F, respectively. The rare CS2- only phenotype in serogroup O6 strains of biotypes B and C reported previously (SMYTH 1982) is likely the result of a defective CFA/II-ST-LT plasmid since introduction of other CFA/II-ST-LT plasmids into these strains results in the expression of both CS2 and CS3 (BOYLAN and SMYTH 1985). Furthermore, DNA isolated from strains producing only CS2 does not hybridize with a CS3-specific DNA probe (BOYLAN et al. 1987). BOYLAN and SMYTH (1985) suggest that possibly the expression of either CS1 or CS2 does not correlate with the ability to ferment rhamnose *per se,* since O6 serotypes other than O6:K15:H16 or H-, but capable of rhamnose fermentation, express only CS3. One exception described so far is a strain of serotype O139:H28 (SCOTLAND et al. 1985).

At present it is not known which chromosomal genes provoke the ability of O6:H16 strains to produce either CS1 or CS2.

2.4 CFA/IV-ST-LT Plasmids

The colonization factor CFA/IV of human ETEC strains, previously designated PCF8775, was also shown to consist of three antigenic components: CS4, CS5, and CS6. Strains of serogroup O25 produce CS4 and CS6, whereas strains of serogroups O6, O92, O115, and O167 produce the antigenic components CS5 and CS6. Antigens CS4 and CS5 were identified as fimbriae, whereas CS6 was reported to be

nonfimbrial in nature (THOMAS et al. 1982, 1985; MCCONNELL et al. 1985). Strains producing only CS6 have been detected (MCCONNELL et al. 1985, 1986).

A plasmid with a molecular mass of 88 Md and coding for CS5, CS6, and ST has been demonstrated in strains of serogroup O167 (THOMAS et al. 1987). After mobilization of this plasmid into *E. coli* K-12, none of the transconjugants appear to cause mannose-resistant hemagglutination (MRHA), indicating that CS5 is not expressed in *E. coli* K-12. Expression of the MRHA-negative CS6 antigen was not tested. Mobilization of the 88-Md plasmid into strains of various serotypes demonstrated that expression of CS5 in wild-type *E. coli* strains is not affected by the serotype of the host. Recent analysis of a larger number of CFA/IV-positive strains indicated that the surface antigens CS4, CS5, and CS6 are usually carried on the same plasmid as the genes coding for ST or LT (MCCONNELL et al. 1988).

KNUTTON et al. (1987b) identified a new fimbrial structure consisting of curly fibrils in human ETEC strains of serotype 0148:H28. They suggest that these fibrils may represent the CS6 antigen. Another new plasmid-encoded fimbrial adhesin was found on ETEC strains belonging to serotype O159:H4 (TACKET et al. 1987).

3 Enteropathogenic *E. coli* (EPEC) Strains

Adherence of EPEC strains to the mucosa of the small bowel is an important step in the infection process. Plasmid-encoded adhesins have been shown to be essential for the adherence of EPEC to cultured HEp-2 cells. BALDINI et al. (1983) demonstrated that HEp-2 adherence was encoded on a 60-Md plasmid (pMAR2) in an EPEC strain of serotype O127:H6. Using a DNA probe derived from this plasmid, the genes for HEp-2 adhesion were detectable in EPEC strains of O serogroups O55, O111, O119, and O127 (BALDINI et al. 1986).

Two patterns of adherence were distinguished: localized adherence, character-ized by the formation of microcolonies on HEp-2 and HeLa cells, and diffuse adherence, in which bacteria are found in a uniform distribution all over the cells (NATARO et al. 1985). The two patterns are associated with distinct adhesins each encoded on plasmids varying in size from 55 to 70 Md. In strains of serogroup O55, the structural genes for the localized adherence phenotype are located on a plasmid also carrying drug resistance markers (LAPORTA et al. 1986). *E. coli* K-12 acquires adhesiveness after receiving this resistance factor or the previously identified plasmid pMAR2. Cells cured of these plasmids lose their ability to adhere (LAPORTA et al. 1986; KNUTTON et al. 1987c). Plasmid-containing *E. coli* K-12 cells, however, do not show the intimate attachment to HEp-2 cells which is characteristic for all wild-type EPEC cells (KNUTTON et al. 1987a). Probably, the pMAR2 plasmid codes for a fimbrial adhesin that promotes HEp-2 adherence but other chromosomally encoded factors are required for the characteristic intimate attachment of EPEC cells. The authors suggest that two steps may be involved in the adherence of EPEC strains to enterocytes: an initial attachment mediated by plasmid-encoded adhesins,

followed by effacement of brush border microvilli and intimate attachment (KNUTTON et al. 1987a). Recently, SCALETSKY et al. (1988) identified the binding factor responsible for localized adherence as a protein doublet with molecular weights of 29 000 and 32 000. Both proteins appear to be components of the bacterial outer membrane.

4 Enteroinvasive *E. coli* (EIEC) Strains

EIEC strains associated with dysentery-like diarrheal disease also adhere to the surface of cultured HEp-2 cells. The genetic determinant(s) for the adhesive phenotype is probably encoded by the bacterial chromosome (NANDADASA et al. 1981).

The mannose-resistant hemagglutinins of two EIEC strains were initially described as nonfimbrial agglutinins essential for adherence to erythrocytes and HEp-2 cells (WILLIAMS et al. 1984). MRHA-deficient mutants have lost their ability to adhere to or to penetrate cultured cells (KNUTTON et al. 1984). Recently, it was demonstrated that the ability to adhere to human colonocytes, originally attributed to nonfimbrial adhesins, was promoted by fine fibrillae (HINSON et al. 1987).

An invasive *E. coli* strain of serotype O15:K + :H21 isolated from a septicemic lamb was shown to possess a virulence plasmid, denoted Vir, which is involved in attachment of Vir-positive strains to intestinal brush borders (MORRIS et al. 1982). The presence of the Vir plasmid could be associated with the ability to produce a fimbrial adhesin (F.K. DE GRAAF, unpublished results).

Another fimbrial adhesin, designated F165, was found on *E. coli* strains of serogroup O115, associated with hemorrhagic enteritis and septicemia in calves and piglets (FAIRBROTHER et al. 1986).

5 Structural Organization of Gene Clusters Involved in the Biosynthesis of Fimbrial Adhesins

5.1 The K88, F41, and 987P Determinants

Analysis of genetic determinants coding for the biosynthesis of fimbriae has evolved rapidly and in particular the gene clusters involved in the production of type 1, P, K88, and K99 fimbriae have been studied in detail. The organization of these gene clusters was analyzed after cloning the respective genetic determinants in a suitable plasmid vector, construction of deletion and transposon-insertion mutants, analysis of gene expression in *E. coli* minicells, and nucleotide sequence analysis.

The genes involved in the biosynthesis of the two K88 variants K88ab and K88ac appeared to be located on an 8-Md DNA fragment, and derived from wild-type K88/Raf plasmids (MOOI et al. 1979; SHIPLEY et al. 1981). Comparison of the

restriction endonuclease cleavage patterns of the cloned fragments and of the parental plasmids suggests that both fragments are essentially the same. Most probably, the K88ab and K88ac encoding plasmids are derived from a common ancestral plasmid. The smallest fragment of cloned K88-DNA that contains sufficient information for the biosynthesis of K88 fimbriae is about 6.5 kb pair in size. *E. coli* K-12 cells harboring either pFM205 (K88ab) or pMK005 (K88ac) agglutinate with anti-K88 antisera, cause MRHA of guinea pig erythrocytes, and adhere to the brush borders of isolated porcine intestinal epithelial cells.

Expression of the recombinant plasmids *E. coli* minicells reveals the synthesis of several proteins ranging from 16 to 82 kd. The fimbrial subunits with a molecular weight of 27000 have been identified by immunoprecipitation with anti-K88 antiserum (MOOI et al. 1981; SHIPLEY et al. 1981).

Subsequently, the identification and the genetic organization of the K88 gene cluster was analyzed by studying the expression of various deletion and transposon-insertion mutants in *E. coli* minicells (KEHOE et al. 1981, 1983; MOOI et al. 1981, 1982, 1984). Six structural genes (*faeC–H*) were identified on the cloned DNA contained in pFM205 (K88ab) encoding polypeptides with apparent molecular weights of 16900, 82100, 26300, 15400, 27600, and 27500 respectively (Fig. 1). Mutational inactivation of *faeC*, *faeD*, or *faeE* results in a $K88^-$, $MRHA^-$, Adh^- phenotype, although some of these mutants are capable of expressing a low level of K88 subunits. Gene *faeG* encodes the K88ab fimbrial subunit. Inactivation of gene *faeH* results in a strong reduction in the biosynthesis of K88ab fimbriae and in the ability of the cells to agglutinate erythrocytes and to adhere to intestinal epithelial cells (MOOI et al. 1981, 1982, 1984). Complementation with FaeH restores normal fimbrial production, indicating that this protein is involved in K88 biosynthesis (D. BAKKER, unpublished results). Nucleotide sequence analysis of a K88ab clone which contains the complete genetic determinant for the synthesis of K88 fimbriae revealed the presence of at least two more K88 genes, designated *faeB* and *faeI*, located upstream of *faeC* and downstream of *faeH*, respectively (D. BAKKER, unpublished results).

Five structural gene (*adhA-E*) were located on the cloned DNA contained in pMK005 (K88ac). The K88ac fimbrial subunits are encoded by *adhD*. The genes *adhE*, *adhA*, *adhB*, and *adhC* correspond, respectively, to *faeC*, *faeD*, *faeE*, and *faeF* in the K88ab gene cluster (Fig. 1). The K88ac gene corresponding to *faeH* was not detected. Expression of all *adh* genes is essential for high-level expression of K88ac fimbriae (KEHOE et al. 1981, 1983).

All the structural genes identified code for polypeptides which contain an amino-terminal leader sequence essential for initiation of their translocation across the cytoplasmic membrane.

The genetic determinant for production of F41 fimbriae was isolated by cosmid cloning (MOSELEY et al. 1986). DNA probes derived from the K88ac-encoded plasmid pMK005 hybridize with the cloned F41-DNA and transposon insertions which inactivate F41 production were mapped to the region of homology, indicating a genetic relatedness between the F41 and K88 determinants. Recently, the genetic organization of the polypeptides involved in F41 biosynthesis was investigated (ANDERSEN and MOSELY 1988). Genes encoding polypeptides with apparent molecular weights of 29000, 30000, 32000, and 86000 were indicated. The 29-kd protein was identified as the F41 fimbrial subunit. Extensive nucleotide sequence homology

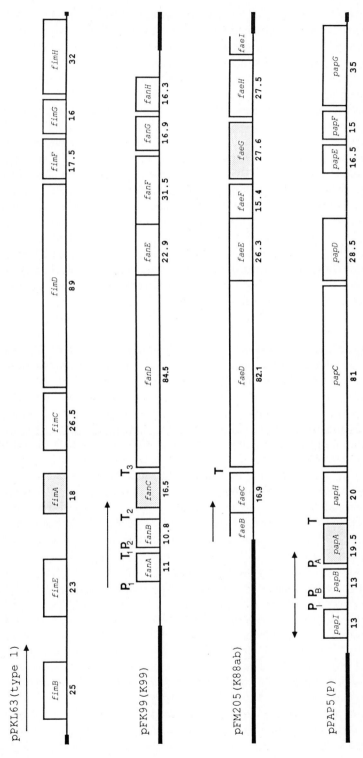

Fig. 1. Structural organization of genetic determinants encoding the biogenesis of fimbrial adhesins. The location of the genes is indicated by *boxes*; the molecular mass of the gene products is printed in kd below the boxes. As far as the nucleotide sequence of the respective genes has been determined, the molecular mass of the proteins has been given on the basis of these data. Promoter (*P*) and terminator (*T*) sequences are indicated. *Arrows* represent the direction of transcription. The genes encoding the major fimbrial subunits are *dotted*

was observed between the region encoding the putative signal sequences of the F41 and K88 subunits and the region immediately upstream of the subunit genes. A K88 probe hybridized at high stringency to all DNA fragments shown to be essential for F41 production. Furthermore, hybridization experiments with the K88 gene probe and plasmid or total DNA prepared from a variety of ETEC strains indicated that F41 is chromosomally encoded.

Also the genetic determinant for the biosynthesis of 987P fimbriae was isolated by cosmid cloning (DE GRAAF and KLAASEN and 1986; MORRISSEY and DOUGAN 1986). Cells of *E. coli* HB101 harboring the recombinant plasmid produced fimbriae which could not be distinguished from the 987P fimbriae produced by the parental strain. A 12.4-kb pair derivative, designated pPK180, was used to analyze the genetic organization of the 987P determinant (DE GRAAF and KLAASEN 1986). Five structural genes encoding polypeptides with apparent molecular weights of 16 500, 20 500, 28 500, 39 000, and 81 000 could be located on pPK180. The 20.5-kd polypeptide was identified as the fimbrial subunit (DE GRAAF and KLAASEN 1987). Recently, BROES et al. (1988) described a new fimbrial antigen (CS 1541), isolated from porcine enterotoxigenic *E. coli* and antigenically related to the 987P antigen. Like 987P fimbriae, the CS 1541 fimbriae possess no hemagglutinating properties. The CS 1541 fimbriae consist of two polypeptides of about 18 and 19 kd.

5.2 The K99 Determinant

The genetic determinant for the biosynthesis of K99 fimbriae is located on a 7.1-kb pair DNA fragment cloned into pBR325 (VAN EMBDEN et al. 1980). *E. coli* K-12 harboring this recombinant DNA synthesizes K99 fimbriae, causes MRHA of horse erythrocytes, and adheres to the brush border of porcine intestinal epithelial cells.

Analysis of the genetic organization of the K99 determinant in minicells revealed the presence of six structural genes, designated *fanC-H* (Fig. 1), and encoding polypeptides ranging in molecular weight from 16 300 to 84 500 (DE GRAAF et al. 1984; ROOSENDAAL 1987). The *fanC* gene product was identified as the K99 fimbrial subunit. Mutational inactivation of *fanC, fanD*, or *fanE* results in a K99$^-$, MRHA$^-$, Adh$^-$, phenotype. Inactivation of *fanF, fanG*, or *fanH* results in a simultaneous decrease in antigen production and adhesive capacity (JACOBS 1987; ROOSENDAAL et al. 1987b). All six polypeptides are synthesized with a leader sequence. Analysis of the nucleotide sequence of the region at the proximal end of the fimbrial subunit gene *fanC* revealed the presence of two open reading frames, designated *fanA* and *fanB* (ROOSENDAAL et al. 1987a). Frame shift mutations in both genes and complementation studies have indicated that *fanA* and *fanB* code for regulatory *trans*-acting polypeptides involved in the biogenesis of K99 fimbriae.

5.3 The CFA Determinants

SMITH et al. (1982) investigated the CFA/I determinant located on the 58-Md, CFA/I-ST plasmid NTP113. They were able to show that two regions of this

growth rates result in a gradual decrease in fimbrial production (VAN VERSEVELD et al. 1985; JACOBS and DE GRAAF 1985). Also the variations in the level of fimbrial production observed in different growth media are probably in part due to the regulatory effects of growth rate on the biosynthesis of fimbriae. At present, little information is available about the genetic background of the regulatory influence of growth rate on the biosynthesis of fimbriae.

Glucose and other fermentable sugars suppress the synthesis of type 1 (EISENSTEIN and DODD 1982) and K99 fimbriae (ISAACSON 1980; OLLIER and GIRARDEAU 1983). Indications have been obtained that this phenomenon is probably not due to the classic mechanism of catabolite repression but to a selective outgrowth of nonfimbriated versus fimbriated cells or a decrease in growth rate at lower pH due to an accumulation of fermentation products (VAN VERSEVELD et al. 1985).

6.2 Phase Variation

Expression of the chromosomally encoded type 1 and 987P fimbriae exhibits phase variation whereby individual *E. coli* cells can switch from a fimbriated to a nonfimbriated state and vice versa (BRINTON 1959; NAGY et al. 1977). A possibly related phenomenon was described for the expression of P fimbriae present on uropathogenic *E. coli* strains (RHEN et al. 1983).

Using a fusion of the *lacZ* gene to the DNA region encoding type 1 fimbriae, EISENSTEIN (1981) was able to demonstrate that phase variation between the fimbriate and non-fimbriate state is under transcriptional control. The transition rate from the fimbriate to the nonfimbriate state is 1.05×10^{-3} per bacterium per generation and 3.12×10^{-3} in the reverse direction. Apparently, the oscillation between both states occurs randomly at a frequency of approximately one switch per 1000 cells per generation. Subsequently, it was demonstrated that the region controlling the phase variation is directly adjacent to the gene encoding the fimbrial subunit and codes for a *cis*-acting element (FREITAG et al. 1985). Furthermore, these authors reported that besides the *cis*- active element, a *trans*-acting permissive factor supplied by the host strain is also required. F factors carrying the *fim* region were able to complement phase-locked mutants, indicating that the *trans*-acting element must map near the *fim* operon at 98 min.

Using Southern blot and DNA sequence analysis ABRAHAM et al. (1985) detected a genomic rearrangement in the switch region immediately upstream of the fimbrial structural gene. The switch consists of a small invertible segment of about 300 base pairs carrying the *fim* promoter flanked by a nine-base pair inverted repeat. The invertible element does not encode its own recombinase and is therefore different from other DNA inversion systems characterized by the site-specific recombinases *hin*, *gin*, *cin* or *pin*, which act as invertases (CRAIG 1985; PLASTERK et al. 1983; ZIEG and SIMON 1980). Similar results were recently reported by KLEMM (1986), who detected that the phase switch is controlled by the products of two regulatory genes, *fimB* and *fimE*, located upstream of the fimbrial subunit gene (Fig. 1). The FimB and FimE proteins direct the phase switch into the "on" and

"off" positions, respectively. Both proteins have a molecular weight of about 23 000 and contain a high number of positively charged amino acid residues. Furthermore, both protein show a striking degree of sequence homology. The proteins contain an unequal number of cysteine residues and it was assumed that they may exist as dimers or multimers in their natural state (KLEMM 1986).

Significant homologies were found between a part of the FimB and FimE proteins and the active sites of site-specific recombinases known as the integrases of various phages (DORMAN and HIGGINS 1987). Therefore, it seems likely that FimB- and FimE- directed phase variation is based on a mechanism that is comparable to the Int-Xis system of phage λ. Further support for such a mechanism was provided by the observation that expression of type 1 fimbrial subunits is dependent on the presence of the integration host factor (IHF), a protein that is also required for the functioning of the λ integrase (EISENSTEIN et al. 1987; DORMAN and HIGGINS 1987). Two nucleotide sequences which match the consensus sequence for the IHF binding site are detected in the region containing the invertible DNA element. IHF is composed of two subunits α and β encoded by the *himA* and *himD* genes, respectively. Insertional inactivation of either of these two genes prevents phase variation and locks expression of *fimA* in either the "on" or the "off" state. In addition to the role of IHF in the inversion of the phase variation switch, DORMAN and HIGGINS (1987) observed that IHF is also required for efficient expression controlled by the *fimA* promoter. It is suggested that IHF facilitates the adoption of a DNA conformation favorable for FimB- and FimE-directed recombination. The conformational change induced by IHF probably involves bending DNA.

6.3 Transcriptional Control of K88 and K99 Expression

Analysis of the nucleotide sequence of the DNA region located upstream of the K99 fimbrial subunit gene (*fanC*) made possible the detection of two open reading frames and several transcriptional signals (Fig. 1). The open reading frames, designated *fanA* and *fanB*, code for positively charged proteins with a molecular mass of about 11 000 (ROOSENDAAL et al. 1987a). Both proteins exhibit a remarkable sequence homology. Furthermore, they show significant homology with another regulatory protein (PapB) encoded by the Pap operon (BAGA et al. 1985). No indications for a leader sequence were detected, suggesting that both proteins reside in the bacterial cytoplasm. Expression of FanA and FanB is very low since neither protein is detectable in minicells harboring the complete K99 operon. Both proteins, however, are clearly detectable in an in vitro DNA-directed translation system (ROOSENDAAL et al. 1988).

The possible role of FanA and FanB was investigated by constructing a frame-shift mutation in each of the respective genes. The mutational inactivation resulted in 8- and 16-fold reductions in K99 expression, respectively. Complementation of the mutations *in trans* restored K99 production to about 75% of the wild-type level. Apparently, FanA and FanB are *trans*-acting regulatory proteins affecting the biosynthesis of K99 fimbriae (ROOSENDAAL et al. 1987).

Putative promoters were observed preceding *fanA*, *fanB*, and *fanC*, respectively. No other promoter consensus sequences were detectable downstream of *fanC*, and

apparently the whole operon is controlled by the regulatory region upstream of *fanC*. The activity of the putative promoters was tested after cloning of the appropriate DNA fragments in a promoterless transcription vector which contains the *E. coli* galactokinase gene as assayable marker (ROOSENDAAL et al. 1988). A very low activity was detected for the putative promoter sequence preceding the fimbrial subunit gene *fanC*. Expression of the regulatory proteins FanA and FanB did not stimulate this putative transcription signal, indicating that the *fanC* promoter is of minor importance in the transcriptional control of the K99 gene cluster (Fig. 1). In this context it should be mentioned that also the putative promoter sequences preceding the gene for the fimbrial subunit-like protein encoded by the K88 operon (*faeC*) or the 987P fimbrial subunit gene exhibit low activity (MOOI et al. 1984; F. K. DE GRAAF, unpublished results). Obviously, the control of expression of gene clusters coding for the biosynthesis of fimbriae is more complicated and requires expression of regulatory genes at the 5′ end of the respective clusters.

The recombinant plasmids pFM205 and pMK005 contain all necessary information for the biosynthesis of K88ab and K88ac fimbriae, respectively, but only some of the regulatory elements were cloned from the original parental plasmids (KEHOE et al. 1983; MOOI et al. 1982). Therefore, expression of K88ab or K88ac fimbriae by both recombinant strains is controlled by the P1 promoter of vector pBR322. An open reading frame strongly homologous to the *fanB* gene of pFK99 was observed in pFM205 upstream of *faeC*. This open reading frame (*faeB*), however, is not complete because the nucleotide sequence encoding the amino-terminal end of the corresponding polypeptide, FaeB, is not contained in pFM205 (Fig. 1). Recently the complete K88ab determinant was cloned into pBR322. This clone exhibits a ten fold higher production of K88 fimbriae, indicating that K88 regulatory proteins also have a positive effect on the synthesis of fimbriae (D. Bakker, unpublished results).

Further analysis of the K99 regulatory region indicated that the promoters P_1 and P_2 possess a high and an intermediate activity, respectively (ROOSENDAAL et al. 1988). The activity of these promoters, cloned into the promoterless transcription vector, is not affected by FanA or FanB, but both regulatory proteins appear to affect the transcriptional activity of a DNA fragment containing P1, *fanA*, and P2, indicating a possible interference with other control elements located within this region.

Factor-dependent terminators of transcription were detected and are probably located in the intercistronic regions between *fanA* and *fanB* (T_1) and between *fanB* and *fanC* (T_2) (ROOSENDAAL et al. 1988). The identity of these terminators (Fig. 1) is not known. The intercistronic regions between *fanA* and *fanB* and between *fanB* and *fanC* do not contain sequences known to be involved in a transcriptional pause (ROOSENDAAL et al. 1987a). Factor-dependent terminators, however, do not appear to correspond to any specific sequence requirements but require additional sequences considerably upstream of the termination endpoints to convey the signal for termination (PLATT 1986). A region showing dyad symmetry that may function as a potential binding site for protein factors that regulate transcription is located within *fanA* (ROOSENDAAL et al. 1987a). This region shows similarities to the Box B region of the lambda *nut*-site which is part of the lambda pN antitermination system

(FRIEDMAN and GOTTESMAN 1983, PALO and SAUER 1984). Most likely, the regulatory proteins FanA and FanB both function as antiterminators of transcription (ROOSENDAAL et al. 1988).

A third terminator of transcription (T_3) is located in the intercistronic region between *fanC* and *fanD* (Fig. 1) and has an efficiency of 90% (ROOSENDAAL et al. 1984; 1988). This terminator is composed of a GC-rich region of dyad symmetry, thus allowing the formation of an intramolecular hairpin structure in the RNA transcript but without the usual series of uridine residues at the 3' end. This might indicate that either T_3 must be considered as a factor (rho)-dependent terminator or the pausing of the RNA-polymerase at the hairpin is sufficient to allow 'translational attenuation.' The efficiency of the termination at T_3 is in agreement with the observation that the fimbrial subunit is expressed at a much higher level than the auxiliary proteins FanD–FanH.

Other indications that the region of dyad symmetry in the intercistronic region between *fanC* and *fanD* is involved in translational control have been derived from the K88 operon, where a comparable region contains the 3' end of *faeC*, the ribosome binding site of *faeD*, and the translation initiation codon of this gene (MOOI et al. 1986; ROOSENDAAL 1987). Translation of *faeC* is terminated within the ribosome-binding site preceding the start codon of *faeD*. Therefore, it is conceivable that a ribosome terminating translation of *faeC* could reinitiate translation at *faeD* without being released from the mRNA molecule (translational coupling). A study of this possible function for translational control of the *faeD* gene has shown that if translation of the 3' end of *faeC* is prevented, the synthesis of FaeD is descreased. Most likely, the ribosome binding site of *faeD* is masked by mRNA secondary structure if the 3' end of *faeC* is not translated (MOOI et al. 1986).

7 Biosynthesis of Fimbriae

The biosynthesis of fimbriae is rather complicated process which requires at least (a) the transport of fimbrial subunits across the cytoplasmic membrane, the periplasm, and the outer membrane; (b) the polymerization of fimbrial subunits at the cellular surface, and (c) the anchoring of fimbriae to the cell envelope. Furthermore, it seems likely that the bacteria are able to regulate the length of their fimbriae. Functionally, the capacity of fimbriae to adhere to their respective receptors on the intestinal mucosa or the underlying enterocytes may be encoded by the fimbrial subunits or specific adhesin molecules attached to the fimbrial structure.

Analysis of the gene clusters responsible for the biosynthesis of various fimbriae has shown that these clusters indeed contain much more information than is required for the production of fimbrial subunits, and in general at least five or six auxiliary or "helper" proteins with distinct functions are encoded by the various genetic determinants for fimbrial production. The subcellular location of the proteins encoded by the K88 and K99 operons has been determined (JACOBS 1987; VAN DOORN et al. 1982).

Comparison of the gene clusters (Fig. 1) shows that each cluster analyzed so far contains a gene encoding a large outer membrane protein (molecular mass of about 85 000). This protein may have several functions in the biosynthesis of fimbriae: as a pore protein that facilitates the translocation of fimbrial subunits across the outer membrane, as an anchor for assembled fimbriae, or as a sort of catalyst for subunit polymerization. Mutants impaired in the synthesis of this protein do not possess fimbriae and accumulate fimbria precursor complexes in their periplasm (MOOI et al. 1982, 1983). The topology of the protein in the outer membrane is not known, but analysis of the secondary structure of the FaeD protein indicates a large central region in the protein with an alternation of turns and β sheets that may form loops in the membrane bilayer (MOOI et al. 1986). Comparable features have been found in the large outer membrane protein FanD encoded by the K99 operon (E. ROOSENDAAL, unpublished results). Both proteins exhibit considerable amino acid sequence homology.

A second gene present in all operons described encodes a smaller periplasmic protein (molecular weight about 26 000, Fig. 1) which probably also has several functions in fimbrial biogenesis. Not only do mutations in this gene abolish the formation of fimbriae, but in the absence of this protein none of the fimbrial subunits are detectable in the periplasm (DE GRAAF and KLAASEN 1986; DE GRAAF et al. 1984; JACOBS 1987; KLEMM et al. 1985; MOOI et al. 1983; ORNDORFF and FALKOW 1984a). Apparently, this protein is involved in the stabilization of nonpolymerized fimbrial subunits. Complexes of FaeE and FaeG have been isolated from K88-producing cells (MOOI et al. 1983). Also the K99 fimbrial subunits (FanC) appear to form a complex with the periplasmic protein FanE encoded by the K99 operon. Immunoprecipitation of ultrasonic extracts of K99-producing cells with anti-K99 antiserum results in a coprecipitation of FanE with the fimbrial subunits (DE GRAAF et al. 1984). The interaction of the 26-kd protein with other proteins is not restricted to the major fimbrial subunit because in the absence of the 26-kd protein other minor components of the fimbriae are also no longer detectable (JACOBS 1987; NORGREN et al. 1984). Apparently, all proteins that are translocated through the cell envelope and assembled into the fimbrial structure are protected by the 26-kd protein. We assume that this periplasmic protein may have the following functions: (a) to prevent premature subunit polymerization in the periplasmic space, (b) to act as a shuttle that transports the major and minor fimbrial subunits from the inner to the outer membrane, and (c) to deliver the energy necessary for transport and/or polymerization of subunits at the outer membrane. The protein may be considered as an "unfoldase" which keeps the fimbrial subunits in an energetically unfavourable extended conformation necessary for export across the outer membrane and the delivery of the conformational energy during the transport and/or polymerization process.

In principle, the synthesis of fimbrial subunits together with the periplasmic carrier protein and the outer membrane pore protein might be sufficient for the biogenesis of fimbriae, as has been observed for type 1 and P fimbriae (KLEMM and CHRISTIANSEN 1987; MAURER and ORNDORFF 1985; NORGREN et al. 1984). Such fimbriae, however, are longer than the fimbriae produced by cells containing the

complete genetic determinant (KLEMM and CHRISTIANSEN 1987; MAURER and ORNDORFF 1987), indicating that other proteins are required to regulate fimbrial length.

Another group of proteins which play a role in the biosynthesis of fimbriae are the so-called fimbrial subunit-like proteins or minor fimbrial subunits, which are supposed to act as initiators or terminators of subunit polymerization. These proteins show a substantial amino acid sequence homology with the major fimbrial subunit, they have a comparable molecular weight, and in some cases they were detected as minor components of fimbriae.

For type 1 fimbriae, the two minor fimbrial subunits FimF (PilD) and FimG (PilF), have been identified. The FimG (PilF) protein regulates the length of the fimbriae. Mutants with a lesion in this gene produce very long fimbriae (MAURER and ORNDORFF 1987; KLEMM and CHRISTIANSEN 1987). The easiest explanation for the regulatory function of this protein is that subunit polymerization stops upon incorporation of a FimG (PilF) molecule in the fimbrial structure. The length of the fimbriae would depend upon the ratio of FimA (PilA) and FimG (PilF) molecules available. In this model FimG (PilF) acts as a competitive inhibitor of fimbrial polymerization: inactivation of the protein results in longer fimbriae, whereas overproduction of the protein results in shorter fimbriae. A similar model has been proposed for the PapH protein, which modulates the length of P fimbriae (BAGA et al. 1987). Little information is available for the role of the second minor fimbrial subunit FimF (PilD). We assume that this minor component acts as an initiator of polymerization and will discuss this possibility in relation to the expression of another gene contained in the genetic determinant of the various fimbriae and encoding a 30-kd protein.

The K99 operon contains two similar genes, designated *fanG* and *fanH*, which encode fimbrial subunit-like proteins showing significant amino acid sequence homology with the major fimbrial subunit FanC (ROOSENDAAL et al. 1987b). Mutational inactivation of *fanG* or *fanH* resulted in a simultaneous decrease in the production of K99 fimbriae and in adhesive capability. FanG and FanH are associated with the bacterial outer membrane but have not been detected so far in purified fimbriae. Their role in K99 biosynthesis is not known but we assume that these proteins are functionally comparable to the minor subunit components of type 1 and P fimbriae.

Analysis of the K88ab determinant contained in pFM205 revealed the presence of *faeH* encoding a polypeptide showing significant sequence homology with the major fimbrial subunit FaeG (D. Bakker, unpublished results). Mutational inactivation of *faeH* results in a simultaneous decreased in the production of K88 fimbriae and adhesive capability (MOOI et al. 1982). A second fimbrial subunit-like protein (FaeI) is probably encoded by the K88 operon but the reading frame of the corresponding gene (*faeI*) is only partially contained in pFM205 (Fig. 1).

As depicted in Fig. 1, all gene clusters analyzed contain an open reading frame encoding a protein of about 30-kd. The *fimH* (*pilE*) gene contained in the genetic determinant for the expression of type 1 fimbriae appeared to be responsible for the mannose-specific adherence of these fimbriae (KLEMM and CHRISTIANSEN 1987; MAURER and ORNDORFF 1985, 1987). Overproduction of the mannose-specific

adhesin FimH results in the formation of 10-nm-diameter rounded structures (fimbriosomes) composed of FimH protein and detectable in association with type 1 fimbriae or in the culture medium (ABRAHAM et al. 1988). Mutants with a lesion in *fimH* (*pilE*) are adhesion-negative and fail to agglutinate erythrocytes. Furthermore, mutational inactivation of FimH (type 1) reduces the amount of fimbriae produced (KLEMM and CHRISTIANSEN 1987), indicating that the protein is involved in the biogenesis of fimbriae. A similar role as described for FimH has been found for the PapG protein, which could be identified as the Gal α (1 → 4) Gal-specific adhesin of P fimbriae (LUND et al. 1987). Mutants defective in the synthesis of the 30-kd FanF (K99) protein are unable to agglutinate horse erythrocytes but are also strongly hampered in the synthesis of K99 fimbriae (JACOBS 1987). Similarly, mutation in the 33-kd protein encoded by the 987P gene cluster results in a strong reduction of 987P production (DE GRAAF and KLAASEN 1986). Unfortunately, the adhesive capability of this mutant was not tested.

The available data clearly indicate that at least some fimbriae, i.e., 1 and P, carry separate adhesin molecules, while in other cases, i.e., K88 and K99 fimbriae, such indications have not yet been obtained. Studies on the structure–function relationship of K88 and K99 fimbrial subunits have indicated that the adhesive capability of these fimbriae is an instrinsic property of the major fimbrial subunit. Three different tripeptides, Ile-Ala-Phe, Ser-Leu-Phe, and Ala-Ile-Phe, derived from the K88 fimbrial subunit, were found to inhibit the binding of K88 fimbriae to guinea pig erythrocytes or pig intestinal epithelial cells in vitro (JACOBS et al. 1987c). Subsequently, it has been shown that in vivo, phenylalanine residue 150 plays an essential role in the binding of K88 fimbrial subunits to guinea pig erythrocytes (JACOBS et al. 1987a). Recently, however, indications were obtained that the high affinity binding of K88ab fimbriae to chicken erythrocytes is not mediated by the fimbrial subunits but most likely by one of the minor components of the K88 fimbriae, either FaeC, or FaeF (D. BAKKER, unpublished results). In vitro mutagenesis of the K99 fimbrial subunit Fan C has demonstrated that lysine residue 132 and arginine residue 136 are essential for the adhesive capability of these fimbriae (JACOBS et al. 1987b).

In this context, the question arises whether (a) the adhesive capability of the 30-kd minor components of type 1 and P fimbriae represents their unique biologic activity or (b) the 30-kd proteins encoded by all gene clusters share another common function in the biosynthesis of fimbriae. Comparison of the primary structure of the 30-kd proteins encoded by the type 1, K99, and P determinants revealed that these proteins are about twice the size of fimbrial subunits and contain four cysteine residues. The distance between two of these residues in the C-terminal domain of the protein is similar to the distance found for the two cysteine residues present in the various fimbrial subunits. Furthermore, the C-terminal domain of the 30-kd proteins shows substantial sequence homology with major and minor fimbrial subunits. We suppose that each of the different fimbrial subunits encoded by a particular operon possesses a distinct but different affinity to each of the other fimbrial subunits and to the 30-kd protein of that operon. In addition it is likely that major and minor fimbrial subunits and the 30-kd protein possess affinity for the pore protein which is involved in their translocation to the cellular surface.

On the basis of these assumptions and the experimental data available, we propose the following model for the biosynthesis of fimbriae:

1. Major and minor fimbrial subunits as well as the 30-kd protein form a complex with the periplasmic 26-kd carrier protein upon their translocation through the cytoplasmic membrane. This interaction prevents preliminary polymerization of subunits and keeps the various polypeptides in a conformation favorable to their translocation across the outer membrane. Furthermore, the interaction with the carrier protein prevents the proteolytic degradation of "unfolded" fimbrial subunits.

2. The 30-kd protein possesses affinity for the outer membrane pore protein and is the first protein to be inserted in the fimbrial growth point. Once detached from the carrier protein and delivered to the pore protein 30-kd protein blocks this pore in the absence of a minor fimbrial subunit, probably because of the formation of disulfide bridges, which changes the conformation of the 30-kd protein to an export-unfavorable form.

   Indications for such a possibility can be derived from an experiment described by KLEMM and CHRISTIANSEN (1987), who observed that fimbriated cells harboring a plasmid pPK5 encoding *fimA, fimC,* and *fim D* became bald when another plasmid was introduced in these cells, coding for the 30-kd FimH protein only.

3. In the presence of a minor fimbrial subunit with high affinity for the C-terminal domain of the 30-kd protein, the transition to an export-unfavorable conformation is prevented and the pore remains open for transport of fimbrial subunits. This minor fimbrial subunit may be considered as an initiator protein, which together with the 30-kd protein forms an initiation complex.

4. Interaction between the 30-kd protein and one of the minor fimbrial subunits does not appear to be sufficient to allow efficient export of the major fimbrial subunits, possibly because the N-terminal domain of the 30-kd protein still interacts with the pore protein at the cell surface and/or because the affinity of the major fimbrial subunit to this initiation complex is relatively low. A second minor fimbrial subunit with a comparable affinity for the first minor as well as the major fimbrial subunit is required to detach the initiation complex from the pore protein and to keep the pore open for subsequent export of the major fimbrial subunits. In addition, this second minor fimbrial subunit may facilitate the translocation of major fimbrial subunits through the outer membrane. The initiation complex remains attached to the tip of the fimbrial structure. It seems likely that the presence of the minor fimbrial subunits in the fimbrial growth point allow not only efficient transport of major fimbrial subunits but also the transport and polymerization of the 30-kd protein depending on the relative concentration of 30-kd protein and major fimbrial subunits. This situation may result in the formation of fimbriosomes (ABRAHAM et al. 1988). Furthermore, the concentration of minor fimbrial subunits may be high enough to allow their integration into the fimbrial structure (ABRAHAM et al. 1987; LINDBERG et al. 1987).

5. As soon as another 30-kd protein or an initiation complex is delivered to a functional growth point we presume that it prevents further subunit export. The

C-terminal domain of the 30-kd protein or the attached initiator protein interacts with the last major fimbrial subunit inserted in the growth point. Further translocation of the 30-kd protein is arrested because it attaches to the growth point in the opposite orientation. In this model the 30-kd protein is a multifunctional protein. In the wild-type situation this protein is part of the initiation complex but it also acts as terminator of subunit polymerization.

The number and length of fimbriae produced depend entirely on the concentration of major subunits versus the other (auxiliary) proteins which are all equally essential for efficient synthesis of fimbriae. This distinction between major subunits on the one hand and other proteins on the other is reflected in the regulation of expression of the fimbrial gene clusters. Mutations is one of the minor fimbrial subunits or the 30-kd protein affect the regulation of the number and length of fimbriae produced. Inactivation of the 30-kd protein, for instance, may allow the synthesis of longer fimbriae at low efficiency because both initiation and termination of the polymerization are hampered. On the other hand overproduction of this protein should reduce the length of the fimbriae without having much effect on the number of fimbriae per cell.

Although our model presents a common pathway in fimbriae biosynthesis, it is likely that variations have developed in the course of the evolution. In some systems, e.g., as described for P fimbriae, an additional minor fimbrial subunit protein may act as terminator of polymerization, for instance the PapH protein encoded by the Pap operon (BAGA et al. 1987). In other systems the expression of major fimbrial subunits may be hampered and the complex of the 30-kd protein with the minor fimbrial subunits remains in contact with the outer membrane, where it serves as nonfimbrial adhesin. An interesting variation on this model is the biosynthesis of K88 fimbriae. In the K88 operon, the open reading frame *faeC* located at the position of the major fimbrial subunit gene in other operons, is expressed at a very low level, while *faeG,* corresponding to the position of a minor fimbrial subunit, is expressed at a high level (MOOI et al. 1984). Consequently, K88 fimbriae may be considered as composed of lectin molecules or of "originally" minor fimbrial subunits which have taken over the function of FaeC. The "originally" major fimbrial subunit (FaeC) is located at the tip of the K88 fimbriae (B. Oudega, unpublished results). Possibly FaeC is responsible for the high affinity of K88 fimbriae to chicken erythrocytes while the major fimbrial subunits (FaeG) confer the adhesive capability for guinea pig erythrocytes.

It seems likely that the variations on the "common" pathway described have developed by a natural selection of mutants with a more efficient and specific adherence for a particular host epithelium.

References

Abraham, JM, Freitag, CS, Clements, JR, Eisenstein BI (1985) An invertible element of DNA controls phase variation of type 1 fimbriae of *Escherichia coli.* Proc Natl Acad Sci USA 82: 5724–5727
Abraham SN, Goguen JD, Sun D, Klemm P, Beachey EH (1987) Identification of two ancillary subunits

of *Escherichia coli* type 1 fimbriae by using antibodies against synthetic oligopeptides of *fim* gene products. J Bacteriol 169: 5530–5536

Abraham SN, Goguen JD, Beackey EH (1988) Hyperadhesive mutants of type 1-fimbriated *Escherichia coli* associated with formation of FimH organelles (fimbriosomes). Infect Immun 56: 1023–1029

Anderson DG, Mosely SL (1988) *Escherichia coli* F41 adhesin: genetic organization, nucleotide sequence, and homology with the K88 determinant. J Bacteriol 170: 4890–4896

Baga M, Göransson M, Normark S, Uhlin BE (1985) Transcriptional activation of a Pap pilus virulence operon from uropathogenic *Escherichia coli* EMBO J 4: 3887–3893

Baga M, Norgren M, Normark S (1987) Biogenesis of E. coli Pap pili: Pap H, a minor pilin subunit involved in cell anchoring and length modulation. Cell 49: 241–251

Bak AL, Christiansen G, Christiansen C, Stenderup A, Orskov I, Orskov F (1972) Circular DNA molecules controlling synthesis and transfer of the surface antigen (K88) in *Escherichia coli*. J Gen Microbiol 73: 373–385

Baldini MM, Kap JB, Levine MM, Candy DCA, Moon HW (1983) Plasmid-mediated adhesion in enteropathogenic *Escherichia coli*. J Pediatr Gastroenterol Nutr 2: 534–538

Baldini MM, Nataro JP, Kaper JB (1986) Localization of a determinant for HEp-2 adherence by enteropathogenic *Escherichia coli*. Infect Immun 52: 334–336

Boylan M, Smyth CJ (1985) Mobilization of CS fimbriae-associated plasmids of enterotoxigenic *Escherichia coli* of serotype O6:K15:H16 or H- into various wild-type hosts. FEMS Microbiol Lett 29: 83–89

Boylan M, Coleman DC, Smyth CJ (1987) Molecular cloning and characterization of the genetic determinant encoding CS3 fimbriae of enterotoxigenic *Escherichia coli*. Microb Pathogen 2: 195–209

Boylan M, Smyth CJ, Scott JR (1988) Nucleotide sequence of the gene encoding the major subunit of CS3 fimbriae of enterotoxigenic *Escherichia coli*. Infect Immun 56: 3297–3300

Brinton CC (1959) Non-flagellar appendages of bacteria. Nature 183: 782–786

Brinton CC, Gemski P, Falkow S, Baron LS (1961) Location of the piliation factor on the chromosome of *Escherichia coli*. Biochem Biophys Res Commun 5: 293–298

Bores A, Fairbrother JM, Jacques M, Larivière S (988) Isolation and characterization of a new fimbrial antigen (CS1541) from a porcine enterotoxigenic *Escherichia coli* 08:KX105 strain. FEMS Microbiol Lett 55: 341–348

Craig NL (1985) Site-specific inversion: enhancers, recombination proteins and mechanism. Cell 41: 649–650

Cravioto A, Scotland SM, Rowe B (1982) Hemagglutination acitivity and colonization factor antigens I and II in enterotoxigenic and non-enterotoxigenic strains of *Escherichia coli* isolated from humans. Infect Immun 36: 189–197

De Graaf FK, Klaasen P (1986) Organization and expression of genes involved in the biosynthesis of 987P fimbriae, MGG 204: 75–81.

De Graaf FK, Klaasen P (1987) Nucleotide sequence of the gene encoding the 987P fimbrial subunit of *Escherichia coli*. FEMS Microbiol Lett 42: 253–258

De Graaf FK, Mooi FR (1986) The fimbrial adhesins of *Escherichia coli*. Adv Microbiol Physiol 28: 65–143.

De Graaf FK, Krenn BE, Klaasen P (1984) Organization and expression of genes involved in the biosynthesis of K99 fimbriae. Infect Immun 43: 508–514

Dorman CJ, Higgins CF (1987) Fimbrial phase variation in *Escheriachia coli*: dependence on integration host factor and homologies with other site-specific recombinases. J Bacteriol 169: 3840–3843

Eisenstein BI (1981) Phase variation of type 1 fimbriae in *Escherichia coli* is under transcriptional control. Science 214: 337–339

Eisenstein BI, Dodd DC (1982) Pseudocatabolite repression of type 1 fimbriae of *Escherichia coli*. J Bacteriol 151: 1560–1567

Eisenstein BI, Sweet DS, Vaughn V, Friedman D (1987) Integration host factor is required for the DNA inversion that controls phase variation in *Escherichia coli*. Proc Natl Acad Sci USA 84: 6506–6510

Evans DG, Silver RP, Evans DJ, Chase DG, Gorbach SL (1975) Plasmid-controlled colonization factor associated with virulence in *Escherichia coli* enterotoxigenic for humans. Infect Immun 12: 656–667

Fairbrother JM, Larivière S, Lallier R (1986) New fimbrial antigen F165 from *Escherichia coli* serogroup O115 strains isolated from piglets with diarrhea. Infect Immun 51: 10–15

Freitag CS, Eisenstein BI (1983) Genetic mapping and transcriptional orientation of the *fimD* gene. J Bacteriol 156: 1052–1058

Freitag CS, Abraham JM, Clements JR, Eisenstein BI (1985) Genetic analysis of the phase variation control of expression of type 1 fimbriae in *Escherichia coli*. J Bacteriol 162: 668–675

Friedman DI, Gottesman M (1983) Lytic mode of lambda development. In: Hendrix RW, Roberts JW, Stahl FW, Weisberg RA (eds) Lambda II. Cold Spring Harbor Lab, New York, pp 21–51

Girardeau JP, Dubourguier HC, Contrepois M (1980) Attachement des *E. coli* entéropathogènes à la muqueuse intestinale. Bull Group Technol Vet 80-4-B-190: 49–59

Girardeau JP, Der Vartanian M, Ollier JL, Contrepois M (1988) CS31A, a new K88-related fimbrial antigen on bovine enterotoxigenic and septicemic *Escherichia coli* strains. Infect Immun 56: 2180–2188

Hinson G, Knutton S, Lam-Po-Tang KL, McNeish HS, Williams PH (1987) Adherence to human colonocytes of an *Escherichia coli* strain isolated from severe infantile enteritis: molecular and ultrastructural studies of a fibrillar adhesin. Infect Immun 55: 393–402

Honda T, Arita M, Miwatani T (1984) Characterization of new hydrophobic pili of human enterotoxigenic *Escherichia coli*: a possible new colonization factor. Infect Immun 43: 959–965

Isaacson RE (1980) Factors affecting expression of the *Escherichia coli* pilus K99. Infect Immun 28: 190–194

Jacobs AAC (1987) Structure-function relationships of the K88 and K99 fibrillar adhesins of enterotoxigenic *Escherichia coli*. Thesis, Krips Repro, Meppel, The Netherlands

Jacobs AAC, de Graaf FK (1985) Production of K88, and F41 fibrillae in relation to growth phase and a rapid procedure for adhesin purification. FEMS Microbiol Lett 26: 15–19

Jacobs AAC, Roosendaal B, van Breemen JFL, de Graaf FK (1987a) Role of phenylalanine 150 in the receptor-binding domain of the K88 fibrillar subunit. J Bacteriol 169: 4907–4911

Jacobs AAC, Simons BH, de Graaf FK (1987b). The role of lysine-132 and arginine-136 in the receptor-binding domain of the K99 fibrillar subunit. EMBO J6: 1805–1808

Jacobs AAC, Venema J, Leeven R, van Pelt-Heerschap H, de Graaf FK (1987c) Inhibition of adhesive activity of K88 fibrillae by peptide derived from the K88 adhesin. J Bacteriol 169: 735–741

Kehoe M, Sellwood R, Shipley P, Dougan G (1981) Genetic analysis of K88-mediated adhesion of enterotoxigenic *Escherichia coli*. Nature 291: 122–126

Kehoe M, Winther M, Dougan G (1983) Expression of a cloned K88ac adhesion antigen determinant: identification of a new adhesion cistron and role of a vector-encoded promoter. J Bacteriol 155: 1071–1077

Klemm P (1986) Two regulatory *fim* genes, *fimB* and *fimE*, control the phase variation of type 1 fimbriae in *Escherichia coli*. EMBO J 5: 1389–1393

Klemm P, Christiansen G (1987) Three *fim* genes required for the regulation of length and mediation of adhesion of *Escherichia coli* type 1 fimbriae. MGG 208: 439–445

Klemm P, Jorgensen BJ, van Die I, de Ree H, Bergmans H (1985) The *fim* genes responsible for synthesis of type 1 fimbriae in *Escherichia coli*, cloning and genetic organization. MGG 199: 410–414

Knutton S, Baldini MM, Kaper JB, McNeish AS (1987c) Role of plasmid-encoded adherence factors in adhesion of enteropathogenic *Escherichia coli* to HEp-2 cells. Infect Immun 55: 78–85

Knutton S, Lloyd DR, McNeish AS (1987a) Adhesion of enteropathogenic *Escherichia coli* to human intestinal enterocytes and cultured human intestinal mucosa. Infect Immun 55: 69–77

Knutton S, Lloyd DR, McNeish AS (1987b) Identification of a new fimbrial structure in enterotoxigenic *Escherichia coli* (ETEC) serotype O148:H28 which adheres to human intestinal mucosa: a potentially new human ETEC colonization factor. Infect Immun 55: 86–92

Knutton S, Williams PH, Lloyd DR, Candy DCA, McNeish AS (1984) Ultrastructural study of adherence to and penetration of cultured cells by two invasive *Escherichia coli* strains isolated from infants with enteritis. Infect Immun 44: 599–608

Laporta MZ, Silva MLM, Scaletsky ICA, Trabulski LR (1986) Plasmids coding for drug resistance and localized adherence to Hela cells in enteropathogenic *Escherichia coli* O55:H- and O55:H6. Infect Immun 51: 715–717

Levine MM, Ristaino P, Marley G, Smyth C, Knutton E, Boedeker R, Black R, Young C, Clements ML, Cheney C, Patnaik R (1984) Coli surface antigens 1 and 3 of colonization factor antigen II-positive enterotoxigenic *Escherichia coli*: morphology, purification, and immune responses in humans. Infect Immun 44: 409–420

Lindberg F, Lund B, Johansson L, Normark S (1987) Localization of the receptor-binding protein adhesin at the tip of the bacterial pilus. Nature 328: 84–87

Lintermans P, Pohl P, Deboeck F, Bertels A, Schlicker C, VandeKerckhove J, van Damme J, van Montagu M, de Greve H (1988) Isolation and nucleotide sequence of the F17-A gene encoding the structural protein of the F17 fimbriae in bovine enterotoxigenic *Escherichia coli*. Infect Immun 56: 1475–1484

Lund B, Lindberg F, Marklund BI, Normark S (1987) The Pap G protein is the α-D-galactopyranosy-(1 $\rightarrow$ 4)β-D-galactopyranose-binding adhesin of uropathogenic *Escherichia coli*. Proc Natl Acad Sci USA 84: 5898–5902

Manning PA, Timmis KN, Stevenson G (1985) Colonization factor antigen II (CFA/II) of enterotoxigenic *Escherichia coli*: molecular cloning of the CS3 determinant. MGG 200: 322–327

Maurer L, Orndorff PE (1985) A new locus, *pilE*, required for the binding of type 1 piliated *Escherichia coli* to erythrocytes. FEMS Microbiol Lett 30: 59–66

Maurer L, Orndorff PE (1987) Identification and characterization of genes determining receptor binding and pilus length of *Escherichia coli* type 1 pili. J Bacteriol 169: 640–645

McConnell MM, Smith HR, Willshaw GA, Field AM, Rowe B (1981) Plasmids coding for colonization factor antigen I and heat-stable enterotoxin production isolated from enterotoxigenic *Escherichia coli*: comparison of their properties. Infect Immun 32: 927–936

McConnel MM, Thomas LV, Day NP, Rowe B (1985) Enzyme-linked immunosorbent assays for the detection of adhesion factor antigens of enterotoxigenic *Escherichia coli*. J Infect Dis 152: 1120–1127

McConel MM, Thomas LV, Scotland SM, Rowe B (1986) The possession of coli surface antigen CS6 by enterotoxigenic *Escherichia coli* of serogroups O25, O27, O148 and O159: a possible colonisation factor? Curr Microbiol 14: 51–54

McConnell MM, Thomas LV, Willshaw GA, Smith HR, Rowe B (1988) Genetic control and properties of coli surface antigens of colonization factor antigen IV (PCF 8775) of enterotoxigenic *Escherichia coli*. Infect Immun 56: 1974–1980

Minion FC, Abraham SN, Beachey EH, Goguen JD (1986) The genetic determinant of adhesive function in type 1 fimbriae of *Escherichia coli* is distinct from the gene encoding the fimbrial subunit. J Bacteriol 165: 1033–1036

Mooi FR, De Graaf FK, van Embden JDA (1979) Cloning, mapping and expression of the genetic determinant that encodes for the K88ab antigen. Nucleic Acids Res. 6: 849–865

Mooi FR, Harms N, Bakker D, De Graaf FK (1981) Organization and expression of genes involved in the production of the K88ab antigen. Infect Immun 32: 1155–1163

Mooi FR, Wouters C, Wijfjes A, De Graaf FK (1982) Construction and characterization of mutants impaired in the biosynthesis of the K88ab antigen. J Bacteriol 150: 512–521

Mooi FR, Wijfjes A, De Graaf FK (1983) Identification and characterization of precursors in the biosynthesis of the K88ab fimbria of *Escherichia coli*. J Bacteriol 154: 41–49

Mooi FR, van Buuren M, Koopman G, Roosendaal B, De Graaf FK (1984) A K88ab gene of *Escherichia coli* encodes a fimbria-like protein distinct from the K88ab fimbrial adhesin. J Bacteriol 159: 482–487

Mooi FR, Claasen I, Bakker D, Kuipers H, De Graaf FK (1986) Regulation and structure of an *Escherichia coli* gene coding for an outer membrane protein involved in export of the K88ab fimbrial subunits. Nucleic Acids Res 14: 2443–2457

Morris JA, Thorns CJ, Scott AC, Sojka WJ (1982) Adhesive properties associated with the Vir plasmid: a transmissible pathogenic characteristic associated with strains of invasive *Escherichia coli*. J Gen Microbiol 128: 2097–2103

Morris JA, Chanter N, Sherwood D (1987) Occurrence and properties of FY (Att25)[+] *Escherichia coli* associated with diarrhoea in calves. Vet Rec 121: 189–191

Morrissey PM, Dougan G (1986) Expression of a cloned 987P adhesion-antigen fimbrial determinant in *Escherichia coli* K-12 strain HB101. Gene 43: 79–84

Moseley SL, Dougan G, Schneider RA, Moon HW (1986) Cloning of chromosomal DNA encoding the F41 adhesin of enterotoxigenic *Escherichia coli* and genetic homology between adhesins F41 and K88. J Bacteriol 167: 799–804

Mullany P, Field AM, McConnell MM, Scotland SM, Smith HR, Rowe B (1983) Expression of plasmids coding for colonization factor antigen II (CFA/II) and enterotoxin production in *Escherichia coli*. J Gen Microbiol 129: 3591–3601

Murray BE, Evans DJ, Penaranda ME, Evand DG (1983) CFA/I-ST plasmids: comparison of enterotoxigenic *Escherichia coli* (ETEC) of serogroups O25, O63, O78 and O128 and mobilisation from an R-factor-containing epidemic ETEC isolate. J Bacteriol 153: 566–570

Nagy B, Moon HW, Isaacson RE (1977) Colonization of porcine intestine by enterotoxigenic *Escherichia coli*: selection of piliated forms in vivo, adhesion of piliated forms to epithelial cells in vitro, and incidence of pilus antigen among porcine enteropathogenic *E. coli*. Infect Immun 16: 344–352

Nandadasa HG, Sargent GF, Brown MGM, McNeish AG, Williams PH (1981) The role of plasmids in adherence of invasive *Escherichia coli* to mammalian cells. J Infect Dis 143: 286–290

Nataro JP, Scaletsky ICA, Kaper JB, Levine MM, Trabulski LR (1985) Plasmid-mediated factors conferring diffuse and localized adherence of enteropathogenic *Escherichia coli*. Infect Immun 48: 378–383

Norgren M, Normark S, Lark D, O'Hanley P, Schoolink G, Falkow S, Svanbor-Eden C, Baga M, Uhlin BE (1984) Mutations in *E. coli* cistrons affecting adhesion to human cells do not abolish Pap pili fiber formation. EMBO J 3: 1159–1165

Ollier JL, Girardeau JP (1983) Structures et fontions hémagglutinantes des pili K99 dont la biosynthèse est glucose-dépendante ou constitutive et des pili F41. Ann Microbiol 134A: 247–254

Orndorff PE, Falkow S (1984a) Organization and expression of genes responsible for type 1 piliation in *Escherichia coli*. J Bacteriol 159: 736–744

Orndorff PE, Falkow S (1984b) Identification and characterization of a gene product that regulates type 1 piliation in *Escherichia coli*. J Bacteriol 160: 61–66

Orskov I, Orskov F (1966) Episome-carried surface antigen K88 of *Escherichia coli*. I. Transmission of the determinant of the K88 antigen and influence on the transfer of chromosomal markers. J. Bacteriol 91: 69–75

Pabo CO, Sauer RT (1984) Protein-DNA interactions. Annu Rev Biochem 53: 293–321

Penaranda ME, Mann MB, Evans DG, Evans DJ (1980) Transfer of an ST:LT:CFA/II plasmids into *Escherichia coli* K-12 strain RR1 by cotransformation with PSC 301 plasmid DNA. FEMS Microbiol Lett 8: 251–254

Penaranda ME, Evans DG, Murray BE, Evans DJ (1983) ST:LT:CFA/II plasmids in enterotoxigenic *Escherichia coli* belonging to serogroups O6, O8, O80, O85 and O139. J Bacteriol 154: 980–983

Plasterk RHA, Brinkman AD, van der Putte P (1983) DNA inversions in the chromosome of *Escherichia coli* and in bacteriophage Mu: relationships to other site-specific recombination systems. Proc Natl Acad Sci USA 80: 5355–5358

Platt T (1986) Transcription termination and the regulation of gene expression. Annu Rev Biochem 55: 339–372

Pohl P, Lintermans P, van Muylen K, Schotte M (1982) Colibacilles entérotoxigènes du veau possédant in antigène d'attachment différent de l'antigène K99. Annu Med Vet 126: 569–571

Reis MHL, Affonso MHT, Trabulski LR, Mazaitis AJ, Maas R, Maas WK (1980) Transfer of a CFA/I-ST plasmid promoted by a conjugative plasmid in a strain of *Escherichia coli* of serotype O128ac:H12. Infect Immun 29:140–143

Rhen M, Mäkelä PH, Korhonen TK (1983) P-fimbriae of *Escherichia coli* are subject to phase variation. FEMS Microbiol Lett 19: 267–271.

Roosendaal B (1987) A molecular study on the biogenesis of K99 fimbriae. Thesis, Tessel Offset, Utrecht

Roosendaal E, Gaastra W, De Graaf FK (1984) The nucleotide sequence of the gene encoding the K99 subunit of enterotoxigenic *Escherichia coli*. FEMS Microbiol Lett 22: 253–258

Roosendaal E, Boots M, De Graaf FK (1987a) Two novel genes, *fanA*, and *fanB*, involved in the biogenesis of K99 fimbriae. Nucleic Acids Res 15:5973–5984

Roosendaal E, Jacobs AAC, Rathman P, Sondermeyer C, Stegehuis F, Oudega B, De Graaf FK (1987b) Primary structure and subcellular localization of two fimbrial subunit-like proteins involved in the biosynthesis of K99 fibrillae. Mol Microbiol 1: 211–217

Roosendaal B, Damoiseaux J, Jordi W, de Graaf FK (1988) Transcriptional organization of the DNA region controlling expression of the K99 gene cluster, MGG (in press)

Scaletsky ICA, Milani SR, Trabulsi LR, Travassos LR (1988) Isolation and characterization of the localized adherence factor of enteropathogenic *Escherichia coli*. Infect Immun 56: 2979–2983

Schmitt R, Mattes R, Schmid K, Altenbuchner J (1979) Raf plasmids in strains of *Escherichia coli* and their possible role in enteropathogeny. In: Timmis KN, Pühler A (eds) Plasmids of medical, environmental and commercial importance.Elsevier, North-Holland Biomedical, New York, pp 199–210

Scotland SM, McConnell MM, Willshaw GA, Rowe B, Field AM (1985) Properties of wild-type strains of enterotoxigenic *Escherichia coli* which produce colonization factor antigen II, and belonging to serogroups other than O6. J Gen Microbiol 131: 2327–2333

Shipley PL, Gyles CL, Falkow S (1978) Characterization of plasmids that encode for the K88 colonization antigen. Infect Immun 20: 559–566

Shipley PL, Dougan G, Falkow S (1981) Identification and cloning of the genetic determinant that encodes for the K88ac adherence antigen. J Bacteriol 145: 920–925

Smith HR, Cravioto A, Willshaw GA, McConnell MM, Scotland SM, Gross RJ, Rowe B (1979) A plasmid coding for the production of colonisation factor antigen I and heat-stable enterotoxin in strains of *Escherichia coli* of serogroup O78. FEMS Microbiol Lett 6: 255–260

Smith HR, Willshaw GA, Rowe B (1982) Mapping of a plasmid, coding for colonization factor antigen I and heat-stable enterotoxin production, isolated from an enterotoxigenic strain of *Escherichia coli*. J Bacteriol 149: 264–275

Smith HR, Scotland SM, Rowe B (1983) Plasmids that code for production of colonization factor antigen II and enterotoxin production in strains of *Escherichia coli*. Infect Immun 40: 1236–1239

Smith HW, Linggood MA (1972) Further observations on *Escherichia coli* enterotoxins with particular regard to those produced by a typical piglet strains and by calf and lamb strains. The transmissible nature of these enterotoxins and of a K antigen possessed by calf and lamb strains. J Med Microbiol 5: 243–250

Smith HW, Parsell Z (1975) Transmissible substrate-utilising ability in enterobacteria. J Gen Microbiol 87: 129–140

Smyth CJ (1982) Two mannose-resistant haemagglutinins on enterotoxigenic *Escherichia coli* of serotype O6:K15:H16 or H-isolated from travellers' and infantile diarrhoea. J Gen Microbiol 128: 2081–2096

Smyth CJ (1984) Serologically distinct fimbriae on enterotoxigenic *Escherichia coli* of serotype O6:K15:H16 or H-. FEMS Microbiol Lett 21: 51–57

So M, Crandall JF, Crosa JH, Falkow S (1974) Extrachromosomal determinants which contribute to bacterial pathogenicity. In: Schlessinger D (ed) Microbiology 1974. American Society for Microbiology, Washington, pp 16–26

Swaney LM, Liu Y-P, Ippen-Ihler K, Brinton CC (1977) Genetic complementation analysis of *Escherichia coli* type 1 somatic pilus mutants. J Bacteriol 130: 506–511

Tacket CO, Maneval DR, Levine MM (1987) Purification, morphology, and genetics of a new fimbrial putative colonization factor of enterotoxigenic *Escherichia coli* O159:H4. Infect Immun 55: 1063–1069

Thomas LV, Cravioto A, Scotland SM, Rowe B (1982) New fimbrial antigenic type (E8775) that may represent a colonization factor in enterotoxigenic *Escherichia coli* in humans. Infect Immun 35: 1119–1124

Thomas LV, McConnell MM, Rowe B, Field AM (1985) The possession of three novel coli surface antigens by enterotoxigenic *Escherichia coli* strains positive for the putative colonization factor PCF 8775. J Gen Microbiol 131: 2319–2326

Thomas LV, Rowe B, McConnell MM (1987) In strains of *Escherichia coli* O167 a single plasmid encodes for the coli surface antigens CS5 and CS6 of putative colonization factor PCF8775, heat-stable enterotoxin, and colicin Ia. Infect Immun 55: 1929–1931

Van Doorn J, Oudega B, Mooi FR, De Graaf FK (1982) Subcellular localization of polypeptides involved in the biosynthesis of the K88ab fimbriae. FEMS Microbiol Lett 13: 99–104

Van Embden JDA, De Graaf FK, Schouls LM, Teppema JS (1980) Cloning and expression of a deoxyribonucleic acid fragment that encodes for the adhesive antigen K99. Infect Immun 29: 1125–1133

Van Verseveld HW, Bakker P, Van der Woude T, Terleth C, De Graaf FK (1985) Production of fimbrial adhesins K99 and F41 by enterotoxigenic *Escherichia coli* as a function of growth-rate domain. Infect Immun 49: 159–163

Williams PH, Knutton S, Brown MGM, Candy DCA, McNeish AS (1984) Characterization of nonfimbrial mannose-resistant protein hemagglutinins of two *Escherichia coli* strains isolated from infants with enteritis. Infect Immun 44: 592–598

Willshaw GA, Smith HR, McConnell MM, Barclay EA, Krnjulac J, Rowe B (1982) Genetic and molecular studies of plasmids coding for colonization factor antigen I and heat-stable enterotoxin in several *Escherichia coli* serotypes. Infect Immun 37: 858–868

Willshaw GA, Smith HR, Rowe R (1983) Cloning of regions encoding colonisation factor antigen I and heat-stable enterotoxin in *Escherichia coli*. FEMS Microbiol Lett 16: 101–106

Willshaw GA, Smith HR, McConnell MM, Rowe B (1985) Expression of cloned plasmid regions encoding colonization factor antigen I (CFA/I) in *Escherichia coli*. Plasmid 13: 8–16

Zieg J, Simon M (1980) Analysis of the nucleotide sequence of an invertible controlling element. Proc. Natl Acad Sci USA 77: 4196–4201

Nature and Organization of Adhesins

K. JANN and H. HOSCHÜTZKY

1 Introduction

The adherence of pathogenic bacteria to epithelial surfaces is an important early even in their interaction with the host, leading to colonization and infection (OFEK and BEACHEY 1980; D.C. SAVAGE 1985). This process provides the bacteria with several advantages, such as resistance to the rinsing and cleaning action of body fluids, evasion of host defenses, and improved acquisition of nutrients from their environment. It may also permit an optimal delivery of exotoxins. In extraintestinal infections the specific adhesion to certain tissues may result in an organ tropism of infectious bacteria (NOWICKI et al. 1986).

The term adhesion, as used in this article, describes a specific interaction of surface-attached bacterial recognition proteins (adhesins) with the carbohydrate moiety of glycoproteins or glycolipids on mammalian cells. Since the receptors for bacteria are often also expressed on erythrocytes, hemagglutination is used as a simple in vitro assay for the adhesive properties of bacteria (LEFFLER and SVANBORG-EDÉN 1986; SALIT and GOTSCHLICH 1977). Thus, adhesins may also be termed hemagglutinins but the more general term lectins is also used. It was found early that some agglutinations/adhesions can be inhibited with α-mannosides, which

Max-Planck-Institut für Immunbiologie, Stübeweg 51, D-7800 Freiburg, FRG

were termed mannose sensitive (MS). Others were not inhibitable with α-mannosides and were thus termed mannose resistant (MR) (SHARON and OFEK 1986).

The carbohydrate specificity of several MR adhesins could be defined in molecular terms: -α-Gal-(1,4)-β-Gal- is recognized by P-specific adhesins of uropathogenic *Escherichia coli* (VÄISÄNEN-RHEN et al. 1981), α-NeuNAc-(2,3 or 2,6)-β-Gal is recognized by S-specific adhesins of *E. coli* causing sepsis and neonatal meningitis (PARKKINEN et al. 1983), and β-GlcNAc-(1,3)-β-GlcNAc is recognized by G-specific adhesins of uropathogenic *E. coli* (VÄISINEN-RHEN et al. 1983). Some uropathogenic bacteria adhere to cells exhibiting an as yet unknown structural arrangement of galactose, sialic acid, and serine. Since the receptor for the latter bacteria is associated with the expression of the human M/N blood group system, their adhesins are termed M/N specific (VÄISÄNEN-RHEN et al. 1982). Human enteropathogenic *E. coli* adhere to cell linings of the small intestine with the aid of colonization factor antigens (mainly CFA/I and CFA/II) that interact with mucosal gangliosides: NeuNAc seems to be essential for the interaction (FARIS et al. 1980).

The adhesins which govern the interaction of bacteria with receptors on host cells are subject to regulation by growth conditions. Thus, most adhesins are expressed above a growth temperature of 20°C and not below. The expression of others is regulated by the presence of certain nutrients such as glucose or alanine (DE GRAAF et al. 1980; EISENSTEIN and DODD 1982). The mannose-specific (type 1) adhesins are produced in large amounts by bacteria grown in liquid culture and in only very small amounts in agar-grown bacteria (EISENSTEIN and DODD 1982); the expression of other fimbriae as well as nonfimbrial adhesins is more pronounced in agar-grown bacteria. Bacterial adhesins may be subject to variation between an expressed and a nonexpressed state with the genetic information, however, constantly present (EISENSTEIN 1981; RHEN et al. 1983).

The adhesiveness of bacteria is frequently correlated with the presence of proteinaceous fibrillar structures on the bacterial surface. These appendages, which are distinct from the sex pili and from the flagella, have been termed fimbriae or pili (BRINTON 1965; DUGUID et al. 1955; DUGUID and OLD 1980). Thus, fimbriae were assumed to be the mediators of adhesion. The nature of the actual recognition protein has been elusive for many years and has been described only recently for some fimbrial types (ABRAHAM et al. 1987a; HOSCHÜTZKY et al. 1989b; MANSON and BRINTON 1988; MOCH et al. 1987; ABRAHAM et al. 1987a). The nature of adhesins at large became seemingly more complex when bacteria were found that were adhesive but did not express fimbriae. It was possible to isolate proteins from these bacteria which agglutinated red blood cells and which did not form electron microscopically recognizable structures (DUGUID et al. 1979). It should, however, be pointed out that a distinction between fimbriae-associated (or fimbrial) and nonfimbrial adhesins may be superficial and in fact be due to the limitations of electron microscopic resolution. Thus, the adhesins of certain enteropathogenic *E. coli* have been described as nonfimbrial and some of them were later found to form very fine fimbrillae on the bacterial surfacc (ØRSKOV et al. 1985). We are using the terms fimbrial and nonfimbrial with this reservation.

Bacterial adhesins and their interactions with receptors on host cells have been

studied with many bacterial genera (for reviews see MIRELMAN and OFEK 1986; ISAACSON 1985). In this article we restrict ourselves to the chemical and topographic characterization of the adhesins of *E. coli*, with special emphasis on P- and S-specific fimbriae and on (blood group M/N specific) nonfimbrial adhesins.

2 Characterization of Adhesins

2.1 Adhesins Associated with Fimbriae

Fimbriae can be detached in a morphologically and functionally unaltered form from the bacterial surface without damage to the cells. SDS–PAGE analysis revealed that fimbrial preparations consist of more than one protein (JANN et al. 1981; HOSCHÜTZKY et al. 1989a). For a long time it remained unclear whether the observed minor proteins were integral components of the fimbriae, or whether they were contaminating proteins. It was also not known which protein is the actual mediator of the adhesive properties. Genetic studies on P, S, and type 1 fimbriae showed that the phenotypes of fimbriation and adhesiveness are encoded by a complex gene cluster but determined by different genes (LINDBERG et al. 1984; HACKER et al. 1985; KLEMM and CHRISTIANSEN 1987; MINION et al. 1986; VAN DIE et al. 1985). This suggested that the protein mediating the adhesive properties of the bacteria is different from that forming the fimbriae. The first genetic system studied in detail was that of the gene complex encoding F13 (pap) fimbriae of uropathogenic *E. coli*. Expression of the genes in minicells showed that the gene complex directed the synthesis of several peptides (A, H, C, D, E, F, G, X, Y) (LINDBERG et al. 1986; NORGREN et al. 1984; TENNENT et al. 1987). Essential peptides concerning the fimbrial structure itself are encoded by the A, E, F, and G genes, whereas the C protein is an outer membrane protein, essential in the passage of the fimbriae through the outer membrane and their anchorage to the cell surface. The D protein seems to be a periplasmic protein, serving as a shuttle in the passage through the periplasm of all proteins forming adhesive fimbriae (TENNENT et al. 1987). It was found that the A peptide is the structural subunit of the fimbrium. Since F, G, and possibly E negative mutants were not adhesive, it was thought that these proteins are involved in the adhesive process. The question remained, however, of whether these proteins (or one of them) are directly responsible for receptor binding, or whether they modify the fimbrial subunits so that they acquire receptor binding properties (LINDBERG et al. 1986).

In our attempts to verify the genetic data on the protein level we have assumed as a working hypothesis that the major fimbrial subunit (A protein) and the adhesin are distinct proteins and that one of the minor proteins we normally detect in preparations of purified fimbriae is responsible for the adhesive properties. The expectation was that the molar ratio of the proteins must be in the order of one adhesin molecule to several hundred fimbrial subunits. We have developed an isolation procedure for these fimbriae-associated adhesins that in principle consists of the following steps: (a) detachment of fimbriae from the bacterial surface, (b) isolation of purified fimbriae, (c) dissociation of the adhesin from the fimbrial

polymer, and (d) final purification of the adhesin by HPLC. This isolation procedure, which is described below, is generally applicable to all fimbriae which carry an adhesive protein different from the major subunit of the polymer (Moch et al. 1987; Hoschützky et al. 1989b).

2.1.1 Isolation of the Fimbriae–Adhesin Complex

The separation of the fimbriae–adhesin complex (FAC) from the bacteria can be achieved by shearing a suspension of fimbriated bacteria in an Omnimixer or a similar device, by their incubation with urea or octyl glucoside, or by heating to 50°–70°C. Since omnimixing concomitantly releases substantial amounts of outer membrane material and gives only a low yield of fimbriae, and detergents or chaotropes interfere with subsequent purification of FACs and their dissociation, heating of bacterial suspensions at low ionic strength to 65°C was the method of choice for the removal of FACs (Moch et al. 1987; Hoschützky et al. 1989a). After cooling, the bacteria are removed by centrifugation and the fimbriae are precipitated from the supernatant with 10% ammonium sulfate or with 500 mM LiCl. The presence of EDTA, glycine, and 5% sucrose prevents coprecipitation of bacterial outer membrane proteins. Lipopolysaccharide (LPS) is then removed from the FAC by incubation with 0.5% sodium desoxycholate at 80°C followed by ultracentrifugation. SDS–PAGE analysis at this point reveals the presence of major fimbrillar subunits and two or three additional faint protein bands. One of these has proved to be the respective adhesin. In the case of the genetically well-characterized F13 fimbriae, the other two proteins had molecular sizes (15.5 kd and 16 kd) (Hoschützky et al. 1989b), corresponding to the E and F proteins proposed to be minor components of fimbriae (Lindberg et al. 1986). In our isolation procedure the adhesin (G protein) and the E protein are isolated in a 1:1 ratio, while the F protein is usually isolated in a five- to tenfold lower concentration.

It should be noted that if the fimbriae are removed from the bacteria with octyl glucoside rather than by heating, a 80-kd protein is coextracted and can be obtained separately (Hoschützky and Jann, unpublished). This seems to be the C protein (anchorage protein) proposed by Normak to be associated with the outer membrane (Norgren et al. 1984).

The purified S- and P-specific FACs disperse readily in water at pH 7–8. They adhere to cultured cells of a human kidney cell line and to HeLa cells, as could be demonstrated by immunofluorescence using specific antibodies. Fimbriae isolated from recombinant *E. coli* strains expressing the adhesive negative phenotype, i.e., lacking the adhesive G protein, were not able to adhere to the tissue culture cells.

The purified S- and P-FACs adhered to different cells in the pH range from 5 to 9, and did so optimally at pH 7–8. However, hemagglutination was not observed with purified FACs at neutral pH. At pH values below 6, as well as in the presence of divalent cations, hemagglutination could be readily demonstrated. We interpret these observations as indicating that near neutrality the isolated FACs are dispersed and monovalent with respect to cell interaction. They can therefore adhere to cells but not agglutinate them. At lower pH as well as in the presence of divalent ions the FACs aggregate either isoelectrically or through ionic interactions. Thus they

become polyvalent and able to agglutinate cells (HOSCHÜTZKY et al. 1989b). The adherence/agglutination could be specifically inhibited with the trisaccharide α-galactoside-(1,4)-lactose in the case of P-specificity (LEFFLER and SVANBORG-EDÉN 1986; HOSCHÜTZKY et al. 1989a) and with α-sialyl-(2,3/6)-lactose in the case of S-specificity (MOCH et al. 1987). Thus, the purified FACs had retained their specific receptor recognition.

2.1.2 Isolation of Adhesins from Fimbriae–Adhesin Complexes

During our studies we observed that the use of mild detergents like octyl glucoside released the FAC together with the 80-kd C protein. The latter protein was not detectable in FACs that had been released from the bacteria by mechanical treatment or by heat extraction. We were also able to demonstrate that with the use of detergents like SDS or some of the Zwittergents, fimbriae could be isolated that had lost their recognition protein and thus the ability to adhere to eukaryotic cells. Based on these observations we developed a method to specifically release the adhesin from the FAC without their dissociation into the major fimbrillar subunits. The best way to achieve this was heating of the purified FAC in the presence of 0.5% Zwittergent C-16 at 80°C. SDS also dissociates the FAC into adhesin and fimbriae. Since this detergent is difficult to remove and interferes with subsequent purification steps, it was not used further. After incubation with Zwittergent C-16 the fimbriae were precipitated with 500 mM LiCl. The supernatant contained the adhesin and the fimbrillar subunit in a ratio of 1:1 as estimated by SDS–PAGE. This is a 50- to 100-fold enrichment of the adhesin, as compared to the protein composition of intact FAC. The adhesins were concentrated from the supernatant of the detergent extraction either by precipitation with ice-cold ethanol/1-butanol or by dialysis against 50 mM NH_4HCO_3 followed by lyophilization. Subsequent high resolution ion exchange chromatography (HPLC) on a MonoQ or a PW 5-DEAE column was performed, preferentially after denaturation of the proteins with 8 M guanidine hydrochloride prior to the separation by HPLC. After treatment with guanidine the adhesins purified in our laboratory could be renatured to functional proteins.

2.1.3 Characterization of Fimbriae-Associated Adhesins

We have isolated and purified the adhesins from S fimbriae and from P fimbriae of different serotypes ($F7_1$, F8, F13) (MOCH et al. 1987; HOSCHÜTZKY et al. 1989b). The general properties of the proteins are summarized in Table 1. To demonstrate the adhesive specificity of the isolated adhesins, we used a hemadhesion assay, in which erythrocytes were incubated together with the immobilized adhesin in the presence or absence of specific inhibitors. The extent to which the red cells attached to the ELISA plate was determined by measuring hemoglobin at OD_{405}, after lysis of the specifically bound red cells. With this assay we were able to demonstrate that the purified adhesins had maintained their receptor-recognizing specificities.

The N-terminal sequence of the F13 (pap) adhesin (Table 1; HOSCHÜTZKY et al. 1989b) proved to be identical with the amino acid sequence derived from the DNA sequence (LUND et al. 1987). The N-terminal sequence of the $F7_1$ adhesin is not

Table 1. Properties of adhesins and fimbrillins from S and P fimbriae

FAC		Fimbrillin		Adhesin	
		MW (10^3 d)	pI	MW (10^3 d)	pI
S		16.5	6	14	4.7
F7	(P)	22	5	35	4.8–5
F8	(P)	18.5	5	35	4.8–5
F13	(P)	18	5	35	4.8–5

related to the F13 adhesin but is homologous with the adhesins from the P-specific F7$_2$ and F11 fimbriae (LUND et al. 1988). These data indicate that at least groups of recognition proteins exist; however, since they have the same Gal–Gal receptor binding specificity, they most probably have a conserved receptor binding site. Thus, the P-specific adhesins represent a group of related recognition proteins which have the binding region in common.

For an immunochemical and functional analysis of P and S fimbriae (FAC) and their corresponding adhesins, as well as for diagnostic purposes, we prepared monoclonal antibodies. Several antifimbrial antibodies reacted only with the homologous F type and others cross-reacted more or less extensively with fimbriae of other F types (HOSCHÜTZKY et al. 1989b). Similarly, several antiadhesin antibodies reacted only with the homologous adhesin and a few reacted with all P or S adhesins isolated from the different FACs (H. HOSCHÜTZKY et al., unpublished material). There was no immunologic cross-reactivity between fimbriae and their adhesins. The monoclonal antibodies reacting with all P or S adhesins were antiadhesive. First results indicate that the (ELISA) titer of their serologic cross-reactivity parallels their capacity to inhibit adherence/agglutination of target cells. This underlines the above interpretation that the adhesins may contain a conserved region which is the receptor binding site.

The question of the location of adhesins on the bacteria was addressed with the aid of immunogold electron microscopy. The S adhesin and the P adhesins from F7$_1$ and F11 and F13 fimbriae were found to be located at the tips of the fimbriae (MOCH et al. 1987; RIEGMAN et al. 1989; LINDBERG et al. 1982), as shown in Fig. 1. Interestingly, the adhesin and another minor protein (corresponding to the E protein of pap fimbriae) form a functional complex attached to the fimbrial rod. This seems, however, not to be the only mode of adhesin presentation on fimbriae. Analysis of the P-specific F9-FAC revealed P-specific adhesin not only at the tip but also at the side of the fimbriae, which had a kinked appearance (RIEGMAN et al. 1989). Using the same technique, BEACHEY and ABRAHAM (1988) obtained a similar picture with an *E. coli* recombinant expressing mannose-specific type 1 fimbriae. The authors showed that the adhesin (H protein) is located alongside the fimbriae as distinct globules which were termed fimbriosomes and which may contain additional minor subunits. Although the clone used by ABRAHAM et al. 1987a overproduced the adhesin and thus may not be representative, the evidence cannot be disregarded; it is possible that in some strains the adhesin may be located on the tips of the fimbriae and in other strains alongside the fimbriae.

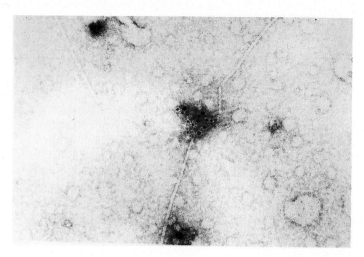

Fig. 1. Immunoelectron micrograph of F7$_1$ fimbriae, double labeled with E- and G-specific antiserum. The larger (11-nm) gold particles adhere to the adhesin; the 7-nm gold particles adhere to the nonadhesive minor subunit E. F7$_2$ and F11 fimbriae show the same labeling pattern. (Courtesy of N. RIEGMAN, Utrecht)

2.1.4 Isolation of adhesins from Outer Bacterial Membranes

Several years ago we found that *E. coli* with mannose-specific fimbriae agglutinated erythrocytes and *S. cerevisiae* even after removal of the fimbriae (ESHDAT et al. 1981). We were also able to show that isolated outer membranes of these bacteria were still agglutinating in an MS way. From the membranes of defimbriated P-specific *E. coli* the adhesin could be solubilized with octyl glucoside or Zwittergent 3-16, but not with Triton X-100 or 4M urea. The P adhesin thus isolated does not associate with the respective fimbriae; it can also be obtained from fimbriated bacteria by direct extraction with octyl glucoside which does not dissociate FAC. Such an extraction leads to a five- to tenfold higher yield of adhesin as compared with the other procedures. The cell wall associated adhesin, which is solubilized with octyl glucoside, does not copurify with the FAC. However, it has the same molecular size, receptor specificity, and serologic specificity as analyzed with monoclonal antibodies (H. HOSCHÜTZKY and K. JANN, in preparation).

These findings, which indicate an FAC-independent adhesin pool in or associated with the outer membrane, are difficult to reconcile with the biogenesis and export assembly of FACs as proposed by NORMARK and co-workers (BAGA et al 1987). These authors postulate that transport of the P adhesin (G protein) is closely linked with that of the other minor subunit proteins (E and F) constituting the functional head of the fimbria and of the major subunit (A protein), which forms the supporting fimbrial rod. Our findings permit the interpretation that the P adhesin is exported independently of the other fimbrial proteins and forms a pool in (or on) the outer bacterial membrane from which the fimbriae-associated adhesin is drawn. Alternatively, the adhesin may be exported by two independent mechanisms, one as proposed by NORMARK et al., and the other using a different export system which

channels the protein into the outer membrane. This holds not only for the P adhesin but for the S- and mannose-specific adhesins as well.

2.2 Fimbriae Consisting of Adhesive Subunits

Fimbriae which contain the receptor-recognizing protein (adhesin) as an associated minor subunit are found with many pathogenic *E. coli*, mainly of extraintestinal origin. In contrast, swine pathogenic *E. coli* of O groups 8 and 148 exhibit the fimbrial K88 antigen, which has a different organization. Genetic studies have indicated that the major subunit of the K88 fimbriae is the adhesin (DE GRAAF 1988). Such fimbriae, consisting of adhesive subunits, may be polyvalent if the receptor binding domains of all subunits are available for receptor interaction, or monovalent if only the terminal subunit is available for receptor binding. Like the P and S fimbriae (see Sect. 2.1.1), the K88 fimbriae are monodispers, adhering but not agglutinating at pH 7-8, but aggregating and thus agglutinating at pH 5-6. We therefore assume that the K88 fimbriae consist of adhesive subunits which have their receptor binding sites blocked by their organization into fimbriae.

M fimbriae of uropathogenic *E. coli* seem to be organized in the same way as the K88 fimbriae, while in the SS142 fimbriae (METT et al. 1983) all subunits can interact with the receptor (H. HOSCHÜTZKY and K. JANN, unpublished results).

2.3 Nonfimbrial Adhesins of *E. coli*

The early work of DUGUID has already shown that, not uncommonly, *E. coli* are isolated which show adhesive and agglutinating properties but are not fimbriated (DUGUID et al. 1979). Systematic studies of these bacteria and their respective adhesins have only recently begun in several laboratories (GOLDHAR et al. 1987;

Table 2. Properties of nonfimbrial adhesins of *E. coli*

Nonfimbrial adhesin	MW of subunit (10^3 d)	Receptor	Reference
GV-12	13.4	MR[a]	SHELADIA et al., 1982
444-3	14.5	MR	WILLIAMS et al. 1984
469-3	14	MR	WILLIAMS et al. 1984
O75X	16	MR	VÄISANEN-RHEN 1984
AFA-1	16	MR	WALZ et al. 1985
ZI	14.4	MR	ØRSKOV et al. 1985
M	21	M[b]	RHEN et al. 1986
2230	16	MR	FORESTIER et al. 1987
NFA-1	21	M/N[b]	GOLDHAR et al. 1987
NFA-2	19	M/N	GOLDHAR et al. 1987
NFA-3	17.5	N[b]	GRÜNBERG et al. 1988
NFA-4	28	M	HOSCHÜTZKY et al. 1989b
NFA-5	23	M	HOSCHÜTZKY and K. JANN, unpublished material

[a] MR, mannose resistant;
[b] Blood group specificity

GRUNBERG et al. 1988; HOSCHÜTZKY et al. 1989a; ØRSKOV I et al. 1985; SKELADIA et al. 1982; WALZ et al. 1985; WILLIAMS et al. 1984; VAISÄNEN-RHEN 1984). Strains which express nonfimbrial adhesins are listed in Table 2. These adhesive structures seem to be subject to temperature regulation (restrictive temperatures below 20°C) and to phase variation, as has been described for the fimbrial adhesins. Most of the clinical isolates also express mannose-specific fimbriae, especially when the bacteria are grown in liquid culture. Two of the nonfimbrial adhesins have been cloned (LABIGNE-ROUSSEL et al. 1984, 1985; HALES et al. 1988). Their gene organization was shown to be similar to that of the fimbrial adhesins. The major difference between fimbriated and nonfimbriated strains seems to be the lack of a transcribed gene coding for the major fimbrial subunit. In this context it should be noted that the fimbriae consisting of adhesive subunits (see Sect. 2.2) have a gene organization analogous to that of the nonfimbrial adhesins.

The most intensive genetic studies have been performed on a nonfimbrial (afimbrial) adhesin (NFA) termed AFA-1 (LABIGNE-ROUSSEL et al. 1984, 1985). This or closely related adhesins are expressed in many *E. coli* strains (LABIGNE-ROUSSEL and FALKOW 1988). Amino acid sequence and receptor specificity indicate that AFA-1 is different from the other non-fimbrial adhesins listed in Table 2.

Whereas receptor structures for the fimbrial adhesins are expressed not only on human but also on animal cells, this is not the case with the nonfimbrial adhesins with blood group M/N specificity. The only animal cell found to express an NFA receptor is the chicken erythrocyte (HOSCHÜTZKY et al. 1989b). Such a specificity for chicken as well as human red blood cells is also known for the sialic acid-specific influenza A virus (MARKWELL 1986). The chemical nature of the NFA receptor(s) is not known. Interestingly, most NFAs which we have isolated have a preference for erythrocytes of MM, MN, or NN blood groups (GOLDHAR et al. 1987; GRUNBERG et al. 1988; HOSCHÜTZKY et al. 1989a).

2.3.1 Isolation

The isolation of NFAs was achieved in several laboratories with very similar methods. We have developed a procedure which is similar to that for the isolation of fimbrial-associated adhesin (see Sect. 2.1.1). Crude preparations of NFA are obtained by heating of the agar-grown bacteria to 50–70°C or by the other methods described in Sect. 2.1.1. Temperature, ionic strength, and pH during heat extraction are critical and may vary from one strain to another. After removal of the bacteria by centrifugation, crude NFAs are obtained by differential ammonium sulfate precipitation in the presence of EDTA and glycine. To remove lipid contamination, the crude NFAs may be treated with 50% ethanol. At this stage the solubility of the NFAs is reduced, possibly due to a change in conformation or loss of a compound which stabilizes the proteins in aqueous solution. The NFAs are dissolved in 8M guanidine hydrochloride and, after its exchange for 8 M urea, purified by high resolution ion exchange chromatography. Using this method we have isolated NFAs from six different *E. coli* strains, with yields ranging from 1 to 10 mg per 10 g wet weight.

Table 3. N-terminal sequences of fimbriae-associated and nonfimbrial adhesins

Adhesin	N-terminal sequence					Reference
	1	6	11	16	21	
M	STVTA	THTVE	SDAEF	TI		RHEN et al. 1986
NFA-5	VTVTA	RHTVE	SDAXF	IDXV		HOSCHÜTZKY et al., unpublished material
2230	GNVLS	GGNGT	QTVTM	PVNAA	TXTVS	FORESTIER et al. 1987
NFA-1	DANGL	NTVNA	GDGKN	LGTAA	A	HOSCHÜTZKY et al., unpublished material
AFA-1	NFTSG	GTNGK	VDLIT	TEECR	VTVES	LABIGNE-ROUSSEL et al. 1985
NFA-4	NTTGD	FNGSF	DMNGA	IAADV	YKG	HOSCHÜTZKY et al., 1989a
K88	WMTGD	FNGSV	DIGGS	ITADD	YRQ	GAASTRA et al. 1981
F1 (typge I)	CKTAN	GTAIP	IGGSA	NVYVN	LAPVV	ABRAHAM et al. 1987
F7₁	XNNIV	FYSLG	NVNSY	QGG		HOSCHÜTZKY et al. 1989
F7₂	WNNIV	FYSLG	NVNSY	QGGNV	VITQR	LUND et al. 1988
F11	WNNIV	FYSLG	DVNSY	QGGNV	VITQR	LUND et al. 1988
F13	GWHNV	MFYAF	NDYLT	TNAGN	FKVID	LUND et al. 1987 HOSCHÜTZKY et al. 1989[b]

2.3.2 Characterization

Data accumulated on NFAs are shown in Table 2 and the known N-terminal amino acid sequences are compared in Table 3. The only sequence homologies seen so far are those between NFA-4 and the fimbrial K88 antigen and between NFA-5 and the M-specific adhesin described by RHEN et al. (1986), HOSCHÜTZKY et al. (1989), and H. HOSCHÜTZKY and K. JANN (unpublished material).

The NFAs have apparent molecular weights in excess of 10^7, as estimated by gel permeation chromatography. SDS–PAGE showed that they consist of noncovalently linked subunits with molecular weights in the range of 15–30 kD, which is

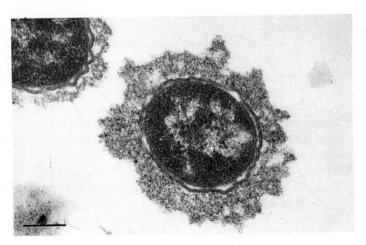

Fig. 2. Electron micrograph of an ultrathin section of *E. coli* 21248 expressing NFA-1. The extracellular adhesin was stabilized with an adhesin-specific monoclonal antibody

comparable to those of fimbrial adhesins and fimbrillins. The NFAs are therefore large polymers consisting of more than 20 subunits. It will be interesting to learn in which way these subunits aggregate and if stable intermediate stages of aggregation exist. No information concerning aggregation states of NFAs in solution and their arrangement on the bacterial cell surface is available at present.

Isolated NFA-1, NFA-2, and NFA-4 were used for the preparation of specific antisera and monoclonal antibodies. Some of the monoclonal antibodies are strongly antiadhesive in the hemadhesion assay. The antibodies were used to elucidate the cellular expression of the NFAs. Electromicroscopic analysis of thin sections from NFA-1, NFA-2, and NFA-4 expressing *E. coli* after stabilization of the adhesins with homologous antibody revealed that these adhesins surround the bacterial cell like a capsule. This is shown in Fig. 2 with NFA-1 as an example. This type of extracellular presentation was also demonstrated by ØRSKOV et al. (1985) and termed an adhesive capsule. Such an extracellular expression of an NFA may be more common that hitherto known.

3 Coexpression of Polysaccharide Capsules and Adhesins

Escherichia coli causing extraintestinal infections frequently express K antigens, which surround the cells as a polysaccharide capsule (JANN and JANN, this volume). With the aid of these capsules the bacteria are able to overcome the nonspecific defense mechanisms of the host, mostly the action of complement and phagocytes. Since several such strains also express adhesive proteins, it is interesting to know whether or not in these extraintestinal bacteria polysaccharide capsules and adhesins are expressed by the same or by different cells of a given population. In immunoelectron microscopic studies of fimbriated and encapsulated *E. coli* we have found evidence that polysaccharide capsules and fimbriae are coexpressed in many but not all cells of the population. K.D. KRÖNCKE and K. JANN, unpublished material). Many cells were seen which seemed to express either one or other of these virulence determinants. This may be due to phase variations and/or mutations in the bacterial population. In a statistical mean time both virulence factors are probably expressed by all cells. There is one additional factor which hitherto has escaped close examination, i.e., the regulation of fimbrial expression in certain stages of an infection. We do not know when fimbriae are essential for the bacteria and when they impede the progress of infection. For instance, it may be that fimbriae are not expressed on bacteria which are in the process of invading a tissue or which are encountering receptor-expressing phagocytes. In these cases, phase variation may provide a selective advantage to the nonfimbriated cells.

The problem of coexpression of adhesins and polysaccharide capsules becomes especially interesting when the adhesin also forms a capsule. In such cases the possibility exists that the bacteria express two types of capsule. We have analyzed this phenomenon with the uropathogenic *E. coli* O7:K98:H6, which exhibits the polysaccharide K98 capsule as well as the nonfimbrial adhesin NFA-4 (KRÖNCKE et al., manuscript in preparation). The bacteria were subjected to immunoelectron

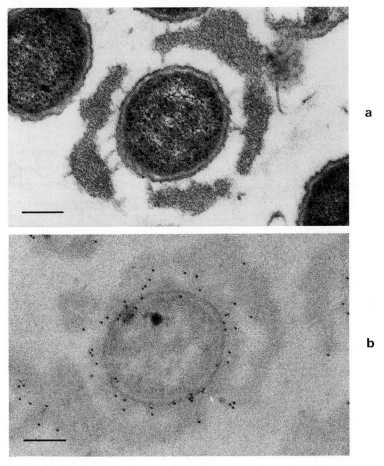

Fig. 3a, b. Coexpression of NFA-4 and the K98 antigen in *E. coli* 21511, a NFA-4 was stabilized with an adhesin-specific monoclonal antibody. **b** NFA-4 was stabilized as in **a**. The 10-nm gold particles indicate the K98-antigen stabilized with a specific polyclonal antiserum

microscopy with a monoclonal anti-NFA-4 antibody, absorbed anti-K98-antiserum, or both. As shown in Fig. 3, the nonfimbrial adhesin NFA-4 surrounds the bacterial cells as a capsule, but without a continuous circumferential contact. There are large gaps between the cell wall and the adhesin, which are bridged in many places. Using only anti K98-antiserum, these structures are not seen. Instead, the bacteria are directly surrounded by a dense layer with the usual appearance of a polysaccharide capsule. Double contrasting with both types of antibody reveals the concentric way in which these extracellular substances are arranged, with the adhesin predominantly on the outside and the polysaccharide more at the cell proximal space. This appearance was seen with practically all cells of the bacterial population. These results show that extraintestinal *E. coli* can express both adhesins and polysaccharide capsules simultaneously. It remains to be analyzed in which way the expression of one or both of these extracellular components is transient during a cell's life span and at different stages of the ineffective process.

4 Conclusions

Within the last two decades our knowledge about the molecular basis of bacterial adhesion and its specificity has increased tremendously. This was to a large measure due to advances in molecular genetics, biochemistry, and immunology as well as to the development of immunoelectron microscopy.

The early interpretation that fimbriae are mediators of bacterial adhesion was corroborated in many cases by genetic and biochemical evidence. It was recently demonstrated that the fimbriae have specific adhesins at their tips. The fimbriae, which were shown to consist of peptide subunits, are more or less rigid structures supporting the adhesins and presenting them to the surrounding of the bacteria.

Other fimbriae, such as the K88 antigen, seem to consist of adhesive subunits. If these block each other in their association to functional fimbriae with only the terminal (tip) one remaining functional, a chemical differentiation between these and the fimbriae with distinct adhesins will not be easy. More recently, adhesins were reported as not being associated with or organized into fimbriae. Although several of them were later shown to be very thin fimbrillae, this demonstration was not possible with others. The latter are operationally termed nonfimbrial. Some of them form adhesive capsules around the bacteria. However, their molecular organization is not known.

It will be interesting to learn why bacterial adhesins serving the same function are so differently expressed on the bacterial surface—ranging from fimbriae to capsules. Perhaps an ancestral adhesin gene has evolved through duplication and variation into a more complex genetic system which expresses the adhesin as part of a functional complex consisting of several different proteins.

Adhesins even of one specificity may in fact be a group of closely related but not identical proteins having a conserved receptor binding domain, as was recently demonstrated for P-specific fimbrial adhesins. This may also be true for several nonfimbrial adhesins, which share the recognition of blood group M and/or N substances.

If one accepts the presence of a conserved receptor binding domain in a group of related adhesins, no matter whether fimbrial or nonfimbrial, a comparison with another group of recognition proteins, namely the antibodies, is interesting. Whereas antibodies have the binding site in a very variable region, the adhesins have a conserved binding site. The structural variability of adhesins outside the binding domain will provide these recognition proteins with a serologic flexibility vis-à-vis the infected host, which in fimbriated bacteria is increased in the structural/serologic variability of the fimbriae.

The specificity or recognition was attributed to complex carbohydrates on host cells and the relevant oligosaccharide structures were elucidated in many cases. Although much knowledge has accumulated in this field, the chemical structures of many receptors, e.g., those associated with bloog group M and/or N substances, remain to be elucidated. A more extended comparative biochemical analysis of adhesins and their receptors will probably reveal that the adhesion of such distinct pathogens as bacteria, viruses, or parasites is governed by their recognition of related, if not identical, host structures—possibly with related recognition systems.

Acknowledgments. The work from the authors' laboratory was in part supported by the Deutsche Forschungsgemeinschaft and the Bundesministerium für Forschung und Technologie/DFVLR.

References

Abraham SN, Goguen JG, Beachey EH (1987a) Analysis of the genetic and structural determinants of the D-mannose sensitive adhesin of *Escherichia coli*. J Cell Biochem 11B: 121

Abraham SN, Goguen JD, Sun D, Klemm P, Beachey EM (1987b) Identification of two ancillary subunits of *Escherichia coli* type 1 fimbriae by using antibodies against synthetic oligopeptides of fim gene products. J Bacteriol 169: 5330–5336

Baga M, Norgren M, Normark S (1987) Biogenesis of *E. coli* pap pili: Pap H, a minor pilin subunit involved in cell anchoring and length modulation. Cell 49: 214–251

Beachey EH, Abraham SN (1988) Biological properties of bacterial surface proteins: type 1 fimbriae of *Escherichia coli*. In: Schrinner E, Richmond PMM, Seibert G, Schwarz U (eds) Surface structures of microorganisms and their interaction with the mammalian host. VCH, Weinheim

Brinton CC (1965) The structure, function, synthesis and genetic control of bacterial pili and a molecular model for DNA and DNA transport in gram-negative bacteria. Trans NY Acad Sci 27: 1003–1054

de Graaf FH (1988) Fimbrial structures of enterotoxigenic *E. coli*. Antonie van Leeuwenhook J Microbiol 54: 395–404

de Graaf FK, Klaasen-Bor P, van Hees JE (1980) Biosynthesis of the K99 surface antigen is repressed by alanin. Infect Immun 30: 125–128

Duguid JP, Old DC (1980) Adhesive properties of Enterobacteriaceae. In: Beachey EH (ed) Bacterial adherence. Chapman and Hall, London, pp 184–217 (Receptors and recognition, series B, vol 6)

Duguid JP, Smith IW, Dempster G, Serol Edmunds PM (1955) Nonflagellar filamentous appendages ("fimbriae") and hemagglutinating acitivity in *Bacterium coli*. J Pathol Bacteriol 70: 335–348

Duguid JP, Clegg S, Wilson MI (1979) The fimbrial and non-fimbrial hemagglutinins of *Escherichia coli*. J Med Microbiol 12: 213–227

Eisenstein BI (1981) Phase variation of type-1 fimbriae in *Escherichia coli* is under transcriptional control. Science 214: 337–339

Eisenstein BI, Dodd D (1982) Pseudocatabolite repression of type 1 fimbriae of *Escherichia coli*. J Bacteriol 151: 1560–1567

Eshdat Y, Speth V, Jann K (1981) Participation of pili and cell wall adhesin in the yeast agglutination activity of *Escherichia coli*. Infect Immun 34: 980–986

Faris A, Lindahl M, Wadström J (1980) GM$_2$-like glycoconjugate as possible erythrocyte receptor for the CFA/1 and K99 hemagglutinins of enterotoxigenic *Escherichia coli*. FEMS Microbial Lett 7: 265–269

Forestier C, Welinder HG, Darfeuille-Michaud A, Klemm P (1987) Afimbrial adhesin from *Escherichia coli* strain 2230: purification, characterization and partial covalent structure. FEMS Lett 40: 47–50

Gaastra E, Movi FR, Stnitje AR, and de Graaf FK (1981) The nucleotide sequence of the gene encoding the K88ab protein subunit of porcine enterotoxigenic *Escherichia coli*. FEMS Microbiol Lett 12: 41–46

Goldhar J, Perry R, Ofek I (1984) Extraction and properties of nonfimbrial mannose-resistant hemagglutinin from a urinary isolate of *Escherichia coli*. Curr Microbiol 11: 49–54

Goldhar J, Perry R, Golecki J, Hoschützky H, Jann B, Jann K (1987) Nonfimbrial, mannose-resistant adhesins from uropathogenic *Escherichia coli*. O83:K1:H4 and O14:K:H11. Infect Immun 55: 1837–1842

Grunberg J, Perry R, Hoschützky H, Jann B, Jann K, Goldhar J (1988) Nonfimbrial blood group N-specific adhesin (NFA-3) from *Escherichia coli* O20:X104:H⁻, causing systemic infection. FEMS Microbiol Lett 56: 241–246

Hacker J, Schmidt G, Hughes G, Knapp S, Marget M, Goebel W (1985) Cloning and characterization of genes involved in production of mannose-resistant, neuraminidase-susceptible (X) fimbriae from a uropathogenic O6:K15:H31 *Escherichia coli* strain. Infect Immun 47: 434–440

Hales BA, Beverly-Clarke H, High NJ, Jann K, Perry R, Goldhar J, Boulnois GJ (1988) Molecular cloning and characterization of the genes for a non-fimbrial adhesin from *Escjerichia coli*. Microbiol Pathogen 5: 9–17

Hoschützky H, Lottspeich F, Nimmich W, Jann K (1989a) Isolation and characterization of the

nonfimbrial adhesin NFA-4 from uropathogenic *Escherichia coli* O7:K98:H6. Microbiol Pathogen 6: 351–359

Hoschützky H, Lottspeich F, Jann K (1989b) Isolation and characterization of the αGal-(1,4)-βGal (P) specific adhesin from fimbriated *Escherichia coli*. Infect Immun 57: 76–87

Isaacson RC (1985) Pilus adhesins In: Savage DC, Fletcher H (ed) Bacterial adhesion. Mechanisms and physiological consequences. Plenum, New York, pp 307–336

Jann K, Jann B, Schmidt G (1981) SDS polyacrylamide gel electrophoresis and serological analysis of pili from *Escherichia coli* of different pathogenic origin. FEMS Microbiol Lett 11: 21–25

Klemm P, Christiansen G (1987) Three fim genes required for the regulation of length and mediation of adhesion of *Escherichia coli* type 1 fimbriae. MGG 208: 439–445

Knutton S, Williams PH, Llyod DR, Candy DCA, McNeish AS (1984) Ultrastructural study of adherence to and penetration of cultured cells by two invasive *Escherichia coli* strains isolated from infants with enteritis. Infect Immun 44: 599–608

Labigne-Roussel AF, Lark D, Schoolnik G, Falkow S (1984) Cloning and expression of an afimbrial adhesin (AFA-1) responsible for P-blood group-independent mannose-resistant hemagglutination from a pyelo-nephritic *Escherichia coli* strain. Infect Immun 46: 251–259

Labigne-Roussel AF, Schmidt MA, Walz W, Falkow S (1985) Genetic organization of the *afa* operon and nucleotide sequence from a uropathogenic *Escherichia coli* gene encoding an afmbrial adhesin (AFA-1). J Bacteriol 162: 1285–1292

Labigne-Roussel AF, Falkow S (1988) Distribution and degree of heterogeneity of the afimbrial-adhesin-encoding operon (*afa*) among uropathogeneic *Escherichia coli* isolates. Infect Immun 56: 640–648

Leffler H, Svanborg-Edén C (1986) Glycolipids as receptors for *Escherichia coli* lectins or adhesins. In: Mirelman D (ed) Microbiol lectins and agglutinins: properties and biological activity. Wiley, New York, pp 83–112

Lindberg FP, Lund B, Normark S (1984) Genes of pyelonephritogenic *E. coli* required for digalactoside-specific agglutination of human cells. EMBO J 3: 1167-1173

Lindberg F, Lund B, Normark S (1986) Gene products specifying adhesion of uropathogenic *Escherichia coli* are minor components of pili. Proc Natl Acad Sci USA 83: 1891–1895

Lindberg F, Lund B, Johannson L, Normark S (1987) Localization of the receptor-binding protein adhesin at the tip of the bacterial pilus. Nature 328: 84–87.

Lund B, Lindberg G, Marklund B-I, Normark S (1987) The papG protein is the α-D-galactopyranosyl-(2-4)-β-D-galactopyranose-binding adhesion of uropathogenic *Escherichia coli*. Proc Natl Acad Sci USA 84: 5898–5902

Lund B, Lindberg F, Normark S (1988) Structure and antigenic properties of the tip-located P pilus proteins of uropathogenic *Escherichia coli*. J Bacteriol 170: 1887–1894

Manson MS, Brinton CC (1988) Identification and characterization of *E. coli* type-1 pilus tip adhesion protein. Nature 332: 265–268

Markwell MAK (1986) Viruses as hemagglutinins and lectins. In: Mirelman D (ed) Microbiol lectins and agglutinins. Properties and biological activity. Wiley, New York, pp 21–53

Mett H, Kloetzlen L, Vosbeck K (1983) Properties of pili from *Escherichia coli* SS142 that mediate mannose-resistant adhesion to mammalian cells. J Bacteriol 153: 1038–1044

Minion FC, Abraham SN, Beachey EH, Goguen JD (1986) The genetic determinant of adhesive function in type 1 fimbriae of *Escherichia coli* is distinct from the gene encoding the fimbrial subunit. J Bacteriol 165: 1033–1036

Mirelman D, Ofek I (1986) Introduction to microbial lectins and agglutinins. In: Mirelman D (ed) Microbial lectins and agglutinins: properties and biological activity. Wiley, New York, pp 1–19

Moch T, Hoschützky H, Hacker J, Kröncke KD, Jann K (1987) Isolation and characterization of the α-sialyl-β-2,3-galactosyl-specific adhesin from fimbriated *Escherichia coli*. Proc Natl Acad Sci USA 84: 3462–3466

Norgren M, Normark S, Lark D, O'Hanley P, Schoolnik G, Falkow S, Svanborg-Edén C, Baga M, Uhlin BE (1984) Mutations in *E. coli* cistrons affecting adhesion to human cells do not abolish pap pili Hiber formation, EMBO J 3:1159–1165

Nowicki B, Holthöfer H, Saraneva T, Rhen M, Väisanen-Rhen V, Korhonen TK (1986) Location of adhesion sites for P-fimbriate and for O75X-positive *Escherichia coli* in the human kidney. Microb Pathogen 1: 169–180

Ørskov I, Birch-Anderson A, Duguid JP, Stenderup J, Ørskov F (1985) An adhesive protein capsule of *Escherichia coli*. Infect Immun 47: 191–200

Ofek I, Beachey EH (1980) General concepts and principles of bacterial adhesion. In: Beachey EH (ed) Bacterial adherence. Chapman and Hall, London, pp 1–29 (Receptors and recognition, series A, vol 6)

Parkkinen J, Finne J, Achtmann M, Väisanen V, Korhonen TK (1983) *Escherichia coli* strains binding neuraminyl α2-3 galactosides. Biochem Biophys Res Commun 111: 456-461

Rhen M, Mäkelä PH, Korhonen TK (1983) P-fimbriae of *Escherichia coli* are subject to phase variation. FEMS Lett 19: 267–271

Rhen M, Klemm P, Korhonen TK (1986) Identification of two new hemagglutinins of *Escherichia coli*, N-acetyl-D-glucosamine-specific fimbriae and a blood group M-specific agglutinin, by cloning the corresponding genes in *Escherichia coli* K12. J Bacteriol 168: 1234-1242

Riegman N, Hoschützky H, Jann K, Bergmans H, Hoekstra W (1989) Immunocytochemical analysis of P-fimbrial structure: localization of the minor subunits and the influence of the minor subunit FSOE on the biogenesis of the adhesion. Mol Microbiol in press

Salit IE, Gotschlich EC (1977) Hemagglutination by purified type 1 *Escherichia coli* pili. J Exp Med 146: 1169–1181

Savage DC (1985) Effects on host animals of bacteria adhering to epithelial surfaces. In: Savage DC, Fletcher M (eds) Bacterial adhesion. Mechanisms and physiological significance. Plenum, New York, pp 437–464

Sharon N, Ofek I (1986) Mannose specific bacterial surface lectins. In: Mirelman D (ed) Microbial lectins and agglutinins: properties and biological activity. Wiley, New York, pp 55–82

Sheladia VL, Chambers JP, Guevara J, Evans DJ (1982) Isolation, purification, and partial characterization of type V–A hemagglutinin from *Escherichia coli* CV-12, O1:H⁻. J Bacterial 152: 757–761

Tennent JM, Baga M, Fossman K, Göransson M, Lindberg F, Lund B, Marklund BI, Norgren M, Uhlin BE, Normaks (1987) Protein interactions essential for the biosynthesis of P pili of uropathogenic *Escherichia coli* In: Schrinner E et al. (eds) Surface structures of microorganisms and their interactions with the mammalian host. Workshop conferences, vol 18 VCH Weinheim

Väisanen-Rhen V (1984) Fimbriae-like hemagglutinin of *Escherichia coli* O75 strains. Infect Immun 46: 401–407

Väisanen-Rhen V, Elo J, Tallgren LG, Siitonen A, Mäkelä PH, Svanborg Edén C, Källenius G, Svenson SB, Hultberg H, Korhonen TK (1981) Mannose-resistant hemagglutination and P-antigen-recognition are characteristic of *Escherichia coli* causing primary pyelonephritis. Lancet ii: 1366–1369

Väisanen-Rhen V, Korhonen TK, Jokinen M, Gahmberg CG, Ehnholm C (1982) Blood group M specific hemagglutinin in pyelonephritogenic *Escherichia coli*. Lancet i: 1192

Väisanen-Rhen V, Korhonen TK, Finne J (1983) Novel cell-binding activity specific for N-acetyl-D-glucosamine in an *Escherichia coli* strain. FEBS Lett 159: 233–236

Van Die I, Spierings G, Van Megen I, Zuidweg E, Hoekstra W, Bergmans H (1985) Cloning and genetic organization of the gene cluster encoding F7$_1$ fimbriae of a uropathogenic *Escherichia coli* and comparison with the F7$_2$ gene cluster. FEMS Microbiol Lett 28: 329–334

Walz W, Schmidt A, Labigne-Roussel A, Falkow S, Schoolnik G (1985) AFA-1, a cloned afimbrial X-type adhesin from a human pyelonephritic *Escherichia coli* strain. Eur J Biochem 152: 315–321

Williams PH, Knutton S, Brown MGM, Candy DCA, McNeish AS (1984) Characterization of nonfimbrial mannose-resistant protein hemagglutinins of two *Escherichia coli* strains isolated from infants with enteritis. Infect Immun 44: 592–598

Serologic Classification of Fimbriae

I. ØRSKOV and F. ØRSKOV

1 Introduction

Many bacteria have the ability to attach to epithelial cells at various sites in man and animal by means of adhesins. The serologically best studied adhesins are those of gram-negative bacteria, particularly Enterobacteriaceae and Neisseria gonorrhoeae. They are proteins (e.g., JONES and ISAACSON 1983) and are commonly structured as filaments of various thickness; if the diameter is wide enough, they are called fimbriae (DUGUID et al. 1955) (synonym: pili (BRINTON 1959)), while very thin filaments are often referred to as fibrils, but no rules exist for the use of these names. Recently adhesive *E. coli* surface proteins have been described consisting of extremely fine filaments which can often be visualized only with great difficulty (HINSON et al. 1987; LEVINE et al. 1984; ØRSKOV et al. 1985).

Fimbriae and adhesins have been classified according to morphology and ability to agglutinate erythrocytes from various animals (DUGUID et al. 1966), and furthermore according to serology (DUGUID et al. 1979; GILLIES and DUGUID 1958). A more recent way of characterizing fimbriae is by their chemical composition, i.e., the sequence of amino acids, or by the receptors to which they adhere (KLEMM 1985). The receptors described to date are carbohydrate constituents of glycoconjugates

International Escherichia and Klebsiella Centre (WHO), Statens Seruminstitut, Amager Boulevard 80, DK-2300 Copenhagen S, Denmark

Current Topics in Microbiology and Immunology, Vol. 151
© Springer-Verlag Berlin·Heidelberg 1990

Table 1. *E. coli* fimbriae groups

Fimbriae group	Antigen types	F antigen number[a]	Ref. to group name
Type 1	Different types	F1A and variants of this	BRINTON 1965; DUGUID et al. 1966
P	Different types	F7–F16 and variants of these	KÄLLENIUS et al. 1981
S	Highly related types[b]		KORHONEN et al. 1984
G	?		RHEN et al. 1986b
M	?		RHEN et al. 1986b
F (= Sex)	Different types		BRINTON et al. 1964
Fib	?		FARIS 1985

[a] ØRSKOV and ØRSKOV (1983a);
[b] Serologically related to F1C, see Table 3 (OTT et al. 1986)

(JONES and ISAACSON 1983; SMYTH 1986). For example, P fimbriae of *E. coli*, particularly from urinary tract infections, bind to the disaccharide Galα(1-4)Gal present on human erythrocytes of the P blood group system and on epithelial cells of the urinary tract (KÄLLENIUS et al. 1980; LEFFLER and SVANBORG-EDEN 1980, 1981). Recent examples of naming fimbriae in *E. coli* according to the receptors are the S fimbriae, which adhere to sialic acid-containing receptors (KORHONEN et al. 1984; PARKKINEN et al. 1986), and the Fib fimbriae, which bind to fibronectin (FARIS 1985) (see Table 1). In this chapter we shall deal with serologic classification of fimbriae and adhesins in some Enterobacteriaceae, particularly *E. coli*. The fimbriae of gonococcal strains are being intensively studied (e.g., SWANSON et al. 1987); antigenically they are extremely heterogeneous, and the fimbriae of each strain can undergo both antigenic variation and phase variation (SPARLING et al. 1986); no serologic classification as such exists; these fimbriae will not be treated here.

2 Organization of Fimbriae and Adhesins

Bacterial adhesion to erythrocytes and cell surfaces is frequently associated with fimbriae (DUGUID et al. 1955; DUGUID and GILLIES 1957; DUGUID and OLD 1980; BRINTON 1965). The adhesion may be sensitive or resistant to inhibition by D-mannose and is referred to as MS or MR, respectively. Type 1 fimbriae are MS. Fimbriae lacking adhering capacity also exist. It has been suggested that the adhesin protein may be distinct from the major subunit of the fimbriae (NORMARK et al. 1983), and recently this has been confirmed regarding type 1, P, and S fimbriae. Gene clusters coding for production and adhesive capacity of these fimbriae have been cloned from *E. coli*, and genetic analyses of the clones have shown that distinct genes code for fimbriation and adhesiveness (HACKER et al. 1985; MAURER and ORNDORFF 1985; MINION et al. 1986; NORGREN et al. 1984; RHEN et al. 1986a; VAN DIE et al. 1986). The MS adhesion of type 1 fimbriae has been suggested to be provided by the product of the *fimH* and either the *fimF* or *fimG* genes (KLEMM and CHRISTIANSEN 1987).

In P fimbriae, a minor protein termed PapG located at the tip of the fimbria is the protein which binds to the Gal-Gal receptor; the major PapA protein is not required for binding (LINDBERG et al. 1987).

Recently the S-specific and P-specific adhesive proteins have been isolated (MOCH et al. 1987; HOSCHÜTZKY et al. 1989). Immunoelectron microscopy (IEM) findings suggested that the S adhesin is located at the tip of the fimbria (MOCH et al. 1987).

Evidence for the presence of an adhesive minor subunit different from a major fimbrial subunit has hitherto not been obtained in K88 *E. coli* fimbriae, which have adhesin molecules as the major component (JACOBS 1987). For K99 fimbriae the situation is not yet clear (JACOBS 1987).

There seem to be two categories of fimbrial structure. The first category, in this chapter referred to as fimbriae I, comprises rigid fimbriae, of about 7 nm in diameter (BRINTON 1965; DUGUID et al. 1966; LEVINE et al. 1984; ØRSKOV et al. 1980). It may be that in all these fimbriae the fimbrial and adhesive subunits are distinct, although forming a functional complex in which the fimbrial subunit is the major protein.

The other category of fimbriae, in this chapter referred to as fimbriae II, comprises flexible thin fibrils or filaments of a diameter well below 7 nm, and sometimes as narrow as 2 nm. They often surround the bacteria as a fur coat, e.g., K88 (STIRM et al. 1967b), which by immunolabeling would look like a capsule. Fimbriae II may consist exclusively of adhesive molecules.

Both fimbriae I and fimbriae II have been serotyped. The major fimbrial protein constitutes the bulk of fimbriae I, thus > 99% of each P fimbria (LUND et al. 1988a), and it is in general believed that only antibodies against the major protein will be demonstrable in polyclonal antisera against fimbriae. The serotypes described to date are thus considered to reflect the antigenic properties of the major fimbrial protein. However, by selective absorption of a polyclonal antiserum against F13 fimbriae, antibodies against minor adhesin protein were demonstrated by a radio-immunoassay (LUND et al. 1988a). Serotyping of fimbriae as carried out today is complicated; if in the future serotyping should include examination of minor proteins present in the fimbria, we can only speculate on the complexity of such an analysis.

The serology dealt with in the following will involve reactions of the major fimbrial protein of fimbriae I and the fimbrial-adhesin protein of fimbriae II.

3 Some Results Obtained by Different Methods

3.1 Introduction

When it appeared that fimbriae in, for example, enterotoxigenic and uropathogenic *E. coli* played a role in attachment of the bacteria to mucosal surfaces, it became of great interest to know whether antigenically different fimbriae existed. In animal husbandry vaccines against K88 and K99 and 987 are in use to avoid diarrhea in young animals (for a review see KLEMM 1985), and it is the aim of many workers to

develop a fimbria-based or partly fimbria-based vaccine against pyelonephritis and traveller's diarrhea in man. With this idea in mind serologic differentiation is important.

3.2 Bacterial Agglutination

Fimbriae are good antigens, and fimbrial antisera are easily obtained that can be used for demonstration of the presence of fimbriae and for serologic differentiation of fimbriae. GILLIES and DUGUID (1958) were the first to examine serologic relatedness between fimbriae by bacterial agglutination. Their report and a later one by DUGUID and CAMPBELL (1969) showed that type 1 fimbrial antigens are shared among *Escherichia*, *Shigella*, and to a lesser extent *Klebsiella*, and similarly among *Salmonella* and *Citrobacter*. There was no sharing of antigens between the two groups (see Sect. 3.3 and Table 2).

The agglutination test is a sensitive method and easy to carry out. It is a reliable test if proper antisera are used, i.e., properly absorbed polyclonal antisera against whole cells or purified fimbriae, or monoclonal antibodies (MAbs). In many cases a single strain will produce fimbriae with different receptors and/or antigenically different fimbriae with the same receptor (DUGUID and OLD 1980; KLEMM et al. 1982; ØRSKOV et al. 1982a, b). In such cases the agglutination technique will only distinguish between different antigens if monospecific antisera are used. The K88 and its variants K88ab and K88ac, and K99, were first demonstrated by means of bacterial agglutination, and this method is still used in our laboratory for differentiation of these antigens (ØRSKOV et al. 1961, 1964, 1975) (Table 3).

PARRY et al. (1982) and PARRY and ROOKE (1985) examined the antigens of seven uropathogenic *E. coli* strains with MR hemagglutinins by agglutination tests with cross-absorbed antisera and demonstrated seven antigens designated a–g. All seven strains expressed P fimbriae and four in addition expressed X adhesin, which is an

Table 2. Fimbriae in Enterobacteriaceae serologically examined

Fimbriae classification	Serologic results	Reference
Type 1[a]	Ten distinct groups[b] within Enterobacteriaceae	ADEGBOLA and OLD 1987
Type 2[a]	Serologically similar to type 1, but not hemagglutinating (*Salmonella paratyphi* B, *Salmonella pullorum*)	OLD and PAYNE 1971
Type 3[a]	Nine distinct groups[c] in Enterobacteriaceae (none in *E. coli* or *Shigella*)	OLD and ADEGBOLA 1985
Other types		For a review see CLEGG and GERLACH 1987

[a]Types 1–3 were defined according to morphology and hemagglutination by DUGUID et al. (1966);
[b]See Sects. 3.2 and 3.3;
[c]See Sect. 3.3

Table 3. *E. coli* fimbriae classified as antigens

Fimbria antigen	Different antigen types	Proposed F antigen number[a]	Reference
1C[b]		F1C	KLEMM et al. 1982
CFA/I		F2	EVANS et al. 1975
CFA/II		F3	EVANS and EVANS 1978
	CS1		CRAVIOTO et al. 1982
	CS2		SMYTH 1982
	CS3		
CFA III			HONDA et al. 1984
PCF 8775			THOMAS et al. 1982
= CFA IV			WILLSHAW et al. 1988
	CS4		
	CS5		THOMAS et al. 1985
	CS6		
K88		F4	ØRSKOV et al. 1961
	K88ab		
	K88ac		ØRSKOV et al. 1964
	K88ad		GUINÉE and JANSEN 1979
K99		F5	ØRSKOV et al. 1975
987P		F6	NAGY et al. 1977
F41			MORRIS et al. 1980
F(y)	F(y)		GIRARDEAU et al. 1980
	Att25 etc.		POHL et al. 1982
			MORRIS et al. 1985b
		F17	LINTERMANS et al. 1988
F165			FAIRBROTHER et al. 1986
Z	Z₁Z₂		ØRSKOV et al. 1985

[a]ØRSKOV and ØRSKOV (1983a);
[b]Serologically ralated to S fimbriae; see Table 1 (OTT et al. 1986)

assembly name for adhesins recognizing unknown epitopes on human erythrocytes (VÄISÄNEN-RHEN et al. 1984). The results of PARRY and ROOKE (1985) did not demonstrate which antigen corresponded to P- or to X-specific fimbriae. Table 4 shows the serologic results obtained with these strains by different methods and by different workers. In this table the unnumbered antigen (marked "?") of SP57 and SP88 is related to or identical with a particular X hemagglutinin present in many O75:K5:H⁻ strains and described as a coil-like structure on the basis of electron microscopy (EM) (VÄISÄNEN-RHEN 1984). This hemagglutinin is probably a fimbria II structure.

There are conflicting results in the literature regarding the usefulness of MAbs for bacterial agglutination. MORRIS et al. (1985a) found the reactions of a MAb against K99 to be identical with those of a polyclonal antiserum. DE REE et al. (1986a) experienced that strains which expressed cloned fimbriae but not wild-type strains were agglutinated by MAbs prepared against purified P fimbriae with different F specificities. A MAb against an F8 preparation from a P-fimbriated strain agglutinated this strain but not another one expressing F8, although it bound ^{125}I-labeled antibody; EM showed that the latter strain was less fimbriated than the agglutinable one (MOSER et al. 1986). SCHMITZ et al. (1986) reported that MAbs against *E. coli* F antigen 1C did not agglutinate F1C-fimbriated strains although

Table 4. Results of serologic examination of fimbriae in uropathogenic *E. coli* obtained by different methods in different different laboratories

O:K:H serotype[a]	Strain no.[b]	Specificity according to receptor[b]	Antigenic composition		
			PARRY	DE REE	ØRSKOV
			Bacterial aggluti-nation[b]	ELISA (MAbs)[c]	CIE[a]
O18ac:K5:H-	SP7	P + X	c, d, e	F8	F8, F1C
O157:H45	SP57	P + X	a, b	F12 rel. (F16)	F16 + ?[d]
O157:H45	SP88	P + X	a, b	F12 rel. (F16)	F16 + ?[d]
O1:K1:H7	SP101	P + X	b, c, e	F11	F11
rough:K1:H7	SP133	P	c, e	F11	F11
O6:K5:H1	SP144	P	f, g		F14, F1C
O75:K5:H-	SP201	P	g, e		F15, F1C

[a]ØRSKOV I and ØRSKOV F (unpublished results);
[b]Results by PARRY and ROOKE (1985);
[c]Results by DE REE et al. (1986a, b);
[d]An unnumbered adhesin, probably of type fimbriae II

they bound to the bacteria, while PERE et al. (1985) reported that a MAb against 1C agglutinated 44 out of 45 1C-fimbriated strains. The usefulness of MAbs for agglutination probably depends on how richly fimbriated the strains are and how accessible the recognized epitopes are.

3.3 Immunoelectron Microscopy

By IEM the antibody-binding sites become visible by being coated with antibody followed by negative staining. This method of direct labeling was introduced by LAWN (1967), and by use of it LAWN and MEYNELL (1970) concluded that four serotypes were present among sex fimbriae of the F type (present on male bacteria of compatibility group F). This conclusion was based on the different extents to which the sex fimbriae were coated with antibody. Since then other reports have appeared dealing with direct IEM studies of fimbriae (e.g., EVANS et al. 1975; ØRSKOV et al. 1980). The difficult interpretation of agglutination tests with fimbriated cultures caused ADEGBOLA and OLD (1982) and OLD and ADEGBOLA (1983) to use the IEM method in distinguishing different kinds of fimbria formed by multifimbriated strains. By this method the same authors demonstrated nine groups of antigenically distinct type 3 fimbriae which are present in all members of Enterobacteriaceae except *E. coli* and *Shigella* (OLD and ADEGBOLA 1985). Type 3 fimbriae is a name coined by DUGUID et al. (1966) for thin fimbriae which cause agglutination of tannic acid-treated erythrocytes, but not of fresh ones (Table 2). Recently IEM was also used to examine antigenic relationships among type 1 fimbriae of 40 Entero-bacteriaceae strains of 19 species of seven genera, and ten distinct groups were distinguished (ADEGBOLA and OLD 1987) (Table 2). Antigenic relationships were found to be more complex than described in previous reports based on findings

from agglutination tests (GILLIES and DUGUID 1958; DUGUID and CAMPBELL 1969; NOWOTARSKA and MULCZYK 1977) (see Sect. 3.2).

Immunoelectron microscopic studies by OLD et al. (1987) of P fimbriae on 37 urinary *E. coli* strains revealed antigenic heterogeneity and marked differences in the extent to which the fimbriae were coated with antibody. Five pure fimbrial antisera were prepared by absorption and used for agglutination tests and IEM, and in this study the degree of activity was reported to be almost identical by both methods. By cross-absorptions of the five antisera, four distinct P antigenic determinants were demonstrated which occurred in different combinations of two in four of the five strains used for preparation of antisera. Unfortunately we cannot compare these results with ours obtained by crossed immunoelectrophoresis (CIE). Our reference strains for F antigens 7, 8, 9, 11, and 12, all antigens of P fimbriae (ØRSKOV and ØRSKOV 1983a, 1985), are included in the material examined, but no results with these strains are reported by OLD et al. (1987).

A fimbriae-containing specimen can, after direct labeling with, for example, rabbit antiserum, be processed further for indirect labeling with anti-rabbit IgG–ferritin, anti-rabbit IgG–gold, or protein A–gold. Indirect labeling is, in contrast to direct labeling, mainly independent of the quality of the negative staining, but it is more time and material consuming (GELDERBLOM et al. 1985).

The indirect immunogold EM method was, for example, used by MOCH et al. (1987) when they showed that the adhesin of an S-fimbriated strain was localized exclusively on the fimbriae with a possible preference for the tips. This method is particularly useful for differentiation when more types of fimbria are present in a culture.

Immunoelectron microscopy is an excellent method for demonstration of antigenic sites on fimbriae. However, for serologic examinations of fimbriae on many strains the present authors would prefer other methods which are less time consuming and easier to evaluate.

3.4 Electron Microscopy, Immunoelectron Microscopy, and Fimbriae II

For demonstration of very fine filaments (Table 5), i.e., fimbriae II, EM is preferable to IEM, because using IEM, whether direct or indirect, these fimbriae will often appear as a mass since they aggregate and are often present in abundance. When LEVINE et al. (1984) showed that antigen CS3, present on some enterotoxigenic *E. coli* and formerly considered to be nonfimbrial (MULLANY et al. 1983), consisted of thin (2 nm), flexible, "fibrillar" fimbriae, this was primarily seen by improved EM examination and then confirmed by indirect IEM. Similarly, an adhesin produced by *E. coli* 469-3 (021:H⁻) from a case of enteritis was first described as nonfimbrial (WILLIAMS et al. 1984), but after technical improvement in EM procedures the adhesive strain was found to produce fine flexible filaments which were identified as the adhesin by indirect IEM (HINSON et al. 1987). LABIGNE-ROUSSEL et al. (1984) reported about an afimbrial adhesin (AFAI) with MR hemagglutinating ability from a pyelonephritic *E. coli* strain of O group 2. No visible fimbriae of this strain were detected by EM. The protein antigen provisionally termed Z_1(ØRSKOV et al. 1985)

Table 5. Some *E. coli* fine filaments or nonfimbrial adhesins (fimbriae II)

Name of fimbria/adhesin	Demonstrable in O:K:H serotype	Reference to morphology
K88[a]	e.g., O149:H10	Stirm et al. 1967b
F41[a]	e.g., O101:K32:H-	de Graaf and Roorda 1982
CS3[a]	e.g., O6:K15:H16	Levine et al. 1984
XO75	O75:K5:H-	Väisänen-Rhen 1974
Z[a,b]	e.g., O21:K4:H4	Ørskov et al. 1985
Fib[c]	Different	Faris 1985
469-3[b]	O21:H-	Hinson et al. 1987
AFAI[b]	O2	Labigne-Roussel et al. 1984
NFAI	O83:K1:H4	Goldhar et al. 1984
NFAII	O14:H11	Goldhar et al. 1987
2230	O25:H16	Darfeuille-Michaud et al. 1986
M[c]	O2	Rhen et al. 1986b

[a] See Table 3;
[b] Serologically identical or strongly related (I. Ørskov, unpublished observations);
[c] See Table 1

was found in three strains earlier described as MR hemagglutinating but non-fimbriated by Duguid et al. (1979) and Ip et al. (1981). EM studies of one of the strains, O21:K4, showed that many but not all bacteria were surrounded by a coat consisting of a mesh of exceedingly fine threads. By indirect IEM the bacteria appeared surrounded by a thick capsule-like brim (Ørskov et al. 1985). By CIE we have found that AFAI and the 469-3 adhesin mentioned above are antigenically identical with or strongly related to the Z_1 antigen.

Other protein adhesins have been described as nonfimbrial by EM, e.g., one present in *E. coli* strain 2230 (O25:K?:H16) isolated from an infant with diarrhea (Forestier et al. 1987; Darfeuille-Michaud et al. 1986). This adhesin is non-hemagglutinating but adheres to human enterocyte brush borders, not to HEp-2 cells. No antigenic relationship was found by double immunodiffusion to CFA/I or CFA/II. Two other nonfimbrial protein adhesins, termed NFA, have been demonstrated on MR hemagglutinating *E. coli* of serotypes O83:K1:H4 and O14:K?:H11 isolated from urine (Goldhar et al. 1984, 1987). Direct IEM with monoclonal as well as polyclonal antisera against purified adhesin followed by embedding showed a capsule-like material around one of the strains and patchy material on the other. The strains and the purified adhesins adhered to cultured human kidney cells as tested by an ELISA type procedure, and inhibition studies of this adhesion showed that the adhesins from the two strains were serologically related but could be differentiated with MAbs. No cross-reactions were found by Goldhar et al. (1987) to the Z antigen and the fimbrial antigens F7–F14.

Since it appears from recent literature (Hinson et al. 1987) that demonstration of very fine threads by EM requires improved technique, it cannot be excluded that new studies would reveal that at least some of the adhesins described as nonfimbrial may also consist of delicate filaments, provided that the thickness is above the size visible by EM.

3.5 Enzyme-Linked Immunosorbent Assay

One of the main methods used today for the study of fimbriae serology is ELISA (ENGVALL and PERLMANN 1972); this was used, for example, by KORHONEN et al. (1982, 1984). The method is sensitive and has the advantage that the result is read in an objective way and that both whole bacteria suspensions and purified fimbrial preparations can be used as antigens. In many cases, however, it has the same disadvantage as the agglutination test, i.e., it does not differentiate between different antigens or different antibodies when such are present in an antigen preparation or a polyclonal antiserum, respectively.

When using MAbs, ELISA is in general the method of choice, e.g., DE REE et al. (1986a) found ELISA better than the agglutination test. McCONELL et al. (1985) examined more than 100 enterotoxigenic *E. coli* strains for presence of fimbrial antigens CFAI and CS1 to CS6 (Table 3). These antigens could be detected in more strains by ELISA than by the double immunodiffusion in gel test, which was normally used (e.g., THOMAS and ROWE 1982).

3.6 SDS–PAGE and Immunoblotting (Western Blotting)

In 1981 JANN et al. examined fimbriae preparations of ten *E. coli* strains of different O:K:H types by sodium dodecyl sulfate–polyacrylamide gel electrophoresis (SDS–PAGE) and found that they all exhibited different patterns of peptide bands, and that there was always more than one band corresponding to each strain. Similar multiple bands were found by KORHONEN et al. (1982) and HANLEY et al. (1985). The molecular weights of the subunits of fimbrial preparations from 14 strains ranged from 14 000 to 19 500. Very limited cross-reactivity between the strains was found by either an ELISA inhibition test or Western blotting (HANLEY et al. 1985).

The Western blotting technique (TOWBIN et al. 1979) is most useful when only a few antigens are to be examined with one or a few antisera, e.g., the examinations of CS1 and CS3 (LEVINE et al. 1984) and of the Z antigens (ØRSKOV et al. 1985) (fimbriae II), or when the reaction of several fimbrial preparations, whether originating from wild-type or recombinant strains, are to be examined with one antiserum (OTT et al. 1986).

3.7 SDS–PAGE of Immunoprecipitates

By immunoprecipitation RHEN et al. (1983a) examined whether the multiple peptides found in an SDS–PAGE analysis of a fimbrial preparation originated from different fimbriae or from the same fimbriae composed of two or three different subunits (KORHONEN et al. 1982). Two preparations of antigenically cross-reacting fimbriae derived from two strains were first precipitated with a nonhomologous antiserum reacting with only some of the peptides, and the supernatants were further precipitated with homologous antisera giving a second precipitate. Both

precipitates were analyzed by SDS–PAGE, where they formed only distinct bands (RHEN et al. 1983a). By EM it was shown that the preparation from the second precipitate consisted of fimbriae, demonstrating that the different bands originally seen in SDS–PAGE originated from different fimbriae. Serologic examination of both P and S fimbriae was later undertaken by SDS–PAGE analysis of immunoprecipitates obtained with different fimbrial antisera, whereby it was demonstrated that S fimbriae of various strains (O18:K1:H7, O6:K$^+$, rough K1:H33, and O2:K2) showed great immunologic cross-reactivity (KORHONEN et al. 1984); in contrast, the serology of P fimbriae was highly complex (PERE 1986; PERE et al. 1986, 1988).

3.8 Gel Precipitation Tests

Double diffusion in gel precipitation tests (OUCHTERLONY 1949) and immunoelectrophoresis (SCHEIDEGGER 1955) have to a great extent been used for serologic analysis of fimbriae, particularly from enterotoxigenic E. coli, e.g., STIRM et al. (1967a) (K88), GUINÉE et al. (1976) (K99), and EVANS et al. (1975) (CFA/I). Both CFA/II (EVANS and EVANS 1978) and the colonization factor PCF 8775 (THOMAS et al. 1982) were resolved into three components in double diffusion, representing different fimbriae called coli surface antigens CS1–3 (CRAVIOTO et al. 1982; SMYTH 1982) and CS4–6 (THOMAS et al. 1985), respectively. CS3 are thin filaments (LEVINE et al. 1984) here named fimbriae II, but the nature of CS6 has not been reported (THOMAS et al. 1985). The other CS fimbriae are fimbriae I.

Another gel precipitation method which has been highly valuable for studies on fimbria serology is CIE because of its high resolving power (AXELSEN 1973, AXELSEN et al. 1973; WEEKE 1973). We used antisera from rabbits immunized with whole bacterial culture subsequently absorbed with culture of the same strain grown at 18°C, at which temperature type 1 fimbriae are expressed, in contrast to most other fimbriae (ØRSKOV et al. 1982b; ØRSKOV and ØRSKOV 1983a). In cases where a nonfimbriated mutant of the strain used for immunization was at hand, the serum was made fimbria-specific by absorption with the mutant grown at 37°C instead of the homologous culture grown at 18°C.

We prepared the fimbrial extract for CIE by heating bacterial suspensions at 60°C for 20 min followed by treatment in an Ultra Turrax apparatus for 2 × 1 min. By experience it was learned at which positions in the gels the different fimbria lines are situated. The relationship between fimbria antigens was examined by crossed line immunoelectrophoresis (CLIE) (KRÖLL 1973), i.e., incorporation of heterologous extract in an intermediate gel of a fimbrial reference system, i.e., a reference fimbrial extract run against its homologous fimbria antiserum. If antigens are related, the precipitation line will be somewhat lifted, i.e., moved anodically. If two antigens are identical, the line from the extract in the intermediate gel will fuse completely with the line or peak of the reference system, and this combined line will be moved upward to an extent depending on the antigen concentration in the intermediate gel.

However, a serologic relationship is more evident when it is examined in the less specific but more sensitive way by incorporation of a heterologous antiserum in the

intermediate gel of a reference system (CLOSS et al. 1975). The relationship will be demonstrated by the formation of the precipitation line or peak at a lower position than when saline is incorporated in the intermediate gel. In a sense this method is an examination of one antigen against two antisera in a competitive way. Even if only some of the antigenic determinants, or epitopes, of the fimbrial protein in the bottom gel fit the antibody or antibodies in the intermediate gel, all the fimbrial molecules will participate in formation of the precipitate, and none will be left to react with the homologous antiserum in the upper gel, provided that only one fimbrial protein is present in the reference antigen in the bottom gel.

For general serotyping of fimbriae we examine fimbrial extracts by rocket immunoelectrophoresis. For confirmation of positive reactions, the extracts are incorporated in the intermediate gels (CLIE) of those reference systems indicated by the reactions in rocket immunoelectrophoresis. Only if the precipitation line of the extract under examination fuses with the reference precipitation line is a certain fimbria serotype reported.

Examination of *E. coli* from urinary tract infections (UTIs), particularly pyelonephritis, by CIE and IEM has shown the presence of different fimbrial antigens which have been termed F antigens and numbered F1B, F1C, and F7 to F16 (ØRSKOV et al. 1980; ØRSKOV and ØRSKOV 1983a and I. ØRSKOV and F. ØRSKOV, unpublished results). Serologically these antigens are easily distinguished from each other if studied by CLIE, while some relationships between F1C and F1B and between F7 to F16 are apparent when heterologous antiserum is incorporated in the intermediate gel. F1C, and probably also F1B, does not cause any agglutination of erythrocytes or adhesion to urinary epithelial cells. F7 to F13, F15, and F16 belong to the group of fimbriae (P) binding to gal-gal receptors.

Two striking features have appeared from the F antigen study: (a) an association between F antigens and O:K:H serotype, a finding which suggests nature's selection of certain virulent clones, and (b) a diversity of fimbriae not only among different O:K:H serotypes but also in the same strain (ØRSKOV et al. 1982b). As examples of these features mention can be made of O6:K2:H1 strains, which in our studies characteristically have shown the presence of either $F7_1$, $F7_2$, and F1C or $F7_2$ and F1C at the same time (ØRSKOV et al. 1981a), and O4:K12:H5 strains, which have mainly been found with the following F antigens: F1C, F13, F14, and F16.

At this juncture we should comment on the numbering of F antigens in the O4:K12:H5 strain C134-73 (Table 6). These antigens were originally given other designations, thus F13 was FC134.3, F14 was FC134.4 or Fy, and F16 was FC134.2 or F12 rel. The change to F13 took place when the FC134.3 antigen by CIE was found to be identical with the antigen of the pap fimbria in strain J96 (O4:K6) cloned by HULL et al. (1981). FC134.4 was difficult to separate from the other F antigens in

Table 6. Fimbriae of *E. coli* C134-73 (O4:K12:H5)

FC134 1 = pseudotype 1 = F1C
      2 = F12 rel. = F16
      3 = F13
      4 = Fy = F14

strain C134 by CIE and was therefore provisionally termed Fy (ØRSKOV and ØRSKOV 1983a), which has no relationship to the F(y) antigen found in strains from calves and first described by GIRARDEAU et al. (1980).

A MAb against a fimbrial preparation of strain 20025 of serotype O4:K12:H⁻, similar to strain C134, was examined in ELISA, immunoblot, and rocket immunoelectrophoresis with various fimbrial preparations, and was shown to react with strains expressing Fy or an Fy-related antigen or the $F7_1$, $F7_2$ antigens (ABE et al. 1987). The fimbrial antigen reacting with this MAb was designated F14, well knowing that it was highly related to but not identical with $F7_2$. F14 was cloned by BOULNOIS (to be published) but its state as a P or an S fimbria is not yet clear.

By CIE the FC134.2 antigen had been found to be related to F12 and was therefore termed F12 rel. An antigen identical with it was detected, also by CIE, in two E. coli UTI strains of serotype O157:H45 (Table 4). By use of ELISA DE REE et al. (1986b) similarly demonstrated a difference between MAbs against F12 rel. and F12 (Table 7). The two O157:H45 strains reacted with the MAb against F12 rel. but not with the one against F12. The two MAbs thus seem to recognize different epitopes. The designation F16 was introduced instead of F12 rel. for this fimbrial antigen, which had first been demonstrated in the C134-73 strain.

In O75:K5:H⁻ strains also from UTIs, another F12 rel. fimbrial antigen was found. This antigen was denoted F15. The relationship to F12 is different from that of F16.

At the beginning of this section it was stated that an antiserum against whole cells can be used for analysis of fimbrial antigens if it is absorbed with the same strain as is used for antiserum production but cultured at 18°C. Such an absorbed antiserum may also contain antibodies against other surface antigens; of particular importance in this respect are antibodies against those of the E. coli polysaccharide K antigens which are not expressed at 18°C (ØRSKOV et al. 1984). In CIE such antibodies can be recognized because the strongly anodic position of the precipitates is characteristic. An example is given in Fig. 1, which shows the K15, CS1, and CS3 precipitates. The form of the CS1 line is characteristic of tight compact fimbriae (fimbriae I). If the serum is diluted or the antigen concentrated, this line will be

Table 7. Comparison between two E. coli MAbs in ELISA with whole bacteria. Results from Table 2 of DE REE et al. (1986b)

Strain	Serotype	MAbs against fimbriae	
		F12 rel.[a] (F16) in strain 20025 (O4:K12:H-)	F12[b] in strain C1979 (O16:K1:H-)
C1979	O16:K1:H-	+	+
C134	O4:K12:H5	+	−
SP57	O157:H45	+	−
SP88	O157:H45	+	−

[a] MAb prepared by ABE et al. (1987);
[b] MAb prepared by DE REE et al. (1986b);
See also Table 4

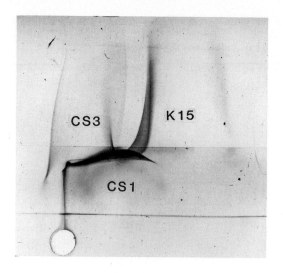

Fig. 1. CIE showing precipitation reactions of strain E1392-75 (06:K15:H16). *Lower gel*: extract E1392; *intermediate gel*: saline; *upper gel*: antiserum E1392 absorbed with culture 1392 grown at 18°C. The high peak to the *left* is the CS3 peak, the high peak to the *right* is the K15 peak, and the almost *horizontal line* is the CS1 line. The anode is to the right in the first dimension and at the top in the second dimension

elevated and form a peak which, however, does not look like the peak of CS3, which is characteristic of fine flexible filaments (fimbriae II). The more anodic position of a fimbriae I line than of a fimbriae II line is also characteristic.

4 Phase Variation

Fimbriae phase variation is a regulatory mechanism affecting phenotypic expression of fimbriae, which means that cells can vary between two alternative forms: fimbriated and nonfimbriated (BRINTON et al. 1954). The role of this change is influenced by cultural conditions (DUGUID and GILLIES 1957; DUGUID et al. 1955).

Based on the hemagglutinating capacity of strains we some years ago separated differently fimbriated organisms of the same strain and were surprised that fimbriae of different antigenic structures could be present on different cells and, although rarely, on the same cell, and that not all cells were fimbriated in a fimbriated culture (ØRSKOV et al. 1982b). Shortly afterward RHEN et al. (1983b) reported that there was a phase variation between P-fimbriated and 1C-fimbriated cells. Differently fimbriated cells were fractionated with specific antifimbria sera, and cells remaining in suspension after this serum treatment were examined for their agglutination properties with the various antisera. The phase variation was very rapid compared with the on-off variation of the *E. coli* type 1 fimbriae (EISENSTEIN 1981). By immunofluorescence microscopy with differently fluorochrome-labeled antibodies specific for either P, type F1C, or type 1 fimbriae it was shown that in a broth culture of the examined strain the different fimbrial types mostly occurred on different cells. Only 9% carried more than one fimbrial type (NOWICKI et al. 1984). A similar fast phase variation was described between S and type 1 fimbriae by the same technique.

The cells of the S-fimbriated strain 3040 (O18ac:K1:H7) changed more rapidly from S-fimbriated or type 1-fimbriated cells into nonfimbriated cells than they shifted from one phase to another (NOWICKI et al. 1985a). Since these phase changes are very fast, overnight culture of fractionated subpopulations carrying only one fimbrial type produces colonies that are heterogeneous in respect of fimbrial antigens (NOWICKI et al. 1985b).

5 Conclusions

What we in the beginning supposed to be distinct antigens of P fimbriae of *E. coli*, i.e., F7–F12, have turned out to be not so distinct. Multiple copies of the pap operon have been found in a high percentage of *E. coli* from the urinary tract (HULL et al. 1985), so it is no wonder that, for example, some strains of serotype O6:K2:H1 express P fimbriae antigen $F7_1$ or $F7_2$, and others $F7_1$ and $F7_2$, etc. (ØRSKOV and ØRSKOV 1983a; ØRSKOV et al. 1982a). By CLIE we can tell when two fimbrial antigens are identical, and when we examine strains of O:K:H serotypes which are frequent in cases of pyelonephritis we find that a high percentage of the strains have F antigens identical with those of our reference strains; such strains often represent clones, i.e., strains of the same bioserotype, electrotype, outer membrane pattern, etc. (ØRSKOV and ØRSKOV 1983b; NIMMICH et al. 1984; NIMMICH and ZINGLER 1984). The F antigens of UTI strains not belonging to these most frequent clones may, upon CLIE examination, show only a relationship to, and not identity with, one or more of the known F antigens. Studies of F7–F12 by CIE with heterologous antiserum in the intermediate gel showed that several of these antigens were related although they were distinct when examined by CLIE (ØRSKOV and ØRSKOV 1983a), a finding which reflects the fact that more than one epitope is present in each F antigen. Results obtained by SDS–PAGE examination of immunoprecipitates have similarly suggested that more antigenic determinants can occur in different P fimbriae in variable combinations, and use of the term "F-specific antigenic determinant" rather than "specific F antigen" was proposed (PERE et al. 1988). Antigenic complexity of *E. coli* fimbrial antigens is reminiscent of the complexity of the Enterobacteriaceae O antigens, where the polysaccharide side chain of the lipopolysaccharide from different O groups often contains similar chemical structures (epitopes) in combinations characteristic for the single O group. Exactly defining which antigenic factors, determinants, or epitopes compose the fimbrial antigens is an important scientific question, and it may be important for the development of a vaccine, independently of what kind of fimbriae we are dealing with. It should be mentioned here that PERE et al. (1988) found that 82 of 84 P-fimbriated *E. coli* reacted in immunoprecipitation with three anti-P-fimbriae sera, and concluded that the antigens used for preparing the antisera might form the basis of a broadly cross-reacting P-fimbrial vaccine. However, recent data have indicated that purified adhesin proteins might be superior vaccines to those prepared from intact fimbriae (LUND et al. 1988a), and that the receptor-binding site of these minor proteins is conserved despite differences

in their primary structures (HOSCHÜTZKY et al. 1989). Furthermore, not only gene clusters determining F13 fimbriae together with the Galα(1-4)Gal binding adhesin can be cloned from strain J96, as LUND et al. (1988b) recently cloned the genes for F13 fimbriae and a GalNAcα(1-3)GalNAc binding adhesin from J96. Strains with P fimbriae agglutinate sheep erythrocytes to various degrees, and this ability has been ascribed to the Forssman antigen, which is present on sheep erythrocytes but also on human erythrocytes. However, the Forssman antigen contains both the Forssman-specific GalNAcα(1-3)GalNAc moiety and the Galα(1-4)Gal moiety, and this antigen has recently been isolated from the human kidney (BREIMER 1985; LUND et al. 1988b). Thus the adhesin binding the Forssman-specific determinant may also have an important function in colonization of the upper urinary tract, and its possible antigenic variability should be examined.

VAN DIE et al. (1988) questioned in a recent paper whether determination of F specificity is sufficient for serologic characterization of fimbriae. The answer is probably that some sort of simplified F typing will suffice for most epidemiologic examinations because of the apparent stability of the main F character in the different pathogenic clones. Of course, for other purposes a more detailed analysis may be necessary. Such a detailed analysis could be a combination of an examination by SDS–PAGE of fimbrial preparations and of immunoprecipitates, and an analysis by CIE, particularly CLIE; the fimbria-specific antisera should include cross-absorbed antisera, and production of many MAbs should be considered.

References

Abe C, Schmitz S, Moser I, Boulnois G, High NJ, Ørskov I, Ørskov F, Jann B, Jann K (1987) Monoclonal antibodies with fimbrial F1C, F12, F13, and F14 specificities obtained with fimbriae from *E. coli* O4:K12:H⁻. Microb Pathogen 2: 71–77

Adegbola RA, Old DC (1982) New fimbrial hemagglutinin in *Serratia* species. Infect Immun 38: 306–315

Adegbola RA, Old DC (1987) Antigenic relationships among type-1 fimbriae of Enterobacteriaceae revealed by immuno-electronmicroscopy. J Med Microbiol 24: 21–28

Axelsen NH (1973) Intermediate gel in crossed and in fused rocket immunoelectrophoresis. Scand J Immunol 2 (Suppl 1): 71–77

Axelsen NH, Bock E, Kröll J (1973) Comparison of antigens: the reaction of identity. Scand J Immunol 2 (Suppl 1): 91–94

Breimer ME (1985) Chemical and immunological identification of the Forssman pentaglycosylceramide in human kidneys. Glycoconjugate 2: 375–385

Brinton CC (1959) non-flagellar appendages of bacteria. Nature 183: 782–786

Brinton CC (1965) The structure, function, synthesis and genetic control of bacterial pili and a molecular model for DNA and RNA transport in gram negative bacteria. Trans NY Acad Sci (Series II) 27: 1003–1054

Brinton CC, Buzell A, Lauffer MA (1954) Electrophoresis and phage susceptibility studies on a filament-producing variant of the *E. coli* B bacterium. Biochim Biophys Acta 15: 533–542

Brinton CC, Gemski P, Camahan J (1964) A new type of bacterial pilus genetically controlled by the fertility factor of *E. coli* K12 and its role in chromosome transfer. Proc Natl Acad Sci USA 52: 776–783

Clegg S, Gerlach GF (1987) Enterobacterial fimbriae. J Bacteriol 169: 934–938

Closs O, Harboe M, Wassum Am (1975) Cross reactions between mycobacteria. Scand J Immunol 2 (Suppl 2): 173–185

Cravioto A, Scotland SM, Rowe B (1982) Hemagglutination activity and colonization factor antigens I and II in enterotoxigenic and non-enterotoxigenic strains of *Escherichia coli* isolated from humans. Infect Immun 36: 189–197

Darfeuille-Michaud A, Forestier C, Joly B, Cluzel R (1986) Identification of a nonfimbrial adhesive factor of an enterotoxigenic *Escherichia coli* strain. Infect Immun 52: 468–475

de Graaf FK, Roorda I (1982) Production, purification, and characterization of the fimbrial adhesive antigen F41 isolated from calf enteropathogenic *Escherichia coli* strain B41M. Infect Immun 36: 751–758

de Ree JM, Schwillens P, van den Bosch JF (1986a) Monoclonal antibodies for serotyping the P fimbriae of uropathogenic *Escherichia coli*. J Clin Microbiol 24: 121–125

de Ree JM, Jann K, van de Bosch JF (1986b) Characterization of the P fimbriae F8 and F12 from uropathogenic *Escherichia coli* with monoclonal antibodies. In: de Ree JM (thesis) Molecular and serological characterization of P fimbriae from uropathogenic *Escherichia coli*. Krips Repro, Meppel

Duguid JP, Campbell I (1969) Antigens of the type-1 fimbriae of salmonellae and other enterobacteria. J Med Microbiol 2: 535–553

Duguid JP, Gillies RR (1957) Fimbriae and adhesive properties in dysentery bacilli. J Pathol Bacteriol 74: 397–411

Duguid JP, Old DC (1980) Adhesive properties of Enterobacteriaceae. In: Beachy EH (ed) Bacterial adherence. Chapman and Hall, London, Chap 7 (Receptors and recognition, series B, vol 6)

Duguid JP, Smith IW, Dempster G, Edmunds PN (1955) Non-flagellar filamentous appendages ("fimbriae") and haemagglutinating activity in *Bacterium coli*. J Pathol Bacteriol 70: 335–348

Duguid JP, Anderson ES, Campbell I (1966) Fimbriae and adhesive properties in salmonellae. J Pathol Bacteriol 92: 107–138

Duguid JP, Clegg S, Wilson MI (1979) The fimbrial and non-fimbrial haemagglutinins of *Escherichia coli*. J Med Microbiol 12: 213–227

Eisenstein BI (1981) Phase variation of type 1 fimbriae in *Escherichia coli* is under transcriptional control. Science 214: 337–339

Engvall E, Perlmann P (1972) Enzyme-linked immunosorbent assay, ELISA. III. Quantitation of specific antibodies by enzyme-labelled anti-immunoglobulin in antigen-coated tubes. J Immunol 109: 129–135

Evans DG, Evans DJ (1978) New surface-associated heat-labile colonization factor antigen (CFA/II) produced by enterotoxigenic *Escherichia coli* of serogroups O6 and O8. Infect Immun 21: 638–647

Evans DG, Silver RP, Evans DJ, Chase DG, Gorbach SL (1975) Plasmid-controlled colonization factor associated with virulence in *Escherichia coli* enterotoxigenic for humans. Infect Immun 12: 656–667.

Fairbrother JM, Larivière S, Lallier R (1986) New fimbrial antigen F165 from *Escherichia coli* serogroup O115 strains isolated from piglets with diarrhea. Infect Immun 51: 10–55

Faris A (1985) Adhesive and hydrophobic adsorptive properties of enterotoxigenic and bovine mastitis *Escherichia coli*. Identification of fibronectin-binding fimbriae (Fib fimbriae). Thesis, Swedish University of Agricultural Sciences, Uppsala

Forestier C, Welinder KG, Darfeuille-Michaud A, Klemm P (1987) Afimbrial adhesin from *Escherichia coli* strain 2230: purification, characterization and partial covalent structure. FEMS Microbiol Lett 40: 47–50

Gelderblom H, Beutin L, Hadjiyiannis D, Reupke H (1985) Rapid typing of pili of pathogenic *Escherichia coli* by dispersive immunoelectron microscopy. In: Habermehl K-O (ed) Rapid methods and automation in microbiology and immunology. Springer, Berlin Heidelberg New York Tokyo

Gillies RR, Duguid JP (1958) The fimbrial antigens of *Shigella flexneri*. J Hyg (Lond) 56: 303–318

Girardeau JP, Doubourguier HC, Contrepois M (1980) Attachment des *Escherichia coli* entéro-pathogènes à la muqueuse intestinale. Bull Groupe Techn Vet 80-4-B-190: 49–60

Goldhar J, Perry R, Ofek I (1984) Extraction and properties of nonfimbrial mannose-resistant hemagglutinin from a urinary isolate of *Escherichia coli*. Curr Microbiol 11:49–54

Goldhar J, Perry R, Golecki JR, Hoschützky H, Jann B, Jann K (1987) Nonfimbrial, mannose-resistant adhesins from uropathogenic *Escherichia coli* O83:K1:H4 and O14:K?: H11. Infect Immun 55: 1837–1842

Guinée PAM, Jansen WH (1979) Behavior of *Escherichia coli* K antigens K88ab, K88ac, and K88ad in immunoelectrophoresis, double diffusion, and hemagglutination. Infect Immun 23: 700–705

Guinée PAM, Jansen WH, Agterberg CM (1976) Detection of the K99 antigen by means of agglutination and immunoelectrophoresis in *Escherichia coli* isolates from calves and its correlation with enterotoxigenicity. Infect Immun 13: 1369–1377

Hacker J, Schmidt G, Hughes C, Knapp S, Marget M, Goebel W (1985) Cloning and characterization of

genes involved in production of mannose-resistant, neuraminidase-susceptible (X) fimbriae from a uropathogenic O6: K15: H31 *Escherichia coli* strain. Infect Immun 47: 434–440

Hanley J, Salit IE, Hofmann T (1985) Immunochemical characterization of P pili from invasive *Escherichia coli*. Infect Immun 49: 581–586

Hinson G, Knutton S, Lam-Po-Tang MK-L, McNeish AS, Williams PH (1987) Adherence to human colonocytes of an *Escherichia coli* strain isolated from severe infantile enteritis: molecular and ultrastructural studies of a fibrillar adhesin. Infect Immun 55: 393–402

Honda T, Arita M, Miwatani T (1984) Characterization of new hydrophobic pili of human enterotoxigenic *Escherichia coli*: a possible new colonization factor. Infect Immun 43: 959–965

Hoschützky H, Lottspeich F, Jann K (1989) Isolation and characterization of the α-galactosyl-1,4-β-galactosyl-specific adhesin (P adhesin) from fimbriated *Escherichia coli*. Infect Immun 57: 76–81

Hull RA, Gill RE, Hsu P, Minshew BH, Falkow S (1981) Construction and expression of recombinant plasmids encoding type 1, or D-mannose-resistant pili from a urinary tract infection *Escherichia coli* isolate. Infect Immun 33: 933–938

Hull S, Clegg S, Svanborg Eden, C, Hull R (1985) Multiple forms of genes in pyelonephritogenic *Escherichia coli* encoding adhesins binding globoseries glycolipid receptors. Infect Immun 47: 80–83

Ip SM, Chrichton PB, Old DC, Duguid JP (1981) Mannose-resistant and eluting haemagglutinins and fimbriae in *Escherichia coli*. J Med Microbiol 14: 223–226

Jacobs AAC (1987) Structure-function relationships of the K88 and K99 fibrillar adhesins and enterotoxigenic *Escherichia coli*. Thesis, Free University, Amsterdam

Jann K, Jann B, Schmidt G (1981) SDS polyacrylamide gel electrophoresis and serological analysis of pili from *Escherichia coli* of different pathogenic origin. FEMS Microbiol Lett 11: 21–25

Jones GW, Isaacson RE (1983) Proteinaceous bacterial adhesins and their receptors. CRC Crit Rev Microbiol 10: 229–260

Källenius G, Möllby R, Svenson SB, Winberg J, Hultberg H (1980) Identification of a carbohydrate receptor recognized by uropathogenic *Escherichia coli*. Infection 8 (Suppl 3): S228–S293

Källenius G, Möllby R, Hultberg H, Svenson SB, Cedergren B, Winberg J (1981) Structure of carbohydrate part of receptor on human uroepithelial cells for pyelonephritogenic *Escherichia coli*. Lancet II: 604–606

Klemm P (1985) Fimbrial adhesins of *Escherichia coli*. Rev Infect Dis 7: 321–340

Klemm P, Christiansen G (1987) Three *fim* genes required for the regulation of length and mediation of adhesion of *Escherichia coli* type 1 fimbriae. MGG 208: 439–445

Klemm P, Ørskov I, Ørskov F (1982) F7 and type 1-like fimbriae from three *Escherichia coli* strains isolated from urinary tract infections: protein chemical and immunological aspects. Infect Immum 36: 462–468

Korhonen TK, Väisänen V, Saxén H, Hultberg H, Svenson SB (1982) P-antigen-recognizing fimbriae from human uropathogenic *Escherichia coli* strains. Infect Immun 37: 286–291

Korhonen TK, Väisänen-Rhen V, Rhen M, Pere A, Parkkinen J, Finne J (1984) *Escherichia coli* fimbriae recognizing sialyl galactosides. J Bacteriol 159: 762–766

Krøll J (1983) Crossed line-immunoelectrophoresis. Scand J Immunol 2 (Suppl 1): 79–81

Labigne-Roussel AF, Lark D, Schoolnik G, Falkow S (1984) Cloning and expression of an afimbrial adhesin (AFA-I) responsible for P blood group-independent, mannose-resistant hemagglutination from a pyelonephritic *Escherichia coli* strain. Infect Immun 46: 251–259

Lawn AM (1967) Simple immunological labelling method for electron microscopy and its application to the study of filamentous appendages of bacteria. Nature 214: 1151–1152

Lawn AM, Meynell E (1970) Serotypes of sex pili. J Hyg 68: 683–684

Leffler H, Svanborg-Edén C (1980) Chemical identification of a glycosphingolipid receptor for *Escherichia coli* attaching to human urinary tract epithelial cells and agglutinating human erythrocytes. FEMS Microbiol Lett 8: 127–134

Leffler H, Svanborg-Edén C (1981) Glycolipid receptors for uropathogenic *Escherichia coli* on human erythrocytes and uroepithelial cells. Infect Immun 34: 920–929

Levine MM, Ristaino P, Marley G, Smyth C, Knutton S, Boedeker E, Black R, Young C, Clements ML, Cheney C, Patnaik R (1984) Coli surface antigens 1 and 3 of colonization factor antigen II-positive enterotoxigenic *Escherichia coli*: morphology, purification and immune responses in humans. Infect Immun 44: 409–420

Lindberg F, Lund B, Johansson L, Normark S (1987) Localization of the receptor-binding protein adhesin at the tip of the bacterial pilus. Nature 328: 84–87

Lintermans PF, Pohl P, Bertels A, Charlier G, Vandekerckhove J, Vandamme J, Schoup J, Schlicker C, Korhonen T, de Greve H, van Montagu M (1989) Characterization and purification of the F17 adhesin present on the surface of bovine enteropathogenic and septicemic *Escherichia coli*. Am J Vet Res

Lund B, Lindberg F, Marklund B-I, Normark S (1988a) Tip proteins of pili associated with pyelonephritis: new candidates for vaccine development. Vaccine 6: 110–112

Lund B, Marklund B-I, Strömberg N, Lindberg F, Karlsson K-A, Normark S (1988b) Uropathogenic *Escherichia coli* express serologically identical pili with different receptor binding specificities. Mol Microbiol 2: 255–265

Maurer L, Orndorff PE (1985) A new locus, *pilE*, required for the binding of type 1 piliated *Escherichia coli* to erythrocytes. FEMS Microbiol Lett 30: 59–66

McConnell MM, Thomas LV, Day NP, Rowe B (1985) Enzyme-linked immunosorbent assays for the detection of adhesin factor antigens of enterotoxigenic *Escherichia coli*. J Infect Dis 152: 1120–1127

Minion FC, Abraham SN, Beachey EH, Goguen JD (1986) The genetic determinant of adhesive function in type 1 fimbriae of *Escherichia coli* is distinct from the gene encoding the fimbrial subunit. J Bacteriol 165: 1033–1036

Moch T, Hoschützky H, Hacker J, Kröncke K-D, Jann K (1987) Isolation and characterization of the α-sialyl-β-2,3-galactosyl-specific adhesin from fimbriated *Escherichia coli*. Proc Natl Acad Sci USA 84: 3462–3466

Morris JA, Thorns CJ, Sojka WJ (1980) Evidence for two adhesive antigens on the K99 reference strain *Escherichia coli* B41. J Gen Microbiol 118: 107–113

Morris JA, Thorns CJ, Boarer C (1985a) Evaluation of a monoclonal antibody to the K99 fimbrial adhesin produced by *Escherichia coli* enterotoxigenic for calves, lambs and piglets. Res Vet Sci 39: 75–79

Morris JA, Sojka WJ, Ready RA (1985b) Serological comparison of the *Escherichia coli* prototype strains for the F(Y) and Att 25 adhesins implicated in neonatal diarrhoea in calves. Res Vet Sci 38: 246–247

Moser I, Ørskov I, Hacker J, Jann K (1986) Characterization of a monoclonal antibody against the fimbrial F8 antigen of *Escherichia coli*. FEMS Microbiol Lett 34: 329–334

Mullany P, Field AM, McConnell MM, Scotland SM, Smith HR, Rowe B (1983) Expression of plasmids coding for colonization factor antigen II (CFA/II) and enterotoxin production in *Escherichia coli*. J Gen Microbiol 129: 3591–3601

Nagy B, Moon HW, Isaacson RE (1977) Colonization of porcine intestine by enterotoxigenic *Escherichia coli*: selection of piliated forms in vivo, adhesion of piliated forms to epithelial cells in vitro, and incidence of a pilus antigen among porcine enteropathogenic *E. coli* Infect Immun 16: 344–352

Nimmich W, Zingler G (1984) Biochemical characteristics, phage patterns, and O1 factor analysis of *Escherichia coli* O1:K1:H7:F11 and O1:K1:H⁻:F9 strains isolated from patients with urinary tract infections. Med Microbiol Immunol 173: 75–85

Nimmich W, Zingler G, Ørskov I (1984) Fimbrial antigens of *Escherichia coli* O1:K1:H7 and O1:K1:H⁻ strains isolated from patients with urinary tract infections. Zentralbl Bakteriol Mikrobiol Hyg [A] 258: 104–111

Norgen M, Normark S, Lark D, O'Hanley P, Schoolnik G, Falkow S, Båga M, Uhlin BE (1984) Mutations in *E. coli* cistrons affecting adhesion to human cells do not abolish Pap pili fiber formation. EMBO J 3: 1159–1165

Normark S, Lark D, Hull R, Norgren M, Båga M, O'Hanley P, Schoolnik G, Falkow S (1983) Genetics of digalactocide-binding adhesin from a uropathogenic *Escherichia coli* strain. Infect Imun 41: 942–949

Nowicki B, Rhen M, Väisänen-Rhen V, Pere A, Korhonen TK (1984) Immunofluorescence study of fimbrial phase variation in *Escherichia coli* KS71. J Bacteriol 160: 691–695

Nowicki B, Rhen M, Väisänen-Rhen V, Pere A, Korhonen TK (1985a) Kinetics of phase variation between S and type-1 fimbriae of *Escherichia coli*. FEMS Microbiol Lett 28: 237–242

Nowicki B, Rhen M, Väisänen-Rhen V, Pere A, Korhonen TK (1985b) Organization of fimbriate cells in colonies of *Escherichia coli* strain 3040. J Gen Microbiol 131: 1263–1266

Nowotarska M, Mulczyk M (1977) Serological relationship of fimbriae among Enterobacteriaceae. Arch Immunol Ther Exp (Warsz) 25: 7–46

Old DC, Adegbola RA (1983) A new mannose-resistant haemagglutinin in *Klebsiella*. J Appl Bacteriol 55: 165–172

Old DC, Adegbola RA (1985) Antigenic relationships among type-3 fimbriae of Enterobacteriaceae revealed by immunoelectronmicroscopy. J Med Microbiol 20: 113–121

Old DC, Payne SB (1971) Antigens of the type-2 fimbriae of salmonellae: "cross-reacting material" (CRM) of type-1 fimbriae. J Med Microbiol 4: 215–225

Old DC, Yakubu DE, Chrichton PB (1987) Demonstration by immunoelectronmicroscopy of antigenic heterogeneity among P fimbriae of strains of *Escherichia coli*. J Med Microbiol 23: 247–253

Ørskov I, Ørskov F (1983a) Serology of *Escherichia coli* fimbriae. In: Hanson LÅ, Kallós P, Westphal O (eds) Host parasite relationships in gram-negative infections. Prog Allergy 33: 80–105

Ørskov F, Ørskov I (1983b) Summary of a workshop on the clone concept in the epidemiology, taxonomy, and evolution of the Enterobacteriaceae and other bacteria. J Infect Dis 148: 346–357

Ørskov I, Ørskov F (1985) *Escherichia coli* in extra-intestinal infections. J Hyg 95: 551–575

Ørskov I, Ørskov F, Sojka WJ, Leach JM (1961) Simultaneous occurrence of *E. coli* B and L antigens in strains from diseased swine. Acta Pathol Microbiol Scand 53: 404–422

Ørskov I, Ørskov F, Sojka WJ, Wittig W (1964) K antigens K88ab(L) and K88ac(L) in *E. coli*. A new O antigen: O147 and a new K antigen: K89(B). Acta Pathol Microbiol Scand 62: 439–447

Ørskov I, Ørskov F, Smith HW, Sojka WJ (1975) The establishment of K99, a thermolabile, transmissible *Escherichia coli* K antigen, previously called "Kco", possessed by calf and lamb enteropathogenic strains. Acta Pathol Microbiol Scand [B] 83: 31–36

Ørskov I, Ørskov F, Birch-Andersen A (1980) Comparison of *Escherichia coli* fimbrial antigen F7 with type 1 fimbriae. Infect Immun 27: 657–666

Ørskov I, Ørskov F, Birch-Andersen A, Klemm P, Svanborg-Edén C (1982a) Protein attachment factors: fimbriae in adhering *Escherichia coli* strains. In: Robbins JB, Hill JC, Sadoff JC (eds) Bacterial vaccines. Part 4. Surface antigens: pili. Thieme-Stratton, New York (Seminars in infectious disease, vol 4)

Ørskov I, Ørskov F, Birch-Andersen A, Kanamori M, Svanborg-Edén C (1982b) O, K, H and fimbrial antigens in *Escherichia coli* serotypes associated with pyelonephritis and cystitis. Scand J Infect Dis [Suppl] 33: 18–25

Ørskov F, Sharma V, Ørskov I (1984) Influence of growth temperature on the development of *Escherichia coli* polysaccharide K antigens. J Gen Microbiol 130: 2681–2684

Ørskov I, Birch-Andersen A, Duguid JP, Stenderup J, Ørskov F (1985) An adhesive protein capsule of *Escherichia coli*. Infect Immun 47: 191–200

Ott M, Hacker J, Schmoll T, Jarchau T, Korhonen TK, Goebel W (1986) Analysis of the genetic determinants coding for the S-fimbrial adhesin (*sfa*) in different *Eschericha coli* strains causing meningitis or urinary tract infections. Infect Immun 54: 646–653

Ouchterlony O (1949) Antigen-antibody reactions in gel. Acta Pathol Microbiol Scand 26: 507–515

Parkkinen J, Rogers GN, Korhonen T, Dahr W, Finne J (1986) Identification of the O-linked sialyloligosaccharides of glycophorin A as the erythrocyte receptors for S-fimbriated *Escherichia coli*. Infect Immun 54: 37–42

Parry SH, Rooke DM (1985) Adhesins and colonization factors of *Escherichia coli*. In: Sussman M (ed) The virulence of *Escherichia coli*. Academic, London (Special publications of the Society for General Microbiology, 13)

Parry SH, Abraham SN, Sussman M (1982) The biological and serological properties of adhesion determinants of *Escherichia coli* isolated from urinary tract infections in children. In: Schulte-Wisserman H (ed) Clinical, bacteriological and immunological aspects of urinary tract infections in children. Thieme, Stuttgart

Pere A (1986) P fimbriae on uropathogenic *Escherichia coli* O16:K1 and O18 strains. FEMS Microbiol Lett 37: 19–26

Pere A, Leinonen M, Väisänen-Rhen V, Rhen M, Korhonen TK (1985) Occurrence of type-1C fimbriae on *Escherichia coli* strains isolated from human extraintestinal infections. J Gen Microbiol 131: 1705–1711

Pere A, Väisänen-Rhen V, Rhen M, Tenhunen J, Korhonen TK (1986) Analysis of P fimbriae on *Escherichia coli* O2, O4, and O6 strains by immunoprecipitation. Infect Immun 51: 618–625

Pere A, Selander RK, Korhonen TK (1988) P fimbriae on O1, O7, O75, rough and nontypable strains of *Escherichia coli*. Infect Immun 56: 1288–1294

Pohl P, Lintermans P, Van Muylen K, Schotte M (1982) Colibacillis entérotoxigènes de veau possedant un antigène d'attachment différent de l'antigène K99. Ann Med Vet 126: 569–571

Rhen M, Wahlström E, Korhonen TK (1983a) P-fimbriae of *Escherichia coli*: fractionation by immune precipitation. FEMS Microbiol Lett 18: 227–232

Rhen M, Mäkelä PH, Korhonen TK (1983b) P-fimbriae of *Escherichia coli* are subject to phase variation. FEMS Microbiol Lett 19: 267–271

Rhen M, Tenhunen J, Väisänen-Rhen V, Pere A, Båga M, Korhonen TK (1986a) Fimbriation and P-antigen recognition of *Escherichia coli* strains harbouring mutated recombinant plasmids encoding fimbrial adhesins of the uropathogenic *E. coli* strains KS71. J Gen Microbiol 132: 71–77

Rhen M, Klemm P, Korhonen TK (1986b) Identification of two new hemagglutinins of *Escherichia coli*, N-acetyl-D-glucosamine-specific fimbriae and a blood group M-specific agglutinin, by cloning the corresponding genes in *Escherichia coli* K-12. J Bacteriol 168: 1234–1242

Scheidegger J-J (1955) Une micro-méthode de l'immuno-électrophorèse. Int Arch Allergy 7: 103–110

Schmitz S, Abe C, Moser I, Ørskov I, Ørskov F, Jann B, Jann K (1986) Monoclonal antibodies against the nonhemagglutinating fimbrial antigen 1C (pseudotype 1) of *Escherichia coli*. Infect Immun 51: 54–59

Smyth CJ (1982) Two mannose-resistant haemagglutinins on enterotoxigenic *Escherichia coli* of serotype O6:K15:H16 or H- isolated from travellers' and infantile diarrhoea. J Gen Microbiol 128: 2081–2096

Smyth CJ (1986) Fimbrial variation in *Escherichia coli*. In: Birkbeck TH, Penn CW (eds) Antigenic variation in infectious diseases. IRL, Oxford (Special publications of the Society for General Microbiology, 19)

Sparling PF, Cannon JG, So M (1986) Phase and antigenic variation of pili and outer membrane. J Infect Dis 153: 196–201

Stirm S, Ørskov F, Ørskov I, Mansa B (1967a) Episome-carried surface antigen K88 of *Escherichia coli*. II. Isolation and chemical analysis. J Bacteriol 93: 731–739

Stirm S, Ørskov F, Ørskov I, Birch-Andersen A (1967b) Episome-carried surface antigen K88 of *Escherichia coli*. III. Morphology. J Bacteriol 93: 740–748

Swanson J, Robbins K, Barrera O, Koomey JM (1987) Gene conversion variations generate structurally distinct pilin polypeptides in *Neisseria gonorrhoeae*. J Exp Med 165: 1016–1025

Thomas LV, Rowe B (1982) The occurrence of colonisation factors (CFA/I, CFA/II and E8775) in enterotoxigenic *Escherichia coli* from various countries in South East Asia. Med Microbiol Immunol 171: 85–90

Thomas LV, Cravioto A, Scotland, SM, Rowe B (1982) New fimbrial antigenic type (E8775) that may represent a colonization factor in enterotoxigenic *Escherichia coli* in humans. Infect Immun 35: 1119–1124

Thomas LV, McConnell MM, Rowe B, Field AM (1985) The possession of three novel coli surface antigens by enterotoxigenic *Escherichia coli* strains positive for the putative colonization factor PCF8775. J Gen Microbiol 131: 2319–2326

Towbin H, Stachelin T, Gordon J (1979) Electrophoretic transfer of proteins from polyacrylamide gels to nitrocellulose sheets: procedure and some applications. Proc Natl Acad Sci USA 76: 4350–4354

van Die I, Zuidweg E, Hoekstra W, Bergmans H (1986) The role of fimbriae of uropathogenic *Escherichia coli* as carriers of the adhesin involved in mannose-resistant hemagglutination. Microb Pathogen 1: 51–56

van Die I, Riegman N, Gaykema O, van Megen I, Hoekstra W, Bergmans H, de Ree H, van den Bosch H (1988) Localization of antigenic determinants on P-fimbriae of uropathogenic *Escherichia coli*. FEMS Microbiol Lett 49: 95–100

Väisänen-Rhen V (1984) Fimbria-like hemagglutinin of *Escherichia coli* O75 strains. Infect Immun 46: 401–407

Väisänen-Rhen V, Elo J, Väisänen E, Siitonen A, Ørskov I, Ørskov F, Svenson SB, Mäkelä PH, Korhonen TK (1984) P-fimbriated clones among uropathogenic *Escherichia coli* strains. Infect Immun 43: 149–155.

Weeke B (1973) General remarks on principles, equipment, reagents and procedure. Scand J Immunol 2 (Suppl 1): 15–35

Williams PH, Knutton S, Brown MGM, Candy DCA, McNeish AS (1984) Characterization of nonfimbrial mannose-resistant protein hemagglutinins of two *Escherichia coli* strains isolated from infants with enteritis. Infect Immun 44: 592–598

Willshaw GA, Smith HR, McConnell MM, Rowe B (1988) Cloning of genes encoding coli-surface (CS) antigens in enterotoxigenic *Eschericia coli*. FEMS Microbiol Lett 49: 473–478

Adhesins as Lectins: Specificity and Role in Infection

I. Ofek[1] and N. Sharon[2]

1 Introduction

The idea that proteins with lectin-like properties on bacterial surfaces serve as adhesins, which bind the organisms to animal cells, was first suggested in 1977 for *Escherichia coli* expressing type 1 fimbriae (or pili) specific for mannose (OFEK et al. 1977). Since then the adhesins of many bacteria studied have been found to be carbohydrate-binding proteins, akin to lectins (Table 1). These lectins have become the focus of interest in research because of the mounting evidence for the crucial role they, like other adhesins, play in infectious disease (SHARON 1987; OFEK and SHARON 1988).

The bacterial surface lectins serve as molecules of recognition in cell–cell interactions. For many of them, only limited information is available on their

[1] Department of Human Microbiology, Sackler School of Medicine, Tel Aviv University, Tel Aviv, and
[2] Department of Biophysics, The Weizmann Institute of Science, Rehovot, Israel

Current Topics in Microbiology and Immunology, Vol. 151
© Springer-Verlag Berlin·Heidelberg 1990

Table 1. Sugar specificity of bacterial surface lectins[a]

Monosaccharide	Bacteria[b]	Fimbriae[c]
Mannose	*Citrobacter freundii, Enterobacter* spp., *Erwinia carotovora, Escherichia coli, Klebsiella aerogenes, Klebsiella pneumoniae, Salmonella* spp., *Serratia marcescens, Shigella flexneri* (1)	Type 1
Galactose	*Escherichia coli* (2), *Fusobacterium nucleatum* (3)	
L-Fucose	*Vibrio cholerae* (4)	
L-Rhamnose, D-fucose	*Capnocytophaga ochracea* (5)	
N-Acetylgalactosamine	*Eikenella corrodens* (6), *Escherichia coli* (7)	
N-Acetylglucosamine	*Escherichia coli* (8)	Type G
Galα4Galβ-	*Escherichia coli* (9)	Type P
Galβ3GalNAc	*Actinomyces naeslundii, Actinomyces viscosus* (10, 11), *Bacteroides* spp. (12), *Clostridia* (12), *Lactobacillus* (12), *Propionibacterium* (12)	Type 2
Galβ4GlcNAc	Erwinia rhapontici (13), Staphylococcus saprophyticus (14)	
GalNAcβ4Gal	*Haemophilus influenzae* (15), *Klebsiella pneumoniae* (15), *Neisseria gonorrhoeae* (16), *Pseudomonas aeruginosa* (17), *Pseudomonas cepacia* (17)	
GlcNAcβ3Gal	*Streptococcus pneumoniae* (18, 19)	
NeuGcα2-3Galβ4Glc-	*Escherichia coli* (20)	K99
NeuAcα2-3Galβ	*Escherichia coli* (21, 22)	Type S
	Bordetella bronchiseptica (23), *Campylobacter pylori* (24), *Mycoplasma gallisepticum* (25), *Mycoplasma pneumoniae* (26), *Streptococcus sanguis* (27)	
(Glcα6)$_{5-8}$	*Streptococcus cricetus* (28), *Streptococcus sobrinus* (29)	

[a] For a more complete listing, as well as for agglutinins of viruses, fungi, and protozoa, the reader is referred to MIRELMAN and OFEK (1986);

[b] References to literature are numbered in parentheses as follows: (1) DUGUID and OLD 1980; (2) NILSSON et al. 1983; (3) MURRAY et al. 1988; (4) JONES and FRETER 1976; (5) WEISS et al. 1987; (6) YAMAZAKI et al. 1981; (7) Faris et al. 1980; (8) VÄISÄNEN-RHEN et al. 1983; (9) LEFFLER and SVANBORG EDÉN 1986; (10) Cisar 1986; (11) BRENNAN et al. 1987; (12) HANSSON et al. 1983; (13) KORHONEN et al. 1988; (14) GUNNARSSON et al. 1984; (15) KRIVAN et al. 1988a; (16) STROMBERG et al. 1988; (17) KRIVAN et al. 1988b; (18) ANDERSSON et al. 1983; (19) PULVERER et al. 1987; (20) SMIT et al. 1984; (21) PARKKINEN et al. 1986; (22) KORHONEN et al. 1984; (23) ISHIKAWA and ISAYAMA 1987; (24) EVANS et al. 1988; (25) GLASGOW and HILL 1980; (26) LOOMES et al. 1984; (27) MURRAY et al. 1982; (28) DRAKE et al. 1988; (29) LANDALE and McCABE 1987;

[c] Type of fimbria is given only for those microorganisms for which a lectin activity has been ascribed.

properties and sugar specificity. Several of the bacterial surface lectins have, however, been studied to a considerable extent with respect to not only their detailed carbohydrate specificity but also to their role in infection. The knowledge obtained has provided insights into various features of the sugar-combining site of the lectins and the nature of the interaction between bacteria and cell surfaces. Eventually, it may lead to the design of highly effective inhibitors that will prevent adhesion, colonization of mucosal surfaces, and infections in humans.

In this chapter we summarize the knowledge about the sugar specificity and role in infection of the better characterized bacterial surface lectins. For a more thorough coverage of bacterial lectins, as well as of lectins or agglutinins whose function as adhesins has not yet been defined, the reader is referred to a recent book on the subject (MIRELMAN 1986).

2 Sugar Specificity

The approaches used to elucidate the sugar specificity of the bacterial lectins are based on procedures commonly used in studies of lectins in general, and of lectin–cell interactions in particular (SHARON et al. 1981; OFEK et al. 1985). The first step involves the testing of the effect of a panel of sugars (monosaccharides, simple glycosides, and oligosaccharides) on bacterial adherence to, or agglutination of, erythrocytes or other cells. This step is based on the well-known hapten inhibition techniques used in the study of the specificity of antibodies and plant lectins (KABAT 1978).

The specificity of the lectin is usually defined by the sugar which is the best inhibitor of the adherence or agglutination reaction (Table 1). Alternatively, agglutination of cells, e.g., yeasts, or synthetic particles, e.g., latex beads carrying defined carbohydrates, may be employed (OFEK and BEACHEY 1978; DE MAN et al. 1987). Important information about the structure of the carbohydrates which serve as attachment sites on cell surfaces for a bacterial lectin, i.e., the lectin receptors, may be obtained by examining the effect on agglutination or adherence of treatment of the cells with enzymes (e.g., glycosidases or galactose oxidase) and chemical reagents (e.g., periodate) which modify carbohydrates (reviewed in OFEK et al. 1985).

For further identification of the receptors, they must be isolated and character-ized. In general, the receptors that carry the sugar structure(s) for which a bacterial lectin is specific are glycoproteins and/or glycolipids. For receptors that are glycoproteins, techniques using affinity chromatography on immobilized bacterial lectins (RODRIGUEZ-ORTEGA et al. 1987; GIAMPAPA et al. 1988), or lectin overlays of blots of electrochromatograms of cell membrane glycoproteins, are used (PRAKOBPHOL et al. 1987). For receptors that are glycolipids, membrane glycolipids are separated on thin layer silica gel plates and the chromatograms are probed with the lectin-carrying bacteria (HANSSON et al. 1985). Although the number of bacterial lectin receptors known is still very small, it is already clear that they may differ among the various cell types which bind the same bacterial lectin (KARLSSON 1986); the term "isoreceptors" was suggested to describe such a family of molecules. This has been shown for the P fimbrial lectin, whose sugar specificity appears to be absolute for Galα4Galβ (galabiose). It is also true for the mannose-specific type 1 fimbrial lectin, which binds to three distinct glycoproteins derived from the cell membrane of human polymorphonuclear leukocytes (RODRIGUEZ-ORTEGA et al. 1987) and to a glycoprotein from guinea pig erythrocytes (GIAMPAPA et al. 1988) which is different from the former ones. The accessibility of such isoreceptors may vary with the type of tissue and, as a consequence, the affinity of different bacterial strains carring the same lectin to various tissues or cells may differ too (SHERMAN et al. 1985; OFEK et al. 1982).

Bacteria which carry the gene coding for a certain lectin may not always express it on their surface. In particular, many lectin-producing bacteria undergo phase variation, i.e., they switch readily back and forth from the phenotype which expresses the lectin to one that does not. Outgrowth of one phenotype over the other may occur in a bacterial population growing under specific conditions. In addition,

bacterial cultures frequently contain two or more types of lectin. This may be the result of either coexpression on the cell surface of multiple types of lectin or the presence of heterogeneous populations of cells, each bearing a different lectin. In such cases, combinations of sugars are more effective inhibitors than individual ones. In addition, the percentage of the total test population of bacteria which express the different lectin may vary (MAAYAN et al. 1985; GOOCHEE et al. 1987).

2.1 Surface Lectins of Enterobacteriaceae

Much of our knowledge of the surface lectins of Enterobacteriaceae is based on the pioneering studies performed in the 1950s and 1960s in the laboratories of DUGUID and of BRINTON (reviewed by DUGUID and OLD 1980; BRINTON 1965). DUGUID was the first to study the agglutination properties of enteric bacteria systematically. He observed that many of them agglutinated erythrocytes of different animal species and classified the agglutinating bacteria into two groups: (a) mannose sensitive (MS) i.e., those that agglutinated guinea pig erythrocytes very strongly and human erythrocytes of all blood groups (A, B, O) moderately to strongly, and whose agglutination activity was inhibited by small concentrations (0.01%–0.5% w/v) of mannose, methyl α-mannoside, and yeast mannan; (b) mannose resistant (MR), i.e., those that agglutinated human erythrocytes strongly and were not inhibited by mannose. It is now well established that many of the latter strains exhibit distinct sugar specificities (Table 1).

Most bacterial strains are genotypically capable of producing more than one type of lectin. This is particularly pronounced in the case of pathogenic enterobacteria which possess the ability to produce type 1 fimbriae as well as one or more additional lectins (usually in the form of fimbriae) or hemagglutinins which may not be sugar specific (GOLDHAR et al. 1984).

In this chapter we focus on those fimbrial lectins of the enteric bacteria for which information is available on sugar specificity.

2.2 Type 1 Fimbriae

Most of the information on the carbohydrate specificity of type 1 fimbriae is based on studies of the inhibitory effect of a variety of glycosides and oligosaccharides of mannose on the agglutination of yeasts by type 1 fimbriated *E. coli*, *Klebsiella pneumoniae*, *Salmonellae* species, and, in the case of *E. coli*, also type 1 fimbriae isolated from this organism (FIRON et al. 1983, 1984) (Table 2). A similar pattern of specificity was subsequently found by NEESER et al. (1986), who used guinea pig erythrocyte instead of yeasts as indicator cells. We have postulated that the combining site of the type 1 fimbrial lectin corresponds to the size of a trisaccharide (Fig. 1) and that it is in the form of a depression or pocket on the surface of the lectin. Extended carbohydrate binding sites have been described for enzymes (e.g., lysozyme), several lectins, and antibodies (KABAT 1978). In the case of the *E. coli*

Table 2. Relative inhibition by mannose derivatives of yeast agglutination by *E. coli* 346 and by the type 1 fimbriae isolated from this organism (Firon et al. 1984)

Sugar	*E. coli* 346	Isolated fimbriae
MeαMan	1.0	1.0
Mannose	0.8	–
Manα6Man	0.5	–
Manα2Man	1.3	1.8
Manα3Man	1.2	–
Manα2Manα2Man	1.4	–
Manβ4GlcNAc	<0.4	–
Manα3Manβ4GlcNAc	21.0	30.0
Manα6Manβ4GlcNAc	0.7	–
Manα2Manα3Manβ4GlcNAc	0.7	5.5
Manα2Manα2Manα3Manβ4GlcNAc	0.7	–

Manα6
Manα6⟍
⟍Manα3⟋ᐳManαOMe   3.5   –
Manα3⟋

Manα2Manα6
Manα6⟍
⟍Manα3ᐳManαOMe   4.7   4.8
Manα3⟋

Manα6⟍
⟍Manα3ᐳManαOMe   10.5   –

Manα6⟍
⟍Manα3⟋Manα6⟍
       ⟍Manα3ᐳManαOMe   30.0   –

Manα6⟍
⟍Manα3⟋Manα6⟍
       ⟍Manα3ᐳManαOMe   30.0   36.0
Manα2Manα3⟋

pNPαMan	30.0	48.0
pNPβMan	1.2	–
Galβ4GlcNAcβ2Manα6Manβ4GlcNAc	0.25	–

Galβ4GlcNAcβ2Manα6⟍
                   ⟍Manβ4GlcNAc   0.6   –
Galβ4GlcNAcβ2Manα3⟋

pNP = *p*-nitrophenyl

lectin, there are probably three adjacent subsites, each of which accommodates a monosaccharide residue.

The presence of a hydrophobic binding region adjacent to the binding site of type 1 fimbriae is indicated by the finding that aromatic α-mannosides are powerful inhibitors of the agglutination of yeasts by *E. coli* and of the adherence of the bacteria to guinea pig ileal epithelial cells (Firon et al. 1984, 1987). In both systems, the best inhibitors were 4-methylumbelliferyl α-mannoside and *p*-nitro-*o*-chlorophenyl α-mannoside (500–1000 times more inhibitory than methyl α-mannoside). 4-Methylumbelliferyl α-mannoside was also more effective than methyl α-mannoside in removing adherent *E. coli* from ileal epithelial cells.

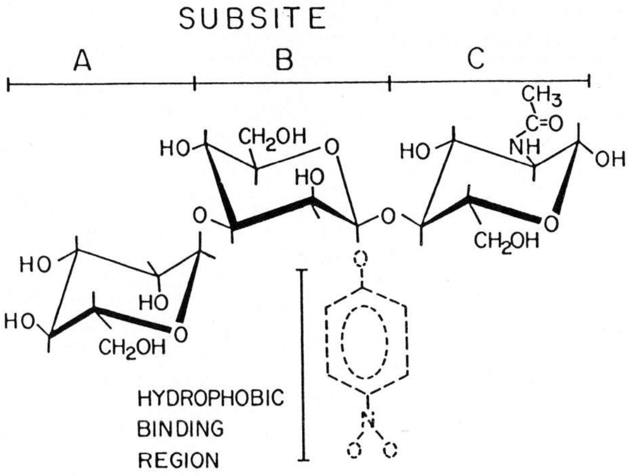

Fig. 1. Scheme of combining site of the mannose-specific lectin (type 1 fimbriae) of *E. coli* (Sharon 1987)

The combining site of type 1 fimbriae appears to differ from that of concanavalin A, a plant lectin with a closely related sugar specificity. The agglutinating activity of concanavalin A is inhibited by both mannose and glucose, whereas that of type 1 fimbriated *E. coli* is not inhibited by glucose. In addition, Manα2Man is a considerably better inhibitor of concanavalin A than is methyl α-mannoside, in contrast to what is found with the *E. coli* lectin.

Although all strains of *E. coli* examined, as well as *K. pneumoniae*, exhibited essentially the same pattern of specificity this is not the case with other enterobacteria (FIRON et al. 1984). For example, with several *Salmonella* species examined, aromatic α-mannosides, as well as the trisaccharide Manα3Manβ4GlcNAc, were weaker inhibitors than methyl α-mannoside. The combining site of different *Salmonellae* species is probably smaller than that of *E. coli* or *K. pneumoniae*, and it is devoid of a hydrophobic region. Although classified under the general term mannose specific (or mannose sensitive), the fimbrial lectins of different genera and species differ in their sugar specificity. Within a given genus, however, all strains tested exhibited the same specificity.

In general, it appears that mannose-specific bacteria preferentially bind structures found in short oligomannose chains (and in hybrid units, see below) of *N*-linked glycoproteins. Such structures are common constituents of many eukaryotic cell surfaces (SHARON and LIS 1982), which accounts for the fact that mannose-specific bacteria bind to a wide variety of cells. Membrane glycolipids are unlikely to serve as receptors for mannose-specific bacteria, since they are devoid of mannose residues.

These conclusions are supported by studies of the binding of mannose-specific *E. coli* to mammalian cells that differ in the level of oligomannose units on their surfaces. Mutants of baby hamster kidney (BHK) cells with increased levels of *N*-linked oligomannose or hybrid units in their glycoproteins bound considerably larger numbers of mannose-specific *E. coli* (FIRON et al. 1985) (Fig. 2). These cells were also more sensitive to agglutination by these bacteria than the parental wild-type cells. The best example is a mutant (Ric^{R}14) that lacks the enzyme *N*-

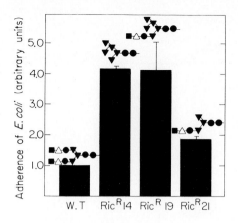

Fig. 2. Mannose-specific binding of type 1 fimbriated E. coli to wild-type and ricin-resistant (Ric) BHK cells. The symbols above each bar denote the predominant N-linked oligosaccharide expressed on the surface of the BHK cells: ▼, mannose; ●, N-acetylglucosamine; △, galactose; ■, sialic acid. (Sharon 1987; data from Firon et al. 1985)

acetylglucosaminyltransferase I, which catalyzes the first step in the conversion of oligomannose units into complex ones. This mutant bound four times more type 1 fimbriated E. coli and was agglutinated at a rate more than ten times faster than the parental BHK cells. Preference for binding to hybrid units was indicated from results of experiments with mutants which express high levels of such units on their surface. The N-linked oligomannosides specific for type 1 fimbrial lectin probably reside on more than one type of molecule on the animal cell surface. For example, type 1 fimbriae bound to three glycoproteins derived from the surface membrane of human polymorphonuclear leukocytes (RODRIGUEZ-ORTEGA et al. 1987).

2.3 P Fimbriae

P fimbriae are specific for the disaccharide Galα4Galβ, whether located in a terminal nonreducing portion or internally (LEFFLER and SVANBORG EDÉN 1980, 1986). Compounds containing this disaccharide were the best inhibitors of agglutination of human erythrocytes by P fimbriated E. coli and of adhesion of these bacteria to epithelial cells (Table 3). Monosaccharides did not inhibit the attachment of the bacteria to the cells. Globotetraose (GalNAcβ3Galα4Galβ4Glc) blocked the agglutination of human type P erythrocytes by the isolated fimbriae.

The receptor for P-specific E. coli on epithelial cells appears to be globotetraosylceramide. Thus, such bacteria did not bind to epithelial cells (e.g., urinary tract cells of p⁻ individuals) lacking this substance. Also, erythrocytes not agglutinated by the bacteria or by the isolated P fimbriae became susceptible to agglutination after they had been coated with globotetraosylceramide (or trihexosylceramide) (LEFFLER and SVANBORG EDÉN 1980, 1986; KORHONEN et al. 1982). Latex beads coated with Galα4Gal, or suitable derivatives of this disaccharide, have been used to detect the presence of P fimbriae in clinical isolates of E. coli (DE MAN et al. 1987). Additional information on the specificity of P fimbriae has been obtained in experiments in which the binding of the bacteria to glycolipids separated by thin layer chromatography has been examined (BOCK et al. 1985; KARLSSON 1986).

Table 3. Inhibition of adherence of P fimbriated *E. coli* 3669 to human urinary epithelial cells[a]

Compound tested	Inhibtory concentration[b]
GalNAcβ3Galα4Galβ4Glcβ1-Cer (globotetraosylceramide)	0.1
Galα4Galβ4GlcβO-(CH$_2$)$_2$-S-(CH$_2$)$_{17}$-CH$_3$	0.2
GalNAcβ3Galα4Galβ4Glc	0.2
Galα4Galβ4GlcNAcβOEt	1.3
Galα4GalβOEt	2
Galα4Galβ4GlcβOEt	2
Galα4Gal	11
GalNAcβ3GalαOMe	> 50
Galα4GlcβOEt	> 50

[a] Data from LEFFLER and SVANBORG EDÉN (1986);
[b] Concentration (mM) required for complete inhibition of the adherence of 50 bacteria/cell.

Computer-based calculations and molecular models of the preferred conformation of the Galα4Gal-containing glycolipids revealed that the disaccharide forms a bend, or knee, in the chain, on which there is a continuous nonpolar surface surrounded by polar oxygens. The sugar-combining site of the P fimbrial lectin seems to bind to the latter side of the disaccharide (BOCK et al. 1985; KARLSSON 1986).

2.4 Fimbriae Specific for Sialic Acid

Enterotoxigenic strains of *E. coli* isolated from human and farm animals express fimbrial hemagglutinins specific for glycoconjugates containing sialic acids. This conclusion was originally based on the observation that hemagglutination caused by fimbriated bacteria was decreased or completely abolished after sialidase treatment of the erythrocytes. Several fimbrial lectins with this type of specificity are known. They include: K99, the adhesin expressed by enterotoxigenic strains isolated from piglets, calves, and lambs suffering from diarrhea; CFA/I and CFA/II expressed by human enterotoxigenic isolates; and type S expressed by strains isolated from newborn infants suffering from sepsis and meningitis.

2.4.1 K99 Fimbriae

The detailed sugar specificity of K99 fimbrial lectin was recently studied by LINDAHL et al. (1987), who examined the effect of various sialic acid-containing oligosaccharides on hemagglutination caused by bacteria carrying K99 fimbriae. The affinity of K99 fimbriae for *N*-glycolylneuraminic acid was found to be twice that of *N*-acetylneuraminic acid, and the monosaccharides were found to be less than one-tenth as effective as inhibitors. SMIT et al. (1984) have isolated, from horse erythrocytes, glycolipids that contain the attachment site for binding the K99 fimbrial lectin. The receptor was identified as the glycolipid NeuGcα2-

3Galβ4Glcβ1-ceramide. The purified glycolipid inhibited hemagglutination caused by the whole bacteria and by the purified fimbrial lectin, as well as adherence of the bacteria to intestinal cells.

2.4.2 CFA/I and CFA/II Fimbriae

The effect of various naturally occurring glycopeptides and oligosaccharides on hemagglutination caused by bacteria carrying CFA/I and CFA/II fimbriae was examined by NEESER et al. (1988). Although simple sugars were not employed to define precisely the specificity of the lectins, several interesting findings emerged. First, only complex-type N-linked or human milk oligosaccharides were inhibitory and this activity was dependent on the presence of sialic acids in the compounds. Second, there was a close analogy between the carbohydrate specificities of the CFA/I and CFA/II fimbrial lectins. Finally, the combining site of the lectins seemed to best fit oligosaccharide structures of glycopeptides derived from human red blood cells, in spite of the fact that CFA/II expressing bacteria do not agglutinate human erythrocytes. Thus, the results obtained emphasize the notion that even though the target cells contain glycoconjugates for which the bacterial lectin is specific, the cells may not be agglutinated by intact bacteria expressing the lectin, probably due to inaccessibility of the receptors on the cells or the lectins on the bacterial surface (OFEK et al. 1982).

2.4.3 Type S Fimbriae of E. coli Causing Sepsis and Meningitis

The specificity of S-fimbrial lectins was investigated using the overlay method in which erythrocyte cell membrane glycoproteins are electrophoresed, blotted, and incubated with radiolabeled E. coli bacteria expressing these fimbriae (PARKKINEN et al. 1986). The only band which bound the bacteria was glycophorin A, suggesting that the latter contains an attachment site for the bacterial lectin. Binding of bacteria to glycophorin A-coated plates was inhibited by several sialylated oligosaccharides, the most active of which was NeuAcα2-3Galβ3GalNAc, also a constituent of glycophorin A.

2.5 Lectins of *Vibrio cholerae* Specific for L-Fucose

Cholera vibrios produce a variety of hemagglutinins (FINKELSTEIN and HANNE 1982). Agglutination of human group O erythrocytes by V. cholerae and adhesion of the organism to brush borders was specifically inhibited by L-fucose and various glycosides of L-fucose, and to a lesser extent by mannose (JONES and FRETER 1976). The bacteria adhered specifically to agarose beads that carried covalently linked L-fucose on their surfaces. It has been suggested that structures containing L-fucose on eukaryotic cell surfaces may function as receptors for the vibrio hemagglutinins and may therefore be an important determinant of host susceptibility to these bacteria.

HANNE and FINKELSTEIN (1982) reported that V. cholerae is capable of producing four different hemagglutinins. The El-Tor biotype produced a cell-associated

mannose-specific hemagglutinin that was inhibited by fructose. This lectin was active on all human (A, B, O) and all chicken erythrocytes tested. A lectin specific for L-fucose was detected transiently in early log-phase growth in several strains of *V. cholerae*, including a number of mutants that were not inhibited by mannose.

2.6 *Mycoplasma pneumoniae* and *Mycoplasma gallisepticum*

Mycoplasma pneumoniae is specific for N-acetylneuraminic acid attached by $\alpha 2 \to 3$ linkage to the terminal galactose residue of the poly-N-acetyllactosamine sequences of blood type I/i antigens (LOOMES et al. 1984, 1985). This conclusion is based in part on measurements of the adherence of sialidase-treated human erythrocytes that have been resialylated by specific sialyltransferases. Highest levels of binding were observed with erythrocytes having the sequence NeuAcα2-3Galβ3/4GlcNAc on their surfaces.

The specificity of the *M. pneumoniae*–erythrocyte interaction was also investigated using oligosaccharides and glycoproteins as inhibitors of binding. A preference for sialic acid $\alpha 2 \to 3$ linked rather than $\alpha 2 \to 6$ linked to galactose was found. In its strong preference for sialic acid $\alpha 2 \to 3$ linked to galactose residues, *M. pneumoniae* differs from *M. gallisepticum*. Since glycophorin is the major sialoglycoprotein of human erythrocyte membranes, it is not surprising that it binds readily to *M. gallisepticum*, and that asialoglycophorin binds poorly (BANAI et al. 1978; GLASGOW and HILL 1980). Other sialoglycoproteins (such as ovine and bovine submaxillary mucins, α_1-acid glycoprotein, and fetuin) bind poorly to *M. gallisepticum* although they inhibit, to varying extents, the binding of glycophorin to the organisms (GLASGOW and HILL 1980). Sialic acid binds equally well to the organisms when linked either $\alpha 2 \to 3$ to galactose or $\alpha 2 \to 6$ to N-acetylgalactosamine.

Clustering of sialic acid residues (like in glycophorin) appears to be required for effective binding to *M. gallisepticum* (GLASGOW and HILL 1980). Thus, among the glycoproteins and glycolipids tested, the most potent inhibitors were the polyglycosyl peptides of human erythrocytes (derived mainly from bands 3 and 4.5) and the bovine erythrocyte glycoprotein GP-2, both of which are rich in branched poly-N-acetyllactosamine sequences of type I antigen. Human glycophorin A and α_1-acid glycoprotein were substantially less active and fetuin was inactive, in accordance with their lack of poly-N-acetyllactosamine sequences. Inhibition experiments with glycolipids have also indicated that sialylated poly-N-acetyllactosamine sequences are the preferred sequences for *M. pneumoniae* binding (LOOMES et al. 1984).

The availability of the variant erythrocytes of i-blood type provided the strongest evidence for the importance of sialylated poly-N-acetyllactosamine sequences as receptors for *M. pneumoniae*. Cells of this blood type have a high content of linear poly-N-acetyllactosamine sequences which are more susceptible to digestion with endo-β-galactosidase than the corresponding branched sequences on erythrocytes of type I. The binding of these cells to *M. pneumoniae* was decreased by 85% following treatment with endo-β-galactosidase although only 5% of the total erythrocyte sialic acid is released by this glycosidase (LOOMES et al. 1985). Thus, minor sialylated oligosaccharides of the poly-N-acetyllactosamine series (such as

those carried by glycoprotein bands 3 and 4.5) and glycolipids are the main receptors for *M. pneumoniae*, rather than the carbohydrate chains of the major sialogly-coproteins, which are not susceptible to digestion by endo-β-galactosidase.

2.7 *Streptococcus pneumoniae*

Among the bacterial species listed in Table 1, only three gram-positive ones were found to express agglutinins with defined sugar activity. Convincing evidence for adhesive function was obtained for the surface lectin of *Streptococcus pneumoniae*, although it has not yet been isolated. N-Acetylglucosamine inhibited binding of the organisms to tissue cells only at relatively high concentrations (25 mM) (BEUTH et al. 1987). The most active inhibitory compound was found to be GlcNAcβ3Gal (ANDERSSON et al. 1983), and the receptor is likely to belong to the neolacto- and lacto-series of glycolipids containing this disaccharide unit. Whole bacteria bind to glycoconjugates bearing structures with the disaccharide. For example, coating of guinea pig erythrocytes, normally not agglutinated by the organisms, with glycolipids containing GlcNAcβ3Gal made them susceptible to agglutination by the streptococci.

The pneumococcal lectin is inhibited strongly by the tetrasaccharide Galβ4GlcNAcβ3Galβ4Glc. This tetrasaccharide is also present in human milk and it has been suggested that it may protect breast-feeding infants from pneumococcal infections (ANDERSSON et al. 1986).

3 Role in Infection

The best experimental approach to assess the role of bacterial lectins in infections caused by lectin-carrying bacteria is by testing whether injection into animals of the organisms together with suitable inhibitory sugars results in lower rates of infection than are caused by the bacteria alone. Another direct approach is to examine the effect on infectivity of antibodies specific for the carbohydrate of the receptors of the lectin. A different approach is to compare the infectivity of variants or phenotypes that differ in their expression of the fimbrial lectins.

The bacterial lectins may influence the infectious process in several ways. First, and foremost, is the ability of the lectins to mediate attachment to epithelial cells of mucosal tissues in order to withstand the cleansing mechanisms which may remove the bacteria at the very early stage of infection before they have had the chance to proliferate (BEACHEY 1981; BEACHEY et al. 1982). Second, the lectin-mediated adherence may confer growth advantage and enhanced toxicity to the adherent pathogen, due to restricted diffusion of products secreted by the target cell and bacteria, respectively (ZAFRIRI et al. 1987). Third, the bacteria may bind via their surface lectins to glycoconjugates on phagocytic cells with resultant killing of the bacteria once the latter invade deep tissue by a process termed lectinophagocytosis

(OFEK and SHARON 1988). Fourth, the bacterial lectins may interact with soluble glycoproteins containing sugar residues specific for the lectin in body fluids, resulting in inhibition of the bacteria–host cell interaction (ØRSKOV et al. 1980; KURIYAMA and SILVERBLATT 1986).

In the following we summarize what is known about the role of surface lectins in infections caused by enteric and oral bacteria, since these have been investigated in considerable detail and they serve as a paradigm for bacterial infections that are initiated on mucosal and smooth surfaces, respectively.

3.1 Adherence to and Colonization of Mucosal Surfaces

Organisms belonging to the family of enterobacteria cause various types of infections, all of which are initiated at mucosal surfaces. Subsequent to colonization, the organisms may cause intestinal and extraintestinal infections by spreading to other sites, such as the urinary tract, blood, meninges, and other tissues, or they may secrete toxins which cause symptomatic infections. The role of enterobacterial lectins in these infectious processes has been best studied in gastrointestinal and urinary tract infections, in particular those caused by *E. coli* (GAASTRA and DE GRAAF 1982; DE GRAAF and MOOI 1986; CLEGG and GERLACH 1987; REID and SOBEL 1987). Almost all of these studies were carried out with mannose or Galα4Gal-specific fimbrial lectins.

In three separate systems, each employing different type 1 fimbriated enterobacterial species, it has been demonstrated that mannose or methyl α-mannoside inhibited experimental infection or mucosal colonization by the organisms (Table 4). In each of these, glucose (or methyl α-glucoside), which is not an inhibitor of type 1 fimbriae, did not affect the infectivity when injected together with the bacteria. Similarly, Galα4Gal-containing sugars were shown to prevent urinary tract infection

Table 4. Inhibitors of sugar-specific adherence that prevent infection

Organism	Animal, site of infection	Inhibitor	Reference
Type 1 fimbriated			
Escherichia coli	Mice, UT	MeαMan	ARONSON et al. 1979
	Mice, GIT	Mannose	GOLDHAR et al. 1986
	Mice, UT	Anti-Man antibody	ABRAHAM et al. 1985
Klebsiella pneumoniae	Rats, UT	MeαMan	FADER and DAVIS 1980
Shigella flexnerii	Guinea pigs, eye	Mannose	ANDRADE 1980
P fimbriated			
Escherichia coli	Mice, UT	Globotetraose	SVANBORG EDÉN et al. 1982b
	Monkeys, UT	Galα4GalβOMe	ROBERTS et al. 1984

UT = urinary tract; GIT = gastrointestinal tract

in both mice and monkeys by P fimbriated *E. coli*. In addition, antimannose antibodies also prevented urinary tract infection in mice by type 1 fimbriated *E. coli*. These findings provide the most convincing evidence for the central role of bacterial lectin in infection, and particularly in mucosal colonization. They also illustrate the great potential of simple sugar in the prevention of infections caused by bacteria that express surface lectins. For example, the studies on the sugars specificity of type 1 fimbrial lectin suggest that aromatic glycosides such as 4-methylumbelliferyl α-mannoside and *p*-nitro-*o*-chlorophenyl α-mannoside can provide a basis for the design of therapeutic agents that may prevent adherence in vivo and infection by *E. coli* strains that express this lectin (FIRON et al. 1987).

Another experimental approach to assess the role of enterobacterial lectins in colonization of mucosal surfaces included the use of animals that were passively or actively immunized against the corresponding lectins. This approach was employed in the case of type 1 and P fimbriated *E. coli*. In all cases infection was prevented in the immunized animals challenged with strains expressing the fimbrial lectin (Table 5). It should be pointed out that, although the antifimbrial antibodies inhibit adherence in vitro (SILVERBLATT and COHÉN 1979; SVANBORG EDÉN et al. 1982a), there is no evidence that these antibodies are directed against the sugar-combining site of the fimbrial lectin.

Comparison between fimbriated phenotypes and nonfimbriated ones showed in all cases that the infectivity of the former was significantly higher. This was found for strains expressing type 1 fimbriae in gastrointestinal infections induced by *Salmonella typhimurium* in mice (DUGUID et al. 1976), as well as in urinary tract infection induced by *K. pneumoniae* in rats (FADER and DAVIS 1982) or in mice (MAAYAN et al. 1985) and by *E. coli* in mice for type 1 fimbriated (IWAHI et al. 1983; HULTGREN et al. 1985), P fimbriated (HAGBERG et al. 1983a, b), and S fimbriated (MARRE and HACKER 1987) strains.

In an interesting study (HAGBERG et al. 1983a, b), mice were injected intraurethrally with mixtures of fimbriated and nonfimbriated, as well as with mixtures of type 1 and P fimbriated isogens. Examination of the bladder 1 day after challenge showed a marked preponderance of type 1 fimbriated bacteria, whereas in the kidney there

Table 5. Prevention of infection caused by enterobacteria carrying fimbrial lectin by antifimbrial immunity

Type of immunity	Fimbrial antigen	Animal, site of infection	Reference
Passive	Type 1	Mice, UT	ABRAHAM et al. 1985
		Pigs, GIT	JAYAPPA et al. 1985
Active	Type 1	Rats, UT	SILVERBLATT and COHEN 1979
		Rats, GIT	GUERINA et al. 1983
		Pigs, GIT	JAYAPPA et al. 1985
	Type P	Monkeys, UT	KAACK et al. 1988
			ROBERTS et al. 1984
		Mice, UT	O'HANLEY et al. 1985
			SCHMIDT et al. 1988
	Type K99	Pigs, GIT	ISAACSON et al. 1980

was a preponderance of P fimbriated bacteria. It was concluded that the type 1 fimbrial lectin confers an advantage to organisms during growth in the bladder. In contrast, in deep tissue (e.g., kidney) the P fimbrial lectin seems advantageous for infectivity.

3.2 Growth Advantage and Enhanced Toxicity

Once the organisms adhere to mucosal cells they start to multiply in order to colonize these tissues. The growing organisms may elaborate toxins that cause tissue damage. Recently ZAFRIRI et al. (1987) examined in tissue culture the growth and toxicity induced by the heat-labile toxin of E. coli using tissue culture cells and a pair of bacterial isogens, one of which was nonfimbriated and the other type 1 fimbriated. Growth advantage and enhanced toxicity were observed with the isogen adherent via type 1 fimbriae to the target tissue cells. It was concluded that this adherence-dependent activity is due to restricted diffusion of products secreted by the cells. Other investigators also found growth advantage of type 1 fimbriated phenotypes in vivo (ALKAN et al. 1986; TANAKA 1982).

3.3 Lectinophagocytosis

Following colonization, the organisms may invade and multiply in deep tissues. While the adherence to cells of these tissues may confer growth advantage to the bacteria, the latter have at the same time to confront the phagocytic cells also present at such sites. If these cells possess receptors for the bacterial lectins, they may bind, engulf, and kill the lectin-carrying bacteria. This process of lectin-mediated phagocytosis was termed "lectinophagocytosis" by us (OFEK and SHARON 1988). There is ample evidence showing that type 1 fimbriae are mediators in lectino-phagocytosis of E. coli expressing these fimbriae by a variety of phagocytic cells. In contrast, P fimbriated bacteria do not undergo phagocytosis by human polymor-phonuclear leukocytes since receptors for these fimbriae are absent from the phagocytic cells (SVANBORG EDÉN et al. 1984). Lectinophagocytosis of the bacteria, however, was observed by leukocytes that were coated with Galα4Gal-containing glycolipids.

The evidence that the recognition of type 1 fimbriated E. coli by phagocytes is mediated by interaction of the fimbrial lectin with mannose-containing glyco-proteins on the surface of the phagocyte is based on various findings: (a) the specificity pattern of inhibition of bacteria–host cell interaction observed is the same for phagocytic and nonphagocytic target cells (FIRON et al. 1983, 1985; BONER et al. 1987); (b) whenever sugars other than mannose or its derivatives were examined, they inhibited poorly (if at all) the interaction of type 1 fimbriated E. coli with mouse peritoneal macrophages or human polymorphonuclear leukocytes (BAR-SHAVIT et al. 1977; SILVERBLATT et al. 1979); (c) a very good correlation was found between the

mannose-binding activity of the bacteria and the extent of their attachment to mouse peritoneal macrophages (BAR-SHAVIT et al. 1980); (d) the finding that pretreatment of type 1 fimbriated bacteria with yeast mannan inhibited their attachment to mouse and human phagocytes, whereas pretreatment of the phagocytes did not have such an effect (BAR-SHAVIT et al. 1977), shows that the receptor for the bacterial lectin is on the surface of the phagocytes; and (e) latex particles coated with purified type 1 fimbriae stimulated human polymorphonuclear leukocytes and this activity was inhibited by mannose (GOETZ and SILVERBLATT 1987).

The lectin-mediated binding of the bacteria to phagocytic cells described above leads to ingestion, stimulation of antimicrobial systems (e.g., oxygen burst, degranulation), and killing of the bacteria, as summarized in Table 6. Maximum stimulation of antimicrobial systems in phagocytes appears to require cross-linking of type 1 fimbriae on the bacterial surfaces (PERRY et al. 1983; SÖDERSTRÖM and ÖHMAN 1984). Such cross-linking may cause aggregation of the receptors on the phagocytic cells. Aggregation of receptors is important for many other membrane-initiated events.

Table 6. Stages of lectinophagocytosis of *E. coli* mediated by type 1 fimbriae

Stage	Temp.	Cell	Assay system	Reference
Attachment	4°C	Macrophage, mouse	CFU	OFEK and SHARON 1988
Ingestion	37°C	PMNL, human	EM	SILVERBLATT et al. 1979; ROTTINI et al. 1979
			FITC-*E. coli*	ÖHMAN et al. 1982, 1985
		Macrophage, mouse	FITC-anti-*E. coli*	BAR-SHAVIT et al. 1980
Stimulation	37°C	PMNL, human	O$_2$ consumption	GOETZ and SILVERBLATT 1987; ROTTINI et al. 1979
			CL	MANGAN and SNYDER 1979; BJÖRKSTÉN and WADSTRÖM 1982; SÖDERSTRÖM and ÖHMAN 1984
			Lysozyme release	SVANBORG EDÉN et al. 1984; MANGAN and SNYDER 1979
			Protein iodination	PERRY et al. 1983
		Macrophage, human	CL	BONER et al. 1987; MHASHILKAR 1988
		Macrophage, rat	CL	BLUMENSTOCK and JANN 1982
Killing	37°C	PMNL, human	CFU	SILVERBLATT et al. 1979; ÖHMAN et al. 1982
		Macrophage, mouse	CFU	OFEK and SHARON 1988
		Macrophage, rat	CFU	BLUMENSTOCK and JANN 1982
		Macrophage, human	CFU	BONER et al. 1989

Abbreviations: CFU, colony forming units; CL, chemiluminescence; EM, electron microscopy; FITC, fluorescein isothiocyanate; PMNL, polymorphonuclear leukocytes

Whereas the occurrence of lectinophagocytosis mediated by mannose-specific bacterial surface lectins has been established unequivocally in vitro, little is known about its occurrence in vivo. Indirect evidence that it may take place in vivo was obtained in experimental infection with mixed bacterial phenotypes (or isogens), one of which expresses type 1 fimbriae while the other does not. Such experiments revealed that, whenever the organisms reached phagocyte-rich sites, the non-fimbriated phenotype survived, while at phagocyte-poor sites the fimbriated one survived, irrespective of the bacterial species or experimental animal employed or of the route or site of the infection (Table 7). The selective survival of the fimbriated phenotype on mucosal surfaces was interpreted as being due to its ability to bind to the epithelial cells, whereas the selective survival of the nonfimbriated phenotype in deep tissues (e.g., kidney or peritoneal cavity) could be explained by the elimination of the fimbriated phenotype by macrophages and/or polymorphonuclear leukocytes usually present in such deep tissues (OFEK et al. 1981; OFEK 1984). It was suggested that phase variation, a random on–off switching process that allows the cells to alternate between fimbriated and nonfimbriated states, is an important virulence trait of type 1 fimbriated *E. coli* (OFEK and SILVERBLATT 1982; OFEK 1984), as well as of other fimbriated bacterial species (SILVERBLATT and OFEK 1978, 1983; OFEK 1984), in the survival of the organisms in phagocyte-rich sites.

Lectinophagocytosis has recently been demonstrated to occur with type 2 fimbriated *Actinomyces* species. The fimbrial lectin of these bacteria is specific for Galβ3GalNAc (Table 1) and for lactose (Galβ4Glc). Attachment, internalization, and killing of *Actinomyces viscosus* T14V and *Actinomyces naeslundii* WVU45, both carrying type 2 fimbriae, by human polymorphonuclear leukocytes was blocked by methyl β-galactoside and lactose, whereas cellobiose of methyl α-galactoside was ineffective (SANDBERG et al. 1986, 1988). Phagocytosis was markedly enhanced (to more than 95%) by pretreating the polymorphonuclear leukocytes with sialidase, which unmasks galactose residues on oligosaccharide units of glycoproteins and glycolipids. Only bacteria expressing the galactose-specific lectin were phagocytosed in the absence of serum; phagocytosis of mutants of *A. viscosus* T14V and *A. naeslundii* WVU45 deficient in type 2 fimbriae was minimal or absent.

Table 7. Survival of mannose-specific fimbriated and nonfimbriated phenotypes or isogens in phagocyte-rich and -poor sites following infection with mixed strains

Organism	Animal	Route of infection	Site of infection	Level of phagocytes at infection site	Fimbriated phenotype or genotype	Reference
E. coli	Mouse	Intravesicular	Kidney	Rich	−	1, 2
			Bladder	Poor	+	
		Oral	Blood	Rich	−	3
			Oral cavity	Poor	+	
		Peritoneal	Peritoneum	Rich	−	4
	Rat	Intravesicular	Kidney	Rich	−	5
		Peritoneal	Blood	Rich	−	6
			Peritoneum	Rich	−	6
K. pneumoniae	Mouse	Intravesicular	Kidney	Rich	−	7
			Bladder	Poor	+	

Key to references: (1) HAGBERG et al. 1983a, b; (2) SCHAEFFER et al. 1987; (3) GUERINA et al. 1983; (4) ALKAN et al. 1986; (5) MARRE and HACKER 1987; (6) SAUKKONEN et al. 1988; (7) MAAYAN et al. 1985

3.4 Interaction with Soluble Glycoconjugates and Lectins in Body Fluids

Soluble glycoconjugates in body fluids may contain sugars to which bacterial lectins bind. Such glycoconjugates may, therefore, inhibit lectin-mediated interaction of bacteria with host cells. A case in point is Tamm-Horsfall glycoprotein, the most abundant glycoprotein in normal human urine, which contains N-linked oligomannose units (SERAFINI-CESSI et al. 1984; DELL'OLIO et al. 1988). It is not surprising, therefore, that it binds type 1 fimbriae and that this binding is inhibited by methyl α-mannoside. Bacteria coated with Tamm-Horsfall glycoprotein were considerably less susceptible to mannose-specific lectinophagocytosis than were the uncoated bacteria (KURIYAMA and SILVERBLATT 1986). However, the glycoprotein did not affect the phagocytosis of opsonized bacteria. It was suggested that these observations may explain the virulence of *E. coli* in the bladder and kidney of a susceptible host, where local serum activity is low and Tamm-Horsfall glycoprotein reaches high concentrations (KURIYAMA and SILVERBLATT 1986).

In bladder colonization, Tamm-Horsfall glycoprotein seems to play a dual role. On the one hand, it may facilitate the persistence of type 1 fim-briated bacteria since it sticks to the epithelial cells and provides a matrix to which these bacteria can readily adhere (CHICK et al. 1981; ØRSKOV et al. 1980). On the other hand, adherence of the bacteria to aggregated Tamm-Horsfall glyco-protein in suspension would facilitate their elimination during micturition (ØRSKOV et al. 1980). Thus, depending on its concentration and physical state in urine, the glycoprotein may either enhance or act as natural host defense against the development of infection from type 1 bacteria. This hypothesis is supported by the finding that significantly lower concentrations of Tamm-Horsfall glycoprotein are excreted by patients suffering from urinary tract infection as compared to controls (ISRAELE et al. 1987). These studies show that interaction of lectin-expressing bacteria with soluble glycoconjugates carrying suitable sugars may affect the infectious process.

4 Concluding Remarks

Studies on bacterial lectins expressed on the surfaces of enterobacteria and, in particular, those associated with type 1 and P fimbriae, clearly demonstrate that they influence the infectious process in more ways than one. This is by virtue of their ability to serve as adhesins which bind the organisms to host cells and to glycoconjugates in body fluids. It should thus be possible to intervene in the infectious process by administering sugars which inhibit the lectins.

Expression of the bacterial lectins during the infectious process is not always beneficial to the survival of the bacteria. For example, any adverse effect of type 1 fimbriae on the survival of the organisms due to their interaction with phagocytes or mannose-containing soluble glycoproteins, such as Tamm-Horsfall glycoprotein,

will not necessarily result in the termination of the infection, since these bacteria may undergo phase variation in vivo (MAAYAN et al. 1985). This would ensure that a nonfimbriated phenotype or a phenotype expressing another surface lectin of the same infecting strain be present to proceed with the infection in an environment hostile to the type 1 fimbriated phenotype. We expect that similar mechanisms of survival may exist in other bacteria that express surface lectins capable of interacting with phagocytes or with soluble glycoconjugates in body fluids.

The bacterial lectins may have additional functions in vivo besides those discussed above. For example, why, among all *E. coli* strains which express the mannose-specific lectin associated with type 1 fimbriae, do only those that also express the Galα4Gal-specific lectin associated with P fimbriae induce pyelonephritis in humans? Clearly, the P fimbrial lectin possesses some role that is unique for the survival of the organisms during the natural course of infection that leads to pyelonephritis. It is also noteworthy that the genes coding for the expression of type 1 fimbriae are conserved among most enteric bacteria, suggesting that this lectin confers advantages not shared by other bacterial lectins. One such advantage may be related to the distribution of receptors on the host tissues. Receptors containing N-linked oligomannosides and hybrid units to which type 1 fimbriae bind are ubiquitous and abundant on many types of cells, whereas those for which other lectins are specific have a more limited distribution. It follows that each bacterial lectin may have several functions, some of which are shared by other types of lectin while others are unique. Further studies are expected to reveal new and exciting functions for these recognition molecules in host–pathogen interactions.

Acknowledgment. We thank Dvorah Ochert for editorial assistance. Part of the work from the authors' laboratories discussed in this review was supported by grant AI23165 from the National Institutes of Health, Bethesda, MD.

References

Abraham SN, Babu JP, Giampapa CS, Hasty DL, Simpson WA, Beachey EH (1985) Protection against *Escherichia coli*-induced urinary tract infections with hybridoma antibodies directed against type 1 fimbriae or complementary D-mannose receptors. Infect Immun 48: 625–628

Alkan ML, Wong L, Silverblatt FJ (1986) Change in degree of type 1 piliation of *Escherichia coli* during experimental peritonitis in the mouse. Infect Immun 52: 549–554

Andersson B, Dahmén J, Frejd T, Leffler H, Magnusson G, Noori G, Svanborg-Edén C (1983) Identification of an active disaccharide unit of a glycoconjugate receptor for pneumococci attaching to human pharyngeal epithelial cells. J Exp Med 158: 559–570

Andersson B, Porras O, Hanson LA, Lagergård T, Svanborg-Edén C (1986) Inhibition of attachment of *Streptococcus pneumoniae* and *Haemophilus influenzae* by human milk and receptor oligosaccharides. J Infect Dis 153: 232–237

Andrade JRC (1980) Role of fimbrial adhesiveness in guinea-pig keratoconjunctivitis by *Shigella flexneri*. Rev Microbiol (S Paulo), 11: 117–125

Aronson M, Medalia O, Schori L, Mirelman D, Sharon N, Ofek I (1979) Prevention of colonization of the urinary tract of mice with *Escherichia coli* by blocking of bacterial adherence with methyl α-D-mannopyranoside. J Infect Dis 139: 329–332

Banai M, Kahane I, Razin S, Bredt W (1978) Adherence of *Mycoplasma gallisepticum* to human erythrocytes. Infect Immun 21: 365–372

Bar-Shavit Z, Ofek I, Goldman R, Mirelman D, Sharon N (1977) Mannose residues on phagocytes as receptors for the attachment of *Escherichia coli* and *Salmonella typhi*. Biochem Biophys Res Commun 78: 455–460

Bar-Shavit Z, Goldman R, Ofek I, Sharon N, Mirelman D (1980) Mannose-binding activity in *Escherichia coli*: a determinant of attachment and ingestion of the bacteria by macrophages. Infect Immun 29: 417–424

Beachey EH (1981) Bacterial cdherence: adhesin-receptor interactions mediating the attachment of bacteria to mucosal surfaces. J Infect Dis 143: 325–345

Beachey EH, Eisenstein BI, Ofek I (1982) Bacterial adherence in infectious diseases. Upjohn, Kalamazoo (Current concepts series)

Beuth J, Ko HL, Uhlenbruk G, Pulverer G (1987) Lectin-mediated bacterial adhesion to human tissue. Eur J Clin Microbiol 6: 591–593

Björkstén B, Wadström T (1982) Interaction of *Escherichia coli* with different fimbriae and poly-morphonuclear leukocytes. Infect Immun 38: 298–305

Blumenstock E, Jann K (1982) Adhesion of piliated *Escherichia coli* strains to phagocytes: differences between bacteria with mannose-sensitive pili and those with mannose-resistant pili. Infect Immun 35: 264–269

Bock K, Breimer ME, Brignole A, Hansson GC, Karlsson KA, Larson G, Leffler H, Samuelsson BE, Strömberg N, Svanborg-Edén C, Thurin J (1985) Specificity of binding of a strain of uropathogenic *Escherichia coli* to Galα1 → 4Gal-containing glycosphingolipids. J Biol Chem 260: 8545–8551

Boner G, Mhashilkar AM, Rodriguez-Ortega M, Sharon N (1989) Lectin-mediated, nonopsonic phagocytosis of type 1 *Escherichia coli* by human peritoneal macro-phages of uremic patients treated by peritoneal dialysis. J Leuk Biol 46: 239–245

Brennan MJ, Joralmon RA, Cisar JO, Sandberg AL (1987) Binding of *Actinomyces naeslundii* to glycosphingolipids. Infect Immun 55: 487–489

Brinton CC (1965) The structure, function, synthesis and genetic control of bacterial pili and a molecular model for DNA and RNA transport in gram negative bacteria. Trans NY Acad Sci 27: 1003–1054

Chick S, Harber MJ, MacKenzie R, Asscher AW (1981) Modified method for studying bacterial adhesion to isolated uroepithelial cells and uromucoid. Infect Immun 34: 256–261

Cisar JO (1986) Fimbrial lectins of the oral actinomyces. In: Mirelman D (ed) Microbial lectins and agglutinins: properties and biological activity. Wiley, New York, pp 183–196

Clegg S, Gerlach GF (1987) Enterobacterial fimbriae. J Bacteriol 169: 934–938

de Graaf FK, Mooi FR (1986) The fimbrial adhesins of *Escherichia coli*. Adv Microb Physiol 28: 65–143

Dell'Olio F, de Kanter FJJ, van den Eijnden DH, Serafini-Cessi F (1988) Structural analysis of the preponderant high-mannose oligosaccharide of human Tamm-Horsfall glycoprotein. Carbohydr Res 178: 327–332

de Man P, Cedergren B, Enerbäck S, Larsson A-C, Leffler H, Lundell A-L, Nilsson B, Svanborg-Edén C (1987) Receptor-specific agglutination tests for detection of bacteria that bind globoseries glycolipids. J Clin Microbiol 25: 401–406

Drake D, Taylor KG, Bleiweis AS, Doyle RJ (1988) Specificity of the glucan-binding lectin of *Streptococcus cricetus*. Infect Immun 56: 1864–1872

Duguid JP, Old DC (1980) Adhesive properties of Enterobacteriaceae. In: Beachey EH (ed) Bacterial adherence. Chapman and Hall, London, pp 185–217 (Receptors and recognition, series B, vol 6)

Duguid JP, Darekar MR, Wheater DWF (1976) Fimbriae and infectivity in *Salmonella typhimurium*. J Med Microbiol 9: 459–473

Evans DG, Evans DJ, Moulds JJ, Graham DY (1988) *N*-Acetylneuraminyllactose-binding fibrillar hemagglutinin of *Campylobacter pylori*: a putative colonization factor antigen. Infect Immun 56: 2896–2906

Fader RC, Davis CP (1980) Effect of piliation on *Klebsiella pneumoniae* infection in rat bladders. Infect Immun 30: 554–561

Fader RC, Davis CP (1982) *Klebsiella pneumoniae*- induced experimental pyelitis: the effect of piliation on infectivity. J Urol 128: 197–201

Faris A, Lindahl M, Wadström T (1980) GM_2-like glycoconjugate as possible receptor for the CFA/I and K99 hemagglutinins of enterotoxic *Escherichia coli*. FEMS Microbiol Lett 7: 265–269

Finkelstein RA, Hanne LF (1982) Purification and characterization of the soluble hemagglutinin (cholera lectin) produced by *Vibrio cholerae*. Infect Immun 36: 1199–1208

Firon N, Ofek I, Sharon N (1983) Carbohydrate specificity of the surface lectins of *Escherichia coli, Klebsiella pneumoniae* and *Salmonella typhimurium*. Carbohydr Res 120: 235–249

Firon N, Ofek I, Sharon N (1984) Carbohydrate-binding sites of the mannose-specific fimbrial lectins of Enterobacteria. Infect Immun 43: 1088–1090

Firon N, Duksin D, Sharon N (1985) Mannose-specific adherence of *Escherichia coli* to BHK cells that differ in their glycosylation patterns. FEMS Microbiol Lett 27: 161–165

Firon N, Ashkenazi S, Mirelman D, Ofek I, Sharon N (1987) Aromatic alpha-glycosides of mannose are powerful inhibitors of the adherence of type 1 fimbriated *Escherichia coli* to yeast and intestinal epithelial cells. Infect Immun 55: 472–476

Gaastra W, de Graaf FK (1982) Host-specific fimbrial adhesins of noninvasive enterotoxigenic *Escherichia coli* strains. Microbiol Rev 46: 129–161

Giampapa CS, Abraham SN, Chiang TM, Beachey EH (1988) Isolation and characterization of a receptor for type 1 fimbriae of *Escherichia coli* from guinea pig erythrocytes. J Biol Chem 263: 5362–5367

Glasgow LR, Hill RL (1980) Interaction of *Mycoplasma gallisepticum* with sialyl glycoproteins. Infect Immun 30: 353–361

Goetz MB, Silverblatt FJ (1987) Stimulation of human polymorphonuclear leukocyte oxidative metabolism by type 1 pili from *Escherichia coli*. Infect Immun 55: 534–540

Goldhar J, Perry R, Ofek I (1984) Extraction and properties of nonfimbrial mannose-resistant hemagglutinin from a urinary isolate of *Escherichia coli*. Curr Microbiol 11: 49–54

Goldhar J, Zilberberg A, Ofek I (1986) Infant mouse model of adherence and colonization of intestinal tissues by enterotoxigenic strains of *Escherichia coli* isolated from humans. Infect Immun 52: 205–208

Goochee CF, Hatch RT, Cadman TW (1987) Some observations on the role of type 1 fimbriae in *Escherichia coli* autoflocculation. Biotech Bioeng 29: 1024–1034

Guerina NG, Kessler TW, Guerina VJ, Neutra MR, Clegg HW, Langermann S, Scannapieco FA, Goldmann DA (1983) The role of pili and capsule in the pathogenesis of neonatal infection with *Escherichia coli* K1. J Infect Dis 148: 395–404

Gunnarsson A, Mårdh PE, Lundblad A, Svensson S (1984) Oligosaccharide structures mediating agglutination of sheep erythrocytes by *Staphylococcus saprophyticus*. Infect Immun 45: 41–46

Hagberg L, Hull R, Hull S, Falkow S, Freter R, Svanborg-Edén C (1983a) Contribution of adhesion to bacterial persistence in the mouse urinary tract. Infect Immun 40: 265–272

Hagberg L, Engberg I, Feter R, Lam J, Olling S, Svanborg-Edén C (1983b) Ascending unobstructed urinary tract infection in mice caused by pyelonephritogenic *Escherichia coli* of human origin. Infect Immun 40: 273–283

Hanne LF, Finkelstein RA (1982) Characterization and distribution of the hemagglutinins produced by *Vibrio cholerae*. Infect Immun 36: 209–214

Hansson GC, Karlsson K-A, Larson G, Lindberg A, Strömberg N, Thurin J (1983) Lactosylceramide is the probable adhesion site for major indigenous bacteria of the gastrointestinal tract. In: Chester MA, Heinegård D, Lundblad A, Svensson S (eds) Glycoconjugates. 7th International symposium on glycoconjugates, Lund Sweden, July 17–23, p 631

Hansson GC, Karlsson D-A, Larson G, Strömberg N, Thurin J (1985) Carbohydrate-specific adhesion of bacteria to thin-layer chromatograms: a rationalized approach to the study of host cell glycolipid receptors. Anal Biochem 146: 158–163

Hultgren SJ, Porter TN, Schaeffer AJ, Duncan JL (1985) Role of type 1 pili and effects of phase variation on lower urinary tract infections produced by *Escherichia coli*. Infect Immun 50: 370–377

Isaacson RE, Dean EA, Morgan RL, Moon HW (1980) Immununization of suckling pigs against enterotoxigenic *Escherichia coli*-induced diarrheal disease by vaccinating dams with purified K99 or 987P pili: antibody production in response to vaccination. Infect Immun 29: 824–826

Ishikawa H, Isayama Y (1987) Evidence for sialyl glycoconjugates as receptors for *Bordetella bronchiseptica* on swine nasal mucosa. Infect Immun 55: 1607–1609

Israele V, Darabi A, McCracken GH (1987) The role of bacterial virulence factors and Tamm-Horsfall protein in the pathogenesis of *Escherichia coli* urinary tract infection in infants. Am J Dis Child 141: 1230–1234

Iwahi T, Abe Y, Nakao M, Imada A, Tsuchiya K (1983) Role of type 1 fimbriae in the pathogenesis of ascending urinary tract infection induced by *Escherichia coli* in mice. Infect Immun 39: 1307–1315

Jayappa HG, Goodnow RA, Geary SJ (1985) Role of *Escherichia coli* type 1 pilus in colonization of porcine ileum and its protective nature as a vaccine antigen in controlling colibacillosis. Infect Immun 48: 350–354

Jones GW, Freter R (1976) Adhesive properties of *Vibrio cholerae*: nature of the interaction with isolated rabbit brush border membranes and human erythrocytes. Infect Immun 14: 240–245

Kaack MB, Roberts JA, Baskin G, Patterson GM (1988) Maternal immunization with P fimbriae for the prevention of neonatal pyelonephritis. Infect Immun 56: 1–6

Kabat EA (1978) Dimensions and specificities of recognition sites on lectins and antibodies. J Supramol Struct 8: 79–88

Karlsson K-A (1986) Animal glycolipids as attachment sites for microbes. Chem Phys Lipids 42: 153–172

Korhonen TK, Väisänen V, Saxén H, Hultberg H, Svenson SB (1982) P-Antigen-recognizing fimbriae from human uropathogenic Escherichia coli strains. Infect Immun 37: 286–291

Korhonen TK, Väisänen-Rehn V, Rehn M, Pere A, Parkkinen J, Finne J (1984) Escherichia coli fimbriae recognizing sialyl galactosides. J Bacteriol 159: 762–766

Korhonen TK, Haahtela K, Pirkola A, Parkkinen J (1988) A N-acetyllactosamine-specific cell-binding activity in a plant pathogen, Erwinia rhapontici. FEBS Lett 236: 163–166

Krivan HC, Roberts DD, Ginsburg V (1988a) Many pulmonary pathogenic bacteria bind specifically to the carbohydrate sequence GalNAcβ1-4Gal found in some glycolipids. Proc Natl Acad Sci USA 85: 6157–6161

Krivan HC, Ginsburg V, Roberts DD (1988b) Pseudomonas aeruginosa and Pseudomonas cepacia isolated from cystic fibrosis patients bind specifically to gangliotetraosylceramide (asialo GM1) and gangliotriaosylceramide (asialo GM2). Arch Biochem Biophys 260: 493–496

Kuriyama SM, Silverblatt FJ (1986) Effect of Tamm-Horsfall urinary glycoprotein on phagocytosis and killing of type I-fimbriated Escherichia coli. Infect Immun 51: 193–198

Landale EC, McCabe MM (1987) Characterization by affinity electrophoresis of an α-1,6-glucan-binding protein from Streptococcus sobrinus. Infect Immun 55: 3011–3016

Leffler H, Svanborg-Edén C (1980) Chemical identification of a glycosphingolipid receptor for Escherichia coli attaching to human urinary tract epithelial cells and agglutinating human erythrocytes. FEMS Microbiol Lett 8: 127–134

Leffler H, Svanborg-Edén C (1986) Glycolipids as receptors for Escherichia coli lectins or adhesins. In: Mirelman D (ed) Microbial lectins and agglutinins: properties and biological activity. Wiley, New York, pp 83–111

Lindahl M, Brossmer R, Wadström T (1987) Carbohydrate receptor specificity of K99 fimbriae of enterotoxigenic Escherichia coli. Glycoconjugate J 4: 51–58

Loomes LM, Uemura K, Childs RA, Paulson JC, Rogers GN, Scudder PR, Michalski J-C, Hounsell EF, Taylor-Robinson D, Feizi T (1984) Erythrocyte receptors for Mycoplasma pneumoniae are sialylated oligosaccharides of Ii antigen type. Nature 307: 560–563

Loomes LM, Uemura K, Feizi T (1985) Interaction of Mycoplasma pneumoniae with erythrocyte glycolipids of I and i antigen types. Infect Immun 47: 15–20

Maayan MC, Ofek I, Medalia O, Aronson M (1985) Population shift in mannose-specific fimbriated phase of Klebsiella pneumoniae during experimental urinary tract infection in mice. Infect Immun 49: 785–789

Mangan DF, Snyder IS (1979) Mannose-sensitive interaction of Escherichia coli with human peripheral leukocytes in vitro. Infect Immun 26: 520–527

Marre R, Hacker J (1987) Role of S- and common-type 1-fimbriae of Escherichia coli in experimental upper and lower urinary tract infection. Microb Pathogen 2: 223–226

Mhashilkar A (1988) Interaction of Escherichia coli, Salmonella typhimurium and Pseudomonas aeruginosa with human polymorphonuclear leukocytes and human peritoneal macrophages — comparative study. MSc thesis, Weizmann Institute of Science, Rehovot

Mirelman D (ed) (1986) Microbial lectins and agglutinins: properties and biological activity. Wiley, New York

Mirelman D, Ofek I (1986) Introduction to microbial lectins and agglutinins. In: Mirelman D (ed) Microbiol lectins and agglutinins: properties and biological activity. Wiley, New York, pp 1–19

Murray PA, Levine MJ, Tabak LA, Reddy MS (1982) Specificity of salivary-bacterial interactions. II. Evidence for a lectin on Streptococcus sanguis with specificity for a NeuAcα2,3Galβ1,3GalNAc sequence. Biochem Biophys Res Commun 106: 390–396

Murray PA, Kern DG, Winkler JR (1988) Identification of a galactose-binding lectin on Fusobacterium nucleatum FN-2. Infect Immun 56: 1314–1319

Neeser J-R, Koellreutter B, Wuersch P (1986) Oligomannoside-type glycopeptides inhibiting adhesion of Escherichia coli strains mediated by type 1 pili: preparation of potent inhibitors from plant glycoproteins. Infect Immun 52: 428–436

Neeser J-R, Chambaz A, Hoang KY, Link-Amster H (1988) Screening for complex carbohydrates inhibiting hemagglutinations by CFA/I- and CFA/II-expressing enterotoxigenic Escherichia coli strains. FEMS Microbiol Lett 49: 301–307

Nilsson G, Svensson S, Lindberg AA (1983) The role of the carbohydrate portion of glycolipids for the adherence of Escherichia coli K88[+] to pig intestine. In: Chester MA, Heinegård D, Lundblad A, Svensson S (eds) Glycoconjugates. 7th International symposium on glycoconjugates, Lund, July 17–23 Sweden, pp 637–638

O'Hanley P, Lark D, Falkow S, Schoolnik G (1985) Molecular basis of *Escherichia coli* colonization of the upper urinary tract in BALB/c mice. J Clin Invest 75: 347–360

Ofek I (1984) Adhesin receptor interaction mediating adherence of bacteria to mucosal tissues: importance of phase transition in the expression of bacterial adhesins. In: Falcon G (ed) Bacterial and viral inhibition and modulation of host defenses. Academic, London, pp 7–24

Ofek I, Beachey EH (1978) Mannose binding and epithelial cell adherence of *Escherichia coli*. Infect Immun 22: 247–254

Ofek I, Sharon N (1988) Lectinophagocytosis: a molecular mechanism of recognition between cell surface sugars and lectins in the phagocytosis of bacteria. Infect Immun 56: 539–547

Ofek I, Silverblatt FJ (1982) Bacterial surface structures involved in adhesion to phagocytic and epithelial cells. In: Schlesinger D (ed) Microbiology 1982. American Society for Microbiology, Washington, pp 296–300

Ofek I, Mirelman D, Sharon N (1977) Adherence of *Escherichia coli* to human mucosal cells mediated by mannose receptors. Nature 265: 623–625

Ofek I, Mosek A, Sharon N (1981) Mannose specific adherence of *Escherichia coli* freshly excreted in the urine of patients with urinary tract infections and of isolates subcultured from the infected urine. Infect Immun 34: 708–711

Ofek I, Goldhar J, Eshdat Y, Sharon N (1982) The importance of mannose specific adhesins (lectins) in infections caused by *Escherichia coli*. Scand J Infect Dis [Suppl] 33: 61–67

Ofek I, Lis H, Sharon N (1985) Animal cell surface membranes. In: Savage DC, Fletcher M (eds) Bacterial adhesion: mechanisms and physiological significance. Plenum, New York, pp 71–88

Öhman L, Hed J, Stendahl O (1982) Interaction between human polymorphonuclear leukocytes and two different strains of type 1 fimbriae-bearing *Escherichia coli*. J Infect Dis 146: 751–757

Öhman L, Magnusson K-E, Stendahl O (1985) Mannose-specific and hydrophobic interaction between *Escherichia coli* and polymorphonuclear leukocytes—influence of bacterial culture period. Acta Pathal Microbiol Immunol Scand [B] 93: 125–131

Ørskov I, Ørskov F, Birch-Andersen A (1980) Comparison of *Escherichia coli* fimbrial antigen F7 with type 1 fimbriae. Infect Immun 27: 657–666

Parkkinen J, Rogers GN, Kornhonen T, Dahr W, Finne J (1986) Identification of the O-linked sialyloligosaccharides of glycophorin A as the erythrocyte receptors for S-fimbriated *Escherichia coli*. Infect Immun 54: 37–42

Perry A, Ofek I, Silverblatt FJ (1983) Enhancement of mannose-mediated stimulation of human granulocytes by type 1 fimbriae aggregated with antibodies on *Escherichia coli* surfaces. Infect Immun 39: 1334–1345

Prakobphol A, Murray PA, Fisher SJ (1987) Bacterial adherence on replicas of sodium dodecyl sulfate-polyacrylamide gels. Anal Biochem 164: 5–11

Pulverer G, Beuth J, Ko HL, Sölter J, Uhlenbruck G (1987) Modification of glycosylation by tunicamycin treatment inhibits lectin-mediated adhesion of *Streptococcus pneumoniae* to various tissues. Zentralbl Bakteriol Mikrobiol Hyg [A] 266: 137–144

Reid G, Sobel JD (1987) Bacterial adherence in the pathogenesis of urinary tract infection: a review. Rev Infect Dis 9: 470–487

Roberts JA, Kaack B, Källenius G, Möllby R, Winberg J, Svenson SB (1984) Receptors for pyelonephritogenic *Escherichia coli* in primates. J Urol 131: 163–168

Rodriguez-Ortega M, Ofek I, Sharon N (1987) Membrane glycoproteins of human polymorphonuclear leukocytes that act as receptors for mannose-specific *Escherichia coli*. Infect Immun 55: 968–973

Rottini G, Cian F, Soranzo MR, Albrigo R, Patriarca P (1979) Evidence for the involvement of human polymorphonuclear leucocyte mannose-like receptors in the phagocytosis of *Escherichia coli*. FEBS Lett 105: 307–312

Sandberg AL, Mudrick LL, Cisar JO, Brennan MJ, Mergenhagen SE, Vatter AE (1986) Type 2 fimbrial lectin-mediated phagocytosis of oral *Actinomyces* spp. by polymorphonuclear leukocytes. Infect Immun 54: 472–476

Sandberg AL, Mudrick LL, Cisar JO, Metcalf JA, Malech HL (1988) Stimulation of superoxide and lactoferrin release from polymorphonuclear leukocytes by the type 2 fimbrial lectin *Actinomyces viscosus* T14V. Infect Immun 56: 267–269

Saukkonen KMJ, Nowicki B, Leinonen M (1988) Role of type 1 and S fimbriae in the pathogenesis of *Escherichia coli* O18:K1 bacteremia and meningitis in the infant rat. Infect Immun 56: 892–897

Schaeffer AJ, Schwan WR, Hultgren SJ, Duncan JL (1987) Relationship of type 1 pilus expression in *Escherichia coli* to ascending urinary tract infections in mice. Infect Immun 55: 373–380

Schmidt MA, O'Hanley P, Lark D, Schoolnik GK (1988) Synthetic peptides corresponding to protective epitopes of *Escherichia coli* digalactoside-binding pilin prevent infection in a murine pyelonephritis model. Proc Natl Acad Sci USA 85: 1247–1251

Serafini-Cessi F, Dall'Olio F, Malagolini N (1984) High-mannose oligosaccharides from human Tamm-Horsfall glycoprotein. Biosci Rep 4: 269–274

Sharon N (1987) Bacterial lectins, cell–cell recognition and infectious disease. FEBS Lett 217: 145–157

Sharon N, Lis H (1982) Glycoproteins. In: Neurath H, Hill RL (eds) The proteins, 3rd edn, vol 5. Academic, New York, pp 1–144

Sharon N, Eshdat Y, Silverblatt FJ, Ofek I (1981) Bacterial adherence to cell surface sugars. In: Elliot K, O'Connor M, Whelan J (eds) Adhesion and micro-organism pathogenicity. Pitman Medical, London, pp 119–135 (Ciba symposium series 80)

Sherman PM, Houston WL, Boedeker EC (1985) Functional heterogeneity of intestinal *Escherichia coli* strains expressing type 1 somatic pili (fimbriae): assessment of bacterial adherence to intestinal membranes and surface hydrophobicity. Infect Immun 49: 797–804

Silverblatt FJ, Cohen LS (1979) Antipili antibody affords protection against experimental ascending pyelonephritis. J Clin Invest 64: 333–336

Silverblatt FJ, Ofek I (1978) Influence of pili on the virulence of *Proteus mirabilis* in experimental hematogenous pyelonephritis. J Infect Dis 138: 664–667

Silverblatt FJ, Ofek I (1983) Interaction of bacterial pili and leukocytes. Infection 11: 235–238

Silverblatt FJ, Dreyer JS, Schauer S (1979) Effect of pili susceptibility of *Escherichia coli* to phagocytosis. Infect Immun 24: 218–223

Smit H, Gaastra W, Kamerling JP, Vliegenthart JFG, de Graaf FK (1984) Isolation and structural characterization of the equine erythrocyte receptor for enterotoxigenic *Escherichia coli* K99 fimbrial adhesin. Infect Immun 46: 578–584

Söderström T, Öhman L (1984) The effect of monoclonal antibodies against *Escherichia coli* type 1 pili and capsular polysaccharides on the interaction between bacteria and human granulocytes. Scand J Immunol 20: 299–305

Stromberg N, Deal C, Nyberg G, Normark S, So M, Karlsson K-A (1988) Identification of carbohydrate structures that are possible receptors for *Neisseria gonorrhoeae*. Proc Natl Acad Sci USA 85: 4902–4906

Svanborg Edén C, Marlid S, Korhonen TK (1982a) Adhesion inhibition by antibodies. Scand J Infect Dis [Suppl] 33: 72–78

Svanborg Edén C, Freter R, Hagberg L, Hull R, Hull S, Leffler H, Schoolnik G (1982b) Inhibition of experimental ascending urinary tract infection by an epithelial cell-surface receptor analogue. Nature 298: 560–562

Svanborg Edén C, Bjursten L-M, Hull R, Hull S, Magnusson K-E, Moldovano Z, Leffler H (1984) Influence of adhesins on the interaction of *Escherichia coli* with human phagocytes. Infect Immun 44: 672–680

Tanaka Y (1982) Multiplication of the fimbriate and nonfimbriate *Salmonella typhimurium* organisms in the intestinal mucosa of mice treated with antibodies. Jpn J Vet Sci 44: 523–527

Väisänen-Rhen V, Korhonen TK, Finne J (1983) Novel cell-binding activity specific for *N*-acetyl-D-glucosamine in an *Escherichia coli* strain. FEBS Lett 159: 233–236

Weiss EI, London J, Kolenbrander PE, Kagermeier AS, Andersen RN (1987) Characterization of lectinlike surface components on *Capnocytophaga ochracea* ATCC 33596 that mediate coaggregation with gram-positive oral bacteria. Infect Immun 55: 1198–1202

Yamazaki Y, Ebisu S, Okada H (1981) *Eikenella corrodens* adherence to human buccal epithelial cells. Infect Immun 31: 21–27

Zafriri D, Oron Y, Eisenstein BI, Ofek I (1987) Growth advantage and enhanced toxicity of *Escherichia coli* adherent to tissue culture cells due to restricted diffusion of products secreted by the cells. J Clin Invest 79: 1210–1216

Tissue Tropism of *Escherichia coli* Adhesins in Human Extraintestinal Infections

T. K. Korhonen[1], R. Virkola[1], B. Westurlund[1], H. Holthöfer[2], and J. Parkkinen[3]

1 Introduction

Mechanical protective factors at epithelial surfaces are an important part of our defenses against invading bacteria. These factors include direct removal by washing, e.g., by the flow of urine in the urinary tract, by peristalsis in the intestine, and by continuous secretion of saliva in the oral cavity. To colonize epithelial surfaces, bacteria have to overcome the washing effect by firmly attaching to the infection site; this is apparently necessary for the bacteria both to cause infectious diseases and to establish themselves as members of our normal flora.

Svanborg-Edén and co-workers (1976) showed that the ability to adhere to epithelial cells of the human urinary tract is a characteristic of *Escherichia coli* strains associated with upper urinary tract infections. Subsequently, a number of epidemiologic (Hagberg et al. 1981: Källenius et al. 1981; Väisänen-Rhen et al. 1984; Johnson et al. 1987) and experimental (Hagberg et al. 1983; Roberts et al. 1984; O'Hanley et al. 1985) studies have led to the conclusion that the ability to adhere to uroepithelium is perhaps the most important single virulence determinant of *E. coli* strains associated with human pyelonephritis and urosepsis. The importance of bacterial adhesion in the pathogenesis of human pyelonephritis is further supported by the fact that susceptibility to *E. coli* adhesion is directly related to an individual's susceptibility to pyelonephritis caused by these bacteria

Departments of General Microbiology[1], Bacteriology and Immunology[2], and Medical Chemistry[3], University of Helsinki, SF-00280, Helsinki, Finland

(KÄLLENIUS and WINBERG 1978). So far the role of bacterial adhesion in the invasive phase of septic infections remains open, but the findings that the E. coli O18:K1 strains associated with neonatal meaningitis have their typical adhesins (KORHONEN et al. 1985) that are expressed in vivo during a systemic infection (NOWICKI et al. 1986b) and have receptors in the brain (PARKKINEN et al. 1988a) suggest that bacterial adhesion is involved in the determination of tissue tropism of neonatal meningitis.

The adhesion assays used to demonstrate the correlation between adhesive capacity and uropathogenicity of E. coli were performed with exfoliated epithelial cells of human urine (SVANBORG-EDÉN et al. 1977; KÄLLENIUS et al. 1980). These cells, however, are heterogeneous in origin, being derived mainly from the lower regions of the ureter, the urinary bladder, and the urethra. Thus the information about the distribution of bacterial receptors that can be obtained with these assays is rather limited. Recent results have shown that the distribution of cell-surface glycoconjugates in the urinary tract, e.g., in the kidney, is strictly limited to various tissue subcompartments, as shown, for example, by histochemical studies with labeled lectins (HOLTHÖFER et al. 1982; HOLTHÖFER 1983; HENNIGAR et al. 1985). Since these glycoconjugates are potential receptors for bacterial adherence, one could expect that various epithelial surfaces along the urinary tract would also show variable reactivity for bacterial adhesins. Information concerning the bacterial adhesion sites in mammalian tissues is important to increase our understanding of the molecular mechanisms of bacterial pathogenicity. Therefore we recently developed methods for determining the precise sites for bacterial adhesion in frozen tissue sections.

2 Types of Adhesins on *Escherichia coli* Strains Causing Extraintestinal Infections

A number of adhesins have been characterized on E. coli strains associated with urinary tract infections or neonatal meningitis (Table 1). These adhesins differ in molecular binding specificities and in serologic properties, and, excepting the type 1 fimbriae, they occur only on certain strain clusters of E. coli. Of these adhesins, only the P and S fimbriae are conclusively associated with strains from infectious diseases, the former with strains from cases of pyelonephritis and the latter with strains from cases of neonatal sepsis and meningitis. The type 1C fimbriae are more common on strains from upper urinary tract infections than on fecal strains, although less frequent than the P fimbriae.

An important feature of adhesins on pathogenic E. coli strains is their multiplicity. A strain can have two or three different adhesin types, and many of the P-fimbriated strains further possess two or three variants of the P fimbria (PERE et al. 1986). The different fimbriae on a strain are under phase variation: they are mostly expressed by separate cells that can rapidly switch their fimbrial synthesis (NOWICKI et al. 1984). This kind of fimbrial phase variation also takes place in vivo during

Table 1. Adhesins of *E. coli* strains associated with urinary tract infections or neonatal meningitis

Adhesin	Binding characteristics	Occurrence/Remarks	Reference
P fimbria	Blood group P-specific glycolipids; minimal receptor for most is DGalα1-4DGal	O1:K1:H7, O4:K12, O4:K-, O6:K2:H1, O16:K1, O18, and O7:K1:H1 strains associated with pyelone-phritis and urosepsis	KÄLLENIUS et al. 1980 VÄISÄNEN-RHEN et al. 1984 ØRSKOV and ØRSKOV 1983 BOCK et al. 1986 JOHNSON et al. 1987
S fimbria	NeuNAcα2-3DGal and NeuNAcα2-3DGalβ1-3-DGalNac sequences in glycoproteins	O18:K1:H7 strains asso-ciated with neonatal sepsis and meningitis	PARKKINEN et al. 1983, 1986 KORHONEN et al. 1985 OTT et al. 1986
Type 1 fimbria	Oligomannoside chains in glycoproteins	About 80% of all strains	DUGUID and OLD 1980 FIRON et al. 1982 NEESER et al. 1986
Type 1C fimbria	Molecular details un-known, not hemag-glutinating	O4 and O6 strains associated with pyelo-nephritis; some O22 and O18 strains	PERE et al. 1985
O75X adhesin	Binds to type IV collagen in basement membranes; binding inhibited by chloram-phenicol	O75 strains	VÄISÄNEN-RHEN 1984 NOWICKI et al. 1988 WESTERLUND et al. 1989a
M agglu-tinin	Binds to glycophorin A^M, terminal serine part of receptor	Rare	JOKINEN et al. 1985 RHEN et al. 1986
G fimbria	Terminal DG1cNAc residues	Rare on human pathogens	VÄISÄNEN-RHEN et al. 1983 RHEN et al. 1986

systemic infection in mice (NOWICKI et al. 1986b) and urinary tract infection in man (PERE et al. 1987). Due to phase variation, the infecting *E. coli* population in the urinary tract is heterogeneous, consisting of cells with different adhesins and of nonfimbriate cells.

3 Tissue Specificity of the Adhesins

3.1 Methodologic Aspects

In our approach we have used two parallel methods to identify the receptor-active domains in tissue samples. The first (NOWICKI et al. 1986a) involves staining of frozen tissue sections with fluorochrome-labeled bacteria. Fimbriated bacteria can be directly labeled with fluorescein isothiocyanate (FITC) or tetramethyl rhodamine (TRITC) without damaging the binding activity of the fimbriae. FITC-tagged bacteria can then be incubated at various cell concentration (10^8–10^{10} per ml, the optimal concentration depending on the strain) on frozen tissue sections, washed,

and examined by fluorescence microscopy. For identification of tissue structures, sections with bound bacteria can be double stained with specific tissue markers, i.e., TRITC-labeled lectins or antibodies.

Using a suitable bacterial concentration, adhesion sites for the bacteria can be identified by this simple procedure (Fig. 1A). Specificity of the adhesion should always be controlled by testing adhesin-specific Fab fragments (Fig. 1B) or receptor-active carbohydrates for inhibition and also by including adhesin-negative strains as controls (NOWICKI et al. 1986a; KORHONEN et al. 1986a). It should be noted that, due to multiplicity of adhesins, pathogenic wild-type strains are only rarely suitable for adhesion tests, and the use of recombinant strains expressing only one fimbrial type is preferable.

The other method involves indirect immunofluorescent staining of tissue sections with purified adhesins (KORHONEN et al. 1986a, b; WESTERLUND et al. 1987). This method, which has the advantage of a more precise localization of the binding sites, can be combined with double staining with TRITC-labeled lectins to identify

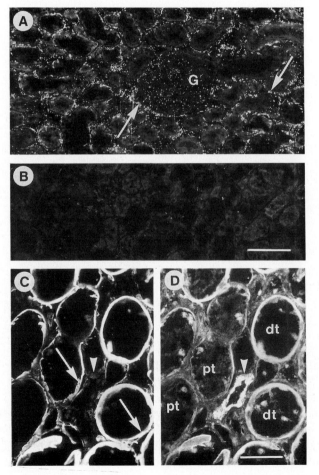

Fig. 1A–C. Binding of the O75X adhesin in kidney. A Adhesion of an O75X-positive strain to frozen sections of kidney; note bacteria on the basement membranes of tubules and on Bowman's capsule (*arrows*). Glomerulus (*G*) is also positive for the bacteria. **B** As in **A**, but in the presence of Fab fragments against the O75X adhesin. Note the almost complete inhibition of the adhesion. **C** and **D** Double staining of the same section with the O75X adhesin (**C**) and FITC-DBA (**D**). The adhesin binds to the basement membranes of both distal (*dt*; positive for FITC-DBA) and proximal (*pt*; negative for FITC-DBA) tubules. *Arrowhead* in **D** indicates a DBA-positive structure, most likely the loop of Henle, that is negative for the adhesin (**C**). *Bars*, 100 μm in **A** and **B**; 40 μm in **C** and **D**

specific tissue elements (Fig. 1C, D). Specificity of the adhesin binding and the common problem of autofluorescence can be controlled by the use of receptor analogs (Fig. 2A, B) and by staining the tissues with the antibodies alone. We have found it necessary to absorb the antibodies with tissue homogenates before using them in the binding tests. In general, a distinct tissue-substructure specificity in fimbrial binding has been observed (Fig. 2), and the results with the recombinant strains and with the corresponding purified adhesins have been in good agreement (Fig. 1).

An alternative approach to localize bacterial receptors in tissue sections is immunofluorescence staining with antibodies raised against receptor-active disaccharides (O'HANLEY et al. 1985) or glycoproteins (DEAN and ISAACSON 1985). This approach is, however, limited by the fact that antibodies and bacterial adhesins can recognize different configurations of the same epitopes, which may lead to different reacitvities at the macromolecular or tissue level. The minimum receptor structure for most P fimbriae is the DGalα1-4DGal disaccharide unit of blood group P-specific glycolipids. P fimbriae recognize this sequence more avidly in an internal

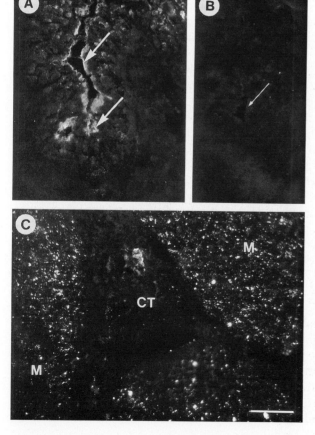

Fig. 2A–C. Fimbrial binding to epithelial cells and to muscular layer. **A** Binding of S fimbriae to epithelial cells of canine urethra (*arrows*). **B** As in **A**, but in the presence of 30 mM sialyl α2-3 lactose. Note complete inhibition of binding (*thin arrow*). **C** Binding of type 1 fimbriae to muscular layer (*M*) of human bladder. Note that connective tissue (*CT*) between the muscle cells is almost negative for the fimbrial binding

position, e.g., in globoside (Bock et al. 1986), but antibodies to the disaccharide bind only to terminal sequences and not to globoside, a major receptor-active glycolipid at the infection site (O'Hanley et al. 1985). Such differences may contribute to the slightly differing distribution of P and type 1 fimbrial receptors in kidneys obtained with antibodies (O'Hanley et al. 1985) or with purified fimbriae and labeled bacteria (Nowicki et al. 1986a; Korhonen et al. 1986b; Virkola 1987). For receptor localization, the methods employing either directly labeled bacteria or indirect staining of tissue sections with purified fimbriae or adhesins are obviously preferable over the use of antibodies raised against receptor-active carbohydrates or glycoproteins.

3.2 Binding Sites in the Urinary Tract

We have used the methods described above to localize binding sites for P, type 1, type 1C, and S fimbriae and for the O75X adhesin in human kidney and bladder (Nowicki et al. 1986a; Korhonen et al. 1986a,b,c; Virkola 1987; Virkola et al. 1988) and along the whole urinary tract of the dog (Westerlund et al. 1987; B. Westerlund, unpublished material). The results have revealed considerable tissue tropism for the E. coli adhesins: they bind differently and selectively to restricted tissue domains (Figs. 1, 2) and various epithelial surfaces of the urinary tract show differences in their reactivity with the adhesins (Table 2).

P and S fimbriae have a closely similar binding pattern in the urinary tract. They bind to epithelial cells of proximal and distal nephron and of urinary bladder, to glomeruli in the kidney, to vascular endothelium in the kidney and bladder, and to exfoliated epithelial cells of human urine (Table 2). The binding of the two fimbrial types seems to differ only with respect to the podocytes in glomeruli (Korhonen et al. 1986a, b) and to connective tissue elements in the bladder. The type 1 fimbriae bind avidly to luminal aspects of proximal tubules but only weakly, or not at all, to other epithelial surfaces in the kidney and bladder. This is in line with their lack of binding to exfoliated uroepithelial cells. Muscular layer of the urinary bladder is strongly stained by the type 1 fimbriae (Fig. 2C). A different pattern was found for the type 1C fimbriae, which bind to epithelial cells of the distal nephron and to vascular endothelium. A strikingly different binding pattern was found for the O75X adhesin, which binds strictly to nonepithelial elements in the kidney (mainly to basement membranes; Fig. 1) but reacts with epithelial cells of the bladder and urine sediment (Table 2).

The results indicate that P fimbriae bind to most, if not all, epithelial surfaces in the human urinary tract, thus giving a physical basis for the colonization of the upper urinary tract by P-fimbriated E. coli strains. Interestingly, however, the P and the S fimbriae, which are associated with different types of infection caused by E. coli (Table 1), show similar tissue binding patterns in the urinary tract (Table 2). This indicated to us that, in addition to the presence of binding sites on uroepithelia, other factors also contribute to the specific pathogenetic role of P fimbriae in human upper urinary tract infections. One such factor might be the presence of inhibitory compounds for bacterial binding, which led us to test this hypothesis further.

Table 2. Binding of the *E. coli* adhesins to human kidney and bladder, to sediment cells, and to inhibitors in normal human urine

Tissue site (inhibitor)	Adhesin binding[a]				
	P fimbria	S fimbria	Type 1 fimbria	Type 1C fimbria	O75X adhesin
Kidney:					
Bowman's capsule	+ + +	+ + +	−	−	+ + +[b]
Glomerulus	+ + +	+ + +	−	−	−
Proximal tubule	+ +	+ +	+ + +	−	+ + +[b]
Distal tubule	+ +	+ +	(+)	+ +	+ + +[b]
Collecting duct	+	+ +	(+)	+ +	+ + +[b]
Vessel walls	+ + +[c]	+ + +[c]	+ + +	+ + +[c]	−
Urinary bladder:					
Epithelium	+	+ +	−	−	+
Vessel walls	+ + +[c]	+ + +[c]	+ +	+ + +[c]	−
Muscular layer	+	+	+ + +	+	+
Connective tissue	−	+ +	−	−	+ + +
Sediment cells[d]:	+	+	−	−	+
Inhibitors in urine[e]:					
Oligosaccharides	−	−	+	ND[f]	+/−[g]
Tamn-Horsfall glycoprotein	−	+	(+)	−	−

[a]Binding to tissues is graded from + + + (intense) to − (not detectable); (+) denotes very weak binding. Data for the tissues is from NOWICKI et al. 1986a; KORHONEN et al. 1986a, b, c; VIRKIOLA 1987; VIRKOLA et al. 1988;
[b]To capsular or tubular basement membranes;
[c]Mainly to endothelial cells;
[d]Data for sediment cells are from KORHONEN et al. 1980, 1981, 1986c; ØRSKOV et al. 1980; VIRKOLA et al. 1988. Only positivity (+) or negativity (−) is shown;
[e]Data are from PARKKINEN et al. 1988b. (+), modest interaction; +, intense interaction; −, no interaction;
[f]Not determined;
[g]Inhibitors observed in 2/11 urine samples originating from different individuals

4 Identification of Inhibitors in Human Urine

In order to gain insight into the capacity of the different *E. coli* adhesins to mediate bacterial adhesion to urinary tract epithelia in vivo, we tested urine from different individuals for inhibition of hemagglutination by recombinant strains carrying different fimbriae genes (PARKKINEN et al. 1988b). Urine was found to inhibit the hemagglutination by S and type 1 fimbriae but not that by P fimbriae. Fractionation of the urine showed that the Tamm-Horsfall glycoprotein, the most abundant protein in normal human urine, was mainly responsible for the inhibitory effect for S fimbriae, whereas the major inhibitors for the type 1 fimbrial binding were identified as low molecular weight mannosides. These urine fractions inhibited hemagglutination by S and type 1 fimbriate bacteria at concentrations found in normal urine, indicating that the interactions have physiologic significance, and no significant individual variation in the inhibitory capacity of different urines was found (PARKKINEN et al. 1988b). S and type 1 fimbriae bound also to immobilized Tamm-Horsfall glycoprotein, whereas no such interaction was found for P and type 1C

fimbriae or the O75X adhesin (Table 2). Some urine samples were found to contain low molecular weight inhibitors against hemagglutination by the O75X adhesin.

5 Role of the Different Adhesins in Human Urinary Tract Infections

The results summarized in Table 2 provide an insight into the role and function of the *E. coli* adhesins in human urinary tract infections. P fimbriae, which by epidemiologic criteria appear important for pyelonephritis and urosepsis (Table 1), probably bind to all epithelial surfaces in the human urinary tract. The identified binding sites suggest an ascending route for the invasion of P-fimbriated *E. coli* into the kidney and subsequently into the circulatory system. Binding properties of P fimbriae thus support their role as a major bacterial virulence factor in pyelonephritis.

S fimbriae, which only rarely can be found on uropathogenic *E. coli* strains, have a similar binding pattern in the urinary tract to that of the P fimbriae. This indicates that the presence of binding sites on uroepithelia is not enough to explain the pathogenetic function of P fimbriae. The two fimbriae differ in that normal human urine contains inhibitors, mainly Tamm-Horsfall glycoprotein, which at concentrations found in urine can interfere with S fimbriae-mediated adhesion in the urinary tract. Such inhibitors have not been found for the P fimbriae (ORSKOV et al. 1980; O'HANLEY et al. 1985; PARKKINEN et al. 1988b). These results suggest an important principle: P fimbriae are important for pyelonephritis because they readily attach to uroepithelia and their binding is not inhibited by compounds secreted by the host in soluble form into the urine.

We have recently observed a novel interaction of P fimbriae that is independent of the DGalα1-4DGal binding. Both as a purified protein and on bacterial cells, P fimbriae interact with immobilized fibronectin (WESTERLUND et al. 1989b). This interaction is not inhibited by DGalα1-4DGal and is as effective with wild-type P fimbriae as with mutated ones lacking the lectin activity. Insoluble fibronectin is a component of the extracellular matrix and basement membranes and is known to be involved in a number of molecular and cellular binding processes. Our observation suggests a further function for the P fimbriae, i.e., interaction in a lectin-independent manner with a component of the extracellular matrix (WESTERLUND et al. 1988a). Such interaction could be useful for the bacteria at later stages of the infection after epithelial trauma and exposure of connective tissue. It could be that in such conditions the lectin activity of the fimbriae is no longer useful.

Our results do not support a pathogenetic function for type 1 fimbriae in human pyelonephritis or cystitis. These fimbriae do not bind to the distal nephron or to the epithelia of the urinary bladder, which are important surfaces for bacterial ascent. Moreover, low molecular weight α-mannosides in normal human urine would effectively prevent their binding to urinary tract components and to precipitated Tamm-Horsfall glycoprotein occurring in urinary casts and slime (PARKKINEN et al.

1988b). It should be noted that the results suggesting a pathogenetic function for type 1 fimbria in cystitis (e.g., KEITH et al. 1986) have been obtained with uroepithelial cells of mice or rats. The latter are known to differ from epithelial cells of human urine in respect of type 1 fimbrial binding (KORHONEN et al. 1981).

The type 1C fimbriae bound to vascular endothelium and to the epithelial cells of proximal tubules and of collecting ducts in the kidney. This fimbrial type is associated with pyelonephritogenic strains that often also carry P fimbriae (Table 1). Binding of the type 1C fimbriae to the lumen of collecting ducts might increase the invasive potential of *E. coli* as P-fimbriated bacteria adhere to collecting ducts only poorly (NOWICKI et al. 1986b). However, the presence of inhibitors in urine for type 1C fimbrial binding has not been determined so far.

In the kidneys, the O75X adhesin binds only to basement membranes (Fig. 1) and we have recently shown that it strongly interacts with type IV collagen, a major basement membrane glycoprotein (WESTERLUND et al. 1989a). Binding of O75X to basement membranes and to purified type IV collagen is specifically inhibited by chloramphenicol and *N*-acetyltyrosine (NOWICKI et al. 1988; WESTERLUND et al. 1989a), which indicates a protein–protein interaction. The active region in type IV collagen is the aminoterminal 7S domain (WESTERLUND et al. 1989a). The O75X adhesin also binds to bladder epithelium and to exfoliated uroepithelial cells, suggesting that it may facilitate colonization of *E. coli* in epithelia of the lower urinary tract. Moreover, binding to basement membranes may be an important factor after epithelial trauma. The epidemiologic data, however, do not support a significant pathogenetic role for the O75X adhesin, nor does the presence of inhibitors for it in urine.

6 Possible Role of S Fimbriae in Neonatal Meningitis

The distinct association of S fimbriae with *E. coli* O18:K1:H7 strains isolated from neonatal sepsis and meningitis (KORHONEN et al. 1985) suggests that S fimbriae might have a pathogenetic function in these infections. Strains of the O18:K1:H7 serotype predominate among the *E. coli* strains isolated from septic neonatal infections and cause experimental meningitis in newborn rats (BORTOLUSSI et al. 1978), which provides an animal model to study the interactions of S fimbriae during the invasive stage of the infection.

The presence of binding sites for S fimbriae in the different tissues of the newborn rat was recently investigated (PARKKINEN et al. 1988a). In the brain, S fimbriae specifically bind to the luminal surface of the vascular endothelium lining the choroid plexuses and brain ventricles (Fig. 3). Interestingly, there was a distinct decrease in the binding of S-fimbriated bacteria to the choroid plexus of rats older than 2 weeks. Investigation of other organs of the newborn rat indicated that S fimbriae bind to the glomeruli and vascular endothelium in kidney and, more weakly, to vascular endothelium and alveolar epithelium in the lung. No binding was observed in liver and spleen.

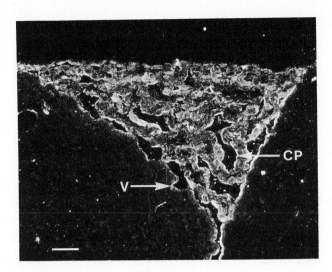

Fig. 3. Binding of S fimbriae to rat brain. The fimbriae bind to the luminal surface of epithelial cells lining the choroid plexuses (*CP*) and brain venticles (*V*). *Bar*, 100 μm

The presence of specific binding sites for S fimbriae in the brain is of particular interest as the bacterial and host factors that, in the pathogenesis on meningitis, result in the invasion of bacteria from circulation into the cerebrospinal fluid are unknown (McGee 1985). In particular, the intensive binding of S fimbriae to the choroid plexuses may be of pathogenic importance since the choroid plexus is regarded as the site of bacterial invasion into the cerebrospinal fluid (McGee 1985; Levine 1987). During invasion into the cerebrospinal fluid, bacteria must first penetrate the vascular endothelium, and the endothelial receptors for S fimbriae could facilitate this process. On the other hand, in animal models infection of the cerebrospinal fluid compartment is a kinetic process, with bacteria entering from blood and being cleared within the cerebrospinal fluid flow through the arachnoid villi to the cerebral venous sinuses (Scheld et al. 1979). In view of this, the ability of S-fimbriated bacteria to adhere to the epithelium lining the choroid plexuses and brain ventricles might provide a means for the bacteria to resist mechanical clearance by the cerebrospinal fluid flow (Parkkinen et al. 1988a).

7 Perspectives

As pointed out earlier, the receptor density for P-fimbriated *E. coli* may determine the susceptibility of certain individuals to pyelonephritis (Källenius and Winberg 1978). There is also evidence suggesting that the expression by calves and rats of sialic acid-containing receptors for *E. coli* is age dependent, perhaps contributing to the suscepitibility of newborns to diarrheal and septic infections by *E. coli* (Runnels et al. 1980; Parkkinen et al. 1988a). Determination of the density and localization of tissue receptors could thus be an important step in the identification of individuals who are prone or susceptible to bacterial infections. Our results show that

immunofluorescence techniques, either with whole bacteria or purified fimbriae or adhesins (Table 2) or possibly with the receptor-binding components of the adhesins (MOCH et al. 1987), can be used for such purposes. With better understanding of the biochemistry and serologic features of the receptor-active macromolecules, antibodies against them could also be utilized in determining receptor density in selected tissue sites. On the other hand, the obvious ability of naturally occurring inhibitors in urine to prevent bacterial adhesion (PARKKINEN et al. 1988b) encourages the development of synthetic receptor analogues to be used to prevent bacterial adhesion in urinary tracts and in septic metastatic infections.

Acknowledgement. This study was supported by the Academy of Finland.

References

Bock K, Breimer ME, Brignole A, Hansson GG, Karlsson K-A, Keffler HA, Samuelsson Bü-E, Strömberg N, Svanborg-Edén C, Thurin J (1986) Specificity of binding of a strain of uropathogenic *Escherichia coli* to Galα(1-4)Gal-containing glycosphingolipids. J Biol Chem 260: 8545–8551

Bortolussi R, Ferrieri P, Wannamaker LW (1978) Dynamics of *Escherichia coli* infection and meningitis in infant rats. Infect Immun 22: 480–485

Dean EA, Isaacson RE (1985) Location and distribution of a receptor for the 987P pilus of *Escherichia coli* in small intestines. Infect Immun 47: 345–348

Duguid JP, Old DC (1980) Adhesive properties of Enterobacteriaceae. In: Beachey EH (ed) Bacterial adherence. Chapman and Hall, London, pp 185–271 (Receptors and recognition, series B, vol 6)

Firon N, Ofek I, Sharon N (1982) Interaction of mannose-containing oligosaccharides with the fimbrial lectin of *Escherichia coli*. Biochem Biophys Res Commun 105: 1426–1432

Hagberg L, Jodal U, Korhonen TK, Lidin-Janson G, Lindberg U, Svanborg-Edén C (1981) Adhesion, hemagglutination and virulence of *Escherichia coli* causing urinary tract infections. Infect Immun 31: 564–570

Hagberg L, Hull R, Hull S, Falkow S, Freter R, Svanborg-Edén C (1983) Contribution of adhesion to bacterial presistence in the mouse urinary tract. Infect Immun 40: 265–272

Hennigar R, Schulte BA, Spicer SS (1985) Hetreogeneous distribution of glycoconjugates in human kidney tubules. Anat Res 211: 376–390

Holthöfer H (1983) Lectin binding sites in kidney. A comparative study of 14 animal species. J Histochem Cytochem 31: 531–537

Holthöfer H, Virtanen I, Pettersson E, Törnroth I, Alfthan O, Linder E, Miettinen A (1982) Lectins as fluorescence markers for saccharides in the human kidney. Lab Invest 45: 391–399

Johnson JR, Roberts PL, Stamm WE (1987) P fimbriae and other virulence factors in *Escherichia coli* urosepsis: association with patient's characteristics. J Infect Dis 156: 225–229

Jokinen M, Ehnholm C, Väisänen-Rhen V, Korhonen T, Pipkorn R, Kalkkinen N, Gahmberg CG (1985) Identification of the major human red cell sialoglycoprotein, glycophorin A^M, as the receptor for *Escherichia coli* IH11165 and characterization of the receptor site. Eur J Biochem 147: 47–52

Källenius G, Winberg J (1978) Bacterial adherence to periurethral cells in girls prone to urinary-tract infections. Lancet ii: 540–543

Källenius G, Möllby R, Winberg J (1980) In vitro adhesion of uropathogenic *Escherichia coli* to human periurethral cells. Infect Immun 28: 972–980

Källenius G, Möllby R, Svenson SB, Helin I, Hultberg H, Cederberg B, Winberg J (1981) Incidence of P-fimbriated *Escherichia coli* in urinary tract infections. Lancet ii: 1369–1371

Keith BR, Maurer L, Spears PA, Orndorff PE (1986) Receptor-binding function of type 1 pili affects bladder colonization of *Escherichia coli*. Infect Immun 53: 693–696

Korhonen TK, Edén S, Svanborg-Edén C (1980) Binding of purified *Escherichia coli* pili to human urinary tract epithelial cells. FEMS Microbiol Lett 7: 237–240

Korhonen TK, Leffler H, Svanborg-Edén C (1981) Binding specificity of piliated strains of *Escherichia*

Colonization Factor Antigens of Human Pathogens

D. J. EVANS, Jr. and D. G. EVANS

1 Introduction

The concept of microbial pathogenesis as a complex process divisible into discrete steps, each mediated by a specific type of virulence factor, is not new. However, within this concept lies the key to future success in preventation and control of diseases for which there is no practical vaccine or prophylactic method at this time. Every pathogen has a characteristic mode of pathogenesis, some more obvious than others and hence more susceptible to human intervention, diphtheria being a classic example. Others such as *Vibrio cholerae* are thought to be well understood and cholera therapy is technically well advanced; however, a cost-effective and practical vaccine rendering complete and long-term protection has yet to be achieved.

Dissecting the infectious process, the first specific event may be visualized as entry of the pathogen through a suitable host portal, such as breathing in a respiratory virus, drinking water contaminated with an enteric pathogen, or being bitten by a rabies-infected animal. Early recognition of this type of event as a prerequisite to illness gave rise to the principles of disinfection, sanitation, quarantine, insect vector control, pasteurization, food preservation, and sewage and

The Bacterial Enteropathogen Laboratory, Digestive Disease Section, Veterans Administration Medical Center, Houston, Texas, and Department of Medicine, Baylor College of Medicine, Houston, Texas, USA

water treatment which are routinely practiced today. Various combinations of these
basic measures designed to prevent pathogen transmission have been remarkably
effective in controlling once devastating pathogens and continue to be the most
important means of disease prevention. Unfortunately, it is also true that on a global
scale most of these basic preventative measures are not practiced, because of lack of
either education or physical resources.

Clearly, if one cannot always prevent exposure to microbial pathogens, then one
must seek means of intervention based on an understanding of events subsequent to
such exposure. In this chapter, we concentrate on the importance of the second step
in the infectious process, which is actually the first specific physical interaction
between pathogen and host, i.e., attachment to a specific host receptor mediated by
specialised macromolecules exposed on the surface of the pathogen. This key step in
pathogenesis is currently the subject of intense investigation for diseases as diverse
as HIV-1 (AIDS virus), malaria, and Asiatic cholera.

Consider the problem of designing vaccines. Most microbial pathogens, whether
parasite, virus, or bacterium, possess unique species- and/or strain-specific surface
antigens which can theoretically be employed as immunogens in a vaccine, and this
approach has had its share of success. However, in reality many pathogens have so
far defied all attempts at artificial immunization, some because they possess
exquisitely complex and/or variable antigenic surface structure(s) and others by
equally exquisite mechanisms for avoiding exposure to antibody attack. We feel that
many of these problems will be resolved by targeting as immunogens the specific
surface-associated antigens which function as adhesins, simply because preventing
colonization by the pathogen is essentially equivalent to aborting the infection.

In this chapter we consider the role of adhesins in the infectious process, using
the enterotoxigenic *Escherichia coli* (ETEC) colonization factor antigens (CFAs) as a
"model" example. We submit some hopefully accurate historical perspectives on this
subject as well as a brief overview of its current status, speculations on the role of
CFAs in the evolution of ETEC as they exist today, and, finally, a few ideas about
those aspects of ETEC CFAs which we feel will be the focus of future research.

2 Recognition of Adhesins as Important Virulence Factors: Historical Perspective

Generally, microbial pathogens possess on their surface specific molecules which
are configured so as to recognize and interact with receptors on the surface of
specific host cells, usually those of the epithelial cell lining of the respiratory,
gastrointestinal, or genitourinary tract. We define colonization as adhesion at a
specific site followed by multiplication at that site. Thus colonization factors
represent the mechanism by which pathogens such as the ETEC recognize and
affix themselves to a specific target tissue. Adhesion, even colonization, rarely
constitutes the entire disease process, a fact which is largely responsible for the
relative delay in appreciating the significance of colonization factors. Historically,

the existence of colonization factors as molecular entities was less obvious than that of the functionally secondary virulence factors which mediate actual damage to the host and therefore are responsible for the overt symptoms of infection. Virulence factors of bacteria include factors facilitating invasion of tissue (invasins), cell death (cytotoxins, cytolysins), neurologic dysfunction (neurotoxins), and diarrhea (enterotoxins).

Interestingly, diseases such as pneumonia, meningitis, and even acute diarrhea may be caused by either viral or bacterial pathogens and even today the task of differentiating between these can be challenging. In practical terms, an intact infectious viral particle is itself an adhesin and replication (colonization) occurs intracellularly. Viruses do possess on their surface specific molecular entities which mediate adhesion to host receptors and these adhesins represent potentially important targets for designing antiviral defenses such as vaccines.

3 Multiplicity of *Escherichia coli* Fimbrial Adhesins and Correlations Between Fimbrial Type and Pathogenicity

Approximately a century ago it was recognized that the common enteric bacillus *Bacterium coli* (*Escherichia coli*) had the property of readily adhering to other cells, including plant cells, yeast cells, and animal erythrocytes. Later it was found that most, if not all, genera of gram-negative enteric bacteria have this property. It became convenient to classify such adherence as either mannose sensitive (MS) (i.e., readily blocked by mannose) or mannose resistant, since the most common type of adherence factor was mannose sensitive, and to employ erythrocytes to detect both MS- and MR-type adhesins. Hemagglutination (HA) tests have an additional attraction in that adhesins can be classified according to the type of erythrocyte producing a positive test. By consensus the current test for common fimbriae, which mediate MSHA, employs guinea pig erythrocytes. Common fimbriae are generally long, thin hair-like projections on the bacterial cell surface but as a group these are somewhat morphologically diverse. Common fimbriae are also quite diverse antigenically, even among individual species such as *E. coli*.

A large variety of functions have been ascribed to common fimbriae, or common pili, including a role in virulence. However, since the receptor for these fimbriae (mannose-containing glycoproteins) appears to be universally distributed, cell- or tissue-specific adherence is an unlikely function for common fimbriae. There is some experimental evidence, from work with animal models, that these fimbriae may play a secondary but important role in colonization of the lower urinary tract (ORNDORFF 1987). It is interesting that ETEC are capable of producing common fimbriae but this is not surprising since (a) production of these fimbriae is encoded by the chromosome and (b) ETEC certainly evolved from *E. coli* of the normal flora, which typically possess common fimbriae. There is no evidence for the role of common fimbriae in ETEC virulence although this possibility has been given serious consideration.

As discussed below, there is evidence that ETEC possess control mechanisms which dictate that either common fimbriae or CFA-type fimbriae will be produced in a particular environment (EVANS et al. 1977a, b). Serologic evidence has shown that CFA-type fimbriae are produced in vivo (DEETZ et al. 1979; STOLL et al. 1986). It is possible that common fimbriae may be one of the ancestral proteins from which evolved one or more of the tissue-specific fimbrial CFAs of the ETEC and/or other gram-negative pathogenic bacteria.

Pathogenic *E. coli* generally fall into one of two large groups, i.e., those serotypes commonly associated with intestinal infections and those associated with extra-intestinal infections (EVANS and EVANS 1983; ORSKOV et al. 1977). There are subdivisions within each major group, each sharing the ability to produce a particular set of virulence factors. Briefly, one hallmark of *E. coli* which cause extraintestinal infection is production of fimbrial colonization factors (PAP, or pyelonephritis-associated pili), the receptor of which is a digalactoside moiety (LEFFLER and SVANBORG-EDEN 1980; BOCK et al. 1985) plus one or more other virulence factors such as hemolysin and/or certain carbohydrate capsular antigens, particularly the K-1 antigen (EVANS et al. 1981). PAP-type fimbriae, like common fimbriae, are an antigenically heterogeneous group (PERE et al. 1986); however they do share a highly conserved region the function of which is receptor recognition. Correlations have been noted between possession of PAP receptors and suscepti-bility to urinary tract infection with this type of *E. coli*. However, not all *E. coli* associated with upper urinary tract infections produce PAP-type fimbriae. There are bioserotypes which possess functionally equivalent fimbriae that recognize different host receptors and also those which possess adhesins that are not fimbrial at all but are actually capsular in morphology (ORSKOV et al. 1985; RHEN et al. 1986; GOLDHAR et al. 1987).

The enteropathogenic group of *E. coli* can be subdivided into at least three subgroups on the basis of mechanism of pathogenesis; these are the ETEC, the *Shigella*-like enteroinvasive *E. coli*, or EIEC, serotypes, and the enteroadherent serotypes which include the classical EPEC serogroups. Some individual isolates of enteropathogenic *E. coli* possess unusual combinations of virulence factors and appear to belong to more than one subgroup, e.g., a classic EPEC serogroup hosting ETEC virulence plasmids (GUTH et al. 1985). These represent exceptional cases since it is well established that the three subgroups of enteropathogenic *E. coli* possess different specialized sites of attachment (ROBINS-BROWNE 1987). Only the ETEC preferentially colonize the small intestine. With the *Shigella*-like *E. coli* it appears that adherence to the intestinal cell may be the trigger which initiates invasion of the host cell by the bacteria.

4 ETEC Colonization Factor Antigens: Historical Perspective

Species-specific CFAs of the ETEC were not originally discovered by prospectively searching for fimbriae with unique adhesive properties (although today this is a well-accepted approach) but rather as surface antigen unique to diarrhea-associated

isolates of *E. coli*. Upon discovery, both K88 (on swine-associated ETEC) and K99 (on calf-associated ETEC) were characterized as heat-labile capsular antigens and only later recognized as a surface layer possessing fimbrial structure (ORSKOV and ORSKOV 1966; ORSKOV et al. 1975; BURROWS et al. 1976). Subsequent studies on K88 and K99 revealed several properties which also helped in defining the CFAs of human-associated ETEC. K88 and K99 both mediate MRHA but are detectable with different species of erythrocytes and thus recognize different receptors, as has been confirmed by studies on their individual adherence properties. Also, the genes determining production of either K88 or K99 were found to be located on plasmids, which explains the close correlation between enterotoxin production (also plasmid mediated) and production of either K88 or K99.

Studies which detected piglets genetically resistant to K88-positive ETEC produced the first evidence that possession of a specific intestinal epithelial cell receptor is a determining factor in susceptibility to ETEC diarrhea (JONES and RUTTER 1972). That the tissue specificity and host specificity of the ETEC is a function of their CFAs has been repeatedly confirmed by epidemiologic observations and by in vivo and in vitro studies on the affinity of ETEC for intestinal epithelial cells of man and animals (BURROWS et al. 1976; SMITH and LINGOOD 1971; EVANS et al. 1978b; KNUTTON et al. 1984; CHENEY and BOEDEKER 1983). The observed pattern of tissue affinity is in accord with the natural host of the ETEC isolates; K88-positive ETEC do not adhere to human intestine and do not cause diarrhea in man.

Colonization factor antigen receptors are di- or trisaccharide sequences, often including sialic acid moieties, which occur on surface-associated sialoglycoproteins of the target cells. (BEACHEY 1981; BOCK et al. 1985, EVANS et al. 1988a). These same receptor sequences often occur on various cell types, including erythrocytes, but it is their occurrence on epithelial cells of the small intestine which is relevant to susceptibility to colonization with ETEC. One can speculate that host-specific receptor recognition is the result of an evolutionary process by which certain *E. coli* bioserotypes evolved the means to maximize their ability to colonize. In essence, potential host diversity appears to have been sacrificed in exchange for efficiency of colonization.

The existence of K88 and K99 led us to speculate that human-associated ETEC might possess plasmid-encoded fimbriae detectable as unique antigens having unique receptor specificity, detectable as MR-type hemagglutinins, and having a demonstrable correlation with enterotoxin production. We searched for, and found within cultures of ETEC isolated from cases of diarrhea, clones possessing a new antigenic type of fimbriae which satisfied the definition of a colonization factor and the production of which correlated with enterotoxin production and possession of a particular plasmid; this fimbrial antigen is CFA/I (EVANS et al. 1975). CFA/II also has these properties.

The major clue to the existence of CFA/II was that ETEC isolates belonging to the commonly isolated ETEC serotype O6:H16 never expressed CFA/I (EVANS and EVANS 1978). It is now known that O6:H16 is the most commonly isolated CFA/II-positive ETEC serotype. Both CFA/I and CFA/II have a specific affinity for attachment to human intestinal epithelial cells and both have been found, associated with different ETEC serotypes, among ETEC isolated from cases of acute diarrhea

found to produce CFA/II. The number of ETEC isolates possessing E8775 is minor compared to those with CFA/I or CFA/II (THOMAS and ROWE 1982). This is simply a reflection of the relative predominance and distribution of ETEC serotypes, which varies from time to time and from one location to another (BACK et al. 1980). DARFEUILLE et al. (1983) described as CFA/III a fimbrial antigen found on an ETEC strain belonging to serogroup O128. However, this putative CFA/III may in fact be a variant of CFA/I since we and at least three other laboratories have reported that isolates of enterotoxigenic O128 produce CFA/I (MURRAY et al. 1983; THOMAS and Rowe 1982; GOTHEFORS et al. 1985; GUTH et al. 1985).

HONDA et al. (1984) reported a new antigenic type of CFA on strains of ETEC. This CFA was described as highly hydrophobic, as are CFA/I, CFA/II, K88, and K99 (WADSTROM et al. 1980), and genetically linked to enterotoxin production. This pilus antigen, designated 260-1, did not produce MRHA with human or bovine erythrocytes but did mediate colonization in both infant rabbits and suckling mice. The relative prevalence of ETEC with 260-1 pili has yet to be tested and the possible association with particular ETEC serotypes also remains to be determined.

With the discovery of the E8775 fimbrial ETEC antigen, only a few frequently isolated ETEC serotypes (namely O148:H28 and O159:H4) were considered unaccounted for in terms of their CFAs. However, SEN et al. (1984) reported that eight of ten ETEC isolates belonging to serotype O148:H28 were positive for CFA/II. Recently, TACKET et al. (1987) examined isolates of ETEC belonging to serotype O159:H4 and negative for MRHA with human erythrocytes and found that six of ten such isolates, from diverse sources, possessed a new fimbrial antigen. This O159:H4-associated fimbriae may represent a new CFA since its production is plasmid encoded with ST and LT genes on the same plasmid. Definitive studies demonstrating a link between colonization activity and this putative CFA have not yet been reported.

KNUTTON et al. (1987) identified a unique fimbrial structure, consisting of very numerous curly fibrils, approximately 3 nm in diameter, on human enterocyte-adhesive ETEC strains belonging to serotype O148:H28. The O148:H28-associated fibrils are apparently nonhemagglutinating; the genetics and further antigenic characterization of this putative CFA have not yet been reported.

6 Role of ETEC Virulence Factors in the Transmission Dynamics of Acute Diarrhea and Speculations on the Evolution of ETEC

In numerous studies of ETEC diarrhea it has been observed that a small number of ETEC serotypes predominate against a background of much less frequently isolated serotypes (EVANS and EVANS 1983; ORSKOV et al. 1976; EVANS et al. 1984b). Serotypes which produce a known CFA are isolated in different regions around the world and are the same ones which predominate in specific locations (ROWE et al. 1983; DANBARA et al. 1987). Also, CFA-positive ETEC are responsible for the most serious cases of ETEC diarrhea. Serologic evidence, cited elsewhere, further

confirms the importance of CFAs in ETEC virulence (STOLL et al. 1986). However, circulating, IgG, antibody against either CFA(s) or LT has proven to be a poor indicator of antigen exposure in the intestine even in cases of acute diarrhea. Specific intestinal secretory IgA responses are a much better measure of exposure to ETEC antigens but appropriate intestinal samples are difficult to obtain except under very convenient circumstances such as in volunteer studies (EVANS et al. 1978; STOLL et al. 1986).

Dependence of ETEC on possession of a CFA for successful colonization of their natural host has broad implications. As is true for many bacterial pathogens, those strains which possess a full complement of virulence factors (in this case, ST, LT, and a CFA) are the ones which infect and successfully colonize the largest number of individual hosts. This is essentially a function of the number of bacteria released from one host and thus available to infect other individuals. ETEC bioserotypes seem to be well adapted to survival in the small intestine but not in the colon which hosts *E. coli* of the normal flora. In fact bacterial enteropathogens in general appear to be at a disadvantage in the ability to take up long-term residence as part of the normal colonic flora. Survival of ETEC in a given population of hosts is well served by the infection–transmission–infection cycle which is driven by the combination of diarrheagenic toxin(s) plus highly efficient colonizing capabilities afforded by the CFAs. If one accepts the premise that with ETEC survival of the "species" is dependent upon virulence then it is not difficult to appreciate the competitive advantage derived from packaging the genetic information for both diarrheagenic toxin(s) and CFA(s) in the same plasmids or in different but coexisting plasmids. Thus the fact that the genes encoding for the ETEC virulence factors are located on extrachromosomal elements, rather than on the chromosome, may be directly related to their combined survival value.

Whether the genetic elements for ST, for LT, and for the individual CFAs evolved separately and later combined into the same plasmids or whether these elements evolved together on a particular type of plasmid is unknown. It is also uncertain why ETEC which produce particular H antigens frequently produce a particular type of CFA. Presuming that all flagellar antigens are functionally equivalent (and observing that H-minus ETEC derivatives are in no way impaired in their expression of CFA fimbriae), one must conclude that the observed CFA–H pairings are based on either indirectly related or coincidental selective factors, akin to the "clonal" hypothesis. On the other hand, there may be direct factors involved in this phenomenon such as interactions between the genetic mechanisms which control expression of these surface structures or even shared accessory elements such as anchor proteins.

If ETEC plasmids evolved from elements such as phage-like particles then it may be that particular O groups, particular O:H combinations, or particular bioserotypes were the preferred hosts for these different ancestral phage-like particles. Even more speculative is the possibility that the different CFAs could have evolved from attachment factors employed by the phage-like elements to infect their bacterial hosts. It is a fact that some bacteriocins, such as pyocins, structurally resemble bacteriophage particles and are thought to have evolved from bacteriophages (HOLLOWAY and KRISHNAPILLAI 1975). Also, not all

transmissible plasmids encode for sex pili which are as large as F-type pili. Many of these sex pili (fimbriae) are in the same size range as CFA fimbriae and many are expressed in large numbers per cell, as are CFA fimbriae. LT may have evolved on the bacterial chromosome and later become incorporated into the extra-chromosomal element(s) encoding for a CFA, with ST being the last to join the system since the identity of ST as a transposon is still evident today. Recently perfected techniques for application to "genetic archeology" (YAMAMOTO et al. 1984; VINAL and DALLAS 1987; TAMIYA and YAGI 1985) may someday provide answers to these questions.

From the above, it can be seen that CFAs, as a functional class of macro-molecules, may be an excellent example of convergent evolution and that different CFAs may have evolved via different pathways as different *E. coli* bioserotypes adapted to their particular species of host. This could well account for the antigenic and morphologic diversity seen among the CFAs. Both CFA/II and E8775 consist of at least three different surface-associated components and these components can be expressed in various combinations, or even alone, by different ETEC strains. This is very unlike CFA/I, which has a single and consistent fimbrial morphology, is composed of only one type of subunit, and behaves like a single antigen. Most CFA/II-positive ETEC produce a fimbrial structure, which has strong MRHA activity with bovine erythrocytes, plus a very narrow (2–3 nm diameter) fibrillar structure. CFA/II fimbriae may be of one or another antigenic type, termed CS1 and CS2. Strains produce either CS1 or CS2 but not both (LEVINE et al. 1984; SMYTH 1984). The CS3 fibrillar antigen is either very weakly positive or negative for MRHA. Evidently CS3 functions to strengthen the attachment of CFA/II-positive ETEC to target cells since CS3-only strains, lacking fimbriae, are also associated with cases of diarrhea.

The three-component CFA/II system is essentially duplicated by the CFA E8775, which also consists of three components, termed the CS4, CS5, and CS6 antigens (THOMAS et al. 1985). CS4 and CS5 have fimbrial morphology whereas CS6 is difficult to visualize by electron microscopy but may also be a 3-nm-diameter curly fibrillar structure (KNUTTON et al. 1987). While the distribution of CS4, CS5, and CS6 among ETEC needs further clarification, the isolation of virulent CS5-only ETEC of serotype O115:H40 has already been documented and the ETEC serogroup O148:H28 (MANNING et al. 1987) may include a CS6-only variety (KNUTTON et al. 1987).

The following may be a reasonable hypothesis about the evolution of the ETEC as they exist today. There is evidence that both ST and LT originated in an ancestral microbe, probably as chromosomal genes, which had as its host one particular animal species, either man or swine. Both ETEC which cause acute diarrhea in man and those which are animal pathogens produce ST and/or LT. With minor variations ST from either type of host and LT from either type of host are basically the same although there are molecular subspecies of each which seem to have been host influenced. This indicates that both ST and LT orginated in one source and divergence has since taken place as the result of host factors such as differences in intestinal receptors in the case of ST or immunologic pressure in the case of LT. This process may have occurred in parallel with evolution of the CFA adhesins. Different

bioserotypes produce different CFAs and associate with different animal species; since host specificity is a function of the CFAs, it follows that each CFA most likely evolved from a different ancestral protein system. Antigenically and morphologically the CFAs are more heterogeneous than are the known varieties of ST and LT. The particular ETEC "clonal" types prevalent today may simply be those bioserotypes (ex: O6:H16:CFA/II; CS1 + CS3) which harbored those plasmids in which a particular physical event occurred, that event being emplacement of an enterotoxin gene in the same plasmid as a CFA operon, or a physical combination of an ST + LT plasmid with a CFA-encoding plasmid. This evolutionary event may still be evident today in that O78:H11 ETEC usually carry a plasmid encoding for both ST and CFA/I but not LT, which coexists in a separate plasmid in this "clone." Further, O6:H16 ETEC carry a plasmid encoding for ST, LT, and CFA/II. One might predict that similar "clonal" evidence will be found in the case of E8775, K88, K99, and other ETEC CFAs. One might argue that size differences between particular types of plasmid carried by the "clones" isolated today are incompatible with the above hypothetical evolutionary events. However, it is only important that virulence factor operons be conserved.

7 Colonization Factor Antigens as the Basis for Anti-ETEC Vaccine(s)

The multiplicity of ETEC, CFAs and the heterogeneity of antigens within particular CFAs such as CFA/II have important consequences. For maximum effectiveness, a CFA-based vaccine should be designed to include all of the major antigens. However, it should be mentioned that although CFAs are seemingly numerous, these antigens are not nearly as numerous as the O groups of ETEC. Also, *E. coli* O antigens would be a poor choice upon which to base an anti-ETEC vaccine since many closely related O groups frequently colonize man as normal flora of the large intestine. The other obvious possibility is an antienterotoxin vaccine and this possibility is under active investigation (KLIPSTEIN et al. 1985; SVENNERHOLM et al. 1984). However, because of the mode of pathogenesis of the ETEC it is possible that those strains capable of heavily colonizing the epithelial surface of the small intestine may overwhelm an antienterotoxin defense. We agree with the generally accepted idea that incorporation of LT (or cholera B subunit) into an anti-ETEC or anticholera CFA or whole-cell vaccine would enhance efficacy (CLEMENTS et al. 1986).

The anti-CFA approach to vaccine development has several theoretically favorable aspects and some of these have already been demonstrated experimentally. The primary consideration is that ETEC do not attain significant, i.e., diarrheagenic, numbers in the small intestine without attachment to the mucosal surface. This has been demonstrated in the laboratory rabbit (EVANS et al. 1981) and also with volunteers in which anti-CFA immunization has prevented illness in the face of challenge with virulent ETEC (EVANS et al. 1984a). Studies with both animals

and man support the premise that intestinal IgA is the immunoglobulin protective against ETEC colonization.

Development of an effective anti-ETEC vaccine is one of our major goals and although it seems clear that an oral vaccine based on CFAs will be the key to long-lasting protection, there is the task of maximizing delivery, via the oral route, of such antigens to the gut immune system. Although purified CFAs were effective in stimulating both intestinal anti-CFA IgA and protection in rabbits it has been difficult to reproduce this result with volunteers (EVANS et al. 1984b). We have concluded that CFAs administered in the form of CFA-positive bacterial cells are for some reason more effective in stimulating a protective antibody response. Whole killed ETEC as a vaccine has another attractive aspect, namely the easy adaptability of this approach for including cells containing all of the important CFAs in combination with other ETEC surface antigens such as plasmid-mediated outer membrane proteins which might contribute to a protective immune response.

We recently reported the results of a double-blind vaccination/challenge study in which two doses, $1 \times 10 \{10\}$ each, of colicin E2-killed ETEC strain H-10407, given orally 1 month apart, protected against challenge 8 weeks later with $3 \times 10 \{9\}$ living H-10407 (EVANS et al. 1988a). Eight of nine volunteers in the placebo group experienced diarrhea upon challenge, whereas only two of ten vaccinated individuals became ill. One of the two vaccinees who were not protected had failed to develop an intestinal IgA anti-CFA/I response and the other showed a weak antibody response and experienced only mild diarrhea. Thus, eight of ten vaccinees had a significant intestinal anti-CFA response and were protected.

The above results do not prove that anti-CFA/I IgA was the protective factor. In fact, more recent volunteer studies (unpublished data) showed that the colicin E2-killed H-10407 vaccine not only protected six of eight vaccinees against challenge with an O63:H-:CFA/I (ST + LT) strain but also protected six of eight vaccinees challenged with an O6:H16:CFA/II (ST + LT) ETEC strain. It is of interest that in recent studies we demonstrated that 19 of 22 vaccinees who had been administered two doses of the colicin E2-killed H-10407 vaccine did exhibit an intestinal anti-LT response. Previously, we had confirmed that colicin E2 (an endonuclease which destroys both the chromosomal and plasmid DNA) kills *E. coli* without damage to the integrity of the cells (KONISKY 1982; EVANS et al. 1988a). For example, lethal treatment with this colicin does not cause the release of LT from the bacterial cells; colicin E2-killed cells and control, untreated, cells released the same amount of LT upon treatment with polymyxin (unpublished results).

The data cited above show that the gut immune system is very effectively stimulated by both CFA/I and LT administered in the form of whole killed ETEC cells. Although the molecular events responsible for this result remain unknown, we believe that our original contention that colicin E2-killed cells would more naturally mimic actual infection than chemically or heat-killed cells has been justified, and that the prospects for development of an effective anti-ETEC vaccine appear to be good although the majority of this work lies in the future.

8 Evidence for Specific Mechanisms Controlling Expression of Colonization Factor Antigens by ETEC

Enterotoxigenic *E. coli* virulence plasmids encoding for a CFA represent an ideal experimental model for elucidating the molecular mechanisms which control expression of plasmid-encoded products in *E. coli*. It is clear that expression of a CFA is in large part dependent on molecular signals mediated either directly or indirectly by products of the bacterial chromosome. For example, expression of both CFA/I and CFA/II in vitro is regulated such that under certain growth conditions the cells express CFA fimbriae but not common fimbriae, and vice versa. Thus expression of CFA and common fimbriae are coordinated in a negative fashion. More direct evidence for such control was found when we isolated a mutant of strain H-10407 which is hyperproductive for CFA/I (unpublished results). This mutant, termed strain SB-3456, produces large amounts of CFA/I even under conditions which favor production of common fimbriae. Common fimbriae were not detectable on this mutant under any growth conditions although revertants of this mutant did show normal control over CFA/I production and did produce common fimbriae under appropriate growth conditions.

It is well known that broth culture favors common fimbriae production whereas agar culture favors CFA production. However, the effect of broth versus agar substrate can be overcome by manipulation of nutrients; for example growth on CFA agar results in CFA production whereas growth on peptone agar results in the production of common fimbriae (EVANS et al. 1977a, b). We have found that expression of CFA/I is regulated in part by the availability of iron in that CFA/I production in a defined medium is maximal when iron is decreased to a concentration which limits growth. Conversely, addition of iron in excess of that required for maximum cell yield, using the same basal medium, significantly decreased CFA/I production. These results seem reasonable since the human small intestine, where CFA/I production is relevant to virulence, is normally a low-iron environment. Individual carbon substrates, particularly acetate, were also found to affect expression of CFA/I. Replacement of glucose by acetate as the substrate in an excess-iron defined medium was found to abolish CFA/I production completely. Interestingly, the above-mentioned mutant (SB-3456) of strain H-10407 is unaffected by acetate. On an agar medium containing excess iron and glucose plus acetate as the major carbon sources strain H-10407 is negative for CFA/I but positive for common fimbriae; on this same medium the derivative strain SB-3456 is negative for common fimbriae and positive for CFA/I.

The above-cited results show that the control mechanism(s) which regulates the expression of common fimbriae, which is a chromosomal function, and that which regulates expression of CFA fimbriae, which is a plasmid-encoded function, are not independent. The location of the mutation responsible for the properties exhibited by the derivative strain SB-3456 (i.e., plasmid versus chromosome) and the exact nature of the gene product(s) or control gene functions involved are being investigated.

9 Summary and a View Toward the Future

In this chapter we have cited only a few of the many researchers who have contributed to the current state of knowledge about the ETEC and their significance as a major human health problem. Furthermore, there are volumes of data which could be cited concerning the economic cost of ETEC infection of domestic animals, CFAs of these animal-associated ETEC other than K88 and K99, and the important strides of progress which have been made in developing an effective vaccine approach to deal with these ETEC.

Our basic message is that the CFAs are the key to survival of the ETEC in any given population, be it man or animal, and we postulate that an anti-ETEC vaccine aimed at the CFAs, especially if combined with an antienterotoxin stimulus, will prove eventually to be very successful. In terms of economic feasibility, one must consider the current cost of ETEC diarrhea in morbidity and mortality in countries with a high endemicity of ETEC diarrhea, not to mention treatment costs, costs to travelers, and the effects of ETEC diarrhea on child development and increased susceptibility to the devastating effects of other pathogens. We also postulate that one major benefit which will be derived from studies on the ETEC CFAs will be elucidation of the CFA(s) of *Vibrio cholerae* and that this achievement will provide the final step in development of an oral vaccine remarkably effective against cholera.

Discovery of the new ETEC CFAs, or putative CFAs, cited here makes it imperative that epidemiologic studies on susceptible populations continue, preferably based on an organised surveillance approach rather than on short-term or retrospective studies. Certainly it would be timely, and hopefully economical, to institute newer, rapid identification techniques such as a battery of gene probes which could account for the known ETEC CFAs as well as the adhesive factors of the non-ETEC enteropathogenic *E. coli*.

Finally, it will be intersting to see the evolutionary history of the ETEC CFAs unfold as newer techniques such as computer-assisted restriction endonuclease analysis and protein/antigen analysis are put to the task. Here, we suggest that the range of *E. coli* fimbriae selected for examination be expanded to include all of the known types of sex pili, i.e., those fimbriae involved in DNA transfer between *E. coli* cells. These seemingly irrelevant pili may prove to be related, in an ancestral fashion, to the fimbrial/fibrillar CFAs. Also, elucidation of the molecular mechanics by which chromosomal and plasmid control mechanisms interact may lead to practical applications, even to completely new approaches to prophylaxis and treatment of diseases caused by pathogenic bacteria which are dependent on plasmid-encoded virulence factors.

References

Back E, Mollby R, Kaijser B, Stintzing G, Wadstrom T, Habte D (1980) Enterotoxigenic *Escherichia coli* and other gram-negative bacteria of infantile diarrhea: surface antigens, hemagglutinins, colonization factor antigens, and loss of enterotoxigenicity. J Infect Dis 142: 318–327

Beachey EH (1981) Bacterial adherence: adhesin-receptor interactions mediating the attachment of bacteria to mucosal surfaces. J Infact Dis 143: 325–345

Bock K, Breimer ME, Brignole A, Hansson GC, Karlsson K-A, Larson G, Leffler H, Samuelsson BE, Stromberg N, Eden CS, Thurin J (1985) Specificity of binding of a strain of uropathogenic *Escherichia coli* to Gal alpha 1-4-Gal-containing glycosphingolipids. J Biol Chem 260: 8545–8551

Burrows MR, Sellwood R, Gibbons RA (1976) Haemagglutinating and adhesive properties associated with the K99 antigen of bovine strains of *Escherichia coli*. J Gen Microbiol 96: 269–275

Cheney CP, Boedeker EC (1983) Adherence of an enterotoxigenic *Escherichia coli* strain, serotype O78:H11, to purified human intestinal brush borders. Infect Immun 39: 1280–1284

Clements JD, Sack DA, Harris JR, Chakraborty J, Khan MR, Stanton BF, Kay BA, Khan MU, Yunus M, Atkinson WA, Svennerholm A-M, Holmgren J (1986) Field trial of oral cholera vaccines in Bangladesh. Lancet 2: 124–129

Danbara H, Komase K, Kirii Y, Shinohara M, Arita H, Makino S, Yoshikawa M (1987) Analysis of the plasmids of *Escherichia coli* O148:H28 from travelers with diarrhea. Microb Pathogen 3: 269–278

Darfeuille A, Lafeuille B, Joly B, Cluzel R (1983) A new colonization factor antigen (CFA/III) produced by enteropathogenic *Escherichia coli* O128:B12. Ann Inst Pasteur Microbiol 134A: 53–64

Deetz TR, Evans DJ, Evans DG, DuPont HL (1979) Serologic responses to somatic O and colonization-factor antigens of enterotoxigenic *Escherichia coli* in travelers. J Infect Dis 140: 114–118

Evans DG, Evans DJ (1978) New surface-associated heat-labile colonization factor antigen (CFA/II) produced by enterotoxigenic *Escherichia coli* of serogroups O6 and O8. Infect Immun 21: 638–647

Evans DJ, Evans DG (1983) Classification of pathogenic *Escherichia coli* according to serotype and the production of antigens. Rev Infect Dis 5 (Suppl): 692–701

Evans DG, Silver RP, Evans DJ, Chase DG, Gorbach SL (1975) Plasmid-controlled colonization factor associated with virulence in *Escherichia coli* enterotoxigenic for humans. Infect Immun 12: 656–667

Evans DG, Evans DJ, DuPont HL (1977a) Virulence factors of enterotoxigenic *Escherichia coli*. J Infect Dis 136 (Suppl): 118–123

Evans DG, Evans DJ, Tjoa W (1977b) Hemagglutination of human group A erythrocytes by enterotoxigenic *Escherichia coli* isolated from adults with diarrhea: correlation with colonization factor. Infect Immun 18: 330–337

Evans DG, Satterwhite TK, Evans DJ, DuPont HL (1978) Differences in serological responses and excretion patterns of volunteers challenged with enterotoxigenic *Escherichia coli* with and without colonization factor antigen. Infect Immun 19: 883–888

Evans DJ, Evans DG, Hohne C, Noble MA, Haldane EV, Lior H, Young LS (1981) Hemolysin and K antigens in relation to serotype and hemagglutination type of *Escherichia coli* isolated from extraintestinal infections. J Clin Microbiol 13: 171–178

Evans DG, Cabada FJ, Evans DJ (1982) Correlation between intestinal immune response to colonization factor antigen/I (CFA/I) and acquired resistance to enterotoxigenic *Escherichia coli* diarrhea in an adult rabbit model. Eur J Clin Microbiol 1: 178–185

Evans DG, Graham DY, Evans DJ (1984a) Administration of purified colonization factor antigens (CFA/I, CFA/II) of enterotoxigenic *Escherichia coli* to volunteers. Response to challenge with virulent enterotoxigenic *Escherichia coli*. Gastroenterology 87: 934–940

Evans DJ, Evans DG, Sack DA, Clegg S (1984b) Entertoxigenic *Escherichia coli* pathogenic for man: biological and immunological aspects of fimbrial colonization factor antigens. In: Boedeker EC (ed) Attachment of organisms to the gut mucosa, vol I. CRC, Boca Raton, chap 8

Evans DJ, Evans DG, Opekun AR, Graham DY (1988a) Immunoprotective oral whole cell vaccine for enterotoxigenic *Escherichia coli* prepared by in situ destruction of chromosomal and plasmid DNA with colicin E2. FEMS Microbiol Immunol 47: 9–18

Evans DG, Evans DJ, Moulds JJ, Graham DY (1988b) *N*-acetylneuraminyllactose-binding fibrillar hemagglutinin of *Campylobacter pylori*: a putative colonization factor antigen. Infect Immun 56: 2896–2906

Evans DJ, Evans DG, Diaz SR, Graham DY (1988c) Mannose-resistant hemagglutination of human erythrocytes by entertoxigenic *Escherichia coli* with colonization factor antigen II. J Clin Microbiol 26: 1626–1629

Goldhar J, Perry R, Golecki JR, Hochutzky H, Jann B, Jann K (1987) Non-fimbrial, mannose-resistant adhesins from uropathogenic *Escherichia coli* O83:K1:H4 and O14:K?:H11. Infect Immun 55: 1837–1842

Gothefors L, Ahren C, Stoll B, Barua DK, Orskov F, Salek MA, Svennerholm A-M (1985) Presence of colonization factor antigens on fresh isolates fecal *Escherichia coli*: a prospective study. J Infect Dis 152: 1128–1133

Guth BEC, Silva MLM, Scaletsky ICA, Toledo MRF, Trabulsi LR (1985) Enterotoxin production, presence of colonization factor antigen I, and adherence to HeLa cells by *Escherichia coli* O128 strains belonging to different O subgroups. Infect Immun 47: 338–340

Holloway BW, Krishnapillai V (1975) Bacteriophages and bacteriocins. In: Clarke PH, Richmond MH (eds) Genetics and biochemistry of *Pseudomonas* Willey, London, pp 99–132

Honda T, Arita M, Miwatani T (1984) Characterization of new hydrophobic pili of human enterotoxigenic *Escherichia coli*: a possible new colonization factor. Infect Immun 43: 959–965

Jones GW, Rutter JM (1972) Role of the K88 antigen in the pathogenesis of neonatal diarrhea caused by *Escherichia coli* in piglets. Infect Immun 6: 918–927

Klipstein FA, Engert RF, Houghten RA (1985) Mucosal antitoxin response in volunteers to immunization with a synthetic peptide of *Escherichia coli* heat-stable enterotoxin. Infect Immun 50: 328–332

Knutton S, Lloyd DR, Candy DCA, McNeish AS (1984) In vitro adhesion of enterotoxigenic *Escherichia coli* to human intestinal epithelial cells from mucosal biopsies. Infect Immun 44: 514–518

Knutton S, Lloyd DR, McNeish AS (1987) Identification of a new fimbrial structure in enterotoxigenic *Escherichia coli* (ETEC) serotype O148:H28 which adheres to human intestinal mucosa: a potentially new human ETEC colonization factor. Infect Immun 55: 86–92

Konisky J (1982) Colicins and other bacteriocins with established mode of action. Annu Rev Microbiol 36: 125–144

Leffler H, Svanborg-Eden C (1980) Chemical identification of a glycosphingolipid receptor for *Escherichia coli* attaching to human urinary tract epithelial cells and agglutinating human erythrocytes. FEMS Microbiol Lett 8: 127–134

Levine MM, Ristaino P, Marley G, Smythe C, Knutton S, Boedeker E, Black R, Young C, Clements ML, Cheney C, Patnaik R (1984) Coli surface antigens 1 and 3 of colonization factor antigen II-positive enterotoxigenic *Escherichia coli*: morphology, purification, and immune responses in humans. Infect Immun 44: 409–420

Manning PA, Higgins GD, Lumb R, Lanser JA (1987) Colonization factor antigens and a new fimbrial type, CFA/V, on O115:H40 and H-strains of enterotoxigenic *Escherichia coli* in Central Australia. J Infect Dis 156: 841–844

Murray BE, Evans DJ, Penaranda ME, Evans DG (1983) CFA/I-ST plasmids: comparison of enterotoxigenic *Escherichia coli* (ETEC) of serogroups O25, O63, O78, and O128 and mobilization from an R factor-containing epidemic ETEC isolate. J Bacteriol 153: 566–570

Orndorff PE (1987) Genetic study of piliation in *Escherichia coli*: implications for understanding microbe–host interactions at the molecular level. Pathol Immunopathol Res 6: 82–92

Orskov I, Orskov F (1966). Episome-carried surface antigen K88 of *Escherichia coli*. I. Transmission of the determinant of the K88 antigen and influence on the transfer of chromosomal markers. J Bacteriol 91: 69–75

Orskov I, Orskov F, Smith HW, Sojka WJ (1975) The establishment of K99, a thermolabile, transmissible, *Escherichia coli* K antigen, previously called "Kco", possessed by calf and lamb enterotoxigenic strains. Acta Pathol Microbiol Scand [B] 83: 31–36

Orskov F, Orskov I, Evans DJ, Sack RB, Sack FA, Wadstron T (1976) Special *Escherichia coli* serotypes among enterotoxigenic strains from diarrhoea in adults and children. Med Microiol Immunol (berl) 162: 73–80

Orskov I, Orskov F, Jan B, Jann K (1977) Serology, chemistry, and genetics of O and K antigen of *Escherichia coli*. Bacteriol Rev 41: 667–710

Orskov I, Birch-Anderson A, Duguid JP, Stenderup J, Orskov F (1985) An adhesive protein capsule of *Escherichia coli*. Infect Immun 47: 191–290

Penaranda ME, Evans DG, Murray BE, Evans DJ (1983) ST:LT:CFA/II plasmids in enterotoxigenic *Escherichia coli* belonging to serogroups O6, O8, O80, O85, and O139. J Bacteriol 154: 980–983

Pere A, Vaisanen-Rhen V, Rhen M, Tenhunen J, Korhonen TK (1986) Analysis of P fimbriae on *Escherichia coli* O2, O4, and O6 strains by immunoprecipitation. Infect Immun 51: 618–625

Rhen M, Klemm P, Korhonen TK (1986) Identification of two new hemagglutinins of *Escherichia coli*, N-acetyl-D-glucosamine-specific fimbriae and a blood group M-specific aglutinin, by cloning the corresponding genes in *Escherichia coli* K-12. J Bacteriol 168: 1234–1242

Robins-Browne RM (1987) Traditional enteropathogenic *Escherichia coli* of infantile diarrhea. Rev Infect Dis 9: 28–53

Rowe B, Gross R, Takeda Y (1983) Serotyping of enterotoxigenic *Escherichia coli* isolated from diarrhoeal travelers from various Asian countries. FEMS Microbiol Lett 20: 187–190

Sen D, Ganguly U, Saha MR, Bhattacharya SK, Datta P, Datta D, Mukherjee AK, Chakravarty R, Pal SC (1984) Studies on *Escherichia coli* as a cause of acute diarrhea in Calcutta. J Med Microbiol 17: 53–58

Smith HR, Cravioto A, Willshaw GA, McConnell MM, Scotland SM, Gross RJ, Rowe B (1979) A plasmid coding for the production of colonisation factor antigen I and heat-stable enterotoxin in strains of *Escherichia coli* of serogroup O78. FEMS Microbiol Lett 6: 255–260

Smith HW, Linggood MA (1971) Observations of the pathogenic properties of the K88, Hly and Ent plasmids of *Escherichia coli* with particular reference to porcine diarrhoea. J Med Microbiol 4: 467–485

Smythe CJ (1984) Serologically distinct fimbriae on enterotoxigenic *Escherichia coli* of serotype O6:K15:H16 or H-. FEMS Microbiol Lett 21: 51–57

Stoll BJ, Svennerholm A-M, Gothefors L, Baura D, Huda S, Holmgren J (1986) Local and systemic antibody responses to naturally acquired enterotoxigenic *Escherichia coli* diarrhea in an endemic area. J Infect Dis 153: 527–534

Svennerholm A-M, Gotherfors L, Sack DA, Bardhan PK, Holmgren J (1984) Local and systemic antibody responses and immunological memory in humans after immunization with cholera B subunit by different routes. Bull WHO 62: 909–918

Tacket CO, Maneval DR, Levine MM (1987) Purification, morphology, and genetics of a new fimbrial putative colonization factor of enterotoxigenic *Escherichia coli* O159:H4. Infect Immun 55: 1063–1069

Tamiya N, Yagi T (1985) Non-divergence theory of evolution: sequence comparison of some proteins from snakes and bacteria. J Biochem 98: 289–303

Thomas LV, Rowe B (1982) The occurrence of colonisation factors (CFA/I, CFA/II, and E8775) in enterotoxigenic *Escherichia coli* from various countries in South East Asia. Med Mcrobiol Immunol 171: 85–90

Thomas LV, Cravioto A, Scotland SM, Rowe B (1982) New fimbrial antigenic type (E8775) that may represent a colonization factor in enterotoxigenic *Escherichia coli* in humans. Infect Immun 35: 1119–1124

Thomas LV, McConnell MM, Rowe B, Field AM (1985) The possession of three novel coli surface antigens by enterotoxigenic *Escherichia coli* strains positive for the putative colonization factor PCF8775. J Gen Microbiol 131: 2319–2326

Vinal AC, Dallas WS (1987) Partition of heat-labile-enterotoxin genes between human and animal *Escherichia coli* isolates. Infect Immun 55: 1329–1331

Wadstrom T, Faris A, Freer J, Habte D, Hallberg D, Ljungh A (1980) Hydrophobic surface properties of enterotoxigenic *E. coli* (ETEC) with different colonization factors (CFA/I, CFA/II, K88 and K99) and attachment to intestinal epithelial cells. Scand J Infect Dis 24 (Suppl): 148–153

Yamamoto T, Nakazawa T, Miyata T, Kaji A, Yokota T (1984) Evolution and structure of two ADP-ribosylation enerotoxins, *Escherichia coli* heat-labile toxin and cholera toxin. FEBS Lett 169: 241–246

Colonization Factor Antigens of Enterotoxigenic *Escherichia coli* in Animals

H. W. MOON

1 Introduction

Colonization factor antigens probably play a critical role in the pathogenesis of most bacterial diseases. Such speculation is warranted because most bacterial infections arise from mucosal or cutaneous surfaces, and when such processes have been investigated the pathogens involved have been found to produce antigens that enable them to survive and multiply in the special environments at these surfaces. This implies that there are myriad colonization factor antigens that act at skin and mucosal surfaces and that have not yet been discovered. In some diseases, the bacterial pathogens (*Mycoplasma, Bordetella, Bacteroides, Campylobacter, Moraxella*, and *Clostridium*, as well as some strains of *Escherichia coli, Salmonella, Streptococcus*, and *Staphylococcus*) are characteristically confined to mucosae or skin and cause localized disease. In other diseases, the pathogens (*Pasteurella, Hemophilus*, and *Yersinia*, as well as some strains of *E. coli. Salmonella, Streptococcus*, and *Staphylococcus*) characteristically invade from mucosae to cause systemic disease. In both groups, subclinical carrier states, with bacteria in or on mucosae, maintain and disseminate the agent in the population. Clinical disease occurs less frequently than the carrier state, and results from opportunistic expansions in these localized bacterial populations (increased bacterial numbers leading to local disease or translocation and systemic infection).

U.S. Department of Agriculture, Agricultural Research Service, National Animal Disease Center, P.O. Box 70, Ames, Iowa, USA

Colonization depends on multiple host–bacterial interactions, and the pathogens have a constellation of attributes which act by different mechanisms to facilitate colonization. Adhesion to epithelial surfaces is one such attribute. Because adhesion is well recognized as critical to colonization by some pathogens, the antigens mediating adhesion are sometimes referred to as colonization factor antigens. This nomenclature is useful to the extent that it emphasizes the role of adhesion. It is misleading to the extent that it oversimplifies the colonization process by ignoring the probability that bacterial antigens that are not involved in adhesion are also necessary for colonization. The colonization factors of enterotoxigenic *E. coli* (ETEC) have been the focus of extensive multidisciplinary research during the last 20 years. As a result, they are comparatively well understood. This chapter will emphasize the adhesive interactions between the colonization factors of ETEC and the intestinal epithelium of their animal hosts. This will illustrate some of the principles involved in the colonization of mucosal surfaces in animals by bacterial pathogens.

2 Enterotoxigenic *Escherichia coli* of Calves and Pigs

Colonization of the small intestine by *E. coli* was recognized as a characteristic of a commonly occurring diarrheal disease in neonatal calves and pigs well before the discovery of *E. coli* enterotoxins or the fulfillment of Koch's postulates with ETEC. This abnormal colonization pattern was apparently the evidence that originally led to the hypothesis that the disease was caused by *E. coli*. The term colonization factor antigen (CFA) was originally applied to fimbriae (pili) of ETEC pathogenic for humans. The role of adhesive CFAs in ETEC infections of animals, and the molecular biology of the fimbrial CFAs, has been comprehensively reviewed (BRINTON et al. 1977; JONES and ISAACSON 1982; KORHONEN et al. 1985; GAASTRA and DE GRAAF 1982; ISAACSON 1985; KLEMM 1985; LEVINE et al. 1983; MOOI and DE GRAAF 1985; MOON et al. 1979b). This chapter presents the author's perspectives on the role of fimbriae and capsules in colonization of pig and calf small intestine by ETEC.

2.1 Fimbriae

Fimbrial CFA types known or suggested to facilitate adhesion and colonization by ETEC in the small intestine of pigs and calves are F1 (type 1), F4 (K88), F5 (K99), F6 (987P), F41, F42, and FY (Table 1).

The evidence that K88, K99, and 987P mediate adhesion in, and are required for colonization of, the small intestine by ETEC is convincing (reviewed, MOON et al. 1979b). For example, wild-type strains which bear one of these antigens adhere and colonize in the small intestine of the appropriate host, and also adhere to intestinal epithelial cells from such hosts in vitro. Isogenic derivatives of the wild-type strains

Table 1. Characteristics of known or putative fimbrial CFAs produced by ETEC isolated from animals

Antigen type	Colonization factor status	Morphology[a]	Hemag-glutinin	Location of genes	Host range of ETEC
F4 or K88	Known	Fine[b] Irregular[c]	Mannose-resistant	Plasmid	Pigs
F5 or K99	Known	Fine Irregular	Mannose-resistant	Plasmid	Calves, lambs, Pigs, mice
F6 or 987P	Known	Thick Straight	None	Chromosome	Pigs
F1 or type 1	Putative	Thick Straight	Mannose-sensitive	Chromosome	Animals, humans
F41	Putative	Fine Irregular	Mannose-resistant	Chromosome	Calves, lambs, Pigs, mice
F42	Putative	Thick Straight	Mannose-resistant	Unknown	Pigs
FY	Putative	Fine	Unknown	Unknown	Calves

[a] See Fig. 1;
[b] Diameter < 7 nm (Fig. 1A);
[c] Frequently kinked or curled (Fig. 1A).

which no longer bear these antigens (via mutation, loss of plasmid, or phase variation) lack the adhesive and colonizing attributes of the wild-type strains. The adhesive and colonizing attributes of K88 and K99 ETEC are transferred to suitable *E. coli* hosts along with K88 or K99 plamids. K88, K99, or 987P antibody inhibits adhesion and colonization in an antigen-specific fashion. The evidence that the other (putative) CFAs listed in Table 1 play a critical role in colonization of the small intestine by ETEC is less convincing than that for K88, K99, and 987P, and will be discussed in more detail.

2.1.1 F41 Fimbriae

F41 (Fig. 1A) was recognized more recently and has been less fully characterized than K88, K99, and 987P; in addition its role in colonization has been less well defined. Although F41 was originally referred to as anionic K99 (MORRIS et al. 1978, 1980), F41 is now recognized to be physically, antigenically, and genetically distinct from K99 (CHANTER 1982, 1983; ISAACSON 1985; MORRIS et al. 1982, 1983; MOSELEY et al. 1986; TO 1984). It is also distinct from K88, although the chromosomal genetic determinant for production of F41 has some sequence homology with the plasmid-born determinant for K88 (MOSELEY et al. 1986). Most F41[+] ETEC belong to serogroups O9 and O101, and produce K99 as well as F41. Several of the strains originally designated as K99[+] and used in experiments to define the role of K99 in colonization (MOON et al. 1977; SMITH and LINGGOOD 1972) were subsequently shown to produce F41 in addition to K99 (MORRIS et al. 1980). Nevertheless, the conclusions about the role of K99 drawn from those experiments are valid because they are based, in part, on K99[+] strains which do not produce F41 and on the effects of curing or transferring the K99 plasmid (SMITH 1976). The fact that K99-facilitated colonization can occur independent of F41 makes it difficult to assess the role of F41 in colonization by K99[+] F41[+] ETEC. Most evidence in this regard is based on

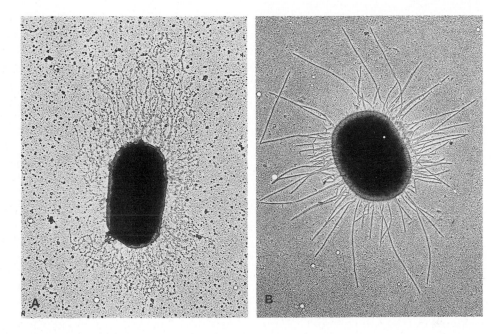

Fig. 1A, B. Electron micrographs of fimbriated *E. coli* (courtesy of Dr. S.M. To). The specimens were prepared for examination by rotary shadowing with platinum (magnification approximately × 28 000). **A** F41 fimbriae, to illustrate the fine irregular morphology characteristic of some fimbriae. **B** Type 1 fimbriae, to illustrate the thick straight morphology characteristic of some fimbriae

the use of phenotypic variant K99$^-$ F41$^+$ ETEC strains (Morris et al. 1983) which carry the gene for K99 (Moseley et al. 1986) but do not express the antigen. However, the possibility that these K99$^-$ F41$^+$ variants produce still another unrecognized fimbrial colonization factor cannot be excluded.

On the one hand, there is strong suggestive evidence that F41 can mediate colonization by adhesion. A K99$^-$ F41$^+$ ETEC strain has been shown to adhere to calf intestinal epithelial cells in vitro (Morris et al. 1982). In vitro adhesion is competitively inhibited by isolated F41 antigen and prevented by growing the bacteria at 18°C to inhibit expression of F41 (and other fimbriae). Both K99$^+$ F41$^+$ and K99$^-$ F41$^+$ ETEC adhere, colonize, and produce F41 antigen in the small intestine of pigs and calves during disease (Morris et al. 1982; Runnels et al. 1987). Vaccination with F41 antigen protects pigs against colonization with K99$^-$ F41$^+$ ETEC (Runnels et al. 1987). Although infant mice are not known to be natural hosts for ETEC infections, they are susceptible to colonization by adhesion and the resultant fatal diarrhea following oral inoculation with K99$^+$ F41$^+$ ETEC (Duchet-Suchaux 1983; Nagy and Ushe 1985). A K99$^-$ F41$^+$ variant ETEC strain was shown to be virulent in infant mice, while a K99$^-$ F41$^-$ derivative from it was not (Bertin 1985).

On the other hand, the preponderance of evidence suggests that F41 is currently of minor importance or practical significance in naturally occurring disease. F41 is less prevalent than K88, K99, or 987P and is usually accompanied by K99 (Morris et al. 1980; Moseley et al. 1986). The few strains originally characterized as naturally

occurring, virulent 3P⁻ or F41 only ETEC (Awad-Masalmeh et al. 1982; Moon et al. 1980), were subsequently shown to carry the K99 gene, even though they do not express it in vitro or in vivo (Moseley et al. 1986). It seems likely that these strains may have expressed K99 at the time of their original isolation and lost that ability during growth in the laboratory. Thus, in naturally occurring disease, most ETEC that produce F41 apparently have redundant fimbrial adhesins (both F41 and K99) to facilitate colonization of the small intestine. In theory, if one of these redundant adhesins is blocked by antibody, then colonization and disease would still result based on adhesion mediated by the other. However, pregnant swine and cattle given purified fimbrial vaccines containing K99 but not F41, protected their suckling newborn pigs (Morgan et al. 1978) and calves (Acres et al. 1979) against challenge with ETEC strains 431 and B44, respectively. Both these strains are now known to produce F41 in addition to K99 (Morris et al. 1980; Runnels et al. 1987). Furthermore, monoclonal antibody against K99 can protect calves and pigs against challenge with the F41⁺ K99⁺ ETEC strains B44 and B41 (Sadowski et al. 1983; Sherman et al. 1983).

Thus, as a practical matter, K99 vaccines can be used to potect against strains that produce both adhesins. There are no known antigenic cross-reactions between F41 and K99. This suggests that vaccine-induced protection acts by mechanisms in addition to or other than, combining directly with the sites on fimbriae that mediate adhesion. Alternatively, there may be some unrecognized antigenic relatedness between F41 and K99, or K99 may be more important or critical to colonization than is F41.

The observation that vaccination with F41 protected pigs against challenge with a K99⁻ F41⁺ ETEC strain, but not against challenge with the K99⁺ F41⁺ ETEC strain 431 (Runnels et al. 1987), is consistent with the notion that K99 is more important than F41 for colonization by strain 431. However, we have recently found that variants of strains 431 that have lost the gene for K99 (Mainil et al. 1987) still carry the gene for and produce F41 and are still virulent for newborn pigs (T.A. Casey and H.W. Moon, unpublished material). Furthermore, F41 is apparently at least as important as K99 in the virulence of K99⁺ F41⁺ ETEC for infant mice and, in contrast to our experience with pigs, vaccination with F41 was more effective than vaccination with K99 in protecting infant mice against K99⁺ F41⁺ ETEC (Duchet-Suchaux 1988). Obviously, more definitive data are needed on the role of F41 in colonization and on the relative importance of K99 and F41 in disease caused by ETEC that produce both antigens. Although F41 may currently be of minor importance, as suggested above, theoretically F41 has the potential to become highly important under the selection pressure of vaccines or other factors directed against K99.

2.1.2 Type 1 Fimbriae

The comparatively thick and straight (Fig. 1B), chromosomally encoded fimbriae which cause mannose-sensitive hemagglutination (MSHA) and are subject to phase variation are designated as type 1 (F1 or common pili). The question as to whether or not type 1 fimbriae are involved in the pathogenesis of ETEC infection is controversial (Brinton et al. 1977, 1983; Karch et al. 1987). The predominance of

the evidence suggests that they are not. Most *E. coli* (pathogens and nonpathogens) produce type 1 fimbriae. In contrast to the other fimbriae listed in Table 1, type 1 is at least as prevalent among non-ETEC as it is among ETEC. Most animal ETEC probably have the capacity to produce type 1 in addition to one or more of the other fimbriae listed in Table 1. However, our results indicate that ETEC which have the capacity to produce type 1 fimbriae in vitro may not produce them in the small intestine during disease (To et al. 1984). The relatively low prevalence of type 1 fimbriae found in surveys of porcine ETEC also suggests that most isolates are in the type 1 negative phase when isolated from the intestine of diseased pigs (Truszczynski and Osek 1987; Wilson and Francis 1986).

However, type 1 fimbriae can mediate adhesion of type 1 positive phase *E. coli* to isolated porcine intestinal epithelial cells in vitro (Isaacson et al. 1978). Furthermore, pigs inoculated orally with ETEC, in the type 1 positive phase, had bacteria bearing type 1 antigen adherent to their intestinal villi 9 h later (Jayappa et al. 1985). One possible explanation for the conflicting reports might be variation among type 1 fimbriae of ETEC (Adegbola and Old 1987; De Graaf and Klassen 1987; Duguid 1985). It has been concluded (based substantially on unpublished data) that there are at least 12 different serotypes in the *E. coli* "type 1 pilus family" (Jayappa et al. 1983). The type 1$^+$ (MSHA) ETEC strain M8 colonizes pig small intestine, while a type 1$^-$ variant derived from it does not (Nakazawa et al. 1986). Strain M8 was subsequently found (E.A. Dean and H.W. Moon, unpublished material) to produce 987P antigen in pig small intestine in vivo. Workers in another laboratory (Broes et al. 1988) found several porcine ETEC strains that caused MSHA and reacted with antisera against both type 1 and 987P fimbriae. It is not known if such strains produce two fimbrial antigens (type 1 and 987P) or variants of type 1 which react with polyclonal 987P antiserum. Nor is it known if impaired colonization by the variant of M8 is due to impaired expression of the type 1 antigen, the 987P antigen, or some other defect. Type 1 and 987P fimbrial antigens share some epitopes (Abraham et al. 1986). However, cross-reactions are not detected in routine serologic tests using polyclonal antisera.

Type 1 and 987P fimbriae appear to be more closely related to each other than to the other fimbriae listed in Table 1. Both are chromosomally encoded and subject to phase variation. They are morphologically identical and have similar physical–chemical properties. They differ in amino acid composition, peptide subunit size, hexosamine content, receptor specificity, and hemagglutinating capability, as well as in antigenicity (Brinton et al. 1977; Dean and Isaacson 1985; Isaacson 1985; Isaacson and Richter 1981). Epidemiologically, type 1 fimbriae are ubiquitous, while 987P is confined to porcine ETEC. 987P fimbriae apparently also differ from the type 1 fimbriae on most *E. coli* in the tendency of 987P$^+$ strains to enter, or be selected for, the fimbriate phase during growth in porcine small intestine. Perhaps 987P and type 1 fimbriae are closely related phylogenetically and intermediates exist, but have not been recognized to be intermediates.

2.1.3 *FY, F42, and Others*

Some *E. coli* from diarrheal calves in Europe (Contrepois et al. 1982) and the United Kingdon (Morris et al. 1985) produce the fimbrial adhesin provisionally

designated as FY or Att 25. FY commonly occurs along with K99 on calf ETEC in this region. The prevalence of FY in other regions of the world or among *E. coli* from other hosts is not known. In addition to ETEC, the enteropathogenic (nonenterotoxigenic, attaching and effacing) calf *E. coli* strain X114/83 has been shown to produce FY (HALL et al. 1988). Although the role (if any) of FY in colonization has not been defined, FY is suspected to facilitate colonization. There is evidence that when combined with K99 and F41 antibodies, FY antibody adds to the protection of calves against challenge with a K99$^+$ F41$^+$ FY$^+$ ETEC strain (CONTREPOIS and GIRARDEAU 1985).

Some porcine ETEC from pigs in Brazil produce fimbriae that are distinct from the others in Table 1 and are provisionally designated as F42. YANO et al (1986) demonstrated that F42 mediates mannose-resistant hemagglutination and adhesion to brush borders from porcine intestinal epithelial cells in vitro. They hypothesized that F42 may function as an adhesive colonization factor. However, data on the colonizing abilities of F42$^+$ ETEC and the role of F42 in the small intestine during ETEC infection are not yet available.

ETEC from calves and pigs produce fimbriae in addition to those listed in Table 1 (ANING and THOMLINSON 1983; CONTREPOIS et al. 1982; FAIRBROTHER et al. 1988; GIRARDEAU et al. 1988). One of them, designated CS31A, appears to be associated with bacteremia rather than intestinal colonization (GIRARDEAU et al. 1988). Furthermore, it seems likely that many such "new" or currently unrecognized fimbriae exist. Most of them can probably mediate adhesion in vitro, because adhesion occurs via both hydrophobic and receptor-mediated interactions. Some of the receptors or their analogues [i.e., mannose for type 1 and sialic acid for K99 (LINDAHL et al. 1987; MOURICOUT and JULIEN 1987; SMIT et al. 1984)] are widely distributed in animal cells. However, experience with K88 (below) demonstrates that, at least for some fimbriae, hydrophobic interactions or interactions with receptor analogues is not sufficient, and that colonization requires highly specific receptors. The experience with type 1 and 987P fimbriae (above) illustrates that, in addition to adhesive capability, in vivo expression of the fimbriae (or selection for the bacterial cells which bear them) is also a critical determinant as to which types of fimbriae facilitate colonization. Economic importance of a specific CFA is also dependent on its prevalence, and probably on whether or not it is redundant (usually accompanied by another CFA). Thus, as a practical matter, at present the diagnostic tests and vaccines based on K88, K99, and 987P are globally adequate for ETEC infections in calves and neonatal pigs. It seems reasonable to expect that other fimbriae will become practically important in time because of immunity, genetic change in livestock populations, or management practices which tend to select for alternative fimbriae or against those that predominate at present.

2.1.4 Host Specificity

The host specificity of ETEC is largely determined by fimbrial CFAs. Naturally occurring disease caused by K88$^+$ and 987$^+$ ETC is essentially confined to pigs. Humans are not susceptible to colonization by K88$^+$ ETEC, even following experimental challenge (DUPONT et al. 1971). Some pigs are genetically susceptible to colonization by K88$^+$ ETEC, and others are genetically resistant (GIBBONS et al.

1977). Genetic susceptibility depends on receptors for K88 on the brush borders of epithelial cells in the small intestine (SELLWOOD 1980). The occurrence of the receptors is controlled by an autosomal dominant gene(s). K88 antigens consist of a constant determinant designated as a, and variable determinants designated as b, c, and d (GUINÉE and JANSEN 1979). Adhesion of K88$^+$ ETEC to the K88-specific receptors on pig intestinal epithelial cell brush borders depends on the variable determinants. Some pigs are susceptible to adhesion by all three subtypes of K88 fimbriae (K88ab, K88ac, and K88ad), some are only susceptible to one or two subtypes, and some are resistant to all three subtypes of K88 (BIJLSMA et al. 1982, 1984; RAPACZ and HASLER-RAPACZ 1986). Thus, the pathogenicity of K88$^+$ ETEC in swine requires highly specific brush border receptors for K88. Furthermore, in vitro tests for these receptors correlate with the susceptibility of the pigs to disease, provided that the tests are conducted under the appropriate conditions (SELLWOOD 1980; SARMIENTO et al. 1988). Thus, as a practical matter, disease caused by K88$^+$ ETEC is narrowly restricted to those genotypes of swine that produce the appropriate subtypes of brush border receptors. The receptors are probably galactosyl-containing residues of glycoproteins (ANDERSON et al. 1980; SELLWOOD 1980).

There is reason to think that genetic intraspecies regulation of susceptibility to ETEC, based on the availability of receptors for fimbriae, extends beyond K88. SMITH and HALLS (1968) found that pigs from an inbred herd were susceptible to colonization by an O141:K85ac strain of ETEC, but that pigs from other herds were not. They suggested that the intestinal epithelium of the pigs in the inbred herd was genetically predisposed to adhesion by ETEC. The O141:K85ac ETEC strain used did not produce K88. However, the nature of the fimbriae that were produced by the strain (if any) was not determined.

In contrast to the specificity required for pathogenicity in swine, under some in vitro conditions K88 mediates adhesion to a variety of cells and cell products. These include erythrocytes from several species, buccal epithelial cells, intestinal epithelial cells from several species, intestinal mucus from mice, brush borders from mouse intestinal epithelial cells, and even from K88-resistant pigs (COX and HOUVENAGHEL 1987; JONES and RUTTER 1974; LAUX et al. 1986; PARRY and PORTER 1978; RUNNELS et al. 1980; SELLWOOD 1980; TZIPORI et al. (1984)). It is not known whether such interactions are mediated by the hydrophobicity of K88, by interactions with analogues to the specific receptor (which exists in the brush border of susceptible pigs), or by other mechanisms.

K88 mediated hemagglutination of porcine erythrocytes does not depend on the receptors that are required for adhesion to intestinal brush borders (COX and HOUVENAGHEL 1987). Thus, hemagglutination tests do not detect the genetically susceptible and resistant pigs. There is suggestive evidence that K88 can facilitate colonization in neonatal mice (DAVIDSON and HIRSH 1975; KÉTYI et al. 1978). The studies cited are based on clearance of K88$^+$ ETEC from the intestine but do not report directly on either adhesion or number of ETEC in the small intestine. Intestinal transit is comparatively sluggish in neonatal mice, and clearance of bacteria from their small intestine is markedly influenced by the ambient temperature (MOON et al. 1979a). These variables may have influenced the results in the

reports cited. Thus, the relevance of the mouse model for K88 mediated adhesion and colonization is unknown. Apparently, horses are resistant to colonization by K88$^+$ ETEC, even though K88 does mediate adhesion to their small intestinal brush borders in vitro (TZIPORI et al. 1984). Perhaps this is because the brush borders do not contain sufficient (qualitatively or quantitatively) receptors to facilitate colonization in vivo.

In contrast to the narrow host species ranges characteristic of K88$^+$ and 987P$^+$ ETEC, K99$^+$ and K99$^+$ F41$^+$ ETEC intensively colonize the small intestines of pigs, calves, lambs, and mice (BERTIN 1985; DUCHET-SUCHAUX 1983; MOON et al. 1977, 1979a; MORRIS et al. 1983; NAGY and USHE 1985; SMITH and HUGGINS 1978). However, the host specificity of K99$^+$ and K99$^+$ F41$^+$ ETEC is sharply age restricted (SMITH and HALLS 1967; reviewed, MOON and RUNNELS 1984; WILSON and FRANCIS 1986). Pigs commonly develop ETEC-induced diarrhea during the immediate neonatal period (< 1 week old) and after weaning ($\geqslant$ 3 weeks old). K88$^+$ ETEC cause disease in both age groups, but K99$^+$ ETEC are confined to the immediate neonatal period. Calves and lambs infrequently develop ETEC-induced diarrhea after the immediate neonatal period. K99$^+$ ETEC, which rapidly colonize and cause fatal diarrhea following inoculation into neonatal calves and pigs, do not colonize or cause disease when given to 1-week-old calves or pigs. There are probably several factors that contribute to this innate age-dependent resistance of calves and pigs to K99$^+$ ETEC (reviewed by MOON and RUNNELS 1984). Age-dependent resistance is apparently due in part to decreased availability of epithelial cell receptors for K99 with age, in that K99$^+$ ETEC (now known to be K99$^+$ F41$^+$) adhere to epithelial cells from 1-day-old pigs, calves, and mice in greater numbers than to epithelial cells from older animals of the same species (RUNNELS et al. 1980).

Age restriction is also characteristic of 987P$^+$ ETEC, in that they are also commonly associated with diarrhea in neonatal pigs, but infrequently associated with diarrhea in pigs after weaning (WILSON and FRANCIS 1986). Experimentally, a strain of 987P$^+$ ETEC that adheres and colonizes intensively and causes fatal disease in neonatal pigs does not colonize or cause diarrhea in 3-week-old pigs (DEAN et al. 1987). In this case, development of resistance with age to 987P$^+$ ETEC does not correlate with decreased availability of brush border receptors [probably galactose or fucose-containing residues of glycoproteins (DEAN and ISAACSON 1985)], in that 987P$^+$ ETEC adhere equally well to brush borders isolated from intestinal epithelial cells from neonatal or 3-week-old pigs. In neonates, 987P$^+$ bacteria appear to adhere directly to epithelium, leaving comparatively few bacteria free in the intestinal lumen (NAGY et al. 1977). In contrast, in 3-week-old pigs, 987P$^+$ bacteria tend to be associated with the mucus and cellular debris in the intestinal lumen (DEAN et al. 1987). One of the hypotheses proposed in explanation was that 987P receptors remain bound to epithelial cells in the neonate, but are released from the epithelium and trapped by mucus in older pigs. Receptors in mucus would then hypothetically compete with those bound to the epithelial cells and protect the older pigs from colonization by 987P$^+$ ETEC.

In addition to the host species specificity, specificity for some genotypes within a host species, and host age specificity, fimbriae also contribute to the site specificity of ETEC. For example, K88$^+$ ETEC colonize throughout the small intestine in

1984). It has been suggested that capsules act by stabilizing or maintaining the in vivo adhesion initiated by fimbriae, or protect the bacteria from antibody, serum factors, or phagocytes in the intestinal lumen (CHAN et al. 1982). Capsular antigens can be protective in vaccines to provide passive immunity of sucklings against ETEC infection (MOON and RUNNELS 1983). Some commercial vaccines include both capsular and fimbrial CFAs. The potential value of capsular antigens in vaccines is limited because many ETEC do not produce capsules and because there are many different capsular antigen types among encapsulated ETEC (ØRSKOV and ØRSKOV 1972, 1978).

3 Concluding Comments

Adhesion mediated by fimbriae is thought to be an essential step in most bacterial infections that arise from mucosal surfaces in animals. This is best understood in ETEC infections. A single CFA (K99) predominates globally among ETEC afflicting calves, while three CFAs (K88, K99, and 987P) predominate globally among those afflicting neonatal pigs. These predominant CFAs are routinely and effectively used as the basis for diagnostic tests and vaccines (to stimulate passive lacteal immunity) to control ETEC infections in suckling neonatal calves and pigs. In addition to these currently predominant CFA types, most ETEC probably produce other fimbriae, and there may be myriad fimbrial antigens among ETEC. There is good evidence that some of these additional or currently less recognized or less prevalent fimbriae (F41, F42, FY, type 1 variants, and others) can also mediate adhesion and facilitate colonization in the intestine of calves and pigs. Thus, current control measures based on the predominant CFA types could conceivably be short-lived, due to vaccine-induced selection pressure. It is argued that this is unlikely to be a major limitation, because such selection pressure has existed in nature for a long time, and yet only a few CFA types predominate. There appear to be unrecognized factors that tend to favor or select for K88, K99, and 987P. Intraspecies genetic regulation of K88 receptor occurrence indicates that K88 infections could be prevented by selective breeding in swine. However, this has not come into practical use because of the technical problems in identification of resistant breeding stock and because K88-resistant pigs still have receptors for K99 and 987P.

In contrast to the situation with the neonatal disease, the current understanding of CFAs has not yet contributed significantly to the control of the ETEC infections that occur in swine after weaning. Existing knowledge of CFAs and related technology can probably be extended to allow control of the disease in these older animals as well. Inhibition of CFA-facilitated colonization via active local immunity, or by feeding analogues of fimbrial CFAs or analogues of their receptors, and genetic selection for swine lacking receptors for CFAs are attractive approaches for research toward that goal.

Acknowledgment. The author thanks Dr S.M. To for the electron micrographs used in Fig. 1.

References

Abraham SN, Schifferli DM, Banks D, Beachey EH (1986) Immunological cross-reactivity between type 1 and 987P fimbriae of *Escherichia coli*. Abstracts, 86th annual meeting of the American Society of Microbiologists, p 84

Acres SD (1985) Enterotoxigenic *Escherichia coli* infections in newborn calves: a review. J Dairy Sci 68: 229–256

Acres SD, Isaacson RA, Babiuk LA, Kapitany RA (1979) Immunization of calves against enterotoxigenic colibacillosis by vaccinating dams with purified K99 antigen and whole cell bacterins. Infect Immun 25: 121–126

Adegbola RA, Old DC (1987) Antigenic relationships among type-1 fimbriae of enterobacteriaceae revealed by immunoelectronmicroscopy. J Med Microbiol 24: 21–28

Anderson MJ, Whitehead JS, Kim YS (1980) Interaction of *Escherichia coli* K88 antigen with porcine intestinal brush border membranes. Infect Immun 29: 897–901

Aning KG, Thomlinson JR (1983) Adhesion factor distinct from K88, K99, F41, 987P, CFAI and CFAII in porcine *Escherichia coli*. Vet Rec 112: 251

Awad-Masalmeh M, Moon HW, Runnels PL, Schneider RA (1982) Pilus production, hemagglutination, and adhesion by procine strains of enterotoxigenic *Escherichia coli* lacking K88, K99, and 987P antigens. Infect Immun 35: 305–313

Bertin A (1985) F41 antigen as a virulence factor in the infant mouse model of *Escherichia coli* diarrhoea. J Gen Microbiol 131: 3037–3045

Bijlsma IGW, De Nijs A, Van Der Meer C, Frik JF (1982) Different pig phenotypes affect adherence of *Escherichia coli* to jejunal brush borders by K88ab, K88ac, or K88ad antigen. Infect Immun 37: 891–894

Bijlsma IGW, De Nijs A, Frik JF (1984) Serological variants of *Escherichia coli* K88 antigen: differences in adhesion and haemagglutination. Rev Sci Tech Off Int Epiz 3: 871–879

Brinton CC, Fusco P, To AC-C, To SC-M (1977) The piliation phase syndrome and the uses of purified pili in disease control. Proc XIIIth US-Japan conference on cholera, Atlanta, Georgia, National Institute of Health, Sept 19–21, pp 33–70

Brinton CC, Fusco P, Wood S, Jayappa HG, Goodnow RA, Strayer RG (1983) A complete vaccine for neonatal swine colibacillosis and the prevalence of *Escherichia coli* pilli on swine isolates. Vet Med Small Anim Clin 78: 962–966

Broes A, Fairbrother JM, Lariviére S, Jacques M, Johnson WM (1988) Virulence properties of enterotoxigenic *Escherichia coli* O8:KX105 strains isolated from diarrheic piglets. Infect Immun 56: 241–246

Chan R, Acres SD, Costerton JW (1982) Use of specific antibody to demonstrate glycocalyx, K99 pili, and the spatial relationships of K99$^+$ enterotoxigenic *Escherichia coli* in the ileum of colostrum-fed calves. Infect Immun 37: 1170–1180

Chanter N (1982) Structural and functional differences of the anionic and cationic antigens in K99 extracts of *Escherichia coli* B41. J Gen Microbiol 128: 1585–1589

Chanter N (1983) Partial purification and characterization of two non K99 mannose-resistant haemagglutinins of *Escherichia coli* B41. J Gen Microbiol 129: 235–243

Contrepois MG, Girardeau J-P (1985) Additive protective effects of colostral antipili antibodies in calves experimentally infected with enterotoxigenic *Escherichia coli*. Infect Immun 50: 947–949

Contrepois M, Girardeau JP, Gouet P, Desmattre P (1982) Vaccination contre L'antigene K99 et D'autres "adhesines" des *Escherichia coli* bovins. Proc XIIth World congress on diseases of cattle, Sept 7–10, Amsterdam, NL, pp 332–338

Cox E, Houvenaghel A (1987) In vitro adhesion of K88ab-, K88ac-, and K88ad-positive *Escherichia coli* to intestinal villi, to buccal cells and to erythrocytes of weaned piglets. Vet Microbiol 15: 201–207

Davidson JN, Hirsh DC (1975) Use of the K88 antigen for in vivo bacterial competition with porcine strains of enteropathogenic *Escherichia coli*. Infect Immun 12: 134–136

Dean EA, Isaacson RE (1985) Purification and characterization of a receptor for the 987P pilus of *Escherichia coli*. Infect Immun 47: 98–105

Dean EA, Whipp SC, Moon HW (1987) The role of epithelial receptors for 987P pili in age-specific intestinal colonization by enterotoxigenic *Escherichia coli*. In: Sack RB, Zinnaka Y (eds) Advances in research on cholera and related diarrheas. Proc US-Japan conference on cholera, Williamsburg, VA, Nov 9–12, 1987. KTK Scientific, Tokyo

De Graaf FK, Klaasen P (1987) Nucleotide sequence of the gene encoding the 987P fimbrial subunit of *Escherichia coli*. FEMS Microbiol Lett 42: 253–258

Dougan G, Morrissey P (1984/85) Molecular analysis of the virulence determinants of enterotoxigenic

Escherichia coli isolated from domestic animals: applications for vaccine development. Vet Microbiol 10: 241–257

Duchet-Suchaux M (1983) Infant mouse model of *E. coli* diarrhoea: clinical protection induced by vaccination of the mothers. Ann Rech Vet 14: 319–331

Duchet-Suchaux M (1988) Protective antigens against enterotoxigenic *Escherichia coli* O101:K99, F41 in the infant mouse diarrhea model. Infect Immun 56: 1364–1370

Duguid JP (1985) Antigens of type-1 fimbriae. In: Stewart-Tull DES, Davis M (eds) Immunology of the bacterial cell envelope. Wiley, New York, chap 11, pp 301–318

DuPont HL, Formal SB, Hornick RB, Snyder MJ, Libonati JP, Sheahan DG, LaBrec EH, Kalas JP (1971) Pathogenesis of *Eschericha coli* diarrhea. New Engl J Med 285: 3–11

Evans DG, Graham DY, Evans DJ, Opekun A (1984) Administration of purified colonization factor antigens (CFA/I, CFA/II) of enterotoxigenic *Escherichia coli* to volunteers. Gastroenterology 87: 934–940

Fairbrother JM, Lariviere S, Johnson WM (1988) Prevalence of fimbrial antigens and enterotoxins in nonclassical serogroups of *Escherichia coli* isolated from newborn pigs with diarrhea. Am J Vet Res 49: 1325–1328

Francis DH, Wilson RA (1985) Concurrent infection of pigs with enterotoxigenic *Escherichia coli* of different serogroups. J Clin Microbiol 22: 457–458

Gaastra W, De Graaf FK (1982) Host-specific fimbrial adhesins of noninvasive enterotoxigenic *Escherichia coli* strains. Microbiol Rev 46: 129–161

Gibbons RA, Sellwood R, Burrows M, Hunter PA (1977) Inheritance of resistance to neonatal *E. coli* diarrhoea in the pig: examination of the genetic system. Theor Appl Genet 51: 65–70

Girardeau JP, der Vertanian M, Ollier JL, Contrepois M (1988) CS31A, a new K88-related fimbrial antigen on bovine enterotoxigenic and septicemic *Escherichia coli* strains. Infect Immun 56: 2180–2188

Guinée PAM, Jansen WH (1979) Behavior of *Escherichia coli* K antigens K88ab, K88ac, and K88ad in immunoelectrophoresis, double diffusion, and hemagglutination. Infect Immun 23: 700–705

Hadad JJ, Gyles CL (1982) The role of K antigens of enteropathogenic *Escherichia coli* in colonization of the small intestine of calves. Can J Comp Med 46: 21–26

Hall GA, Chanter N, Bland AP (1988) Comparison in gnotobiotic pigs of lesions caused by verotoxigenic and non-verotoxigenic *Escherichia coli*. Vet Pathol 25: 205–210

Isaacson RE (1985) Pili of enterotoxigenic *Escherichia coli* from pigs and calves. Adv Exp Med Biol 185: 83–99

Isaacson RE, Richter P (1981) *Escherichia coli* 987P pilus: purification and partial characterization. J Bacteriol 146: 784–789

Isaacson RE, Fusco PC, Brinton CC, Moon HW (1978) In vitro adhesion of *Escherichia coli* to porcine small intestinal epithelian cells: pili as adhesive factors. Infect Immun 21: 392–397

Isaacson RE, Dean EA, Morgan RL, Moon HW (1980) Immunization of suckling pigs against enterotoxigenic *Escherichia coli*-induced diarrheal disease by vacinating dams with purified K99 or 987P pili: antibody production in response to vaccination. Infect Immun 29: 824–826

Jayappa HG, Strayer JG, Goodnow RA, Fusco PC, Wood SW, Haneline P, Cho H-J, Brinton CC (1983) Experimental infection and field trial evaluations of a multiple-pilus phase-cloned bacterin for the simultaneous control of neonatal colibacillosis and mastitis in swine. Proceedings 4th Int symp on neonatal diarrhea, Vet Infect Disease Organization, University of Saskatchewan, Canada, Oct 3–5, pp 518–535

Jayappa HG, Goodnow RA, Geary SJ (1985) Role of *Escherichia coli* type 1 pilus in colonization of porcine ileum and its protective nature as a vaccine antigen in controlling colibacillosis. Infect Immun 48: 350–354

Jones GW, Isaacson RE (1982) Proteinaceous bacterial adhesins and their receptors. CRC Crit Rev Microbiol 10(3): 229–260

Jones GW, Rutter JM (1974) The association of K88 antigen with haemagglutinating activity in porcine strains of *Escherichia coli*. J Gen Microbiol 84: 135–144

Karch H, Heesemann J, Laufs R, Kroll H-P, Kaper JB, Levine MM (1987) Serological response to type 1-like somatic fimbriae in diarrheal infection due to classical enteropathogenic *Escherichia coli*. Microb Pathog 2: 425–434

Kétyi I, Kuch B, Vertényi A (1978) Stability of *Escherichia coli* adhesive factors K88 and K99 in mice. Acta Microbiol Acad Sci Hung 25: 77–86

Klemm P (1985) Fimbrial adhesins of *Escherichia coli*. Rev Infect Dis 7: 321–340

Korhonen TK, Rhen M, Vaisanen-Rhen V, Pere A (1985) Antigenic and functional properties of enterobacterial fimbriae. In: Stewart-Tull DES, Davies M (eds) Immunology of the bacterial cell envelope. Wiley, New York, pp 319–354

Larsen JL (1976) Differences between enteropathogenic *Escherichia coli* strains isolated from neo-natal *E. coli* diarrhoea (N.C.D.) and post weaning diarrhoea (P.W.D) in pigs. Nord Vet Med 28: 417–429

Laux DC, McSweegan EF, Williams TJ, Wadolkowski EA, Cohen PS (1986) Identification and characterization of mouse small intestine mucosal receptors for *Escherichia coli* K-12(K88ab). Infect Immun 52: 18–25

Levine MM, Kaper JB, Black RE, Clements ML (1983) New knowledge on pathogenesis of bacterial enteric infections as applied to vaccine development. Microbiol Rev 47: 510–550

Levine MM, Ristaino P, Marley G, Smyth C, Knutton S, Boedeker E, Black R, Young C, Clements ML, Cheney C, Patnaik R (1984) Coli surface antigens 1 and 3 of colonization factor antigen II-positive enterotoxigenic *Escherichia coli*: morphology, purification, and immune responses in humans. Infect Immun 44: 409–420

Lindahl M, Brossmer R, Wadstrom T (1987) Carbohydrate receptor specificity of K99 fimbriae of enterotoxigenic *Escherichia coli*. Glycoconjugate 4: 51–58

Linggood MA, Porter P (1981) The antibody-mediated elimination of adhesion determinant from enteropathogenic strains of *Escherichia coli*. In: Berkeley RCW, Lynch JM, Melling J, Rutter PR, Vincent B (eds) Microbial adhesion to surfaces. Horwood, Chichester, chap 24, pp 441–453

Mainil JG, Sadowski PL, Tarsio M, Moon HW (1987) In vivo emergence on enterotoxigenic *Escherichia coli* variants lacking genes for K99 fimbriae and heat-stable enterotoxin. Infect Immun 55: 3111–3116

Mooi FR, De Graaf FK (1985) Molecular biology of fimbriae of enterotoxigenic *Escherichia coli*. In: Goebel W (ed) Genetic approaches to microbiol pathogenicity. Springer, Berlin Heidelberg New York, pp 119–138 (Current topics in microbiology and immunology, vol 118)

Moon HW (1978) Pili as protective antigens in vaccines for the control of enterotoxigenic *Escherichia coli* infections. Proceedings, 2nd Intl symp on neonatal diarrhea, Vet Infect Disease Organization, University of Saskatchewan, Canada, Oct 3–5, pp 393–410

Moon HW (1981) Protection against enteric colibacillosis in pigs suckling orally vaccinated dams: evidence for pili as protective antigens. Am J Vet Res 42: 173–177

Moon HW, Runnels PL (1981) Prospects for development of a vaccine against diarrhea caused by *Escherichia coli*. In: Tholme T, Holmgren J, Merson MH, Mollby R (eds) Acute enteric infections in children. New prospects for treatment and prevention. Elsevier North-Holland Biomed, Amsterdam, pp 477–491

Moon HW, Runnels PL (1983) Trials with somatic (O) and capsular (K) polysaccharide antigens of enterotoxigenic *Escherichia coli* as protective antigens in vaccines for swine. Proceedings, 4th Int symp on neonatal diarrhea, Vet Infect Disease Organization, University of Saskatchewan, Canada, Oct 3–5, pp 558–569

Moon HW, Runnels PL (1984) The K99 adherence system in cattle. In: Boedeker EC (ed) Attachment of organisms to the gut mucosa, vol I. CRC, Boca Raton, pp 31–37

Moon HW, Nagy B, Isaacson RE, Ørskov I (1977) Occurrence of K99 antigen on *Escherichia coli* isolated from pigs and colonization of pig ileum by K99 + enterotoxigenic *E. coli* from calves and pigs. Infect Immun 15: 614–620

Moon HW, Fung PY, Isaacson RE, Booth GD (1979a) Effects of age, ambient temperature, and heat-stable *Escherichia coli* enterotoxin on intestinal transit in infant mice. Infect Immun 25: 127–132

Moon HW, Isaacson RE, Pohlenz J (1979b) Mechanisms of association of enteropathogenic *Escherichia coli* with intestinal epithelium. Am J Clin Nutr 32: 119–127

Moon HW, Kohler EM, Schneider RA, Whipp SC (1980) Prevalence of pilus antigens, enterotoxin types, and enteropathogenicity among K88-negative enterotoxigenic *Escherichia coli* from neonatal pigs. Infect Immun 27: 222–230

Moon HW, Rogers DG, Rose R (1988) Effects of a live oral pilus vaccine on duration of lacteal immunity to enterotoxigenic *Escherichia coli* in swine. Am J Vet Res 49(12): 2068–2077

Morgan RL, Isaacson RE, Moon HW, Brinton CC, To C-C (1978) Immunization of suckling pigs against enterotoxigenic *Escherichia coli*-induced diarrheal disease by vaccinating dams with purified 987 or K99 pili: protection correlates with pilus homology of vaccine and challenge. Infect Immun 22: 771–777

Morris JA, Stevens AE, Sojka WJ (1978) Anionic and cationic components of the K99 surface antigen from *Escherichia coli* B41. J Gen Microbiol 107: 173–175

Morris JA, Thorns CJ, Sojka WJ (1980) Evidence for two adhesive antigens on the K99 reference strain *Escherichia coli* B41. J Gen Microbiol 118: 107–113

Morris JA, Thorns CJ, Scott AC, Sojka WJ, Wells GA (1982) Adhesion in vitro and in vivo associated with an adhesive antigen (F41) produced by a K99 mutant of the reference strain *Escherichia coli* B41. Infect Immun 36: 1146–1153

164 H. W. Moon

Morris JA, Thorns CJ, Wells GAH, Scott AC, Sojka WJ (1983) The production of F41 fimbriae by piglet strains of enterotoxigenic *Escherichia coli* that lack K88, K99 and 987P fimbriae. J Gen Microbiol 129: 2753–2759

Morris JA, Sojka WJ, Ready RA (1985) Serological comparison of the *Escherichia coli* prototype strains for the F(Y) and AH 25 adhesins implicated in neonatal diarrhoea in calves. Res. Vet Sci 38: 246–247

Moseley SL, Dougan G, Schneider RA, Moon HW (1986) Cloning of chromosomal DNA encoding the F41 adhesin of enterotoxigenic *Escherichia coli* and genetic homology between adhesins F41 and K88. J Bacteriol 167: 799–804

Mouricout MA, Julien RA (1987) Pilus-mediated binding of bovine enterotoxigenic *Escherichia coli* to calf small intestinal mucins. Infect Immun 55: 1216–1223

Nagy B, Ushe TC (1985) Colonization of infant mice by K99 + *Escherichia coli* and lack of colonization by *Streptococcus faecium* M74. Acta Vet Hung 33: 143–147

Nagy B, Moon HW, Isaacson RE (1976) Colonization of porcine small intestine by *Escherichia coli*: ileal colonization and adhesion by pig enteropathogens that lack K88 antigen and by some acapsular mutants. Infect Immun 13: 1214–1220

Nagy B, Moon HW, Isaacson RE (1977) Colonization of porcine intestine by enterotoxigenic *Escherichia coli*: selection of piliated forms in vivo, adhesion of piliated forms to epithelial cells in vitro, and incidence of a pilus antigen among porcine enteropathogenic *E. coli*. Infect Immun 16: 344–352

Nakazawa M, Haritani M, Sugimoto C, Kashiwazaki M (1986) Colonization of enterotoxigenic *Escherichia coli* exhibiting mannose-sensitive hemagglutination to the small intestine of piglets. Microbiol Immunol 30: 485–489

Ørskov F, Ørskov I (1972) Immunoelectrophoretic patterns of extracts from *Escherichia coli* O antigen test strains O1 to O157 examinations in homologous OK sera. Acta Pathol Microbiol Scand [B] 80: 905–910

Ørskov F, Ørskov I (1978) Significance of surface antigens in relation to enterotoxigenicity of *E. coli*. Proceedings, cholera and related diarrheas, 43rd Nobel symposium, Stockholm, pp 134–141

Parry SH, Porter P (1978) Immunological aspects of cell membrane adhesion demonstrated by porcine enteropathogenic *Escherichia coli*. Immunology 34: 41–49

Rapacz J, Hasler-Rapacz J (1986) Polymorphism and inheritance of swine small intestinal receptors mediating adhesion of three serological variants of *Escherichia coli*-producing K88 pilus antigen. Anim Genet 17: 305–321

Riising H-J, Svendsen J, Larsen JL (1975) Occurrence of K88-negative *Escherichia coli* serotypes in pigs with post weaning diarrhoea. Acta Pathol Microbiol Scand [B] 83: 63–64

Runnels PL, Moon HW (1984) Capsule reduces adherence of enterotoxigenic *Escherichia coli* to isolated intestinal epithelial cells of pigs. Infect Immun 45: 737–740

Runnels PL, Moon HW, Schneider RA (1980) Development of resistance with host age to adhesion of K99 + *Escherichia coli* to isolated intestinal epithelial cells. Infect Immun 28: 298–300

Runnels PL, Moseley SL, Moon HW (1987) F41 pili as protective antigens of enterotoxigenic *Escherichia coli* that produce F41, K99, or both pilus antigens. Infect Immun 55: 555–558

Rutter JM, Jones GW (1973) Protection against enteric disease caused by *Escherichia coli*–a model for vaccination with a virulence determinant? Nature 242: 531–532

Sadowski PL, Acres SD, Sherman DM (1983) Monoclonal antibody for the protection of neonatal pigs and calves from toxic diarrhea. In: Hollaender A, Laskin AI, Rogers P (eds) Basic biology of new developments in biotechnology. Plenum, New York, pp 93–99 (Basic Life Sciences, vol 25)

Sadowski PL, Hermanson V, Hoffsis G (1984) Protection of pigs from fatal colibacillosis through the use of "a" and "c" specific monoclonal antibodies to the K88 pilus. Proceedings, 65th Annual Meeting of the Conference of Research Workers in Animal Disease, Chicago, Illinois, p 52

Sarmiento JI, Casey TA, Moon HW (1988) Postweaning diarrhea in swine: experimental model of enterotoxigenic *Escherichia coli* infection. Am J Vet Res 49(7): 1154–1158

Schneider RA, To SCM (1982) Enterotoxigenic *Escherichia coli* strains that express K88 and 987P pilus antigens. Infect Immun 36: 417–418

Sellwood R (1980) The interaction of the K88 antigen with porcine intestinal epithelial cell brush borders. Biochim Biophys Acta 632: 326–335

Sherman DM, Acres SD, Sadowski PL, Springer JA, Bray B, Raybould TJG, Muscoplat CC (1983) Protection of calves against fatal enteric colibacillosis by orally administered *Escherichia coli* K99-specific monoclonal antibody. Infect Immun 42: 653–658

Simonson RR, Isaacson RE, Jacob CR, Newman KZ (1983) The class specific antibody in passive protection against *Escherichia coli* diarrhea in pigs using a subunit genetically engineered pili vaccine. Proceedings, 4th Int symp on neonatal diarrhea, Vet Infect Disease Organization, University of Saskatchewan, Canada, Oct 3–5, pp 548–557

Smit H, Gaastra W, Kamerling JP, Vliegenthart JFG, De Graaf FK (1984) Isolation and structural characterization of the equine erythrocyte receptor for enterotoxigenic *Escherichia coli* K99 fimbrial adhesin. Infect Immun 46: 578–584

Smith HW (1976) Neonatal *Escherichia coli* infections in domestic mammals: transmissibility of pathogenic characteristics. Ciba Found Symp 42: 45–72

Smith HW, Halls S (1967) Observations by the ligated intestinal segment and oral inoculation methods on *Escherichia coli* infections in pigs, calves, lambs and rabbits. J Pathol Bacteriol 93: 499–529

Smith HW, Halls S (1968) The production of oedema disease and diarrhoea in weaned pigs by the oral administration of *Escherichia coli*: factors that influence the course of the experimental disease. J Med Microbiol 1: 45–59

Smith HW, Huggins MB (1978) The influence of plasmid-determined and other characteristics of enteropathogenic *Escherichia coli* on their ability to proliferate in the alimentary tracts of piglets, calves and lambs. J Med Microbiol 11: 471–492

Smith HW, Linggood MA (1972) Further observations on *Escherichia coli* enterotoxins with particular regard to those produced by atypical piglet strains and by calf and lamb strains: the transmissible nature of these enterotoxins and of a K antigen possessed by calf and lamb strains. J Med Microbiol 5: 243–250

Soderlind O, Olsson E, Smyth CJ, Mollby R (1982) Effect of parenteral vaccination of dams on intestinal *Escherichia coli* in piglets with diarrhea. Infect Immun 36: 900–906

Sojka WJ, Wray C, Morris JA (1977) Passive protection of lambs against experimental enteric colibacillosis by colostral transfer of antibodies from K99-vaccinated ewes. J Med Microbiol 11: 493–499

Svennerholm A-M, Vidal YL, Holmgren J, McConnel MM, Rowe B (1988) Role of PCF 8775 antigen and its coli surface subcomponents for colonization, disease, and protective immunogenicity of enterotoxigenic *Escherichia coli* in rabbits. Infect Immun 56: 523–528

To SCM (1984) F41 antigen among porcine enterotoxigenic *Escherichia coli* strains lacking K88, K99, and 987P pili. Infect Immun 43: 549–554

To SC-M, Moon HW, Runnels PL (1984) Type 1 pili (F1) of porcine enterotoxigenic *Escherichia coli*: vaccine trial and tests for production in the small intestine during disease. Infect Immun 43: 1–5

Truszczyński M, Osek J (1987) Occurrence of mannose resistant hemagglutinins in *Escherichia coli* strains isolated from porcine colibacillosis, Comp Immun Microbiol Infect Dis 10: 117–124

Tzipori S, Withers M, Hayes J (1984) Attachment of *E. coli*-bearing K88 antigen to equine brush-border membranes. Vet Microbiol 9: 561–570

Wilson MR, Hohmann AW (1974) Immunity to *Escherichia coli* in pigs: adhesion of enteropathogenic *Escherichia coli* to isolated intestinal epithelial cells. Infect Immun 10: 776–782

Wilson RA, Francis DH (1986) Fimbriae and enterotoxins associated with *Escherichia coli* serogroups isolated from pigs with colibacillosis. Am J Vet Res 47: 213–217

Yano T, Leite DDS, de Carmargo IJB, de Castro AFP (1986) A probable new adhesive factor (F42) produced by enterotoxigenic *Escherichia coli* isolated from pigs. Microbiol Immunol 30: 495–508

Inhibition of Bacterial Attachment: Examples from the Urinary and Respiratory Tracts

C. Svanborg Edén, B. Andersson, G. Aniansson, R. Lindstedt, P. de Man, A. Nielsen, H. Leffler, and A. Wold

1 Introduction

Bacterial attachment to components of mucosal surfaces promotes bacterial persistence in vivo and thus guides the colonization of mucosal sites (BEACHY 1981). Attachment is also the first in a series of pathogenetic events leading to disease. Bacterial binding enhances the tissue-damaging effect of exo- and endotoxins, and the subsequent tissue invasion by whole bacteria (FRETER 1969; SMITH and LINGGOOD 1971; JONES and RUTTER 1972; SVABORG EDÉN et al. 1982c) (Fig. 1).

Inhibition of attachment in vivo can modify bacterial colonization or interrupt infection (FRETER 1969; JONES and RUTTER 1972; WILLIAMS and GIBBONS 1972; SVANBORG EDÉN and SVENNERHOLM 1978). The detailed information on mechanisms

Department of Clinical Immunology, University of Göteborg, Guldhedsgatan 10, S-413 46 Göteborg, Sweden

Current Topics in Microbiology and Immunology, Vol. 151
© Springer-Verlag Berlin·Heidelberg 1990

Fig. 1. Attachment of bacteria to target cells is mediated via bacterial adhesins specifically recognizing target cell receptors

of attachment which has been generated over the past decade should be used to examine the protective potential of adhesion inhibition in humans. This chapter describes approaches to inhibition of bacterial adhesion based on in vitro studies, animal experiments, and clinical studies and discusses the feasibility of applying this knowledge to prophylaxis and treatment of infections in man.

2 Approaches to Adhesion Inhibition

Attachment may be inhibited by substances that block the interaction between the binding site of the bacterial adhesin and the target cell receptor (Fig. 1). These include: the soluble form of the receptor-binding site (Fig. 2b), antibodies against the receptor-binding site of the adhesin (Fig. 2a), and antireceptor antibodies that occupy the receptor site or soluble adhesins. The synthesis of bacterial adhesins is influenced by, for example, antibiotics. Antibacterial agents thus may be used not only for their antibacterial effect but also to interfere with bacterial attachment. Compounds that alter the glycosylation of the host cells can change the receptor phenotype.

2.1 Blocking of the Adhesin with Soluble Receptor Oligosaccharides

The ability of soluble receptor oligosaccharides to inhibit attachment to the receptor-bearing target cell in vitro has been demonstrated in several systems.

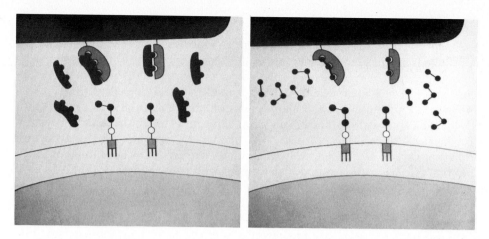

Fig. 2. Adhesion inhibition by blocking of the bacterial adhesin with **a** antibodies against the receptor-binding site and **b** soluble receptors which competitively block adhesin binding to the receptor

2.1.1 Mannose-Specific Binding

It has been recognized for several decades that the simple sugar mannose, or derivatives thereof, can inhibit bacterial binding to different target cells (COLLIER et al. 1955). The ability of bacteria to induce agglutination of erythrocytes from guinea pig or other species which is inhibited or reversed by mannose, provided the basis for the classification of adhesins on Enterobacteriaceae as mannose sensitive (MS) or mannose resistant (MR) (for review see DUGUID and OLD 1980).

Bacteria with mannose-reversible binding reactions are variably inhibited by different mannose-containing oligosaccharide structures (FIRON et al. 1982, 1983; SHARON and OFEK 1986; NEESER et al. 1986; SVANBORG EDÉN et al. 1983b). This variation in receptor specificity within the group with mannose-containing oligosaccharide structures, has also been shown by heterogeneity in the spectrum of target cells to which bacteria with type 1 fimbriae bind. The nature of the cell-bound receptors has recently been the focus of investigation. The trisaccharide Manαl-3[Man]αl-6Man occurs on asparagine-linked oligosaccharide chains of cell surface glycoproteins. The branched core is substituted in various ways, either with mannose residues alone or with N-acetylglucosamine, galactose, and sialic acid. The result is complex, high-mannose or hybrid types of oligosaccharide chains. So far, the oligosaccharide sequences of cell-bound glycoprotein receptors have not been identified. Glycoproteins from human polymorphonuclear leukocytes (PMNLs) and the BHK cell line have been shown to bind *Escherichia coli* fimbriae. Studies on mutants from the BHK cell line, defective in processing of the N-linked oligosaccharide chains, indicate that the complex type of N-linked chains are less effective as receptors than the oligomannose or hybrid types (GIAMPAPA et al. 1988; RODRIQUEZ-ORTEGA et al. 1987).

2.1.1.1 Receptor Activity of Secreted Glycoproteins

Secreted glycoproteins interact with type 1 fimbriae. The Tamm-Horsfall gly-coprotein is synthesized in the kidney and is secreted into the urine. It contains N-glycosidic chains both of the tetra-antennary complex and of the high-mannose type (SERAFINI-CESSI et al. 1984a, b). The Tamm-Horsfall glycoprotein binds type 1 fimbriae in a mannose-sensitive manner (SVANBORG EDÉN et al. 1982a; ØRSKOV et al. 1980; DULAWA et al. 1988) and blocks the attachment to uroepithelial cells. Recently, the Tamm-Horsfall glycoprotein was shown to opsonize for phagocytosis (SILVERBLATT et al. 1986) and to inhibit bacterial hemagglutination. The inhibitory activity was reduced by treatment with mannosidase (PARKKINEN et al. 1988).

Immunoglobulin molecules of all classes, as well as secretory component, possess N-linked oligosaccharide chains (KORNFELD and KORNFELD 1976). We recently demonstrated that secretory IgA, especially of the IgA2 subclass, functions as a receptor for mannose-specific bacterial lectins (SVANBORG EDÉN et al. 1987; WOLD et al. 1988a). This was first shown using myeloma proteins lacking antibody specificity against the *E. coli* strains used. Whereas IgG and IgM myeloma proteins were inactive, proteins of the IgA isotype agglutinated the bacteria with MS adhesins. The specificity for mannose was shown by inhibition with methyl-α-D-mannoside and by the lack of reactivity with bacteria without MS adhesins. Half of the polymeric IgA2 myelomas displayed strong reactivity and half of the IgA1 myelomas moderate activity. This was explained by truncation of the oligosac-charide with exposure of mannose in a terminal position.

Receptor activity for MS adhesins was also shown for total secretory IgA isolated from human milk and secretory IgA2, which is the predominant im-munoglobulin in the large intestine. Secretory IgA as well as IgA2 myeloma inhibited the attachment of mannose-binding *E. coli* strains to human colonic epithelial cells. Attachment mediated by adhesins specific for Galα1-4Galβ-containing receptors was unaffected. By providing oligosaccharide binding sites for mannose-specific bacterial lectins, secreted immunoglobulins may promote bacter-ial colonization, when bound to the mucus layer, and protect the host against bacterial attachment directly to the tissues—all without any need for specificity of the antigen-combining site against each bacterial antigen. Indeed, the myeloma IgA2 proteins which inhibited attachment of type 1 fimbriated *E. coli* to intestinal epithelial cells also protected mice against experimental urinary tract infection (UTI).

2.1.1.2 Consequences of Mannose-Specific Binding

The human large intestine is an important ecological niche for Enterobacteriaceae, of which, for example, *E. coli*, *Klebsiella*, and Enterobacter express MS adhesins. Human colonic epithelial cells carry mannose-containing receptors (DUGUID and OLD 1980) in both membrane-bound and surface-associated form (WOLD et al. 1988b), which may contribute to bacterial persistence in the large intestine.

The urinary tract is a second niche for the gram-negative species which frequently express mannose-specific adhesins (HAGBERG et al. 1981). The mannose-

specific attachment to urinary tract epithelial cells is species dependent (HAGBERG et al. 1983a). Mannose-containing receptors mediate attachment to rat cells but less so to mouse cells. MS attachment has been shown to contribute to bacterial persistence in kidneys and bladders of rats and mice (ARONSON et al. 1979; HAGBERG et al. 1983b; FADER and DAVIS 1980; IWAHI et al. 1983), including after experimental infection with *E. coli* genetically manipulated to express the MS adhesins (HAGBERG et al. 1983b; IWAHI et al. 1983). Bacteria with MS adhesins bind variably, but mostly poorly, to human uroepithelial cells (SVANBORG EDÉN and HANSSON 1978).

Attempts have been made to deduce the role of MS binding for human UTI from the frequency of expression of mannose-specific adhesins in clinical isolates of different origins. A majority of clinical isolates contain chromosomal DNA homologous to *pil*, the chromosomal DNA region of the *E. coli* strain SH1 required for the expression of fimbriae and MS adhesins (HULL et al. 1981). MS adhesins are expressed by 95% of laboratory-grown acute cystitis isolates compared to about 60% of fecal strains (HAGBERG et al. 1981). It has, however, been claimed that all *E. coli* can be induced to express MS adhesins given the right culture conditions (C. BRINTON, personal communication). The frequency estimates based on phenotype are therefore difficult to interpret.

Mannose-containing receptors also mediate the binding of bacteria to, for example, PMNLs, macrophages, and lymphocytes (BAR-SHAVIT et al. 1977; BLUMENSTOCK and JANN 1972; SVANBORG EDÉN et al. 1984). Binding of MS adhesins to human PMNLs triggers a chemoluminescence signal. The degree of phagocytosis and killing depends, however, on the capsule and lipopolysaccharide of the bacteria. Phagocytosis is likely to reduce the survival of mannose-specific bacteria in compartments where PMNLs are active (HAGBERG et al. 1983a, b; SVANBORG EDÉN et al. 1987).

2.1.1.3 Protection

It is probably not a coincidence that the glycoproteins which are secreted in the large intestine and the urinary tract express oligosaccharide sequences which expose mannose and enable them to interact with enterobacterial adhesins. Mucosal membranes other than the large intestine and the urinary tract mainly produce IgA1, which showed poor reactivity with the mannose-specific bacterial adhesins (WOLD et al. 1988a). The reason for the association of type 1 fimbriae with colonization rather than disease may be that secreted glycoproteins provide continuous protection of the tissues as well as superficial mucosal binding sites. This hypothesis may be examined by analysis of the colonic flora and UTI rate in individuals lacking IgA2 or Tamm-Horsfall glycoprotein, respectively.

The protective potential of soluble methyl-α-D-mannoside has been analyzed in experimental UTI models (ARONSON et al. 1979; FADER and DAVIS 1980; SVANBORG EDÉN et al. 1982c). Using the diuresing mouse infection model, a reduction in bacterial excretion was demonstrated. Similar results were obtained in a rat UTI model. With a different end point, i.e., the number of bacteria in kidneys and bladders of mice 24 h after infection, no protective effect of mannose could be documented (SVANBORG EDÉN et al. 1982c).

2.1.2 Binding to the Globoseries of Glycolipids

The globoseries of glycolipids were the first cell-bound receptor molecules for attaching bacteria to be identified, and the specificity has been characterized extensively (LEFFLER and SVANBORG EDÉN 1986). Their identification as members of the globoseries is based on the presence of the Galα1-4Galβ disaccharide, which confers a bent conformation to the oligosaccharide chain (BOCK et al. 1985). The function of the globoseries of glycolipids as receptors has been derived from several lines of evidence:

Bacteria bind selectively to cells carrying the globoseries of glycolipids, e.g., to erythrocytes from individuals of blood group P1 and P2, but not of blood group P̄ with a genetic defect in the synthesis of these glycolipids (KÄLLENIUS et al. 1980; LEFFLER and SVANBORG EDÉN 1980). Purified glycolipids not only confer receptor activity either to cells or to inert surfaces (LEFFLER and SVANBORG EDÉN 1980, 1981: BOCK et al. 1985; DE MAN et al. 1987) but also inhibit bacterial binding to receptor-bearing target cells (LEFFLER and SVANBORG EDÉN 1980).

The fact that Galα1-4Galβ was the only structural unit shared by the components with receptor activity led to the proposal of Galα1-4Galβ as the recognition site. This was subsequently confirmed using synthetic disaccharides (DE MAN et al. 1987; LEFFLER and SVANBORG EDÉN 1986). The Galα1-4Galβ disaccharide did not, however, provide the optimal receptor conformation. Most Galα1-4Galβ-recognizing E. coli reacted more strongly with globotetraosylceramide, and globotetraose was about tenfold more active than Galα1-4Galβ as an inhibitor of attachment (ENERBÄCK et al. 1987; LEFFLER and SVANBORG EDÉN 1980) (see Table 1).

Recently, it has become apparent that E. coli may recognize components of the

Table 1. Adhesion inhibition by soluble receptor molecules

Structure	Concentration (mM) required for 50% inhibition, compared to the saline control
GalNAcβ1-3Galα1-4Galβ1-4Gelβ-O-Et	0.22
Galα1-4Galβ1-4Glcβ-O-Et	0.52
Galα1-4Galβ1-4GlcNAcβ-O-Et	0.71
Galα1-4Galβ-O-Et	0.88
Galα1-4Galβ-O-⟋⟍⟋ OH (OH)	0.32
Galα1-4Galβ	2.13
2Deoxy-Galα1-4Galβ-O-Et	2.05
GalAα1-4GalA	2.10
Galα1-4Galβ-O-(CH₂)₂—S—C₆H₅NH₂	>3.5
Glcα1-4Galβ-O-Et	>3.5
GalNacβ1-3Galα-O-Me	>3.5
Galβ1-4Galcβ-O-Me	>3.5

E. coli 2914 were preincubated for 30 min at 37°C with soluble saccharides at concentrations varying from 3.5 to 0.1 mg/ml. Urinary tract epithelial cells were subsequently added, and adherence testing performed as described. The number of attached bacteria was counted by interference contrast microscopy, and inhibition given in % of the saline control

globoseries other than Galα1-4Galβ. The second copy of the *pap* gene cluster in J96 encodes adhesins that reacts with sheep erythrocytes (LUND et al. 1988; HULL and HULL, in press) and binds to globotetraosylceramide and to the Frossman antigen on thin-layer chromatogram plates. Bacterial isolates from the urinary tract of dogs bound specifically to the globo-A structure, but not to Galα1-4Galβ or other disaccharide components of this structure (SENIOR et al. 1988; LINDSTEDT et al. 1989). Their specificity was indeed the same as that of the second copy of *pap* homologous DNA from *E. coli* J96 (SENIOR et al. 1988; LINDSTEDT et al. 1989). This did not, however, recognize GalNAcα1-3GalNAcβ as initially suggested (LUND et al. 1988), but rather the GalNAc terminal together with Galα1-4Galβ disaccharide in a binding site possibly provided by the approximation of the terminal and internal saccharides in the bent globo-A and α Forssman structures (LINDSTEDT et al. 1989). It remains to be shown whether these specificities confer functions on the bacteria different from those of the Galα1-4Galβ-recognizing strains.

These observations have considerable importance for the selection of receptor analogues for inhibition of attachment in vivo. Inhibition of binding to the globoseries of glycolipids is likely to be best achieved using more complete oligosaccharides or combinations of Galα1-4Galβ and other saccharide sequences (Table 1).

2.1.2.1 Functional Consequences

In contrast to the mannose-specific adhesins, which are widely distributed, the ability to bind to the globoseries of glycolipids is restricted to certain *E. coli* clones. These are identified by certain O:K:H serotypes, and are typical of isolates with the ability to colonize the large intestine and infect extraintestinal sites (for review see SVANBORG EDÉN and DE MAN 1987).

We recently obtained evidence for the presence of a receptor in the human large intestine mediating the attachment of Galα1-4Galβ-specific *E. coli* (WOLD et al. 1988b). The intestinal cell line HT-29 as well as surgical specimens of human colon specifically bound *E. coli* strains transformed with *pap*, i.e., the chromosomal DNA fragment encoding pili and adhesins with specificity for Galα1-4Galβ-containing receptors. The bacteria bound primarily to a material loosely associated with the surface of the intestinal cells, which is in contrast to the attachment to uroepithelial cells. Therefore, the Galα1-4Galβ-containing receptor may be associated with a mucin-like glycoprotein rather than with glycolipids in the large intestine. This may explain the ability of Galα1-4Galβ-binding clones to become quantitatively dominating and resident, e.g., to colonize the large intestine for extended periods of time. If this can be confirmed it is plausible that the evolutionary advantage provided by the recognition of the globoseries of glycolipids is related to colonization of the intestine rather than or in addition to the spread to the urinary tract and other sites.

The globoseries of glycolipids occur in epithelial and nonepithelial components of the urinary tract (LEFFLER and SVANBORG EDÉN 1980; BREIMER et al. 1985). Binding to these receptors explains the attachment to uroepithelial cells of uropathogenic *E. coli*. The specific attachment has several consequences. Attach-

ment increases bacterial persistence in kidneys and bladders (HAGBERG et al. 1983b). This has been most clearly demonstrated in experimental UTI models using *E. coli* strains genetically manipulated to differ in adhesins. The advantage for attaching strains over nonattaching mutants or transformants was about tenfold. In man, the role of adherence for persistence is more difficult to evaluate. Persisting bacteriuria occurs mainly in the asymptomatic state, where the frequency of attaching *E. coli* strains is low (20%) (SVANBORG EDÉN et al. 1976).

The injection of attaching *E. coli* into the mouse urinary tract provokes inflammation. Adhesins and the lipid A moiety of endotoxin have a special role. Isolated lipid A coaggregated with adhesins specific for the globoseries of glycolipids induce inflammation synergistically. Since the signal was triggered by injection into the urinary tract of the isolated bacterial components, this implies that the epithelial cells when stimulated can mediate signals to the systemic inflammatory responses. Bacterial metabolism or invasion was not required for this to occur (LINDER et al. 1988). The crucial role of endotoxin for inflammation was also shown by the lack of inflammation in lipopolysaccharide nonresponder mice, and their consequent inability to clear the infection (HAGBERG et al. 1985; SHAHIN et al. 1987).

The role of Galα1-4Galβ-specific binding in the induction of inflammation has been confirmed in patients with UTI; those infected with *E. coli* with Galα1-4Galβ-specific adhesins had higher inflammation than those infected with other strains (MÅRILD et al. 1988; DE MAN et al. 1988). Since acute pyelonephritis is diagnosed by inflammatory signs, this may explain the association between attachment, binding to the globoseries of glycolipid receptors, and severity of disease in man, which was the initial observation leading to the elucidation of this problem complex (SVANBORG EDÉN et al. 1976).

From the two examples of colonic colonization and induction of inflammation it appears that the nature of the carrier may determine the functional consequences of adherence (SVANBORG et al. 1989). The Galα1-4Galβ-containing receptor material on colonic epithelial cells was shown to be loosely associated with the cells, giving a different adherence pattern than that to the uroepithelial cells, where the receptor is anchored in the membrane via the ceramide portion of the glycolipid receptor. In contrast to the membrane-bound form of the receptor, which may mediate inflammation, the secreted form may provide protection against tissue contact and facilitate colonization.

2.1.2.2 Protection

From the above it is clear that inhibition of binding to the globoseries of glycolipids or their analogues has a protective potential. Peroral administration of receptor bound to a solid phase might decrease bacterial persistence in the large intestine. A protective effect against UTI may be secondary to a more rapid turnover of the uropathogenic *E. coli* in the large intestine and a secondarily reduced satistical chance of spread to extraintestinal sites.

The protection of the urinary tract by globotetraose and Galα1-4Galβ-O-Et has been tested in mouse and primate UTI models, respectively (SVANBORG EDÉN et al.

1982c; ROBERTS et al. 1984). In mice, the infection, measured as bacterial persistence, was reduced but not abolished. In primates there was a transient decrease in the degree of infection, as measured by the leukocyte response. Since adherence in the urinary tract has a dual function in promoting both bacterial persistence and clearance through inflammation it is difficult to predict the protective potential of receptor analogues. In view of the clear-cut association of binding with clinical disease, and the well-defined receptor specificity, the UTI complex should be used as a model system to address these questions in man.

2.1.3 Lactoseries of Glycolipids

Attaching strains of *Streptococcus pneumoniae* interact with the lactoseries of glycolipids (ANDERSSON et al. 1983). The receptor function has been demonstrated in three ways: (a) Coating of epithelial cells with lactotetraosylceramide and neolacto-tetraosylceramide increased the attachment to those cells. (b) Soluble, natural or synthetic oligosaccharides inhibited attachment of pneumococci to, for example, epithelial cells, the most effective inhibitors being lactotetraose and neolacto-tetraose. (c) The oligosaccharides functioned as receptors when coupled to a solid phase. Pneumococci agglutinated latex beads covalently coupled with synthetic GlcNAcβ1-3Gal and Galβ1-3GlcNAc. These disaccharides provided the minimal receptor requirement.

2.1.3.1 Natural Occurrence of Receptor Saccharides in Human Milk

The lactoseries oligosaccharides occur in human milk. Consistent with this (ANDERSSON et al. 1986), the oligosaccharide fraction of milk was shown to inhibit the attachment of pneumococci to respiratory tract epithelial cells. The inhibitory activity of the oligosaccharides was higher than that of specific antipneumococcal antibodies, which also occur in milk. Inhibition of *Haemophilus influenzea* and *S. pneumoniae* was also associated with the k-casein component (ANIANSSON et al., in press).

The ability to attach to nasopharyngeal epithelial cells characterizes the majority of pneumococcal and *H. influenzae* isolates from that site (ANDERSSON et al. 1981, 1988). Also the majority of strains causing acute otitis media are adhering. Attachment thus appears to promote bacterial persistence in the nasopharynx, and secondary to that the spread of the isolates present in the nasopharynx to the middle ear when host resistance is reduced, e.g., by a viral infection. Accordingly, reduction of the nasopharyngeal colonization might secondarily reduce the frequence of acute otitis media.

Although the structure of the nasopharyngeal epithelial cell receptors for *S. pneumoniae* and *H. influenzae* has not been characterized, the finding of highly active inhibitors of attachment in milk provided the basis for an assessment of antiadherence in vivo. We have analyzed the ability of receptor analogues in milk to protect against bacterial colonization in the respiratory tract (ANIANSSON et al. 1987). Human milk is an excellent vehicle for antiadhesive substances, since it is

Table 2. Adhesion inhibition in vivo. Preliminary evidence for protection by antiadhesive components in human milk ($n = 271$)

Age of child (months)[a]	Feeding pattern	Colonization frequency (%) Hi[b]	Pnc[c]	Acute otitis media (%)	Px
0–3	BM	4	10	1	<0.001
	Mixed	2	13	9	NS
	Other	8	8	4	
4–6	BM	6	19	8	
	Mixed	3	25	7	NS
	Other	4	22	12	
7–12	BM	0	11	0	NS
	Mixed	0.001 9	29	14	<0.001
	Other	8	20	19	
Total	BM	4	11	2	<0.01
	Mixed	4	23 0.001	8	<0.001
	Other	7	21 0.001	20	

[a] Data from 271 children;
[b] *H. influenzae*;
[c] Pneumococci

administered onto the site of bacterial colonization, e.g., the nasopharynx, several times daily.

The acquisition of the nasopharyngeal flora was followed prospectively from birth with cultures at 2, 6, and 10 months of age. Milk samples were collected and episodes of otitis media were recorded. The protection afforded by the milk was calculated as the difference in bacterial colonization and otitis media of breast-fed versus non-breast-fed babies and correlated to the content of oligosaccharide inhibitors of the individual milks. Some preliminary results are shown in Table 2. Breast-fed babies receiving milk with high antiadhesive activity had reduced nasopharyngeal colonization and frequency of otitis compared to non-breast-fed controls or children receiving milk with low inhibitory activity (not shown).

2.2 Adhesion Inhibition by Antibacterial Antibodies

Adhesion may be inhibited either directly by antibodies to the adhesin or indirectly by antibodies to other bacterial surface components, which may inhibit adherence by, for example, agglutination or steric hindrance (FRETER 1969; JONES and RUTTER 1972; WILLIAMS and GIBBONS 1972; SVANBORG EDÉN and SVENNERHOLM 1978; SVANBORG EDÉN et al. 1982a). For instance, IgG antibodies against the O antigen of *E. coli* lipopolysaccharides agglutinate bacteria and thereby reduce the number of bacteria available for attachment. Agglutinating antibodies may thus contribute to the immune-mediated protection of mucosal surfaces. F(ab) fragments have no such

effect. Antibodies to bacterial surface antigens adjacent to the adhesin may sterically hinder access to the receptor. This effect is, in many systems, difficult to separate from the effect of adhesin-specific antibodies.

Antiadhesin antibodies appear to be a simple and straightforward means of blocking bacterial adhesion which has been successfully tested in veterinary praxis (see other contributors, this volume). This concept has, however, several major problems.

2.2.1 Different Antigenicity of Fimbriae and Adhesins

The adhesins of, for example, *E. coli* are associated with pili/fimbriae but are distinct from the fimbrial subunit (LUND et al. 1987; MOCH et al. 1987; HOSCHÜTZKY et al. 1989). The immune response against whole fimbriated bacteria or against isolated fimbriae is dominated by antibodies directed towards the fimbrial subunit (fimA of type 1 fimbriae, papA of Galα1-4Galβ-binding adhesins). Although polyclonal antifimbrial antisera were reported by several investigators to block adherence (ISAACSON 1977; KORHONEN et al. 1980), monoclonal antibodies to the structural protein did not. Monoclonal antiadhesin antibodies inhibited attachment. Antibodies from patients with acute pyelonephritis, although active against the fimbrial subunit, failed to block adhesion (DE REE et al. 1987). To achieve antiadhesive antibodies, the adhesin should thus be used to induce an immune response.

2.2.2 Antigenic Diversity

Several bacterial surface components vary their antigenic properties while retaining a common function. The *E. coli* lipopolysaccharides share the toxicity afforded by lipid A but vary the structure and antigenicity of the O polysaccharide (ØRSKOV et al. 1977). In analogy, fimbriae which share the receptor specificity vary in antigenicity. Fimbriae with adhesins specific for the Galα1-4Galβ-containing receptors express several fimbrial (F) antigens, including $F7_1$, $F7_2$, and F8–F14. The F antigens are conserved among strains of the same O:K:H serotype (ØRSKOV and ØRSKOV 1983). The extent of antigenic variation for the adhesins remains to be defined.

2.2.3 Antigenic Repertoire

The antigenic properties vary between isolates infecting different patient populations. Both the frequency of attaching strains and the receptor specificity of the adhesins and the serotypes of the fimbrial antigens are variable. The selection of antigens for the induction of antiadhesive antibodies thus needs to be based on information about the strains infecting the population for which the antiadhesive treatment will be targeted. Most of the work on bacterial vaccines has assumed that the selection of vaccine antigens should be based on the most virulent strains. In contrast, patients with recurrent bacterial infections often appear to be reinfected with bacteria different from those causing the primary infection and with reduced virulence. For example, patients with recurrent pyelonephritis, reflux, and renal

scarring had about 30% attaching *E. coli*, compared with about 80% in those without reflux (LOMBERG et al. 1984). When such patient populations are the target of vaccination programs, antiadhesive immunity may not be the optimal choice (SVANBORG EDÉN et al. 1982a, b).

2.2.4 Induction of Antiadhesive Mucosal Immunity

The concept of adhesion inhibition presumes that the antiadhesive antibodies exert their action at mucosal surfaces, by preventing contact between bacteria and, for instance, epithelial cells. The dominating mucosal immunoglobulin class, secretory IgA (SIgA), is assembled by selective coupling of dimeric IgA to secretory component during transport through the epithelial cells into the lumen (KRAEHENBUHL et al. 1987). The mucosal immune responses require local antigenic stimulation. The plasma cells are recruited from the site of mucosal priming, e.g., in the Peyer's patches or the respiratory tract, to sites of antigenic stimulation and are induced to produce specific antibodies. Once induced, mucosal immune responses are short-lived (for references, see HANSON and SVANBORG EDÉN 1988).

The induction of stable antiadhesive immunity requires administration of intact adhesins and/or fimbrial antigens to the mucosal immune system. Soluble protein antigens administered to the surface mostly are poor immunogens. For this reason alternative modes of administration are being tested, including the use of live bacteria as antigen presentors. For example, a hybrid between *E.coli* and *Salmonella*, which colonizes the Peyer's patches, may be genetically manipulated to produce adhesins and act as a vehicle delivering these antigens to antigen-presenting cells in the mucosal immune system (KATZ et al. 1987).

An attempt to induce local antiadhesive immunity in the urinary tract of humans was recently made by deliberate installation into the urinary tract of bacteria which had been genetically manipulated in vitro. We selected a wild-type *E. coli* strain which had been carried in the urinary tract of one child for more than 3 years without giving rise to symptoms. The strain, which was highly sensitive

Table 3. Antibody response of patients receiving genetically manipulated *E. coli* in the urinary tract

Patient	Days after colonization	Urinary antibodies, ELISA titer[a]	
		IgA	IgM
EKJ	2	0.59	1.1
LEA	5	0.20	0.26
EJ	30	0.78	0.3
BL	4	0.53	0.26
JE	4	0.13	0.19

[a]Optical density at 405 nm after incubation for 100 min with substrate for alkaline phosphatase conjugated to antihuman IgA or IgM. A heat extract from the transformant strain 506 MR, containing lipopolysaccharide, fimbriae, and other heat-stable proteins, was used as antigen. Patients were colonized with *E. coli* 506 MR, introduced via a catheter into the urinary bladder

to antibacterial agents and had one small plasmid, was transformed with the chromosomal DNA fragments *pap* or *pil* encoding Galα1-4Galβ-specific and mannose-specific adhesins respectively. The transformants and the parent strain were introduced into the urinary bladders of patients by catherterization. The five patients who consented to participate all had neurogenic bladder disorders and recurrent pyelonephritis. The immune response to the introduced strains was measured by ELISA using as antigens heat extracts of whole bacteria containing fimbriae and lipopolysaccharide (Table 3). No serum antibody response was recorded. In contrast, a significant urinary antibody response was observed in the three patients who were stably colonized with the *E. coli* strain (EKJ, EJ, BC).

2.2.5 Protection by Antiadhesive Antibodies

Experimental UTI has been used as a model for the study of antiadhesive immunity. The advantages of the model include the fact that adherence is important both for bacterial persistence and for the induction of disease. In addition, the urinary tract is normally sterile and infections are caused by a single strain, which makes it easy to evaluate the antigens inducing or acting as targets for immunity and to detect protection. Protection against homologous bacterial challenge in experimental UTI models has been achieved using different vaccine antigens: whole bacteria, lipopolysaccharides, capsular polysaccharides, and fimbriae (KAIJSER et al. 1978; ROBERTS et al. 1981; SILVERBLATT 1974; for review see SVANBORG EDÉN et al. 1988a). The fimbrial preparations used have been contaminated with lipopolysaccharide, and in spite of extensive controls using either heterogeneous challenge or parallel induction of immunity to the O antigen, it has been difficult to evaluate the contribution of antifimbrial immunity per se. In addition, the protection has not been defined in terms of mucosal antibodies and antiadherence in vivo. The protective power of mucosal antibodies in the urinary tract thus remains to be defined. In view of the complications involved in the induction of antiadhesive immunity and since the receptor structure recognized by the adhesins is shared by antigenically different strains, the use of receptor molecules for competitive inhibition of binding appears as a more straightforward strategy for antiadherence.

2.3 Receptor Blockade with Antireceptor Antibodies

A large proportion of naturally occurring antibodies are directed against carbohydrate antigens. Such antibodies may reognize cell-bound glycoconjugates, e.g., in epithelial and nonepithelial tissues. Binding to structures which are receptors for bacterial adhesins may competitively inhibit bacterial binding to the receptor-bearing cell. The extent to which such antibodies modify bacterial attachment has not been studied.

The antibodies to the globoseries of glycolipids have been studied in relation to the P blood group system (WATKINS 1978). Individuals of blood group P2 produce antibodies to the P1 antigen. Antibodies to the P blood group antigen occur in both P1 and P2 individuals. Neither of these antibodies has specificity for the Galα1-

4Galβ disaccharide. Still, binding of antibodies to an adjacent determinant of the oligosaccharide might influence the access of bacterial adhesins to the Galα1-4Galβ disaccharide.

Another source of antireceptor antibodies is anti-idiotypes. Antibodies against the binding site of the bacterial adhesin resemble the combining site on the receptor. A subset of the antiantibodies may, in turn, recognize the receptor. In this way, an immune response triggered by the bacterial adhesin may lead to receptor blockade.

Monoclonal antibodies to Galα1-4Galβ have been used to map the distribution of receptors in the urinary tract (O'HANLEY et al. 1985; LARK et al. 1984). Their protective potential has, however, not been investigated. The binding of antibodies to host tissues involves the risk of triggering autoimmune events.

2.4 Phenotypic Changes of Bacteria or Target Cells

Antibacterial agents influence the expression of adhesins. This has been shown not only for inhibitors of protein synthesis, e.g., chloramphenicol, but also for streptomycin and penicillins. The contribution of adhesion inhibition compared to bacteriostatic or bactericidal effects of antibacterial agents in vivo has not been defined. It is possible that antiadhesive effects contribute to the positive effects of low-dose prophylaxis against UTIs (SANDBERG et al. 1979; for review see VOSBECK et al. 1982).

The receptor expression of the target cell may be altered by pharmacologic means. It is well established that agents affecting the glycosylation, such as tunicamycin, modify the cell surface if added to cells in culture. Commonly used drugs which affect glycosylation of cell surface glycoconjugates may influence the receptor expression in man. These effects have not been analyzed in relation to bacterial adherence.

3 Concluding Remarks

Adhesion inhibition is an attractive concept for prophylaxis and protection against infection. By interrupting the initial contact between bacteria and mucosal surfaces, the subsequent events in the disease process are aborted. In principle, inhibition of adherence may be achieved in all the ways described in this review. The blocking of binding by receptor analogues is easily achieved in vitro. The suggested relationship between respiratory tract infections and the antiadhesive effect of milk components, may provide the evidence required for larger scale testing of antiadhesive substances as a complement to the currently used antimicrobial agents. Antiadhesive immunity is a simple and attractive concept. In view of the complications involved in the induction of antiadhesive immunity, and since the receptor structures recognized by the adhesins are shared regardless of antigenicity, the use of receptor molecules appears to be the most straightforward approach.

References

Andersson B, Eriksson B, Falsen E, Fogh A, Hanson LÅ, Nylén O, Peterson H, Svanborg Edén C (1981) Adhesion of *Streptococcus pneumoniae* to human pharyngeal epithelial cells in vitro. Differences in adhesive capacity among strains isolated from subjects with otitis media, specticemia, or meningitis or from healthy carriers. Infect Immun 32: 311–317

Andersson B, Dahmén J, Frejd T, Leffler H, Magnusson G, Noori G, Svanborg Edén C (1983) Identification of a disaccharide unit of a glycoconjugate receptor for pneumococci attaching to human pharyngeal epithelial cells. J Exp Med 158: 559–570

Andersson B, Porras O, Hanson LÅ, Lagergård T, Svanborg-Edén C (1986) Inhibition of attachment of *Streptococcus pneumoniae* and *Heamophilus influenzae* by human milk and receptor oligosaccharides. J Infect Dis 153: 232–237

Andersson B, Gray BM, Dillon HC, Bahrmand A, Svanborg Edén C (1988) Role of adherence of *S. pneumoniae* in acute otitis media. Pediatr Inf Dis 7: 476–480

Aniansson G, Andersson B, Alm B, Larsson P, Nylén O, Pettersson H,Ringér P, Svanborg Edén C (1987) Protection by breastfeeding against bacterial colonization of the nasopharynx: a pilot study.

Aniansson G, Andersson B, Lindstedt R, Svanborg edén C (in press) Receptor activity of human casein for *S. pneumoniae* and *H. influenzae*

Aronson M, Medalia O, Schori L, Mirelman D, Sharon N, Ofek I (1979) Prevention of colonization of the urinary tract of mice with *Escherichia coli* by blocking of bacterial adherence with methyl α-D-mannopyranoside. J Infect Dis 139: 329–332

Bar-Shavit Z, Ofek I, Goldman R, Mirelman D, Sharon N (1977) Mannose residues on phagocytes as receptors for the attachment of *Escherichia coli* and Salmonella typhi. Biochem Biophys Res Commun 78: 455–460

Beachey EH (1981) Adhesin-receptor interactions mediating the attachment of bacteria to mucosal surfaces. J Infect Dis 143: 325–345

Blumenstock B, Jann K (1982) Adhesion of piliated *Escherichia coli* strains to phagocytes: difference between with mannose-sensitive pili and those with mannose-resistant pili. Infect Immun 35: 264–269

Bock K, Brignole A, Breimer Me et al. (1985) Specificity of binding of a strain of uropathogenic *Escherichia coli* to Galα1-4Gal containing glycosphingolipids. J Biol Chem 260: 8545–8551

Breimer M, Hansson GC, Leffler H (1985) The specific glycosphingolipid composition of human ureteral epithelial cells. J Biochem 98: 1169–1180

Collier WA, de Miranda G, von Loeuwenhoek AJ (1955) Microbiol Serol 21: 135–140

de Mann P, Cedergren B, Enerbäck S et al. (1987) Receptor-specific agglutination tests for detection of bacteria that bind the gnoboseries glycolipids. J Clin Microbiol 25: 401–407

de Mann P, Jodal U, Lincoln K, Svanborg Edén C (1988) Bacterial attachment and inflammation in the urinary tract. J Infect Dis 158: 29–35

de Ree IM, Schwillens P, van den Bosch JF (1987) Monoclonal antibodies raised against Pap fimbriae recognize minor component(s) involved in receptor binding. Microb Pathogen 2: 113–121

Duguid JP, Old DC (1980) Adhesive properties of Enterobacteriaceae. In: Beachey EH (ed) Bacterial adherence. Champman and Hall, New York, pp 187–215

Dulawa J, Jann K, Thomsen M, Rambausek M, Ritz E (1988) Tamm Horsfall glycoprotein interfers with bacterial adherence to human kidney cells. Eur J Clin Invest 18: 87–91

Enerbäck S, Larsson AC, Jodal U et al. (1987) Binding to galactoseα1-4galactoseβ-containing receptors as potential diagnostic tool in urinary tract infection. J Clin Microbiol 25: 407–411

Fader RC and Davis C (1980) Effect of piliation on *Klebsiella pneumaniae* infection in rat bladders. Infect Immun 30: 554–561

Firon N, Ofek I, Sharon N (1982) Interaction f mannose-containing oligosaccharides with the fimbrial lectin of *Escherichia coli*. Biochem Biophys Res Commun 105: 1426–1432

Firon N, Ofek I, Sharon N (1983) Carbohydrate specificity of the surface lectins of *Escherichia coli*, *Klebsiella pneumoniae* and *Salmonella typhimurium*. Carbohydr Res 120: 235–249

Freter R (1969) Studies of the mechanism of action of intestinal antibody in experimental cholera. Texas Rep Biol Med 27 (Suppl 1): 299–316

Giampapa CS, Abraham SN, Chiang TM, Beachy EH (1988) Isolation and characterization of a receptor for type 1 fimbriae of *Escherichia coli* from guinea-pig erythrocytes. J Biol Chem 263: 5362–5367

Hagberg L, Jodal U, Korhonen TK et al. (1981) Adhesion hemagglutination and virulence of *Escherichia coli* causing urinary tract infections. Infect Immun 31: 564–574

Hagberg L, Engberg I, Freter R et al. (1983a) Ascending unobstzucted urinary tract infection in mice caused by pyelonephritogenic *Escherichia coli* of human origin. Infect Immun 40: 273–283

Hagberg L, Hull R, Hull S et al. (1983b) Contribution of adhesion to bacterial persistence in the mouse urinary tract. Infect Immun 40: 265–272

Hagberg L, Briles D, Svanborg Edén C (1985) Evidence for separate genetic defects in C2H/HeJ and C3HeB/FeJ micm, that affect the susceptibility to gram-negative infection. J Immunol 134: 4118–4122

Hanson LÅ, Svanborg Edén C (eds) (1988) In: Mucosal immunology. Nobel symposium no 68. Monogr Allergy

Hoschützky H, Lottspeich F, Jann K (1989) Iso,ation and characterization of the α-Galactosyl-1,4-β-Galactosyl specific adhesin (Padhesin) from fimbriated *Escherichia coli*. Infect Immun 57: 76–81

Hull S, Hull R (in press) Linkage and duplication of copies of genes encoding P fimbriae and hemolysin in the chromosome of a uropathogenic *E. coli* isolate. In: Svanborg Edén C, Kass EH (eds) Host parasite interaction in the urinary tract. Chicago University Press, Chicago

Hull RA, Gill RE, Hsu P et al. (1981) Construction and expression of recombinant plasmids encoding type I or D-mannose resistant pili from a urinary tract infection *Escherichia coli* isolate. Infect Immun 33: 933–938

Isaacson RE (1977) K99 surface antigen on *Escherichia coli*: Purification and partial characterization. Infect Immun 15: 272–279

Iwahi T, Abe Y, Nakao H, Imada A, Tsuchiya K (1983) Role of type 1 fimbriae in the pathogenesis of ascending urinary tract infection induced by *Escherichia coli* in mice. Infect Immun 39: 1307–1315

Jones GW, Rutter JM (1972) Role of the K88 antigen in the pathogenesis of neonatal diarrhoea caused by *Escherichia coli* in piglets. Infect Immun 6: 918–927

Kaijser H, Larsson P, Olling S (1978) Protection against ascending *Escherichia coli* pyelonephritis in rats and significance of loca immunity. Infect Immun 20: 78–81

Källenuius G, Möllby R, Svensson SB et al. (1980) The p^k antigen as receptor for the haemagglutination of pyelonephritic *E. coli*. FEMS Microbiol Lett 7: 297–302

Katz J, Michalek SM, Curtiss R, Harmon C, Richardsson G, Mestecky J (1987) Novel oral vaccines: the effectiveness of cloned gene products on inducing secretory immune responses. In: McGhee JR, Mestecky J, Ogra Pl, Bienenstock J (eds) Recent advances in mucosal immunology. Plenum, New York, pp 1741–1747

Korhonen TK, Nurmiaho EL, Ranta H, Svanborg Edén C (1980) New method for isolation of immunologically pure pili from *Escherichia coli*. Infect Immun 27: 569–575

Kornfeld R, Kornfeld S (1976) Comparative aspects of glycoprotein structure. Annu Rev Biochem 45: 217–233

Kraehenbuhl J-P, Schaerer E, Weltzin K, Solari R (1987) Receptor-mediated transepthelial transport of secretory antibodies and engineering of mucosal antibodies. In; Mc Ghee Jr, Mestecky J, Ogra Pl, Bienenstock J (eds) Recent advances in mucosal immunology. Plenum, New York, pp 1053–1069

Lark DL, O'Hanley P, Weinstein WM, Schoolnik G (1984) Human uroepithelia: the distribution and density of receptor analogues for pyelonephritic *E. coli* pili. Clin Res 32: 379

Leffler H, Svanborg Edén C (1980) Chemical identification of a glycosphingolipid receptor for *E. coli* attaching to human urinary tract epithelial cells and agglutinating human erythrocytes. FEMS Microbiol Lett 8: 127–134

Leffler H, Svanborg Edén C (1981) Glycolipid receptors for uropathogenic *Escherichia coli* on human erythrocytes and uroepithelial cells. Infect Immun 34: 920–929

Leffler H, Svanborg Edén C (1986) Glycolipids as receptors for *Escherichia coli* lectins or adhesins. In: Mirelman D (ed) Microbial lectins. Wiley, New York pp 84–96

Linder H, Engberg I, Mattsby-Baltzer I, Jann K, Svanborg-Edén C (1988) Induction of inflammation by *Escherichia coli* on the mucosal levels: requirement for adherence and endotoxin. Infect Immun 56: 1309–1313

Lindstedt R, Falk P, Larsson G, Svanborg Edén C (1989) Comparative binding of ONAP and *prs* to the globoseries of glycolipids. Carbohydr Res (submitted for publication)

Lomberg H, Hellström M, jodal U, Leffler H, Lincoln K, Svanborg Edén C (1984) Virulence associated traits in *E. coli* causing first and recurrent episodes of urinary tract infections in children with or without vesicoureteric reflux. J Infect Dis 150: 561–569

Lund B, Lindberg F, Marklund B-I, Normark S (1987) The PapG protein is the α-D-galactopyranosol-(1-4)-β-D-galactopyranose-binding adhesin of uropathogenic *Escherichia coli*. Proc Natl Acad Sci USA 84: 5898–5902

Lund B, Marklund B-I, Strömberg N, Lindberg F, Karlsson K-A, Normark S (1988) Uropathogenic *E. coli* express srologically identical pili with different receptor binding specificities. Mol Microbiol 2: 255–263

Mårlid S, Wettergren B, Hellström M, Jodal U, Lincoln K, Orskov I, Orskov F, Svanborg Edén C (1988)

Bacterial virulence and inflammatory response in infants ith febrile urinary tract infection or screening bacteriuria. J Pediatr 112: 398–

Moch T, Hoschutzky H, Hacker J, Kröncke K-D, Jann K (1987) Isolation and characterization of the α-sialyl-β-2,3-galactosyl-specific adhesin from fimbriated *Escherichia coli*. Proc Natl Acad Sci USA 84: 3462–3466

NesserJ-R, Koellreutter B, Wuersch P (1986) Oligomannoside-type glycopeptides inhibiting adhesion of *E. coli* strains mediated by type 1 pili: preparation of potent inhibitors of plant glycoproteins. Infect Immun 52: 428–436

O'Hanley P, Lark D, Falkow S, Schoolnik G (1985) Molecular basis of *Escherichia coli* colonization fo the upper urinary tract in BALB/c mice. J Clin Invest 75: 347–360

Ørskov I, Ørskov F, Jann B, Jann K (1977) Serology, chemistry and genetics of O and K antigens of *Escherichia coli*. Bacteriol Rev 41: 667–710

Ørskov I, Ferencz A, Ørskov F (1980) Tamm-Horsfall protein or uromucoid is the normal urinary slime that traps type 1 fimbriated *Escherichia coli*. Lancet 1: 887

Ørskov I, Ørskov F (1983) Serology of *Escherichia coli* fimbriae. Prog Allergy 33: 80–105

Parkkinen J, Virkola R, Korkonen TK (1988) Identification of inhibitors in human urine for binding of *E. coli* adhesins. Infect Immun (in press)

Porras O, Dillon H, Gray B, Svanborg Edén C (1987) Lack of correlation of in vitro adherence of *Haemophilus influenzae* to epithelial cells with frequent occurrence of otitis media. Pediatr Infect Dis J 6: 41–45

Roberts JA, Domingue GJ, Martin LN, Kim JCS, Rangan SRS (1981) Immunology of pyelonephritis in the primate model. II. Effect of Immunosuppression. Invest Uro 19: 148–153

Roberts JA, Kaack B, Källenius G Et al. (1984) Receptors for pyelonephritogenic *Escherichia coli* in primates. Invest Urol 131: 163–168

Rodriguez-Ortega M, Ofek I, Sharon N (1987) Infect Immun 35: 968–973

Sandberg T, Stenquvist K, Svanborg Edén C (1979) Effects of subminimal inhibitory concentrations of ampicillin, chloramphenicol and nitrolmantoin on the attachment of *E. coli* to human uroepithelial cells in vitro. Rev Infect Dis 1: 838–844

Senior D, Baker N, Cedergren B, Falk P, Larsson G, Lindstedt R, Svanborg Edén C (1988) Globo A—A new receptor specificity for attaching *E. coli*. FEBS Lett 237: 123–127

Serafini-Cessi F, Malagolini N, Dall'Olio F (1984a) A tetraantennary glycopeptide from human Tamm-Horsfall glycoprotein inhibits agglutination of desialylated erythrocytes induced by leucoagglutinin. Biosci Rep 4: 973–978

Serafini-Cessi F, Dall'Olio F, Malagoni N (1984b) High-mannose oligosackharides from human Tamm-Horsfall glycoprotein. Biosci Rep 4: 269–274

Shahin R, Engberg I, Hagberg L, Svanborg Edén C (1987) Neutrophil recruitment and bacterial clearance correlated with non-responsiveness in local gram-negative infection. J Immunol 10: 3475–3480

Sharon N, Ofek I (1986) Mannose specific bacterial surface lectins. In: Miselman D (ed) Microbial lectins and agglutinins. Wiley, New York, pp 56–79

Silverblatt FJ (1974) Host-parasite interaction in the rat renal pelvis. A possible role for pili in the pathogenesis of pyelonephritis. J Exp Med 140: 1696–1711

Silverblatt FJ, Cohen L (1979) Anti-pili antibody affords protection against experimental, ascending pyelonephritis. J Clin Invest 64: 333–336

Smith HW, Lingood MA (1971) Observations on the pathogenic properties of the K88, HLY and Ent plasmids of *Escherichia coli* with particular reference to porcine diarrhoea. J Med Microbiol 4: 467–485

Svanborg Edén C, Hansson HA (1978) *Escherichia coli* pili as possible mediators of attachment to human urinary tract epithelial cells. Infect Immun 21: 229–237

Svanborg Edén C, de Man P (1987) Bacterial virulence in urinary tract infection. In:Andriole V (ed) Urinary tract infections. Infectious disease clinics of North America, vol 1. Karger, Base, pp 731–750

Svanborg Edén C, Svennerholm A-M (1978) Secretory immunoglobulin A and G antibodies prevent adhesion of *Escherichia coli* to human urinary tract epithelial cells. Infect Immun 22: 790–797

Svanborg Edén C, Hanson LÅ, Jodal U, Lindberg U, Sojl Åkerlund A (1976) Variable adherence to normal urinary tract epithelial cells of *Escherichia coli* strains associated with various forms of urinary tract infection. Lancet II: 490–492

Svanborg-Edén C, Hanson LÅ, Jodal U, Leffler H, Mårild S, Korhonen T, Brinton C, Jann B, Jann K, Silverblatt F (1982b) Receptor analogs and antipili antibodies as inhibitors of attachment of uropathogenic *Escherichia coli*. In: sell K, Hanson LÅ, Strobel W (eds) Recent advances in mucosal immunity. Raven, New York, pp 355–369

Svanborg Edén C, Fasth A, Hagberg L, Hanson LÅ, Korhonen TK, Leffler H (1982b) Host interaction

with *Escherichia coli* in the urinary tract. In: Robbins J, Hill J, Sadoff J (eds) Bacterial vaccines. IV. Thieme, Stuttgart, pp 113–131

Svanborg Edén C, Freter R, Hagberg L et al. (1982c) Inhibition of experimental ascending urinary tract infection by receptor analogue. Nature 298: 560–562

Svanborg Edén C, Andersson B, Hagberg L, Hanson LÅ, Leffler H, Magnusson G, Noori G, Dahmén J, Söderström T (1983a) Receptor analogues and antipili antibodies as inhibitors of attachment in vivo and in vitro. Ann NY Acad Sci 409: 580–595

Svanborg Edén C, Hull R, Falkow S, Leffler H (1983b) Target cell specificity of wild type *E. coli* and mutants and clones with genetically defined adhesions. Prog Food Nutr Sci Res 7; 75–89

Svanborg Edén C, Bjursten LM, Hull R et al. (1984) Influence of adhesins on the interaction of *Escherichia coli* with human phagocytes. Infect Immun 44: 407–413

Svanborg Edén C, Andersson B, Aniansson G, Leffler H, Lomberg H, Mesteckley J, Wold AE (1987) Glycoconjugate receptors for bacteria attaching to mucosal sites. In: Mestecley J, McGhee JR, Bienenstock J, Ogra PJ (eds) Recent advances in mucosal immunology. B. New York, Plenum, New York, pp 937–939

Svanborg Edén C, de Man P, Linder H, Lomberg H (1988a) Natural versus induced resistance to urinary tract infection. In: Savanborg Edén C, Kass EA (eds) Host parasite interaction in the urinary tract. Chicago University Press, Chicago

Svanborg Edén C, Linder H, de Man P (1988b) Consequences of specific attachment of *E. coli* to Galα1-4Galβ-containing receptors. In: Schrinner E, Richmond MH, Seibert G, Schwartz U (eds) Surface structures of microorganisms and their interaction with the mammalian host. NCH Verlagsgesellschaft, pp 185–196 (workshop conferences, Hoechst, vol 18)

Svanborg Edén C, Hull S, Leffler H, Norgren S, Plos K, Wold A (1989) The large intestine as a reservoir for *Escherichia coli* causing extraintestinal infections. In: Midtredt T (ed) B. Gustavsson symposium (in press)

Vosbeck K, Mett H, Huber U, Bohn J, Petiquant m (1982) Effects of low concentrations of antibiotics on *E. coli* adhesion. Antimicrob Agents. Chemother 21: 864–869

Watkins WM (1978) Gnetics and biochemistry of some human blood groups. Proc R Soc Lond [Biol] 202: 31–53

Williams RC, Gibbons RJ (1972) Inhibition of bacterial adherence by secretory immunoglobulin A: a mechanism of antigenic disposal. Science 177: 697–699

Wold AE, Mestecky J, Svanborg Edén S (1988a) Agglutination of *Escherichia coli* by secretory IgA: a result of interaction between bacterial mannose-specific adhesins and immunoglobulin carbohydrate Monogr Allergy 24: 307–309

Wold AE, Thorssen M, Hull S, Svanborg Edén C (1988b) Attachment of *Escherichia coli* to mannose- or Galα1-4Galβ-containing receptors in human colonic epithelial cells. Infect Immun (in press)

Synthetic Peptides: Prospects for a Pili (Fimbriae)-Based Synthetic Vaccine

M. A. SCHMIDT

1 Introduction

Pathogenic bacteria owe their capacity to cause disease to the combined effects of their repertoires of virulence factors. These factors, in interaction with the various defense mechanisms of the host, are involved in triggering a succession of events leading from colonization and infection of local epithelia to the onset of disease which in most cases afflicts the host as a whole. In mucosal infections adherence of the pathogens to host epithelial cells is regarded as the essential first step. Adhesion is mediated by surface-associated proteinaceous *adhesins* which recognize and bind specific carbohydrate structures on the epithelial cell surface (GIBBONS 1977; BEACHEY 1981; FRETER 1981). Most of the adhesin systems described so far have been found to be associated with filamentous protein structures, fibrillar or fimbrial, though a few examples of afimbrial adhesins have been reported. The possibility of interfering with the adherence of pathogenic microorganisms to epithelial cell receptors might open up new ways of combating infectious diseases at a very early stage of the infectious process.

In this chapter some general aspects of the use of synthetic peptides for the induction of protective immunity will be discussed, as well as more recent

Zentrum für Molekulare Biologie Heidelberg (ZMBH), Im Neuenheimer Feld 282, D-6900 Heidelberg, FRG

one might have expected to find proteins with identical functions to be more conserved as they seem not to be exposed to the selective pressure of the immune system to a large extent. This may also dampen current hopes of employing the receptor-binding PapG proteins as the basis for the development of a subunit vaccine directed against the actual adhesin complex, though a cross-reactive mono-clonal antibody has been described (HOSCHÜTZKY et al. 1989).

3 Synthetic Peptides and Antigen Presentation

The investigation of the antigenic make-up of proteins has been the focus of intense research efforts for several decades. Nearly 30 years ago evidence had already been accumulated (JERNE 1960; SELA 1969) suggesting that antiprotein antibodies specifically recognize rather short, distinct segments of the protein sequence and that antibodies against these determinants can be induced by short synthetic peptides corresponding in sequence to these domains (LERNER 1982). With the advent of DNA sequencing and the availability of deduced amino acid sequences of a fast growing number of proteins, interest in synthetic peptide technology increased even more. Synthetic peptides serve as "immunologic tools," i.e., to study the antigenicity of proteins, the interaction of the immune system, and the possible expression of proteins from unidentified reading frames. Furthermore, synthetic peptides are investigated regarding their potential use as synthetic vaccines (ROWLANDS 1986).

With regard to the antigenicity of proteins the term "immunogenic epitope" is used to describe a particular domain in the native protein that is recognized by the immune system and gives rise to antibodies able to bind synthetic peptides corresponding to this domain. "Antigenic epitope" refers to domains that are recognized in the native protein by antibodies engendered by synthetic peptides corresponding to that particular region of the protein.

Antibodies induced by native proteins can recognize two types of determinant: either sequential (also termed "continuous" or "primary") or conformational (also termed "discontinuous," "assembled," or "topographic"). While sequential epitopes are made up of linear amino acid sequences, conformational determinants are introduced by the juxtaposition of two or more segments which are separated on the linear sequence due to the three-dimensional folding of the amino acid chain. Both types of determinant occupy discrete regions of the protein surface and are thus subject to conformational changes (VAN REGENMORTEL 1986, 1987). Though experimental evidence suggests that most of the determinants establishing the overall antigenicity of a given protein are made up of conformational epitopes (BARLOW et al. 1986), synthetic peptides have been applied successfully for the elucidation of linear antigenic structures of several proteins (ATASSI 1984; NIMAN et al. 1983). More recently, a technique has been developed to synthesize peptides designed to mimic conformational epitopes in the form of "mimotopes" (GEYSEN et al. 1985, 1986). A mimotope is a sequence of amino acids which mimics the ability

of a conformational determinant to bind a specific monoclonal antibody without necessarily bearing any resemblance to the sequence of the epitope (STEWARD and HOWARD 1987). An additional feature of the application of synthetic peptides is the possibility of engendering cross-reactive antibodies against areas of the protein found to be inaccessible to the immune system when the native protein is used as the immunogen (WILSON et al. 1984). This could have important implications for the development of synthetic vaccines, as discussed below.

A basic problem concerning the general application of synthetic peptides as immunogens still remains, i.e., how to select segments of a protein sequence for synthesis which are likely to encompass antigenic determinants and might be used to trigger protective immunity. Despite intensive efforts by numerous groups, only a few minimal properties concerning the nature of antigenic sites could be agreed on. For a region likely to be recognized as an antigenic determinant the prospective antigenic sites should be localized on the surface of the protein and should be accessible to the components of the immune system. There is a continuing debate on whether these regions present defined conformations (NOVOTNY et al. 1987) or represent areas of relatively high flexibility and mobility of the amino acid chain (TAINER et al. 1984, 1985). The latter argument might offer an explanation for the surprisingly frequent induction of cross-reactive antibodies by synthetic peptides (NIMAN et al. 1983; WILSON et al. 1985; JEMMERSON 1987), as very few short peptides (less than 20 amino acids) adopt a defined conformation in aqueous solutions.

Thus, for the prediction of possible antigenic determinants for the induction of cross-reactive antibodies there is no particular "best" method available. Rather, prediction is based on a combination of several available methods, or algorithms (Table 1; STEWARD and HOWARD 1987), supported if possible by additional experimental information.

The activation of B cells to synthesize and secrete specific antibodies is in most cases coincident with and dependent on the activation of antigen-specific helper T cells (T_h) to release B cell growth and differentiation factors. Unlike the B cell receptor (antibody), which directly recognizes native proteins free in solution, T_h

Table 1. Available methods for the prediction and detection of antigenic determinants (according to STEWARD and HOWARD 1987)

Hydrophilicity plots
Acrophilicity plots
Prediction of secondary structure (β-turns, β-sheets, α-helices)
Protrusion index plots
Segmental or atomic mobility analysis
Solvent accessibility
Knowledge-based modeling of amino acid sequences
Analysis of immunologic properties of purified fragments
Reactivity with monoclonal antibodies
Affinity of antibodies to native protein for peptides
Analysis of substitutions, deletions in variant proteins
Synthesis of overlapping peptides and mimotopes

cells usually cannot recognize foreign antigens in their native state. Rather, the antigen must be processed and presented on the surface of antigen presenting cells (APCs) in association with the Ia molecule, a class II major histocompatibility complex (MHC) antigen (MALE et al. 1987; BROWN et al. 1988; JANEWAY 1988; WATTS and DAVIDSON 1988). Processing in most cases involves antigen uptake, denaturation, and proteolysis in endosomes (UNANUE 1984; ALLEN 1987; PIERCE and MARGOLIASH 1988; CRESSWELL 1987). To enlist T cell help most short peptides have therefore to be conjugated to a larger carrier protein which serves as a source for T cell epitopes (ADA 1988).

The elucidation of the molecular basis for T cell recognition, a major goal in molecular immunology, has very recently seen a dramatic development. As a result of the description of the first crystallographic structure of an MHC glycoprotein (HLA-A2) (BJORKMAN et al. 1987a, b), more detailed investigation of possible contact sites as well as the molecular modeling of other class I and class II MHC antigens will be possible (PARHAM 1988; BROWN et al. 1988). Sequence analysis of T cell epitopes as well as the characterization of antigen-Ia complexes (BUUS et al. 1986; SETTLE et al. 1987; LAMB et al. 1987; ALLN et al. 1987; BABBITT et al. 1985) led to the proposal of a simple sequential motif for the prediction of T cell determinants (ROTHBARD et al. 1988; ROTHBARD and TAYLOR 1988) as well as to the suggestion of amphipathic α-helices as well-suited T cell epitopes (DELISI and BERZOFSKY 1985; BERZOFSKY 1988).

Thus, the exciting possibility of combining B cell epitopes recognized in the particular antigen with known or prospective T cell determinants for the respective MHC antigens in one synthetic peptide might open up new avenues for the development of highly efficient synthetic vaccines. Initial studies investigating this possible application for the malaria circumsporozoite protein (GOOD et al. 1987) as well as for the gp120 envelope protein of HIV (CEASE et al. 1987) have been reported.

4 Selection, Synthesis, and Conjugation of Fimbriae-Based Peptides as Immunogens

Synthetic peptides have so far been applied for the detection and identification of linear B cell epitopes in fimbriae of urinary tract infective *E. coli* and of *N. gonorrhoeae*. The straightforward use of synthetic peptides to identify antigenic or immunogenic epitopes is applicable only to such determinants which are encoded by linear amino acid sequences. In most proteins continuous epitopes represent only a fraction of the overall antigenicity. Nevertheless, antibodies induced by synthetic peptides can be successfully used as reagents for the identification of antigenic determinants and also as sequence-specific probes for structure–function analysis if they cross-react with high enough affinity with the native protein. The induction of such antibodies will only occur frequently if (in solution) the peptide adopts or can be induced to adopt a conformation that is identical or at least very similar to the

conformation of the corresponding segment in the parent protein (ARNON 1986a, b, VAN REGENMORTEL 1987; SHINNIK et al. 1983). Of the basic secondary structures commonly found in proteins [α-helices, β-pleated sheets, and β (reverse)-turns], β-turns have the highest probability of being mimicked in a short isolated synthetic peptide of about 15 amino acid residues. Strands of a β-pleated sheet require interaction with the adjacent strand to be stabilized (CHOTIA et al. 1977). Helices can form in an isolated peptide but the amino acid chain must be long enough for sufficient intrahelical interaction to occur. Further stabilization of helices is often the result of additional intramolecular interactions with neighboring protein regions (CHOTIA et al. 1977). The forces involved in the formation of β-turns, however, are thought to be inherent in the linear amino acid sequence of the oligopeptide chain and are in particular dependent on the nature of the four residues actually forming the reverse turn (RICHARDSON 1981; ROSE et al. 1985; LESZCZYNSKI and ROSE 1986). Turns have been found in immunologically interesting regions of proteins (ROSE et al. 1985). Furthermore, short peptides have been demonstrated to be able to adopt β-turns as preferred conformations in aqueous solutions (DYSON et al. 1985). For the fimbriae-based synthetic peptides these considerations lead to the selection of regions of the protein sequence predicted to contain preferably hydrophilic reverse turns as prime targets for peptide synthesis.

For the prediction of regions with a high probability for hydrophilic β-turns, a variety of algorithms are available for the prediction of secondary structures as well as hydrophilic and acrophilic domains (e.g., ROBSON and SUZUKI 1976; CHOU and FASMAN 1978; HOPP and WOODS 1981; KYTE and DOOLITTLE 1982).

The choice of peptides corresponding to *N. gonorrhoeae* or *E. coli* fimbriae sequences followed the arguments discussed above and was biased with regard to secondary structure and hydrophilicity predictions according to the algorithms of CHOU and FASMAN (1978) and HOPP and WOODS (1981). Regions were selected that were predicted to contain hydrophilic reverse turns at either end of the peptide sequence. The methods employed to conjugate oligopeptides to carrier protein molecules have a critical influence on the ability of the synthetic peptide to adopt the desired conformation (BRIAND et al. 1985; DYRBERG and OLDSTONE 1986) and thus also on the specificity of the antipeptide antibodies induced. During synthesis of selected fimbrial sequences a natural or additional cystein residue was therefore placed at the N- or C-terminal end distal to the predicted reverse turn, so that the peptide could be coupled in a unique orientation via heterobifunctional cross-linking agents to the respective carrier protein (SCHMIDT et al. 1984; DYRBERG and OLDSTONE 1986).

Peptides are synthesized by standard Merrifield solid phase techniques (BARANY and MERRIFIELD 1980; STEWARD and YOUNG 1984). Each peptide is conjugated after reduction to thyroglobulin and bovine serum albumin (BSA) using *m*-malein-imidobenzoyl *N*-hydroxysuccinimide ester (MBS) and succinimidyl 4-(*N*-mileinimido-methyl) cyclohexane-1-carboxylate (SMCC), respectively, as hetero-bifunctional cross-linking agents. Peptide specific antibodies are induced with the thyroglobulin conjugates while the resulting antisera are tested with the corresponding BSA conjugates.

5 *Neisseria gonorrhoeae* Fimbriae-Based Synthetic Peptides as Prospective Vaccines

Among the sexually transmitted diseases gonorrhea has reached pandemic proportions in many parts of the world, reawakening intensive research efforts regarding various aspects of the gonococcus (GOTSCHLICH 1984). Gonococcal fimbriae have been demonstrated to be mediators of gonococcal adherence to epithelial cells (BRITIGAN et al. 1985). Fimbriae have therefore been proposed as essential constituents of any acellular gonorrhea vaccine (ROBBINS 1978). However, the serologic diversity of gonococcal fimbriae remains a problem, though it has been suggested that fimbriae from antigenically heterologous strains possess a common conserved determinant which is immunorecessive in the native protein (BRINTON et al. 1978; SCHOOLNIK et al. 1983). Thus, considerable efforts have been directed towards the characterization of fimbrial structure, receptor binding domains (SCHOOLNIK et al. 1984), and the possibility of employing fimbriae, subfragments, and corresponding synthetic peptides for the induction of protective immunity.

The complete 159 amino acid fimbrillin sequence from strain MS11 has been determined. Subfragments generated by CNBr and tryptic cleavage were analyzed for the presence of functional regions. TC-2 (31-111), a fragment overlapping with the CNBr-2 fragments (9-92), was found to bind to human endocervical cells but not to buccal or HeLa cells (SCHOOLNIK et al. 1983, 1984). Thus, these fragments were suggested to contain the receptor binding domain of the gonococcal fimbriae. Furthermore, sequence comparison with the corresponding fragments of heterologous strains (R10 and 2686) indicated that these regions are highly conserved among gonococcal fimbriae. However, as suspected, these regions were shown to be immunorecessive in the native fimbriae. When fragment CNBr-2 of the fimbrillin was used as an immunogen, the common fimbriae determinant became immunodominant. The resulting antibodies cross-reacted with fimbriae from heterologous strains (SCHOOLNIK et al. 1983), thus raising the possibility of circumventing the serologic diversity among gonococcal fimbriae.

Based on these results, synthetic peptides corresponding to conserved as well as variable regions of the MS11 fimbrillin sequence were used to map the antigenic structure of the fimbrillin more precisely as well as to identify linear regions of the protein that would elicit cross-reactive antisera possibly inhibiting the binding of gonococci to eukaryotic cells (ROTHBARD et al. 1984). Results of these studies supported the earlier finding that type-specific and conserved cross-reactive determinants are separated in different regions of the fimbrillin sequence.

The selection and synthesis of peptides followed the lines discussed in the two preceding paragraphs. Eight peptides were synthesized corresponding to amino acid sequences 21–35, 41–50, 48–60, 69–84, 95–107, 107–121, 121–134, and 135–151. Antisera to whole MS11 or R10 fimbriae bound only the regions corresponding to residues 48–60, thus indicating this region to contain the common immunorecessive epitope identified earlier in the TC-2 and CNBr-2 subfragments. The binding was significantly less than that of homologous antiserum to the strain-specific immuodominant epitopes in the cystein loop (R121–134 and R135–151). Less than

15% of the immunogenicity of the whole fimbriae was found to reside in the common determinant (R48–60). The results of these studies in combination with similar experiments employing monoclonal antibodies as probes (EDWARDS et al. 1984) supported the clustering of type-specific and conserved epitopes in different regions of the fimbrillin sequence. However, when the central CNBr-2 fragment (residues 8–92) was used as immunogen a much stronger cross-reactive response was generated. Antisera raised against the CNBr-2 fragment did not recognize R48–60 but bound to R69–84 and R41–50. This indicates that the immunogenicity of this region is determined by interactions in the whole intact fimbriae which are absent in the isolated fragments. Furthermore, it shows that peptides can elicit antibody populations that are different from those obtained using the intact protein as immunogen.

The antipeptide antisera were assessed for cross-reactivity with intact fimbriae of homologous and heterologous strains as well as for their ability to inhibit the binding of whole bacteria to human endometrial carcinoma cells (ROTHBARD et al. 1985). As shown in Fig. 1, the antipeptide antisera varied in their ability to recognize the homologous MS11 as well as the heterologous R10 fimbriae. Especially peptide R69–84 was effective in evoking a cross-reactive response. In Western blotting all antipeptide antisera cross-reacted with MS11 and most also recognized fimbriae from strain R10. Anti-R69–84 antiserum additionally recognized fimbriae from the heterologous strains F62, 1896, and 2686. Antisera raised against residues 21–35, 41–50, 48–60, and 69–84 immunoprecipitated the TC-2 fragment of MS11 fimbriae containing the proposed receptor-binding domain. Thus, these antisera were screened for their ability to block adherence of strain F62 to the human endometrial carcinoma cell line ENCA-4. Only antisera to residues 41–50 and 69–84 corresponding to the proposed conserved receptor-binding domain inhibited adherence (about 90%). Cross-reactive antibodies directed against the region containing type-specific epitopes (R135–151) were not able to reduce the binding of gonococci to ENCA-4 endometrial cells.

The peptides eliciting cross-reactive antibodies have been proposed as candidate immunogens for the prevention of gonorrhea (ROTHBARD et al. 1985) under the assumption that they would evoke the formation of antiadhesive antibodies. Success of any synthetic vaccine is clearly linked to the conservation of the respective antigenic epitope in the in vivo situation. As no animal model exists for gonorrhea, this question was addressed in a model of experimental gonorrhea in male volunteers (SWANSON et al. 1987). All reisolates from an infection with a defined strain MS11 expressed pili distinct from the strain used for infection and thus corroborated earlier results found with other MS11 variants and clinical isolates (HAGBLOM et al. 1985). Furthermore, amino acid changes have also always been found in the 69–84 oligopeptide region, suggesting that this region is not conserved in the in vivo situation and that therefore the peptide 69–84 will not be effective as a gonorrhea vaccine (SWANSON et al. 1987). Thus, the mechanism of chromosomal rearrangement involving recombination of minicassettes (SEGAL et al. 1985) gives rise to novel pili whose antigenic differences stem from amino acid changes in multiple regions so that the possible existence of a truly conserved domain needs to be reinvestigated.

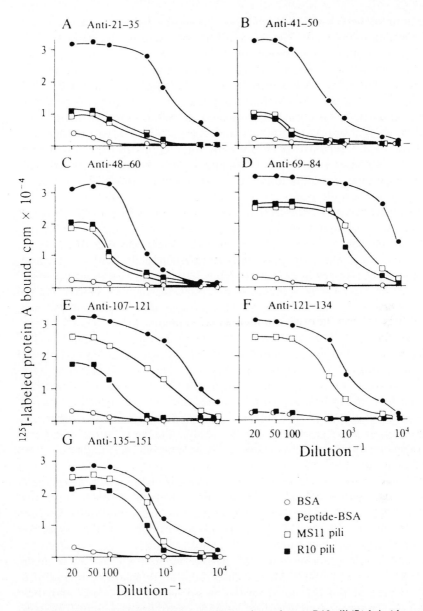

Fig. 1. Recognition of either homologous MS11 or heterologous R10 pili (fimbriae) by antipeptide sera in solid phase binding assays. Antisera elicited by peptide–thyroglobulin conjugates corresponding to residues 21–35 (*A*), 41–50 (*B*), 48–60 (*C*), 69–84 (*D*), 107–121 (*E*), 121–134 (*F*), and 135–151 (*G*) of MS11 pili were incubated with homologous peptide–BSA conjugate (●), isolated intact MS11 (□) and R10 (■) pili, or BSA (○). (ROTHBARD et al. 1985)

6 Synthetic Peptides Based on P-Specific Fimbriae of Uropathogenic *Escherichia coli* as Vaccines

Urinary tract infections caused by uropathogenic strains of *E. coli* represent one of the most common types of infectious disease, afflicting about 20% of all women at least once (ANDRIOLE 1987). About 80%–90% of all pyelonephritis isolates express P-specific fimbriae recognizing the α-Gal-(1-4)-β-Gal digalactoside as receptor. Though P-specific fimbriae from heterologous uropathogenic *E. coli* strains are structurally and functionally closely related and have also been shown to be protective immunogens for homologous infections in animal models (O'HANLEY et al. 1985; ROBERTS et al. 1982, 1984b; KAACK et al. 1988), their pronounced serologic diversity has so far impeded the development of a fimbriae-based vaccine. A way of circumventing this obstacle might be the development of synthetic peptides corresponding to possibly conserved sequences of the immunodominant fimbrillin.

N-terminal amino acid sequences of a number of fimbrillin proteins associated with P-specific fimbriae have been elucidated (Table 2), indicating conserved segments among heterologous strains. These regions, however, are immunorecessive when native isolated fimbriae are used as immunogens (SCHMIDT et al. 1984). Synthetic peptides corresponding to selected regions of the HU 849 fimbrillin (J96) sequence have been applied to map linear antigenic and immunogenic determinants (SCHMIDT et al. 1984). Three specific immunogenic epitopes (R25–38, R38–50, R48–61) were identified which jointly constitute the N-terminal cystein loop of the fimbrillin. Two prominent antigenic determinants were localized on peptides corresponding to R5–12 and R93–104 whereas R65–75 and R119–131 represented two minor antigenic determinants. However, only antisera raised against thyroglobulin conjugates of R5–12 and R93–104 cross-reacted with fimbriae from heterologous *E. coli* strains. Anti-R5–12 antiserum recognized about 85% of all P-specific fimbriae investigated so far by Western blotting (Fig. 2). Thus, the synthetic peptide R5–12 corresponds to a highly conserved antigenic determinant which was furthermore shown to be immunorecessive in the native fimbriae (SCHMIDT et al. 1984) and should thus not be prone to antigenic variation due to the selective pressure of the host's immune system.

Peptides corresponding to antigenic epitopes were assayed for their protective effect when applied as immunogens in the model of experimental pyelonephritis in mice. (O'HANLEY et al. 1985). Groups of Balb/c mice were immunized and boostered with peptide–thyroglobulin conjugates in Freund's adjuvant and subsequently challenged by intra-bladder inoculations of 10^8 colony-forming units (CFU) of the wild-type pyelonephritogenic *E. coli* strain J96. Two days later colonization of urine and kidneys with J96 bacteria was assessed as a measure of infection. It was shown that immunization with the synthetic peptides R5–12 and R65–75 protected against homologous infection just as efficiently as immunization with homologous isolated fimbriae (SCHMIDT et al. 1988). Thus peptides R5–12 and R65–75 correspond to "protective" epitopes (Fig. 3). Furthermore, as R5–12 encompasses a highly conserved cross-reactive epitope, these results suggest that this region might also be

Table 2. Comparison of N-terminal amino acid sequences[a] of UTI *E. coli* pilins and (afimbrial) adhesins

Bacteria	Protein	Isolate	N-terminal amino acid sequence
UTI *E. coli*	*Afimbrial*		
	AFA-I	KS52	N F T S S G T N G K V D L T I T E E C R V T V E
	AFA-V	MIR2194	A N Q G Q G V V N S K G T V I D A T C G I D P D
	Fimbrial		
	F7$_1$	C1212	A A T I P Q G Q G E V A F K G T V V D A P
	F7$_2$	AD110	A P T I P Q G Q G K V T F N G T V V D A P C G
	F9	3669	A P S Q G S G Q V N F K G T V I D A P C G I E T Q S A N Q T I D F
	F11		A P T I P Q G Q G K V T F N G T V V D A P C S I S Q K S A D Q S I
	F12	C1979	A P T I P E G Q G K V T F N G T V V
	F13	J96	A P T I P Q G Q G K V T F N G T V V D A P C S I S Q K S A D Q S I
	PapA		V D N L T F R G K L I I P A C T V S N T T V D W Q D
	PapE		D V Q I N I R G N V Y I P P C T I N N G Q N I V V D
	PapF		
	PapG		G W H N V M F Y A F N D Y L T T N A G N V K V I D Q
Type 1	Type 1A	K12	A A T T V N G – G T V H F K G E V V N A A C A
	Type 1A	J96	A A T T V N G – G T V H F K G E V V N A A C A
	Type 1A	C1214	A A T T V N G – G T V H F K G E V V N A A X A
	Type 1B	C1214	A T T V N G – G T V H F K G E V V V
	Type 1B	C1023	V T T V N G – G T V H F K G E V V D

UTI = Urinary tract infective

[a] References from which the N-terminal amino acid sequences have been obtained: AFA-I (WALZ et al. 1985; LABIGNE-ROUSSEL et al. 1985), AFA-V (Ruffing and Schmidt 1988, unpublished work), F7 (KLEMM 1985), F7$_2$ (RHEN et al. 1985; VAN DIE and BERGMANS 1984), F9 (KLEMM 1985), F11 (VAN DIE et al. 1986), F12 (KLEMM et al. 1983), F13 (BAGA et al. 1984), PapE, F (LINDBERG et al. 1986), PapG (LUND et al. 1987), Type 1A, B, C (KLEMM 1985; RHEN et al. 1985)

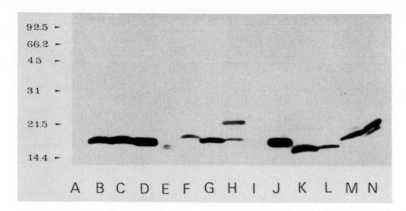

Fig. 2. Western blot of P-specific *E. coli* strains or purified P-specific pili (fimbriae) probed with anti-R5–12 antiserum diluted 1:200. Bound antibody was detected with ^{125}I-labeled protein A after an 8-h autoradiographic exposure. *Lane A*, nonpiliated K-12 strain HB101; *lane B*, strain J96 (F13); *lane C*, pap5 (HB 101) (F13); *lane D*, purified pili from recombinant strain HU849 (F13); *lane E*, C1979 (F12); *lane F*, AM 1727 carrying plasmid pPIL110-75 (expresses $F7_1$ of AD 110); *lane G*, AM 1727 carrying pPIL110-35 (expresses $F7_2$ of AD 110); *lane H*, C1212 (AD 110) ($F7_1$ and $F7_2$); *lane I*, 3669 (F9); *lane J*, pilin purified from pap5 (HB 101); *lanes K–N*, pyelonephritis strains P21, A42, A50, and A8. Positions and sizes (kd) of standard proteins run in parallel are shown at *left*. (SCHMIDT et al. 1988).

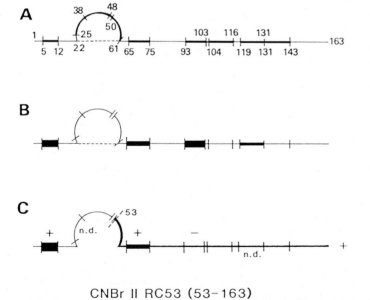

CNBr II RC53 (53–163)

Fig. 3. Linear antigenic and protective epitopes of the HU 849 pilin. The linear depiction of the pilin shows the location of the peptides synthesized (*A*), the identified linear antigenic determinants (*B*), and the synthetic peptides corresponding to protective epitopes (*C*) in the experimental pyelonephritis model

protective against heterologous challenge. This study demonstrated that a small selected peptide corresponding to a linear conserved immunorecessive epitope (R5–12) is able to confer protection on a mucosal surface in a relevant animal model against homologous bacterial infection equal to that obtained with the intact protein.

The molecular basis for the efficacy of peptides R5–12 and R65–75 as vaccines, however, was not addressed. In sera of immunized animals only fimbriae-specific IgG antibodies could be detected. In light of the identification and localization of the adhesin complex at the tip of the pilus filament (LINDBERG et al. 1987; HOSCHÜTZKY et al. 1989), a model for the efficacy of antipeptide antibodies directed against the N-terminal region of the fimbrillin protein is difficult to envisage. However, preliminary results using immunogold labeling of bacteria incubated with antibodies directed against the N-terminal sequence of the HU 849 pilus suggest a selective binding at the tip of the filament, thus offering a possible explanation for the protective effect (M. A. SCHMIDT, unpublished data). It remains to be seen from further experiments whether the protection demonstrated with *fimbrillin*-based synthetic peptides against homologous infections in an animal model can be extended to urinary tract infections due to heterologous strains. Although the employed animal model exhibits properties very close to the human situation, a real test of efficacy for any candidate vaccine can only be conducted in human trials.

7 Conclusion and Outlook

The possibility of employing fimbriae-based synthetic peptides for the development of synthetic vaccines has so far been investigated for fimbriae of *N. gonorrhoeae* and of uropathogenic P-specific *E. coli*. In both cases synthetic peptides were used to characterize the linear antigenicity of the immunodominant structural fimbrillin as a prerequisite for functional studies. Synthetic peptides corresponding to conserved antigenic determinants were assayed for their capacity to induce antibodies able to interfere with binding of the respective bacteria.

Synthetic peptides corresponding to a proposed conserved region of MS11 fimbriae induced cross-reactive antibodies which reduced the number of MS11 and R10 gonococi adhering to endometerial cells used in a tissue cultue adherence assay to about 10%. Studies in human volunteers, however, showed that the extensive antigenic variation found in gonococcal fimbriae is even more pronounced in the in vivo situation and furthermore always affected the proposed conserved region. Thus, the induction of protective immunity in humans by those synthetic peptides characterized so far seems rather unlikely.

In P-specific fimbriae of *E. coli* a conserved highly cross-reactive linear epitope has been identified. It could be shown that this determinant induces protective immunity towards homologous infection in an animal model relevant to the situation in humans. Though it remains to be seen whether these results can be extended to infections with heterologous strains, these studies showed that a small

synthetic peptide corresponding to a linear antigenic fimbrial determinant is able to confer protection on a mucosal surface against bacterial infection. A similar approach is currently being applied to proteins more directly involved in the adhesive complex of P-specific fimbriae.

In considering possible applications of synthetic peptides as vaccines, one has to keep in mind that so far the theoretical basis for the selection of linear domains for synthesis is still rather crude. Detection and selection of peptide sequences likely to be employed as mimotopes are still largely based on trial and error. With the rapidly increasing knowledge of the molecular geometry of antigen-presenting MHC antigens as well as the corresponding T cell receptors, a more knowledge-based selection of antigenic domains might be possible, perhaps even leading to a predictive analysis of possible mimotopes. The incorporation of synthetic T_h and B cell sites in one synthetic antigen (CELADA and SERCARZ 1988) might also be a possible way of overcoming genetic restrictions (GOOD et al. 1987; FRANCIS et al. 1987). Furthermore, synthetic peptides can now be synthesized with inbuilt conformational restrictions (SATTERTHWAIT et al. 1988) so that the probability of eliciting cross-reactive antibodies will be highly increased. One of the more practical advantages of synthetic vaccines in general is that they can be obtained free of reactogenic contaminants which often present problems in vaccines derived from biologic sources. Synthetic peptides enjoy excellent prospects of being incorporated into semisynthetic or fully synthetic vaccines in the near future, including also the development of synthetic peptide vaccines on the basis of adhesion-linked proteins of pathogenic bacteria.

Acknowledgments. I like to thank Ms. Johanna Grosser for secretarial assistance and Dr. Inga Benz for the critical reading of the manuscript.

References

Abe C, Schmitz S, Moser I, Boulnois G, High NJ, Ørskov I, Jann B, Jann K (1987) Monoclonal antibodies with fimbrial FIC, F12, F13 and F14 specificities obtained with fimbriae from *E. coli* 04:K12:H⁻. Microb Pathogen 2: 71–77

Acres SD, Isaacson RE, Babiuk LA, Kapitany RA (1979) Immunization of calves against enterotoxigenic colibacillosis by vaccinating dams with purified K99 antigen and whole cell bacterins. Infect Immun 25: 121–126

Ada GL (1988) What to expect of a good vaccine and how to achieve it. Vaccine 6: 77–79

Allen PM (1987) Antigen processing at the molecular level. Immunol Today 8: 270–273

Allen PM, Matsueda GR, Evans RJ, Dunbar JB, Marshall GR, Unanue ER (1987) Identification of the T-cell and Ia contact residues of a T-cell antigenic epitope. Nature 327: 713–715

Andriole VT (1987) Urinary tract infections: recent developments. J Infect Dis 156: 865–869

Arnon R (1986a) Peptides as immunogens—prospects for a synthetic vaccine. In: Koprowski H, Melchers F (eds) Peptides as immunogens. Springer, Berlin Heidelberg New York, pp 1–12 (Current topics in microbiology and immunology, vol 130)

Arnon R (1986b) Synthetic peptides as the basis for future vaccines. Trends Biochem Sci (TIBS) 11: 521–524

Atassi MZ (1984) Antigenic structures of proteins. Eur J Biochem 145: 1–20

Babbitt BP, Allen PM, Matsueda G, Haber E, Unanue ER (1985) Binding of immunogenic peptides to Ia histocompatibility molecules. Nature 317: 359–361

Baga M, Normark S, Hardy J, O'Hanley P, Lark D, Olsson O, Schoolnik G, Falkow S (1984) Nucleotide sequence of the papA gene encoding the Pap pilus subunit of human uropathogenic *Escherichia coli*. J Bacteriol 157: 330–333

Barlow DJ, Edwards MS, Thornton JM (1986) Continuous and discontinuous protein antigenic determinants. Nature 322: 747–748

Beachey EH (1981) Bacterial adherence: adhesin-receptor interactions mediating the attachment of bacteria to mucosal surfaces. J Infect Dis 143: 325–345

Berzofsky JA (1988) Features of T-cell recognition and antigen structure useful in the design of vaccines to elicit T-cell immunity. Vaccine 6: 89–93

Bjorkman PJ, Saper MA, Samraoui B, Bennett WS, Strominger JL, Wiley DC (1987a) Structure of the human class I histocompatibility antigen, HLA-A2. Nature 329: 506–512

Bjorkman PJ, Saper MA, Samraoui B, Bennett WS, Strominger JL, Wiley DC (1987b) The foreign antigen binding site and T cell recognition regions of class I histocompatibility antigens. Nature 329: 512–518

Briand JP, Muller S, Van Regenmortel MHV (1985) Synthetic peptides as antigens: pitfalls of conjugation methods. J Immunol Methods 78: 59–69

Brinton CC, Bryan J, Dillon JA, Guerina N, Jacobson LJ, Kraus S, Labik A, Lee S, Levene A, Lim S, McMichael J, Polen S, Rogers K, To ACC, To SCM (1978) Uses of pili in gonorrhea control. Role of pili disease, purification and properties of gonococcal pili, and progress in the development of a gonococcal pilus vaccine for gonorrhea. In: Brooks GF, Gotschlich EC, Holmes KK, Sawyer WD, Young FE (eds) Immunology of *Neisseria gonorrhea*. American Society for Microbiology, Washington, pp 155–178

Britigan EB, Cohen MS, Sparling PF (1985) Gonococcal infection: a model of molecular pathogenesis. N Engl J Med 312: 1683–1694

Brown JH, Jardetzky T, Saper MA, Samraoui B, Bjorkman PJ, Wiley DC (1988) A hypothetical model of the foreign antigen binding site of class II histocompatibility molecules. Nature 332: 845–850

Buus S, Sette A, Colon SM, Jenis DM, Grey HM (1986) Isolation and characterization of antigen-Ia complexes involved in T-cell recognition. Cell 47: 1071–1077

Cease KB, Margalit H, Cornette JL, Putney SD, Robey WG, Ouyang C, Streicher HZ, Fischinger PJ, Gallo RC, Delisi C, Berzofsky JA (1987) Helper T cell antigenic site identification in the AIDS virus gp 120 envelope protein and induction of immunity in mice to the native protein using a 16-residue synthetic peptide. Proc Natl Acad Sci USA 84: 4249–4253

Celada F, Sercarz EE (1988) Preferential pairing of T-B specificities in the same antigen: the concept of directional help. Vaccine 6: 94–98

Chothia C, Levitt M, Richardson D (1977) Structures of proteins: packing of α-helices and β-pleated sheets. Proc Natl Acad Sci USA 74: 4130–4134

Chou PY, Fasman GD (1978) Empirical predictions of protein conformation. Annu Rev Biochem 47: 251–276

Contrepois M, Girardeau JP (1985) Additive protective effects of colostral antipili antibodies in calves experimentally infected with enterotoxigenic *Escherichia coli*. Infect Immun 50: 847–849

Cravioto A, Scotland SM, Rowe B (1982) Hemagglutination activity and colonization factor antigens I and II in enterotoxigenic and non-enterotoxigenic strains of *Escherichia coli* isolated from humans. Infect Immun 36: 189–197

Cresswell P (1987) Antigen recognition by T lymphocytes. Immunol Today 8: 67–69

de Graaf FK, Roorda I (1982) Production, purification and characterization of the fimbrial adhesive antigen F41 isolated from calf enteropathogenic *Escherichia coli* strain B41M. Infect Immun 36: 751–758

de la Cabada FJ, Evans DG, Evans DJ (1981) Immunoprotection against enterotoxigenic *Escherichia coli* diarrhea in rabbits by peroral administration of purified colonization factor antigen I(CFA/I). FEMS Microbiol Lett 11: 303–7

DeLisi C, Berzofsky JA (1985) T-cell antigenic sites tend to be amphipathic structures. Proc. Natl Acad Sci USA 82: 7048–7052

Dyrberg T, Oldstone MBA (1986) Peptides as antigens—importance of orientation. J Exp Med 164: 1344–1349

Dyson HJ, Cross KJ, Houghten RA, Wilson IA, Wright PE, Lerner RA (1985) The immunodominant site of a synthetic immunogen has a conformational preference in water for a type-II reverse turn. Nature 318: 480–483

Edwards, McDade RL, Schoolnik G, Rothbard JB, Gotschlich EC (1984) Antigenic analysis of gonococcal pili using monoclonal antibodies. J Exp Med 160: 1782–1791

Evans DG, Evans DJ (1978) New surface associated heat-labile colonization factor antigen (CFA/II) produced by enterotoxigenic *Escherichia coli* of serogroups O6 and O8. Infect Immun 21: 638–647

Evans DG, Evans DJ, Tjoa WS, DuPont HL (1978) Detection and characterization of the colonization

factor antigen of enterotoxigenic *Escherichia coli* isolated from adults with diarrhea. Infect Immun 19: 727–736

Evans DG, Evans DJ, Clegg S, Pauley JA (1979) Purification and characterisation of the CFA/I antigen of enterotoxigenic *Escherichia coli*. Infect Immun 25: 738–748

Evans DG, de la Cabada FJ, Evans DJ (1982) Correlation between intestinal immune response to colonization factor antigen/I and acquired resistance to enterotoxigenic *Escherichia coli* diarrhea in an adult rabbit model. Eur J Clin Microbiol 1: 178–85

Evans DG, Graham BY, Evans DJ, Opekun A (1984) Administration of purified colonization factor antigens (CFA/I, CFA/II) of enterotoxigenic *Escherichia coli* to volunteers. Gastroenterology 87: 934–940

Francis MJ, Hastings GZ, Syred AD, McGinn B, Brown F, Rowlands DJ (1987) Non–responsiveness to foot-and-mouth disease virus peptide overcome by addition of foreign helper T-cell determinants. Nature 300: 168–170

Freter R (1981) Mechanism of association of bacteria with mucosal surfaces. Ciba Found Symp 80: 36–55

Gaastra W, Klemm P, de Graaf FK (1982) Prediction of antigenic determinants and secondary structures of the K88 and CFA/I fimbrial proteins from enteropathogenic *Escericia coli*. Infect Immun 38: 41–45

Geysen HM, Rodda SJ, Mason TJ (1985) The delineation of peptides able to mimic assembled epitopes. Ciba Found Symp 119: 130–149

Geysen HM, Rodda SJ, Mason TJ (1986) *A priori* delineation of a peptide which mimics a discontinuous antigenic determinant. Mol Immunol 23: 709–715

Gibbons RJ (1977) Adherence of bacteria to host tissue. In: Schlessinger D (ed) Microbiology. American Society for Microbiology, Washington, pp 395–406

Good MF, Maloy WL, Lunde MN, Margalit H, Cornette JL, Smith GL, Moss B, Miller LH, Berzofsky JA (1987) Construction of a synthetic immunogen: use of a new T-helper epitope on malaria circumsporozite protein. Science 235: 1059–1062

Gotschlich EC (1984) Development of a gonorrhoea vaccine: prospects, strategies and tactics. Bull WHO 62: 671–680

Gross RJ, Rowe B (1985) *Escherichia coli* diarrhoea. J Hyg 95: 531–550

Hagblom P, Segal E, Billyard E, So M (1985) Intragenic recombination leads to pilus antigenic variation in *Neisseria gonorrhoeae*. Nature 315: 156–158

Hopp TP, Woods KR (1981) Prediction of protein antigenic determinants from amino acid sequences. Proc Natl Acad Sci USA 78: 3824–3828

Hoschützky H, Lottspeich F, Jann K (1989) Isolation and characterization of the α-galactosyl-1,4-β-galactosyl specific adhesin (P adhesin) from fimbrial *Escherichia coli*. Infect Immun 57: 76–81

Isaacson RE (1977) K99 surface antigen of *Escherichia coli*: purification and partial characterization. Infect Immun 15: 272–279

Isaacson RE, Dean EA, Morgan RL, Moon HW (1980) Immunization of suckling pigs against enterotoxigenic *Escherichia coli*-induced diarrheal disease by vaccinating dams with purified K99 or 987P pili: antibody production in response to vaccination. Infect Immun 29: 824–826

Janeway CA (1988) Frontiers of the immune system. Nature 333: 804–806

Jemmerson R (1987) Antigenicity and native structure of globular proteins: low frequency of peptide reactive antibodies. Proc. Natl Acad Sci USA 84: 9180–9184

Jerne NK (1960) Immunological speculations Annu Rev Microbiol 14: 341–358

Kaack MB, Roberts JA, Baskin G, Patterson GM (1988) Maternal immunization with P fimbriae for the prevention of neonatal pyelonephritis. Infect Immun 56: 1–6

Kaper JB, Levine MM (1988) Progress towards a vaccine against enterotoxigenic *Escherichia coli*. Vaccine 6: 197–199

Klemm P (1985) Fimbrial adhesins of *Escherichia coli*. Rev Infect Dis 7: 321–340

Klemm P, Mikkelsen L (1982) Prediction of antigenic determinants and secondary structures of the K88 and CFA/I fimbrial proteins from enteropathogenic *Escherichia coli*. Infect Immun 38: 41–45

Klemm P, Ørskov I, Ørskov F (1983) Isolation and characterization of F12 adhesive fimbrial antigen from uropathogenic *Escherichia coli* strains. Infect Immun 40: 91–96

Kyte J, Doolittle RF (1982) A simple method for displaying the hydropathic character of a protein. J Mol Biol 157: 105–132

Labigne-Roussel A, Schmidt MA, Walz W, Falkow S (1985) Genetic organization of the afimbrial adhesin operon and nucleotide sequence from a uropathogenic *Escherichia coli* gene encoding an afimbrial adhesin. J Bacteriol 162(3): 1285–1292

Lamb JR, Ivanyi J, Rees ADM, Rothbard JB, Howland K, Young RA, Young DB (1987) Mapping of T cell epitopes using recombinant antigens and synthetic peptides. EMBO J 6: 1245–1249

Lerner LA (1982) Tapping the immunological repertoire to produce antibodies of predetermined specificity. Nature 299: 592–596

Leszczynski JF, Rose GD (1986) Loops in globular proteins: a novel category of secondary structure. Science 234: 849–855

Levine MM, Kaper JB, Black RE, Clements ML (1983) New knowledge on pathogenesis of bacterial enteric infections as applied to vaccine development. Microbiol Rev 47: 510–550

Levine MM, Ristaino P, Marley G, Smyth C, Knutton S, Boedecker E, Blanck R, Young C, Clements ML, Cheney C, Patnaik R (1984) Coli surface antigens 1 and 3 of colonization factor antigen II-positive enterotoxigenic *Escherichia coli*: morphology, purification, and immune responses in humans. Infect Immun 44; 409–420

Lindberg F, Lund B, Normark S (1986) Gene products specifying adhesion of uropathogenic *Escherichia coli* are minor components of pili. Proc Natl Acad Sci USA 83: 1891–1895

Lindberg F, Lund B, Johansson L, Normark S (1987) Localization of the receptor-binding protein adhesin at the tip of the bacterial pilus. Nature 328: 84–87

Lund B, Lindberg F, Marklund BI, Normark S (1987) The PapG protein is the α-D-galactopyranosyl-(1-4)-β-D-galactopyranose-binding adhesin of uropathogenic *Escherichia coli*. Proc Natl Acad Sci USA 84: 5898–5902

Lund B, Lindberg F, Normark S (1988) Structure and antigenic properties of the tip-located P pilus proteins of uropathogenic *Escherichia coli*. J Bacteriol 170: 1887–1894

Male D, Champion B, Cooke A (1987) Advanced immunology. Gower Medical, London

Mimion FC, Abraham SN, Beachey EH, Gogen JD (1986) The genetic determinant of adhesive function in type 1 fimbriae of *Escherichia coli* is distinct from the gene encoding the fimbrial subunit. J Bacteriol 165: 1033–1036

Moch T, Hoschützky H, Hacker J, Kröncke KD, Jann K (1987) Isolation and characterization of the α-sialyl-β-2,3-galactosyl-specific adhesin from fimbriated *Escherichia coli*. Proc Natl Acad Sci USA 84: 3462–3466

Morgan RL, Isaacson RE, Moon HW, Brinton CC, To CC (1978) Immunization of suckling pigs against enterotoxigenic *Escherichia coli*-induced diarrheal disease by vaccinating dams with purified 987 or K99 pili: protection correlates with pilus homology of vaccine and challenge. Infect Immun 22; 771–777

Morris JA, Thorns C, Scott AC, Sojka WC, Wells GA (1982) Adhesion in vitro and in vivo associated with an adhesive antigen (F41) produced by a K99 mutant of the reference strain *Escherichia coli* B41. Infect Immun 36: 1146–1153

Nagy B, Moon HW, Isaacson RE, To CC, Brinton CC (1978) Immunization of suckling pigs against enteric enterotoxigenic *Escherichia coli* infection by vaccinating dams with purified pili. Infect Immun 21: 269–274

Niman HL, Houghten RA, Walker LE, Reisfeld RA, Wilson IA, Hogle JM, Lerner RA (1983) Generation of protein-reactive antibodies by short peptides is an event of high frequency: implications for the structural basis of immune recognition. Proc Natl Acad Sci USA 80: 4949–4953

Normark S, Båga M, Göranson M, Lindberg FP, Lund B, Norgen M, Uhlin BE (1986) Genetics and biogenesis of *Escherichia coli* adhesins. In: Mirelman D (ed) Microbial lectins and agglutinins (properties and biological activity). Wiley, New York, pp 113–145

Novotny J, Handschumacher M, Bruccoleri RE (1987) Protein antigenicity: a static surface property. Immunol Today 8: 26–31

O'Hanley P, Lark D, Falkow S, Schoolnik G (1985) Molecular basis of *Escherichia coli* colonization of the upper urinary tract in BALB/c mice—Gal-Gal pili immunization prevents *Escherichia coli* pyelonephritis in the Balb/c mouse model of human pyelonephritis. J Clin Invest 75: 347–360

Ørskov I, Ørskov F (1983) Serology of *Escherichia coli* fimbriae. Prog Allergy 33: 80–105

Parham P (1988) Presentation and processing of antigens in Paris. Immunol Today 9: 65–68

Pierce SK, Margoliash (1988) Antigen processing: an interim report. Trends Biochem Sci (TIBS) 13: 27–29

Rhen M, van Die I, Rhen V, Bergmans H (1985) Comparison of the nucleotide sequences of the genes encoding the KS71A and $F7_1$ fimbrial antigens of uropathogenic *Escherichia coli*. Eur J Biochem 151: 573–577

Richardson JS (1981) The anatomy and taxonomy of protein structure. Adv Protein Chem 34: 167–339

Robbins JB (1978) Disease control for gonorrhea by vaccine immunoprophylaxis: the next step? In: Brooks GF, Gotschlich EC, Holmes KK, Sawyer WD, Loung FE (eds) Immunobiology of Neisseria gonorrhoeae. American Society Microbiology, Washington, pp 391–394

Roberts JA, Kaack B, Korhonen TK, Källenius G, Svenson SB, Winberg J (1982) Protection against pyelonephritis by immunization with bacterial fimbriae of *Escherichia coli* in the primate model (Abstract no 243). In: Proceedings of the 7th international congress on infections and parasitic disease, Stockholm

Roberts JA, Kaack B, Kallenius G, Mollby R, Winberg J, Svenson SB (1984a) Receptors for pyelonephritogenic *Escherichia coli* in primates. J Urol 131: 163–168

Roberts JA, Hardaway K, Kaack B, Fussell EL, Baskin G (1984b) Prevention of pyelonephritis by immunization with P-fimbriae. J Urol 131: 602–607

Robson B, Suzuki E (1976) Conformational properties of amino acid residues in globular proteins. J Mol Biol 107: 327–356

Rose GD, Gierasch LM, Smith JA (1985) Turns in peptides and proteins. Adv Protein Chem 37: 1–109

Rothbard JB, Fernandez R, Schoolnik GK (1984) Strain-specific and common epitopes of gonococcal pili. J Exp Med 160: 208–221

Rothbard JB, Fernandez R, Wang L, Teng NNH, Schoolnik GK (1985) Antibodies to peptides corresponding to a conserved sequence of gonococcal pilins block bacterial adhesion. Proc Natl Acad Sci USA 82: 915–919

Rothbard JB, Taylor WR (1988a) A sequence pattern common to T cell epitopes. EMBO J 7: 93–100

Rothbard JB, Lechler RI, Howland K, Bal V, Eckels DD, Sekaly R, Long EO, Taylor WR, Lamb JR (1988b) Structural model of HLA-DR1 restricted T cell antigen recognition. Cell 52: 515–523

Rowlands DJ (1986) Vaccines—the synthetic antigen approach. In: Silver S, Silver S, Broda P, Chakrabarty AM, Collins J, Davies JE, Hopwood DA, Knowles CJ, Starlinger P, van Montagu M (eds) Biotechnology: potentials and limitations. Report of the Dahlem workshop 1985. Springer, Berlin Heidelberg New York, pp 139–154 (Dahlem workshop reports, vol 35)

Runnels PL, Moseley SL, Moon HW (1987) F41 pili as protective antigens of enterotoxigenic *Escherichia coli* that produce F41, K99 or both pilus antigens. Infect Immun 55: 555–558

Rutter JM, Jones GW (1973) Protection against enteric disease caused by *Escherichia coli*—a model for vaccination with a virulence determinant? Nature 242: 531–532

Sack RB (1980) Enterotoxigenic *Escherichia coli*: identification and characterization. J Infect Dis 142: 279–286

Satterthwait AC, Arrhenius T, Hagopian RA, Zavala F, Nussenzweig V, Lerner RA (1988) Conforma tional restriction of peptidyl immunogens with covalent replacements for the hydrogen bond. Vaccine 6: 99–103

Schmidt MA, O'Hanley P, Schoolnik GK (1984) Gal-Gal pyelonephritis *Escherichia coli* pili linear immunogenic and antigenic epitopes. J Exp Med 161: 705–715

Schmidt MA, O'Hanley P, Lark D, Schoolnik PA (1988) Synthetic peptides corresponding to protective epitopes of *Escherichia coli* digalactoside-binding pilin prevent infection in a murine pyelonephritis model. Proc. Natl Acad Sci USA 85: 1247–1251

Schoolnik GK, Tai JY, Gotschlich EC (1983) A pilus peptide vaccine for the prevention of gonorrhea. Prog Allergy 33: 314–331

Schoolnik GK, Fernandez R, Tai JY, Rothbard JB, Gotschlich EC (1984) Gonococcal pili—primary structure and receptor binding domain. J Exp Med 159: 1351–1370

Segal E, Billyard E, So M, Storzbach S, Meyer TF (1985) Role of chromosomal rearrangement in *N. gonorrhoeae* pilus phase variation. Cell 40: 293–300

Sela M (1960) Antigenicity: some molecular aspects. Science 166: 1365–1374

Settle A, Buus S, Colon S, Smith JA, Miles C, Grey HM (1987) Structural characteristics of an antigen required for its interaction with Ia and recognition by T-cells. Nature 328: 395–399

Shinnik TM, Sutcliffe JG, Green N, Lerner RA (1983) Synthetic peptide immunogens as vaccines. Annu Rev Microbiol 37: 425–446

Sojka WJ, Wray C, Morris JA (1978) Passive protection of lambs against experimental enteric colibacillosis by colostral transfer of antibodies from K99-vaccinated ewes. J Med Microbiol 11: 493–499

Steward MW, Howard CT (1987) Synthetic peptides: a next generation of vaccines? Immunol Today 8: 57–58

Stewart JM, Young JD (1984) Solid phase peptide synthesis. 2nd edn. Pierce Chemical, Rockford, Illinois

Svennerholm AM, Lopez Vidal Y, Holmgren J, McConnel MM, Rowe B (1988) Role of PCF8775 antigen and its coli surface subcomponents for colonization, disease, and protective immunogenicity of enterotoxigenic *Escherichia coli* in rabbits. Infect Immun 56(2): 523–528

Swanson J, Robbins K, Barrera O, Corwin D, Boslego J, Ciak J, Blake M, Koomey JM (1987) Gonococcal pilin variants in experimental gonorrhea. J Exp Med 165: 1344–1357

Tainer JA, Getzoff ED, Alexander H, Houghten RA, Olson AJ, Lerner RA, Hendrickson WA (1984) The reactivity of antipeptide antibodies is a function of the atomic mobility of sites in a protein. Nature 312: 127–134

Tainer JA, Getzoff ED, Paterson YA, Olson AJ, Lerner RA (1985) The atomic mobility component of protein antigenicity. Annu Rev Immunol 3: 501–535

Thomas LV, Cravioto A, Scotland SM, Rowe B (1982) New fimbrial antigenic type (E8775) which may represent a colonization factor in enterotoxigenic *Escherichia coli* in humans. Infect Immun 35: 119–1124

Thomas LV, McConnell MM, Rowe B, Field AM (1985) The possession of three novel coli surface antigens by enterotoxigenic *Escherichia coli* strains positive for the putative colonization factor PCF8775. J Gen Microbiol 131: 2319–2326

Thomas LV, Rowe B, McConnell MM (1987) In strains of *Escherichia coli* O167 a single plasmid encodes for the coli surface antigens CS5 and CS6 of putative colonization factor PCF8775, heat-stable enterotoxin and colicin Ia. Infect Immun 55: 1929–1931

Unanue ER (1984) Antigen-presenting function of the macro-phage. Annu Rev Immunol 2: 395–428

Van Die I, Bergmans H (1984) Nucleotide sequence of the gene encoding the $F7_2$ fimbrial subunit of a uropathogenic *Escherichia coli* strain. Gene 32: 83–90

Van Die I, Zuidweg E, Hockstra W, Bergmans H (1986) The role of fimbriae of uropathogenic *Escherichia coli* as carriers of the adhesin involved in mannose resistant hemagglutination. Micro Pathogen 1: 51–56

Van Regenmortel MHV (1986) Which structural features determine protein antigenicity? Trends Biochem Sci (TIBS) 11: 36–39

Van Regenmortel MHV (1987) Antigenic cross-reactivity between proteins and peptides: new insights and applications. Trends Biochem Sci (TIBS) 12: 237–240

Watts C, Davidson HW (1988) Endocytosis and recycling of specific antigen by human B cell lines. EMBO J 7: 1937–1945

Wilson IA, Niman HL, Houghten RA, Cherenson AR, Conolly ML, Lerner RA (1984) The structure of an antigenic determinant in a protein. Cell 37: 767–778

Wilson IA, Haft DA, Getzoff ED, Tainer JA, Lerner RA, Brenner S (1985) Identical short peptide sequences in unrelated proteins can have different conformations: a testing ground for theories of immune recognition. Proc Natl Acad Sci (USA) 82: 5255–5259

Subject Index